ENCYCLOPEDIA OF COMPUTER SCIENCE AND TECHNOLOGY

VOLUME 45

ENCYCLOPEDIA OF COMPUTER SCIENCE AND TECHNOLOGY

EXECUTIVE EDITORS

Allen Kent   *James G. Williams*

UNIVERSITY OF PITTSBURGH
PITTSBURGH, PENNSYLVANIA

ADMINISTRATIVE EDITOR

Carolyn M. Hall

ARLINGTON, TEXAS

VOLUME 45
SUPPLEMENT 30

MARCEL DEKKER, INC.   NEW YORK • BASEL

Headquarters
Marcel Dekker, Inc.
270 Madison Avenue, New York, NY 10016
tel: 212-696-9000; fax: 212-685-4540

Eastern Hemisphere Distribution
Marcel Dekker AG
Hutgasse 4, Postfach 812, CH-4001 Basel, Switzerland
tel: 41-61-261-8482; fax: 41-61-261-8896

World Wide Web
http://www.dekker.com

LIBRARY OF CONGRESS CATALOG CARD NUMBER: 74–29436
ISBN: 0-8247-2298-1

Current Printing (last digit)
10 9 8 7 6 5 4 3 2 1

PRINTED IN THE UNITED STATES OF AMERICA

CONTENTS OF VOLUME 45

CONTRIBUTORS TO VOLUME 45

AMY APON   Department of Computer Science and Computer Engineering, University of Arkansas, Fayettesville, Arkansas: *Cluster Computing and Applications*

MARK BAKER   School of Computer Science, University of Portsmouth, Portsmouth, United Kingdom: *Cluster Computing and Applications*

REINHOLD BEHRINGER, Ph.D.   Senior Scientist, Rockwell Scientific Company, Thousand Oaks, California: *Augmented Reality*

ATHMAN BOUGUETTAYA   Department of Computer Science, Virginia Polytechnic Institute and State University, Falls Church, Virginia: *Wards and UPGMA Clustering of Data with Very High Dimensionality*

HELMAR BURKHART   University of Basel, Basel, Switzerland: *Parallel Computing*

RAJKUMAR BUYYA   School of Computer Science and Software Engineering, Monash University, Melbourne, Victoria, Australia: *Cluster Computing and Applications*

TIZIANA CATARCI   Universitá di Roma La Sapienza, Rome, Italy: *Visual Information Querying*

ANTHONY Y. CHANG, Ph.D.   Department of Computer Science and Information Engineering, Tamkang University, Tamsui, Taipei Hsien, Taiwan, Republic of China: *Multimedia Abstract Machine*

ALEX DELIS   Department of Computer and Information Science, Polytechnic Institute University, Brooklyn, New York: *Wards and UPGMA Clustering of Data with Very High Dimensionality*

IVO DÜNTSCH, Ph.D.   Professor of Computing Science, School of Information and Software Engineering, University of Ulster, Newtownabbey, Northern Ireland: *Evaluation of Software Systems*

GÜNTHER GEDIGA, Ph.D.   Chief Executive Officer, Institute for Evaluation and Market Research, Jeggen, Germany: *Evaluation of Software Systems*

KAI-CHRISTOPH HAMBORG, Ph.D.   Fachbereich Psychologie, Universitat Osnabrhck, Osnabrhck, Germany: *Evaluation of Software Systems*

JASON C. HUNG, Ph.D.   Department of Computer Science and Information Engineering, Tamkang University, Tamsui, Taipei Hsien, Taiwan, Republic of China: *Multimedia Abstract Machine*

PAO-ANN HSIUNG   Department of Computer Science and Information Engineering, National Chung Cheng University, Chiayi, Taiwan, Republic of China: *Real-Time Constraints*

HAI JIN   University of Southern California, Los Angeles, California: *Cluster Computing and Applications*

LAKS V. S. LAKSHMANAN   Professor, Department of Computer Science, University of British Columbia, Vancouver, British Columbia, Canada: *Logic Programming and Deductive Databases with Uncertainty: A Survey*

KIN HONG LEE   Associate Professor, Department of Computer Science, The Chinese University of Hong Kong, Hong Kong: *Chinese Text Spelling Check and Segmentation*

QIN LU, Ph.D.   Associate Professor, Department of Computing, The Hong Kong Polytechnic University, Hong Kong: *Chinese Text Spelling Check and Segmentation*

AKIRA MARUOKA   Professor, Graduate School of Information Sciences, Tohoku University, Sendai, Japan: *Algorithmic Learning Theory*

MAU KIT MICHAEL NG   Research Assistant, Department of Computer Science, The Chinese University of Hong Kong, Hong Kong: *Chinese Text Spelling Check and Segmentation*

JE-HO PARK   Department of Computer and Information Science, Polytechnic Institute University, Brooklyn, New York: *Wards and UPGMA Clustering of Data with Very High Dimensionality*

ALEXANDER PASKO   Professor, Department of Digital Media, Faculty of Computer and Information Sciences, Hosei University, Tokyo, Japan: *Shape Modeling*

JENNIFER PITTMAN, Ph.D.   Research Fellow, National Institute of Statistical Sciences (NISS), Research Triangle Park, North Carolina: *Multilayer Perceptrons and Fractals*

HONGMING QI   Department of Computer Science, Virginia Polytechnic Institute and State University, Falls Church, Virginia: *Wards and UPGMA Clustering of Data with Very High Dimensionality*

VLADIMIR SAVCHENKO   Professor, Department of Digital Media, Faculty of Computer and Information Sciences, Hosei University, Tokyo, Japan: *Shape Modeling*

TIMOTHY K. SHIH   Professor, Department of Computer Science and Information Engineering, Tamkang University, Tamsui, Taipei Hsien, Taiwan, Republic of China: *Multimedia Abstract Machine*

NEMATOLLAAH SHIRI   Assistant Professor, Department of Computer Science, Concordia University, Montreal, Quebec, Canada and Department of Electrical and Computer Engineering, Tarbiat Modares University, Tehran, Iran: *Logic Programming and Deductive Databases with Uncertainty: A Survey*

ELVIRA I. SICILIA-GARCIA   School of Computer Science, Queen's University Belfast, Belfast, Northern Ireland: *Statistical Language Modeling*

SANJAY SINGH   Software Specialist, Electrical and Computer Engineering, University of Waterloo, Waterloo, Ontario, Canada: *Systems Documentation*

F. JACK SMITH   Professor of Computing Science, School of Computer Science, Queen's University Belfast, Belfast, Northern Ireland: *Statistical Language Modeling*

STEFANO SPACCAPIETRA   Professor, Swiss Federal Institute of Technology, Lausanne, Switzerland: *Visual Information Querying*

EIJI TAKIMOTO   Associate Professor, Graduate School of Information Sciences, Tohoku University, Sendai, Japan: *Algorithmic Learning Theory*

JENS VOLKERT   Department of Graphics and Parallel Processing, Institute of Technical Computer Science and Telematics, Johannes Kepler University Linz, Linz, Austria: *Parallel Computing*

ALGORITHMIC LEARNING THEORY

INTRODUCTION

Humans appear to have a remarkable ability to extract underlying general rules from what they observe. This ability is mysterious in that once a human obtained such a rule, he can recognize unseen objects of the same category and he can obtain such rules by only observing a certain number of objects without explicitly being told the general rules. The rules he obtained apparently do not seem to be strictly implied from his observations. It is a challenging research problem to understand the possibilities and limitations of such ability. It is also worth studying this kind of phenomenon from the engineering point of view because we would have great advantage if we could build a computing machine that automatically extract useful knowledge from a large amount of data as general rules. This machine would be completely different from the conventional computers in the sense that the intended machine could obtain, in feasible a time, rules that have not been described explicitly as a program.

L. G. Valiant thought of the computational aspects of the phenomenon as learning and provided the methodology to study the phenomenon (1). The computational learning theory he introduced seeks a deep understanding of learning based on the methodology. From a computational viewpoint, he addressed the following questions: What is a relevant framework to the computational phenomenon of learning? What are the limits of what can be learned within feasible computational resources? There has been a large body of work on computational learning theory. References 1 and 2 give excellent reviews of the theory. Although we are far from having understood computational possibilities and limitations of learning, we have succeeded, on the other hand, in obtaining a large number of results on the topics. A number of new computational mechanisms for learning have been evolved and have been shown to have provably guaranteed performance. Exploring the information-gathering mechanism is the subject of not only computational learning but also machine learning and data mining. Ambitious research on scientific discovery is also ongoing along those lines (2,5).

In this article, we survey the field from algorithmic aspects. Instead of trying to give an exhaustive overview of such mechanisms, we try to survey fundamental learning algorithms, focusing on computational mechanisms behind them and hopefully bringing out underlying relationships between them. For ease of exposition, we did not make efforts in presenting the results that are the strongest in terms of generality of the models and performance of the algorithms referred to. To extract useful information from data, the learner somehow has to interact with data. In the case of *batch* learning, all the data are given to the learner at the start of learning, whereas in the case of *on-line* learning, the learner repeats trials to receive data and process them somehow. We mainly focus on the on-line learning. If we consider the agent to give data as the *adversary* or the *environment*, learning can be discussed in the framework of game theory. In fact, many of the results in this article are formalized in the game-theoretic framework.

The first section describes the computational model of learning, focusing on the definition of the so-called a Probably Approximately Correct model. Based on this model, a *strong leaning algorithm* is defined to be one that produces as output a *strong hypothesis* with arbitrarily high accuracy, whereas a *weak learning algorithm* is one that yields a *weak hypothesis*, with performance just slightly better than random guessing. *Boosting* is defined as transforming a weaking learning algorithm to a strong learning algorithm. The first section presents a number of preliminary definitions necessary for the subsequent sections. The second section presents the subsampling boosting algorithm due to Freund. The section is divided into two subsections. In the first subsection, we describe a two-player game, denoted **MajoGame**, which is played by the learner and the adversary, each aiming at conflicting goals. In the second subsection, it is shown that playing **MajoGame** can be seen to be essentially the same as boosting weak hypotheses into a strong hypothesis. The third section describes a two-person game, denoted **Repea-Game**, which will be referred to later in order to solve learning problems such as boosting and on-line prediction. The repeated game is analyzed to give an upper bound on the cumulative loss of the game relative to that of the best strategy. It is also noted that **RepeaGame** can be thought of as one seeking the minmax strategy approximately. In the fourth section, the repeated game given in the third section is shown to serve as the underlying scheme both for an on-line prediction algorithm and a boosting algorithm, which are presented in the two subsections of this section. The performance of these algorithms is also analyzed based on the theorem that gives the bound of the repeated game. In the fifth section, an on-line prediction algorithm based on experts' prediction is given. In this expert model, a loss function is introduced to measure the discrepancy between the predictions and real outcomes. The loss of the on-line prediction algorithm relative to that of the best expert is given again by applying the theorem on the bounds of the repeated game for a large variety of loss functions satisfying the convexity condition. The sixth section describes another boosting algorithm which, unlike the boosting algorithms mentioned so far, adapts to the accuracy of each weak hypothesis and hence overcomes many of the practical difficulties of the earlier boosting algorithms. The seventh section presents still another boosting algorithm which, as output, yields a decision tree that performs as a strong hypothesis; a decision tree is a tree with weak hypotheses at internal nodes and output values at the leaves. The proposed boosting algorithm performs in a top-down fashion, growing a tree from the root to the leaves repeatedly; the existing top-down algorithms such as CART and C4.5 can be thought of as special cases of the boosting algorithm. An information-theoretic criterion is incorporated into the algorithm to choose a weak hypothesis that is associated with each internal nodes.

PROBABLY APPROXIMATELY CORRECT LEARNING

In order to study the computational phenomenon of learning, Valiant introduced a so-called PAC (Probably Approximately Correct) model, which is basically a model for learning a concept or function from its examples (1). Consider, for instance, learning Boolean functions from examples. Let us suppose that the function to be learned, which is called the target function, is the majority function f of five variables. The learner is required to yield a function h, called an hypothesis, which approximates the target function. To do so, the learner is allowed to observe a certain number of examples, such as (10001, 0), (10000, 0), (11010, 1), (00010, 0), and (10111, 1) which are drawn according to some fixed probability distribution D over $\{(x, f(x)) \,|\, x \in \{0, 1\}^5\}$. If the learner knows in advance that the target function comes from the collection of the threshold functions, then, after observing the examples, he can decide that the target is the threshold function with threshold 3, namely the majority function. In fact, the first and the third of the five examples is enough for that decision in this case. The knowledge about possible targets is usually given as a class of Boolean formulas representing the targets (e.g., a class of disjunctions of length three conjunctions). On the other hand, if the learner has no knowledge about the target, then he cannot say anything for sure unless he could observe all 32 distinct examples in our case, because the domain consists of 32 vectors. The goal of the *learning algorithm* is to find an *hypothesis h* that approximates the unknown *target function f* by observing feasibly few *examples* drawn independently according to an unknown probability distribution over the instance space. We are interested in knowing how accurate the hypothesis is in approximating the target on instances that do not appear in the examples the learning algorithm receives.

Let B denote the *instance space* or *domain*, which can be thought of as a set of encodings of instances or objects in the real world. Throughout this article, we assume that the instance space is discrete. Typically, when the objects are encoded as a collection of attributes, the instance space consists of vectors whose components take the values of the attributes. We are mainly concerned with learning classification, so both the target function f and the hypothesis h are assumed to be functions from B to $\{0, 1\}$. A target function f together with a hypothesis is sometimes treated as the subset of B, namely $\{x \in B \,|\, f(x) = 1\}$, which is called a *concept*. An *example of* a target function f takes the form $(x, f(x))$ for $x \in B$. How do we measure the accuracy of a hypothesis? To measure its accuracy, we define the error of a hypothesis h, denoted error (h), to be the probability that the hypothesis disagrees with the target on an instance drawn according to the distribution D over B; that is, error$(h) = \Pr_{x \in D}[h(x) \neq f(x)]$. Throughout this article, $\Pr_{x \in D}[E(x)]$ denotes the probability that event $E(x)$ holds with respect to the random draw of x according to distribution D. When points x are indexed like x_i, the same probability will also be denoted by $\Pr_{i \sim D}[E(x_i)]$. When no confusion arises, subscripts $x \in D$ or $i \sim D$ in the notation may be omitted. Although error (h) depends implicitly on f and D, we omit these in the notation for brevity when no confusion arises. It is a crucial point of the PAC model that the same distribution D is used both for drawing examples and evaluating the error of the hypothesis obtained.

We should list a number of remarkable features concerning the PAC model before going into its formal definition:

- Because the learner is supposed to receive a feasibly few number of examples drawn randomly, we cannot hope that he yields a hypothesis with no error. Because we cannot hope for perfection in this sense, we should instead require that the error of a hypothesis produced can be made arbitrarily small as the amount of computational resources spent, such as time or the number of the examples, is increased.
- Learning should be done efficiently. In another words, we require a feasible amount of computational resources to be used to learn a hypothesis. The quantitative requirement is described that the time the learner spends has to be bounded by a fixed polynomial in the relevant parameters such as the size of

the minimal description of the target and the inverse of the quantity of the error we allow.

- Examples are supposed to be drawn according to an arbitrarily fixed probability distribution which is unknown to the learner. Because the performance of the learner should be insensitive to the arbitrariness of distributions, the error of the hypothesis produced should be evaluated according to the same distribution from which the examples are drawn.

In the formal definition of the PAC model, we consider the learnability of a class F of functions rather than that of a single function. We give the model in its most basic version, which will be relevant to what we discuss in the later sections.

Let F and H denote a class of target functions and that of hypotheses, respectively, both being functions from B to $\{0, 1\}$. We may think of F and H classes of representations expressing the corresponding functions. For brevity, we will often identify functions with their representations when no confusion arises. Let f be any function in F. A set of examples of f is called a sample, which is denoted by $S = ((x_1, f(x_1)), \ldots, (x_N, f(x_N)))$. We define a *learning algorithm* for F with respect to H to be one that takes a sample of a function $f \in F$ as input and produces a function $h \in H$ as output. Examples in sample S are assumed to be drawn independently according to some unknown arbitrarily fixed probability distribution D over B. Hence, a sample of size N is chosen according to the product probability distribution D^N over B^N. We are now ready to give the definition of *Probably Approximately Correct learning*, or simply *PAC learning*. Roughly speaking, a successful learning algorithm is one that with a high probability (with respect to D^N) produces a hypothesis whose error is small. To be more precise, we introduce two parameters: the error parameter ε measuring the error of hypotheses and the confidence parameter δ corresponding to tolerance for the probability of failing to produce a sufficiently accurate hypothesis. Let size (f) denote some complexity measure of a function f (e.g., the minimal description length of f). F is *polynomially learnable* with respect to H if there exists a learning algorithm for F with respect to H and a polynomial $p(\cdot, \cdot, \cdot)$ such that the followings hold:

1. For any $f \in F$ and any distribution D over B, given a random sample S of size $p(1/\varepsilon, 1/\delta,$ size $(f))$, the algorithm produces a hypothesis h with error at most ε with probability at least $1 - \delta$.
2. The algorithm produces its hypothesis in $p(1/\varepsilon, 1/\delta,$ size $(f))$ steps as output.

Such an algorithm is called a *polynomial learning algorithm*. When F is *polynomially learnable*, we often simply say F is *learnable*. Similarly, we also call such an algorithm a learning algorithm. In the PAC model we have described so far, the learning algorithm is only allowed to obtain an example drawn according to an unknown distribution. The basic model can be made to have more power by allowing a learning algorithm to ask more general questions and assuming oracles to answer these questions. One such oracle is MEMBER, which, given an instance x chosen by the learner, returns "yes" or "no" depending on whether $f(x) = 1$, where f is the target function. Another oracle called EQUIVALENCE returns an answer indicating whether or not a hypothesis and the target is equivalent; that is, given a hypothesis h, EQUIVALENCE returns "yes" if $h \equiv f$ and a counterexample otherwise.

A learning algorithm is required to achieve arbitrarily high accuracy. In contrast with this notion of learnability, Refs. 4 and 6 introduced the notion of *weak learnability*:

A weak learning algorithm is roughly one that produces a weak hypothesis which performs just slightly better than random guessing. To define the weak learnability, we drop the requirement that the hypothesis produced is arbitrarily accurate by simply fixing the parameter ε to $\frac{1}{2} - \gamma$ for some constant $\gamma > 0$. Furthermore, omitting the phrases concerning the confidence parameter δ, we modify the definition for learnability by requiring that a weak learning algorithm produces a weak hypothesis with absolute certainty. After all, a *weak learning algorithm* is defined as an algorithm that produces a hypothesis whose error is at most $\frac{1}{2} - \gamma$, where $\gamma > 0$ is a constant. It will be seen that for the purpose of this article, it is relevant to adopt this definition for weak learning. We denote a weak learning algorithm in this sense by the genetic name **WeakLearn** and refer to a hypothesis produced by **WeakLearn** as a *weak hypothesis*. In particular, a hypothesis whose error is at most $\frac{1}{2} - \gamma$ is called $\gamma - weak\ hypothesis$, where $\gamma > 0$ is a constant. We will refer to the original definition of PAC learning as *strong learning* when we need to distinguish it from the weak learning.

Having defined the notions of strong and weak learnabilities, we are faced with the problem of whether a weak learning algorithm can be "boosted" into a strong learning algorithm. This problem posed by Kearns and Valiant (4,6) was first settled by Schapire, who presented a polynomial-time boosting algorithm in Ref. 7. Then, Freund developed a simpler and more efficient boosting algorithm (15). Because Schapire's boosting algorithm works recursively, the final hypothesis it generates can be represented as a circuit which consists of many levels of three-input majority gates. On the other hand, because Freund's construction does not involve recursive calls, the final hypothesis can be represented as a single multi-input majority gate. Finally, Ref. 8 presents a boosting algorithm, called **AdaBoost**, which overcomes certain practical drawbacks of the two previous algorithms. Because Freund's algorithm has a construction more similar to **AdaBoost** than Schapire's algorithm, we will explain the former in detail in this article. It should be noted that all of these boosting algorithms fully exploit the power of the weak learning algorithms which are guaranteed to work for all distributions D.

Learning algorithms somehow generate hypotheses during the learning process. Generally, the accuracy of the hypotheses is improved gradually through the process. Let X be a subset of the instance space B and D_X be a distribution over X. The error of h with respect to D_X, denoted by $\mathrm{error}_{D_X}(h)$, is defined by

$$\mathrm{error}_{D_X}(h) = \mathrm{Pr}_{x \in D_X}[h(x) \neq f(x)],$$

where f denotes the target function. Let a learning algorithm be fed with sample $S = ((x_1, y_1), \ldots, (x_N, y_N))$, which is considered to be a training set to yield a hypothesis. Let X be the set $\{x_1, \ldots, x_N\}$ and D_X be a distribution over X. The *training error* of h with respect to D_X is defined to be $\mathrm{error}_{D_X}(h)$. Subscript D_X in the notation will be omitted when it is clear from the context.

A hypothesis h is said to be *consistent* with sample $S = ((x_1, y_1), \ldots, (x_N, y_N))$ (or simply consistent when S is clear from the context) if $h(x_i) = y_i$ holds for any $1 \leq i \leq N$. Therefore, if D_X is such that $D_X(x) \neq 0$ for any $x \in X$, then the condition of hypothesis h being consistent with the sample S is equivalent to $\mathrm{error}_{D_X}(h) = 0$. The ultimate goal of learning algorithms is to produce a final hypothesis whose error is small outside the training set as well. Thus, we need to define the generalization error, taking into account the entire space B. Given distribution D_B over B, the *generalization error* with respect to D_B is defined to be $\mathrm{error}_{D_B}(h)$. Note that the generalization error is exactly the one that we are concerned with in defining the learnability. Given sample S, a learning algorithm typically produces a hypothesis consistent with S as output. However, a hypothesis that is consistent with the training set might not be accurate on examples outside the training set. A hypothesis that is constructed from a training set might "overfit" statistical irregularities of distribution D_X over the training set. A general strategy for avoiding overfitting is to somehow restrict the hypotheses to be simple.

Thus far, a hypothesis is evaluated in terms of its error. However, this is not the only way to measure goodness of hypotheses. There are other two parameters which measure how good a hypothesis is. The first is the length of description for hypotheses. This parameter leads to the notion of an *Occam learning algorithm*, which, after seeing a number of examples, yields a consistent hypothesis that is somewhat shorter to describe than the number of examples seen. The precise definition of an Occam learning algorithm is given in Ref. 9. It has been shown that Occam learning is essentially equivalent to PAC learning (10). Generalizing the description length for a hypothesis to the VC dimension, another characterization for PAC learning is given in terms of the VC dimension in Ref. 11. In the same spirit as looking for a hypothesis with somewhat shorter description length, Ref. 12 gives an algorithm which produces decision trees.

The second of the alterative parameters to measure goodness of hypotheses is information that a hypothesis gains about the target. Based on information gained, the notion of an *entropy-based learning algorithm* is introduced in Ref. 13. Let us suppose that an instance $x \in B$ is drawn according to distribution D. Then, given a target function f and hypothesis h, these are considered to be random variables $f(x)$ and $h(x)$, respectively. Then, the conditional entropy $H(f(x)|h(x))$ measures the uncertainty about the value of $f(x)$ remaining after knowing the value of $h(x)$. An entropy-based learning algorithm is defined essentially the same way as PAC learning except that "h with error at most ε" is replaced by "h with $H(f(x)|h(x)) \leq \varepsilon$." It is shown (13) that the notion of entropy-based learning is equivalent to that of PAC learning. The fact that definitions of learnability based on three different parameters are essentially equivalent can be interpreted as showing that PAC learning is a robust notion. Reference 14 gives still another variety of definitions for learnability which are shown equivalent each other.

MAJORITY-VOTE GAME AND SUBSAMPLING BOOSTING

The majority-vote game is a game that is played in a sequence of rounds by two players called the learner and the environment, each aiming at conflicting goals. The game-theoretic framework captures essential aspects of a learning problem, boosting. In the first subsection, we present a particular game called the majority-vote game, and in the second subsection, we transform the learner's strategy for the game into the boosting algorithm working on a sample.

Majority-Vote Game

Consider a two-player game called the majority-vote game (15). The players of a two-person game are generally called the *learner* and the *adversary*, whereas in the particular game we consider in this subsection, we may call them the *weightor* and *chooser*, respectively, so as to reflect the roles they play in the game. We assume that a probability distribution D over the instance space B and a parameter $0 < \gamma < \frac{1}{2}$ are given. The majority-vote game is played repeatedly in a sequence of T rounds. On each round t:

1. The weightor chooses a distribution W_t over B
2. The chooser selects a subset M_t of B such that $W_t(M_t) \geq \frac{1}{2} + \gamma$

where $W_t(M_t)$ denotes the probability that an instance drawn according to W_t belongs to M_t, namely $W_t(M_t) = \Pr_{x \in W_t}[x \in M_t] = \sum_{x \in M_t} W_t(x)$. A distribution W_t is called a weight distribution. An instance is said to be *marked* when the instance is selected by the chooser. After the whole T rounds are over, the *loss set* of the game is defined to be the set of instances that are marked in less than or equal to half of the T rounds and an instance in the loss set is called a *loss instance*. The probability that an instance drawn according to the distribution D falls in the loss set is defined to be the *loss* of the game (or sometimes referred to as the loss of the learner), which will be denoted by *Loss*. In particular, when the number of rounds is even, an instance being marked if exactly half of the entire rounds falls in the loss set. The set of instances in B outside the loss set is the *reward* set and the probability of a point falling in the reward set according to distribution D is defined to be the *reward* of the game.

The learner's goal is to minimize the loss, whereas the adversary's goal is to maximize it. Therefore, in each round, the learner tries to choose a weight distribution W so that the loss is minimized no matter how the adversary makes marks on instances. As long as the sum of the weights of the marked instances is equal to or larger than $\frac{1}{2} + \gamma$ on each round, the adversary can choose instances anyway he likes so as to maximize the loss after seeing the weights chosen by the learner. How should the learner choose distributions in each round to achieve his goal? We will show how the learner should behave in such a setting by giving an algorithm that describes the learner's behavior. Before going into the details of the learner's strategy, we need some notation.

For $1 \leq t \leq T + 1$ and $0 \leq r \leq t - 1$, let $X_t(r)$ denote the set of instances that have been marked r times during the first $t - 1$ rounds, and let $q_r(t)$ denote the probability of $X_t(r)$ with respect to D; that is,

$$X_t(r) = \{x \in B \mid |\{t' \in [t - 1] \mid x \in M_{t'}\}| = r\},$$
$$q_r(r) = D(X_t(r)).$$

In particular, $X_1^0 = B$ and $q_1(0) = 1$. Throughout the article, for a natural number n, let $[n]$ denote $\{1, \ldots, n\}$.

As shown in Figure 1, the chooser selects a subset of $X_t(r)$ which will fall into X_{t+1} $(r + 1)$ in the next round, and the rest of $X_t(r)$ will fall into $X_{t+1}(r)$. Recall that $M_t \subseteq B$ is a subset chosen by the adversary in round t. Then, for $1 \leq t \leq T$ and $0 \leq r \leq t$, we have

$$X_{t+1}(r) = (X_t(r) \cap \bar{M}_t) \cup (X_t(r - 1) \cap M_t),$$

where the overbar denotes the complement with respect to the domain B. Let $\gamma_t(r)$ be such that the fraction of instances in $X_t(r)$ that are marked in round t is $\frac{1}{2} + \gamma_t(r)$ with respect to the distribution D; that is,

$$\frac{D(X_t(r) \cap M_t)}{D(X_t(r))} = \frac{1}{2} + \gamma_t(r).$$

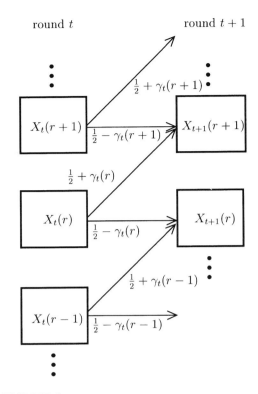

round t round $t+1$

FIGURE 1   Transition from round t to round $t+1$.

Therefore, the real number associated with an arrow in Figure 1 indicates the fraction of points that flow along the arrow, where the fraction is calculated based on the distribution D.

Let $\beta_t(r)$ be defined to be

$$\beta_t(r) = \sum_{j=0}^{\lfloor T/2 \rfloor - r} \binom{T-t+1}{j} \; (\tfrac{1}{2}+\gamma)^j (\tfrac{1}{2}-\gamma)^{T-t+1-j}.$$

In particular, we set

$$\beta_{T+1}(r) = \begin{cases} 1 & \text{for } 0 \le r \le \lfloor \tfrac{T}{2} \rfloor \\ 0 & \text{for } \lfloor \tfrac{T}{2} \rfloor < r \le T. \end{cases}$$

To see what $\beta_t(r)$ means, consider Bernoulli trials, each with probability of success $\tfrac{1}{2} + \gamma$. Then, $\beta_t(r)$ gives the probability that there are at most $\lfloor T/2 \rfloor - r$ successes in $T - t$ Bernoulli trials. Suppose that in each round, an instance in B is marked independently with probability $\tfrac{1}{2} + \gamma$. Then, if we correspond success in the trials to being marked, $\beta_t(r)$ gives exactly the probability that an instance in $X_t(r)$ is marked at most $\lfloor T/2 \rfloor$ times through the remaining $T - t$ rounds and hence ends up as a loss point. Clearly, letting $\gamma_t(r)$ in Figure 1 be γ for any $1 \le t \le T$ and $0 \le r \le t$, we can consider the Bernoulli trials that correspond to the game.

Assuming that $\gamma_t(r)$ is set to γ for all $1 \leq t \leq T$ and $0 \leq r \leq t$, we can give an interpretation about how to choose the weight distribution in each round. The quantity $\beta_{t+1}(r) - \beta_{t+1}(r + 1)$ is exactly the difference between the probabilities of an instance in the corresponding sets [i.e., $X_{t+1}(r)$ and $X_{t+1}(r + 1)$], ending up as a loss point. Thus, we can interpret this quantity as the measure of "benefit" of making an instance in $X_t(r)$ in the sense that the instance in $X_t(r)$ reduces the probability of eventually falling in the loss set by $\beta_{t+1}(r) - \beta_{t+1}(r + 1)$.

We are now ready to explain how the weightor chooses distribution W in each round. For $1 \leq t \leq T$ and $0 \leq r \leq t - 1$, set

$$\alpha_t(r) = \beta_{t+1}(r) - \beta_{t+1}(r + 1).$$

Because by the definition of $\beta_t(r)$ we can easily verify that

$$\alpha_t(r) = \binom{T - t}{\lfloor \frac{T}{2} \rfloor - r} (\tfrac{1}{2} + \gamma)^{\lfloor T/2 \rfloor - r} (\tfrac{1}{2} - \gamma)^{(T-t)-(\lfloor T/2 \rfloor - r)},$$

$\alpha_t(r)$ gives the probability that there exist exactly $\lfloor T/2 \rfloor - r$ successes in $T - t$ Bernoulli trials described earlier. As mentioned previously, we see that this probability reflects the measure of benefit of an instance in $X_t(r)$ being marked. The weightor defines weight W_t in round t as follows: For $x \in X_t(r)$,

$$W_t(x) = D(x)\alpha_t(r) \tag{1}$$

and

$$\bar{W}_t(x) = \frac{D(x)\alpha_t(r)}{\sum_{r'=0}^{t-1} q_t(r')\alpha_t(r')},$$

where $1 \leq t \leq T$ and $0 \leq r \leq t - 1$. Throughout this article, the overbar means the normalization unless stated otherwise. Note that the denominator of the above equation is just to make a distribution. Summarizing what we mentioned so far, in Figure 2 we give the algorithm for playing the majority-vote game. From the interpretation of $\alpha_t(r)$ mentioned earlier, the weight-update rule $W_t(x) := D(x)\alpha_t(r)$ can be interpreted as forcing the adversary to focus on such instances with a large benefit. To see this, consider an extreme

MajoGame

1. **for** $r \in \{0, \cdots, t - 1\}$ **do**

   for $x \in X_t(r)$ **do**

   $$W_t(x) := D(x)\alpha_t(r);$$

2. Receive a subset $M_t \subseteq B$ satisfying

   $$\bar{W}_t(M_t) \geq \tfrac{1}{2} + \gamma.$$

FIGURE 2   The algorithm playing the majority-vote game with the loss set written as $X_{T+1}(0) \cup \cdots \cup X_{T+1}(\lfloor T/2 \rfloor)$.

case of round T. Because, by definition, $\beta_{T+1}(r) = 1$ for $0 \leq r \leq \lfloor T/2 \rfloor$ and $\beta_{T+1}(r) = 0$ for $\lfloor T/2 \rfloor < r \leq \lfloor T \rfloor$, we have $\alpha_T(\lfloor T/2 \rfloor) = \beta_{T+1}(\lfloor T/2 \rfloor) - \beta_{T+1}(\lfloor T/2 \rfloor + 1) = 1$ and $\alpha_T(r) = 0$ for any $r \neq \lfloor T/2 \rfloor$, and hence $\bar{W}(X_T(\lfloor T/2 \rfloor)) = 1$ and $\bar{W}(X_T(r)) = 0$ for any $r \neq \lfloor T/2 \rfloor$. In words, the weightor gives all the weight on instances in $X_T(\lfloor T/2 \rfloor)$. It is intuitively reasonable because on round T, it is only the set $X_T(\lfloor T/2 \rfloor)$ that contains instances for which it has not been determined whether or not they fall in the loss set.

Clearly, the loss in **MajoGame** is written as

$$
\begin{aligned}
\text{Loss} &= \sum_{r=0}^{\lfloor T/2 \rfloor} D(X_{T+1}(r)) \\
&= \sum_{r=0}^{T} q_{T+1}(r)\beta_{T+1}(r).
\end{aligned}
$$

We will show that the loss is upper bounded by the quantity $\sum_{r=0}^{t-1} q_t(r)\beta_t(r)$ for any $1 \leq t \leq T+1$ by backward induction in rounds.

Lemma 1 *For any $1 \leq t \leq T$,*

$$
\sum_{r=0}^{t} q_{t+1}(r)\beta_{t+1}(r) \leq \sum_{r=0}^{t-1} q_t(r)\beta_t(r).
$$

Proof. By the weight-update rules, we have $W_t(X_t(r)) = D(X_t(r))\alpha_t(r) = q_t(r)\alpha_t(r)$. Because the fraction of instances in $X_t(r)$ marked in round t is given by $\frac{1}{2} + \gamma_t(r)$, we have $W(X_t(r) \cap M_t) = D(X_t(r) \cap M_t)\alpha_t(r) = (\frac{1}{2} + \gamma_t(r))D(X_t(r))\alpha_t(r) = (\frac{1}{2} + \gamma_t(r))q_t(r)\alpha_t(r)$. On the one hand, by the requirement for the marked points in round t, we have

$$
\sum_{r=0}^{t-1} W(X_t(r) \cap M_t)) \geq (\tfrac{1}{2} + \gamma) \sum_{r=0}^{t-1} W(X_t(r)).
$$

Noting that $\alpha_t(r) = \beta_{t+1}(\mathrm{r}) - \beta_{t+1}(r+1)$, we therefore have

$$
\begin{aligned}
&\sum_{r=0}^{t-1} q_t(r)(\tfrac{1}{2} + \gamma_t(r))(\beta_{t+1}(r) - \beta_{t+1}(r+1)) \\
&\qquad \geq (\tfrac{1}{2} + \gamma) \sum_{r=0}^{t-1} q_t(r)(\beta_{t+1}(r) - \beta_{t+1}(r+1)),
\end{aligned}
$$

which is further rewritten as

$$
\begin{aligned}
&\sum_{r=0}^{t-1} q_t(r)\gamma_t(r)(\beta_{t+1}(r) - \beta_{t+1}(r+1)) \\
&\qquad \geq \gamma \sum_{r=0}^{t-1} q_t(r)(\beta_{t+1}(r) - \beta_{t+1}(r+1)).
\end{aligned}
$$

Thus, using the last inequality, we have

$$
\begin{aligned}
&\sum_{r=0}^{t} q_{t+1}(r)\beta_{t+1}(r) \\
&= \sum_{r=0}^{t-1} q_t(r)\{(\tfrac{1}{2} + \gamma_t(r))\beta_{t+1}(r+1) + (\tfrac{1}{2} - \gamma_t(r))\beta_{t+1}(r)\} \\
&= \sum_{r=0}^{t-1} q_t(r)(\tfrac{1}{2}\beta_{t+1}(r+1) + \tfrac{1}{2}\beta_{t+1}(r)) - \sum_{r=0}^{t-1} q_t(r)\gamma_t(r)(\beta_{t+1}(r) - \beta_{t+1}(r+1))
\end{aligned}
$$

$$\leq \sum_{r=0}^{t-1} q_t(r)(\tfrac{1}{2}\beta_{t+1}(r+1) + \tfrac{1}{2}\beta_{t+1}(r)) - \gamma \sum_{r=0}^{t-1} q_t(r)(\beta_{t+1}(r) - \beta_{t+1}(r+1))$$

$$= \sum_{r=0}^{t-1} q_t(r)\{(\tfrac{1}{2} + \gamma)\beta_{t+1}(r+1) + (\tfrac{1}{2} - \gamma)\beta_{t+1}(r)\}$$

$$= \sum_{r=0}^{t-1} q_t(r)\beta_t(r).$$

Theorem 2   *Let $\gamma > 0$ be a constant and assume that the weightor plays* **MajoGame** *for T rounds, choosing the weight given by Eq. (1). Then, if the chooser selects instances satisfying the condition of the game, then the loss of the game is given by*

$$\mathrm{Loss} \leq \sum_{j=0}^{\lfloor T/2 \rfloor} \binom{T}{j} (\tfrac{1}{2} + \gamma)^j (\tfrac{1}{2} - \gamma)^{T-j}.$$

Proof. By Lemma 1, we have

$$\mathrm{Loss} = \sum_{r=0}^{\lfloor T/2 \rfloor} D(X_T(r))$$

$$= \sum_{r=0}^{T} q_T(r)\beta_T(r)$$

$$\leq \sum_{r=0}^{T-1} q_{T-1}\beta_{T-1}(r)$$

$$\leq \sum_{r=0}^{T-2} q_{T-2}\beta_{T-2}(r)$$

$$\vdots$$

$$\leq q_0(0)\beta_0(0)$$

$$= \sum_{j=0}^{\lfloor T/2 \rfloor} \binom{T}{j} (\tfrac{1}{2} + \gamma)^j (\tfrac{1}{2} - \gamma)^{T-j}.$$

Corollary 3   *If the number of rounds satisfies*

$$T > \frac{1}{2\gamma^2} \ln\left(\frac{1}{2\varepsilon}\right),$$

then we have

$$\mathrm{Loss} < \varepsilon.$$

Proof. It suffices to show that

$$2^{T-1}\{(\tfrac{1}{2} + \gamma)(\tfrac{1}{2} - \gamma)\}^{T/2} < \varepsilon, \qquad\qquad [2]$$

because if the inequality (2) holds, we can verify

$$\mathrm{Loss} \leq \sum_{j=0}^{\lfloor T/2 \rfloor} \binom{T}{j} (\tfrac{1}{2} + \gamma)^j (\tfrac{1}{2} - \gamma)^{T-j}$$

$$\leq 2^{T-1}\{(\tfrac{1}{2} + \gamma)(\tfrac{1}{2} - \gamma)\}^{T/2} < \varepsilon.$$

The first inequality above comes from Theorem 1. The second one can be easily seen if we note that $\sum_{j=0}^{\lfloor T/2 \rfloor} \binom{T}{j}(\frac{1}{2}+\gamma)^j(\frac{1}{2}-\gamma)^{T-j}$ gives the probability of having at most $\lceil T/2 \rceil$ successes in the Bernoulli trials with probability $\frac{1}{2}+\gamma$ of success and that there are at most 2^{T-1} such events with probability at most $(\frac{1}{2}+\gamma)(\frac{1}{2}-\gamma)^{T/2}$. To verify the third one, we consider the inequality equivalent to Eq. (2):

$$\frac{T}{2} > \frac{\ln(1/2\varepsilon)}{-\ln(1-4\gamma^2)} \, ,$$

which can be derived from the assumption of the corollary and the fact that $-\ln(1-x) \geq x$ for $0 \leq x < 1$. $\qquad\square$

It should be noted that we can verify that the weighting strategy for the weightor is the best possible in the sense that, provided that there is some technical condition on the probability space (B, D), there exists a strategy for the chooser such that the loss is lower bounded by the quantity given in Theorem 2, written as $\sum_{j=0}^{\lfloor T/2 \rfloor} \binom{T}{j}(\frac{1}{2}+\gamma)^j(\frac{1}{2}-\gamma)^{T-j}$, no matter how the weightor behaves. In this sense, we cannot expect to improve the bound given by Theorem 2 (15). To see the idea of the chooser's strategy, we should note that being marked corresponds to the success of the Bernoulli trials, and not being marked corresponds to failure. The condition on (B, D) we need to assume is just to guarantee that in each round, there exists an *eligible* subset A' of each region A consisting of instances with the same history of how they are marked in previous rounds. By an eligible subset A' of A, we mean that given the weight distribution W, both $D(A') = (\frac{1}{2}+\gamma)D(A)$ and $W(A') \geq (\frac{1}{2}+\gamma)W(A)$ hold, where W is the weight distribution chosen by the weightor. The chooser that achieves the error bound is one who marks instances in the union of the all the eligible subsets. It turns out that if such eligible subsets for an instances always exist with the same history in each round, then we can see that the Bernoulli trials correspond to the majority-vote game in the manner mentioned earlier. In fact, we assumed the above-mentioned technical condition on the probability space (B, D) in order to guarantee the existence of such eligible subsets. Then, it is easy to see that for any weightor and the chooser described earlier the loss of the game is lower bounded by the quantity given in Theorem 2. The history of an instance up to round t is represented by the binary sequence of length t such that the ith bit indicates whether or not the instance is marked on round i. As the game goes on, the whole domain B will be divided more and more into smaller regions, each instance in a region having the same history. It should be noted that the condition we need in order to achieve error bound is satisfied only when the domain B is infinite.

Subsampling Boosting as Majority-Vote Game

Applying the results of the majority-vote game, we will design a boosting algorithm based on subsampling, denoted **SubsampBoost** (15). As is illustrated in Figure 3, the subsampling boosting consists of **Boost**, which plays the game as the weightor, and **WeakLearn**, which plays as the chooser. **WeakLearn**, which is called by **Boost**, returns a weak hypothesis. **Boost** draws N examples independently from the domain B according to the distribution D and produces a sample

$$S = ((x_1, \, f(x_1)), \, \ldots, \, (x_N, \, f(x_N))),$$

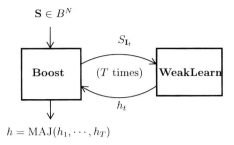

$$\mathbf{S} \in B^N$$

$S_{\mathbf{I}_t}$

Boost $(T \text{ times})$ **WeakLearn**

h_t

$$h = \mathrm{MAJ}(h_1, \cdots, h_T)$$

FIGURE 3   Subsampling boosting algorithm.

where N will be determined later. Set $X = \{x_1, \ldots, x_N\}$. Once a sample S is chosen, **Boost** works on X with the uniform distribution U over X. Therefore, the instance space B and distribution D over B in **MajoGame** are replaced with X and the uniform distribution U, respectively, in the subsampling boosting algorithm. Taking T appropriately, **Boost** calls **WeakLearn** T times. Corresponding each call to a round of the game, we consider the subsampling boosting as the majority-vote game. On each round t, **Boost** updates the weight distribution W_t according to Eq. (1) and **WeakLearn** returns a hypothesis h_t, where hypothesis h_t is assumed to be γ-weak with respect to $\bar{W}_t$. To compute h_t, **WeakLearn** is given a subsample of S together with the distribution $\bar{W}_t$. The subsample is obtained by drawing N_0 examples independently from S according to the distribution $\bar{W}_t$, where N_0 is a sufficiently large constant number for **WeakLearn** to produce a γ-weak hypothesis and, hence, depends solely on the parameter γ. Let set M_t be the set of the examples on which the weak hypothesis h_t gives the right value [i.e., $M_t = \{x \in X \mid h_t(x) = f(x))\}$]. Let the subsampling boosting compute the final hypothesis by taking the majority of all these hypotheses $h_1, \ldots, h_T$, which is denoted by $\mathrm{MAJ}(h_1, \ldots, h_T)$. With the correspondence between the game and the subsampling boosting in mind, we can easily see that the probability that the final hypothesis is incorrect in an example drawn from S according to D is upper bounded by the quantity given by Theorem 2, provided that each hypothesis h_t satisfies the corresponding condition on M_t, namely the condition that h_t is γ-weak with respect to $\bar{W}_t$.

Before going into more detail of our performance analysis for **SubsampBoost** given in Figure 4, we need to explain more about our setting. Because the distribution D over B in **MajoGame** is replaced by the uniform distribution U over X in **Subsamp-Boost**, $D(x)$ in the weight-update rule $W_t(x) := D(x)\alpha_t(r)$ of **MajoGame** is dropped in that of **SubsampBoost**. By definition, in **SubsampBoost**, $X_t(r)$ is rewritten as $\{x \in X \mid |\{t' \in \{1, \ldots, t-1\} \mid h_{t'}(x) = f(x)\} | = r\}$. Given round t's indices $I_t \in [N]^{N_0}$ and sample $S = ((x_1, f(x_1)), \ldots, (x_N, f(x_N)))$, the subsample of S consisting of examples corresponding to I_t is denoted by $S(I_t)$. The collection of such sets of indices over all the rounds is denoted by $I \in [N]^{N_0 T}$, whereas the collection of corresponding subsamples is denoted by $S_I = (S(I_1), \ldots, S(I_T))$. Because **WeakLearn** is assumed to be deterministic, $S(I_1), \ldots, S(I_T)$ uniquely determine weak hypotheses $h_1, \ldots, h_T$, respectively. Therefore, sample S and the collection of indices $I = (I_1, \ldots, I_T)$ determine the final hypothesis $\mathrm{MAJ}(h_1, \ldots, h_T)$, which will be denoted by $h_{S,I}$. Recall that examples of the sample S are drawn independently from the domain B according to distribution D before the first round and that indices of collec-

SubsampBoost

Draw N examples from B independently according to D to form sample

$$S = ((x_1, f(x_1)), \cdots, (x_N, f(x_N))).$$

Set T to be the smallest integer satisfying

$$\sum_{j=0}^{\lfloor \frac{T}{2} \rfloor} \binom{T}{j} \left(\frac{1}{2} + \gamma\right)^i \left(\frac{1}{2} - \gamma\right)^{T-i} < \frac{1}{N}.$$

for $t \in \{1, \cdots, T\}$ **do**

1. Choose W_t such that

$$W_t(x) = \alpha_t(r).$$

for $r \in \{0, 1, \cdots, t-1\}$ and $x \in X_t(r)$.

2. Draw $I_t \in [N]^{N_0}$ according to $\bar{W}_t$.

3. $h_t := \mathbf{WeakLearn}(S(I_t), \bar{W}_t);$

Output $h := \mathrm{MAJ}(h_1, \cdots, h_T)$.

FIGURE 4   Subsampling boosting algorithm corresponding to the majority-vote game. $S(I_t)$ denotes the subsample of S consisting of examples corresponding to indices in I_t.

tions $I_1, \ldots, I_T$ are drawn independently from $[N]$ according to distributions $\bar{W}_1, \ldots, \bar{W}_T$, respectively. When we consider these as the random variables, S, $I = (I_1, \ldots, I_T)$, and I_t are written as $\mathbf{S}$, $\mathbf{I}$, and $\mathbf{I}_t$, respectively. Similarly, the final hypothesis determined by random variables $\mathbf{S}$ and $\mathbf{I}$ is written as $h\mathbf{S},\mathbf{I}$, which is also a random variable. It should be noted that $\mathbf{S}$ corresponds to distribution D^N, whereas $\mathbf{I}$ relies not only on D^N but also on $\bar{W}_t$ for $1 \leq t \leq T$. Thus, we may think that a pair $(S, I) \in B^N \times [N]^{N_0 T}$ is drawn according a certain distribution.

As mentioned previously, **WeakLearn** yields a hypothesis h_t using a subsample $S(\mathbf{I}_t)$ drawn randomly out of the whole sample S. Therefore, it is not reasonable to assume that hypothesis h_t produced by **WeakLearn** is γ-weak with respect to $\bar{W}_t$ with absolute certainty. However, for ease of explanation, we make that assumption. This is because we can verify that if we let **WeakLearn** rerun an appropriate number of times, then at least one of the hypotheses obtained this way is γ-weak with sufficiently high probability, provided that **WeakLearn** produces γ-weak hypothesis with a certain constant probability. In fact, knowing $S = ((x_1, f(x)), \ldots, (x_N, f(x_N)))$ and $\bar{W}_t$, we can find a γ-weak hypothesis, if it exists, from these hypotheses that **WeakLearn** returns.

By theorem 2 and the condition required on T in **SubsampBoost**, we have

$$\mathrm{Loss} \leq \sum_{i=0}^{\lfloor T/2 \rfloor} \binom{T}{i} (\tfrac{1}{2} + \gamma)^i (\tfrac{1}{2} - \gamma)^{T-i} < \frac{1}{N}.$$

On the other hand, because our distribution U is uniform over X, we have

$$\text{Loss} = \frac{1}{N} \left| \left\{ x_i \in X \; \middle| \; \sum_{t=1}^{T} [\![h_t(x_i) = f(x_i)]\!] \leq \left\lfloor \frac{T}{2} \right\rfloor \right\} \right|$$

$$< \frac{1}{N},$$

and, hence, for any $x_i \in X$,

$$\sum_{t=1}^{T} [\![h_t(x_i) = f(x_i)]\!] > \left\lfloor \frac{T}{2} \right\rfloor,$$

which implies that for any $x_i \in X$,

$$h(x_i) = \text{MAJ}(h_1(x_i), \ldots, h_T(x_i))$$
$$= f(x_i),$$

where we define $[\![E]\!]$ to be 1 if E holds, and 0 otherwise. Thus, we have the following theorem.

Theorem 4 *If all the hypotheses h_t's that* **WeakLearn** *returns are γ-weak with respect to $\bar{W}_t$, then the final hypothesis that* **SubsampBoost** *produces is consistent with the sample S.*

Theorem 4 states that if all of the hypotheses that **WeakLearn** returns are γ-weak, then the final hypothesis that **SubsampBoost** yields is consistent, namely its training error is zero. Theorem 5 states that if the number of examples in the sample is sufficiently large, then, with a sufficiently large probability, the generalization error of the final hypothesis is sufficiently small. Thus, we can say that **SubsampBoost** "boosts" weak hypotheses to a strong hypothesis in the sense of the PAC model. The statement of Theorem 5 stems from the fact that only an exponentially small fraction of the examples in the sample are actually used by **WeakLearn** in **SubsampBoost**. In fact, because we only need to run the subsampling boosting for $T \geq (\frac{1}{2}\gamma^2) \ln(\frac{1}{2}\varepsilon)$ rounds with $\varepsilon = 1/N$, the number of examples used by **WeakLearn** during the entire T rounds is given by $N_0 T = O(\log N)$, provided that **WeakLearn** uses the constant number of examples N_0 in each round.

Before proceeding to proving theorem 5, we give an intuitive idea behind the proof of the theorem. Assume that the number T of rounds is "large," so that the final hypothesis h that the subsampling boosting produces is consistent with random sample **S**. Only $O(\log N)$ examples in **S** are used by **WeakLearn** to yield a consistent final hypothesis, and the rest of the examples in **S** have to be consistent with the final hypothesis. Therefore, most of the examples in **S** have to escape from falling in the error region written as $\{ x \in B \mid h(x) \neq f(x) \}$. This is possible only when the probability that an example drawn according to D falls in the error region is "small." In other words, this is the case that the generalization error of the final hypothesis [i.e., $D(\{ x \in B \mid h(x) \neq f(x) \})$], is "small." This is what we want to verify.

Theorem 5 *Assume that using a subsample of length N_0* **WeakLearn** *produces a γ-weak hypothesis which is uniquely determined by the subsample. Then, there exists a constant $k_0 > 0$ such that for any $\varepsilon, \delta > 0$ if*

$$N \geq k_0 \left\{ \left[\frac{1}{\varepsilon} \ln\left(\frac{1}{\delta}\right) + \frac{N_0}{\varepsilon \gamma^2} \left[\ln\left(\frac{N_0}{\varepsilon \gamma^2}\right) \right] \right] \right\},$$

then

$$\Pr[\mathrm{error}(h\mathbf{S}_{,\mathbf{I}}) > \varepsilon] < \delta,$$

where N is the size of the sample $\mathbf{S}$.

Proof. Assume that sample S and sequence $I \in [N]^{N_0 T}$ of indices are arbitrarily chosen. By the assumption of the theorem, sample S together with sequence I determines uniquely the final hypothesis denoted by $h_{S,I}$. By Theorem 4 and the assumption that **WeakLearn** produces a γ-weak hypothesis, the final hypothesis $h_{S,I}$ is consistent with the sample S. If the sample is considered as the random variable $\mathbf{S}$, then the corresponding final hypothesis becomes the random variable denoted $h_{\mathbf{S},I}$, which will be given as follows. A sequence of indices I is divided into T subsequences $I_1, \ldots, I_T$, each having length N_0, namely $I = (I_1, \ldots, I_T)$. Let the subsample of $\mathbf{S}$ corresponding to I_t be denoted by $\mathbf{S}(I_t)$ for $1 \leq t \leq T$. Then, subsamples $\mathbf{S}(I_1), \ldots, \mathbf{S}(I_T)$ specify T weak hypotheses, which we denote by $h_1, \ldots, h_T$, suppressing the subsamples $\mathbf{S}(I_1), \ldots, \mathbf{S}(I_T)$ in the notation. Then, the hypothesis $h_{\mathbf{S},I}$ is given by $\mathrm{MAJ}(h_1, \ldots, h_T)$, where MAJ is defined as

$$MAJ(h_1, \ldots, h_T)(x) = \begin{cases} 1 & \text{if } |\{t \in [T] \mid h_t(x) = 1\}| \geq \dfrac{T}{2} \\ 0 & \text{otherwise.} \end{cases}$$

We shall prove that the probability that the generalization error of $h_{\mathbf{S},I}$ is larger than ε is less than δ, namely $\Pr[\mathrm{error}(h_{\mathbf{S},I}) > \varepsilon] < \delta$. Denoting by $P(S, I)$ the probability that a pair of S and $I = (I_1, \ldots, I_T)$ is chosen in **SubsampBoost**, $\Pr[\mathrm{error}(h_{\mathbf{S},I}) > \varepsilon]$ is written as $\Sigma_{S,I} [\mathrm{error}(h_{S,I}) > \varepsilon] P(S, I)$, where the summation is over $S \in \{(x, f(x)) \mid x \in B\}^N$ and $I \in [N]^{N_0 T}$. On the other hand, Theorem 4 states that we only need to take the summation over S and I such that $h_{S,I}$ is consistent with S. Let us denote such a summation by $\Sigma_{S,I:\mathrm{consist.}}$. Then, denoting by $P(I \mid S)$ the conditional probability of I given S, we have

$$\Pr[\mathrm{error}(h\mathbf{S},\mathbf{I}) > \varepsilon] = \sum_{S,I:\mathrm{consist.}} [\mathrm{error}(hS,I) > \varepsilon] P(S, I)$$

$$= \sum_{S,I:\mathrm{consist.}} [\mathrm{error}(hS,I) > \varepsilon] P(S) P(I \mid S)$$

$$\leq \sum_{S,I:\mathrm{consist.}} [\mathrm{error}(hS,I) > \varepsilon] P(S)$$

$$= \sum_{I} \sum_{S:\mathrm{consist.}} [\mathrm{error}(hS,I) > \varepsilon] P(S)$$

$$= \sum_{I} \Pr[\text{``}\mathrm{error}(h\mathbf{S},I) > \varepsilon\text{'' and ``}h\mathbf{S},I \text{ is consistent with } \mathbf{S}\text{''}],$$

where $[E]$ is defined to be 1 if E holds, and 0 otherwise. The above inequality comes from the fact that $P(S, I) = P(S)P(I \mid S) \leq P(S)$ holds for any sample S and sequence I. Let $I \in [N]^{N_0 T}$ be fixed arbitrarily. Then, hypothesis $h_{\mathbf{S},I}$ is completely determined by $\mathbf{S}(I)$. Therefore, we can upper bound the probability as follows:

$$\Pr[\text{``}\mathrm{error}(h\mathbf{S}_{,I}) > \varepsilon\text{'' and ``}h\mathbf{S},I \text{ is consistent with } \mathbf{S}\text{''}]$$

$$= \sum_{S' \in B^{N_0 T}} \Pr[\mathbf{S}(I) = S'] \Pr[\text{``}\mathrm{error}(h\mathbf{S},I) > \varepsilon\text{''}}$$

and "$h\mathbf{S}\,I$ is consistent with $\mathbf{S}([N] - I)$" $\mid \mathbf{S}(I) = S'$]

$$\leq (1 - \varepsilon)N^{-}N^{0}T,$$

where, for brevity of notation, we denote the set of subsamples S''s by $B^{N_0 T}$ rather than $\{(x, f(x)) \mid x \in B\}^{N_0 T}$. This is because regardless of what subsample $S' \in B^{N_0 T}$ is, the following holds: Under the condition that $\mathbf{S}(I) = S'$, if "error$(h_{S,I}) > \varepsilon$" holds, then the probability that an example in $\mathbf{S}$ with indices outside I falls in the set $\{x \in B \mid h_{S,I}(x) = f(x)\}$ (i.e., "$h_{S,I}$" is consistent with the example) is at most $1 - \varepsilon$. Note that hypothesis $h_{S,I}$ varies according to $\mathbf{S}(I)$, but the above statement still holds. Because I ranges over $[N]^{N_0 T}$, we have

$$\sum_I \text{Pr}[\text{``error}(h_{S,I}) > \varepsilon\text{'' and ``}h_{S,I} \text{ is consistent with } \mathbf{S}\text{''}]$$
$$\leq N^{N_0 T}(1 - \varepsilon)^{N - N_0 T}.$$

By elementary calculations (15), we can show that there exists a constant k_0 such that for any $\varepsilon, \delta > 0$, if

$$N \geq k_0 \left[\frac{1}{\varepsilon} \ln\left(\frac{1}{\delta} \right) + \frac{N_0}{\varepsilon\gamma^2} \ln\left(\frac{N_0}{\varepsilon\delta^2} \right) \right],$$

then

$$N^{N_0 T}(1 - \varepsilon)^{N - N_0 T} < \delta,$$

where we set $T = \ln(N/2) (2\gamma^2)^{-1}$. Thus, we have

$$\text{Pr}[\text{error}(h\mathbf{S},\mathbf{I}) > \varepsilon] < \delta$$

for N satisfying the inequality of the theorem.

REPEATED GAME AND MINMAX STRATEGY

We begin by reviewing briefly a basic part of game theory that we use to study our problems from learning theory (16). We consider two-person games which are played by two players, called the row player and the column player. The game is specified in terms of a *loss matrix* $\mathbf{M}$. In the game, when the row player chooses a row i and the column player chooses a column j, the loss that the row player suffers is given by the entry $\mathbf{M}(i, j)$ of the loss matrix. The row player's goal is to minimize its loss, whereas the column player's goal is to maximize this loss. To explain how the row player's goal is achieved, choose the largest loss in each row and associate them with the corresponding rows. The row player chooses the row that is associated with the smallest of the largest losses chosen. Clearly, this is the best choice for the row player, provided that the column player plays so as to maximize the loss. This is the minmax strategy for the game in which the players choose a single row or column.

Figure 5 illustrates an example of a loss matrix. In the column labeled with max$_j$, are the largest losses associated with each row. In this case, the row player chooses the second row with the smallest of the largest losses chosen, i.e., 4 in this case. The largest losses associated with each row i is written as max$_j$ $\mathbf{M}(i, j)$; thus, the smallest of the

	1	2	3	$\max_j$
1	3	4	5	5
2	1	3	4	4
3	6	5	2	6
$\min_i$	1	3	2	

FIGURE 5   An example of a loss matrix.

largest losses chosen is written as $\min_i \max_j \mathbf{M}(i, j)$, which takes the value of 4 in this case.

By a synmetrix argument, we can think of the strategy in which the column player chooses the column that has the largest of the smallest losses of each column. In Figure 5, the smallest losses of each column are given in the row labeled with $\min_i$. This strategy is called a *maxmin strategy*, whose loss is written as $\max_j \min_i \mathbf{M}(i, j)$, which takes the value of 3 in our case. It is easy to see that, in general, we have for any loss matrix $\mathbf{M}$,

$$\min_i \max_j \mathbf{M}(i, \ j) \geq \max_j \min_i \mathbf{M}(i, \ j).$$

in the case of the loss matrix given in Figure 5, for instance, we have $\min_i \max_j \mathbf{M}(i, j) = 4 \geq \max_j \min_i \mathbf{M}(i, j) = 3$. One may say that the reason why the maxmin strategy achieves the smaller loss as compared to the minmax strategy is that in the former strategy, the row player, whose goal is to minimize its loss, can take advantage of playing after knowing the column player's choice.

So far, we considered the case where the players choose a single row or column. Von Neumann's well-known minmax theorem states the surprising fact that if we allow the choice of the players to be randomized, then the loss of the minmax strategy is equal to that of the maxmin strategy. For ease of explanation, we use a few assumptions. Because a simple scaling leads to a more general case, we assume that all of the entries in a loss matrix is in the range [0, 1]. We also assume that the number of rows or columns is finite so that we can take the maximum or the minimum over all probability distributions over columns or rows without making any further assumptions. Most of the results, however, can be generalized with mild additional assumptions to the infinite cases. In a randomized game, the players choose a probability distribution over rows or over columns rather than a single row or column. Distribution $\mathbf{P}$ over rows chosen by the row player indicates that the probability of each row i being selected is given by $\mathbf{P}(i)$. Similarly, distribution $\mathbf{Q}$ chosen by the column player indicates that the probability of each column j is given by $\mathbf{Q}(j)$. These distributions $\mathbf{P}$ and $\mathbf{Q}$ are called strategies because they specify how the players behave. When we deal with randomized games, the loss is given by the expected loss, which is written as

$$\sum_{i,j} \mathbf{P}(i)\mathbf{M}(i, \ j)\mathbf{Q}(j) = \mathbf{P}^T\mathbf{M}\mathbf{Q}.$$

When the players choose a single row or column deterministically, the corresponding strategy is called a *pure strategy*. In other words, a pure strategy is a distribution $\mathbf{P}$ such that $\mathbf{P}(i) = 1$ for some i and $\mathbf{P}(j) = 0$ for any $j \neq i$. On the other hand, a distribution over rows or columns with no restriction is called a *mixed strategy*. For ease of notation, the expected loss $\Sigma_{i,j} \mathbf{P}(i)\mathbf{M}(i,j)\mathbf{Q}(j)$ is denoted by $\mathbf{M}(\mathbf{P}, \mathbf{Q})$. In particular, when one player uses a pure strategy and the other a mixed strategy, the expected loss $\mathbf{M}(\mathbf{P}, \mathbf{Q})$ is denoted by $\mathbf{M}(\mathbf{P}, j)$ or $\mathbf{M}(i, \mathbf{Q})$. For example, $\mathbf{M}(\mathbf{P}, j) = \Sigma_i \mathbf{P}(i, j)\mathbf{M}(i, j)$.

We are now ready to generalize the minmax and maxmin strategies for the deterministic case to ones for the randomized case. As for the minmax strategy, suppose that fist the row player chooses a mixed strategy $\mathbf{P}$ and then, taking advantage of knowing the chosen strategy $\mathbf{P}$, the column player chooses a mixed strategy $\mathbf{Q}$. Given a distribution $\mathbf{P}$, the maximum loss obtained by varying the column player's strategy $\mathbf{Q}$ is written as $\max_{\mathbf{Q}} \mathbf{M}(\mathbf{P}, \mathbf{Q})$. A *minmax strategy* for the randomized case is the one that minimizes this quantity $\max_{\mathbf{Q}} \mathbf{M}(\mathbf{P}, \mathbf{Q})$ over distributions $\mathbf{P}$; that is, the minmax strategy, denoted $\mathbf{P}^*$, is defined by

$$\mathbf{P}^* = \arg \min_{\mathbf{P}} \max_{\mathbf{Q}} \mathbf{M}(\mathbf{P}, \mathbf{Q}).$$

Putting it another way, the minmax strategy $\mathbf{P}^*$ is a strategy that satisfies

$$\max_{\mathbf{Q}} \mathbf{M}(\mathbf{P}^*, \mathbf{Q}) = \min_{\mathbf{P}} \max_{\mathbf{Q}} \mathbf{M}(\mathbf{P}, \mathbf{Q}).$$

We can argue the symmetric case where first the column player chooses a mixed strategy $\mathbf{Q}$, and then the row player, knowing the chosen strategy $\mathbf{Q}$, chooses a mixed strategy $\mathbf{P}$, each pursuing its own goal. We define the *maxmin strategy* to be the one that maximizes $\min_{\mathbf{P}} \mathbf{M}(\mathbf{P}, \mathbf{Q})$ over distributions $\mathbf{Q}$. Thus, denoting the maxmin strategy by $\mathbf{Q}^*$, we have

$$\min_{\mathbf{P}} \mathbf{M}(\mathbf{P}, \mathbf{Q}^*) = \max_{\mathbf{Q}} \min_{\mathbf{P}} \mathbf{M}(\mathbf{P}, \mathbf{Q}).$$

Clearly, $\mathbf{M}(\mathbf{P}, \mathbf{Q}) \leq \max_{\mathbf{Q}} \mathbf{M}(\mathbf{P}, \mathbf{Q})$ holds for any distributions $\mathbf{P}$ and $\mathbf{Q}$. Applying $\min_{\mathbf{P}}$ to both sides of this inequality, we have $\min_{\mathbf{P}} \mathbf{M}(\mathbf{P}, \mathbf{Q}) \leq \min_{\mathbf{P}} \max_{\mathbf{Q}} \mathbf{M}(\mathbf{P}, \mathbf{Q})$, which implies $\max_{\mathbf{Q}} \min_{\mathbf{P}} \mathbf{M}(\mathbf{P}, \mathbf{Q}) \leq \min_{\mathbf{P}} \max_{\mathbf{Q}} \mathbf{M}(\mathbf{P}, \mathbf{Q})$. As we noted earlier, there exists a loss matrix $\mathbf{M}$ for which the above inequality is strict when we restrict distributions $\mathbf{P}$ and $\mathbf{Q}$ to pure strategies. Von Neumann's well-known minmax theorem states that this is no longer the case when we consider all probability distributions for $\mathbf{P}$ and $\mathbf{Q}$:

$$\max_{\mathbf{Q}} \min_{\mathbf{P}} \mathbf{M}(\mathbf{P}, \mathbf{Q}) = \min_{\mathbf{P}} \max_{\mathbf{Q}} \mathbf{M}(\mathbf{P}, \mathbf{Q})$$

holds for every matrix $\mathbf{M}$. The equality of the minmax theorem can be rewritten as

$$\max_{\mathbf{Q}} \mathbf{M}(\mathbf{P}^* \mathbf{Q}) = \min_{\mathbf{P}} \mathbf{M}(\mathbf{P}, \mathbf{Q}^*).$$

So, we immediately have

$$\mathbf{M}(\mathbf{P}^*, \mathbf{Q}) \leq \mathbf{M}(\mathbf{P}, \mathbf{Q}^*)$$

for any distributions $\mathbf{P}$ and $\mathbf{Q}$. Restricting the strategies to pure strategies, we therefore have

$$\mathbf{M}(\mathbf{P}^*, j) \leq \mathbf{M}(i, \mathbf{Q}^*)$$

for any row i and column j, which will be referred to later.

We see that many problems from learning theory, such as on-line prediction and boosting, can be formulated based on the game-theoretic model. Letting the learner play as the row player and the adversary as the column player, we consider the game specified by a loss matrix $\mathbf{M}$. The learner tries to choose the strategy $\mathbf{P}$ over the rows to minimize the loss, whereas the adversary returns the strategy $\mathbf{Q}$ over the columns in a way unknown to the learner. When we apply the game model to problems from learning theory, we have to consider a few problems which we did not face so far in discussing the game-theoretic issues. First, the loss matrix $\mathbf{M}$ may not be known for the learner. Therefore, the learner who is not permitted to observe the entire matrix $\mathbf{M}$ has to somehow obtain information about matrix $\mathbf{M}$ during the process of the game. Second, the adversary does not necessarily try to maximize the loss, whereas the goal of the learner is to minimize the loss. Therefore, although the best thing for the learner to do is to choose the minmax strategy $\mathbf{P}^*$ as long as the adversary chooses the maxmin strategy $\mathbf{Q}^*$, it might happen that the learner could choose $\mathbf{P}'$ rather than $\mathbf{P}^*$ such that $\mathbf{M}(\mathbf{P}', \mathbf{Q}')$ is significantly smaller than $\mathbf{M}(\mathbf{P}^*, \mathbf{Q}^*)$ when the adversary who is not truly adversarial chooses $\mathbf{Q}'$.

These considerations lead us to the notion of the repeated game, denoted **Repea-Game**, which is given in Figure 6. The game is specified by a matrix $\mathbf{M}$ with n rows and m columns which are not known to the learner. For the repeated game, the row player corresponds to the learner, and the column player corresponds to the environment. The game is played repeatedly in a sequence of T rounds. Its scheme is described as follows. In round $t = 1, \ldots, T$, the following three steps are done sequentially:

1. The learner chooses strategy $\mathbf{P}_t$.
2. The environment chooses $\mathbf{Q}_t$.
3. The learner updates $\mathbf{P}_t$ to obtain $\mathbf{P}_{t+1}$ by observing the loss $\mathbf{M}(i, \mathbf{Q}_t)$ for each row i.

How to update the strategy, $\mathbf{P}_t$ is left unspecified in the above scheme. It is only through observing $\mathbf{M}(i, \mathbf{Q})$ in Step 3 that the learner can obtain (partial) information on $\mathbf{M}$. The (learner's) loss of the game is defined to be the cumulative loss over the rounds, which is given by

$$\sum_{t=1}^{T} \mathbf{M}(\mathbf{P}_t, \mathbf{Q}_t).$$

The goal of the learner is to make the loss as small as possible no matter what sequence of strategies $\mathbf{Q}_1, \ldots, \mathbf{Q}_T$ the environment returns through the rounds. So, we must evalu-

RepeaGame

> **for** $i \in \{1, \cdots, n\}$ **do**
>
> $\quad \boldsymbol{w}_1(i) := 1;$
>
> **for** $t \in \{1, \cdots, T\}$ **do**
>
> $\quad$ **for** $i \in \{1, \cdots, n\}$ **do**
>
> $\quad\quad \mathbf{P}_t(i) := \bar{\boldsymbol{w}}_t(i);$
>
> $\quad\quad \boldsymbol{w}_{t+1}(i) := \boldsymbol{w}_t(i) \cdot \beta^{\mathbf{M}(i,\mathbf{Q}_t)}$

FIGURE 6   Algorithm playing the repeated game associated with matrix $\mathbf{M}$ with n rows.

ate the performance of the learner in terms of the loss relative to the strategies $\mathbf{Q}_1, \dots, \mathbf{Q}_T$ that the environment actually returns. To specify the repeated game, all we have to do is to describe how to update the strategy $\mathbf{P}_t$. The crucial point in **RepeaGame** is that for the weight update, the learner maintains a weight for each row of the matrix. The weight for row i on round t is denoted by $\mathbf{w}_t(i)$. Initially all the weights are set to unity. In each round t, the learner updates the weight by the multiplicative rule given by

$$\mathbf{w}_{t+1}(i) := \mathbf{w}_t(i)\beta^{\mathbf{M}(i, \mathbf{Q}_t)}$$

for each row i, where the parameter $0 < \beta < 1$ will be specified later. Note that the learner can do the update because it is assumed that he obtained the quantity of $\mathbf{M}(i, \mathbf{Q}_t)$. Theorem 6 states that no matter what strategies $\mathbf{Q}_1, \dots, \mathbf{Q}_T$ the environment returns, the cumulative loss $\Sigma_{t=1}^T \mathbf{M}(\mathbf{P}_t, \mathbf{Q})$ determined by strategies $\mathbf{P}_t, \dots, \mathbf{P}_T$ that **RepeaGame** produces can be made arbitrarily close to the loss of the *best strategy* written as

$$\min_{\mathbf{P}} \sum_{t=1}^T \mathbf{M}(\mathbf{P}, \mathbf{Q}_t).$$

Theorem 6 *Let* $\mathbf{M}$ *be a loss matrix that specifies* **RepeaGame**. *Furthermore, let* $\mathbf{Q}_1, \dots, \mathbf{Q}_T$ *be a sequence of strategies returned by the environment and* $\mathbf{P}_1, \dots, \mathbf{P}_T$ *be the sequence of strategies produced by* **RepeaGame** *for the environment's strategies. Then, if* β *is set to*

$$\frac{1}{1 + \sqrt{(2 \ln n/T,}}$$

then

$$\frac{1}{T} \sum_{t=1}^T \mathbf{M}(\mathbf{P}_t, \mathbf{Q}_t) \le \min_{\mathbf{P}} \frac{1}{T} \sum_{t=1}^T \mathbf{M}(\mathbf{P}, \mathbf{Q}_t) + \Delta_T,$$

where

$$\Delta_T = O\left(\sqrt{\frac{\ln n}{T}}\right).$$

Proof. For $t = 1, \dots, T$, we have

$$\sum_{i=1}^n \mathbf{w}_{t+1}(i) = \left(\sum_{i=1}^n \mathbf{w}_t(i)\right)\beta^{\mathbf{M}(i, \mathbf{Q}_t)}$$

$$\le \left(\sum_{i=1}^n \mathbf{w}_t(i)\right)[1 - (1 - \beta)\mathbf{M}(i, \mathbf{Q}_t)]$$

(by $\beta^x \le 1 - (1 - \beta)x$ for $\beta > 0$ and $0 \le x \le 1$)

$$= \left(\sum_{i=1}^n \mathbf{w}_t(i)\right)[1 - (1 - \beta)\mathbf{M}(\mathbf{P}_t, \mathbf{Q}_t)]$$

(by the definition of $\mathbf{P}_t$).

Because $\mathbf{w}_1(i) = 1$, unwrapping this recurrence gives

$$\sum_{i=1}^{n} w_{T+1}(i) \leq n \prod_{t=1}^{T} [1 - (1 - \beta)\mathbf{M}(\mathbf{P}_t, \mathbf{Q}_t)].$$

On the other hand, we have for any $1 \leq j \leq n$,

$$\sum_{i=1}^{n} w_{T+1}(i) \geq w_{T+1}(j) = \beta^{\sum_{t=1}^{T} \mathbf{M}(j, \mathbf{Q}_t)}.$$

By combining these inequalities and taking logs we have

$$\ln(\beta)\left(\sum_{t=1}^{T} \mathbf{M}(j, \mathbf{Q}_t)\right) \leq \ln n + \sum_{t=1}^{T} \ln[1 - (1 - \beta)\mathbf{M}(\mathbf{P}_t, \mathbf{Q}_t)]$$

$$\leq \ln n - (1 - \beta)\sum_{t=1}^{T} \mathbf{M}(\mathbf{P}_t, \mathbf{Q}_t)$$

$$(\text{by } \ln(1 - x) \leq -x \text{ for } x < 1)$$

for any $1 \leq j \leq n$ which, in virtue of the lemma in the Appendix, can be rewritten as

$$\sum_{t=1}^{T} \mathbf{M}(\mathbf{P}_t, \mathbf{Q}_t) \leq \frac{\ln(1/\beta)\sum_{t=1}^{T} \mathbf{M}(\mathbf{P}_t, \mathbf{Q}_t) + \ln n}{1 - \beta}$$

$$\leq \sum_{t=1}^{T} \mathbf{M}(j, \mathbf{Q}_t) + 3\sqrt{\frac{T \ln n}{2}} + \ln n.$$

This completes the proof because these inequalities hold for any j and the strategy that achieves the minimum in the bound of the theorem must be a pure strategy j; that is, $\min_{\mathbf{P}} \Sigma_{t=1}^{T} \mathbf{M}(\mathbf{P}, \mathbf{Q}_t) = \min_j \Sigma_{t=1}^{T} \mathbf{M}(j, \mathbf{Q}_t)$. □

ON-LINE PREDICTION AND BOOSTING BASED ON REPEATED GAME

On-line prediction and boosting are seemingly different topics, and hence have different motivations in the context of learning. The algorithms to solve these problems, however, turn out to have the same computational schema behind them (16). In the two subsections of this section, we present two algorithms to solve these problems in their simplest form and show that these algorithms can be thought of as variants of the same algorithm playing the repeated game.

On-Line Prediction as Repeated Game

An on-line prediction algorithm is one that makes, depending on past observations, binary prediction in a sequence of rounds (16). More specifically, the on-line prediction proceeds in a sequence of rounds as follows. In round $1 \leq t \leq T$:

1. The learner observes an instance $x_t \in X$;
2. The learner makes a randomized prediction $\hat{y}_t \in \{0, 1\}$ for x_t's label;
3. The learner observes the correct label, denoted $f(x_t) \in \{0, 1\}$, for the x_t,

where X is a finite set of instances. Let the correct label for an instance x be given by $f(x)$, where f is a target function from X to $\{0, 1\}$. The learner keeps a finite set of hypotheses $h : X \rightarrow \{0, 1\}$ which is denoted by H. When the learner makes a prediction, he first chooses a hypothesis h in H according to a certain distribution over H and makes the prediction $h(x)$ for the instance x given (by the environment). The goal of the learner is to minimize the expected number of mistakes it makes relative to the number of mistakes the best hypothesis in H makes throughout the rounds.

To get an idea about how to reduce the on-line prediction to a special case of the repeated game, let us consider an example of weather forecast. In this case, X is taken to be a set of weather measurements and H is taken to be a set of rules for the weather forecast. We make no assumption about the relationship between the weather measurement x_t and the actual weather outcome $f(x_t)$ (e.g., either raining or not raining). In fact, unlike the actual weather forecast, the learner does not take into account measurement x_t, but just outputs $\hat{y}_t = h_t(x_t)$, where h_t is drawn according to distribution $\mathbf{P}_t$ over H produced by the learner. To specify the distribution $\mathbf{P}_t$, the learner maintains a weight for each hypothesis in H and updates the weights so that good hypotheses are more likely to be chosen. The corresponding game matrix $\mathbf{M}$ has $|H|$ rows, indexed by $h \in H$ and $|X|$ columns, indexed by $x \in X$. The matrix $\mathbf{M}$ is defined by

$$\mathbf{M}(h, x) = \begin{cases} 1 & \text{if } h(x) \neq f(x) \\ 0 & \text{otherwise} \end{cases}$$

for $h \in H$ and $x \in X$.

It is easy to see that if we only add a statement to **RepeaGame** that indicates how to make prediction in each round, then we can immediately obtain an on-line algorithm for the prediction. Let $x_1, \ldots, x_T$ be a sequence of instances produced by the environment in the context of the game-theoretic model. These $x_1, \ldots, x_T$ correspond to $\mathbf{Q}_1, \ldots, \mathbf{Q}_T$, respectively, so, in this case, the environment is supposed to yield pure strategies. Setting $\mathbf{P}_t = w_t$ as in **RepeaGame**, the learner makes the prediction given by

$$\hat{y}_t = h_t(x_t),$$

where h_t is drawn according to distribution $\mathbf{P}_t$. The update rule $w_{t+1}(i) := w_t(i)\beta^{\mathbf{M}(i, \mathbf{Q}_t)}$ in **RepeaGame** can be rewritten in this case as follows:

$$w_{t+1}(h) = \begin{cases} w_t(h)\beta & \text{if } h(x_t) \neq f(x_t) \\ w_t(h) & \text{otherwise,} \end{cases}$$

where β is assumed to be specified as indicated in Theorem 6. It should be noted that the learner needs to know the value of $f(x_t)$ as well as that of $h(x_t)$ only when he updates the weights according to the above rule. Because $0 < \beta < 1$, the weight of the bad hypothesis h that yields the wrong prediction $h(x_t)$ in round t is decreased by the weight-update rule so that good hypotheses rather than bad hypotheses are more likely to be chosen in the next round $t + 1$. Because

$$\mathbf{M}(\mathbf{P}_t, x_t) = \sum_{h \in H} \mathbf{P}(h)\mathbf{M}(h, x_t)$$
$$= \Pr_{h \sim \mathbf{P}_t}[h(x_t) \neq f(x_t)]$$
$$= \Pr[\hat{y}_t \neq f(x_t)]$$

holds, the loss in round t can be interpreted as the probability of the learner making a mistake in the round. Therefore, by Theorem 6, the expected number of mistakes made by the learner throughout all the rounds is given by

$$\sum_{t=1}^{T} \mathbf{M}(\mathbf{P}_t, x_t) \leq \min_{h \in H} \sum_{t=1}^{T} \mathbf{M}(h, x_t) + O(\sqrt{T \ln |H|}).$$

The above inequality states that the amount by which the expected number of mistakes made by the learner exceeds that of the best hypothesis in H is bounded by $O(\sqrt{T \ln |H|})$.

Boosting as Repeated Game

We move on to the next topic: boosting. Boosting is a method of forming a highly accurate hypothesis by combining many moderately accurate hypotheses called "weak" hypotheses. It is surprising to see that there exists the common computational scheme behind the boosting and the on-line prediction which seemingly looks quite different from each other (16). In fact, the boosting algorithm and the on-line prediction algorithm can both be thought of as variants of the repeated game with the same multiplicative weight-update rule.

    We first explain the underlying basic idea behind the boosting algorithm referring to the minmax theorem and then extend the arguments to describe how to transform the idea into the actual algorithm based on the repeated game. Performance of the resultant boosting algorithm will be analyzed again using Theorem 6.

    When we refer to the repeated game, we adhere to our convention that the learner plays as the row player so as to minimize the loss, whereas the environment plays as the column player in a way that the learner cannot control. Suppose that we are somehow given a collection of instances X, each corresponding to a row of a game matrix, and a collection of hypotheses H, each corresponding to a column of the matrix. Therefore, rows of the matrix are indexed by $x \in X$ and columns are indexed by $h \in H$. The entry of the matrix for boosting is defined by

$$\mathbf{M}(x, h) = \begin{cases} 1 & \text{if } h(x) = f(x) \\ 0 & \text{otherwise,} \end{cases}$$

where f is the target function from X to $\{0, 1\}$. So each column of the matrix consists of the truth values indicating whether or not the corresponding weak hypothesis takes the correct values on the instances, whereas each row consists of the truth values indicating whether or not the weak hypotheses take the correct values in the corresponding instance.

    There are obvious differences between the game matrix for boosting and that for on-line prediction. First, the roles of rows and columns for boosting are reversed compared to those for on-line prediction. We can see that the reversed correspondence is relevant if we note that what the environment chooses is a weak hypothesis in the case of boosting, whereas it is an instance in the case of on-line prediction. In fact, a column of the game matrix is the truth values of a hypothesis in the instances in the former case, whereas it is the correctness of the hypotheses in an instance in the latter case. Another point of difference is that an entry of the matrix is set to 1 when $h(x) = f(x)$ holds in the case of boosting, whereas that happens when $h(x) \neq f(x)$ holds in the case of on-line prediction. According to the weight-update rule $w_{t+1}(i) := w_t(i)\beta^{\mathbf{M}(i, \mathbf{Q}_t)}$ with $0 < \beta < 1$, the weights for rows corresponding to the condition $h(x) = f(x)$ are decreased in the former case, whereas those corresponding to $h(x) \neq f(x)$ are decreased in the latter case. Roughly speaking, these facts mean that in the former case, distribution $\mathbf{P}_t$ is focused on the instances having been often mistaken so that such instances will have a chance to be classified correctly by later weak hypotheses, whereas in the latter case, distribution $\mathbf{P}_t$ is focused on the hypotheses with less mistakes so that these hypotheses have more of an effect in making a prediction in each round.

Let $\mathbf{P}^*$ and $\mathbf{Q}^*$ denote the minmax and maxmin strategies for matrix $\mathbf{M}$, respectively. The crucial point in analyzing the performance of the boosting algorithm is that, as the minmax theorem states, the weighted sum of elements in any row with respect to $\mathbf{Q}^*$ is equal to or larger than the weighted sum of elements in any column with respect to $\mathbf{P}^*$; that is, for any row x and any column h, we have

$$\mathbf{M}(\mathbf{P}^*, h) \leq \mathbf{M}(x, \mathbf{Q}^*).$$

Therefore, if $\frac{1}{2} + \gamma \leq \mathbf{M}(\mathbf{P}^*, h)$ for some h, then we can conclude that $\frac{1}{2} + \gamma \leq \mathbf{M}(x, \mathbf{Q}^*)$ for any row x. This can be interpreted as saying that if h is a γ-weak hypothesis with respect to $\mathbf{P}^*$, then the hypothesis h_{final}, defined as the weighted majority of hypotheses in H with respect to $\mathbf{Q}^*$, gives the correct output $f(x)$ for any x in X. To see this, note that the weighted majority of hypotheses with respect to $\mathbf{Q}^*$ is defined by

$$h_{\text{final}}(x) = \begin{cases} 1 & \text{if } \Pr_{h \sim \mathbf{Q}^*}[h(x) = 1] \geq \frac{1}{2} \\ 0 & \text{otherwise.} \end{cases}$$

Then, we have

$$\frac{1}{2} + \gamma \leq \mathbf{M}(x, \mathbf{Q}^*)$$
$$= \sum_{h \in H} \mathbf{M}(x, h)\mathbf{Q}^*(h)$$
$$= \Pr_{h \sim \mathbf{Q}^*}[h(x) = f(x)]$$

for any $x \in X$.

However, as we mentioned in the section Repeated Game and Minmax Strategy, we cannot expect to have algorithms that yield the minmax and maxmin strategies. What we can have instead is the repeated game whose performance is guaranteed by Theorem 6. Because the inequality still holds if we replace $\min_\mathbf{P}$ in the inequality by $\min_{x \in X}$ and $\mathbf{Q}_t$'s by the pure strategies concentrated on the hypotheses h_t's, we have

$$\frac{1}{T} \sum_{t=1}^{T} \mathbf{M}(\mathbf{P}_t, h_t) \leq \min_{x \in X} \frac{1}{T} \sum_{t=1}^{T} \mathbf{M}(x, h_t) + \Delta_T,$$

where the $\mathbf{P}_t$'s are the strategies produced by the repeated game with the $\mathbf{Q}_t$'s being the pure strategies h_t's. Then, as it will be shown, we can develop an argument analogous to the above one based on the minmax theorem. If h_t is a γ-weak hypothesis with respect to $\mathbf{P}_t$, then we have

$$\mathbf{M}(\mathbf{P}_t, h_t) = \Pr_{x \sim \mathbf{P}}[h_t(x) = f(x)]$$
$$\geq \frac{1}{2} + \gamma$$

for any $t \in \{1, \dots, T\}$. Therefore, by the above inequality, we have

$$\tfrac{1}{2} + \gamma \le \frac{1}{T} \sum_{t=1}^{T} \mathbf{M}(\mathbf{P}_t, h_t) \le \min_{x \in X} \frac{1}{T} \sum_{t=1}^{T} \mathbf{M}(x, h_t) + \Delta_T.$$

Therefore, for any $x \in X$,

$$\frac{1}{T} \sum_{t=1}^{T} \mathbf{M}(x, h_t) \ge \tfrac{1}{2} - \gamma - \Delta_T > \tfrac{1}{2},$$

where the last inequality holds for sufficiently large T because $\Delta_T = O(\sqrt{\ln |X|/T})$. In fact, it can be verified that if we set $T = \lceil (4/\gamma^2) \ln |X| \rceil$, then $\Delta_T < \gamma$ holds (15). Analogously, the final hypothesis h_{final} for this case is written as

$$h_{\text{final}}(x) = \begin{cases} 1 & \text{if } | \{h \in H \mid h(x) = 1\} | \ge T/2 \\ 0 & \text{otherwise,} \end{cases}$$

which is alternatively written as $\mathrm{MAJ}(h_1, \ldots, h_T)$.

We are now ready to present the boosting algorithm **MajoBoost** based on the majority vote, which is given in Figure 7. **MajoBoost** is obtained by simply adding to **RepeaGame** the statement to call **WeakLearn** and to output the majority of the hypotheses as the final hypothesis. Note that, in this case, the multiplicative weight-update rule is rewritten as

$$\mathbf{w}_{t+1}(x) = \begin{cases} \mathbf{w}_t(x)\beta & \text{if } h_t(x) = f(x) \\ \mathbf{w}_t(x) & \text{otherwise.} \end{cases}$$

The weight associated with an instance is decreased if h_t is correct in the instance and is increased otherwise. Thus, as boosting proceeds in rounds, the distribution tends to focus on the instance more often misclassified.

MajoBoost

$T := \lceil \frac{4}{\gamma^2} \ln N \rceil;$

$\beta := \frac{1}{1 + \sqrt{\frac{2 \ln N}{T}}};$

for $x \in X$ **do**

    $\mathbf{w}_1(x) := 1;$

for $t \in \{1, \cdots, T\}$ **do**

    $h_t := \mathbf{WeakLearn}(S, \bar{\mathbf{w}}_t);$

    for $x \in X$ **do**

        $\mathbf{w}_{t+1}(x) := \mathbf{w}_t(x)\beta^{\mathbf{M}(x, h_t)};$

Output $h_{final} = \mathrm{MAJ}(h_1, \cdots, h_T).$

FIGURE 7   The boosting algorithm based on the majority vote.

ON-LINE PREDICTION USING EXPERTS' PREDICTIONS

An on-line prediction using experts' predictions, which will be called the *expert model*, is another variant of the on-line prediction discussed in the subsection On-Line Prediction as Repeated Game. Although these problems are mostly the same, technically they are different in that the loss functions introduced to measure the discrepancy between the predictions and real outcomes are more explicitly taken up in the expert model as compared to the prediction model based on hypotheses' predictions. There is a large body of work that evaluates the performance of various prediction algorithms based on various loss functions (2,17,18). In this section, we give an algorithm for the expert model that makes, for a large class of loss functions, the prediction which is "not much worse" than that of the best expert among the experts assumed (18).

The algorithm makes the prediction in a sequence of rounds, observing experts' predictions and taking the weighted average of their predictions. Because we assume that there exist N experts, each predicting a real number in $[0, 1]$, we put the instance space to be $X = [0, 1]^N$. Thus, an instance consisting of experts' predictions is given by $\boldsymbol{x}_t = (\boldsymbol{x}_t(1), \ldots, \boldsymbol{x}_t(N)) \in [0, 1]^N$, where $\boldsymbol{x}_t(i) \in [0, 1]$ denotes the prediction that the ith expert makes in round t. In each round, the learner receives the experts' predictions and makes its own prediction. After producing the prediction, the learner receives the correct output. The goal of the algorithm is to perform roughly as well as the best expert with no a priori knowledge about which expert performs the best. Performance of the algorithm is evaluated over all the rounds in terms of a loss function. The prediction proceeds in a sequence of rounds. In each round $t = 1, \ldots, T$ the following are performed sequentially:

1. The learner observes an instance $\boldsymbol{x}_t \in X$.
2. The learner makes a prediction $\hat{y}_t \in [0, 1]$ for the instance $\boldsymbol{x}_t$.
3. The learner observes the correct outcome $y_t \in \{0, 1\}$ for the instance $\boldsymbol{x}_t$.

To measure the discrepancy between predictions and actual outcomes, a number of loss functions $L : \{0, 1\} \times [0, 1] \to [0, 1]$ have been introduce in literature (2). The *square loss* function, defined as $L(y, \hat{y}) = (y - \hat{y})^2$, is such a typical function. If one wants to deal with a binary prediction and concerns about the number of mistakes that a prediction algorithm makes, then one should introduce the loss function $L : \{0, 1\} \times \{0, 1\} \to \{0, 1\}$ defined as $L(y, \hat{y}) = 1$ if $y \neq \hat{y}$ and $L(y, \hat{y}) = 0$ otherwise. On the other hand, if a prediction $\hat{y} \in [0, 1]$ is interpreted as the probability of predicting outcome 1 and $1 - \hat{y}$ as the probability of predicting outcome 0, then $|y - \hat{y}|$ is the probability that the prediction is incorrect when the actual outcome is y. In that case, we should adopt the *absolute loss function* defined as $L(y, \hat{y}) = |y - \hat{y}|$. In this way, we should choose a loss function, depending on how we evaluate the real loss incurred by the discrepancy between predictions and actual outcomes.

The total loss of predictions made by the learner or the experts is measured by the accumulated loss incurred throughout the rounds; that is, given a sample $S = ((\boldsymbol{x}_1, y_1), \ldots, (\boldsymbol{x}_T, y_T))$, the total loss for prediction algorithm A is defined by

$$L_A(S) = \sum_{t=1}^{T} L(y_t, \hat{y}_t).$$

Similarly, the total loss for the ith expert $\mathcal{E}_i$ is defined by

$$L_{\mathcal{E}_i}(S) = \sum_{t=1}^{T} L(y_t, x_t(i)).$$

In what follows, the total loss will be called simply the loss.

As in the case of the on-line prediction described so far, we evaluate the performance of prediction algorithm A by the quantity $L_A(S) - \min_i L_{\mathcal{E}_i}(S)$, which is the additional loss the algorithm incurs compared to that of the best expert. We can say that we measure the performance by the *relative loss*, but not by the "absolute" loss. Because we make no assumption on how the outcomes $y_1, \ldots, y_T$ relate to the instances $x_1, \ldots, x_T$, the relative loss is a reasonable performance measure, which we explain as follows. If we consider the extreme case where outcomes y_t are totally random, clearly the prediction algorithm cannot do better than random guessing. However, in this case, none of the experts can do well. On the other hand, if the outcomes y_t are exactly the same as the predictions made by one of the experts, the learner could note that one of the experts is doing well and might try to pay attention to that expert and mimic its predictions. These considerations lead us to adopt the relative loss as the performance measure. After all, the prediction algorithm's goal is to predict almost as well as the best expert regardless of what outcome sequence $(y_1, \ldots, y_T)$ we are given.

A large body of work has been done to show how to construct on-line prediction algorithms to achieve the goal. Among such prediction algorithms is a simplified algorithm **Predict** illustrated in Figure 8. For each expert i, the algorithm keeps a weight, denoted $w_t(i)$, which is updated so that the weight decreases exponentially as a function of the loss suffered by the expert. The constant $0 < \beta < 1$ in the update rule $w_{t+1}(i) := w_t(i)\beta^{L(y_t, x_t(i))}$ is set as in Theorem 6.

The prediction that the algorithm makes is simply the weighted average of the experts' predictions with respect to the normalized weights of the experts. The weighted average is expressed as

$$\bar{w}_t \cdot x_t = \sum_{i=1}^{N} \bar{w}_t(i)x_t(i).$$

Predict

> **for** $i \in \{1, \cdots, N\}$ **do**
>
> > $w_1(i) := 1;$
>
> **for** $t \in \{1, \cdots, T\}$ **do**
>
> > 1. Receive an instance $x_t = (x_t(1), \cdots, x_t(N))$.
> >
> > 2. Output the prediction $\hat{y}_t = \bar{w}_t \cdot x_t$.
> >
> > 3. **for** $i \in \{i, \cdots, N\}$ **do**
> >
> > > $w_{t+1}(i) := w_t(i)\beta^{L(y_t, x_t(i))}$

FIGURE 8   Prediction algorithm **Predict** based on the weighted average of experts' predictions.

We are now ready to see that the prediction algorithm can be thought of as a repeated game. In view of Theorem 6, we shall verify that the algorithm **Predict** performs roughly as well as the best expert for a large class of loss functions satisfying the *convexity* condition. Suppose that we are given N experts $\mathcal{E}_1, \ldots, \mathcal{E}_N$, each corresponding to a row of loss matrix $\mathbf{M}$, and that the prediction algorithm works through T rounds, each corresponding to a column. With the correspondence in mind, an entry $\mathbf{M}(i, t)$ of the loss matrix is specified in terms of a loss function as follows:

$$\mathbf{M}(i, t) = L(y_t, \boldsymbol{x}_t(i))$$

for $1 \leq i \leq N$ and $1 \leq t \leq T$.

In order to bound the loss of the prediction algorithm, we need to make an assumption on loss functions. Given a loss function $L(y, \hat{y})$, we can introduce the function L_y of one variable, which is defined by

$$L_y(\hat{y}) = L(y, \hat{y}).$$

The assumption we need is that the function L_y is convex; that is,

$$L\left(y, \sum_{i=1}^{N} \bar{w}(i)x(i)\right) \leq \sum_{i=1}^{N} \bar{w}(i)L(y, x(i)) \tag{3}$$

for any probability distribution $\bar{w} = (\bar{w}(1), \ldots, \bar{w}(N))$. By Theorem 6 and the convexity of the loss function, we can upper bound the loss of the prediction algorithm, denoted $L_{\mathbf{Pred}}$, as follows:

$$\frac{1}{T} L_{\mathbf{Pred}}(S) = \frac{1}{T} \sum_{t=1}^{T} L(y_t, \bar{w}_t \cdot \boldsymbol{x}_t)$$

$$= \frac{1}{T} \sum_{t=1}^{T} L\left(y_t, \sum_{i=1}^{N} \bar{w}_t(i)\boldsymbol{x}_t(i)\right)$$

$$\leq \frac{1}{T} \sum_{t=1}^{T} \sum_{i=1}^{N} \bar{w}_t(i)L(y_t, \boldsymbol{x}_t(i))$$

[by the convexity of the function $L(y_t, \cdot)$]

$$= \frac{1}{T} \sum_{t=1}^{T} \sum_{i=1}^{N} \bar{w}_t(i)\mathbf{M}(i, t)$$

[by the definition of $\mathbf{M}(i, t)$]

$$= \frac{1}{T} \sum_{t=1}^{T} \mathbf{M}(\bar{w}_t, t)$$

$$\leq \frac{1}{T} \min_{i} \sum_{t=1}^{T} M(i, t) + \Delta_T$$

(by Theorem 6 with $\mathbf{P}_t$ being replaced by $\bar{w}_t$)

$$= \frac{1}{T} \min_{i} \sum_{t=1}^{T} L(y_t, \boldsymbol{x}_t(i)) + \Delta_T$$

[by the definition of $\mathbf{M}(i, t)$]

$$= \frac{1}{T} \min_{i} L_{\mathcal{E}_i}(S) + \Delta_T.$$

Thus, we have

$$\frac{1}{T} L_{\mathbf{Pred}}(S) \le \frac{1}{T} \min_i L_{\mathcal{E}_i}(S) + \Delta_T,$$

which says that the average per-round loss suffered by the prediction algorithm is larger than that suffered by the best expert by at most Δ_T. Because $\Delta_T \to 0$ when $T \to \infty$, as shown in Theorem 6, we can conclude that if the number of the rounds is sufficiently large, then our goal of the on-line prediction is achieved by the algorithm given by Figure 8, provided that the loss function is convex. Thus, **Pred** predicts almost as well as the best expert.

ADAPTIVE BOOSTING

Boosting is a method of combining many weak hypotheses—moderately accurate hypotheses—to obtain a strong hypothesis—a highly accurate hypothesis, where weak hypotheses are produced by a weak algorithm. In this section, we present a boosting algorithm which adjusts much more adaptively to the errors of the weak hypotheses combined as compared to the boost-by-majority algorithms and, hence, overcomes the practical difficulties of the previous boosting (8,19).

There are two ways that a boosting algorithm exploits the power of the weak learning algorithm which produces weak hypotheses. First, a boosting algorithm adjusts for each round a weight for each instance after knowing the correct outcome for the instances so that the algorithm forces the weak learning algorithm to focus on harder instances. In addition to weights for instances, in each round t, a boosting algorithm may maintain weights (parameters) α_t's for weak hypotheses h_t's and adjust a weight for a weak hypothesis after computing its error so that more accurate weak hypotheses having larger weights have more influences on the final strong hypothesis. The boost-by-majority algorithms only adjust the weights for instances. In this section, we consider a more adaptive boosting algorithm, called **AdaBoost**, which adjusts not only the weights for instances but also those for weak hypotheses. "Ada" (short for "adaptive") means that the algorithm works adaptively to the error rates of the individual weak hypotheses. Because **AdaBoost** adjusts the weights both ways, it has a couple of advantages not shared by the boost-by-majority algorithm. Therefore, we can say **AdaBoost** take advantage more fully of hypotheses computed by **WeakLearn** so that the accuracy of the final hypothesis improves as any of the weak hypotheses are improved. This contrasts with the fact that the boost-by-majority algorithm cannot take advantage of weak hypotheses even when the error of some the hypotheses is significantly smaller than the presumed bias of $\frac{1}{2} - \gamma$. The boost-by-majority algorithm requires that the parameter γ must be known in advance. This causes difficulties when applying the boosting algorithm to practical problems because in real situations we usually do not know in advance how accurate the weak hypotheses are. **AdaBoost** overcomes the drawback, adjusting adaptively to the error ε_t of the weak hypotheses h_t returned by **WeakLearn** in round t. As our analysis shows, the error of the final hypothesis **AdaBoost** produces is upper bounded in terms of the error ε_t's of weak hypotheses, where $0 < \varepsilon_t < 1.\backslash$

AdaBoost is described in Figure 9. We assume that a sample $S = ((x_1, y_1), \ldots, (x_N, y_N))$ chosen arbitrarily from $B \times \{-1, +1\}$ is given. Set $X = \{x_1, \ldots, x_N\}$. Throughout this section, we adopt the convention that the range of hypothesis, as well as that of the

AdaBoost

for $i \in \{1, \cdots, N\}$ **do**

$\qquad w_1(i) := 1$;

for $t \in \{1, \cdots, T\}$ **do**

$\qquad$ Receive weak hypothesis $h_t : X \rightarrow \{0, 1\}$.

$\qquad \epsilon_t := \text{Pr}_{i \sim \bar{w}_t}[h_t(x_i) \neq y_i]$;

$\qquad \alpha_t := \frac{1}{2}\ln(\frac{1 - \epsilon_t}{\epsilon_t})$;

$\qquad$ **for** $i \in \{1, \cdots, N\}$ **do**

$\qquad\qquad w_{t+1}(i) := w_t(i) \exp(-\alpha_t y_i h_t(x_i))$;

$\qquad$ output $H(x) = \text{sign}(\sum_{t=1}^{T} \alpha_t h_t(x))$.

FIGURE 9   Adaptive boosting algorithm.

target function, is given by $\{-1, +1\}$ rather than $\{1, 0\}$. **AdaBoost** proceeds in a series of rounds $t = 1, \ldots, T$. As in the case of other boosting algorithms, **AdaBoost** maintains a weight $w_t = (w_t(x_1), \ldots, w_t(x_N))$ over the sample. In each round t, **AdaBoost** calls a weak learning algorithm which, given as input sample S and distribution $\bar{w}_t$ over S, returns an hypothesis $h_t : X \rightarrow \{-1, +1\}$, where $\bar{w}_t$ is computed in the previous round. Given $\bar{w}_t$ and h_t, the algorithm computes the error ε_t of h_t, which is the probability of h_t making a mistake with respect to $\bar{w}_t$:

$$\varepsilon_t = \text{Pr}_{i \sim \bar{w}_t}[h_t(x_i) \neq y_i].$$

The parameter α_t is defined in terms of ε_t as follows:

$$\alpha_t = \ln\left(\frac{1 - \varepsilon_t}{\varepsilon_t}\right).$$

The parameter $\alpha_t > 0$ gets larger as h_t becomes more accurate, so that h_t has much more influence in the final hypothesis that **AdaBoost** produces. Thus, we can consider α_t as the parameter measuring the confidence of hypothesis h_t.

Finally, **AdaBoost** updates the distribution w_t for the next round according to the update rule $w_{t+1}(i) := w_t(i) \exp(-\alpha_t y_i h_t(x_i))$ so that the algorithm increases weights for instances x_i on which h_t makes a mistake [i.e., $y_i h_t(x_i) = -1$] and, hence, forces the weak learning algorithm in the next round to generate a hypothesis that makes fewer mistakes on these instances. After T such rounds, **AdaBoost** outputs the final hypothesis $h_{\text{final}}(x)$. The hypothesis $h_{\text{final}}(x)$ is a weighted majority vote of the T hypothesis, where α_t is the weight assigned to h_t; that is,

$$h_{\text{final}}(x) = \text{sign}(\alpha_1 h_1(x) + \cdots + \alpha_T h_T(x)),$$

where sign(z) is 1 if $z \geq 0$, and -1 otherwise. In words, the final hypothesis is the sign of the weighted majority of weak hypotheses with respect to the confidence parameters α_t's. It should be noted that the final hypothesis produced by the boost-by-majority algorithm is just the one obtained by setting $\alpha_1 = 1, \ldots, \alpha_T = 1$ in the above formula.

We will upper bound the training error ε of the final hypothesis h_{final}, which is bounded by

$$\frac{1}{N} \mid \{i \mid h_{\text{final}}(x_i) \neq y_i\} \mid \leq \frac{1}{N} \sum_{i=1}^{N} \exp\left(-y_i \sum_{t=1}^{N} \alpha_t h_t(x_i)\right). \qquad [4]$$

The inequality holds because $h_{\text{final}}(x_i) = \text{sign}(\Sigma_t \; \alpha_t h_t(x_i)) \neq y_i$ implies $y_i \; \Sigma_{t=1}^{N} \alpha_t h_t(x_i) \leq 0$; hence, $\exp(-y_i \Sigma_{t=1}^{N} \alpha_t h_t(x_i)) \geq 1$. Let W_t be the normalization factor to make w_{t+1} a distribution; that is, W_t is defined by

$$W_t = \sum_{i=1}^{N} w_t(i) \, \exp(-\alpha_t y_i h_t(x_i)).$$

By definition of normalization, $\bar{w}_{t+1}(i)$ is written as

$$\bar{w}_{t+1}(i) = \frac{w_{t+1}(i)}{W_t}$$

$$= \frac{w_t(i) \, \exp(-\alpha_t y_i h_t(x_i))}{W_t}$$

for $1 \leq i \leq N$. By unraveling the recursive definition for $w_t(i)$, we have

$$\sum_{i=1}^{N} \frac{1}{N} \frac{\exp^{[-\alpha_1 y_i h_1(x_i)]}}{W_1} \cdots \frac{\exp^{[-\alpha_T y_i h_T(x_i)]}}{W_T} = \frac{(1/N) \, \Sigma_{i=1}^{N} \, \exp(-y_i \, \Sigma_{t=1}^{T} \alpha_t h_t(x_i))}{\prod_{t=1}^{T} W_t} = 1,$$

which together with Eq. (4) implies

$$\frac{1}{N} \mid \{i \mid h_{\text{final}}(x_i) \neq y_i\} \mid \leq \frac{1}{N} \sum_{i=1}^{N} \exp\left(-y_i \sum_{t+1}^{T} \alpha_t h_t(x_i)\right)$$

$$= \prod_{t=1}^{T} W_t. \qquad [5]$$

Thus, we can minimize the error of h_{final} by minimizing each factor W_t separately. To make the error of the final hypothesis small, we specify α_t as follows. The normalization factor W_t is approximated by the inequality

$$W_t = \sum_{i=1}^{N} w_t(i) \exp^{[-\alpha_t y_i h_t(x_i)]}$$

$$\leq \sum_{i=1}^{N} w_t(i) \left(\frac{1 + y_i h_t(x_i)}{2} e^{-\alpha_t} + \frac{1 + y_i h_t(x_i)}{2} e^{\alpha_t} \right), \qquad [6]$$

which holds for $y_i h_t(x) \in [-1, 1]$. By simple calculation, we can verify that setting

$$\alpha_t = \tfrac{1}{2} \ln\left(\frac{1 - \varepsilon_t}{\varepsilon_t} \right)$$

as in **AdaBoost** minimizes the right-hand side of the above inequality (8). Then, it is easy to see that plugging $\alpha_t = \frac{1}{2} \ln[(1 - \varepsilon_t)/\varepsilon_t]$ into the right-hand side of Eq. (6) gives an upper bound on W_t as follows:

$$W_t \le 2\sqrt{\varepsilon_t(1 - \varepsilon_t)} = \sqrt{1 - 4\gamma_t^2} \le \exp(-2\gamma_t^2), \qquad [7]$$

where

$$\varepsilon_t = \frac{1}{2} - \gamma_t.$$

Note that because a hypothesis that makes an entirely random guess has an error of $\frac{1}{2}$, $\gamma_t > 0$ can be considered to measure the accuracy of hypothesis h_t relative to random guessing. By Eqs. (5) and (7), we have

$$\frac{1}{N} \, | \, \{ i \mid h_{\mathrm{final}}(x_i) \ne y_i \} \, | \le \prod_{t=1}^{T} W_t$$

$$\le \exp\!\left(-2 \sum_{t=1}^{T} \gamma_t^2\right).$$

So, if the biases γ_t's of the weak hypothesis are lower bounded by some positive constant, then the training error drops exponentially fast. Furthermore, it can be seen that as an hypothesis h_t becomes more accurate and, hence, γ_t gets larger, the training error drops faster accordingly. This is in contrast to the boosting algorithm by majority, which cannot take advantage of hypotheses that have significantly smaller errors than the presumed worst-case error of $\frac{1}{2} - \gamma$.

DECISION-TREE BOOSTING

Many algorithms that infer a decision tree in a top-down fashion from a collection of examples have been studied so far (20–22). Such top-down algorithms grow a tree from the root to the leaves by repeatedly replacing an existing leaf ℓ somehow chosen by a tree with the internal node ℓ with its two child leaves ℓ_0 and ℓ_1. Furthermore, the internal node ℓ is labeled with an hypothesis h chosen appropriately. By the replacement data reaching the node ℓ are split into ones going to ℓ_0 and the others going to ℓ_1, depending on the values that the hypothesis h takes on the data. There are many works that present heuristics to infer decision trees, but only a few of them give theoretical guarantees for their performance. In this section, we present a general scheme for such top-down algorithms, which employ information-theoretic criteria for choosing a leaf split. The schema includes the top-down algorithms such as CART and C4.5 as special cases, each having its own criterion for splitting. It will be shown that given an information-theoretic criterion appropriately, such an algorithm yields, as output, the decision trees that achieve any desired level of accuracy relying on the accuracy of splitting at internal nodes, which is slightly better than random guessing. In this sense, one may consider the top-down algorithm as a boosting. We can interpret this fact as a theoretical performance guarantee for apparent empirical success of the top-down algorithms, such as CART and C4.5. For ease of explanation, in this section, we restrict ourselves to the case of the binary classification problem. The arguments in this section can be naturally generalized to the multiclass case, which is made possible for the first time by introducing a pseudoentropy function (22).

We start by defining decision trees. Let a sample $S = ((x_1, f(x_1)), \ldots, (x_N, f(x_N)))$ be given arbitrarily and set $X = \{x_1, \ldots, x_N\}$. A target function $f: X \to \{0, 1\}$ will be fixed throughout this section. We assume that we are given a set H of hypotheses $h: X \to \{0, 1\}$ which are used to label internal nodes of decision trees. A decision tree is a rooted binary tree such that two edges from any internal node are labeled with 0 and 1, respectively, and that each internal node is labeled with a hypothesis in H. Given a tree T, the set of its leaves is denoted by leaves (T). For $x \in X$, there corresponds a path from the root to a leaf in an obvious way; namely, for any node with label h, the path leaves the node along the edge with label $h(x)$. So, we can think of a decision tree T as a function from X to leaves (T), which will also be denoted by T.

Let $x \in X$ be drawn according to distribution D over X. For each $\ell \in$ leaves (T) and $i \in \{0, 1\}$, w_ℓ denotes the probability that an instance x reaches leaf ℓ and $q_{i|\ell}$ denotes the conditional probability that $f(x) = i$ holds provided that x reaches ℓ; that is,

$$w_\ell = \Pr_{x \in D}[T(x) = \ell],$$
$$q_{i|\ell} = \Pr_{x \in D}[f(x) = i \mid T(x) = \ell].$$

Recall that a decision tree T also represents the corresponding function from X to leaves (T). With the decision tree T, we also associate a function from X to $\{0, 1\}$ that approximates the target function f. The approximate function is defined by associating with each instance $x \in X$ reaching leaf ℓ, the most likely binary value that the target function takes on the instances that reach the leaf ℓ. More precisely, we define the function M: leaves $(T) \to \{0,1\}$ by

$$M(\ell) = \arg \max_{i \in \{0, 1\}} q_{i|\ell}.$$

Then, the approximate function corresponding to T is given by $M(T(x))$. Although we can put the value $M(\ell)$ arbitrarily when $q_{0|\ell} = q_{1|\ell}$ holds, we let $M(\ell) = 0$ in that case. In the context of learning, the function $M(T(x))$ is considered as a hypothesis which approximates the target function f. The error of the function written as $M(T(x))$ is defined to be the probability that $M(T(x)) \neq f(x)$ on x drawn according to the distribution D, which is easily seen to be given by

$$\Pr_{x \in D}[M(T(x)) \neq f(x)] = \sum_{\ell \in \text{leaves}(T)} w_\ell \min\{q_{0|\ell}, q_{1|\ell}\}.$$

Assuming that x drawn according to D reaches leaf ℓ, we can interpret the error probability $\min\{q_{0|\ell}, q_{1|\ell}\}$ as the quantity representing a sort of uncertainty about the value of $f(x)$. So, the quantity $\Sigma_{\ell \in \text{leaves}(T)} w_\ell \min\{q_{0|\ell}, q_{1|\ell}\}$, which gives the error probability of the approximate function $M(f(x))$, is considered to give the weighted average of such uncertainty.

We will shortly define a function which we substitute for $\min\{q_{0|\ell}, q_{1|\ell}\}$. The function, denoted $G(q_0, q_1)$, is called the *pseudoentropy function*. The pseudoentropy function will be used not only to bound the error of the approximate function but also to find a leaf to be split. We should choose such a leaf ℓ to be split such that the leaf ℓ has the largest contribution in the weight average of uncertainty (hence, in the error) measured in terms of the pseudoentropy function. This is because splitting such a leaf may lead to the largest reduction of the uncertainty. The pseudoentropy function is defined to be a function $G : [0, 1]^2 \to [0, 1]$ having the following three properties (22). We could say that the notion of the pseudoentropy function is the weakest one for our purpose because, as long as we follow the arguments below, we need all three properties:

1. There exist constants $a > 0$ and $0 < b \leq 1$ such that for any $(q_0, q_1) \in [0, 1]^2$ with $q_0 + q_1 = 1$,

$$\min\{q_0, q_1\} \leq aG(q_0, q_1)^b.$$

2. For any $(q_0, q_1) \in [0, 1]^2$ with $q_0 + q_1 = 1$,

$$G(q_0, q_1) = 1 \Leftrightarrow q_i = 1 \quad \text{for some } i \in \{0\ 1\}.$$

3. G is concave.

It is easy to see that the Shannon entropy function

$$H(q_0, q_1) = -q_0 \log q_0 - q_1 \log q_1$$

is an example of the pseudoentropy function. In the following, G is assumed to be an arbitrary pseudoentropy function.

As in the case of the Shannon entropy, we can define notions of the entropy, the conditional entropy and the mutual information based on G. The G-entropy of f with respect to D, denoted $H_D^G(f)$, is defined as

$$H_D^G(f) = G(q_0, q_1),$$

where $q_i = \Pr_{x \in D}[f(x) = i]$ for $i \in \{0, 1\}$. The G-entropy measures uncertainty about the values the target function f takes. We let the same notation h represent a hypothesis $h: X \to \text{leaves}(\mathcal{T})$ in the conditional entropy as well as an hypothesis h labeled with an internal node. Thus, denoting the range of these functions as Z, we write the hypothesis h as $h: X \to Z$. The *conditional G-entropy* of f given h with respect to D, denoted $H_D^G(f|h)$, is defined as

$$H_D^G(f \mid h) = \sum_{z \in Z} \Pr_{x \in D}[h(x) = z]G(q_{0|z}, q_{1|z}),$$

where $q_{i|z} = \Pr_{x \in D}[f(x) = i \mid h(x) = z]$ for $i \in \{0, 1\}$. The conditional G-entropy measures the uncertainty of the values of f remaining after receiving the values of h. Finally, the *mutual G-entropy* between f and h with respect to D, denoted $I_D^G(f; h)$, is defined as

$$I_D^G(f; h) = H(f) - H(f \mid h).$$

The mutual G-entropy measures the information about the values of f brought by the values of h. Note that because G is concave, we always have $I_D^G(f; h) \geq 0$. In words, any function h brings a non-negative amount of information on f. We omit G in the notations $H_D^G(f)$, $H_D^G(f|h)$, and $I_D^G(f; h)$ when it is clear from the context.

Now, we show that the error of the function $M(\mathcal{T}(x))$ can be bounded in terms of the conditional G-entropy. Recall that the maximum likelihood estimator $M: Z \to \{0, 1\}$ is defined by

$$M(z) = \arg \max_{i \in \{0, 1\}} q_{i|z},$$

where $q_{i|z} = \Pr_{x \in D}[f(x) = i \mid h(x) = z]$. By definition, we can upper bound the error in terms of the conditional entropy as follows:

$$\Pr_{x \in D}[M(h(x)) \neq f(x)] = \sum_{z \in Z} \Pr_{x \in D}[h(x) = z] \; \Pr_{x \in D}[M(h(x)) \neq f(x) \mid h(x) = z]$$

$$= \sum_{z \in Z} \Pr_{x \in D}[h(x) = z] \; \min\{q_{0|z}, q_{1|z}\}$$

(by definition of M)

$$\leq \sum_{z \in Z} \Pr_{x \in D}[h(x) = z] a G(q_{0|z}, q_{1|z})^b$$

(by Property 1 of the pseudoentropy function)

$$\leq a \left(\sum_{z \in Z} \Pr_{x \in D}[h(x) = z] G(q_{0|z}, q_{1|z}) \right)^b$$

[by the concavity of the function $g(x) = x^b$]

$$= a H_D^G(f \mid h)^b,$$

where $a > 0$ and $0 < b \leq 1$. Therefore, in order to find a function h having small error, it suffices to minimize the conditional G-entropy of f given h.

The next theorem states what we have verified.

Theorem 7 *Let D be a distribution over the sample and G be a pseudoentropy function. Then,*

$$\Pr_{x \in D}[M(h(x)) \neq f(x)] \leq a H_D^G(f \mid h)^b$$

holds, where $a > 0$ and $0 < b \leq 1$ are the constants associated with the pseudoentropy function G.

Figure 10 gives the algorithm **TopDown** which, working based on G-entropy, produces a decision tree that approximates the target function f. In what follows, the distribution D over a sample S is assumed to be the uniform distribution, which is denoted by U. Recall that the pseudoentropy function G is fixed arbitrarily. **TopDown** receives, as

TopDown(S, ϵ)

Let $\mathcal{T}$ be the single–leaf tree.

$T := \left(\frac{1}{\epsilon}\right)^{\frac{2}{\gamma}};$

for T times do

1. $\ell := \arg \max_{\ell \in \text{leaves}(\mathcal{T})} w_\ell G(q_{0|\ell}, q_{1|\ell});$

2. $S_\ell := \{(x_1, f(x)) \in S | x \text{ reaches leaf } \ell\};$

3. Let U_ℓ be the uniform distribution over S_ℓ.

4. $h := \textbf{WeakLearn}(S_\ell, U_\ell);$

5. $\mathcal{T} := \mathcal{T}(\ell, h)$

FIGURE 10   Boosting based on top-down decision-tree learning algorithm.

input, a sample S and accuracy parameter $\varepsilon > 0$ and produces as output a decision tree $\mathcal{T}$ with $H_U(f \mid \mathcal{T}) \le \varepsilon$. The algorithm proceeds in a series of trials, starting with a single-leaf tree; Namely at each trial, the algorithm chooses a leaf $\ell \in$ leaves$(\mathcal{T})$, receives an hypothesis $h : X \to \{0, 1\}$ in a way which will be explained shortly, and replaces the existing leaf ℓ by an internal node ℓ with two child leaves, where the internal node ℓ is labeled with hypothesis h. The tree obtained in this way is denoted by $\mathcal{T}(\ell, h)$.

How should the algorithm choose leaf ℓ and hypothesis h that labels the leaf ℓ? The idea is roughly to choose ℓ and h so that the conditional G-entropy of f given a decision tree is reduced the most. Starting with the single-leaf tree, the algorithm repeatedly makes the local modification to the current tree, choosing a leaf ℓ at each trial and receiving a hypothesis h to label the leaf ℓ. Later, we will explain the algorithm **WeakLearn**, which produces a hypothesis h that correlates with the target function more than random guessing so that the local modification from $\mathcal{T}$ to $\mathcal{T}(\ell, h)$ decreases the conditional G-entropy to a certain degree. The goal of the algorithm is to produce, as output, a decision tree whose conditional G-entropy is no more than ε, which implies that the error of the decision tree is "small." The details of the algorithm are given in Figure 10.

To explain how to choose leaf ℓ and hypothesis h in an attempt to reduce the conditional G-entropy, we need to recall that the conditional G-entropy of f given $\mathcal{T}$ is written as

$$H(f \mid \mathcal{T}) = \sum_{\ell \in \text{leaves}(\mathcal{T})} w_\ell G(q_{0 \mid \ell}, q_{1 \mid \ell}), \qquad [8]$$

where $G(q_{0 \mid \ell}, q_{1 \mid \ell})$ measures uncertainty of the value that f takes provided that an example drawn according to D reaches leaf ℓ. As shown in Figure 10, our strategy to choose a leaf is simply to find the leaf ℓ that maximizes $w_\ell G(q_{1 \mid \ell}, q_{1 \mid \ell})$ so that splitting the leaf ℓ reduces the conditional G-entropy hopefully the most. Let h be the hypothesis somehow chosen to label the internal node ℓ in $\mathcal{T}(\ell, h)$. Let S_ℓ denote the collection of examples in S that reaches leaf ℓ and let U_ℓ denote the uniform distribution over S_ℓ. It is easy to see that we have

$$H_U(f \mid \mathcal{T}) - H_U(f \mid \mathcal{T}(\ell, h)) = w_\ell (H_{U_\ell}(f) - H_{U_\ell}(f \mid h))$$

$$= w I_{U_\ell}(f; h), \qquad [9]$$

which is the amount of the conditional G-entropy that is reduced when $\mathcal{T}$ is modified into $\mathcal{T}(\ell, h)$. To guarantee a certain amount of reduction in the modification, we need to require that $H_{U_\ell}(f \mid h)$ is "not large," namely hypothesis h is at least slightly correlated with the target function f. We define a notion of a weak learning algorithm in terms of the entropy, which is contrasted with the same notion defined earlier in terms of error. A *weak learning algorithm* (based on G-entropy) is an algorithm that, when given a sequence S of example and a probability distribution D over S, produces a function h satisfying

$$H_D(f \mid h) \le (1 - \gamma) H_D(f)$$

for some positive constant $\gamma > 0$.

As is shown in Figure 10, algorithm **TopDown** calls the weak learning algorithm **WeakLearn** by setting the sample and the distribution to S_ℓ and U_ℓ, respectively. The next theorem says that the conditional G-entropy of the decision tree produced by **Top-Down** is less than or equal to ε, which together with Theorem 7 implies that **TopDown** produces as output a decision tree with "small" error.

Theorem 8 *Let* **WeakLearn** *be a weak learning algorithm with the associated constant* γ. *Then, for any sequence of examples of* f *and any* $\varepsilon > 0$, *algorithm* **TopDown**(S, ε) *produces* T *with* $H_U(f \mid T) \leq \varepsilon$.

Proof. Let T be the tree at the beginning of the tth iteration of algorithm **TopDown** (S, ε), and let H_t denote the conditional G-entropy $H_U(f \mid T)$. Note that the number of leaves of T is t. Thus, by Eq. (8), there must exist a leaf ℓ such that

$$w_\ell G(q_{0 \mid \ell}, q_{1 \mid \ell}) = w_\ell H_{U_\ell}(f) \geq H_t/t,$$

where U_ℓ is the uniform distribution over S_ℓ. Hence, because h is produced by the weak learning algorithm **WeakLearn**(S_ℓ, U_ℓ).

$$H_t - H_{t+1} = w_\ell (H_{U_\ell}(f) - H_{U_\ell}(f \mid h))$$

$$\geq \gamma w_\ell H_{U_\ell}(f)$$

$$\geq \frac{\gamma H_t}{t}$$

or, equivalently,

$$H_{t+1} \leq \left(1 - \frac{\gamma}{t}\right) H_t \leq e^{-\gamma/t} H_t.$$

Because $H_1 \leq 1$, we have

$$H_{T+1} \leq \exp^{\left(-\gamma \sum_{t=1}^{T} \frac{1}{t}\right)} \leq \exp^{(-\gamma \ln T)} \varepsilon,$$

as desired. $\square$

We should mention that the boosting for the binary class discussed so far in this section can be extended to that for the multiclass case in which the range of the target functions is any finite set. Because the arguments so far for the error-based boosting primarily assume that the target functions are binary valued, the standard approach to boosting for the multiclass case has been to convert the given multiclass problem into several binary problems, and then to use boosting separately on each of the binary problems. On the other hand, it turns out that the information-based setting described in this section is really compatible with the multiclass case. In fact, Theorems 7 and 8, as well as algorithm **TopDown**, can be naturally generalized to the multiclass case (22). For example, the three properties for a pseudoentropy function are given as follows:

1. There exist constants $a < 0$ and $0 < b \leq 1$ such that for any $(q_0, \ldots, q_{N-1}) \in [0, 1]^N$ with $\Sigma_i q_i = 1$,

$$\min_{i \in \{0, \ldots, N-1\}} (1 - q_i) \leq a G(q_0, \ldots, q_{N-1})^b.$$

2. For any $(q_0, \ldots, q_{N-1}) \in [0, 1]^N$ with $\Sigma_i q_i = 1$,

$$G(q_0, \ldots, q_{N-1}) = 0 \Leftrightarrow q_i = 1 \quad \text{for some } i \in \{0, \ldots, N-1\}.$$

3. G is concave.

We have presented a boosting algorithm in an information-based setting. Specifically, this is an information-based algorithm that converts weak hypotheses into a strong hypothesis in an information-based setting. It is worth mentioning that we can derive an error-based boosting algorithm from the information-based boosting algorithm (22). The error-based boosting algorithm converts weak hypotheses into a strong hypothesis in the error-based setting. Therefore, if we assume that an information-based weak learning algorithm also works as an error-based weak learning algorithm and that an information-based strong hypothesis is also an error-based strong hypothesis, then we can claim that an information-based boosting algorithm essentially implies an error-based boosting algorithm. In fact, we can verify the former in the assumption by some technical arguments and prove the latter in view of Theorem 7. Therefore, designing an efficient information-based boosting algorithm might lead to developing a good error-based boosting algorithm.

BIBLIOGRAPHIC NOTES

Since Valiant published the seminal paper "A Theory of the Learnable" (1), a large volume of work has been done to explore the computational possibilities and limitations of learning. The model he proposed is referred to as the PAC model, PAC being an acronym for Probably Approximately Correct. Among the results on the PAC model are the followings. The notion of Occam learning is defined to be one that finds a hypothesis that is consistent with a sample and somewhat shorter to describe than the number of examples in the sample (9). Occam learning and PAC learning are shown to be essentially equivalent to each other (23). In Ref. 13, the mutual information for learning is introduced as being a more appropriate parameter for measuring the discrepancy between targets and hypotheses, and the relationship between mutual information gaining and PAC learning was investigated. The VC dimension is another relevant parameter for measuring the complexity of target classes. In Ref. 11, it is shown that the number of examples in a sample needed to learn a target class of infinite cardinality is given in terms of the VC dimension of the target class. There are many results which give learning algorithms for target classes represented by Boolean formulas (3,24–26), whereas the target classes which are hard to learn are also reported (4). An excellent introduction to the computational learning theory is provided in Ref. 3.

Starting from the framework on computational learning theory, a new family of algorithms has been developed. These algorithms are based on the multiplicative weight-update rule, which are the main focus of this article. Kearns and Valiant posed the question of whether boosting can be done within the framework of computational learning theory (4,6). Schapire first gives a provable polynomial-time boosting algorithm (7). Freund also developed a much more efficient boosting algorithm (15), which constitutes the section majority-vote game and subsampling boosting. In Ref. 16, a close relationship between boosting and on-line prediction is revealed within the framework of game theory. The sections Repeated Game and Minmax Strategy and On-Line Prediction and Boosting based on repeated game contain their work on game-theoretic aspects of boosting and on-line prediction. There are many results on the expert model. The section On-Line Prediction Using Expert's Prediction is from Ref. 18. Adaptive boosting is another topic extensively studied so far. The section Adative Boosting is from Ref. 19, which presents the most simplified framework for the boosting. The section Decision-Tree

Boosting contains the results on another type of boosting, which is from Refs. 20 and 22. Pruning a decision tree which typically over-fits the data used to build the decision is another important topic which can be treated based on the expert model as well (4). Many algorithms to prune decision trees are presented (4, 5, 6) as well as the ones to build decision trees (12,21).

We omitted related work on support vector machines that have been recently studied extensively and proved to outperform most other learning systems developed so far (27). In this model, a hypothesis which classifies the instance space is written as linear functions in a high-dimensional feature space. Reference 27 surveys more recent related work on support vector machines. Another related topic omitted in this article is the margin which is the parameter for measuring the discrepancy between a hypothesis and the target function on given training examples (28). In the case of majority voting by weak hypotheses, the margin of the training examples is simply the difference between the number of correct weak hypotheses and that of incorrect weak hypotheses. In Ref. 28, a bound is given which upper bounds the generalization error in terms of the training error and the margin, where a hypothesis is assumed to take the form of a linear combination of base hypotheses.

The proceedings of an Annual Workshop on Computational Learning Theory, the proceedings of International Workshop on Algorithmic Learning Theory, and the proceedings of European Conference on Computational Learning Theory cover work in this field.

APPENDIX

Lemma *Set*

$$\beta = \frac{1}{1 + \sqrt{(2 \ln n/T)}} \, .$$

For any $0 < L \le T$ and $0 < \beta < 1$,

$$\frac{[\ln (1/\beta)] L + \ln n}{1 - \beta} \le L + 3\sqrt{\frac{T \ln n}{2}} + \ln n.$$

Proof. Applying Taylor expansion to $f(x) = -x \ln x$ at $x = 1$ gives

$$f(x) \le -(x - 1) - \frac{(x - 1)^2}{2} = \frac{1 - x^2}{2} \, .$$

For $\tilde{L} > 0$ and $\tilde{R} > 0$, we therefore have

$$\frac{[\ln(1/\beta) \tilde{L} + \tilde{R}}{1 - \beta} \le \frac{[(1 - \beta)^2/2\beta] \tilde{L} + \tilde{R}}{1 - \beta}$$

$$= \frac{1 + \beta}{2\beta} \tilde{L} + \frac{\tilde{R}}{1 - \beta} \, .$$

The right-hand side of the above equality is minimized when

$$\beta = \frac{1}{1 + \sqrt{2\tilde{R}/\tilde{L}}} \, .$$

Thus, because setting

$$\beta = \frac{1}{1 + \sqrt{(2 \ln n)/T}} \, .$$

gives

$$\ln\left(\frac{1}{\beta}\right) = \ln\left(1 + \sqrt{\frac{2 \ln n}{T}}\right) \le \sqrt{\frac{2 \ln n}{T}} \, ,$$

$$\frac{1}{1 - \beta} = \frac{1 + \sqrt{(2 \ln n)/T}}{\sqrt{(2 \ln n)/T}} = 1 + \sqrt{\frac{T}{2 \ln n}} \, ,$$

we have

$$\frac{[\ln 1/\beta)] L + \ln n}{1 - \beta} \le \left(1 + \sqrt{\frac{2 \ln n}{T}}\right)L + \sqrt{\frac{T \ln n}{2}} + \ln n$$

$$\le L + 3\sqrt{\frac{T \ln n}{2}} + \ln n.$$

$\square$

ACKNOWLEDGMENT

This work was partially supported by Grant-in-Aid for Scientific Research on Priority Areas (Discovery Science), 2000, the Ministry of Education, Science, Sports and Culture in Japan.

REFERENCES

1. L. G. Valiant, "A Theory of the Learnable," *Commun. Assoc. Computing Mach.*, *27*(11), 1134–1142 (1984).
2. M. Kearns and U. Vazirani, *An Introduction to Computational Learning Theory*, MIT Press, Cambridge, MA, 1994.
3. L. A. Valiant, "A View of Computational Learning Theory," in *Computation & Cognition: Proceedings of the First NEC Research Symposium*, 1991.
4. S. Arikawa, M. Sato, T. Sato, A. Maruoka, S. Miyano, and Y. Kanada, "The Discovery Science Project," *J. Jpn. Soc. Artif. Intell.*, *15*, 595–607 (2000).
5. O. Watanabe, "From Computational Learning Theory to Discovery Science," Lecture Notes in Computer Science Vol. 1644, Springer-Verlag, Berlin, 1999, pp. 134–148.
6. M. Kearns and L. G. Valiant, "Learning Boolean Formulae or Finite Automata Is as Hard as Factoring," Technical Report TR-14-88, Harvard University Aiken Computational Laboratory (1988).
7. M. Kearns and L. G. Valiant, "Gryptographic Limitations on Learning Boolean Formulae and Finite Automata," *J. Assoc. Computing Mach.*, *41*(1), 67–95 (1994).
8. R. Schapire, "The Strength of Weak Learnability," *Machine Learn.*, *5*, 157–227 (1990).

9.   Y. Freund, "Boosting a Weak Learning Algorithm by Majority," *Inform. Computat.*, *121*, 256–285 (1995).

10. Y. Freund and R. Schapire, "A Decision-Theoretic Generalization of On-Line Learning and an Application to Boosting," *J. Computer Syst. Sci.*, *55*(1), 119–139 (1997).

11. A. Blumer, A. Ehrenfeucht, D. Haussler, and M. Warmuth, Occam's Razor. *Information Processing Letters*, 24, pp. 377–380, 1987.

12. R. Board and L. Pitt, "On the Necessity of Occam Algorithm," in *Proc. 22nd Annual ACM Symposium on Theory of Computing*, 1990.

13. A. Blumer, A. Ehrenfeucht, D. Haussler, and M. Warmuth, "Learnability and the Vapnic-Chervonenkis Dimension," *J. Assoc. Computing Mach.*, *36*, 929–965 (1989).

14. J. R. Quinlan and R. L. Rivest, "Inferring Decision Trees Using the Minimum Description Length Principle," *Inform. Computat.*, *80*, 227–248 (1989).

15. E. Takimoto, I. Tajika, and A. Maruoka, "Mutual Information Gaining Algorithm and Its Relation to PAC-Learning Algorithm," Lecture Notes in Artificial Intelligence Vol. 872, Springer-Verlag, Berlin, 1994, pp. 547–559.

16. D. Haussler, M. Kearns, N. Littlestone, and M. Warmuth, "Equivalence of Models of Polynomial Learnability," in *Annual Conference on Computational Learning Theory*, 1988, pp. 45–55.

17. Y. Freund and R. Schapire, "Game Theory, On-Line Prediction and Boosting," in *Proc. 9th Annual Conference on Computational Learning Theory*, 1996, pp. 325–332.

18. N. Cesa-Bianchi, Y. Freund, D. Haussler, D. Helmbold, R. Schapire, and M. Warmuth, "How to Use Expert Advice," *J. Assoc. Computing Mach.*, *44*(3), 427–485 (1997).

19. J. Kivinen and M. Warmuth, "Averaging Expert Prediction," in *Proceedings of Eurocomputational Learning Theory Workshop*, 1999, pp. 153–167.

20. N. Littlestone and M. Warmuth, "The Weighted Majority Algorithm," *Inform. Computat.*, *108*, 212–261 (1994).

21. V. Vovk, "Aggregating Strategies," in *Proc. 3rd Annual Conference on Computational Learning Theory*, 1990, pp. 371–383.

22. R. E. Schapire and Y. Singer, "Improved Boosting Algorithms Using Confidence Rated Predictions," in *Annual Conference on Computational Learning Theory*, 1988, pp. 80–91.

23. M. Kearns and Y. Mansour, "On the Boosting Ability of Top-Down Decision Tree Learning Algorithms," in *J. Comput. Syst. Sci.*, *58*, 109–128 (1999).

24. J. R. Quinlan, *C4.5: Programs for Machine Learning*, Morgan Kaufmann, San Mateo, CA, 1993.

25. E. Takimoto and A. Maruoka, "On the Boosting Algorithm for Multiclass Functions Based on Information-Theoretic Criterion for Approximation," Lecture Notes in Artificial Intelligence Vol. 1532, Springer-Verlag, Berlin, 1998. pp. 256–267.

26. R. Board and L. Pitt, "On the Necessity of Occam Algorithms," *Theoret. Computer Sci.*, *100*, 157–184 (1992).

27. J. Jackson, "An Efficient Membership-Query Algorithm for Learning DNF with Respect to the Uniform Distribution," *J. Computer Syst. Sci.*, *55*, 414–440 (1997).

28. N. Linial, Y. Mansour, and N. Nisan, "Constant Depth Circuits, Fourier Transform, and Learnability," *J. Assoc. Computing Mach.*, *40*(3), 607–620 (1993).

29. Y. Sakai and A. Maruoka, "Learning Monotone Log-Term DNF Formulas Under the Uniform Distribution," *Theory Computat. Syst.*, *33*, 17–33 (2000).

30. E. Takimoto, A. Maruoka, and V. Vovk, "Predicting Nearly as Well as the Best Pruning of a Decision Tree Through Dynamic Programming Schema," *Theoret. Computer Sci.* (in press).

31. D. P. Helmbold and R. Schapire, "Predicting Nearly as Well as the Best Pruning of Decision Tree," *Machine Learn.*, *27*(1), 51–68 (1997).

32. M. Kearns and Y. Mansour, "A Fast, Bottom-Up Decision Tree Pruning Algorithm with Near Optimal Genelarization," in *Proceedings of 15th International Conference on Machine Learning*, 1998.

33. N. Cristianini and J. Shawe-Taylor, *An Introduction to Support Vector Machines*, Cambridge University Press, Cambridge, 2000.
34. R. E. Schapire, P. Bartlete, and W. S. Lee, "Boosting the Margin: A New Explanation for the Effectiveness of Voting Methods," *Ann. Statist.*, *26*, 1651–1686 (1998).

AKIRA MARUOKA

EIJI TAKIMOTO

AUGMENTED REALITY

INTRODUCTION

Brief Definition

"Augmentare" is the Latin word for "enlarge, enhance, enrich." In that sense, the term "Augmented Reality" (AR) describes a technology used to provide a user with information which enriches his/her perception of the real world in such a way that this information is perceived to be a part of the spatial environment of the user.

Historical Development

The idea of such a technology was already born in the 1960s, when the first head-mounted displays (HMDs) were built by the visionary Ivan Sutherland (1). The original application of such displays was telepresence—the display would show imagery, captured by remote servo-controlled infrared (IR) cameras, which were moved according to the user's head motion. This allowed the user to change his viewing direction very naturally and provided an immersive feeling. In 1966, the live camera images were replaced by computer-synthesized images—and the technology of "Virtual Reality" (VR) was born. During the following decades, much technical development was done in this area of VR, which provided the means of complete immersion in a virtual environment, generated by increasingly powerful computers with more and more advanced graphics capabilities. Implementations of such immersive VR technology could be found in simulation (aircraft and cars), training, design and prototyping, and entertainment [e.g., three-dimensional (3D) shows in Las Vegas]. Applications which were mixing the real-world perception with information in the sense of augmented reality were mostly implemented in military applications, where helmet-mounted displays provided overlay graphics for target selection and night vision. For use in other domains, these applications were too cumbersome, requiring heavy head-worn displays and precise tracking systems.

Progress in many enabling research areas related to VR has brought an increased focus on AR in the past 10 years, when it was realized that AR could have benefits in much broader areas than the narrow applications of VR technology. With the increased capabilities of VR systems, the concept of placing these synthesized renditions into the perception of the real world became intriguing. This was much more challenging than a purely immersive visualization, because the registration precision for AR has to be much higher—the user would immediately notice misalignment of virtual objects when he also sees the real world. The benefits of this approach to "augment" the reality in many areas are obvious: Information can be presented to the user as if it is part of the real world. Therefore, the user can intuitively understand the information in the current context. Applications which can utilize this immediate intuitive visualization concept are, for example, navigation in an unknown city, where names of streets or landmarks can be shown directly on the relevant objects and where directions can be given directly into the user's view. Architects can see prototypes of their buildings right on the scene where they are to be built, plumbers can see the installations behind closed walls ("virtual x-ray vision"), and physicians can overlay medical imaging data directly onto the patients body. Maintenance and manufacturing are other important applications of AR technology, which allow instructions to be overlaid directly onto the parts of the objects. The first time that such an AR system was tested on a larger scale in a realistic manufacturing environment was in the 1990s in a Boeing airplane factory for assembling wire bundles (2). Many inherent hurdles such as wearability and precise information alignment (registration) still have to be overcome in order to help AR applications to a breakthrough success.

Augmented reality research evolved from the areas of virtual reality, wearable and ubiquitous computing, and human–computer interface. One of the most relevant technical issues in developing AR applications is solving the registration problem; registration means aligning the virtual information with the real world so that it appears to be a part of the real environment. This registration must occur in real time, otherwise the user will experience an unacceptable lag of the visualization when he moves. Another issue is how to share these virtual spaces with other users in collaboration. Human factors research is being done in how to present the information in such a way that the user is not confused about what is real and what is virtual information. Recently, the field of AR is evolving as its own discipline, with strong ties to these related research areas. In 1998, the First International Workshop on Augmented Reality (IWAR'98) (3) attracted 64 attendees, 1 year later the 2nd IWAR'99 had 177 attendees. This is a sign of the increased attention this new field is receiving.

Broader Definition of the Term "Augmented Reality"

Although AR is often perceived to be in the visual domain, it actually includes the other senses as well. Three-dimensional audio, for example, which is based on the concept of head-related transfer functions (4), can be used to provide an immersive sound field, in which the user can precisely locate events and communication streams (5). Also, haptic "displays," which provide a tactile user force feedback (6), or general tangible interfaces (7) can be considered as a part of AR technology. This wide cross-disciplinary aspect of the field of AR leads to the question, What actually can be considered AR, and where are the boundaries? It is, in general, considered as a subdomain within the area of "Virtual Environments." In his survey about AR in 1997, Azuma (8) defined the following three elements to be essential for AR: combining real and virtual, being interactive in real time, and being registered three dimensions. This definition includes AR applications based on head-worn display systems, but excludes the kind of 2D overlays in movies, which match synthetic rendering with real-world footage, because the real-time interactive aspect is not given here. The registration problem for these matching algorithms is, however, the same as for other typical AR applications, and the technologies developed for this problem will eventually find their way in real-time interactive AR applications (9). The experts in the AR community still argue about the "gray zone" on what can still be considered under that term AR. Also bordering the AR domain are applications on hand-held computers, which provide a context-sensitive display content but are not truly registered to the surroundings.

In the context of AR, the term "Mixed Reality (MR)" is often used. It is a superset of AR and covers the reality–virtuality continuum between completely real environments and completely virtual environments, a concept introduced by Milgram and Colquhoun (10), which encompasses both augmented reality and augmented virtuality (AV). The degree to which both elements—virtual and real objects—are within an MR application define its classification as either AR or AV.

For AR visualization, two different modes are possible: the *optical see-through* AR, in which a see-through display overlays synthetically rendered information/objects directly onto the live view of a scenery, and *video see-through* AR, which employs video cameras to capture live images of a scene and performs the merging of both camera imagery and synthetic rendering into a completely opaque display. The video see-through AR has the advantage of providing a more seamless integration of real and virtual worlds, because the video can be matched in its perception (color, intensity) to the virtual rendering and because computer vision techniques can be applied to eliminate jitter of the overlay. However, the resolution of the video is lower and the quality of the perception of the real world is limited to the quality of the optical system (camera, display, etc.) (11). A special case of video see-through displays is the use of hand-held computers with an attached camera, which provides a video image of the display of the hand-held computer, which can be augmented with either annotations or other information.

This article tries to give an overview of augmented reality and the current state of the art of research and application implementations as of the year 2001.

STATE OF THE ART OF CURRENT AR APPLICATIONS

The technological hurdles, which will be discussed in the third section, have so far prevented that and we see large numbers of existing AR applications. However, much progress has been made in the past years in demonstrating solutions to certain problems of AR applications. This section will give a brief overview of the achievements, issues, and benefits in various application areas of AR technology.

Manufacturing, Maintenance, and Repair

Manufacturing, maintenance, and repair are fields which are very promising for utilizing the benefits of AR technology. Its applications would reduce training time, speed up prototype development, and reduce errors in design, maintenance, and repair, and therefore lead to cost savings, which will be a trigger for industrial applications of such AR technology (12). Instructions for assembly or disassembly can be given directly into the user's view, pointing to specific object parts and providing not only textual manuals but also 3D drawings and animations superimposed on real objects. The interactivity allows step-by-step instructions to be displayed, depending on the progress (see Figure 2). Such a system was tested in a pilot experiment in an actual airplane factory at Boeing: The system could provide information to the users on the assembly of wire harnesses (13). Using this AR system, the result was that an untrained person could perform the wiring assembly task faster than an experienced worker who used the conventional method. However, several shortcomings of the current technology still prevent employing such systems on a larger scale: Human interface issues, ergonomics, and overall comfort still leave something to be desired. Other explored applications in an industrial context are the evaluation and optimization of assembly sequences (14). AR visualization can utilize the computer-aided design (CAD) design datasets of modules, which must be integrated into an existing real object [e.g., a car door lock assembly (15)]. Government-funded initiatives worldwide, such as the research project in Germany, ARVIKA (http://www. arvika.de), are trying to stimulate research and development in AR for such industrial applications. With improvements in the human–computer interface, such systems will find their way onto the factory floor of the future.

Medical

For the medical community, AR applications would bring the benefit of visualizing three-dimensional data from noninvasive sensors such as magnetic resonance imaging (MRI), computer tomography (CT), and ultrasound imaging directly projected onto the patient, so that the physician is able to see virtually into the patient ("x-ray vision"). This helps the physician during diagnosis to get more data, but could also be used as an aid for surgery to improve the precision (16), especially in minimal invasive surgery. Problematic in overlaying information on a patient's body is the registration problem; one approach is to place markers on the body for visual tracking. Another problem is how to show the information to the physician without obstructing his clear view of the patient. Collaborations between universities and hospitals such as between MIT and the Brigham and Women's Hospital are exploring the technical issues in such applications. GE and Siemens (17) are developing medical equipment which will provide the capability of using this "x-ray vision" on real patients.

Architecture

The fusion of the real environment and virtual renditions of objects will find a very useful application in architecture, where CAD models of planned buildings can be overlaid directly on the view of the proposed site (18). This allows one to study the impact of the architecture right in the environment. Also, for interior design, this technology can be used in order to design room decor and furnishing by placing virtual furniture into a real room. In general, construction, inspection, and renovation are prime application candidates for AR technology in architecture (19). A problem in architectural AR is how to implement occlusion: The synthetic object, that is placed into the real scene, may occlude

FIGURE 1   AR in architecture: real scene (left), synthetic building (middle) with correct occlusion attributes, and merged result (right). (Courtesy Kiyoshi Kiyokawa, Communications Research Laboratory, Tokyo.)

real objects and also may be occluded partially by other buildings or structures (see Figure 1 and ref. 34).

Military and Aviation

The military area has long been the primary application area of AR technology, although it was not specifically labeled as such. The implementation of head-up displays (HUD) and helmet-mounted displays (HMD) in fighter jets and helicopters provided visual target and threat cues to the pilot, registered with the real world. In recent years, research programs have been funded by DARPA, ARL, and ONR to explicitly develop AR technology with the goal of increasing the situational awareness of soldiers and commanders in outdoor scenarios and under water. Examples of such research programs are the DARPA-funded "Warfighter Visualization" program (initiated in 1997) with its subprogram "Geospatially Registered Information for Dismounted Soldiers," which focused on research for outdoor registration. The U.S. Army Research Lab (ARL) funded a "Federated Laboratory for Advanced Displays and Interactive Displays" from 1996 to 2000 with significant portion in AR for outdoor applications, and ONR is funding a project "Mobile AR" for applications in an urban battlefield. The latest developments in this area focus on fusing VR visualization with AR displays using a common-scenario representation (20). This involves filtering and tailoring the information display for avoiding clutter in the AR display (21). Telerobotics and telepresence is another important military application; for example, Thomson–CSF Corporate Research Laboratories is developing AR system prototypes for military observation of low-intensity battlefields (22).

In commercial airplane cockpits, HUD displays are also being increasingly used to provide visual navigation cues directly into the pilot's view (see Figure 2). The latest developments have targeted the improvement of safety on the ground during taxiing operations (23). NASA is funding further developments using "Enhanced Vision" and "Synthetic Vision," which are targeted toward improving cockpit displays. These developments may also include AR technology (e.g., overlaying synthetically rendered terrain onto image background, captured by a camera, which is mounted outside the airplane).

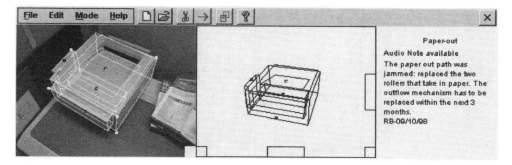

FIGURE 2   Screen shot from a hand-held PC. The wireframe model is aligned with the image of the printer. Clicking on "hot spots" on the printer image allows retrieval of actual information, displayed in the text window on the right. (Courtesy Rockwell Scientific Company.)

FIGURE 3   HUD displays in commercial airplane cockpits: current HUD with data display (left) and future HUD with registered information (right). (Courtesy Bob Wood, Rockwell Collins Flight Dynamics.)

Entertainment/Infotainment

The paradigm of mixing virtual objects with the real world has a very large potential in entertainment applications, which is not yet tapped. Games could be developed which would provide real-time interaction with both real objects and virtual simulation. The Mixed Reality Laboratory (Yokohama) has developed prototypes of such games (24), involving several players in a highly interactive game in which the users can play in a real environment, augmented by virtual objects (e.g., AR Hockey, or shooting games).

This concept of augmenting the real world can be used in museums and art galleries, where information could be shown to the user, linked to the real art works and explaining and highlighting certain aspects. In expanding this concept to showing video clips and information, aligned with real buildings, Feiner introduced the concept of "situated documentaries" in a wearable AR system that was able to show historic multimedia documentaries about the student revolt in 1968 on the campus of Columbia University (25). It was based on the "Touring Machine" (26), which provided, in a backpack solution, navigation instructions in an urban environment. A different concept is employed by the prototype "NaviCam," developed by Rekimoto at SONY Computer Science Laboratory (27). This system uses a hand-held computer with an attached camera; the display shows video from the camera, annotated with information, which is obtained from visual readouts of ID markers in the scene.

TECHNOLOGICAL HURDLES AND POSSIBLE SOLUTIONS

The idea of AR is very intriguing for many possible applications. However, with the current technology, there are still several hurdles to be overcome to make those applications become a reality. This section describes the major hurdles and possible solutions.

Registration

The main challenge in AR applications is to ensure that the displayed information is aligned with the user's view of the surrounding world, because the human visual system is very sensitive to misalignment. This alignment is often referred to as "registration."

Registration must be achieved with a high precision and must be maintained over time when the user is moving and changing his/her viewpoint without noticeable lag. This requires that the user's head be tracked in all six degrees of freedom during the use of the AR system. Such trackers can be external trackers, which require a certain "infrastructure" in the environment and, therefore, are usually limited to fixed locations. Other tracking systems can be more "autonomous," only being mounted on the user and, therefore, being independent of cooperative infrastructure installations. Significant research effort is put into this field of registration, indicated by the number of research papers presented at AR conferences. Related to registration is the problem of calibrating a head-worn display and dealing with slight shifts of the HMD relative to the eye, which result in noticeable misalignment.

Computer Vision

Registration for AR can leverage from the vast amount of effort put into computer vision research. One of the goals of computer vision (CV) is to reconstruct the orientation and position of a camera in real time from video camera image sequences. The methods in computer vision employ image processing techniques for extraction of visual features, which are used to determine the structure of the environment. If the camera is mounted on a user's head, such a system can determine the head position and orientation relative to the environment. In order to assist such a vision tracking system, one can use specifically designed visual markers which are placed into the environment (28) or attached to objects (29). However, this is not always possible and feasible. Other methods have been developed to use natural visual features of objects to reconstruct the spatiotemporal relationship of the real world both for environments with supportive infrastructure (e.g., cameras mounted externally for tracking movable objects and subjects) (30) and for natural environments without any external man-made infrastructure.

The main challenges in computer vision for AR are real-time performance, which requires significant computing power, and robustness toward visual disturbances, such as low contrast and feature occlusion. The weight of high-performance workstations does not permit them to be used as wearable systems; however, the increasing computation power of wearable computers may eventually bring enough capability to such systems. A possible solution with current hardware is to employ a stationary high-performance computer to do the image processing from videos, transmitted from the mobile user. The results are then transmitted back to the user for visualization. This, of course, introduces a noticeable lag. Progress in wearable computing technology and software algorithms will pave the way for the use of computer vision in personal AR applications; however, there are still many problems to be solved.

Other Sensors

For outdoor use, the predominant sensor for locating position is the Global Positioning System (GPS). Since the "selected availability" of the U.S. system, which prevented precise nonmilitary use of the GPS signal, was switched off in Summer 2000, the signals could be received without distortion worldwide, providing precision of typically 1 m without the need of differential GPS. Orientation can be obtained from GPS only when the user (receiver) is in motion. A magnetic compass can provide orientation, but as Azuma pointed out (31), the compass errors due to magnetic distortions of the Earth's magnetic field can be up to 20–30°. However, in combination with an inclinometer, which measures the angle between the gravity vectors and can provide a pitch-and-roll angle, this type of sensor can work without any external sources in any environment. Therefore, it is very well suited for providing at least a "rough estimate" of the orientation. Problems occur during motion due to sensor relaxation time and communication lag. Here, the use of inertial sensors, which measure linear acceleration and angular velocity, can help to improve the registration precision significantly. Intelligent processing of these sensor data helps to overcome their tendency to drift (32).

Ideally, a registration system for an outdoor AR application will combine several sensors for optimal fusion: computer vision, GPS, compass, inclinometer, and inertial sensors. In that way, the shortcomings of each of these sensors can be compensated and a relatively high precision can be obtained. Such systems are being developed in several research labs with the goal of achieving real-time performance. Also, for indoor tracking, a sensor fusion approach promises to improve tracking precision significantly (33).

Occlusion

When mixing real-world perception with synthetically rendered objects, the problem of occlusion occurs. Simple head-worn displays in use for optical see-through AR only "fuse" the synthetic display and the real world by merging them with a semitransparent mirror. In this case, both renditions appear simultaneously, but the synthetic rendition appears to be transparent. Video see-through AR systems have the potential to block out parts of the real-world imagery to make the synthetic renditions nontransparent, e.g., using color cueing. In most cases, this is what is supposed to be achieved: that the synthetic information shall stay "on top" of the real scene and be always visible. However, in some cases (e.g., in a complex structured real scenario), it is appropriate to occlude the virtual object partially by real objects to achieve a realistic impression. Possible solutions were addressed by creating a depth map of the surrounding environment and using either an active sensor at the user location (34) or stereo cameras for a large-scale outdoor scene for creating this depth image. This depth map can then be analyzed for intersection with the object representation, and parts of the virtual object can be rendered as being "behind" the real objects. Another way of calculating the occlusion effect without an active sensor is to use an existing 3D model of the environment for determining the correct occlusion.

Wearability and Other Human Factors

Physical hurdles have so far prevented the widespread use of AR technology in wearable computers. The weight of AR capable systems (15–20 lbs) is still only acceptable for prototype developers in research laboratories. In most cases, such systems are implemented on backpacks, which provides the easiest weight distribution. Wearable vests provide an alternative to those backpacks, distributing the weight more evenly on the user. Usability of such wearable system is another factor. The MIT Media Lab "Wearable Group" has addressed these factors in their research in the past few years.

Wearable Displays

Users generally object to wearing "head-mounted" displays, which cause discomfort and strain. Developments are underway to develop displays which can be integrated into standard eyeglasses. MicroOptical Corporation (http://www.microopticalcorp.com/) is leading the miniaturization efforts (see Figure 4). An alternative technology for head-

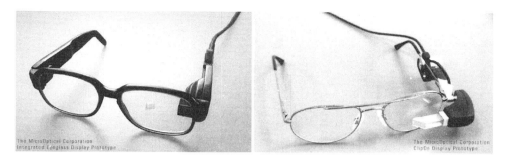

FIGURE 4   Head-worn displays, integrated into standard eye glasses. (Courtesy Mark Spitzer, MicroOptical Corporation.)

worn see-through displays is pursued by Microvision (http://www.mvis.com/): the virtual retinal display. This type of display does not rely on a conventional display chip, but instead uses a low-energy laser beam to "draw" and image on the eye's retina by scanning, analog to a tube cathode ray. This technology was developed at the University of Washington and promises high contrast, wide viewing angle, and omnifocus. Limitations in current design, however, force compromises in these capabilities. A monochrome red version, is commercially available but color displays are in development.

Wearable Computer

Technology development of wearable computers suitable for AR is still in its infancy. Although there are quite a few hand-held/PDA devices on the market, they are not suitable for handling the complex computations required for adequate AR visualization. In some cases, the wearable computer platforms are high-end laptops, mounted on a backpack. The computer manufacturers VIA and Xybernaut sell ruggedized wearable PCs, running Windows 98 on Pentium CPUs with up to 233 MHz. Nonruggedized wearable PCs are available in the ranges from the TIQIT PC (35) with its 66-MHz 486 processor up to the SaintSong "Espresso" PC with its Pentium III (700 MHz). The trend in hardware miniaturization is not yet stopped; we will see amazing miniature computers appear on the market in the next few years, which will help to bring AR applications to larger groups of users.

Usability and Human Factors

An important issue in developing AR applications is to investigate how a suitable interface for these can be developed. The conventional interface currently employed by most computing systems is the Windows–Icons—Mouse-Pointing (WIMP) paradigm. This does not work well in a wearable mobile system, where the main focus of the user's attention is on the real world. Speech input is seen as seamless means for controlling the information display of an AR system, in conjunction with context-sensitive awareness of the system.

Researchers also investigate how to present the information in the real world. One way of avoiding head-worn displays is to project the imagery in the environment by external projects (Spatially Augmented Reality) and to provide correct perspective by tracking the user (36). This, however, allows only one user to see the displayed information in the correct perspective. Linking AR visualization to physical objects is an interesting method for enhancing the real world with information. This exploits the intuitively learned abilities of users to handle real-world objects like ink and paper (37). In general, one may differentiate between *task-specific* AR applications, where the user may compromise certain conveniences as a price for more efficient performance of his/her task with the help of an AR system, and *user-centric* AR applications, which are tailored to the user's abilities in dealing with daily life tasks.

An important issue arose with the advent of more sophisticated rendering and tracking capabilities: the user may no longer be able to differentiate between the real world and the virtual representation and may confuse both. Depending on the applications, ways may have to be found to uniquely indicate what is part of the virtual world and what is real.

User Collaboration

The collaboration between users in virtual spaces has been an important research topic in the past years. Examples of such collaborative environments include the "Studierstube" (38), a project for scientific 3D visualization and "shared spaces", and a collaborative communication tool with video transmission and a common white-board (39). The issue of mutual privacy among those participants in a virtual shared space has been addressed by allowing users to "hide" some of the objects within their "work space" from other users (40). The interface between the users and such collaborative AR systems must not only provide ways of handling/interacting with the information but also among the users themselves. Speech input is used as the most seamless method of user input, but gesture recognition is also a nonintrusive way of interacting with information and users. It is important that such collaborative systems retain the "usual" interaction modes between human users, so that these systems augment the capabilities in a way that provides intuitive extension of these human capabilities.

SUMMARY, CONCLUSION, AND OUTLOOK

The prime time for augmented reality has yet to come; currently, many technological hurdles have to be overcome before AR will play a significant role. However, within the next 10 years, AR will surpass the importance of VR, because VR by its very nature is limited to certain applications, whereas AR will encompass the whole range of user applications, in daily work and even in daily life. This will help users in many tasks, but also may have significant social implications (41).

REFERENCES

1. I. E. Sutherland, "A Head-Mounted Three-Dimensional Display," AFIPS Conf. Proc., *33*(Part I), 757–764 (1968).
2. T. Caudell and D. Mizell, "Augmented Reality: An Application of Heads-Up Display Technology to Manual Manufacturing Processes," in *Proc. of the Hawaii International Conference on System Science (HICSS)*, 1992, Vol. 2, pp. 659–669.

3. R. Behringer, G. Klinker, and D. Mizell (eds.), "Augmented Reality—Placing Artificial Objects in Real Scenes," *Proceedings of the First International Workshop on Augmented Reality 1998*, Peters, 1999.

4. J. Blauert, *Spatial Hearing: The Psychoacoustics of Human Sound Localization*, MIT Press, Cambridge, MA, 1997.

5. E. D. Mynatt, M. Back, R. Want, and R. Frederick, "Audio Aura: Light-Weight Audio Augmented Reality," in *Proceedings of ACM UIST'97*, 1997, pp. 210–212.

6. H. Iwata, "Feel-through: Augmented Reality with Force Feedback," in *Mixed Reality—Merging Real and Virtual Worlds*, Y. Ohta and H. Tamura (eds.), Springer-Verlag, New York, 1999.

7. H. Ishii, "Tangible Bits: Coupling Physicality and Virtuality Through Tangible User Interfaces," in *Mixed Reality—Merging Real and Virtual Worlds*, T. Ohta and H. Tamura (eds.), Springer-Verlag, New York, 1999.

8. R. Azuma, "A Survey of Augmented Reality," *Presence*, 6(4), 355–385 (1997).

9. G. Simon, V. Lepetit, and M. O. Berger, "Computer Vision Methods for Registration: Mixing 3D Knowledge and 2D Correspondence for Accurate Image Composition," in *Proceedings of the First International Workshop on Augmented Reality (IWAR '98)*, Peters, 1999.

10. P. Milgram and H. Colquhoun, "A Taxonomy of Real and Virtual World Display Integration," in *Mixed Reality—Merging Real and Virtual Worlds*, Y. Ohta and H. Tamura (eds.), Springer-Verlag, New York, 1999.

11. H. Tamura, H. Yamamoto, and A. Katayama, "Steps Towards Seamless Mixed Reality," in *Mixed Reality—Merging Real and Virtual Worlds*, Y. Ohta and H. Tamura (eds.), Springer-Verlag, New York, 1999.

12. K. Sato, Y. Ban, and K. Chihara, "MR Aided Engineering: Inspection Support Systems Integrating Virtual Instruments and Process Control," in *Mixed Reality—Merging Real and Virtual Worlds*, Y. Ohta and H. Tamura (eds.), Springer-Verlag, New York, 1999.

13. D. Curtis, D. Mizell, P. Gruenbaum, and A. Janin, "Several Devils in the Details: Making an AR Application Work in the Airplane Factory," in *Proceedings of the First International Workshop on Augmented Reality (IWAR '98)*, Peters, 1999.

14. R. Sharma and J. Molineros, "Interactive Visualization and Augmentation of Mechanical Assembly Sequences," in *Graphics Interface '96*, 1996, pp. 230–237.

15. D. Reiners, D. Stricker, G. Klinker, and S. Müller, "Augmented Reality for Construction Tasks: Doorlock Assembly," in *Proceedings of the First International Workshop on Augmented Reality (IWAR '98)*, Peters, 1999.

16. W. E. L. Grimson, M. E. Leventon, G. Ettinger, A. Chabrerie, F. Ozlen, S. Nakajima, H. Atsumi, R. Kikinis, and P. Black, "Clinical Experience with a High Precision Image-Guided Neurosurgery System," in *Proc. of the First International Conference on Medical Image Computing and Computer-Assisted Intervention (MICCAI)*, 1998, pp. 63–73.

17. N. Navab, A. Bani-Hashemi, and M. Mitschke, "Merging Visible and Invisible: Two Camera-Augmented Mobile C-arm (CAMC) Applications," in *Proceedings of the 2nd International Workshop on Augmented Reality (IWAR '99)*, 1999.

18. G. Klinker, D. Stricker, and D. Reiners, "Augmented Reality for Exterior Construction Applications," in *Augmented Reality and Wearable Computing*, W. Barfield and T. Caudell (eds.), Lawrence Erlbaum Press, 1998.

19. A. Webster, S. Feiner, B. MacIntyre, W. Massie, and T. Krueger, "Augmented Reality in Architectural Construction, Inspection, and Renovation," in *Computing in Civil Engineering*, 1996, pp. 913–919.

20. W. Piekarski, B. Gunther, and B. Thomas, "Integrating Virtual and Augmented Realities in an Outdoor Application," in *Proceedings of the 2nd International Workshop on Augmented Reality (IWAR '99)*, 1999.

21. S. Julier, M. Lanzagorta, Y. Baillot, L. Rosenblum, S. Feiner, T. Höllerer, and S. Sestito,

"Information Filtering for Mobile Augmented Reality," in *Proc. Symposium on Augmented Reality (ISAR 2000)*, 2000.

22. P. Bisson, S. Kakez, C. Poulet-Mathis, X. Pouteau, and M. Cavazza, "Augmented Reality for Telepresence," in *Proceedings of Montpellier Informatique '95: Interfaces to Real and Virtual Worlds*, 1995, pp. 115–124.

23. P. Proctor, "New Head-Up Tool Aims to Cut Runway Incidents," *Aviation Week*, 48–50 (August 14, 2000).

24. T. Ohsima, K. Satoh, H. Yamamoto, and H. Tamura, "AR^2 Hockey: A Case Study of collaborative Augmented Reality," in *Proc. VRAIS '98*, 1998, pp. 268–275.

25. T. Höllerer, S. Feiner, and J. Pavlik, "Situated Documentaries: Embedding Multimedia Presentation in the Real World," in *Proceedings of the 3rd International Symposium on Wearable Computing (ISWC'99)*, 1999, pp. 79–86.

26. S. Feiner, B. MacIntyre, T. Höllerer, and A. Webster, "A Touring Machine: Prototyping 3D Mobile Augmented Reality Systems for Exploring the Urban Environment," in *Personal Technol.*, *1*(4), 208–217 (1997).

27. J. Rekimoto, "NaviCam: A Magnifying Glass Approach to Augmented Reality," *Presence*, 6(4), 399–412 (1997).

28. Y. Cho, J. Lee, and U. Neumann, "A Multi-Ring Fiducial System and an Intensity Invariant Detection Method for Scalable Augmented Reality," in *Proceedings of the First International Workshop on Augmented Reality (IWAR '98)*, Peters, 1999.

29. R. Behringer, S. Chen, V. Sundareswaran, K. Wang, and M. Vassiliou, "A Distributed Device Diagnostics System Utilizing Augmented Reality and 3D Audio," *Computers Graphics*, *23*, 821–825 (1999).

30. T. Kanade, P. Rander, S. Vedula, and H. Saito, "Virtualized Reality: Digitizing a 3D Time-Varying Event as It Is in Real Time," in *Mixed Reality—Merging Real and Virtual Worlds*, Y. Ohta and H. Tamura (eds.), Springer-Verlag, New York, 1999.

31. R. Azuma, "The Challenge of Making Augmented Reality Work Outdoors," in *Mixed Reality—Merging Real and Virtual Worlds*, Y. Ohta and H. Tamura (eds.), Springer-Verlag, New York, 1999.

32. E. Foxlin, M. Harrington, and Y. Altshuler, "Miniature 6-DOF Inertial System for Tracking HMDs," in *Proceedings of SPIE Aerosense'98*, 1998.

33. A. State, G. Hirota, D. T. Chen, W. F. Garret, and M. A. Livingston, "Superior Augmented-Reality Registration by Integrating Landmark Tracking and Magnetic Tracking," in *Proc. SIGGRAPH '96*, 1996, pp. 429–438.

34. K. Kiyokawa, Y. Kurata, and H. Ohno, "An Optical See-Through Display for Mutual Occlusion of Real and Virtual Environments," in *Proceedings of ISAR 2000*, 2000.

35. G. DeFouw and V. Pratt, "The Matchbox PC: A Small Wearable Platform," in *Proc. ISWC'99*, 1999, pp. 79–86.

36. R. Raskar, G. Welch, and W. C. Chen, "Table-Top Spatially-Augmented Reality: Bringing Physical Models to Life with Projected Imagery," in *Proceedings of the 2nd International Workshop on Augmented Reality (IWAR '99)*, 1999.

37. W. E. Mackay and A. L. Payard, "Designing Interactive Paper: Lessons from Three Augmented Reality Projects," in *Proceedings of the 2nd International Workshop on Augmented Reality (IWAR '99)*, 1999.

38. Zs. Szalavari, D. Schmalstieg, A. Fuhrmann, and M. Gervautz, "Studierstube—An Environment for Collaboration in Augmented Reality," *Virtual Res.: Res. Dev. Applic.*, *3*, 37–48 (1998).

39. M. Billinghurst, S. Weghorst, and T. Furness, "Shared Space: An Augmented Reality Approach for Computer Supported Cooperative Work," *Virtual Reality*, *3*(1), 25–36 (1998).

40. A. Butz, T. Höllerer, S. Feiner, B. MacIntyre, and C. Besher, "Enveloping Users and Com-

puters in a Collaborative 3D Augmented Reality," in *Proceedings of the 2nd International Workshop on Augmented Reality (IWAR '99)*, 1999.

41. S. K. Feiner, "The Importance of Being Mobile: Some Social Consequences of Wearable Augmented Reality Systems," in *Proceedings of the 2nd International Workshop on Augmented Reality (IWAR '99)*, 1999.

REINHOLD BEHRINGER

CHINESE TEXT SPELLING CHECK AND SEGMENTATION

INTRODUCTION

In alphabet-based languages such as English, each word is composed of a sequence of letters and each letter is represented by a unique code. To spell check an English word, the word is checked against the entries in an English dictionary. However, Chinese text has no natural delimiters such as spaces between words, which are meaningful sequences of characters. Every Chinese character input must be a valid ideograph, but the sequence of Chinese characters may not make sense. For example, if the word 時間 (which means time) is mistyped as 時聞, both characters 時 and 聞 are correct characters, although the character sequence 時聞 is not a correct word. Spell checking in Chinese text is designed to identify the wrong use or misuse of characters in text composition. In other words, it is error correction at the word (a meaningful sequence of characters) level rather than at the character level. Chinese spell checking is usually divided into two steps: segmentation of text and error detection. Segmentation is a process that divides a string of characters into words. The segmented text is then checked against a dictionary or thesaurus. Grammatical rules are sometimes used to segment Chinese text. The principle of a Chinese spelling checker is based on the fact that most common errors in Chinese writing are due to the misuse of similar sound or similar shaped characters. It is also true that there is a large but manageable set of Chinese words. We can compare the input with a Chinese word dictionary. If such a word does not exist, the system will generate some possible combinations based on the similarity table. All legal combinations, those can be found in the word dictionary, will be returned to the users.

In this article, common Chinese text errors are introduced. An outline of the spelling checker is in the third section, and the fourth section will discuss the Chinese Text Segmentation Methods. The fifth section is the conclusion.

COMMON ERRORS IN CHINESE WORDS

Illegal characters (錯字) refereed in most literature (1,2) are those characters that cannot be found in any Chinese dictionaries. This is because the structure of a Chinese character is composed of many strokes (筆劃). If a user writes one or more strokes incorrectly, the Chinese character will become illegal. However, in any Chinese system, it is not possible to input illegal characters by keyboard or others input devices because all characters that the user can input are those defined in the input methods dictionaries. To design a computerized spelling checker, we will concentrate on the misuse of similar characters (別字), not illegal Chinese characters.

In English, there are only 26 alphabets (characters) in its character set. However, there are more than 20,000 characters in Chinese although only about 3000–4000 of them are frequently used characters (常用字) (3). The techniques such as tree search algorithm used in an English spelling checker may be employed in a Chinese spelling checker. However, the way intelligent guesses are generated when an illegal character is encountered is quite different. In order to generate intelligent suggestions, we have to study the fault model of Chinese words. This fault model is based on seven common causes of faults found in Chinese writings. The following is a discussion on the common causes of faults.

Similar Shape (字形相近)

Chinese characters are composed of three levels of parts. They are strokes (筆劃), components (部件), and radicals (部首). The relationships among these three parts is shown in Figure 1. Basically, strokes contain 橫、豎、撇、點、折. Then, components are constructed by these basic strokes. For example, in the Chinese character 益, there are four components: 八、一、八、皿. Finally, these components construct radicals. For example, in the Chinese characters 錫 and 橋, their radicals are 金、易 and 木、喬 respectively.

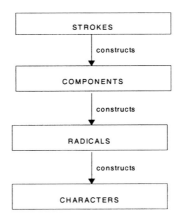

FIGURE 1   Composition of Chinese characters.

First, there are many Chinese characters that differ by one or two strokes. Although the meaning and the usage of these characters are quite different, it is very easy to get confused. For example,

Character sets	Difference
剌 ----> 剌	剌字缺少一橫
酩 ----> 酩	一點變成一撇
印 ----> 卬	印字缺少一橫
衷 ----> 哀	哀字缺少一豎
止 ----> 上	上字缺少一豎

Second, there are also many Chinese characters that differ by one or two components. For example,

Character sets	Difference
裹 裏	部件「果」變成部件「里」

Among the three levels of basic structures, the number of characters which are similar in shape on the basis of radicals are more than that of the others. The main reason of this phenomenon is due to the fact that Chinese characters are created by four different methods:

1. Implied shape   象形
2. Implied event   指事
3. Implied meaning   會意
4. Implied shape and sound   形聲

Among these four methods, the ability to create characters by the method of shape and sound (形 聲) is the strongest. From statistics, over 90% of Chinese characters were created by this method (1). The radical shape (形旁) means the category of the character. The radical of sound (聲 旁) means the pronunciation of the character. For example,

Characters	Category	Sound
搬	手	般
踩	足	采
蝗	虫	皇
湖	水	胡

There are about 400 different radicals in Chinese (1). In the latest ISO/IEC 10646 coding standard (4), 300 radicals are assigned unique codes. Many Chinese characters are composed of similar radicals. A user will easily mistake these similar characters. There are many frequently mistaken words because they share some identical radicals. For example,

Character sets	Common radical
仿彷	方
采彩綵	采
孤弧狐	瓜
催摧	崔

Same Sound and Similar Sound (同音或近音)

Each Chinese character has its pronunciation and tone. The following discussion and examples will be based on Cantonese (廣東話) pronunciations, although the same principle can also be applied to Putonghua (普通話) and other dialects.

Because 90% of Chinese characters are created by the method of shape and sound (形 聲), the pronunciation of each character is often implied by the radical of sound (聲旁). The problem is that the position of the radical of pronunciation is not fixed in each character. There are six main positions of sound radical in a Chinese character (1):

1. 左形右聲: 站 , 枯 , 模 , 經 , 坊
2. 左聲右形: 故 , 郭 , 鄞 , 頸 , 放

3. 上形下聲: 寛 , 芳 , 萱 , 翁 , 蔓
4. 上聲下形: 摹 , 架 , 弊 , 基 , 壟
5. 內形外聲: 問 , 聞 , 闔 , 辨 , 辯
6. 內聲外形: 衷 , 闌 , 圓 , 赴 , 囤

The pronunciation of Chinese characters has changed after several thousands of years of development (1). The ability to represent the pronunciation of characters created by the method of shape and sound (形 聲) is only about 39% nowadays. However, the writer often tries to guess those forgotten words by inserting the radicals of sound. As the result, the chance of writing another similar character with the same pronunciation is very high.

Finally, we want to point out that there are many characters with the same pronunciations. For illustration, there are total 19 consonants, 53 vowels, and 9 tones in Cantonese. There should be about 9000 different sounds of Chinese characters in theory. Even if we discount the nonexistence of some consonant, vowel, and tone combinations, there are, on average, 4 same-sound characters among the 20,000 odd common Chinese characters (5)《索音字彙》. Here, we list some commonly used characters which have same pronunciation Cantonese pronunciations:

Character sets	Pronunciation
師 詩 司 思 斯	si 1
伸 呻 紳 身 新	san 1
沙 砂 紗 鯊	sa 1

In the worst case, from our investigation, there are 25 characters in the following same sound characters set for Cantonese (6):

儒 , 如 , 孺 , 予 , 余 , 俞 , 娛 , 愉 ,

愚 , 榆 , 漁 , 渝 , 瑜 , 盂 , 竽 , 臾 ,

與 , 虞 , 諛 , 輿 , 餘 , 魚 , 嶼 , 隅 , 逾

For the problem of similar pronunciation, the situation is more complicated because one character may have more than one pronunciation. Therefore, the probability that the user mistypes characters because of similar pronunciation is also very high. For example,

Character	Pronunciations
重	chung, jung
降	gong, kong

Hybrid Cases

1. *Similar shape and similar meaning*: For example, both characters 待 (accompany with or serving somebody) and 侍 (waiting for or serving somebody) have very similar shape, and their meanings are very similar too.

2. *Similar shape and same sound*: For example, the pronunciation of both characters 忙 and 忘 are "mong4." Also, they both have an identical radical 「亡」, so their shape are very similar too.

3. *Same sound and similar meaning*: For example, the pronunciation of both characters 刷 (a noun, means a brush) and 擦 (a verb means to clean or rub something) are "chaat3."

Misuses of Characters due to Similar Meanings: (近意字)

There are many Chinese idioms for which the use of the exact character is not clear because two similar characters will form perfectly meaningful idioms. The following are examples:

名「符」其實 should be corrected to 名副其實 (an idiom which means not just in name only, but also in reality). The character 符 means "in accordance with" and 名符其實 can be interpreted as "the name is in accordance with the reality." Some people argue that both are correct in meaning, but it is incorrect because the original characters must be preserved in an idiom.

既往不「究」 should be corrected to 既往不咎 (an idiom which means let bygones be bygones). The character 究 means "to investigate" and 既往不究 can be interpreted as "not to investigate for somebody's past misdeeds." However, it is incorrect because the original characters must be preserved in an idiom.

Wrong Order

There are many examples in Chinese language that even if the order of characters is reversed, the words are still legal phrases in the dictionary. In some cases, their meanings maybe totally different. For example,

Character sets	Meanings
言 語	speech
語 言	language
污 染	pollution
染 污	pollute
悲 傷	sad
傷 悲	sad

Missing Character (缺字)

One of the characters is missing.

Excess Character (多字)

One extra character is entered. There are many phrases in Chinese which contain four or even more characters. The chances to mistype or forgetting one or more characters is high.

Based on these six common faults, we would be able to design an algorithm to make intelligent guesses for incorrect words.

THE SPELLING CHECKER DESIGN

The flowchart (Fig. 2) summarizes the algorithm of the Chinese "spell checker." A string of Chinese characters is checked against a word dictionary. If the word is not found in the dictionary, it will trigger the nonexact match module and try to find suitable matches from the word dictionary. For each character, characters with similar shapes, the same sound, or similar sounds will be compared. Results will be returned to the user to correct the original text. If this nonextract match function still cannot find the correct word, the system will try to generate guesses based on characters in reverse order, similar sound, and shape characters.

There are three main databases: the word dictionary files, the Chinese Character table, and the Chinese Character Position Index table. The word dictionary files hold all the legal words, the Chinese Character table stores all the shape and pronunciation information of a character, and the Position Index table stores the information on how characters can be linked to form legal words.

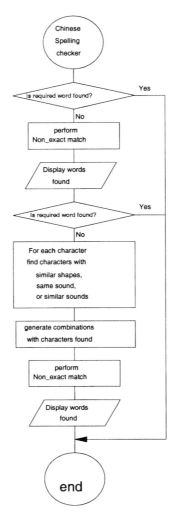

FIGURE 2   The word checker algorithm.

CHINESE TEXT SEGMENTATION

In the previous sections, we explained that Chinese spell checking refers to how to identify the misuse of characters in text composition. In other words, it is error correction at the word level rather than at the character level. Chinese spell checking is divided into two steps: segmentation of text and error detection/correction. Segmentation is a process that divides a string of characters into words. Error detection can then be carried out on the segmented text based on thesaurus and grammar rules. Segmentation is not a trivial process because of ambiguities in the Chinese language and errors in texts. Because it is not practical to define all Chinese words in a dictionary, one must deal with words not predefined. The number of word combinations increases exponentially with the length of the sentence. In this section, a Block-of-Combinations (BOC) segmentation method based on the frequency of word usage is proposed to reduce the word combinations from exponential growth to linear growth. From experiments carried out on Hong Kong newspapers, BOC can correctly solve 10% more ambiguities than the Maximum Match segmentation method.

Segmentation is not a trivial process because of morphological complexities and ambiguities in the Chinese language (7). A sentence may be segmented in several legitimate ways, yielding different meanings. It is not easy to determine which of the possible segmentations is the best. Chinese segmentation problems have been reported in many information-retrieval systems. Also, there is a problem with unknown words. Unknown words are words that are not predefined in the system. It is not practical to define all Chinese words in a dictionary because new words can be created by combining characters or words (8). For example, 足球場 (football field) is a combination of 足球 (football) and 場 (place). Among the unknown words, there are morphologically derived words, personal names, and transliterated foreign names (9).

However, unlike text analysis for translation or semantic analysis, it is sometimes not necessary for a spelling checker to find a unique segmentation solution. For example, the sentence 發展中國家用電器換取外匯 may be segmented as follows:

1. 發展　　中國　家用電器　　　　　換取　　　外匯

   develop/China/household-appliance/exchange/foreign currency

   The translation is "to develop China's household-appliance industry to exchange for foreign currency."

2. 發展中國家　　　　用　　電器　　換取　　　外匯.

   developing country/use/appliance/exchange/foreign currency

   The translation is "developing countries use appliances to exchange foreign currency."

Both segmentation results are correct from the point of view of spell checking and there is no need to solve the ambiguity.

Many segmentation methods exist (7,8,10–14). Most segmentation methods find a unique solution without interacting with the user, even if suspected errors occur. Some of these methods assume that the texts to be segmented are correct; others automatically choose the most likely segmentation as the solution. They are suitable for applications such as semantic analysis for information retrieval. However, they are not suitable for spell checking in text processing because errors and unknown words are not dealt with. Because there is no accurate way to distinguish errors from unknown words, the best solutions obtained may not match the original writer's intended meaning, as in the above example.

In this section, a block-of-combinations (BOC) segmentation method based on the frequency of word usage is described. In order to make the method more suitable for spell checking, user interaction is also introduced into the system. Interaction is possible because the spell checker is intended for on-line text checking. When suspected errors occur, the system will allow the user to make the final decision. Based on the user's response, the segmentation can be refined to fit the user's interpretation, and unknown words can also be learned by the system during the spell checking process.

The following subsections are organized as follows. The first subsection discusses related work in segmentation; the second subsection gives an overview of the segmentation process and the interactive model of this system. The details of our word-frequency based segmentation method (BOC) and some examples are shown in the third and fourth subsections respectively.

Related Work

There are many different approaches to Chinese text segmentation. Basically, they can be classified into rule-based, statistics-based, or hybrid methods based on the combination of rules and statistics.

In rule-based segmentation approaches, dictionaries are often used. However, the arrangement of the dictionaries varies from one design to another. Some segmentation methods use dictionaries of words. The sequences of characters to be segmented are checked against the dictionaries. Among those methods, maximum match (13) is the most commonly used because it is simple and efficient. The idea of maximum match is to select the longest word among all possibilities when there is an ambiguity. On the other hand, some methods use dictionaries of word components. It is based on the idea that most of the words exceeding two characters can be formed by one-character or two-character words. Grammatical rules can be incorporated to combine the word components (7).

In addition to dictionaries of words, other information is also considered in some designs. In the segmentation method proposed by Chang and co-workers (9,12), a character table for similar shape, sound, meaning, and input-method-code characters are proposed. In Chang et al.'s method, all the combinations are proposed based on the character table and scores are given to the combinations. This approach tries to "guess" all the possible errors. The problem with this method is its limitations in handling errors other than single substitution errors. Also, the performance is highly dependent on the size of the character table. A knowledge base containing grammatical and semantic knowledge for word segmentation is suggested by Liang and Zheng (13). However, it is not easy to construct a complete knowledge base for all Chinese words. The semiword method was introduced by Bai (10). A semiword is a one-character word that is seldom used as a word. Instead, semiwords are used to form words with other characters. Examples of semiwords are 確 (real), 實 (real), and 理 (reason). They are seldom used as words on their own, but they form words such as 確實 (really) and 真理 (the truth), which are used more often. A set of semiwords was compiled by Bai (10). The best segmentation is chosen using a set of scoring principles.

In statistics-based methods, probabilities such as word frequency and character co-occurrence frequency are considered. Lua (3) proposed using information theory in word formation. New words are formed if there is a significant change in entropy, in terms of word frequency. A method based on mutual information was proposed by Sproat and Shih (14). This method gives a measure of how strongly two characters are associated based on the probability of the occurrence of the characters. Also, bigrams are considered in finding word boundaries. An *n*-gram is a string of *n* adjacent characters which may or may not be words (in some other approaches (15) an *n*-gram is defined as a string of *n* adjacent words). In particular, a bigram is a string of two adjacent characters and is often used in statistical and hybrid approaches. Bigrams and trigrams were used in Ref. 15 for classifying Chinese words. Markov models and bigrams are used together as an evaluation of a segmentation solution in Yeh and Lee's method (16). Gao and Chen (12) considered all the combinations of *n*-grams, in which *n* is a variable, in performing segmentation.

Some articles suggested that it might be better to solve the problem of segmentation together with other goals. The integration of word segmentation and part-of-speech tagging was proposed by Chang and Chen (11). From their results, it was found that the segmentation-dominated approach is better than the tagging-dominated approach. Thus, a good segmentation can improve tagging. Nie et al. (8) suggested that unknown word detection could be integrated with segmentation. The phrase to be handled is first segmented as much as possible based on a dictionary. The unsegmented portions are then examined and candidate unknown words are proposed.

Quite a number of these efforts at segmentation achieve a high level of accuracy in tests. However, most of the methods assume that there are no unknown words and automatically choose a segmentation among the possibilities as the solution without interacting with the user, even if there are suspected errors. This approach should not be applied to spell checking because the segmentation chosen may not match the original writer's intentions.

The Segmentation Process and System Interaction Model

The proposed segmentation process BOC is dictionary based. It makes use of the statistical data about Chinese words published by the Education Department of Hong Kong (17). The dictionary in BOC contains 60,000 words, in which the 2000 most frequently used words are grammatically tagged. BOC also includes a user dictionary and a temporary dictionary for the storage of unknown words. The user dictionary stores user-defined words, which are not predefined in the system and can be updated from time to time, whereas the temporary dictionary automatically stores the unknown words until the whole segmentation process terminates.

The target of text is first divided into sentences. Punctuation marks are used as delimiters to separate sentences. Some of the sentences may contain symbols, alphabetic symbols, and numerals. These types of characters are skipped without checking and are used as unnatural delimiters to further divide sentences into phrases. The phrases are then segmented into words by the BOC method. Because incorrect characters such as mistyped characters often cannot form a multicharacter word with adjacent characters (18), single-character words are considered as suspected errors. Table 3.1 of Ref. 3 shows, however, monosyllabic words have the highest frequencies, although the number of different monosyllabic words (i.e., single-character words) is much less than that of disyllabic words (i.e., words consisting of two characters) (see Table 1).

In fact, a number of single-character words are used quite frequently. If all the single-character words are treated as suspected errors and presented to the user, there will be many false alarms. In order to reduce false alarms, occurrences of the first 200 most frequently used single-character words such as 的 (of), 一 (one), 是 (is), 不

TABLE 1   Distribution of Monosyllabic and
Polysyllabic Words

Word length	Number	Usage
Monosyllabic	12.1%	64.3%
Disyllabic	73.6%	34.3%
Trisyllabic	7.6%	0.4%
Four syllabic	6.4%	0.4%
Five syllabic or more	0.2%	0%

(not), 有 (have), 在 (in), 我 (I), and 個 (unit, quantity) should not be considered suspected errors.

When a suspected error is detected, it is presented to the user for clarification. A continuous string of suspected errors is considered as one suspicious unit and is highlighted for the user. Words that are similar to a suspicious unit are fetched from the dictionaries and displayed as suggested corrections. Because a suspicious unit may not correspond to a word, the user can adjust the boundaries of the suspicious unit by highlighting it again. The corresponding list of suggested corrections is then obtained.

A suspected error may be an error or an unknown word. Errors can be corrected at once. The user can replace a suspicious unit by a suggested correction or edit the erroneous sentence directly. On the other hand, unknown words are automatically stored in the temporary dictionary or they can also be stored in the user dictionary for future use based on the user's indication. When those words are encountered again in the text, they will not be treated as suspected errors because they are not unknown words any more. After a suspected error is handled, the segmentation process continues at the position immediately after the word handled.

BOC Segmentation Method

Before describing the BOC method, let us consider the following phrase first:

誰都不知道它的確實用途   (No one knows its real use)

Assume that the words 知道 (know), 的確 (really), 確實 (really), 實用 (practical), and 用途 (use) are in the dictionary. Then, there are several possible combinations:

1. 誰　都　不　知道　它　<u>的確</u>　<u>實用</u>　途
2. 誰　都　不　知道　它　<u>的確</u>　實　<u>用途</u>
3. 誰　都　不　知道　它　的　<u>確實</u>　<u>用途</u>

The correct segmentation should be combination 3:

誰　都　不　知道　它　的　確實　用途

(No one knows its real use)

The word-by-word translation is who/also/not/know/it/of/real/use

The other two segmentations are not meaningful. This may be deduced from so-called word formation power (17) in which the word formation power of the character 實 is higher than that of the character 的, and so it is more likely that the character sequence 確實 is a word. Also, the co-occurrence probability suggested by Sproat and

Shih (14) can be used to choose the correct segmentation. However, the correct segmentation would be totally different if one of the characters is changed. For example,

誰都不知道它的確實用嗎   (the last character is changed from 途 to 嗎)

(Does no one know that it is really practical?)

The correct segmentation of this phrase should be

誰 · 都   不   知道 它 的確   實用   嗎

(who/also/not/know/it/really/practical/question tag)

which is very different from the previous example.

In fact, the segmentation can be viewed in another way. The first phrase is segmented as above because it is unlikely that either the character 實 or the character 途 is a single-character word. Therefore, the segmentation can be considered as choosing the combination that has the smallest number of "unusual" single-character words. This is similar to the semiword method proposed by Bai (10). Recall that a semiword is a one-character word that is seldom used as a word. However, in the semiword method, a character is either in the set of semiwords or not and takes a binary value. For the BOC method proposed, word frequency is considered rather than binary value.

In the BOC segmentation method proposed, the single-character-word function U is defined as

$$U(f) = \begin{cases} 1 & \text{if } f \geq f\text{SAT} \\ \dfrac{f - f_{CUT}}{f\text{SAT} - f\text{CUT}} & \text{if } f\text{CUT} < f < f\text{SAT} \\ 0 & \text{if } f \leq f\text{CUT}, \end{cases}$$

where f is the occurrence frequency of the character as a single character word, f_{CUT} is the threshold frequency below the range in which the characters are considered as semiwords, and f_{SAT} is the threshold frequency above which the characters often appear as single-character words. $U(f)$ can be visualized as in Figure 3.

The score of a segmentation is defined as

Score-S = $\Sigma (1 - U(f_j))$,

where j is a single character appearing in the segmentation. Thus, the best segmentation is the one with the smallest Score-S.

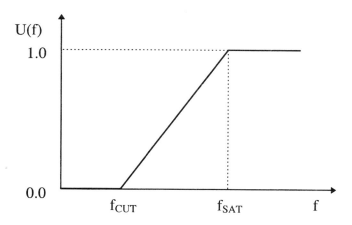

FIGURE 3   The relationship between single-character-word function $U(f)$ and word frequency f.

Heuristic for Finding the Best Segmentation

In order to find the segmentation with the smallest Score-S, all the possible combinations of the words are considered. Theoretically, any sequence of Chinese characters can form a word, if unknown words are also considered. For a phrase of L characters, if the maximum word length is restricted to m, then there are m possible words starting with the first character. For example, in the phrase 天鵝湖是 . . . (swan lake is . . .), when $m = 3$, at most three words can be formed with the first character 天: 天鵝湖 (swan lake), 天鵝 (swan), and 天 (sky).

If the first character 天 is segmented as a monosyllabic word, the number of combinations of the phrase is reduced to that of the remaining $L-1$ characters 鵝湖是. . . . Similarly, for the case that the first two characters 天鵝 are segmented as a disyllabic word, the number of combinations is dependent on the $L-2$ characters 湖是. . . . If the first m characters are segmented as one word, the number of combinations of the phrase will be reduced to that of the $L-m$ characters. Hence, the following hold:

1. For a phrase of length 1 (i.e., a character), the maximum number of different segmentation is 1.

2. From Figure 4, for a phrase of L characters, the maximum number of segmentations is

    Max. no. of segmentation of $L-1$ characters

       + Max. no. of segmentation of $L-2$ characters

       ⋮

       + Max. no. of segmentation of $L-m$ characters.

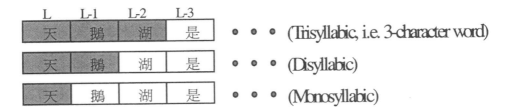

FIGURE 4   The words formed with the first character in a phrase.

Thus, the maximum number of segmentations for a phrase of L characters is

$$N_L = \sum_{i=1}^{i=m} N_{L-i},$$

where $N_{L-i} = 0$ if $L - i < 0$ and $N_{L-i} = 1$ if $L = i$. For the case of maximum word length $m = 7$, the maximum number of segmentations N_L for phrase length L are computed and plotted in Figure 5. From Figure 5, it can be observed that the maximum number of segmentations increases exponentially with the phrase length, and there is a risk of combinatory explosion. Therefore, segmentation will cause long delays if L is large.

In order to avoid the risk of combinatory explosion, a heuristic is designed. It is observed that although there are long-distance dependency phenomena in Chinese, most of the ambiguities can be solved by considering a few adjacent characters. Also, from

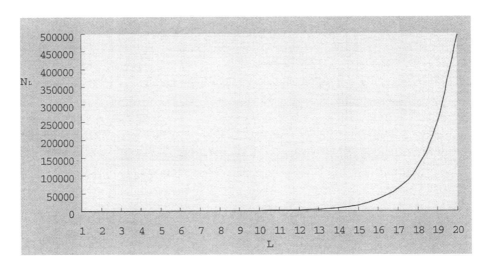

FIGURE 5   Exponential growth of the number of segmentations.

Table 1, most of the words in Chinese are monosyllabic and disyllabic words. Thus, the probability of ambiguities involving long words is much lower than those involving disyllabic words or trisyllabic words. The exception is when long words are composed of shorter ones; for example, 交通工具 (vehicle) is composed of 交通 (transportation) and 工具 (tool). The heuristic proposed is based on these assumptions.

Instead of considering all the combinations of a long phrase at one time, the segmentation process considers text under a sliding window. For each iteration, the process looks ahead several characters and generates combinations in order to choose the best solution. Because there may be several ambiguities adjacent to each other, it may not be able to find a common ending position for evaluation without considering a long series of characters. Here, we have to refine the concept of Terminators. A Terminator is the starting position of the words that follow the words considered in the current iteration. Informally speaking, they are words that will be considered in the next iteration. For example, when considering the phrase 筆畫就是構成漢字字形的各種點和線 (strokes are the dots and lines that construct the shape of the Chinese characters), if the current iteration initially considers the first five characters, then the Terminators are the starting positions of the words located behind the first five characters. Because 漢字 (Chinese character) and 字形 (character shape) are words, the phrase becomes

筆 畫 就 是 構 成 漢 字 字 形 的 各 種 點 和 線

where the arrows indicate two of the possible Terminators.

In order to perform an evaluation of a word combination, a Score-S is calculated from the starting position of the current iteration to the nearest Terminator behind the combination. Thus, if a combination terminates immediately before a Terminator, then the combination matches well with a potential solution in the next iteration. Note that even in the same iteration, the number of characters considered in calculating the Scores for different combinations may be different but are restricted to a certain range. The details of the heuristic are described as follows:

1. The segmentation process scans the phrase from left to right.
2. A number Max_W is predefined (e.g., $Max_W = 5$), which is the maximum length of character strings that will be considered in solving ambiguities. Whenever a word longer than Max_W is encountered, the word is chosen as the result. Thus, in the following steps, the lengths of all the words are assumed to be Max_W or less.

3. At a certain position P of the phrase, all the words beginning with character P are found. (For simplicity, "words" means "multicharacter words".)

    (a) If there is no word beginning at P, it is segmented as a single character and the next iteration starts.

    (b) Otherwise, for the longest word W starting at P, its length L_W is found. All the words starting within P and $P + (L_W - 1)$ inclusively are found. They are denoted as $\{W_{\leq L_W}\}$. If there is only one word, W will be accepted as the result. Then the next iteration begins. If there is more than one word, it is considered to be ambiguous and further analysis is carried out in the following steps.

4. All the words starting within P and $P + (Max_W - 1)$ inclusively are found. This set is denoted by $\{W_{\leq max}\}$. Because all the words under consideration are within Max_W characters, the maximum extent they can span is from P to $P + 2(Max_W - 1)$. For example, if $Max_W = 5$, the maximum extent the words can span is from P to $P + 8$. This is illustrated in Figure 6.

5. All the possible combinations of the words in $\{W_{\leq max}\}$ are generated so that each of these combinations starts at P and ends between $P + (Max_W - 1)$ and $P + 2(Max_W - 1)$. In particular, if $Max_W = 5$, the number of combinations is upper-bounded by 65, which will be explained in Section 4.2.

6. All the words starting within $P + Max_W$ and $P + (Max_W - 1) + Max_W$ inclusively are found and used as Terminators. For $Max_W = 5$, the Terminators are within $P + 5$ and $P + 9$.

7. For each of the combinations generated, the corresponding Score-S is evaluated from P to the smallest Terminator after the combination.

8. After considering all the combinations generated, the one with the smallest Score-S is chosen as the best solution, and the word combination from P to the first word starting between P and $P + (Max_W - 1)$ is the segmentation result of the current iteration. Ties in the smallest Score-S are broken by first choos-

Max. length of first word is 5 (i.e. to P+4)

The longest word starting at P+4 spans to P+8

FIGURE 6   If $Max_W = 5$, the maximum extent the words can span is from P to $P + 8$.

ing the longest word combination, and then the combination consisting of the smallest number of words.

Maximum Number of Combinations in Each Iteration

We have assumed that the length of all the words is less than Max_W and P is the first character considered in the current iteration. For a phrase of L characters, if $L \le Max_W$, then the number of possible word combinations C_L is 2^{L-1}. For example, the phrase ABC can be segmented as {A/B/C, A/BC, AB/C, ABC}; that is, $L = 3$ and $C_L = 2^{3-1} = 4$.

According to Point 4 of the BOC, the number of possible combinations in an iteration is maximum when the words can span from P to $P + 2(Max_W - 1)$; that is,

$$L \ge P + 2(Max_W - 1) - (P + 1)$$
$$\ge 2Max_W - 1.$$

For a phrase of L characters where $L \ge 2\,Max_W - 1$, because all the combinations start at P and end between $P + (Max_W - 1)$ and $P + 2(Max_W - 1)$ as mentioned in Point 5 of the BOC, the maximum number of combinations is

$$Max - C = \sum_{i=Max_W}^{2Max_W - 1} \text{number of combinations of length } i.$$

Recall that all combinations are formed by words in $\{W_{\le max}\}$.

1. For any combination longer than Max_W, the last word in the combination must start with a character within $P + 1$ and $P + Max_W - 1$. If the last word starts at position $P + 1$, the number of combinations equals $C_1 \times 1$, as follows:

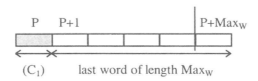

(C_1) last word of length Max_W

   If the last word starts at position $P + 2$, the number of combinations equals $C_2 \times 2$, as follows:

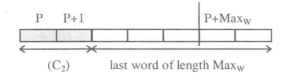

(C_2) last word of length Max_W

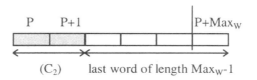

$$(C_2) \qquad \text{last word of length } \text{Max}_W\text{-}1$$

Similarly, if the last word starts at position $P + (\text{Max}_W - 1)$, the number of combinations is $C_{\text{Max}_{W-1}} \times (\text{Max}_W - 1)$. Thus, the total number of combinations is longer than

$$\text{Max}_W = \sum_{j=1}^{\text{Max}_W-1} jC_j$$

2. The number of combinations of length $\text{Max}_W = C_{\text{Max}_W}$. Therefore, the maximum number of combinations is

$$\text{Max} - C = C_{\text{Max}_W} + \sum_{j=1}^{\text{Max}_W-1} jC_j$$

For example, if $\text{Max}_W = 5$,

$$\text{Max} - C = 2^{5-1} + \sum_{j=1}^{5-1} j2^{j-1} = 65.$$

The maximum length of words involving ambiguities (i.e., Max_W) determines the maximum number of combinations Max-C. The larger the maximum length, the more combinations have to be considered and, hence, the more computation time is needed. Therefore, the value of Max_W should be kept as small as possible. Fortunately, most Chinese words are monosyllabic and disyllabic, and most of the ambiguities involve disyllabic words. An ambiguity of two disyllabic words consists of three characters. As the algorithm uses adjacent multicharacter words for solving ambiguities, at least two more characters have to be considered. Therefore, the preferable value of Max_W should be at least 5. It is also a fact that there are not many Chinese words consisting of six of more characters. If such words are encountered, it is very likely that they are desired even when ambiguities occur because long words are often composed of shorter ones. Thus, the maximum length of words involving ambiguities (i.e., Max_W) is set to 5.

For each iteration, if $\text{Max}_W = 5$, the maximum number of combinations is 65 when there are ambiguities. For the worst case, the result of each iteration is a disyllabic word (i.e., word consisting of two characters). Therefore, for a long phrase of 30 characters, 15 iterations are needed and the number of combinations is 65×15 (i.e., 975). The exponential growth of combinations when considering all the possibilities at one time is reduced to linear by this BOC method.

Example

Assume that the phrase 發展中國家庭電器換取外匯 (to develop China's household-appliance industry to exchange for foreign currency) is to be segmented. The corresponding words in the dictionary are 發展中國家 (developing country), 發展 (develop), 中國 (China), 國家 (country), 家庭電器 (household-appliance), 家庭 (family), 電器 (appliance), 換取 (exchange), and 外匯 (foreign currency). Also, $Max_W = 5$ throughout the iterations (refer to Step 2); that is, if a word of six or more characters is encountered, the word will be chosen as the result of that iteration.

Iteration 1: The first character 發 is considered ($P = 1$). There are two words starting with it: 發展中國家 and 發展. The longest word $W =$ 發展中國家 and its length $L_W = 5$ (refer to Step 3b). All the words starting within P (i.e., 1) and $P + (L_W - 1)$ (i.e., 5) inclusively are put in $\{W_{\leq L_W}\}$:

$$\{W_{\leq L_W}\} = \{發展中國家，發展，中國，國家，家庭電器，家庭\}.$$

There are six words in $\{W_{\leq L_W}\}$, so it is considered ambiguous.

Then, because $P = 1$ and $P + (Max_W - 1) = 5$, all the words starting between the first character 發 and the fifth character 家 are found (refer to Step 4). There are six words denoted by

$$\{W_{\leq max}\} = \{發展中國家，發展，中國，國家，家庭電器，家庭\}.$$

Combinations of words are generated based on $\{W_{\leq max}\}$ (refer to Step 5). Examples are the following:

1. 發展中國家
2. 發展　中　國家
3. 發展　中國　家庭電器
4. 發展　中國　家庭

Terminators are then found. Since $P + Max_W = 6$ and $P + (Max_W - 1) + Max_W = 10$, the Terminators start between the 6th character and the 10th character in the iteration (refer to Step 6). Therefore, the Terminators are within the underlined portion of the sentence: (發展中國<u>家庭電器換取</u>外匯). Thus, the Terminators are at the characters (電) and (換), because (電器) and (換取) are words in the dictionary.

In order to evaluate the Score-S, the Terminators are used to limit the length of the combinations (refer to Step 7). The corresponding combinations to be evaluated are as follows:

1. 發展中國家　　庭 ↑Terminator

    $U(f) = 0.0025,$ Score-S $= 0.9975$

2. 發展　　中　　國家　　庭 ↑Terminator

    $U(f) = 0.0915, 0.0025,$ Score-S $= 1.9060$

3. 發展　　中國　　家庭電器 ↑Terminator

    Score-S $= 0.0$

4. 發展　　中國　　家庭 ↑Terminator

    Score-S $= 0.0$

Because the single character 庭 appears in combinations 1 and 2, their Score-S will be higher. Recall that the best combination is the one with the lowest Score-S, combinations 3 and 4 are better. Because combination 3 is longer, it is considered the best combination (refer to Step 8). The segmentation result of this iteration is the first word, 發展. The next iteration starts immediately after this word, and is at the character 中.

Iteration 2: The character 中 is considered and thus P = 3. The only word starting with 中 is 中國. Therefore, W = 中國 and $L_W = 2$ (refer to Step 3b).

Then, because P = 3 and P + (L_W − 1) = 4, all the words starting between the third character (中) and the fourth character (國) are found. There are two words, denoted by

$$\{W_{\leq Lw}\} = \{(\text{中國},\ \text{國家})\}.$$

Thus, the sequence is ambiguous.

Because P = 3 and P + (Max_W − 1) = 7, all the words starting between the third character (中) and the seventh character 電 are found (refer to Step 4). There are five words denoted by

$$\{W_{\leq max}\} = \{\text{中國},\ \text{國家},\ \text{家庭電器},\ \text{家庭},\ \text{電器}\}.$$

Combinations are generated based on $\{W_{\leq max}\}$ (refer to Step 5):

1. 中國　　家庭　　電器
2. 中　　國家　　庭　　電器
3. 中國　　家庭電器

Because $P + \text{Max}_W = 8$ and $P + (\text{Max}_W - 1) + \text{Max}_W = 12$, the Terminators are words starting between the 8th character 器 and the 12th character 匯 in the iteration (refer to Step 6). Thus, the Terminators are at the starting position of the words 換取 and 外匯. Therefore, the evaluation results are (refer to Step 7) as follows:

1. 中國　　家庭　　電器 ↑Terminator

   Score-S = 0.0

2. 中　　國家　　庭　　電器 ↑Terminator

   $U(f) = 0.0915,\ 0.0025,$　Score-S = 1.9060

3. 中國　　家庭電器 ↑Terminator

   Score-S = 0.0

After evaluating the Score-S of the combinations, it is found that combinations 1 and 3 are equally good. Because combination 3 consists of fewer words, it is the best combination (refer to Step 8). The segmentation result of this iteration is the word) 中國. Then, in the next iteration, it will start with the character 家.

Iteration 3: Character considered: 家 and $P = 5$ (Step 3). Words beginning at $P = 5$ are 家庭電器 and 家庭. Therefore, $W = $ 家庭電器 and $L_W = 4$ (Step 3b).

   $\{W_{\leq L_W}\} = \{$家庭電器，家庭，電器$\}$; thus, ambiguous.
   $\{W_{\leq \max}\} = \{$家庭電器，家庭，電器，換取$\}$ (Step 4).

Combinations based on $\{W_{\leq \max}\}$ are generated (Step 5):

1. 家庭電器　　換取
2. 家庭　　電器　　換取

The Terminator is at the starting position of 外匯 (Step 6). After consideration, combination 1 is better and the result of this iteration is 家庭電器 (Steps 7 and 8).

Iteration 4: Character considered: 換 and $P = 9$. The only word starting at $P = 9$ is 換取. Thus, $W = $ 換取 and $L_W = 2$. $\{W_{\leq L_W}\} = \{$換取$\}$. Therefore, it is not ambiguous (Step 3b). The result of this iteration is 換取.

Iteration 5: Character considered: 外 and $P = 11$. The only word starting at $P = 11$ is 外匯. Thus, $W = $ 外匯 and $L_W = 2$. $\{W_{\leq L_W}\} = \{$外匯$\}$. Therefore, it is not ambiguous (Step 3b). The result of this iteration is 外匯.

The final segmentation result of the phrase will be 發展 中國 家庭電器 換取 外匯. The translation is "to develop China's household-appliance industry to exchange for foreign currency."

With this method, the large number of combinations for a long phrase is broken down into blocks of combinations of shorter phrases. Thus, combinatory explosion is avoided.

Performance

The BOC segmentation method proposed is evaluated in terms of accuracy and speed. A segmentation method called Forward Maximum Match (13) is used as a control for comparison. Forward Maximum Match scans sentences from left to right. Character sequences consisting of the first character are first checked against a dictionary. If only one word is matched, it is considered a segment. It is ambiguous if more than one word is matched. Ambiguities are resolved by choosing the longest word among all the possibilities. The process continues after the word is matched. Forward Maximum Match is simple and efficient. However, it is not designed to handle unknown words and errors.

Accuracy

Tests have been performed with articles retrieved over the Internet from the newspaper *Ming Pao* in Hong Kong. Eleven pieces of articles, which are main news, with a total of 6518 characters are segmented. The BOC segmentation method is compared with the Forward Maximum Match segmentation method. We found a total of 100 ambiguities. Among the 100 ambiguities, 68 of them can be solved correctly by both methods, and 5 of them cannot be solved correctly by both methods. Among the remaining 27 ambiguities, 19 of them can only be solved by BOC, whereas 8 of them can only be solved by Forward Maximum Match. Therefore, among the 100 ambiguities, BOC can solve 87 of them, but the Forward Maximum Match can only solve 76 of them. Thus, BOC can solve more ambiguities than Maximum Match by more than 10%. Some examples from the articles are as follows:

1. 可 為 乘客 帶來 更 多 方便 (by BOC, correct). (It can bring more convenience to the passengers)
   可 為 乘客 帶來 更 多方 便 [by Forward Maximum Match (FMM), incorrect]

2. 港 府 上述 提議 仍然 有效 (by BOC, reasonable)
   (The suggestion, which is proposed by the Hong Kong government, mentioned is still valid)

港 府上 述 提議 仍然 有效 (by FMM, incorrect)

where 港府 is an unknown word to the system which means "Hong Kong Government." Note how an unknown word affects the segmentation result.

3. 美 聯 物 業 主席 黃 建業 表示 (by BOC, reasonable) (Mr. Wong, the chairperson of Midland Realty, said)

美 聯 物 業主 席 黃 建業 表示 (by FMM, incorrect)

where 美聯物業 (Midland Realty) is a company name and 黃建業 (the full name of Mr. Wong) is a person name. Both of them are unknown words in the system.

4. However, some ambiguities cannot be solved correctly by BOC:

以便 七月 一 日後 (by BOC, incorrect)

以便 七月 一日 後 (by FMM, correct)

(in order to . . . after the first of July)

The incorrect resolution of ambiguities is because the character □ often appears as a single-character word.

5. Further experiments are performed with errors randomly injected into the articles. Original sentence: 該 批 貨 當時 分別 存放 在 十一 個 箱內. (Those goods were separately placed in eleven boxes at that time)

Error injected:

該 批 貨 人 時 分別 存放 在 十一 個 箱 內 (by BOC, reasonable)

該 批 貨 人 時分 別 存放 在 十一 個 箱 內 (by FMM, incorrect)

where the character 人 is a substitution error randomly injected. Note how an error affects the segmentation result.

Speed

As a segmentation process of an on-line spell checker, speed is important. The computing time of the tests is recorded. In the test, the program is run on a Pentium 100-MHz personal computer with 32M RAM. The operating system is UNIX. The BOC approach is compared with the Forward Maximum Match method, which is very simple and efficient. Each set of data is tested twice. The results are shown in Table 2. From the results, it is observed that the time performance of BOC and FMM are very close to each other. Note that words in the dictionary are fetched by sequential search in the experiment. The speed can be significantly improved through indexing the dictionary or hashing.

TABLE 2   Speeds of the FMM and BOC Segmentation Methods

Case	No. of characters	FMM method time (s)			BOC method time (s)		
		Test 1	Test 2	Mean	Test 1	Test 2	Mean
1	610	135.49	135.21	135.350	135.29	135.35	135.320
2	806	165.99	166.04	166.015	166.21	166.19	166.200
3	293	68.51	68.77	68.640	68.66	68.49	68.575
4	250	57.53	57.62	57.575	57.47	57.51	57.490
5	740	167.85	168.25	168.050	168.05	167.91	167.980
6	1299	304.59	304.99	304.790	304.71	304.80	304.755
7	505	104.00	103.76	103.880	103.89	104.00	103.945
8	486	108.23	108.61	108.420	108.19	108.62	108.405
9	569	120.77	120.89	120.830	120.62	120.71	120.665
10	593	131.12	131.44	131.280	131.55	131.30	131.425
11	367	75.76	75.78	75.770	75.77	75.88	75.825
Total	6518			1440.600			1440.585

CONCLUSIONS

In this article, we have analyzed the common mistakes made by Chinese writers. Based on this analysis, we have devised an algorithm to make intelligent guesses to correct wrong Chinese words. We have proved through experiment that this spelling checker is a workable and invaluable tool to Chinese word processing.

Although our word dictionary is in complex writings, we do not foresee any problem in extending this design to cover simplified writings. Moreover, the sound table should not be restricted to Cantonese pronunciations. As long as suitable data dictionaries is available, user should be given the choice to customize the system.

The main problem with this spelling checker is that the number of combinations generated can be large. The search time can be long if we have a dictionary including all the known Chinese words. However, the memory requirement and response time up to now seems to be reasonable.

An effective text checker relies on an effective segmentation algorithm. In this article, we have also presented a block-of-combinations (BOC) segmentation method based on single-character word occurrence frequency. In order to find the best solution, a long phrase is broken into shorter ones, and a small number of word combinations are considered in each iteration so as to avoid the risk of combinatory explosion. The result of tests on newspapers retrieved over the Internet shows that BOC is more accurate than the Forward Maximum Match approach. The computing time of BOC and Maximum

Match are found to be very close to each other. With BOC, unknown words and errors can be taken into consideration during segmentation.

Segmentation relies on the correct text, but the text checker also relies on good segmentation results. Both processes are inseparable. Although these two processes are described separately in this article, these two processes are intermixed. The next natural development for a better checker may include an element of natural language understanding. However, a good natural language analyzer also relies on a good segmentation algorithm. In this article, we have left out the natural language part to avoid confusion.

REFERENCES

1. 柴世森著 "漫談錯別字問題" 語文出版社

2. 寒莊編著 "漫畫常見錯別字手冊" 明華出版公司

3. K. T. Lua "From Character to Word—An Application of Information Theory," *Computer Process. Chin. Orient. Lang.*, *4*(4), 304–313 (1990).

4. *ISO/IEC 10646*-1, 2nd ed., 2000-09-15, pp. 166–171.

5. 張勵奸,張賽洋編著 "索音字彙" 聯合出版集團

6. 余秉昭司鐸著 "同音字彙" 新亞洲出版社

7. Z. Wu and G. Tseng, "ACTS: An Automatic Chinese Text Segmentation System for Full Text Retrieval," *J. Am. Soc. Inform. Sci.*, *46*(2), 83–96 (1995).

8. J. Y. Nie, M. L. Hannan, and W. Jin, "Unknown Word Detection and Segmentation of Chinese Using Statistical and Heuristic Knowledge," *Commun. COLIPS*, *5*(1&2), 47–57 (1995).

9. N. Chang, R. Sproat, C. Shih, and W. Gale, "A Stochastic Finite-State Word-Segmentation Algorithm for Chinese," *Proceedings of ACL 94*, 1994.

10. S. Bai, "Semi-Word Method for Chinese Word Segmentation," *International Conference on Chinese Computing '94 (ICC94)*, 1994, pp. 304–309.

11. C. H. Chang and C. D. Chen, "A Study on Integrating Chinese Word Segmentation and Part-of Speech Tagging," *Commun. COLIPS*, *3*(2), 69–77 (1993).

12. J. Gao and X. Chen, "Automatic Word Segmentation of Chinese Texts Based on Variable Distance Method," *Commun. COLIPS*, *6*(2), 87–94 (1996).

13. N. Liang and Y. Zheng, "A Chinese Word Segmentation Model and a Chinese Word Segmentation System PC–CWSS," *Commun. COLIPS*, *1*(1), 51–55 (1991).

14. R. Sproat and C. Shih, "A Statistical Method for Finding Word Boundaries in Chinese Text," *Computer Process. Chin. Orient. Lang. 4*(4), 336–351 (1990).

15. C. H. Chang and C. D. Chen, "A Study on Corpus-Based Classification of Chinese Words," *International Conference on Chinese Computing '94 (ICCC94)*, 1994, pp. 310–316.

16. C. L. Yeh and H. J. Lee, "Rule-Based Word Identification for Mandarin Chinese Sen-

tence—A Unification Approach," *Computer Process. Chin. Orient. Lang.*, 5(2), 97–118 (1991).

17.   香港初中學生中文詞匯研究. (1986) 教育研究處. 香港教育署.

18.   C. H. Leung and W. K. Kan, "Difficulties in Chinese Typing Error Detection and Ways to the Solution," *Computer Process. Orient. Lang.* 10(1), 97–113 (1996).

KIN HONG LEE

QIN LU

MAU KIT MICHAEL NG

CLUSTER COMPUTING AND APPLICATIONS

INTRODUCTION

The needs and expectations of modern-day applications are changing in the sense that they not only need computing resources (be they processing power, memory, or disk space) but also the ability to remain available to service user requests almost 24 h a day and 365 days a year. These needs and expectations of today's applications result in challenging research and development efforts in both the areas of computer hardware and software.

It seems that as applications evolve, they inevitably consume more and more computing resources. To some extent, we can overcome these limitations. For example, we can create faster processors and install larger memories. However, future improvements are constrained by a number of factors, including physical ones, such as the speed of light and the constraints imposed by various thermodynamic laws, as well as financial ones, such as the huge investment needed to fabricate new processors and integrated circuits. The obvious solution to overcoming these problems is to connect multiple processors and systems together and coordinate their efforts. The resulting systems are popularly known as parallel computers and they allow the sharing of a computational task among multiple processors.

Parallel supercomputers have been in the mainstream of high-performance computing for the last 10 years. However, their popularity is waning. The reasons for this decline are many, but include being expensive to purchase and run, potentially difficult to program, slow to evolve in the face of emerging hardware technologies, and difficult to upgrade without, generally, replacing the whole system. The decline of the dedicated parallel supercomputer has been compounded by the emergence of commodity-off-the-shelf clusters of personal computers (PCs) and workstations. The idea of the cluster is not new, but certain recent technical capabilities, particularly in the area of networking, have brought this class of machine to the vanguard as a platform to run all types of parallel and distributed applications.

The emergence of cluster platforms was driven by a number of academic projects, such as Beowulf (1), Berkeley NOW (2), and HPVM (3). These projects helped to prove the advantage of clusters over other traditional platforms. Some of these advantages included low entry costs to access supercomputing-level performance, the ability to track technologies, an incrementally upgradable system, an open source development platform, and not being locked into particular vendor products. Today, the overwhelming price/performance advantage of this type of platform over other proprietary ones, as well as the other key benefits mentioned earlier, means that clusters have infiltrated not only the traditional science and engineering marketplaces for research and development but also the huge commercial marketplaces of commerce and industry. It should be noted that this class of machine is not only being used as for high-performance computation but

also increasingly as a platform to provide highly available services, for applications such
Web and database servers.

A cluster is a type of parallel or distributed computer system, which consists of a
collection of interconnected stand-alone computers working together as a single integrated computing resource (4,45). The typical architecture of a cluster computer is shown
in Figure 1. The key components of a cluster include multiple stand-alone computers
(PCs, workstations, or symmetric multi processors (SMPs)), an operating systems, a
high-performance interconnect, communication software, middleware, and applications.
All of these components, their functionality, and representative examples are discussed
in the remaining sections of this article.

This article is divided broadly into two parts. In the first part (the second through
eighth sections), we explore and discuss the hardware and software components that
make up a cluster. In the second part (the ninth section), we discuss five cluster-based
applications. The second and third sections look at networking and operating system
solutions. In the fourth section, we discuss and explain why the concept of having a
Single System Image is so important to clusters. In the fifth section, we review a range
of possible middleware technologies that may be used to provide a range of services to
applications. In the sixth section, we briefly outline the current parallel I/O solutions that
are being used with clusters. The seventh section deals with the important area of high
availability and how this is becoming an increasingly popular role for clusters. In the
eighth section, we sketch out how tools and libraries for clusters are being adapted and
developed for these heterogeneous platforms. Finally, in the ninth section, we discuss a
number of cluster applications, including a Web server, a speech–to–e-mail service, a
data mining service, an ad hoc network simulation, and an image-rendering system.

INTERCONNECTION TECHNOLOGIES

A key component in cluster architecture is the choice of interconnection technology.
Interconnection technologies may be classified into four categories, depending on
whether the internal connection is from the I/O bus or the memory bus and depending

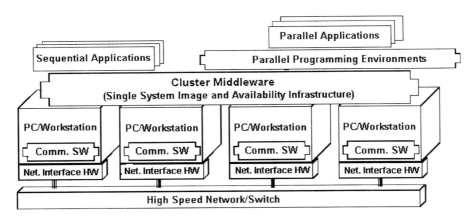

FIGURE 1   A cluster architecture. (From Ref. 45.)

on whether the communication between the computers is performed primarily using messages or using shared storage (4). Table 1 illustrates the four types of interconnections.

Of the four interconnect categories, I/O-attached message-based systems are by far the most common. This category includes all commonly used wide-area and local-area network technologies and includes several recent products that are specifically designed for cluster computing. I/O-attached shared storage systems include computers that share a common disk subsystem. Memory-attached systems are less common, as the memory bus of an individual computer generally has a design that is unique to that type of computer. However, many memory-attached systems are implemented in software or with memory-mapped I/O, such as Reflective Memory (5). Hybrid systems that combine the features of more than one category also exist, such as the Infiniband standard (6), which is an I/O-attached interconnection that can be used to send data to a shared-disk subsystem as well as to send messages to another computer. Similarly, SCI (7) may also be used for both shared memory and message passing.

The choice of interconnect technology for a cluster depends on a number of factors, including compatibility with the cluster hardware and operating system, price, and performance. Performance is usually measured in terms of latency and bandwidth. Latency is the time to send data from one computer to another and includes overhead for the software to construct the message as well as the time to transfer the bits from one computer to another. Bandwidth is the number of bits per second that can be transmitted over the interconnect hardware. Ideally, distributed applications are designed to minimize the amount of remote data that need to be accessed. However, in general, applications that utilize small messages will have better performance, particularly as the latency is reduced, and those that send large messages will have better performance, particularly as the bandwidth increases. The latency in message passing is a function of both the communication software and network hardware. The remainder of this section describes protocols for cluster communication and provides a survey of available interconnection hardware products.

Protocols for Cluster Communication

Traditional networks use the standard Transmission Control Protocol/Internet Protocol (TCP/IP) (8). The TCP/IP protocol is adequate for many cluster applications and is the easiest to use when building a cluster with inexpensive Fast Ethernet products (8). However, TCP/IP was designed for a wide-area network environment where errors are common. TCP/IP includes mechanisms to measure the round-trip time and attempts to optimize the number of bits that are sent in a single message or before an acknowledgment

TABLE 1   Categories of Cluster Interconnection Hardware

	Message based	Shared storage
I/O attached	Most common type, includes most high-speed networks; VIA, TCP/IP	Shared-disk subsystems
Memory attached	Usually implemented in software as optimizations of I/O attached message based	Global shared memory, distributed shared memory

is received. Although these optimizations can reduce the number of times that a message must be resent in an error-prone wide-area network, they increase the overall latency in cluster applications where errors are uncommon and the physical distance is small. For good performance, clusters generally utilize interconnection technologies that are specifically designed for cluster computing and that generally use specialized software and extra hardware for reducing the latency in messages.

Several academic research projects during the 1990s developed low-latency messaging protocols, including Active Messages (9), Fast Messages (10), VMMC (11), BIP (12), and Unet (13). Active Messages (later extended to Generic Active Messages, or GAM) was the low-latency protocol used in the Berkeley Network of Workstations (NOW) project (2). Active Messages allows messages to be sent from one computer to another without intermediate system buffering. Network hardware transfers the data directly from a pinned location in user memory to the network and then to a pinned user location in user memory on the receiving side. Because no copies from user to system memory are required, this type of protocol is called a "zero-copy" protocol. In GAM, a copy sometimes occurs to a buffer in system memory on the receiving side so that user buffers can be reused more efficiently. Fast Messages extends Active Messages by guaranteeing that all messages arrive in order and reliably, even if the underlying network hardware is not reliable.

Virtual Memory-Mapped Communication (VMMC) is the communication protocol used in the Princeton SHRIMP system (14) (Scalable High-Performance Really Inexpensive Multiprocessor system). SHRIMP is based on commodity processors and special communication hardware. VMMC works by mapping a page of user virtual memory to physical memory in the nodes of the cluster. The specially designed hardware allows the network interface to snoop writes to local host memory and allows updates to take place on remote host memory. VMMC is an example of Distributed Shared Memory (DSM), in which memory is physically distributed among the nodes in the system, and falls in the category of memory-attached shared storage.

Basic Interface for Parallelism (BIP) is a low-level message layer for Myrinet (15) and was developed at the University of Lyon. In addition to blocking and nonblocking low-latency messaging, BIP provides multiplexing between Myrinet and shared memory under a single API, for users of clusters of symmetric multiprocessors.

The Unet network interface architecture allows zero-copy messaging where possible and extends Active Messages by adding the concept of a virtual network interface. Each communication endpoint is viewed as a virtual network interface that is mapped to a real set of network buffers and queues on demand. The mapping requires system operations, but once the mappings are defined, the communication can take place without requests to the operating system. The result is that communication can take place with very low latency.

The Virtual Interface Architecture (16) (VIA) standard combines the best features of various academic projects for low-latency messaging. VIA is a standard for low-latency communication that was developed with consortium that includes Compaq, Microsoft, IBM, and other industrial and academic institutions. The VIA standard has been adopted for use by all major cluster application vendors. In addition to products offered by hardware vendors, VIA implementations that are available include M-VIA (17), which is a modular VIA that runs in Linux, and Berkeley VIA (18), which is available for x86PC and Sparc processors and Linux, Windows, and Solaris operating systems. Although VIA can be used directly for application programming, it is considered to be too low level for most applications, and so most users write applications in a messaging-passing language such as MPI (19) (Message Passing Interface) that runs over VIA.

A large consortium of industrial partners, including Compaq, Dell, Hewlett-Pack-ard, IBM, Intel, Microsoft and Sun Microsystems, support the InfiniBand standard. The InfiniBand architecture replaces the shared bus that is standard for I/O on current computers with a high-speed serial, channel-based, message-passing, scalable-switched fabric. All systems and devices attached to the fabric through channel adaptors. A single InfiniBand link operates at 2.5 Gbps point-to-point in a single direction. Data are sent in packets, and six types of transfer methods are available, including reliable and unreliable connections, reliable and unreliable datagrams, multicast connections, and raw packets. In addition, InfiniBand supports remote direct memory access (RDMA) read or write operations, which allows one processor to read or write the contents of memory at another processor, and also directly supports IPv6 messaging for the Internet. Because InfiniBand replaces the standard shared bus, new equipment is needed to introduce Infini-Band into the network, although this can be done incrementally. InfiniBand requires that new system software be implemented in the operating system of the host platforms and that embedded logic be included within the enclosures and devices that attach to the fabric.

Network Topologies

In general, switched networks are preferred for cluster applications over shared implementations of the same type of network. Ethernet, Fast Ethernet, and some Gigabit Ethernet (20) products are based on the concept of a collision domain. When the network is a shared hub, all nodes connected to the hub share the same collision domain and only one computer on the network can send a message at a time. With a switched hub, each computer is in a different collision domain. In this case, two sets of nodes may be communicating at the same time as long as they are not sending to the same receiver. For cluster computing, switched networks are preferred because it allows multiple simultaneous messages to be sent, which can improve overall application performance.

The topology of the network is generally determined by the selection of the specific network hardware. Some networks, such as Ethernet types of networks, only allow a configuration that can be viewed as a tree because of the hardware-implemented transparent routing algorithm. Other networks, such as Myrinet (21), allow a configuration with multiple redundant paths between pairs of nodes. In general, the primary factor with respect to topology that may affect the performance of the cluster is the maximum bandwidth that can be sustained between pairs of nodes in the cluster simultaneously. This is a function of both the topology and the capability of the switches in the network and depends on the specific network product that is chosen.

Network Hardware Products

Most clusters are built using a network technology that is attached to the I/O bus because this interface to the computer is well understood. The I/O bus provides, at least, a hardware interrupt that can inform the processor that data are waiting for it. How this interrupt is handled may vary, depending on the firmware or software stack that is used to receive the data. Networks that are build specifically for cluster computing have additional hardware support for lowering the latency in communication.

Networks that are traditionally used for local-area and campus-area networks, including Ethernet, Fast Ethernet, Gigabit Ethernet (20), and ATM (22), can provide basic functionality for small clusters. Higher-performance products in this category can be competitive for high-performance clusters. Networks that are designed for traditional applications generally have minimal additional hardware support specifically for cluster computing, but can be less expensive. The trade-off is that the messaging latency may be somewhat higher.

Table 2 compares several commonly used networks products for high-performance clusters as of Fall 2000. Products are listed in alphabetic order across the table. Because new products are continually becoming available, this list will be incomplete, but it is representative of the capabilities typically found for network products of this type.

Gigabit Ethernet products are available for low-cost Linux and Microsoft Windows platforms. Although Gigabit Ethernet does not have hardware support for VIA, M-VIA provides an emulated implementation of VIA for several Gigabit Ethernet adaptors and MPI is available with the MVICH (23) implementation over M-VIA.

Giganet (131) cLAN products were developed with the goal of supporting VIA in hardware. It has hot-pluggable links, automatic network mapping, and node detection. Software support includes drivers for VIA and management tools for NT and Linux.

Myrinet (21) is one of the first networks developed for cluster computing. Myrinet technology has several features that make it ideal for cluster computing. Myrinet consists of high-speed, low-latency switches that can be connected in a hierarchical fashion. When connected using a fat-tree configuration (24), multiple paths between nodes can help to reduce contention on the links. Myrinet uses wormhole routing (25), which ensures that a message is delivered without buffering at intermediate nodes and thus reduces latency across the cluster. Myrinet uses a slack buffer for flow control on each link. Unlike the flow control between links in ATM, bits are not dropped. Because most cluster applications require that data be delivered reliably between nodes, this improvement in reliability means that messages do not have to be resent, and the overall performance of the cluster is improved. Myrinet products have been available commercially since the mid-1990s and are a well-established cluster interconnection technology.

QsNet (26) is a high-bandwidth, low-latency interconnect for commodity-symmetric multiprocessing computers. The network switches include a network processor with memory management unit, cache, and local memory interface and are connected in a fat tree. QSnet supports a true zero-copy (virtual-to-virtual memory) protocol and has excellent performance.

ServerNet (27) has been a product from Tandem (now a part of Compaq) since 1995. ServerNet II offers direct support for VIA in hardware, 12-port nonblocking switches, and fat links between switches. Up to four physical links can be mapped into one logical link. Software support includes VIA drivers for NT and Linux. Although ServerNet II is a well-established project, it is only available from Compaq as a packaged cluster solution, not as single components, which may limit its use in general-purpose clusters.

Scalable Coherent Interface (SCI) (28) was the first interconnection technology to be developed as a standard specifically for the purposes of cluster computing. The IEEE 1596 standard for SCI was published in 1992 and specifies the physical and data link layers of the network as well as higher layers for distributed shared memory across a network. Many commercial products are developed using the lower layers only. At higher

TABLE 2 Comparison of Several Interconnection Products

	Gigabit Ethernet	Giganet	Myrinet	Qsnet	ServerNet2	SCI
Bandwidth (MBytes/s)	85	105	140–33 MHz 215–66 MHz	208	65	80
MPI latency (us)	30–200	20–40	16.5–33 MHz 11–66 MHz	5	20.2	6
List price per port	$1.5K	$1.5K	$1.5K	$6.5K	$1.5K	$1.5K
Hardware availability	Now	Now	Now	Now	Summer 2000	Now
Linux support	Now	Now	Now	Late 2000	Summer 2000	Now
Maximum No. of nodes	1000s	1000s	1000s	1000s	64K	1000s
Protocol implementation	Implemented in hardware	Firmware on adaptor	Firmware on adaptor	Firmware on adaptor	Implemented in hardware	Firmware on adaptor
VIA support	NT/Linux	NT/Linux	Soon	None	In hardware	Software
MPI support	MPICH over MVIA, TCP	Third party	Third party	Quadrics/Compaq	Compaq/third party	Third party

layers, SCI defines a directory-based cache coherence scheme that implements distributed shared memory.

The Atoll (29), or Atomic Low Latency network, is one of the newest networks for cluster computing. Atoll has four independent network interfaces (NIs), an 8×8 crossbar switch, and four link interfaces in a single chip. Message latency is as low as 4 μs and the bandwidth between two nodes approaches 200 Mbytes/s. Atoll is available for Linux and Solaris operating systems and supports MPI over its own low-latency protocol. The price per node is expected to be around $700, with product release sometime in 2001.

Shared storage systems are an important cluster interconnection for many commercial systems. The IBM Sysplex interconnection between mainframes is an example of an I/O-attached shared storage system (1). Also, many commercial clusters are interconnected via shared-disk subsystems. These subsystems, often called Storage Area Networks (SANs), are often constructed with a combination of SCSI and Fibre Channel (30) interconnections. Fibre Channel is a set of standards that defines a high-performance data transport connection technology that can transport many kinds of data at speeds up to 1 Gbps, through copper wire or fiber-optic cables. Like SCI, the Fibre Channel standard is defined in layers, beginning at the physical layer, and many commercial products are developed using the lower layers only.

Except for what are really large symmetric multiprocessors, true memory-attached architectures are rate. The illusion of memory-attached interconnections can be created through software or using memory-mapped I/O on I/O-attached interconnections. Reflective memory (31) is an example of a memory-attached interconnection of this type in which nodes write to local memory locations on the NIC and have the data broadcast on the network so that it is available to all other nodes in the network. The broadcast of the data happens automatically, so that all nodes in the network have a shared view of the reflective memory. Reflective memory products have been available since the 1980s and are available from several vendors. Reflective memory is often used in a real-time fault-tolerant environment. In these environments, the replication of the data in the reflective memory gives a higher level of fault tolerance. Because each memory location has to be physically replicated on each node in the system, reflective memory products tend to be more expensive than other types of network, and their cost grows as the size of the shared memory and the number of nodes in the system grows.

OPERATING SYSTEMS

The operating system in the individual nodes of the cluster provides the fundamental system support for cluster operations. Whether the user is opening files, sending messages, or starting additional processes, the operating system is always present. The primary role of an operating system is to multiplex multiple processes onto hardware components that comprise a system (resource management and scheduling), as well as provide a high-level software interface for user applications. These services include protection boundaries, process/thread coordination, interprocess communication, and device handling.

Operating System Features for Clusters

The desirable features of a cluster operating system include the following:

- *Manageability*: Intuitive facilities for local and remote administration; this is often associated with a Single System Image (SSI). These facilities can be realized at different levels, ranging from a high-level set of `Perl` management scripts, down to an internode state sharing via operating-system-level extensions.
- *Stability*: An important characteristic is robustness against system crashes, failure recovery by dynamic reconfiguration, and usability under heavy load.
- *Performance*: Performance is critical to all facets of an operating system. Important parts of the operating system, such as memory management, process and thread scheduler, file I/O, and communication protocols should work as efficiently as possible. A user, such as a programmer or system administrator, should be able to transparently optimize the relevant parameters to fine-tune the operating system for the varying demands of specific applications.
- *Extensibility*: An operating system should allow the easy integration of cluster-specific extensions (e.g., user-loadable device drivers).
- *Scalability*: The scalability of a cluster is primarily determined by the properties of the node interconnect. This may include support by the operating system for low-level, high-performance communications protocols to access the network.
- *Support*: User and system administrator support is an underrated but an essential element to the success or failure of any computer system. Fast and timely support is crucial for the successful deployment of a cluster operating system.
- *Heterogeneity*: By its very nature, a cluster consists of heterogeneous hardware components. An operating system is much more likely to be useful in a cluster if the same operating system can run across multiple architectures, or at least the operating systems can support a set of standardized APIs that simplify the development of middleware layers. Middleware layers enable the seamless usage of heterogeneous components across the cluster.

To date, there has been little work on operating systems specifically for clusters. Most turnkey clusters are provided with versions of the companies' mainline products (4), usually with little or no modification. Generally, however, there may be some form of SSI integrated into a conventional operating system. Two variants are typically encountered: that for system administration and/or job scheduling purposes and that found at the system call level. The former is usually some type of middleware and enables each node to deliver the required services, whereas the latter may offer features like transparent remote device usage or to use a distributed storage facility that is seen by users as a single standard file system.

Another approach to sharing computational resources is via software-enabled distributed shared memory (DSM) (138). This programming paradigm allows the distributed resources of the cluster be used in a similar fashion to a shared-memory system, such as an SGI Origin. DSM is normally realized via user-level libraries (33) and not as a service offered by the operating system. Integration of DSM into an operating system has rarely been done (34,35), as the performance for general-purpose use (requiring strict sequential consistency) is often to low. The use of a relaxed consistency models improves performance, but it presents the possibility that data consistency may not be strictly correct.

Alternatively, Network RAM (36) is an approach to using memory on a remote node. Here, the operating systems manage the remote memory and take advance of a current-day high-speed, low-latency interconnect such as Myrinet or SCI. Technologies such as these allow access to remote RAM faster then for local secondary storage. Network RAM offers the use of remote memory instead of the local hard disk for purposes like swapping or paging.

Heterogeneity

Clusters, by their very nature, are heterogeneous. A cluster may originally be only slightly heterogeneous, where, for example, memory or disk speeds may vary. As new nodes are added or old ones are replaced, the cluster may become moderately heterogeneous when, for example, different generations of components, such as CPUs, are added. In the longer term, a cluster may be potentially highly heterogeneous when, for example, it consists of mixture of different hardware and software components.

Heterogeneity in a cluster can cause problems. The lowest level on which heterogeneity causes problems is the data representation—big-endian versus little-endian. If such systems are to be connected, the adaptation of the different representations should be done on the lowest level possible to gain suitable performance. Obviously, the fastest approach to do endian conversion would be in hardware, but no hardware support currently exists. Middleware approaches to masking heterogeneous systems are currently the most common and successful.

Heterogeneous clusters may not perform as well as homogeneous clusters. In general, a parallel system performs best when all nodes are kept busy an equal amount of the time and communication is minimized. If one node finishes its work before the others, either because it was given less work to do or because it runs at a faster speed, then the time that it spends waiting for the others to complete is time that it does not spend computing. Balancing the load of an application across a cluster that has homogeneous nodes is difficult and becomes even more difficult when the nodes are heterogeneous.

Current State of the Art

The single most popular cluster operating system for clusters is Linux (37,38). This is primarily for three reasons:

- It is free.
- It is an open source. The source code is available and anyone is free to customize the kernel to suit his needs.
- It is easy. A large user community of Linux users and developers have created an abundant number of tools, Web sites, and documentation, so that Linux installation and administration is straightforward enough for a typical cluster user.

MOSIX (39) is a set of extensions for the Linux kernel that provides support for transparent process migration in a cluster environment. In this system, a user can launch jobs on their home node, and the MOSIX will automatically load balance by potentially migrating jobs to lightly loaded nodes. Under MOSIX, a user sees a single process space, making the tracking of migrated jobs easy. Like Linux, MOSIX is free and is distributed under the GNU Public License.

For users who desire to use an operating system that has been developed commercially, several products are available. Commercial clusters often run proprietary operating systems, such as IBM's AIX, Sun's Solaris, SGI's IRIX, Tandem's Non-Stop Unix and Unixware 7, Compaq's Tru64, and Windows NT/2000. Sun Microsystems has developed a multicomputer version of their Solaris operating system called Solaris MC (40). Solaris MC incorporates some advances made by Sun, including an object-oriented methodology and the use of CORBA IDL in the kernel. Solaris MC consists of a small set of kernel extensions and a middleware library. Solaris MC provides a SSI to the level of the device; that is, processes running on one node can access remote devices as if they are local. Solaris MC also provides a global file system and a global process space.

Future

Symmetric multiprocessors (SMPs) are becoming more popular as cluster nodes. High-performance SMP clusters are generally connected via a low-latency and high-bandwidth interconnect. Federated Clusters of SMPs, connected by gigabit-speed wide-area networks, are also emerging with some recent Grid computing testbeds (41). The nature of these Federated Clusters will have its impact on scheduling, both in terms of task placement and in terms of selecting a process to run from a ready queue. In this environment, scheduling, which is traditionally seen as an operating system activity, is carried out in middleware.

New operating systems for clusters may offer a minimalist approach by using microkernels. The Exokernel operating system is an example of a microkernel operating system (32). With this approach to operating systems, only the minimal amount of system functionality is in the kernel. This allows the user to only load services when, and if, they are needed. In addition to maximizing the available physical memory by removing undesirable functionality, the user can alter the characteristics of the service. For example, a scheduler specific to the cluster application may be loaded that helps the application run more efficiently. Operating system microkernels bring up the issue of operating system configuration. In particular, why provide a node operating system with the ability to provide more services to applications than they are ever likely to use? For example, a user may want to alter the personality of the local operating system (e.g., "strip down" to a minimalist kernel to maximize the available physical memory and remove undesired functionality). Possible mechanisms to achieve this range from the use of a new kernel to the dynamically linking service modules into the kernel.

SINGLE SYSTEM IMAGE

The view of a distributed system as a single unified computing resource is often known as a Single System Image (SSI). This property hides the distributed and heterogeneous nature of the available resources and presents them to users as a single, powerful, unified computing resource (41). The ability to realize SSI can be achieved through one or several mechanisms implemented in hardware or software at various levels of abstraction, from the kernel to application layers.

A system with SSI means that users have a system view of the resources available to them irrespective of the node to which they are physically associated. These resources can range from access and manipulation of remote processes to the use of a global file system. Furthermore, SSI can provide a system with other features, including the ability to continue to operate after some failure (high availability) or the ability to ensure that the nodes are evenly loaded. Load balancing is provided through resource management and scheduling.

The design goals for SSI cluster-based systems are mainly focused on complete transparency of resource management, scalable performance, and system availability in supporting user applications (41–45). The following are among some of the key SSI attributes that are generally considered desirable: point of entry, user interface, process space, I/O and memory space, job-management system, and point of management and control.

The most important benefits of SSI (41) include the following:

- It frees the end user from having to know where in the cluster an application will run.
- It allows the use of resources in a transparent way irrespective of their physical location.
- It offers the same command syntax as in other systems and thus reduces the risk of operator errors, with the result that end users see an improved performance, reliability, and higher availability of the system.
- It greatly simplifies system management and thus reduces the cost of ownership.
- It promotes the development of standard tools and utilities.

Single System Image can be realized in one or more of the following levels:

- Hardware: Systems such as the Digital/Compaq Memory Channel (46) and hardware such as distributed shared memory (DSM) (47) allow a user to view a cluster as a shared-memory system.
- Operating System: Achieved by either modifying/extending the operating system kernel [i.e., SCO UnixWare (43) and Sun Solaris-MC (40)] or building a layer [i.e., GLUnix (48)] that integrates the operating systems running on each node;
- Middleware: Use of this layer to provide SSI is common in present-day clusters. Middleware solutions include run-time and programming environments such as PVM (49) and job-management and scheduling systems such as CODINE (50) and Condor (51).
- Application: Application-level SSI is the highest and, in a sense, most important because this is what the end user sees. At this level, multiple cooperative components of an application are presented to the user as a single application. For instance, a GUI-based tool such as PARMON (52) offers a single window representing all the resources or services available. Another solution for providing SSI at this level is application-specific Problem Solving Environments (PSEs). These PSEs consist of all the tools and utilities required to develop, implement, and run scientific and commercial applications, bound into one environment. The distributed nature of the run-time environment is masked from the application developer (53).

It is important to remember that a good SSI is usually obtained by a cooperation among all these levels, as a lower level can simplify the implementation of a higher one. The level at which SSI is developed, the interaction of SSI layers, and the degree of sophistication and complexity of SSI all affect its performance, flexibility, scalability, and usability.

The use of SSI can greatly enhance the acceptability and usability of clusters by hiding the physical distribution and potential complex interaction of multiple independent computers by presenting them as a single, unified resource. SSI can be realized using hardware and/or software techniques, each of them have their own advantages and disadvantages. The designers of software for clusters must always consider SSI (transparency) as one of their important design goals in addition to scalable performance and enhanced availability.

MIDDLEWARE

Middleware is generally considered the layer of software sandwiched between the operating system and applications. Middleware has been around since the 1960s and provides various services to applications. More recently, middleware has reemerged as a means of integrating software applications that run in a heterogeneous environment. There is large overlap between the infrastructure that is provided to a cluster by high-level SSI services and those provided by the traditional view of middleware.

Middleware has the ability to help a developer overcome three potential problems with developing applications on a heterogeneous cluster:

- The integration of software from different sources
- Access to software inside or outside their site
- Rapid application development

In addition, the services that middleware provides are not restricted to application development. Middleware also provides services for the management and administration of a heterogeneous system.

Message-Based Middleware

Message-based middleware is a technology that uses a common communications protocol to exchange data between applications. The communications protocol hides many of the low-level message-passing primitives from the application developer. Message-based middleware software can pass messages directly between applications, send messages via software that queues waiting messages, or use some combination of the two. Examples of this type of middleware are the three upper layers of the OSI model (54): the session, presentation, and applications layers. Other examples are DECmessageQ (55) from Digital, MQSeries (56) from IBM, and TopEnd (57) from NCR.

RPC-Based Middleware

For many applications, the overwhelming numbers of interactions between processes in a distributed system are remote operations, often with a return value. For these applications, the implementation of the client/server model in terms of Remote Procedure Call (RPC) allows the code of the application to remain the same whether the procedures are the same or not. Interprocess communication mechanisms serve four important functions (58):

- They allow communications between separate processes over a computer network.
- They offer mechanisms against failure and provide the means to cross administrative boundaries.
- They enforce clean and simple interfaces, thus providing a natural aid for the modular structure of large distributed applications.
- They hide the distinction between local and remote communication, thus allowing static or dynamic reconfiguration.

Client and server do not execute in the same address space, so there are no global variables, and pointers cannot be used across the interface. Marshaling is the term used for transferring data structures used in RPC (59) from one address space to another. Marshaling is required, as two goals need to be achieved: The data must be serialized for transport in messages and the data structures must be converted from the data representation on the sending end and reconstructed on the receiving end.

Middleware tools built over RPC include Network Information Services (60) (NIS) and Network File Services (61) (NFS). Both NIS and NFS were originally developed by Sun Microsystems, but versions of each of them have been released into the public domain. NIS is a network naming and administrative tool for smaller networks that allows users to access files or applications on the network with a single log-in name and password. NFS allows files and directories to be exported from the server computer to client computers on the network. With NFS, users can have the same view of the file system from any computer in the network. With NFS and NIS, users can log-in; access an application that resides on the file server, and save files into a home directory on the file server from any computer on the network.

Object Request Broker

An Object Request Broker (ORB) is a middleware that supports the remote execution of objects. CORBA (Common Object Request Broker Architecture) is an international ORB standard supported by more than 700 groups and managed by the Object Management Group (OMG) (62). The OMG is a nonprofit organization whose objective is to define and promote standards for object orientation in order to integrate applications based on existing technologies.

The Object Management Architecture (OMA) is characterized by the following:

- The Object Request Broker (ORB). The broker forms the controlling element of the architecture because it supports the portability of objects and their interoperability in a network of heterogeneous systems.
- Object services. These are specific system services for the manipulation of objects. Their goal is to simplify the process of constructing applications.
- Application services. These offer a set of facilities for allowing applications access databases, to printing services, to synchronize with other application, and so on.
- Application objects. These allow the rapid development of applications. A new application can be formed from objects in a combined library of application services. Adding objects belonging to the application can extend the library itself.

OLE/COM

The term COM has two meanings. It stands for Component Object Model (63), which forms the object model underpinning Object Linking and Embedding (OLE) version 2.0. It also stands for the Common Object Model, after an agreement between Microsoft and Digital. The first version of OLE was designed to allow composite documents (text and images) to be handled. The second version of OLE introduced a highly generic object model whose use can be extended well beyond the handling of composite documents. OLE2 offers a set of interfaces (object oriented) that allows applications to intercommunicate. The first version of OLE2 required applications to run on the same machine. OLE2 was later extended to run in a distributed fashion on Windows and UNIX platforms.

The COM model defines mechanisms for the creation of objects as well as for the communication between clients and objects that are distributed across a distributed environment. These mechanisms are independent of the programming languages used to implement objects. COM defines an interoperability standard at the binary level in order to make it independent of the operating system and machine.

Internet Middleware

The Internet is based on the Internet Protocol (IP), which provides datagram services between devices that have an IP address, and the Transmission Control Protocol (TCP), which provides a connection-oriented reliable service over IP. Although many applications use TCP/IP directly, a number of middlewarelike technologies are built over TCP/IP. The HyperText Transport Protocol (HTTP) allows text, graphics, audio, and video files to be mixed together and accessed through a web browser. The Common Gateway Interface (CGI) standard enables retrieved files to be executed as a program, which allows web pages to be created dynamically. For example, a CGI program can be used to incorporate user information into a database query and then display the query results on a web page. CGI programs can be written in any programming language.

Because users access some web pages and applications frequently, some web servers will send a small amount of information back to the web client to be saved between sessions. This information is stored as a "cookie" and saved on the local disk of the client machine. The next time that the web page is accessed, the client will send the cookie back to the server. Cookies allow users to avoid retyping identification information for repeated sessions to the same server and allow sessions to be restarted from a saved state.

Java Technologies

The Java Remote Method Invocation (RMI) (64) allows communications between two or more Java entities that are located in distinct Java Virtual Machines (JVMs). Java RMI is similar to RPC, except that Java RMI allows a Java applet or application access another remote object and invokes one of its methods. In order to access the remote object, the calling application must obtain its address. This is obtained by access to a Registry, where the object's name was registered. The Registry acts as a name server for all objects using RMI. The Registry contains a table where each object is associated with a reference—this is the object's interface and unique address of the object.

Jini (65) from Sun Microsystems is an attempt to resolve the interoperability of different types of computer-based device. These devices, which come from many different vendors, may need to interact over a network. Jini is designed for a network in which devices and services are added and removed regularly. Jini provides mechanisms to enable the addition, removal, and discovery of devices and services attached to the network. Jini also provides a programming model that is meant to make it easier for programmers to enable devices to interact.

Jini objects move around the network from virtual machine to virtual machine. Built on top of Java, object serialization, and RMI, Jini is a set of APIs and network protocols that can be used to create and deploy distributed systems that are organized as federations of services. A Jini service can be anything that is connected to the network and is ready to perform some useful task. The services can consist of hardware devices, software, communications channels, and even interactive users. A federation of services, then, is a set of services currently available on the network that a client (meaning some program, service, or user) can bring together to help it accomplish some task.

In addition to Java RMI and Jini, Sun Microsystems has produced a plethora of Java-based technologies that can be considered as middleware (66). These technologies range from the Java Development Kit (JDK) product family that consists of the essential tools and APIs for all developers writing in the Java programming language to APIs such as for telephony (JTAPI), database connectivity (JDBC), 2D and 3D graphics, security, as well as electronic commerce. These technologies enable Java to interoperate with many other devices, technologies, and software standards.

Cluster Management Software

Cluster Management Software (CMS) is primarily designed to administer and manage application jobs submitted to workstation clusters. More recently, CMS has also been extended to manage other underlying resources as well as software licenses [e.g., CODINE/GRD (50)]. The job can be a parallel or sequential application that needs to run interactively or in the background. This software encompasses the traditional batch and queueing systems. CMS can be used to help manage clusters in a variety of ways:

- Optimize the use of the available resources for parallel and sequential jobs
- Prioritize the usage of the available resources
- Manage mechanisms to "steal" CPU cycles from cluster machines
- Enable check-pointing and task migration
- Provide mechanisms to ensure that tasks complete successfully

Cluster management software is widely available in both commercial and public-domain offerings. There are several comprehensive reviews of their functionality and usefulness (67).

Factors in Choosing Middleware

The purpose of middleware is to provide services to applications running in distributed heterogeneous environments. The choice of which middleware may best meet an organization's needs is difficult, as the technology is still being developed and it may be some time before it reaches maturity. The risk of choosing one solution over another can be reduced if the following occur (68):

- The approach is based on the concept of a high-level interface.
- The concept of a service is associated with each interface.
- The product conforms to a standard and supports its evolution.

In addition to these, a key criterion is ensuring that the middleware is interoperable with the other current and emerging middleware standards. Older software for providing middleware services, such as DCE, is being replaced by a new generation of object-oriented software such as CORBA/COM and Java, and these are being developed to be interoperable with each other. Jini, Sun Microsystems' latest distributed environment, is a promising middleware, as it has been developed with the goal of interoperability.

PARALLEL I/O

The scalability of an application refers to its ability to effectively use additional resources as the size of the cluster and the application grow. In many cases, the scalability of a high-performance application is more limited by the performance of the I/O system than by the performance of the CPUs in a cluster. Scaling such applications is not a case of merely increasing the number of processors but also increasing the available bandwidth of the I/O subsystem. A cluster can potentially provide a large data storage capacity because each node in the cluster will typically have at least one disk attached. These disks can produce a large, common storage subsystem. This storage subsystem can be more effectively accessed using a parallel I/O system.

The general design goals of a parallel I/O system are as follows (69):

- Maximize the use of available parallel I/O devices to increase the bandwidth
- Minimize the number of disk read/write operations per device
- Minimize the number of I/O-specific operations between processes to avoid unnecessary and costly communication
- Maximize the hit ratio (ratio between accessed data to requested data) to avoid unnecessary data accesses

Types of Parallel I/O Systems

Three types of parallel I/O systems can be identified (70):

1. Application level
2. I/O level
3. Access anticipation methods

Application-level methods (based around so-called buffering algorithms) try to organize the main memory and mapping the disk space (e.g., buffer) to make disk accesses efficient. Typically, these methods are realized by run-time libraries, which are linked to the application programs. Thus, the application program performs the data accesses itself without the need for dedicated I/O server programs. Examples for this group are the two-phase method (71), the Jovian framework (132), and the extended two-phase method (73).

The I/O level methods try to reorganize the disk access requests of the application programs to achieve better performance. This is done by independent I/O node servers which collect the requests and perform the accesses. Therefore, the disk requests (of the application) are separated from the disk accesses (of the I/O server). A typical representative of this group is the disk-directed I/O method (74).

Access anticipation methods extend the I/O operations into the time dimension and are based around data prefetching. These methods anticipate data access patterns by using hints from the code in advance of its execution. Hints can be embedded by the programmer into the application or can be delivered automatically by appropriate tools (e.g., compiler). Examples for this group are informed prefetching (75), the PANDA project (76), and the two-phase data administration (77).

Technological Issues

Several technological issues that arise in a cluster can have an impact on the performance of a parallel I/O system. These issues include interconnection latency, heterogeneity of the cluster, parameters of the I/O system, and the user need for optimization.

The latency of the interconnection is not as much of a problem for I/O intensive applications as it is for computational-bound applications. In general, a high-speed, low-latency network can turn the network bottleneck for clusters into the known I/O bottleneck (78). In that case, the already developed methods and paradigms to reduce this I/O bottleneck on massively parallel systems can similarly be used on cluster systems.

A heterogeneous environment leads to the following issues for cluster I/O:

- Hardware Architecture: Each node can exhibit a unique hardware configuration (e.g., various types and numbers of disks and I/O bus and controller characteristics). To understand the behavior of such systems requires complex analytical models and, consequently, makes understanding factors like performance prediction and system optimization very difficult.
- Data Representation: Heterogeneous operating systems and processors can result in different physical representations of the primitive data types. This is not a problem so far if data are stored without semantics, but modern applications use this property (e.g., database tasks). Thus, respective conversion routines and/or a standardized I/O formats have to be implemented.
- Load Balancing: Clusters support a multiuser, multitasking environment. These factors accompanied by the heterogeneous nature of the cluster hardware and software lead to the situation that the overall distribution of the workload of a cluster is hard to predict at any particular moment. The static approach to I/O planning is, consequently, almost useless.

The most crucial parameters for a parallel I/O system are the following:

- Distribution of data on disks
- Data layout on disks
- Latencies and transfer rates of media (disks)
- Communication network latency and transfer rate
- Sizes of disk blocks, memory, and communication buffers
- Transfer rates for memory to memory copy
- I/O scheduling
- Caching, prefetching, and write-behind policies
- Contention

These parameters are essentially the same for clusters as for traditional computers. The (possible) heterogeneity in cluster systems, however, tends to increase the number of parameters dramatically. For example, the characteristics of different disks may vary considerably. Further, the speed of communication may vary, dependent on which nodes are communicating. Many of the parameter values (like latencies and transfer rates) are strongly influenced by the underlying hardware. Nonetheless, these parameters are not constant but can change significantly if other parameters are slightly modified. Given the huge number of possible parameter combinations, finding a near-optimal I/O strategy for a specific application on a given hardware configuration is a difficult task.

In order to gain broad acceptance by the users (application programmers), a parallel I/O system must not only offer a simple API but also deliver a high I/O throughput with little or no user intervention. The I/O system should therefore automatically optimize I/O operations based on information about the underlying hardware and the client application. The need of automatic optimizations implies building an I/O model that sufficiently describes the interdependencies of all the I/O parameters in order to evaluate different characteristics exhibited by applications. Several such models exist that primarily focus on special aspects (e.g., check-pointing) and/or only use a subset of the parameters and, consequently, have limited use.

Because of the complex nature of I/O and even if a complete I/O model was produced, that optimization of the I/O parameters in itself would be a demanding task. The huge number of possible parameter settings will inhibit an exhaustive search. So, intelligent algorithms are needed that only generate parameter sets that seem promising with respect to I/O performance and select the best one based on the model evaluation. These algorithms should produce the optimal (or a near optimal) result and they should not take longer to run than the time that can be gained.

Some potential candidates to help solve the I/O optimization problem are artificial intelligence algorithms and neural networks. Artificial intelligence algorithms are capable of finding near-optimum configurations in large search spaces and have already been successfully used to find partial solutions of the problem (using simulated annealing and genetic algorithms). Neural networks have been used to spot regular patterns in I/O accesses to help understand the optimization problem.

It should also be remembered that I/O requests are dynamic and, consequently, the optimum I/O configuration will be changing with time due to factors like contention or maybe failure of a network connection or a disk. I/O optimization in this case must be done autonomously (i.e., the system detects the changes itself) and in a transparent manner that does not impact the client applications.

Future Aspects for Parallel I/O

The availability of data storage systems capable of storing huge datasets is rapidly increasing. The doubling in the sales of storage system each year can be seen as evidence of this. The support of fast and efficient access of data on these systems is crucial. The demand of new applications, such as multimedia, knowledge engineering, and large-scale scientific computing, is increasing at an astonishing rate.

Cluster-based platforms can provide a practical solution for I/O intensive applications. Past experience of massively parallel processing systems, however, does not provide all the answers of how to configure and optimize clusters for the new generation of I/O-intensive applications. It is evident that new approaches and I/O models will need to be studied to cope with the demands of these applications. Cluster I/O will be a stimulating research area research for some time.

HIGH AVAILABILITY

Highly available (HA) systems for traditional mission critical application have been around for almost as long as modern computers have been around. More recently, the need for highly available systems has increased as electronic commerce and other Internet-based applications have become widely used with the burgeoning web usage. Traditionally, HA systems consist of proprietary hardware and software components. However, the price/performance advantages of commodity-off-the-shelf (COTS)-based clusters have had a compelling effect on HA vendors and their marketplace. The move to COTS-based HA components has driven down the entry price to buy a HA system, and as such, the HA market is expanding and more users, both commercial and many academic, demand minimal downtime for their systems.

In general, systems can provide different types of availability, including the following:

- High Availability (79): The provision of a less expensive alternative to fault tolerance by providing software solutions using COTS hardware components
- Continuous Availability: The provision of a nonstop service, representing an ideal state
- Fault Tolerance: The provision of high levels of availability by employing redundant hardware for various system components

Today, a typical HA solution consists of software modules that run on a system consisting of two or more nodes comprising off-the-shelf computers. The failure of a node or its components results in all applications that were running on that node being migrated over to another node in the system.

The current generation of HA solutions range from two to eight node-clusters, although products for larger clusters are available. A typical HA solution consists of the following:

1. A software infrastructure that enables the cluster to appear as a single system
2. Cluster monitoring software
3. Applications that use the services provided by the infrastructure that provide HA

Highly available solutions are generally implemented at one of two levels, above or integrated within the operating system. HA solutions that are implemented above the operating system (middleware) often provide SSI and are critical to a system's ease of use. The important elements of SSI include global file systems, devices, and networking. SSI also impacts the functionality and usage of cluster management tools.

Integrating HA functionality into the underlying operating system has a number of advantages, such as better performance and ease of use. One of the main advantages of the middleware HA solution is the independence with respect to the underlying operating system. A middleware solution leads to better portability across heterogeneous platforms and often a smaller application-development cycle for the HA functionality in the system.

There are an increasing number of commonly used and commercial highly available applications. The most common ones are the various databases (Oracle, Informix, Sybase), file systems, web servers, and mail servers. Many of these come prepackaged with HA solutions and others can be developed with the HA infrastructure in mind. In addition, a custom application may use an HA–API to convert an application into an HA version. Although each particular HA–API has its own specific functionality, most have methods to start, monitor, or stop an application. Highly available cluster systems are an active area of research (80).

NUMERICAL LIBRARIES AND TOOLS FOR SCALABLE PARALLEL CLUSTER COMPUTING

An essential element for a successful cluster is an effective and efficient suite of numerical libraries and programming tools that is available to application developers. Clusters, especially heterogeneous ones, present tool and library developers a range of problems to solve in order to achieve adequate levels of performance. Tools and libraries that have been developed for existing parallel supercomputers, such as MPI (19) or PVM, will, in most cases, operate adequately on clusters. However, acceptable levels of efficiency or effectiveness may not be achieved. This problem will typically be exasperated if the cluster consists of SMP nodes. Currently, there is little software that exists that offers the mixed-mode parallelism. Nevertheless, there is much interest in this form of mixed-mode programming.

Currently, message passing, using MPI, is the most popular paradigm for developing parallel and distributed application. MPI provides the communication layer of the library or package, which may or may not be revealed to the user. Both free and vendor-supported versions of MPI ensure its widespread availability. More importantly, MPI ensures portability of application codes across all distributed and parallel platforms.

OpenMP (81) is an emerging standard that provides a portable API for the development of applications that used a shared-memory–programming paradigm. This standard has an obvious important implication for Cluster SMP nodes. It is clear that a mixed programming paradigm based on MPI and OpenMP will have an important impact on SMP-based clusters in the near future.

Clusters that consist of small and large SMPs, sometimes called constellations, represent a popular and fast-growing area of the computing market. The depth of the memory hierarchy with its different access primitives and costs at each level makes clusters of SMPs more challenging to design and use effectively than their single SMP and cluster predecessors. It is envisaged that to take advantage of clusters of SMPs, some abstract programming model that is not dependent on implementation details of the underlying machine would be needed. It is probable that some layered programming model that allows the underlying machine to be exposed at varying levels of detail will be used. Such a model would consist of a communication library, various data structure libraries, and numerical algorithms. An important aspect is to build libraries that are parameterized and can take advantage of the architectural features that most influence performance. Such features may include cache sizes, network latency, and bandwidth, for example. Identifying the parallelization strategies for combining distributed and shared-memory programming paradigms is an active area of research (82).

Numerical Libraries

Numerical libraries are an essential tool for scientific application programmers. The categories of libraries that are generally available include linear algebra, iterative solvers, optimization, and partial differential equation solvers. The majority of the available numerical packages in this area are for linear algebra. Both direct solvers and iterative solvers are well represented. Direct solver packages include ScaLAPACK (83) and PLA-PACK (84) both of which are based on the parallelized version of LAPACK (84), but using different approaches.

The majority of iterative solvers packages use MPI as the underlying communications layer and include Aztec (85), Blocksolve (86), and PSPARSLIB (87). Packages for eigenvalue problems include PARPACK (88) and PeIGS (89).

Optimatization and partial differential equation (PDE) solvers include freely available packages from Netlib (133). Several machine vendors produce commercial packages and NAG (90) provides a commercial, supported, a general parallel library (91) based on MPI and also on SMP library (92) based on OpenMP.

PETSc (92) provides a set of tools for solving PDE problems, including iterative methods. PETSc is an object-based interface to the suite of C algorithms. The underlying implementation of algorithms or communications does not need to be known by the application developer. PETSc works well with C++-based packages such as ISIS++ and ELLPACK (93).

In general, cluster applications can take advantage of a legacy of numerical libraries of tools that were originally developed for parallel supercomputer, including both publicly available and commercially supported packages. These legacy packages may not, in general, provide the most effective software for clusters, but they provide a good starting point. Abstract frameworks for developing cluster applications that can exploit complex memory hierarchies as well as heterogeneous clusters of SMPs are still some way in the future. Certainly, the impetuous behind all types of scientific and engineering applications will drive the development of fast and efficient numerical libraries and tools for clusters.

SCIENTIFIC AND COMMERCIAL APPLICATIONS OF CLUSTER COMPUTING

INTRODUCTION

The availability of commodity high-performance microprocessors and high-speed networks has made the use of clusters an appealing vehicle for low-cost commodity supercomputing (45). Clusters provide a computational platform for all types of resource-hungry parallel and distributed applications whether they are scientific or commercial.

One of the classes of application that a cluster can typically cope with would be considered grand challenge or supercomputing applications. GCAs (Grand Challenge Applications) (94) are fundamental problems in science and engineering with broad economic and scientific impact. They are generally considered intractable without the use of state-of-the-art supercomputers. The scale of their resource requirements, such as processing time, memory, and communication needs distinguishes GCAs from other applications. For example, the execution of scientific applications used in predicting life-threatening situations such as earthquakes or hurricanes requires enormous computational power and storage resources. If we try to forecast an earthquake using a single PC, we would probably end up predicting it only after it had occurred, with all the inevitable consequences. In the past, these applications would be run on vector or parallel computing supercomputers costing millions of dollars in order to perform predictions well in advance of actual events. Such applications can be migrated to run on commodity off-the-shelf-based clusters of computers and deliver comparable performance at low cost. In fact, on a few occasions, expensive supercomputers have been replaced by low-cost commodity clusters such as Linux clusters in order to reduce maintenance costs and increase overall computing resources (95).

A typical example of a grand challenge problem is the simulation of some phenomena that cannot be measured through physical experiments. GCAs (96) include complex crystallographic and microtomographic structural problems, protein dynamics and biocatalysis (97), relativistic quantum chemistry of actinides, virtual materials design and processing including crash simulations (98), and global-climate modeling. This section describes commercial and Internet applications that demand both high availability and performance. This section also describes the use of clusters in image-rendering applications, from television and movie animations, to architectural and web-page design.

Clusters are increasingly being used for running commercial applications. In a business environment, for example in a bank, many of its activities are automated. However, a problem arises if the server that is handling customer transactions fails. The bank's activities could come to halt and customers would not be able to deposit or withdraw money from their account. Such situations can cause a great deal of inconvenience and result in loss of business and confidence in a bank. This is where clusters can be useful. A bank could continue to operate even after the failure of a server by automatically isolating failed components and migrating activities to alternative resources as a means of offering an uninterrupted service.

With the escalating popularity of the web, computer system availability is becoming critical, especially in e-commerce application. Popular and free e-mail service providers such as Hotmail (99) and search engines such as Hotbot (95)—that use Inktomi solutions (134)—are hosted by clusters. Cluster-based systems can be used to execute many Internet applications: web servers, search engines, e-mail, security, proxy, and database servers. In the commercial environment, these servers can be consolidated (see Fig. 2) to create what is known as an enterprise server. They can be optimized, tuned, and managed for increased efficiency and responsiveness depending on the workload through load-balancing techniques. A large number of low-end machines (PCs) can be

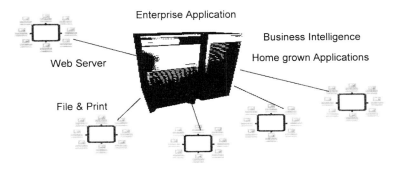

FIGURE 2   Enterprise cluster (server consolidation). (From Ref. 100.)

clustered along with storage and applications for scalability, high availability, and performance. The leading companies building these types of systems are Compaq (ProLiant, AlphaServer, and NonStop Himalaya systems) (100), Hewlett-Packard (HyperFabric technology) (101), IBM (IBM S/390 server) (102), Microsoft (Application Center) (103), and Sun (Data Centre) (104).

In the following subsections, we discuss the use of cluster technologies in the following application areas:

- Web serving
- Audio processing (voice-based e-mail)
- Data mining
- Network simulation
- Image processing

Linux Virtual Server: A Cluster-Based Web Server

A cluster of servers, connected by a fast network, provides a viable platform for building highly scalable and available Internet services. This type of loosely coupled architecture is highly scalable, cost-effective, and more reliable than a tightly coupled multiprocessor system (45) because failed components can be easily isolated and the system can continue to operate without any disruption.

The Linux Virtual Server (105) directs clients' network connection requests to multiple servers that share their workload, which can be used to build scalable and highly available Internet services. Prototypes of the Linux Virtual Server have already been used to build many sites that cope with heavy Internet loads, such as Linux portal (106) and UK National JANET Web Cache Service (105).

The Linux Virtual Server directs clients' network connection requests to the different servers according to scheduling algorithms and makes the parallel services of the cluster appear as a single virtual service with a single IP address. The Linux Virtual Server extends the TCP/IP stack of Linux kernel to support three IP load-balancing techniques:

1. NAT (Network Address Translation): Maps IP addresses from one group to another. NAT is used when hosts in internal networks want to access the Internet and be accessed in the Internet.
2. IP Tunneling: Encapsulates IP datagram within IP datagrams. This allows datagrams destined for one IP address to be wrapped and redirected to another IP address.
3. Direct Routing: Allows route response to the actual user machine instead of the load balancer.

The Linux Virtual Server also provides four scheduling algorithms for selecting servers from cluster for new connections:

1. Round Robin: Directs the network connections to the different server in a round-robin manner.
2. Weighted Round Robin: Treats the real servers of different processing capacities. A scheduling sequence will be generated according to the server weights. Clients' requests are directed to the different real servers based on the scheduling sequence in a round-robin manner.

3. Least Connection: Directs clients' network connection requests to the server with the least number of established connections.
4. Weighted Least Connection: A performance weight can be assigned to each real server. The servers with a higher weight value will receive a larger percentage of live connections at any time.

Client applications interact with the cluster as if it were a single server. The clients are not affected by the interaction with the cluster and do not need modification. The application performance scalability is achieved by adding one or more nodes to the cluster. Automatically detecting node or demon failures and reconfiguring the system appropriately achieve high availability.

The Linux Virtual Server that follows a three-tier architecture is shown in Figure 3. The functionality of each tier is as follows:

- Load Balancer: The front end to the servicer as viewed by connecting clients. The load balancer directs network connections from clients who access a single IP address for a particular service, to a set of servers that actually provide the service.
- Server Pool: Consists of a cluster of servers that implement the actual services, such as Web, Ftp, mail, DNS, and so on.
- Back-End Storage: Provides the shared storage for the servers, so that it is easy for servers to keep the same content and provide the same services.

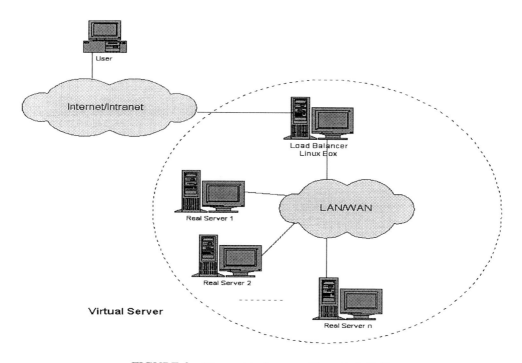

FIGURE 3   Linux virtual server. (From Ref. 105.)

The load balancer handles incoming connections using IP load-balancing techniques. The load balancer selects servers from the server pool, maintains the state of concurrent connections, and forwards packets, and all the work is performed inside the kernel, so that the handling overhead of the load balancer is low. The load balancer can handle much larger numbers of connections than a general server; therefore, the load balancer can schedule a large number of servers and it will not be a potential bottleneck in the system.

The server nodes may be replicated for either scalability or high availability. When the load on the system saturates the capacity of the current server nodes, more server nodes can be added to handle the increasing workload. One of the advantages of a clustered system is that it can be built with hardware and software redundancy. Detecting a node or demon failure and then reconfiguring the system appropriately so that its functionality can be taken over by the remaining nodes in the cluster is a means of providing high system availability. A cluster monitor demon can run on the load balancer and monitor the health of server nodes. If a server node cannot be reached by ICMP (Internet Control Message Protocol) or there is no response of the service in the specified period, the monitor will remove or disable the server in the scheduling table, so that the load balancer will not schedule new connections to the failed one and the failure of a server node can be masked.

The back-end storage for this system is usually provided by distributed and fault-tolerant file system. Such a system also takes care of the availability and scalability issue of file system accesses. The server nodes access the distributed file system in a similar fashion to that of accessing a local file system. However, multiple identical applications running on different server nodes may access shared data concurrently. Any conflicts between applications must be reconciled so that the data remain in a consistent state.

Talking E-Mail: Evoke's Reliable and Scalable Speech–to–E-Mail Service

Evoke Communications (136) is one of the service providers for Internet communication. They have developed a broad range of services to meet the diverse communication needs of businesses and consumers. One of Evoke's most popular applications is a speech–to–e-mail system, called *talking e-mail*. Evoke Talking Email (108) allows users to record a free voice message of up to 30 s in duration and send it as an e-mail message. The service has the capability to deliver the message to thousands of users simultaneously. Additionally, users can post their voice message as a link embedded on a web page. As the popularity of this service grew, meeting the demand required a scalable computing platform architecture. The resulting architecture utilizes both pipelined and multiple levels of parallel processing to meet the requirements of processing speed, reliability, and scalability. At the core of the system is a very large (200 CPUs) cluster of Linux systems, integrated with a very large disk storage array.

Figure 4 shows the simplified message flow pipeline in speech–to–e-mail service. The basic steps to record a speech message from a user and deliver it to the recipient are as follows.

- A user's call is answered.
- The user keys a series of preassigned DTMF (Dual-Tone Multi-Frequency) digits to match the message to appropriate database records.
- Then, the message is digitally recorded, compressed, and stored.

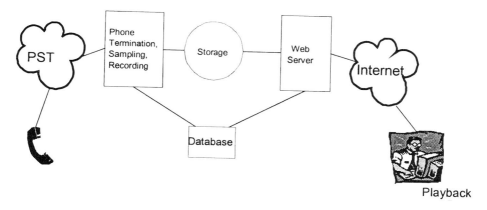

FIGURE 4   Simplified message flow pipeline in speech-to-E-mail service. (From Ref. 108.)

- An e-mail is sent to the recipient, along with a URL to retrieve the stored voice message.

Evoke's speech–to–e-mail system uses two separate servers with an intermediate short-term storage in between. In the initial step, the e-mail message is sampled and stored digitally by a dedicated telephony processor. The selection of number of processors in this stage largely determines the number of simultaneous calls to handle. This stage of the process does not require a great deal of computational power; however, it does require specialized functions and a continuous connection to the user and real-time capture of the voice message. To accomplish this, a large number of small proprietary telephony processors are assigned the task of answering and recording the incoming calls. The recorded messages are stored as uncompressed digital audio files on a shared disk array.

The heart of the system is the transcoding server. This takes the digital audio files and performs processing and compression to create a format suited for long-term storage and streaming playback over an Internet server. This step uses the cluster of Linux systems to perform transcoding to meet the real-time requirement. The number of parallel processors needed for this stage is primarily determined by the workload-generation capability of the telephony processors, and overall throughput and ensuring excess capacity. The current transcoding application is able to convert a message in approximately one-tenth of the time taken to record it, but other transcoding and processing may be added in the future without requiring additional transcoding processors. This asynchronous and faster processing allows the number of Linux nodes to be significantly less than the number of incoming voice channels.

A key element of the system is the storage of the compressed audio files for streaming playback on demand, when a recipient selects the URL sent to them in e-mail. The storage system must be capable of holding a large amount of data, be reliable, and be upgradable. The system chosen by Evoke was a commercial network file server that appears as a shared disk to each of the transcoding nodes.

The speech–to–e-mail service is designed as an engine that may be integrated and used to enhance other services. An example of this is Blue Mountain Arts (109), which uses Evoke's talking e-mail engine to allow senders to add speech messages to their electronic greeting cards.

Parallel and Distributed Data Mining: Terabyte Challenge

Clusters have proved themselves to be very effective for a variety of data mining applications. The data mining process involves both compute and data-intensive operations. Clusters provide two fundamental roles:

- Data clusters provide the storage and data-management services for the data sets being mined.
- Compute clusters provide the computational services required by the data filtering, preparation, and mining tasks (110).

The Terabyte Challenge (111) is an open, distributed testbed for experimental work related to managing, mining, and modeling large, massive, and distributed datasets. The Terabyte Challenge is sponsored by the National Scalable Cluster Project (NSCP) (112), the National Center for Data Mining (NCDM) (113), and the Data Mining Group (DMG) (114). Figure 5 shows the NSCP architecture that connects clusters at multiple sites in different organizations using ATM networks to create a cluster of clusters (also known as a hypercluster). The Terabyte Challenge's testbed is organized into work-group clusters connected with a mixture of traditional and high-performance, broad-band networks. A metacluster is a cluster of work-group clusters connected over the Internet. A supercluster is a cluster of workstations connected with a high-performance network such as Myrinet.

The NSCP philosophy is to use commodity components with high-performance networking to build a virtual platform with supercomputing potential. Currently, the NSCP meta-cluster consists of approximately 100 nodes and 2 TBytes of disk, with two robotic tape libraries. The clusters at University of Illinois at Chicago (UIC), University of Pennsylvania (Upenn), and the University of Maryland (UMD) are linked by an ATM OC-3 (155 Mbps) network to form a single supercluster. The NSCP has demonstrated the effectiveness of local and campus clusters of workstations linked using ATM and Ethernet connections. The NSCP has used the vBNS (very high-performance Backbone Network Service) (137) to create wide-area clusters of workstations for a variety of applications. The main applications of Terabyte Challenge include the following:

- EventStore: Data mining for high-energy physics data with 30 nodes distributed at 6 sites. The data size is 480 GBytes and 79 million events. The underlying architectures are Papyrus distributed data clusters (116), distributed compute clusters (116), Cluster Resource Markup Language (113), and aglet agents (117) to manage data and compute clusters. The performance of EventStore can achieve 30 MBytes/s in moving data between clusters.
- MedStore: Data mining for distributed health care data with four U.S. sites and two international sites. The data size is less than 1 GByte and 600,000 records. This is the first distributed data mining application over an international network. It uses Predictive Model Markup Language (118) built independently and combined with Papyrus, Cluster Resource Markup Language, and aglets used to manage distributed computation.
- Alexa Crawler: Data mining for web documents with 2.1 MBytes of reachable web sites (119). Figure 6 shows the system architecture of Alexa. It is composed for four layers. The first layer gathers more than 80 GBytes of information per day, from more than 2000 different web sites at a time. Alexa uses many commodity off-the-shelf disks that work together in terabyte clusters in the second layer. Up to May 1999, Alexa had collected more than 13 TBytes

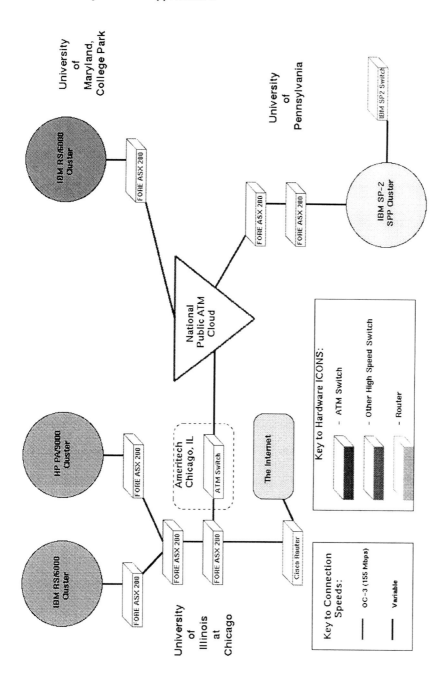

FIGURE 5   National Scalable Cluster Project—ATM connectivity. (From Ref. 115.)

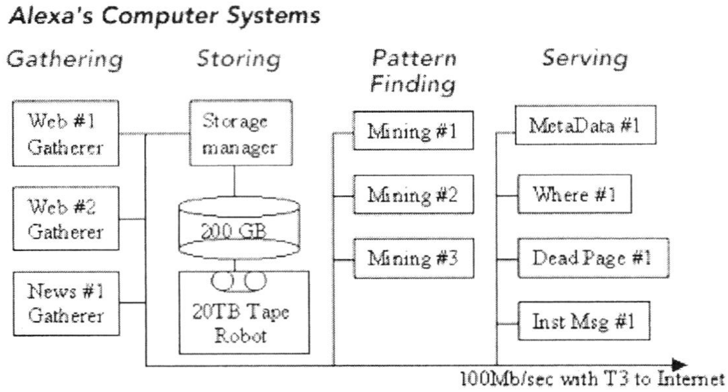

Alexa's Computer Systems

FIGURE 6   Alexa system architecture. (From Ref. 119.)

of information from the web (119). Alexa use a number of data mining techniques in the third layer to find information about web sites. Alexa displays the metadata and clusters web sites in Related Links through the last layer of Alexa service.

- TrajectoryStore: Data mining for simulation data with 4 nodes, 3 GBytes data size, and 800,000 trajectories. Trajectories can be returned in constant time, independent of store size. It uses Papyrus to store complex data, and dyadic decomposition of phase space for scalability.
- Other applications include distributed BLAST search, textural data mining, economic data mining, and so forth.

An underlying technology of NSCP is Papyrus (116). Papyrus is a layered infrastructure for high-performance, wide-area data mining and predictive modeling. Papyrus is specifically designed to support various clusters configurations. Papyrus is designed to support different data, task, and model strategies. These data strategies include local learning, centralized learning, and hybrid learning. Task strategies refer to independent learning or coordinated learning. Model strategies can be meta-learning or knowledge probing. Papyrus is built over a data-warehousing layer, which can move data over both commodity and proprietary networks.

Papyrus applications can be designed to access any of the following four layers:

1. Data management layer, called Osiris
2. Data mining layer
3. Predictive modeling layer
4. Agent layer, called Bast

Currently, Papyrus has two modes:

- It can use Osiris to move segments of data from node to node.
- It can also use Bast to move predictive models from node to node.

Papyrus is the first distributed data mining system to be designed with the flexibility of moving data, moving predictive, or moving the results of local computations.

Ad Hoc Network Simulation: Parametric Computing

Parametric computational experiments are becoming increasingly important in science and engineering as a means of exploring the behavior of complex systems. For example, an engineer may explore the behavior of an aircraft wing by running a computational model of the airfoil multiple times while varying key parameters such as angle of attack or air speed. The results of these multiple experiments yield a picture of how the wing behaves in different parts of parametric space. Parametric computing is suitable for problems in which a single program must be executed repeatedly with different initial conditions (120). Such applications can be easily modeled and executed on clusters using software tools such as Nimrod (121). Nimrod [or its commercial version, Clustor (122)] allows specifying an experiment using a simple GUI and then performing the work on the nodes of the cluster. It provides automatic generation of input parameters and distribution of jobs, as well as the collection of results. The next generation of Nimrod, called Nimrod/G, supports parametric processing over computational Grids (123) with the addition of factors such as computational economy and deadline-based scheduling (124).

One case for parametric computing on clusters is ad hoc network simulations. An ad hoc network can be considered an autonomous system of routers (nodes), interconnected via wireless links, which are free to roam in an arbitrary fashion. Figure 7 illustrates an example of an ad hoc network. The simulation models a multicast protocol known as the Ad Hoc Multicast Protocol (AMP) (125). The purposes of the simulation are to explore achievable network performance at different microwave frequencies under different weather conditions, consider local tropospheric refraction and propagation im-

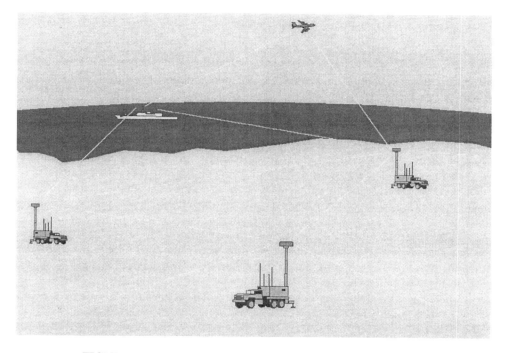

FIGURE 7   An example of the Ad Hoc Network. (From Ref. 125.)

pairments, and analyze global network performance. For example, network simulation under 100 different microwave frequencies and 4 types of weather conditions produce 400 different scenarios. Nimrod allows parameterization of these two parameters (in input file) and automatically creates 400 jobs and manages their processing cluster nodes. If each of these jobs takes 2 h of CPU time, then completing all of them on a single node takes 800 h. Instead, if we run these jobs on clusters of 25 nodes, all jobs can be completed by 16 h with some overhead time. That means that clusters offer (almost) linear performance scalability when used to run such embarrassingly parallel applications.

Persistence of Vision: Parallel Image Rendering

Rendering is a technique for generating a graphical image from a mathematical model of a two- or three-dimensional object or scene. A common method of rendering is ray tracing (126). Ray tracing is a technique used in computer graphics to create realistic images by calculating the paths taken by rays of light entering the observer's eye at different angles. The paths are traced backward from the viewpoint, through a point (a pixel) in the image plane until they hit some object in the scene or go off to infinity. Objects are modeled as collections of abutting surfaces, which may be rectangles, triangles, or more complicated shapes. The optical properties of different surfaces (color, reflectance, transmittance, refraction, and texture) also affect how it will contribute to the color and brightness of the ray. The position, color, and brightness of light sources, including ambient lighting, is also taken into account.

Ray tracing is an ideal application for parallel processing because there are many pixels, each of whose values are independent and can be calculated in parallel. The Persistence of Vision Ray Tracer (POV-Ray) is an all-round three-dimensional ray-tracing software package (127). It takes input information and simulates the way light interacts with the objects defined to create 3D pictures and animations. In addition to the ray-tracing process, newer versions of POV can also use a variant of the process known as radiosity (sophisticated lighting) to add greater realism to scenes, particularly those that use diffuse light. POV-Ray can simulate many atmospheric and volumetric effects (such as smoke and haze).

Given a number of computers and a demanding POV-Ray scene to render, there are a number of techniques to distribute the rendering among the available resources (128). If one is rendering an animation, then, obviously, each computer can render a subset of the total number of frames. The frames can be sent to each computer in contiguous chunks or in an interleaved order; in either case, a preview (every Nth frame) of the animation can generally be viewed as the frames are being computed.

In many cases, even single frames can take a significant time to render. This can occur for all sorts of reasons, such as a complicated geometry, a sophisticated lighting (e.g., radiosity), high antialiasing rates, or, simply, a large image size. The usual way to render such scenes on a collection of computers is to split the final image up into chunks, rendering each chunk on a different computer and reconstructing the chunks together at the end. POV-Ray supports this rendering by the initial file directives.

There are several ways an image may be split up into chunks: by row, column, or in a checker pattern. The basic procedure to render a scene on an N-node cluster is to create N initial files, each one rendering the appropriate row chunk. Processing of each initial file (image chunk) creates one output image file. When all the row chunks are rendered, the image files are reconstructed together.

With regard to performance and efficiency, if each row chunk takes about the same time to render, then one gets a linear improvement with the number of processors available. (This assumes that the rendering time is much longer compared to the scene loading time.) Unfortunately, this is not always the case; the rows across the sky might take a trivial length of time to render, whereas the rows that intersect the interesting part of the scene might take a lot longer. In this case, the machines that rendered the fast portions will stand idle for most of the time. This can be overcome by load-balancing techniques.

One way around this is to split the scene into many more row chunks than there are computers and write a utility that submits jobs to machines as they become free. Another and perhaps neater way is to create row chunks of different heights according to the estimated rendering time. The script used to render the final image can be modified to render a much smaller image with the same number of row chunks. An estimate of the time for the different rows can be used to create narrow row chunks in the complex regions and wide row chunks in the fast-rendering regions. Figure 8 gives an example of composing a ray-tracing image in movie production by using MegaPov (129) and MPI (130) software by executing them on clusters.

SUMMARY AND CONCLUSIONS

In this article, we have discussed the motivation for using clusters as well as the technologies available for building cluster-based systems. There is much emphasis placed on using the commodity-based hardware and software components to achieve high performance and scalability and, at the same time, keep the ratio of price versus performance low. A number of emerging basic building blocks, such as a network technologies, oper-

FIGURE 8   An image that is divided into multiple parts for quick rendering by processing them concurrently on a cluster. [Courtesy of D. Miller (42); *Water Sun* was used as part of a multimedia concert event in which animations were projected onto dancers during the performance.]

ating systems, and middleware, have been discussed. A number of software solutions for providing a Single System Image for clusters are emerging, yet there are still many opportunities for integrating various cluster tools and techniques and making them work together and so help create more usable and better unified clusters.

Clusters are being used to solve many scientific, engineering, and commercial applications. We have discussed a sample of these application areas and how they benefit from the use of clusters. The applications studied include a web server, an audio processing system (voice-based e-mail), data mining, network simulations, and image processing. Many large international web portals and e-commerce sites use clusters to process customer requests quickly and maintain high availability for 24 h a day and throughout the year. The capability of clusters to deliver high performance and availability on a single platform is empowering many existing and emerging applications and making clusters the platform of choice!

REFERENCES

1. Beowulf, http://www.beowulf.org
2. T. Anderson, D. Culler, and D. Patterson, "A Case for Network of Workstations," *IEEE Micro*, *15*(1), 54–64 (1995); http://now.cs.berkeley.edu/
3. High Performance Virtual Machine, http://www-csag.ucsd.edu/projects/hpvm.html
4. G. F. Pfister, *In Search of Clusters*, 2nd ed., Prentice-Hall, Englewood Cliffs, NJ, 1998, p. 29.
5. M. G. Jacunski et al., "Low-Latency Message Passing for Reflective Memory Networks," in *Workshop on Communication, Architecture and Applications for Network-Based Parallel Computing (CANPC)*, 1999.
6. InfiniBand Architecture, http://www.infinibandta.org
7. D. B. Gustavson and Q. Li, "The Scalable Coherent Interface (SCI)," *IEEE Commun. Mag.*, *34*(8), 52–63 (1996).
8. L. L. Peterson and B. S. Davie, *Computer Networks, A Systems Approach*, 2nd. ed., Morgan Kaufmann, San Mateo, CA, 2000.
9. A. M. Mainwaring and D. E. Culler, "Active Messages: Organization and Applications Programming Interface," Technical Report, UC Berkeley (1995); http://now.cs.berkeley.edu/
10. S. Pakin, M. Lauria, and A. Chien, "High Performance Messaging on Workstations: Illinois Fast Messages (FM) for Myrinet, Supercomputing '95," http://www.supercomp.org/sc95/proceedings/567_SPAK/SC95.HTM
11. M. A. Blumrich, C. Dubnicki, E. W. Felten, K. Li, and M. R. Mesarine, "Virtual Memory Mapped Network Interfaces," *IEEE Micro*, 15 (1995).
12. L. Prylli and B. Tourancheau, "BIP: A New Protocol Designed for High Performance Networking on Myrinet," in *Workshop PC-NOW, IPPS/SPDP98*, 1998.
13. A. Basu, M. Welsh, and T. von Eicken, "Incorporating Memory Management into User-Level Network Interfaces," in *Hot Interconnects V*, Stanford University, 1997; also available as Technical Report TR97-1620, Department of Computer Science, Cornell University, http://www2.cs.cornell.edu/U-Net/papers.html
14. M. A. Blumrich et al., "Design Choices in the SHRIMP System: An Empirical Study," in *Proceedings of the 25th Annual ACM/IEEE International Symposium on Computer Architecture*, 1998.
15. N. Boden, D. Cohen, R. Felderman, A. Kulawik, C. Seitz, J. Seizovic, and W-K. Su, "Myrinet–A Gigabit-per-Second Local-Area Network," *IEEE Micro*, 15 (1995).
16. "Virtural Interface Architecture," http://www.viarch.org/

17. "M-VIA: A High Performance Modular VIA for Linux," http://www.nersc.gov/research/FTG/via/

18. P. Buonadonna, A. Geweke, and D. Culler, "An Implementation and Analysis of the Virtual Interface Architecture," in *Proceedings of SC98*, 1998.

19. "Message Passing Interface," *MPI Forum*. http://www.mpi-forum.org/docs/docs.html

20. The Gigabit Ethernet Alliance, http://www.gigabit-ethernet.org/

21. Myricom, Inc., http://www.myri.com/

22. ATM Forum, *ATM User-Network Interface Specification*, Prentice-Hall, Englewood Cliffs, NJ, 1993.

23. "MVICH—MPI for VIA," http://www.nersc.gov/research/FTG/mvich/

24. A. DeHon, "Fat-Tree Routing for Transit," Technical Report, MIT, http://www.ai.mit.edu/people/andre/sb.html

25. E. Leonardi, F. Neri, M. Gerla, and P. Palnati, "Congestion Control in Asynchronous, High-Speed Wormhole Routing Networks," *IEEE Commun. Mag.*, *34*(11), 58–69 (1996).

26. Qsnet, http://www.quadrics.com/web/public/fliers/qsnet.html

27. Server Net II, http://www.servernet.com/

28. SCI Association, http://www.SCIzzL.com/

29. "Atoll: A Network on a Chip," http://www.atoll-net.de/

30. Fibre Channel Industry Association, http://www.fibrechannel.com/

31. "VMIC Reflective Memory," http://reflectivememory.vmic.com/

32. D. R. Engler, M. F. Kaashoek, and J. O'Toole, Jr., "Exokernel: An Operating System Architecture for Application-Level Resource Management," in *Proceedings of the 15th ACM Symposium on Operating Systems Principles* (SOSP '95), 1995, pp. 251–266.

33. K. Scholtyssik and M. Dormanns, "Simplifying the Use of SCI Shared Memory by Using Software SVM Techniques," in *Cluster-Computing*, *Proc. 2nd Workshop*, W. Rehm and T. Ungerer (eds.), Universität Karlsruhe, 1999; http://www.tu-chemnitz.de/informatik/RA/CC99/

34. C. Amza, A. L. Cox, S. D. Warkadas, P. Kelehr, H. Lu, R. Rajamony, W. Yu, and W. Zwaenepoel, "TreadMarks: Shared Memory Computing on Networks of Workstations," *IEEE Computer*, *29*(2), 1996; http://standards.ieee.org/regauth/oui/tutorials/sci.html

35. G. Cabillic, T. Priol, and I. Puaut, "MYOAN: An Implementation of the KOAN Shared Virutal Memory on the Intel Paragon," Technical Report RR-2258, Institute National de Recherche en Informatique et en Automatique (1994).

36. E. Anderson, A. Mainwaring, J. Neefe, C. Yoshikawa, T. Anderson, D. Culler, and D. Patterson, "Experience with Two Implementations of Network RAM," Internal Report, Computer Science Division, University of California at Berkeley; http://http.cs.berkeley.edu/~eanders/projects/netram/

37. D. H. Brown Associates, *Linux—How Good Is It?* D. H. Brown Associates Inc., 1999; http://www.dhbrown.com

38. "Extreme Linux," http://www.extremelinux.org/

39. "MOSIX," http://www.mosix.cs.huji.ac.il.

40. "Solaris MC," http://www.sunlabs.com/research/solaris-mc

41. "DS-Online Grid Computing," http://computer.org/channels/ds/gc/

42. K. Hwang, H. Jin, E. Chow, C.-L. Wang, and Z. Xu, "Designing SSI Clusters with Hierarchical Checkpointing and Single I/O Space," *IEEE Concurrency*, *7*(1), 60–69 (1999).

42. D. H. Miller (http://www.casdn.neu.edu/~dmiller/); image available at http://www.swin.edu.au/supercomputing/rendering/watersun/

43. B. Walker and D. Steel, "Implementing a Full Single System Image UnixWare Cluster: Middleware vs. Underware," in *Proceedings of the International Conference on Parallel and Distributed Processing Techniques and Applications* (PDPTA'99), 1999.

44. G. Popek and B. J. Walker (eds.), *The Locus Distributed System Architecture*, MIT Press, Cambridge, MA, 1996.

45. R. Buyya (ed.), *High Performance Cluster Computing: Architectures and Systems*, Prentice-Hall, Englewood Cliffs, NJ, 1999, Vol. 1.

46. "Memory Channel," http://www.digital.com/info/hpc/systems/symc.html

47. "Distributed Shared Memory Systems," http://www.cs.umd.edu/~keleher/dsm.html

48. "GLUnix: A Global Layer Unix for a Network of Workstations," http://now.cs.berkeley.edu/Glunix/glunix.html

49. "Parallel Virtual Machine (PVM)," http://www.epm.ornl.gov/pvm/

50. "CODINE Resource-Management System," http://www.genias.de/products/codine/

51. "Condor," http://www.cs.wisc.edu/condor/

52. "PARMON: A Portable and Scalable Monitoring System for Clusters," http://www.csse.monash.edu.au/~rajkumar/parmon/

53. D. Abramson, I. Foster, J. Giddy, A. Lewis, R. Sosic, R. Sutherst, and N. White, "The Nimrod Computational Workbench: A Case Study in Desktop Metacomputing," in *Australian Computer Science Conference (ACSC 97)*, 1997.

54. International Organization for Standardization, http://www.iso.ch/

55. "DECmessageQ Documentation," http://www.digital.com/info/decmessageg

56. "MQseries," http://www.software.ibm.com/ts/

57. "TopEnd," http://www.ncr.com/

58. Mullendar, S. (ed.), *Distributed Systems*, 2nd ed., Addison-Wesley, Reading, MA, 1993.

59. The Open Group, http://www.opengroup.org/

60. "Using Name Services," Sun Microsystems, http://www.sun.com/smcc/solaris-migration/docs/transition-guide_2.5/nis.html

61. "The NFS Distributed File Service," NFS White Paper, Sun Microsystems (March 1995); http:www.sun.com/software/white-papers/wp-nfs/

62. Object Management Group, http://www.omg.org/

63. Microsoft, http://www.microsoft.com/com/tech/com.asp

64. "Java RMI," http://www.javasoft.com/products/jdk/rmi/

65. "Jini," http://www.sun.com/jini/

66. "Javasoft," http://www.javasoft.com/products/

67. M. A. Baker, G. C. Fox, and H. W. Yau, "Review of Cluster Management Software," *NHSE Rev.*, *1*(1) (1996); http://www.nhse.org/NHSEreview/96-1.html

68. D. Serain, *Middleware*, Springer-Verlag, New York, 1999.

69. N. Galbreath, W. Gropp, and D. Levine, "Applications-Driven Parallel I/O," in *Supercomputing '93*, IEEE Computer Society Press, Los Alamitos, CA, 1993.

70. E. Schikuta and H. Stockinger, *"Parallel I/O for Clusters: Methodologies and Systems,"* in *High Performance Cluster Computing: Architectures and Systems*, R. Buyya (ed.), Prentice-Hall, Englewood Cliffs, NJ, 1999.

71. R. Bordawekar, J. del Rosario, and A. Choudhary, "Design and Evaluation of Primitives for Parallel I/O," in *Supercomputing '93*, IEEE Computer Society Press, Los Alamitos, 1993, pp. 452–461.

72. "Linux Virtual Server Project," http://www.LinuxVirtualServer.org/

73. R. Thakur and A. Choudhary, "An Extended Two-Phase Method for Accessing Sections of Out-of-Core Arrays," *Sci. Program.*, *5*(4) (1996).

74. D. Kotz, "Disk-Directed I/O for MIMD Multiprocessors," *ACM Trans. Computer Syst.*, *15*(1) (1997).

75. R. H. Patterson, G. A. Gibson, E. Ginting, D. Stodolsky, and J. Zelenka, "Informed Prefetching and Caching," in *Fifteenth ACM Symposium on Operating Systems Principles*, ACM Press, New York, 1995, pp. 79–95.

76. Y. Chen et al., "Performance Modeling for the Panda Array I/O Library," in *Supercomputing '96*, ACM Press/IEEE Computer Society Press, Los Alamitos, CA, 1996.

77. E. Schikuta, T. Fuerle, and H. Wanek, "ViPIOS: The Vienna Parallel I/O System," in *Euro-Par'98*, Springer-Verlag, New York, 1998.

78. T. Sterling, D. J. Becker, D. Savarese, M. R. Berry, and C. Res, "Achieving a Balanced Low-cost Architecture for Mass Storage Management Through Multiple Fast Ethernet Channels on the Beowulf Parallel Worksatation," in *International Parallel Processing Symposium*, 1996.

79. "The D. H. Brown Reports," http://www.dhbrown.com

80. I. Pramanick, "High Availability," *Int. J. High-Perform. Applica. Supercomputing*, *15*(2), 169–174 (2001).

81. L. Dagum and R. Menon, "OpenMP: An Industry-Standard API for Shared-Memory Programming," *IEEE Computat. Sci. Eng.*, *5*(1) (1998).

82. S. A. Salvini, B. Smith, and J. Greenfield, "Towards Mixed Mode Parallelism on the New Model F50-Based IBM SP System," Albuquerque HPCC Report AHPCC98-003, 1998.

83. L. S. Blackford, J. Choi, A. Cleary, E. D'Azevedo, J. Demmel, I. Dhillon, J. Dongarra, S. Hammarling, G. Henry, A. Petitet, D. Walker, and R. C. Whaley, *ScaLAPACK Users' Guide*, SIAM, Philadelphia, 1997; http://www.netlib.org/scalapack

84. P. Alpatov et al., "PLAPACK: Parallel Linear Algebra Libraries Design Overview," in *SC97*, 1997; http://www.cs.utexas.edu/users/rvdg/plapack

85. S. A. Hutchinson, L. V. Prevost, Tuminaro, and J. N. Shadid, *AZTEC Users' Guide: Version 2.0*. Sandia National Laboratories, 1998; http://www.cs.sandia.gov/CRF/aztec1.html

86. M. T. Jones and P. E. Plassman, "Blocksolve V1.1: Scalable Library Software for Parallel Solution of Sparse Linear Systems," ANL Report 92/46, Argonne National Laboratory (December 1992); http://www-unix.mcs.anl.gov/sumaa3d/BlockSolve

87. Y. Saad and M. Sosonkina, "Solution of Distributed Sparse Linear Systems Using Psparslib," in *Applied Parallel Computing, Proc. PARA'98*, Lecture Notes in Computer Science Vol. 1541, Springer-Verlag, Berlin, 1998; http://www.cs.umn.edu/Research/arpa/p_sparslib/psp-abs.html

88. R. B. Lehoucq, D. C. Sorensen, and C. Yang, *ARPACK Users' Guide: Solution of Large-scale Eigenvalue Problems with Implicitly-Restarted Arnoldi Methods*, SIAM, Philadelphia, 1998; http://www.caam.rice.edu/software/ARPACK

89. D. Elwood, G. Fann, and R. Littlefield, *Parallel Eigensolver System User Manual*, Batelle Pacific Northwest Laboratory; Available from anonymous@ftp://pnl.gov

90. Numerical Algorithms Group, http://www.nag.co.uk

91. *The NAG Parallel Library Manual, Release 2*, Numerical Algorithms Group Ltd, Oxford, 1997.

92. S. Salvini and J. Waniewski, "Linear Algebra Subprograms on Shared Memory Computers: Beyond LAPACK," in *Applied Parallel Computing Industrial Computation and Optimization, 3rd International Workshop, PARA'96*, Springer-Verlag Lecture Notes in Computer Science Vol. 1184, J. Waniewski, J. Dongarra, K. Madsen, and D. Olesen (eds.), Berlin, 1996.

93. S. Weerawarana, E. N. Houstis, R. J. Rice, A. C. Catlin, C. L. Crabill, and C. C. Chui, "Pdelab: An Object-Oriented Framework for Building Problem Solving Environments for PDE-Based Applications," Technical Report CSD-TR-94-021, Purdue University (March 1994); http://ziggurat.ca.sandia.gov/isis

94. Argonne National Laboratory, "Grand Challenge Applications," http://www-fp.mcs.anl.gov/grand-challenges/

95. "Hotbot," http://www.hotbot.com

96. R. Buyya (ed.), *High Performance Cluster Computing: Programming and Applications*, Prentice-Hall, Englewood Cliffs, NJ, 1999, Vol. 2.

97. S. Bhandarkar, S. Chirravuri, and S. Machaka, "Biomedical Applications Modelling," in *High Performance Cluster Computing: Programming and Applications*, Prentice Hall, Englewood Cliffs, NJ, 1999, Vol. 2.

98. F. Ferstl, "Global Resource Director (GRD): Customer Scenarios for Large Multiprocessor Environments," in *IEEE International Workshop on Cluster Computing*, 1999.

99. Hotmail, http://www.hotmail.com

100. "COMPAQ Server Consolidation," http://www.compaq.com/solutions/serverconsolidation/
101. "Hewlett-Packard System Consolidation," http://www.unixsolutions.hp.com/solutions/sc/
102. "IBM S390 Server Consolidation," http://www.s390.ibm.com/sc/
103. "Microsoft Application Center 2000," http://www.microsoft.com/applicationcenter/
104. "Sun Data Center Consolidation," http://www.sun.com/datacenter/consolidation/
105. Linux Virtual Server, http://www.LinuxVirtualServer.org/
106. Linux Portal, http://www.linux.com
107. S. Horman, "Creating Redundant Linux Servers," in *Proceedings of the 4th Annual Linux-Expo Conference*, 1998.
108. R. Brumbaugh and T. Vernon, "Design of a Very-Large Linux Cluster for Providing Reliable and Scalable Speech-to-Email Service, in *4th Annual Linux Showcase & Conference, Extreme Linux: Clusters and High Performance Computing Workshop*, 2000.
109. Blue Mountain, http://www.bluemountain.com
110. D. B. Skillicorn, "Data Mining: Parallelism's Killer Application," in *7th Australian Conference on Parallel and Real-time Systems* (*PART 2000*), 2000.
111. The Terabyte Challenge, http://www.ncdm.uic.edu/TC2000.htm
112. National Scalable Cluster Project, http://www.ncsp.uic.edu/
113. National Center for Data Mining, http://www.ncdm.uic.edu
114. Data Mining Group, http://www.dmg.org
115. NSCP, http://www.lac.uic.edu/nscp_atm.gif
116. S. M. Bailey, R. L. Grossman, H. Sivakumar, and A. L. Turinsky, "Papyrus: A System for Data Mining over Local and Wide Area Clusters and Super-Clusters," in *Proceedings of Supercomputing'99 Conference*, 1999
117. D. Lange and M. Oshima, *Programming and Deploying Java Mobile Agents with Aglets*, Addison-Wesley, Reading, MA, 1998.
118. R. L. Grossman et al., "The Management and Mining of Multiple Predictive Models Using the Predictive Modelling Markup Language (PMML)," *Inform. Software Technol.* (1999).
119. Alexa Technology, http://www.alexa.com/support/technology.html
120. "Nimrod," http://www.csse.monash.edu.au/~davida/nimrod/
121. D. Abramson, R. Sosic, J. Giddy, and B. Hall, "Nimrod: A Tool for Performing Parameterised Simulations using Distributed Workstations," *The 4th IEEE Symposium on High Performance Distributed Computing*, 1995.
122. "Active Tools Clustor," http://www.activetools.com
123. I. Foster and C. Kesselman (eds.), *The Grid: Blueprint for a New Computing Infrastructure*, Morgan Kaufmann, San Mateo, CA, 1999.
124. R. Buyya, D. Abramson, and J. Giddy, "Nimrod/G: An Architecture for a Resource Management and Scheduling System in a Global Computational Grid," in *International Conference on High Performance Computing in Asia–Pacific Region* (*HPC Asia 2000*), IEEE Computer Society Press, Los Alamitos, CA, 2000.
125. C. Kopp, "Supercomputing on a Shoestring—Practical Experience with the Monash PPME Linux Cluster," in *Proceedings of Open Source–AUUG'99*, 1999.
126. P. Shirley, *Realistic Ray Tracing*, A K Peters Ltd., 2000.
127. "POVRay," http://www.povray.org/
128. P. Bourke, "Parallel Rendering: Using POVRAY on a Computer Farm, Swinburne Astrophysics and Supercomputing Centre," 2000; http://www.swin.edu.au/astronomy/pbourke/povray/parallel/
129. "MegaPov," http://nathan.kopp.com/patched.htm
130. W. Gropp, E. Lusk, N. Doss, and A. Skjellum, "A High-Performance, Portable Implementation of the Message Passing Interface (MPI) Standard," *Parallel Computing J.*, 22(6) (1996).
131. Giganet, Inc., http://www.giganet.com
132. R. Bennett, K. Bryant, A. Sussman, R. Das, and J. Saltz, "Jovian: A Framework for Opti-

mizing Parallel I/O," in *Scalable Parallel Libraries Conference*, IEEE Computer Society Press, Los Alamitos, CA, 1994.

133. "Netlib," http://www.netlib.org

134. Inktomi Corporation "A Whitepaper on the INKTOMI Technology behind HOTBOT," 2000, http://www.inktomi.com/products/network/traffic/tech/clustered.html

135. W. Zhang, "Linux Virtual Servers for Scalable Network Services," in *Proceedings of 2000 Ottawa Linux Symposium*, 2000.

136. Evoke Communication, http://www.evoke.com/

137. VBNS, http://www.vbns.net/

138. J. Protic, M. Tomaevic, and V. Milutinovic (eds.), *Distributed Shared Memory: Concepts and Systems*, IEEE Computer Society Press, Los Alamitos, CA, 1997.

MARK BAKER

AMY APON

RAJKUMAR BUYYA

HAI JIN

EVALUATION OF SOFTWARE SYSTEMS

INTRODUCTION

Evaluation as a general endeavor can be characterized by the following features (1):

- Evaluation is a task which results in one or more reported outcomes.
- Evaluation is an aid for planning; therefore, the outcome is an evaluation of different possible actions.
- Evaluation is goal oriented. The primary goal is to check the results of actions or interventions, in order to improve the quality of the actions or to choose the best action alternative.
- Evaluation is dependent on the current knowledge of science and the methodological standards.

Evaluation as an aid for software development has been applied since the last decade, when the comprehension of the role of evaluation within human–computer interaction had changed. In one of the most influential models of iterative system design, the Star Life Cycle Model of Hix and Hartson (2), the activities

> Task analysis
> Requirement specification
> Conceptual and formal design
> Prototyping
> Implementation

are each supplemented by an activity "Evaluation" which helps to decide progression to the next step. Software can be evaluated with respect to different aspects (e.g., functionality, reliability, usability, efficiency, maintainability, portability) (3). In this survey, we concentrate on the aspect of usability from an ergonomic point of view. This aspect has gained particular importance during the last decade with the increasing use of interactive software.

Whereas, in earlier times, evaluation of software took place at the end of the developing phase, using experimental designs and statistical analysis, evaluation is, nowadays, used as a tool for information gathering within iterative design:

> Explicit human-factors evaluations of early interactive systems (when they were done at all) were poorly integrated with development and therefore ineffective. They tended to be done too late for any substantial changes to the system to still be feasible and, in common with other human-factors contributions to development, they were often unfavorably received [. . .] This situation has been improved in recent years in a number of ways. (4)

Within this context, instruments for evaluation are not primarily used for global evaluation of an accomplished product, but these instruments are applied during the development of a product. Indeed, most experts agree nowadays that the development of usable software can only be done by a systematic consideration of usability aspects within the life-cycle model. One prominent part is the evaluation of prototypes with respect to usability aspects, employing suitable evaluation techniques in order to find usability errors and weaknesses of the software at an early stage (2,5–7).

GOALS AND RESULTS OF EVALUATION

Any evaluation has pragmatically chosen goals. In the domain of software evaluation, the goal can be characterized by one or more of three simple questions:

1. Which one is better? The evaluation aims to compare alternative software systems (e.g., to choose the best fitting software tool for given application) for a decision among several prototypes, or for comparing several versions of a software system. An example of such a strategy can be found in Ref. 8.
2. How good is it? This goal aims at the determination of the degree of desired qualities of a finished system. The evaluation of the system with respect to "Usability Goals" (7,9) is one of the application of this goal. Other examples are the certification of software and the check on conformity with given standards.
3. Why is it bad? The evaluation aims to determine the weaknesses of a software such that the result generates suggestions for further development. A typical instance of this procedure is a system-developing approach using prototypes or a reengineering of an existing system (2).

The first two goals can be subsumed under the concept of *summative evaluation*; the third goal is an instance of the *formative evaluation* approach.

In general, summative evaluation is concerned with the global aspects of software development and does not offer constructive information for changing the design of the system in a direct manner. It is performed when the development of the system is almost or entirely accomplished (2). Summative evaluation is also applied to prototypes in case there is a need for controlling the effect of design changes in comparison to a preceding version of the system.

In contrast, the goals of formative evaluation are the improvement of software and design supporting aspects (10). It is considered the main part of software evaluation and plays an important role in iterative system development. In every development cycle, formative evaluation results in the following:

*   Quantitative data for the description of the progress of the realization of usability goals
*   Qualitative data which can be used to detect the usability problems of the system

The resulting data can be classified by the following criteria (2):

Objective: Directly observable data; typically user behavior during the use of the interface or the application system

Subjective: Opinions, normally expressed by the user with respect to the usability of the interface or the application system

Quantitative: Numerical data and result (e.g., user performance ratings)

Qualitative: Non-numerical data (e.g., lists of problems, suggestions for modifications to improve the interaction design)

EVALUATION CRITERIA

In the human-factors community, it is a matter of some debate about what constitutes an evaluation criterion. We follow Dzida (11), who advised that "criteria" should mean the measurable part of attributes of design or evaluation. Although this seems clear enough, the literature on software evaluation shows only a few attempts to achieve general principles of design and evaluation criteria.

The concept of *usability*, which is a general quality concept for software systems, is often used for the determination of evaluation criteria (12–14).

The International Standard ISO 9241 (Part 11), which is the methodological foundation of the HCI standard "Ergonomic requirements for office work with visual display terminals" (ISO 9241), states,

> Usability of a product is the extent to which the product can be used by specific users to achieve specific goals with effectiveness, efficiency, and satisfaction in a specific context of use.

Note that the characterization of usability by "effectiveness," "efficiency," and "satisfaction" is not a breakdown to measurable criteria, but only a first step toward reaching such criteria (15, p. 6). The same is true for ISO 9241 (Part 10) (12,16) and for other general guidelines and design principles as well. These standards give no advice on how to achieve trustworthy criteria which will fit into the needs of a specific software evaluation task. For a concrete evaluation project, there needs to be a proper operationalization of the general guidelines and standards, which takes into account the context in which the system will be applied. The context of use is defined in ISO 9241 (Part 11) in terms of the user, the task, the equipment, and the environment. Following this description of the components of the context of use, every evaluation has to take into account the following restrictions:

A. The characteristics of a product's users such as experience, age, gender, or other more specific features
B. The types of activity or tasks that the user will perform
C. The environment of the study itself, ranging from controlled laboratory conditions to largely unstructured field studies
D. The nature of the evaluation object, which can be a paper prototype, a software mock-up, a partially functional prototype, or an accomplished system

Even an expert-based evaluation should consider all of these four contextual restrictions in order to achieve a valid evaluation result.

In principle, there are (at least) four approaches for the derivation of criteria:

1. The successive division of principles into a hierarchy using specialization, until the leaves can be measured by a set of known procedures (top-down I).
2. The successive division of principles into a hierarchy using specialization, until the leaves cannot be subdivided any more. This level will then be operationalized by a tailored technique (top-down II).
3. A classification of known and/or commonly applied methods, and their map-

ping to criteria, or, alternatively, an empirical assignment of items to criteria (bottom up).

4. A direct operationalization of principles, which takes into consideration the measurable demands and the qualities of the object under study.

An advantage of the first strategy is that it is based on known and tried methods. However, known methods will be applicable only to part of the actual problem, namely the final level; therefore, the problem arises that the results may be misinterpreted due to a divergence artifact (17).

The second strategy has the advantage that it intends to measure everything that the evaluation requires. Its disadvantage are the huge amount of labor required for the construction of tailored instruments and that the results usually cannot be compared to the findings of other studies.

The third strategy is expensive as well, including the risk that only some of the basic principles are well covered while others are not.

The fourth strategy not only offers an operationalization but also attempts a more precise formulation of the criteria and the underlying principles as well. Its disadvantage is its cost; furthermore, empirical studies following this procedure offer results which are, in most cases, too general and not sufficiently specific for a concrete application (12).

Tyldesley (18) argues that "objective measurements" such as the time required for learning a system are preferred measurements and should be used as criteria for software evaluation. Although objectivity and reliability of such measures are generally accepted, there are doubts about their validity:

> . . . the so-called objective measurements of performance, for example the number of problems completed within a fixed time span, are widely applied; they are, however, rarely valid as criteria, since the underlying causal relationships are not sufficiently investigated or stated. (translated from Ref. 12)

The derivation of "subjective" criteria such as acceptable levels of human cost in terms of tiredness, discomfort, frustration and personal effort, or even an operational definition of attitude is much harder, and Whitefield et al. (4) come to the pessimistic conclusion that there is, at present, no support for the specification and operationalization of such criteria.

The bottom-up approach offered by Strategy 3 can be a starting point for criteria derivation: At the beginning, one collects "standard" operationalizations with known validity and reliability. From this collection, the designer can choose those instruments which can be subsumed as a set of criteria for the principles under study. At least for the "subjective" criteria, an operationalization via a well-analyzed questionnaire or a survey instrument may be a successful way to cope with the problem.

There seems to be no problem for operationalization on the principles of *heuristic evaluation* proposed by Nielsen (14) and comparable techniques. These are performed by auditors who evaluate the system, given a set of general design principles. In this case, the concretization will be done by the auditor in interaction with the system; therefore, the burden of proper operationalization is put on the auditor. Such methods demand well-educated and well-trained evaluators, and it is no wonder that specialists who are usability *and* task experts perform better with this techniques than usability experts who are not task experts (19).

EVALUATION TECHNIQUES

Evaluation techniques are activities of evaluators which can be precisely defined in behavioral and organizational terms. It is important not to confuse "evaluation techniques" with "evaluation models," which usually constitute a combination of evaluation techniques.

We classify evaluation techniques into two categories: the *descriptive evaluation techniques* and the *predictive evaluation techniques*, both of which should be present in every evaluation:

Descriptive evaluation techniques are used to describe the status and the actual problems of the software in an objective, reliable, and valid way. These techniques are user based and can be subdivided into several approaches:

Behavior-based evaluation techniques record user behavior while working with a system which "produces" some kind of data. These procedures include observational techniques and "thinking-aloud" protocols.

Opinion-based evaluation methods aim to elicit the user's (subjective) opinions. Examples are interviews, surveys, and questionnaires.

Usability testing stems from classical experimental design studies. Nowadays, usability testing (as a technical term) is understood to be a combination of behavior- and opinion-based measures with some amount of experimental control, usually chosen by an expert.

Observe that all descriptive evaluation techniques require some kind of prototype and at least one user. Note, furthermore, that the data gathered by a descriptive technique need some further interpretation by one or more experts in order to result in recommendations for future software development.

Predictive evaluation techniques have as their main aim to make recommendations for future software development and the prevention of usability errors. These techniques are expert-based or, at least, expertise-based, such as walkthrough or inspection techniques. Even though the expert is the driving power in these methods, users may also participate in some instances.

Note that predictive evaluation techniques must rely on "data." In many predictive evaluation techniques, such "data" are produced by experts who simulate "real" users. The criteria *objectivity* and *reliability*, which are at the basis of descriptive techniques, are hard to apply in this setting. Because validity must be the major aim of evaluation procedures, there are attempts to prove the *validity* of predictive evaluation techniques directly (e.g., by comparing "hits" and "false alarm" rates of the problems detected by a predictive technique) (20).

At the end of the section we shall briefly discuss evaluation techniques which can be used either for predictive or descriptive evaluation (e.g., formal usability testing methods) and those which do not fit into the predictive/descriptive classification, such as the "interpretative evaluation techniques" (21).

Behavior-Based Evaluation Techniques

Behavior-based techniques rely on some form of observation in order to detect usability problems. Because the user is confronted with a prototype of the system, these techniques can only be applied in the later stages of system development.

As a first indicator of the expense of the technique, we offer the ratio "analysis time" (time to process the data, by experts after data elicitation) to "time of users' interaction with the system" (time to elicit the data which will be analyzed).

Observational Techniques

User observation as a method of software evaluation takes place directly or indirectly by a trained observer (12), and it can produce quantitative as well as qualitative data (2, p. 306). The techniques try to avoid subjectivity as much as possible by standardizing procedures and documentation, as well as by training the observer. They are applied, for example, if the user's behavior is of interest, especially when the user cannot tell how well (or badly) (s)he behaves using a prototype (14, p. 207).

It turns out that direct observation is not a well-suited technique (22, p. 617), mainly because the observer cannot deal with the amount of information which has to be processed. Therefore, indirect techniques using a video recording of the user's behavior are commonly used. In human-factor laboratories, several parallel video loggings (hands, screen, face, whole body), together with log files, are synchronized and used by the observers; an example is the VANNA system of Harrison (23).

Observational techniques show a ratio of 5:1 of analysis time to recording time (22, p. 620). This ratio does not seem to be reduced by using automated procedures. The main reason is that computerized systems offer more information to the observer, which works against the effect of the rationalization.

Thinking-Aloud Protocols

The method of thinking aloud provides the evaluator with information about cognitions and emotions of a user while (s)he performs a task or solves a problem; examples can be found in Refs. 14 and 24–26. The user is instructed to articulate what (s)he is thinks and what (s)he feels while working with the prototype. The utterances are recorded either using paper and pencil (6,27) or with more modern techniques using audio or video recording (25,26). In connection with synchronized log-file recordings, the evaluator has the chance to interpret the user's reaction based on contextual information (25). Nielsen (6, p. 72) expressed the opinion that a large amount of overhead is unnecessary and that simple paper–pencil recordings suffice to elicit the relevant contextual information.

A slightly different approach are the *preevent* and *postevent* thinking-aloud procedures, in which the user thinks aloud before a task has started or after a task has been completed. The postevent technique is useful if the tasks require careful concentration. Their protocols are based on the comments evoked by thinking aloud, while the user observes the video recorded interaction with the system. Postevent protocols were criticized because the user might rationalize her/his own actions. Some researchers, however, point out that the more rational style of postevent protocols provides the evaluator with useful context information which event protocols cannot deliver (28). The empirical comparison of postevent protocols with event protocols shows that the information provided by postevent protocols are of higher quality, although the amount of information is reduced in comparison to event protocols (29,30).

The procedure of analyzing thinking-aloud protocols has not much changed since the seminal paper by Lewis (26) in 1982: The protocols are scanned and those episodes are extracted which describe the users' problems and their complaints. The episodes are listed and coded by a user number and an episode number. Afterward, the episodes are matched with one "feature" of the system. These "features" define the grouping criteria for the episodes. The design aspect of the "feature" and the frequency information provide further help with the interpretation of the results.

By using thinking-aloud techniques, the evaluator obtains information about the whole user interface. This type of evaluation is oriented toward the investigation of the user's problem behavior and decision behavior while working with the system (12, p. 99). The procedures to transform the lingual information into evaluation criteria is only weakly standardized, which may be problematic.

The expense of the method varies. In our experience, the concurrent-event technique requires a user time factor near 1 : 1 and an evaluator time factor of about 3 : 1 for a trained evaluator. The video-based postevent technique needs more time, with a user time factor of at least 3 : 1 and an evaluator time factor of at least 5 : 1.

Video Confrontation

In the area of human–computer interaction, the video confrontation technique has been in use since the mid-1980s (31,32). It is based on the postevent thinking-aloud technique, but differs in the way the video recordings of the user-system interaction are analyzed. The evaluator picks out interesting recorded episodes and interviews the user about these. The interview is guided by pragmatic or theoretical goals, such as finding usability problems or examining the relationship between user errors and emotional reactions. The questions concern cognition, emotions, or problems which have occurred during the use of the system (32). The main result of the process is the interview protocol. Because the frame for the analysis is set by the evaluator before performing the interview, the questions are concentrated on the salient points, and the protocol is much easier to analyze than a thinking-aloud protocol. Furthermore, the interview questions can be standardized and, thus, they can lead to an operationalization of evaluation criteria, which establish a direct relation to the evaluation goals. It is also possible not only to arrive at a list of problems but also to obtain an indication of the reasons for these problems. Other sources of information such as other recorded sequences and log files may also help the evaluator to interpret the outcome of the procedure (33).

The video confrontation technique is rather costly: A rough estimation of the user time ratio is 5 : 1 and of the evaluator time ratio is 7 : 1.

Opinion-Based Evaluation Methods

Oral or written interview techniques are commonly used to evaluate the user's opinion about software systems. The difference between oral interview techniques and questionnaire-based techniques lies mainly in the effort for setup, evaluating the data, and standardization of the procedure. The development of an interview is more economic than for questionnaires, whereas carrying out and evaluating a questionnaire procedure can be done with less effort and costs. Standardization and accuracy are also better for questionnaires.

The advantage of an interview in comparison with the observational methods of the subsection Observational Techniques is that an interview helps to obtain an insight into the user's opinion of the system which cannot be gathered by observation alone (14, p. 209ff). Furthermore, these techniques are not as expensive as observational techniques.

Oral interviews are held in a flexible manner after the user had come into contact with the system and in a more structured way if the user was faced with unforeseen aspects (14,34).

Another aspect are "critical incidents" (2,14,34) (e.g., examples of worst-case situations created by experts), which can be used to evoke oral responses.

Because there is no standardization of oral interviews as a software evaluation technique, we shall not discuss the various approaches in more detail. As an introduction, we invite the reader to consult the checklist of Nielsen et al. (22,35).

Interviews and questionnaires are primarily used in the specification, design, or reengineering phase, or as a means of system comparison (summative approach), where different techniques have different focal points. In the sequel, we shall discuss three types of questionnaire in more detail: the Questionnaire for User Interface Satisfaction (36, p. 482ff), the Software Usability Measurement Inventory (37), and the IsoMetrics questionnaire (38).

QUIS: Questionnaire for User Interface Satisfaction

The Questionnaire for User Interface Satisfaction (QUIS) aims to provide a measure of overall satisfaction; additionally, it evaluates some aspects of the user interface based on user opinions. The original version [QUIS 5.0 (39)] consists of five scales:

- "Overall User Reactions" with attributes such as the following:

  Terrible/wonderful
  frustrating/satisfying
  dull/stimulating
  inadequate power/adequate power
  rigid/flexible

- "Screen," which evaluates the display appearance
- "Terminology and System Information," which evaluates the distinctiveness of terminology and message display
- "Learning," which evaluates the suitability of the system for learning
- "System Capabilities," which evaluates the efficiency and related aspects of the system in terms of speed and reliability

The current version of QUIS is enhanced by the scales "Technical Manuals and On-line Help," "On-line Tutorials," "Multimedia," "Teleconferencing," and "Software Installation" (40). A short (47 Items) and a long version (126 Items) of QUIS are available. The short version should be used if there are only few time resources or if motivational problems of the user can be anticipated. In the long version, there are more concrete questions explaining and complementing the "leading items" (which constitute the short version) of each scale. At the beginning, there are questions about the properties of the system under study (in terms of the user's opinions) and the characteristics of the user.

The scaling of the items ranges from 1 to 9, and an additional "no answer" option. The end points of the scales are anchored by pairs of adjectives (e.g., difficult/easy). User comments about the system can be expressed at the end of each scale.

Reliability and validity of QUIS(5.0) have been investigated by Chin et al. (39). They could show that its overall reliability is good, but no separate reliability measures for the five subscales were reported. Validity was shown in terms of differentiation of "like" and "dislike" for a software product, and the results of QUIS can be used to differentiate command line systems and menu-driven applications. The predicted dimensionality of QUIS(5.0) is questionable and there should be more analysis for construct validity as well, as " . . . no attempt to establish any construct or predictive validity was done" (39, p. 218). For the new version of QUIS, psychometric results are not (yet) available.

SUMI: The Software Usability Measurement Inventory

SUMI (37,41) was developed primarily as a summative instrument which measures a user's perception of the usability of a software. SUMI consists of 50 items, which are assigned to five scales. Additionally, a "global" scale was constructed consisting of those 25 items which show a high correlation with an overall usability factor. The "global" scale was constructed to present the perceived quality of the software as one index.

The answer format for the items consists of "agree", "don't agree," and "disagree." In a SUMI evaluation, the recommended number of users is 10–12. The headings of the scales are as follows:

- Global (25 items)
- Efficiency (10 items)
- Affect (10 items)
- Helpfulness (10 items)
- Control (10 items)
- Learnability (10 items)

The efficiency scale evaluates how well the software supports the user while working on the tasks. The affect scale measures the user's general emotional reaction to the software. Helpfulness is intended to measure the degree to which the software is self-explanatory and the suitability of the help system. The control scale is used to measure the degree of the user's feeling that (s)he controls the software. Finally, learnability measures time and effort for learning the handling of the software (or parts of it) from the user's point of view.

For formative evaluation, SUMI was supplemented by the "Item Consensual Analysis" (ICA), which enables the evaluator to locate usability problems more precisely than with the analysis of the scales profiles. ICA needs a "Standardization Database" which consists of expected pattern of responses for any SUMI item. A comparison of expected and observed frequencies for the items (using a χ^2 test) shows which item signals a demand for change.

A second variant of the ICA should be used if a more detailed problem analysis is required. In this case, the first step consists of a sample of at least 12 users who are confronted with the standard SUMI. Based on the ICA analysis of the user data, an interview script is constructed, and interviews are held to obtain explanations for the discrepancies of expected and observed frequencies.

The subscales of SUMI show reliabilities which range from satisfactory to good. Validation studies of SUMI have shown that the questionnaire has the capability to distinguish software of different ergonomic quality (37,41). The usefulness of SUMI in consultancy-based studies as well as in case studies has been exemplified in Refs. 37 and 41.

IsoMetrics

The IsoMetrics usability inventory provides a user-oriented, summative as well as formative approach to software evaluation on the basis of ISO 9241 (Part 10) (38). There are two versions of IsoMetrics, both based on the same items: IsoMetrics[S] (short) supports summative evaluation of software systems, whereas IsoMetrics[L] (long) is best suited for formative evaluation purposes.

The current version of IsoMetrics comprises 75 items operationalizing the 7 design principles of ISO 9241 (Part 10). The statement of each item is assessed on a five-point rating scale starting from 1 ("predominantly disagree") to 5 ("predominantly agree"). A further category ("no opinion") is offered to reduce arbitrary answers. IsoMetrics^L consists of the same items as IsoMetrics^S and uses the same rating procedure. Additionally, each user is asked to give a second rating, based on the request

> Please rate the importance of the above item in terms of supporting your general impression of the software.

This rating ranges from 1 ("unimportant") to 5 ("important"), and a further "no opinion" category may also be selected. In this way, each item is supplied with a weighting index. To evoke information about malfunctions and weak points of the system under study, the question

> Can you give a concrete example where you can (not) agree with the above statement?

is posed. This gives users the opportunity to report problems with the software, which they attribute to the actual usability item.

The IsoMetrics design provides information that can be used within an iterative software development. In summary, these are as follows:

- Scores of the usability dimension to measure the progress of development
- Concrete information about malfunctions and their user-perceived attributes
- Mean weight of any user-perceived attribute, given a class of system malfunctions

IsoMetrics has proved its practicability in several software development projects. Its reliability was examined in two studies for five software systems and could be justified for each of the seven design principles. In order to validate the IsoMetrics inventory, the scale means of the five different software systems analyzed in the reliability studies were compared. It could be shown that programs with different ergonomic qualities were discriminated in the corresponding scales (38).

Given 10 evaluating users, IsoMetrics^L evokes approximately 100 remarks. [The validity of this procedure has been reported elsewhere (42)]. These are prioritized by their rated importance and their frequency. The content analysis of the remarks results in the identification of weak points of the evaluated software and provides the input to a usability review. In such a review, users, software engineers, and human-factor specialists develop remedies for the system's weak points and discuss its (re)design. This procedure has been highly accepted by developers as well as the users. A version of IsoMetrics which is applicable in group settings is discussed in Ref. 43.

Another summative evaluation method based on ISO 9241 (Part 10) has been adopted as a formative instrument in a system called "Qualitative Software Screening" (44,45).

Usability Testing

Usability Testing is a name for a systematic and—more or less rigid—experimentally based gathering of information about a product or a prototype using user representatives (46,47). A rough classification by Rubin (47, p. 22) can be used to characterize different approaches to Usability Testing:

- "Formal tests conducted as true experiments." This approach is characterized by the use of classical experimental designs for testing hypotheses and for deriving causal dependencies (see also Ref. 48).
- The second class of usability tests, describe to be "a less formal" one, employs an iterative cycle of tests intended to expose usability deficiencies and gradually shape or mold the product in question.

Whereas both approaches differ in their proximity to classical experimental designs in terms of the accuracy of the description of the independent factors, the problem of defining dependent variables—the measurables—is common to both approaches. The dependent variables are chosen pragmatically according to the evaluation goals. Techniques described earlier, including

- Questionnaires and interviews
- Observational methods
- Think-aloud technique
- Video confrontation

are used to measure the impact of differences in system design or different versions of a prototype on the usability of the product. Additionally, so-called measurement criteria (18) are used. These are task-specific measures such as "time to complete a task" or "percentage of tasks completed," which can be easily applied if tasks are accurately described. The thinking-aloud technique is "perhaps the most common technique for qualitative data generation . . . " (2, p. 306); indeed, many other authors emphasize the use of thinking-aloud methods in usability testing (5,7,13,14,25,26,47).

However, Nielsen (14, p. 165) advocates

> User testing with real users is the most fundamental usability method and is in some sense irreplaceable, since it provides direct information about how people use computers and what their exact problems are with the concrete interface being tested.

This approach has been criticized because of its expense and its low cost–benefit relation (49). As a possible remedy, inspection-based methods are being discussed as an alternative evaluation approach (20). These are predominantly used to uncover general usability problems in the interface and consist of a combination of predictive techniques, described more fully below, such as heuristic evaluation, Walkthrough, or group discussions with other quality assurance tools like standard inspection or feature inspection (20,50).

Virzi (50) calls usability inspection a "nonempirical" method and points out that this method has the typical weaknesses of a purely predictive technique, because it relies mainly on the ability of the inspectors to predict problems of users with the software.

Because Usability Testing requires a large amount of expertise for the following:

- To set up the experimental design
- To choose the suitable tasks for comparison
- To select the users and the number of users
- To define the measurables properly

it is perhaps best suited for usability engineers. It is certainly not a suitable technique for untrained evaluators.

Predictive Evaluation Techniques

Because predictive evaluation techniques aim to achieve results which can be used in practice, these methods are related to problem-solving techniques which are used for the same reasons in other contexts, such as requirements analysis.

Whereas observational and opinion-based methods require a (more or less) sophisticated prototype, the predictive evaluations do not need a built system, because empirical methods are replaced by a theory or the contribution of experts. Consequently, user involvement is not as dominant as in the empirical evaluation techniques. Nevertheless, user participation could be more prominent in predictive techniques, because user representatives have the opportunity to influence the development process actively, whereas in descriptive techniques, the user plays a more passive role.

Usability Walkthrough

There are different variants of Walkthrough methods in human–computer interaction (13,47,51–53). The object of a Walkthrough is either the system design, a paper prototype (e.g., Ref. 13, p. 698), a built prototype (e.g., Ref. 47), or a completed system.

The main feature is a set of instructions to check, step by step, the artifact under development. For each step, the participants note problems with the task or screen design–in the case of a paper prototype—or with the user interface of a built prototype. After the data collection, problems are discussed and improvements of the system are proposed. The task sequence of a Walkthrough must be fixed, otherwise the simulation is not meaningful for evaluation purposes.

Walkthrough methods for software evaluation are often performed in a group (13,51,52), mainly because group Walkthrough has proved to be more effective than comparable individual Walkthroughs (22, p. 706). The participants of a group Walkthrough come from different areas (e.g., representatives of the expected user population, product developers, and human-factor specialists). Because of the heterogeneous composition of the group, one also speaks of "Pluralistic Walkthrough" (52).

Walkthroughs are well suited to detect those usability problems caused by a discrepancy of system behavior and a user's habits or expectations (54, p. 107). Furthermore, they are an aid to ascertain whether the user interface is perceived to be adequate. Examples for such Walkthroughs are checking the wordings in the user interface, the distinction of buttons, commands, or menus, or the analysis of small task sequences.

As a general method, Walkthroughs are limited because of their cost. A whole user interface cannot be evaluated by Walkthroughs with a reasonable cost–benefit relation and, therefore, only selected features are usually taken into consideration. A further limitation is the fact that explorative behavior can only be simulated in a limited way; therefore, unexpected errors or misfits cannot be detected by usability Walkthroughs (52). Another problem is the fact that the success of a Walkthrough, if applied as a group technique, depends on the combination and the psychological fit of the group members (13, p. 698ff).

A prominent example is the Cognitive Walkthrough (CW). It is a method for evaluating user interfaces by analyzing the mental processes required of a user (53, p. 717ff). Its scope is the ease of learning—in particular, of learning by exploration—and it can be carried out by individual experts or by a group of peers. Details for a peer group evaluation can be found in Ref. 54 (p. 106).

The CW is guided by four questions, which the evaluator should answer at every task step:

- Will the user try to achieve the right effect?
- Will the user notice whether the correct action is available?
- Will the user associate the correct action with the effect to be achieved?
- If the correct action is performed, will the user see that progress is being made toward a solution of the task?

Input to a CW session consists of a detailed design description of the interface such as a paper mock-up or a working prototype. Additional input may be a task scenario, the precise description of prospective users, the context of system use, and a correct sequence of actions that a user should successfully perform to complete the designated task. Additionally, there must be a mapping of the task steps to corresponding "interface states." The evaluator simulates the task steps according to the limited possibilities of the intended users and judges whether the system offers suitable tools for each step of the task sequence. In particular, it is noted whether all necessary information is presented in a complete and appropriate manner; the evaluator will record other usability problems as well.

For each action within the task sequence, a "success story" is constructed, which contains the reason(s) why a user will or will not perform the action. If a difficulty is identified, a reason is assigned, for example, that a required menu items does not seem related to the user's goal. Problems and their causes are recorded. Finally, the analyst reports alternatives to the proposed design. In this way, the method utilizes factors which influence mental processes such as a user's background knowledge.

The advantage of the CW is that it can be applied in early stages of the development and that not only usability weaknesses of the system are reported but other problems as well.

One of the restrictions of the CW is the fact that the simulated sequence of actions has to be correct. This requirement puts a high demand on the qualification of the analyst, because (s)he has be familiar with the tasks and the environment in which the tasks will be performed. However, whether a user will perform according to the "correct" way cannot be checked beforehand. Therefore, the analyst should have a profound knowledge of human factors and should be aware of the intended user profile; furthermore, the analyst should be familiar with at least the basics of system development.

It has also been criticized that the focus of analysis of the CW sacrifices other important usability information such as overall consistency (50, p. 707).

Inspection by Experts and Heuristic Reviews

Usability inspection by experts can be subdivided into free, structured, or model-based variants. These are used for the generation of problem lists and they form the basis for system optimization (14). The usability inspection is carried out by a human-factor specialist, who is not directly involved in the development of the system. If there are several inspections of the same subject, they will be done independently of each other. The object of the evaluation can be the whole user interface or some of its components (12, p. 100). The technique can be used at an early stage of the life cycle in which paper prototypes will be used.

In case of a free expert inspection, the evaluator checks the software system using only a few general guidelines. Structured expert inspection, like standard inspection or consistency inspection, is based on detailed criteria or standards and uses checklists as a tool. Model-based inspection commences with a model of the user interface and includes a defined evaluation procedure (12, p. 101).

Heuristic Evaluation (HE) is a special adaptation of a free expert evaluation (19). Unlike the expensive and detailed expert evaluation by standard or consistency inspections, the HE uses the following usability heuristics:

- Provide a simple and natural dialogue
- Speak the user's language
- Minimize user memory load
- Be consistent
- Provide feedback
- Provide clearly marked exits
- Provide shortcuts
- Provide informative error messages
- Prevent errors

The heuristics are general principles which guide the evaluator through the inspection process. A number of evaluators inspect the user interface in individual sessions. Nielsen (19, p. 26) recommended three to five evaluators, because in his studies using HE, a larger number of evaluators will not result in additional relevant information. The degree of standardisation is not very high, and

> In principle, the evaluators decide on their own how they want to proceed with evaluating the interface. (19, p. 29)

Heuristic evaluation is normally carried out by a double inspection of the user interface. In the first round, the evaluator obtains a feeling for the system and its potential. The second inspection allows the evaluator to concentrate on those elements of the interface which are relevant for evaluation purposes. The evaluator steps through the interface design and checks the dialogue elements on the basis of the heuristics. Results of the HE are either fixed in a protocol by the evaluator or the evaluator reports the findings to an observer while checking the system.

An HE session should not last longer than 2 h. If the evaluation of a larger or complicated system requires more time, it is necessary to split the HE into several sessions, which will fit the time restriction.

Inspection methods share a problem with the cognitive Walkthrough: The evaluators must be user *and* task experts. A further disadvantage of the method is that

> ... it sometimes identifies usability problems without providing direct suggestions for how to solve them. The method is biased by the current mindset of the evaluators and normally does not generate breakthroughs in the evaluated design. (55, p. 255)

Although HE is part of the so-called "discount usability engineering methods" (27,56), there are more pessimistic results as well: The main argument for the "discount"—that there is a need for only a few experts to achieve acceptable results—has been questioned by a comparative study of Gediga and Hamborg (57). The authors show that the number of required experts depends on several variables, including the task, the layout of the evaluation, the quality of the evaluator, and the definition of a "usability problem."

Group Discussion

The object of the evaluation using group discussion is the complete user interface of the system, and different criteria can be used for the evaluation. Perhaps the most interesting aspect of group discussion is the possibility of using it as a creativity technique to generate evaluation criteria as a first step of the evaluation. Group discussion is quite flexible in its orientation: It may be user, task, or organisation oriented (12, p. 101). The application of the technique tends to be more efficient in the early stages of development.

Group discussion among user representatives and/or system designers is not a stand-alone technique, and it must be supported by other means. In the "Group Design Reviews" (50), several users discuss the user interface. The discussion has to be moderated by a human-factor expert; other experts such as designers, training experts, marketing experts, and so forth should complete the group if it seems necessary. A combination with a Walkthrough is straightforward (52) and more effective than a Walkthrough on its own (22, p. 706).

Other Techniques

Although we have listed quite a number of techniques, there are more variants and combinations which have been used in the past two decades.

A very interesting different point of view is taken by the *interpretative evaluation techniques* (21), which have moved away from the evaluator-controlled forms of evaluation to more informal techniques derived from anthropology and sociology. The techniques *contextual inquiry* (58), *cooperative evaluation* (28), and *participative evaluation* (59) advocate a more holistic treatment of evaluation. Up to now, no comparative study includes these techniques, but we are confident that at least the idea of the interpretative evaluation techniques will find its way into the HCI laboratories.

Modeling approaches aim at a formal description or prediction of the human–computer interaction. Their historic root is a model of an abstract human processor which sets the frame for a task description, given a more or less abstract system in a concrete environment (60). The concept has resulted in a number of developments such as the GOMS and NGOMSL approach (61), the task knowledge structure (TKS) and the knowledge analysis of tasks (KAT) (62), the task action grammars (TAG) (63), the external tasks–internal task mapping (ETIT) (64), and the yoked state space (YSS) (65). All these models share some characteristics. They offer convincing results (e.g., the comparison of aspects of the PC-DOS and the Macintosh interface using NGOMSL by Kieras (66), and they are used for comparatively small-scaled applications. Even though their advocates have asserted for the past decade that the models will be more applicable, if computer speed and memory are sufficient to fit the requirements of the models, there are some reservations concerning the validity of such methods for larger applications. It was noted that the human processor model does not take into consideration the huge individual differences among human subjects, as well as results from the large body of results in reaction-time research (67). Finally, it was shown that known results on learning or chunking processes is only considered if they fit smoothly into the proposed model. Because the human processor is therefore, at best, a rough approximation of human behavior, one can conclude that the results may well be acceptable for small-scaled examples but will run into problems if the model is applied to more demanding systems.

Comparison of Software Evaluation Techniques

There is a plethora of studies which deal with the comparison of evaluation techniques in terms of effectivity, efficiency, or utility (57,68–76). It is also investigated whether the information gathered by different methods are the same or not. Frequently, some of the "cheaper" predictive methods such as Heuristic Evaluation or Walkthroughs are benchmarked with a usability test method.

The results reported in the literature lead to the conclusion that an empirical comparison of software evaluation techniques is a minefield. First, researchers are faced with the usual problems encountered in empirical comparisons, such as finding adequate and representative testing subjects, objects, and situations, and a suitable methodology for analyzing the results. Second, as Gray and Salzman (77) pointed out, up to now, no study fulfills the rigorous standards of experimental design. In benchmark studies, confounding variables may intervene (e.g., different testing situations, different time of contact, different number of subjects performing the methods, etc.); therefore, it may not be appropriate to interpret the results in terms of difference of methods alone. Carroll (78, p. 309) commented,

> In their focus on conventional experiments, Gray and Salzman underestimate the importance and the distinctiveness of rare evaluation events.

The main argument in favor of comparison is that if one perceives the confounding variables as specific properties of the methods, comparison is a valuable evaluation of techniques, which may help practitioners to choose the "best" method for evaluating software. However, this pragmatic view puts heavy restrictions on the empirical studies, because a valid benchmarking is only feasible if the methods are applied exactly as they will be used in practice. Gray and Salzman (77) have shown that some studies do not fulfill these restrictions.

The situation is complicated because the definition of some methods is not very precise. If, for example, "the" technique of Usability Testing is compared with other methods, it is often not clear what is really meant. One can argue that there is no Usability Testing method as such, because the technique has shown high variability and evolution over the past two decades. The same holds—to some extent—for other techniques as well. Two classical studies shall demonstrate the problem:

- Jeffries et al. (72) compared Heuristic Evaluation with Software Guidelines, Cognitive Walkthrough, and Usability Testing. They showed that Heuristic Evaluation is more effective and efficient than Usability Testing (Rank 2) and the other two techniques in terms of detection of severe problems and of costs.
- Karat et al. (74) compare a variant of Heuristic Evaluation, Walkthroughs, and Usability Testing. They show, to the contrary, that most of the problems are detected by Usability Testing in a shorter time than by the other methods.

Taken together, the results of both studies (and of other cited studies as well) are inconclusive. Reviewing empirical comparison studies, Karat (79, p. 233) summarized as follows:

> Usability evaluation methods act as different types of filters of user interaction with a computer system.

This statement describes the state of knowledge about evaluation technique benchmarking well. Nevertheless, some lessons can be learned:

- Heuristic Evaluation offers at least satisfactory results. A combination of Heuristic Evaluation with a thinking-aloud technique seems to be a very effective strategy (72).
- Usability Testing procedures—and other descriptive techniques as well—often result in more information than predictive techniques. The findings show that predictive techniques, like Heuristic Evaluation, concentrate on severe problems only, whereas problems discovered by a descriptive technique address more specific—and sometimes "cosmetic"—aspects of the software.
- Usability Testing often needs more effort and equipment than comparable predictive techniques.
- Predictive evaluation techniques can be applied earlier in the life cycle than Usability Testing procedures.
- The goal of evaluation needs to be taken into account:

  If the evaluation goal is summative ("which one is better" or "how good"), the behavioral evaluation procedures applied in Usability Testing are the methods of choice.

  Neither Usability Testing nor pure expert-based techniques support participatory design (80). To achieve this, collaborative Walkthroughs or other group discussion techniques which include user representatives are necessary, because in these techniques, the user has the chance to be an active part of system development.

The decision of which evaluation technique(s) should be used has to be based on the concrete demands of the software development schedule, human-factor considerations, and cost–benefits issues (13, p. 699). The results of the above-mentioned comparison studies can only constitute a limited basis for such a decision. A systematic investigation of the "Return of Investment" (81,82) of usability activities in the software life cycle is still missing:

> The relative cost-effectiveness of usability testing and inspection methods, based on return of investment in implemented changes, is not clearly established at this time. (79).

EVALUATION MODELS

In contrast to software evaluation *techniques*, which were presented in the preceeding section, software evaluation *models* determine the frame of the evaluation, which consists of the following:

- Choosing techniques appropriate for the life cycle
- Setting the focus with respect to the objects under study and the measurement criteria

Evaluation models may provide a standardized treatment of establishing (potentially) successful procedures in the practice of evaluation and are a necessary tool for a comparing different types of software evaluation. Any descriptive evaluation procedure must be combined with some kind of predictive technique to result in an applicable evaluation model; furthermore, some preparatory steps are necessary. For example, the evaluation model, which consists of the IsoMetric^L questionnaire as a basic technique, standardizes the preparatory steps "choosing the tasks" and "choosing the user group(s)"; it also standardizes the preparation of the report by an expert and the structure of a "usability review", which consists of a standardized result presentation and a Walkthrough technique (43).

There are three classes of evaluation model:

Method-driven models: These models offer a frame for software evaluation based on a collection of techniques. The models are only applicable if the evaluation procedures fits the problems encountered by the user and the system developers perfectly.

Criteria-driven models: More or less abstract criteria are defined and refined; the evaluation in these models aims at a measurement of the criteria.

Usability Engineering: These are evaluation models which are driven by the needs of a specific life-cycle model.

Method-Driven Evaluation Models

The center of method-driven evaluation models consists of the arrangement of evaluation techniques, amended by the regulation of preparatory and subsequent tasks. A method-driven evaluation model can be perceived as a complex evaluation technique as well. An example is EVADIS II (83,84), which is well tested for office automatization software. The EVADIS II model combines interviews, simplified task analysis, and expert judgment in the following steps:

1. Installation and exploration of the software
2. Analysis and relevance weightings of the tasks; construction of test tasks
3. Analysis of the user characteristics; selection of relevant ergonomic test items
4. Evaluation of the software, based on the results of the first three steps
5. Interpretation of the results and composing a test report

The first three preparatory steps can be handled in parallel; they result in testing tasks and a list of ranked ergonomic evaluation criteria, mainly based on the principles of ISO 9241 (Part 10). The ranks of the criteria are deduced from the user profile and they determine the test items which are chosen from an item database. In Step 4, the testing tasks are evaluated by an expert who steps through the tasks and answers the questions formulated in the ergonomic items. The recorded answers form the basis for the test report. Every step of EVADIS II is supported by a large amount of supporting material such as databases and guidelines, which allows a domain expert with only a small amount of knowledge of software evaluation to form a well-founded opinion on the topic.

Criteria-Driven Evaluation Models

Criteria-driven evaluation models start with assumptions about the structure of the design process in which criteria are defined and give advice on how to derive measurables form the criteria. Because these models focus on criteria and measurables, there is no close connection to a design model. Standards such as ISO 9241 or ISO/IEC 9126 can constitute a basis for a criteria-driven evaluation model. As an example, we discuss the "Evaluation Process Model" ISO/IEC 9126 (1991) (3,85), which is the basis for many software quality assurance procedures. The standard ISO/IEC 9126 aims at a product evaluation from a software quality point of view. It defines a specific process model and some general quality characteristics; for example, the following:

- Functionality
- Reliability
- Usability
- Efficiency
- Maintainability
- Portability

Although "Usability" appears as a criterion, ISO/IEC 9126 does not aim at the ergonomic quality of the software:

> Usability defined in this International Standard as a specific set of attributes of software product differs from the definition from an ergonomic point of view, where other characteristics such as efficiency and effectiveness are also seen as constituents of usability. (3, p. 3)

After the relevant quality characteristics and their weightings have been selected, the evaluation process is performed in three steps.

1. Fixing the requirements: The requirements are derived from the application context of the system. The quality characteristics are formulated concretely in terms of observables, which operationalize the criteria and meet the requirements.
2. Preparation of the evaluation: This step comprises the operationalization of the criteria into metrics and composite measurables.
3. The evaluation step: The evaluation of the product or a part of the product is performed on the basis of the derived requirements and chosen metrics.

Because ISO/IEC 9126 offers a general framework for software evaluation within the context of software quality assurance, we present the tasks accompanying the three steps of evaluation in more detail in Figure 1.

Usability Engineering

Usability Engineering is concerned with the systematic integration of methods and techniques of building usable software in the system development process. It can be characterized as a process which covers the definition and the measure of product usability in general (7, p. 654). Usability Engineering models coordinate the "Usability Engineering activities" and do not replace traditional models of the software engineering process. The evaluation of software is a prominent part of any Usability Engineering model (7,14,86,87).

The models are committed to the approach of the User-Centered Design (88), which is based on the assumption of an iterative system design with user participation (80,86). In this process, the user is regarded not as a producer of usability data, but should be directly and actively involved in the design process:

> I strongly recommend that all team members carry out life-cycle tasks jointly, so that they develop a shared understanding of the requirements and designed issues. In addition, it can be extremely effective to have users participate in many Usability Engineering tasks, not just as objects of study or sources of information, but as active participants. (87, p. 22)

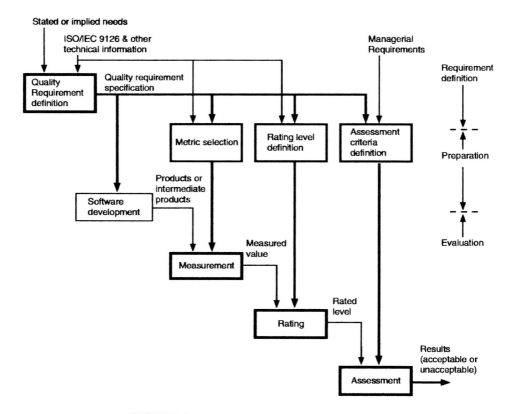

FIGURE 1   The ISO/IEC 9126 evaluation model.

Usability Engineering requires a software engineering model, which allows revisions and feedback loops. These models include the prototyping approaches, iterative system design, and user involvement (5,7,14,87).

Models of Usability Engineering are usually subdivided in three phases (5,14,87,89):

Phase 1: Analysis and specification. The first step—the "Gearing-up Phase"—starts with preparatory activities, such as choosing general principles for the design (e.g., relevant standards, development models, and tools). The next step—the "Initial Design Phase" or "Requirements Analysis"—is concerned with the characterization of users and the setup of user profiles; additionally, task and workflow have to be analyzed. The obtained information is used to plan the activities of the "Work Reengineering" and for the design of the user interface. As a result of this process, usability specifications are developed, which consist of goals for user-oriented design and behavior-oriented measurables of these goals. The outcome of this phase is summarized in a product style guide (87).

Phase 2: Iterative development. The results of the preceding phase are used to design the organizational and workflow part of the system. Conceptual models are developed which can be used to produce paper-and-pencil or prototype mock-ups. Using an iterative design, the prototypes are evaluated and changed continuously. This helps to identify and remove major usability bugs. If the conceptual model shows satisfactory results, the screen design is developed, using screen design standards, and evaluation of the screen design takes place with the aid of a prototype. As in Phase 1, the results are summarized in a product style guide.

Phase 3: System installation. The final phase is concerned with "system installation" and "user training." Furthermore, the acceptance of the system has to be assured, and system support and maintenance must be organized. Software evaluation procedures in the application phase have to be planned in order to obtain feedback about the usability of system. This information can be used for the design of new releases.

The standard ISO/DIS 13407 (90) is closely connected to the Usability Engineering approach. It describes three different usability activities in system design:

1. Analysis and specification of the context of usage and the needs of the users and organizational needs
2. The system design
3. The evaluation of the system design using user-oriented criteria

Similar to the Usability Engineering approach, ISO/DIS 13407 uses the principles

- Prototyping, iterative design, direct user participation, iterative evaluation, quality enhancement of the system

in all phases of the design process.

In case that the evaluation cannot be performed by users, ISO/DIS 13407 recommends evaluation by experts, but it is advocated that a user-based evaluation is done at a later step of system development. The evaluation–(re)design cycle is repeated until the goals of the user-centered design are fulfilled. The product can be evaluated to ascertain whether it fulfills the user-oriented requirements and/or whether it is in accordance with other international standards such as ISO 9241 (91).

A Problem: The Integration of Software Evaluation Models and Software Design Models

It is pointed out in ISO/DIS 13407 that "user-oriented activities" have to be integrated into the system development process, and the standard gives some advice how this can be done. This is an urgent need, because, in classical approaches, the combination of system design with software evaluation models, in general, and the Usability Engineering models, in particular, seems to be more an art than a science. Although some case studies show that an effective combination of both model types can be achieved (92–94). Mayhew (87, p. 4) points out that " . . . Gould and Lewis did not specify exactly how these global usability strategies could be integrated into an overall software development life-cycle . . . " and recommends her own approach as an alternative. She admits, however, that

> . . . the exact overlapping of the two types of tasks is not completely clear. The most appro-

priate relationship between them is probably not absolute, but is most likely dependent on various project-specific factors and on the particular software development methodology with which the life-cycle is integrated . . . For example, traditional systems analysis and Contextual Task Analysis are highly related tasks, but they are not the same thing and require very different kinds of expertise. Exactly how to integrate them to avoid duplication of effort and yet produce the intended and necessary outputs of both is a topic for future work. (87, p. 17)

To date, there are only loose connections of activities of Usability Engineering and the object-oriented design methodology. These are concentrated in the requirements analysis and in the design/testing/development cycle. The generation of an object-oriented "Requirement model" can be supported by user profiles, which can be obtained by task and workflow analysis. "Work Reengineering Tasks" correspond to the construction of an "Analysis Model" in object-oriented design. The design and programming of the user interface in the object-oriented model (the "Design Model") can be supported by conceptual models (87, p. 30).

FUTURE TASKS

There are many evaluation techniques and few evaluation models which can be applied in practice. Although much has been achieved, there is a dire need to devote more effort to developing applicable models for practical use—in particular, if nonexperts evaluate software as in smaller companies. EVADIS is an instance of such a model, as it combines several evaluation techniques to a coherent evaluation model in the domain of office automation.

At present, the differences in effectiveness, efficiency, and the cost–benefit relation of software evaluation techniques and models are not satisfactory. Due to the huge number of techniques and their variants, the labor of comparing these techniques—and models using them—would be tremendous. An empirical stock-taking of frequently used models should be done to form a basis for future comparison studies. These should not only consider effectiveness, efficiency, and return of investment but other effects on the software as well, such as time efficiency, suitability for learning, or user satisfaction (49).

For a number of techniques, there is a need to investigate where they will fit into a software development cycle. The rule of thumb "early → predictive & late → descriptive" should be replaced by a more differentiated rule system. Because most findings demonstrate that the techniques produce a large amount of overlapping results, the effect of combining evaluation techniques needs to be evaluated as well. Inspecting the evaluation models, we see that there should be a higher integration of models as well. In particular, the goals and techniques of Requirements Analysis overlap with the goals and techniques of software evaluation in such a way that unified approach would save time and money.

Most software evaluation techniques we have presented aim at the operationalization of "Usability" of the software. The investigation of how "Usability" can be described in theoretical terms is still ongoing. "Usability" is a combination of at least two different kinds of construct: the "ease of use" and the "enjoyment to use". Whereas older studies and methods had a closer look at the "ease of use" component, the "enjoyment to use" component has been the focus of newer studies (at least since SUN and SAP proclaimed that even office software should be enjoyable). There is some evidence that both components vary independently, which implies that there is also a need for an independent measure of both aspects.

Even though much effort and research are still necessary to develop efficient software evaluation procedures, we hope that the article has demonstrated that there is not only a large body of techniques but also that these techniques are applicable and valuable in the development of software systems.

REFERENCES

1. E. A. Suchman, *Evaluation Research*: *Principles and Practices in Public Service and Social Action Programs*, Russel, New York, 1967.
2. D. Hix and H. R. Hartson, *Developing User Interfaces*: *Ensuring Usability Through Product and Process*, John Wiley & Sons, New York, 1993.
3. ISO/IEC, *ISO/IEC 9126. Information technology—Software product evaluation—Quality characteristics and guidance for their use*, ISO, Geneva, 1991.
4. A. Whitefield, F. Wilson, and J. Dowell, "A Framework for Human Factors Evaluation," *Beh. Inform. Technol.*, *10*, 65–79 (1991).
5. J. D. Gould, "How to Design Usable Systems," in *Handbook of Human Computer Interaction*, M. Helander (ed.), Elsevier, Amsterdam, 1988, pp. 757–789.
6. J. Nielsen, "The Usability Life Cycle," *IEEE Computer*, *25*, 12–22 (1992).
7. D. Wixon and C. Wilson, "The Usability Engineering Framework for Product Design and Evaluation," in *Handbook of Human–Computer Interaction*, 2nd ed., M. Helander, T. Landauer, and P. Prabhu (eds.), Elsevier, Amsterdam, 1997, pp. 653–688.
8. T. L. Roberts and T. P. Moran, " The Evaluation of Text Editors: Methodology and Empirical Results," *Commun. ACM*, *26*, 265–283 (1983).
9. J. M. Carroll and M. B. Rosson, Usability Specifications as a Tool in Iterative Development," in *Advances in Human–Computer Interaction*, H. R. Hartson (ed.), Ablex, Norwood, NJ, 1985, pp. 1–28.
10. M. Scriven, "The Methodology of Evaluation," in *Perspectives of Curriculum Evaluation*, R. Tyler, Gagne, and M. Scriven (eds.), Rand McNally, Chicago, 1967, pp. 39–83.
11. W. Dzida, "Qualitätssicherung durch software-ergonomische Normen," in *Einführung in die Software-Ergonomie*, E. Eberleh, H. Oberquelle, and R. Oppermann (eds.), de Gruyter, Berlin, 1994, pp. 373–406.
12. W. Hampe-Neteler, *Software-ergonomische Bewertung zwischen Arbeitsgestaltung und Software-Entwicklung*, Lang, Frankfurt, 1994.
13. J. Karat, "User-Centered Software Evaluation Methodologies," in *Handbook of Human–Computer Interaction*, 2nd ed., M. Helander, T. K. Landauer, and P. Prabhu (eds.), Elsevier, Amsterdam, 1997, pp. 689–704.
14. J. Nielsen, *Usability Engineering*, AP Professional, Boston, 1993.
15. ISO, *EN ISO 9241-11. Ergonomic requirements for office work with visual display terminals (VDT's)*. Part 11, ISO, Geneva, 1997.
16. ISO, *EN ISO 9241-10. Ergonomic requirements for office work with visual display terminals (VDT's)*. Part 10, ISO, Geneva, 1996.
17. G. Gigerenzer, *Messung und Modellbildung in der Psychologie*, Birkhäuser, Basel, 1981.
18. D. A. Tyldesley, "Employing Usability Engineering in the Development of Office Products," *Computer J.*, *31*, 431–436 (1988).
19. J. Nielsen, "Heuristic Evaluation," in *Usability Inspection Methods*, J. Nielsen and R. Mack (eds.), John Wiley & Sons, New York, 1994, pp. 25–62.

20. J. Nielsen and R. L. Mack, *Usability Inspection Methods*, John Wiley & Sons, New York, 1994.

21. G. Walsham, *Interpreting Information Systems in Organisations*, John Wiley & Sons, Chichester, 1993.

22. J. Preece, *Human–Computer Interaction*, Addison-Wesley, Harlow, U.K., 1999.

23. B. L. Harrison, "Video Annotation and Multimedia Interfaces: From Theory to Practice," in *Proceedings of the Human Factor Society 35th Annual Meeting*, 1991, pp. 319–322.

24. J. M. Carroll and R. Mack, "Learning to Use a Word Processor: By Doing, by Thinking and by Knowing," in *Human Factors in Computing Systems*, J. Thomas and M. Schneider (eds.), Ablex, Norwood, NJ, 1984, pp. 13–52.

25. A. H. Jørgensen, "Using the Thinking-Aloud Method in System Development," in *Designing and Using Human–Computer Interfaces and Knowledge Based Systems*, G. Salvendy and M. J. Smith (eds.), Elsevier, Amsterdam, 1989, pp. 743–750.

26. C. Lewis, "Using the "Thinking Aloud" Method in Cognitive Interface Design," IBM Research Report RC 9265 (40713), IBM Thomas J. Watson Research Center (1982).

27. J. Nielsen, "Usability Engineering at a Discount," in *Designing and Using Human–Computer Interfaces and Knowledge Based Systems*, G. Salvendy and M. Smith (eds.), Elsevier, Amsterdam, 1989, pp. 394–401.

28. A. Monk, P. Wright, J. Haber, and L. Davenport, *Improving Your Human–Computer Interface*: *A Practical Approach*, Prentice-Hall, Englewood Cliffs, NJ, 1993.

29. V. A. Bowers and H. L. Snyder, "Concurrent vs Retrospective Verbal Protocol for Comparing Window Usability," in *Proceedings of the Human Factors Society 34th Annual Meeting of the Human Factors Society*, 1990, pp. 1270–1274.

30. K. R. Ohnemus and D. W. Biers, "Retrospective vs Concurrent Thinking out Loud in Usability Testing," in *Proceedings of the Human Factors and Ergonomics Society 37th Annual Meeting*, 1993, pp. 1127–1131.

31. S. Greif, "Organizational Issues and Task Analysis," in *Human Factors for Informatics Usability*, B. Shackel and S. Richardson (eds.), Cambridge University Press, Cambridge, 1991, pp. 247–266.

32. K.-C. Hamborg and S. Greif, "Heterarchische Aufgabenanalyse," in *Handbuch psychologischer Arbeitsanalyseverfahren*, H. Dunckel (ed.), VDF, Zürich, 1999, pp. 147–177.

33. S. Greif, "The Role of German Work Psychology in the Design of Artifacts," in *Designing Interaction. Psychology at the Human–Computer Interface*, J. M. Carroll (ed.), Cambridge University Press, Cambridge, 1991, pp. 203–226.

34. J. Kirakowski and M. Corbett, *Effective Methodology for the Study of HCI*, North-Holland, Amsterdam, 1990.

35. J. Nielsen, R. L. Mack, K. H. Bergendorff, and N. L. Grischkowsky, "Integrated Software Usage in the Professional Work Environment: Evidence from Questionnaires and Interviews," in *Human Factors in Computing Systems, CHI'86 Conference Proceedings*, M. Mantei and P. Obertson (eds.), ACM, New York, 1986, pp. 162–167.

36. B. Shneiderman, *Designing the User Interface. Strategies for Effective Human–Computer Interaction*, 2nd ed., Addison-Wesley, Reading, MA, 1992.

37. J. Kirakowski and M. Corbett, "SUMI: The Software Usability Measurement Inventory," *Br. J. Educ. Technol.*, *24*, 210–212 (1993).

38. G. Gediga, K.-C. Hamborg, and I. Düntsch, "The IsoMetrics Usability Inventory: An Operationalisation of ISO 9241-10," *Beh. Inform. Technol.*, *18*, 151–164 (1999).

39. J. P. Chin, V. A. Diehl, and K. L. Norman, "Development of an Instrument Measuring User Satisfaction of the Human–Computer Interface," in *Proceedings of SIGCHI '88*, ACM/SIGCHI, New York, 1988, pp. 213–218.

40. B. Shneiderman, *Designing the User Interface. Strategies for Effective Human–Computer Interaction*, 3rd ed., Addison-Wesley, Reading, MA, 1998.

41. J. Kierakowski, "The Use of Questionnaire Methods for Usability Assessment," 2000; http://www.ucc.ie/hfg/questionnaires/sumi/sumipapp.html

42. H. Willumeit, G. Gediga, and K.-C. Hamborg, "Isometrics^L: Ein Verfahren zur formativen Evaluation von Software nach ISO 9241/10," *Ergon. Inform., 27,* 5–12 (1996).

43. G. Gediga, K.-C. Hamborg, and H. Willumeit, *The IsoMetrics Manual (Version 1.15)*, Universität Onabrück, Fachbereich Psychologie, Osnabrück, 1997; http://www.eval-institut.de/isometrics

44. M. Burmester, C. Görner, P. H. Vossen, T. M. Zolleis, and V. Zouboulides, "Qualitatives software screening," in *Das SANUS-Hanbuch. Bildschirmarbeit EU-konform,* M. Burmester, C. Görner, W. Hacker, M. Kärcher, P. Kurtz, U. Lieser, W. Risch, R. Wieland-Eckelmann, and H. Wilde (eds.), Dortmund. Schriftenreihe der Bundesanstalt für Arbeitsschutz und Arbeitsmedizin, FB 760, 1997, Teil II, 2.

45. J. Prümper, "Software-Evaluation Based upon ISO 9241 Part 10," in *Human–Computer Interaction. Vienna Conference, VCHCHI '93,* T. Grechening and M. Tescheligi (eds.), Springer-Verlag, Berlin, 1993.

46. P. A. Holleran, "A Methodological Note on Pitfalls in Usability Testing," *Beh. Inform. Technol., 10,* 345–357 (1991).

47. J. Rubin, *Handbook of Usability Testing,* John Wiley & Sons, New York, 1994.

48. C. Robson, "Designing and Interpreting Psychological Experiments," in *Human–Computer Interaction,* J. Preece and L. Keller (eds.), Prentice-Hall, Hemel Hempstead, U.K., 1990, pp. 357–367.

49. C.-M. Karat, "Cost–Benefit and Business Case Analysis of Usability Engineering," in *Bridges Between Two Worlds, INTERCHI '93. Tutorial Notes 23,* S. Ashlund, K. Mullet, A. Henderson, E. Hollnagel, and T. White (eds.), Addison-Wesley, Reading, MA, 1993.

50. R. A. Virzi, "Usability Inspection Methods," in *Handbook of Human–Computer Interaction,* 2nd ed., M. Helander, T. Landauer, and P. Prabhu (eds.), Elsevier, Amsterdam, 1997, pp. 705–715.

51. R. Bias, "Walkthroughs: Efficient collaborative testing," *IEEE Software, 8,* 94–95 (1991).

52. R. Bias, "The Pluralistic Walkthrough: Coordinated Empathies," in *Usability Inspection Methods,* J. Nielsen and R. Mack (eds.), John Wiley & Sons, New York, 1994, pp. 63–76.

53. C. Lewis and C. Wharton, "Cognitive Walkthroughs," in *Handbook of Human–Computer Interaction,* 2nd ed., M. Helander, T. Landauer, and P. Prabhu (eds.), Elsevier, Amsterdam, 1997, pp. 717–732.

54. C. Wharton, J. Rieman, C. Lewis, and P. Polson, "The Cognitive Walkthrough Method: A Practitionert's Guide," in *Usability Inspection Methods,* J. Nielsen and R. Mack (eds.), John Wiley & Sons, New York, 1994, pp. 105–140.

55. J. Nielsen and R. Molich, "Heuristic Evaluation of User Interfaces," in *Chi'90 Conference Proceedings, Empowering People,* J. Chew and J. Whiteside (eds.), ACM, New York, 1990, pp. 249–256.

56. K. Potosnak, "Big Paybacks from 'Discount' Usability Engineering," *IEEE Software,* 107–109 (1990).

57. G. Gediga and K.-C. Hamborg, "Heuristische Evaluation und IsoMetrics: Ein Vergleich," in *Software-Ergonomie '97,* R. Liskowsky, B. Velichkovsky, and W. Wünschmann (eds.), Teuber, Stuttgart, 1997, pp. 145–155.

58. J. Whiteside, J. Bennett, and K. Hotzblatt, "Usability Engineering: Our Experience and Evolution," in *Handbook of Human–Computer Interaction,* M. Helander (ed.), Elsevier, Amsterdam, 1988, pp. 791–817.

59. J. Greenbaum and M. Kyng, *Design at Work: Cooperative Design of Computer Systems,* Lawrence Erlbaum, Hillsdale, NJ, 1991.

60. S. Card, T. P. Moran, and A. Newell, *The Psychology of Human–Computer Interaction,* Lawrence Erlbaum, Hillsdale, NJ, 1983.

61. D. Kieras, "A Guide to GOMS Model Usability Evaluation Using NGOMSL," in *Handbook*

of Human–Computer Interaction, 2nd ed., M. Helander, T. Landauer, and P. Prabhu (eds.), Elsevier, Amsterdam, 1997, pp. 733–766.

62.   P. Johnson, *Human–Computer Interaction*: *Psychology, Task Analysis and Software-Engineering*, McGraw-Hill, Maidenhead, U.K., 1992.

63.   S. J. Payne and T. R. G. Green, "Task-Action Grammar: The Model and Its Development," in *Task Analysis for Human–Computer Interaction*, D. Diaper (ed.), Ellis Horwood, Chichester, 1989.

64.   T. P. Moran, "Getting into System: External Task–Internal Task Mapping Analysis," in *Human Factors in Computing CHI'83 Conference Proceedings*, A. Janda (ed.), ACM, New York, 1983.

65.   S. J. Payne, "Complex Problem Spaces: Modelling the Knowledge Needed to Use Interactive Devices," in *Proceedings of the IFIP Conference on Human–Computer Interaction*, H.-J. Bullinger and B. Shackel (eds.), North-Holland, Amsterdam, 1987.

66.   D. Kieras, "Bridges Between Worlds," in *INTER CHI'93. Tutorial Notes 5*, S. Ashlund, K. Mullet, A. Henderson, E. Hollnagel, and T. White (eds.), Addison-Wesley, Reading, MA, 1993.

67.   S. Greif and G. Gediga, "A Critique and Empirical Investigation of the 'One-Best-Way-Models,' in Human–Computer Interaction," in *Psychological Issues of Human Computer Interaction in the Work Place*, M. Frese, E. Ulich, and W. Dzida (eds.), Elsevier, Amsterdam, 1987, pp. 357–377.

68.   H. Desurvire, D. Lawrence, and M. E. Atwood, "Empiricism Versus Judgement: Comparing User Interface Evaluation Methods," *ACM SIGCHI Bull.*, *23*, 58–59 (1991).

69.   H. W. Desurvire, J. M. Kondziela, and M. Atwood, "What Is Gained and Lost When Using Evaluation Methods Other Than Empirical Testing," in *Proceedings of HCI '92, People and Computers VII*, Cambridge University Press, Cambridge, 1992, pp. 89–102.

70.   K.-C. Hamborg, G. Gediga, M. Döhl, P. Janssen, and F. Ollermann, "Softwareevaluation in Gruppen oder Einzelevaluation: Sehen zwei Augen mehr als vier?" in *Software-Ergonomie '99: Design von Informationswelten*, U. Arend and K. Pitschke (eds.), Teubner, Stuttgart, 1999, pp. 97–109.

71.   R. D. Henderson, M. C. Smith, J. Podd, and H. Varela-Alvarez, "A Comparison of the Four Prominent User-Based Methods for Evaluating the Usability of Computer Software," *Ergonomics*, *38*, 2030–2044 (1995).

72.   R. Jeffries, J. R. Miller, C. Wharton, and K. M. Uyeda, "User Interface Evaluation in the Real World: A Comparison of Four Techniques," in *Proceedings AMC CHI '91 Conference on Human Factors in Computing Systems*, ACM, New York, 1991, pp. 119–124.

73.   R. J. Jeffries and H. W. Desurvire, "Usability Testing vs Heuristic Evaluation: Was There a Contest?" *ACM SIGCHI Bull.*, *4*, 39–41 (1992).

74.   C. Karat, R. L. Campbell, and T. Fiegel, "Comparison of Empirical Testing and Walkthrough Methods in User Interface Evaluation," in *Proceedings ACM CHI '92 Conference*, P. Bauersfield, J. Bennet, and G. Lynch (eds.), ACM, New York, 1992, pp. 397–404.

75.   E. D. Smilowitz, M. J. Darnell, and A. E. Bensson, "Are We Overlooking Some Usability Testing Methods? A Comparison of Lab, Beta, and Forum Tests," *Beh. Inform. Technol.*, *13*, 183–190 (1994).

76.   R. A. Virzi, J. F. Sorce, and L. B. Herbert, "A Comparison of Three Usability Evaluation Methods: Heuristic, Think Aloud, and Performance Testing," in *Designing for Diversity: Proceedings of the Human Factors and Ergonomics Society 37th Annual Meeting 1993*, Human Factors and Ergonomics Society, Santa Monica, CA, 1993, pp. 309–313.

77.   W. D. Gray and M. C. Salzman, "Damaged Merchandise? A Review of Experiments That Compare Usability Evaluation Methods," *Human–Computer Interact.*, *13*, 203–261 (1998).

78.   J. M. Carroll, "Review Validity, Causal Analysis, and Rare Evaluation Events," *Human–Computer Interact.*, 13, 308–310 (1998).

79.   C.-M. Karat, "A Comparison of User Interface Evaluation Methods," in *Usability Inspection*

Methods, J. Nielsen and R. L. Mack (eds.), John Wiley & Sons, New York, 1994, pp. 203–233.

80. M. J. Muller, J. H. Halkswanter, and T. Dayton, "Participatory Practices in the Software Lifecycle," in *Handbook of Human–Computer Interaction*, 2nd ed., M. Helander, T. Landauer, and P. Prabhu (eds.), Elsevier, Amsterdam, 1997, pp. 255–313.

81. C.-M. Karat, "Cost-Justifying Usability Engineering in the Software Life Cycle," in *Handbook of Human–Computer Interaction*, 2nd ed., M. Helander, T. K. Landauer, and P. Prabhu (eds.), Elsevier, Amsterdam, 1997, pp. 767–777.

82. M. M. Mantei and T. J. Teorey, "Cost/Benefit Analysis for Incorporating Human Factors in the Software Lifecycle," *Commun. ACM*, *31*, 428–439 (1988).

83. H. Reiterer, *User Interface Evaluation and Design. Research Results of the Projects Evaluation of Dialogue Systems (EVADIS) and User Interface Design Assistance (IDA)*, Oldenburg, München, 1994.

84. H. Reiterer and R. Oppermann, "Evaluation of User Interfaces. EVADIS II—A Comprehensive Evaluation Approach," *Beh. Inform. Technol.*, *12*, 137–148 (1993).

85. R. C. Williges, B. H. Williges, and J. Elkerton, "Software Interface Design," in *Handbook of Human Factors*, G. Salvendy (ed.), John Wiley & Sons, New York, 1987, pp. 1416–1449.

86. J. M. Carroll, "Human–Computer Interaction: Psychology as a Science of Design," *Int. J. Human–Computer Studies*, *46*, 501–522 (1997).

87. D. Mayhew, *The Usability Engineering Lifecycle. A Practitionert's Handbook for User Interface Design*, Morgan Kaufmann, San Francisco, 1999.

88. J. Karat, "Evolving the Scope of User-Centered Design," *Commun. ACM*, *40*, 33–38 (1997).

89. J. D. Gould, S. J. Boies, and J. Ukelson, "How to Design Usable Systems," in *Handbook of Human–Computer Interaction*, 2nd ed., M. Helander, T. Landauer, and P. Prabhu (eds.), Elsevier, Amsterdam, 1997, pp. 705–715.

90. ISO, *ISO 13407. Human centered design processes for interactive displays*, ISO, Geneva, 1997.

91. A. Çakir and W. Dzida, "International Ergonomic HCI Standards," in *Handbook of Human–Computer Interaction*, 2nd ed., M. Helander, T. Landauer, and P. Prabhu (eds.), Elsevier, Amsterdam, 1997, pp. 407–420.

92. J. D. Gould, S. J. Boies, S. Levy, J. T. Richards, and J. Schoonard, "The 1984 Olympic Message System: A Test of Behavioral Principles of System Design," *Commun. ACM*, *30*, 758–769 (1987).

93. J. D. Gould, S. J. Boies, and C. Lewis, "Making Usable, Useful, Productivity Enhancing Computer Applications," *Commun. ACM*, *34*, 74–85 (1991).

94. J. Nielsen, "Iterative User-Interface Design," *IEEE Computer*, *26*, 32–41 (1993).

GÜNTHER GEDIGA

KAI-CHRISTOPH HAMBORG

IVO DÜNTSCH

LOGIC PROGRAMMING AND DEDUCTIVE DATABASES WITH UNCERTAINTY: A SURVEY

INTRODUCTION

Most available information about the real world is *imperfect*. In fact, most decisions are made under conditions where the available information is incomplete, imprecise, not completely reliable, and possibly inconsistent. Examples include satellite image data analysis, programs for matching faces to a mugshot database (1), information integration (2,3), and multimedia databases (4), to name a few. To model the real world, we need the ability to represent and manipulate data featuring the various forms of imperfection mentioned here. Although most of the literature on (deductive) databases and logic programming assumes perfect information, significant advances have been made in recent years concerning the modeling and manipulation of uncertainty in this context. It is the goal of this article to survey this work and to point out important directions for future work.

There are several types of imperfection often considered in information systems. Parsons (5) provides a classification of imperfection in artificial intelligence (AI) and database systems and discusses sources of these imperfection. Examples of these types include *incompleteness*, *imprecision*, and *uncertainty* (6). Each of these represents some sort of deficiency in data and is defined and distinguished as follows.

Incompleteness arises from the absence of a value. It has been modeled in various ways, including the use of *null* values in relational (and deductive) databases (7), the use of disjunction in deductive databases (8) and the use of open-world assumption in place of the traditional closed-world assumption.

Imprecision arises when the exact value of an attribute is not known for sure but is known to be among the elements in a range or set of possible values. Using sets to represent possible values stems from various reasons and may represent various states. For instance, this set could be finite or infinite, or it could be discrete or continuous, as in an interval. To give an example, if we know that *John* has a car which is either red or blue but do not know which one, we may represent this state of imprecision by the set {*red, blue*} to represent the color of *John*'s car. As another example, suppose we know that *Mary* is a top manager in a company, but not her exact salary. Based on her rank, however, we may know the range of her salary, say [70000, 90000]. We may then use this interval to represent her salary, with the attendant imprecision. Imprecision may also be used to represent fuzzy or vague concepts in linguistics (e.g., the adjective young could be associated with an age say, between 25 and 29). As can be seen, imprecision arises from lack of granularity and may be disjunctive, existential, or universal (5).

Uncertainty arises when the truth of a piece of information is not established definitely. To be more precise, (un)certainty is the "degree" of truth of some information as estimated by an individual or a sensor. To represent this uncertainty, we associate with the information a value coming from an appropriate domain. The domain can range from lattices with special properties, to possibilities, to probabilities. Both subjective and objective notions of certainty have been considered in the literature.

Inconsistency is a well-known notion in classical logic. In a large knowledge base, particularly one which assimilates information from a variety of sources, it is quite possible that the available information is conflicting and hence inconsistent. For example, different sources may associate different colors with John's car. In classical logic, an inconsistent theory entails everything and, hence, is regarded as useless. Such a rigid approach may not be suitable for large knowledge bases. A better approach is to "localize" the effect of inconsistency while still making valid inferences from the knowledge base. Specific logics for dealing with inconsistency have been proposed (9). As pointed out in Ref. 10, inconsistency-tolerant logics are particularly useful when dealing with uncertain information.

So far, we have considered separate types of imperfection in information sources. However, in some applications, it is quite meaningful and useful to consider combinations of these types to model the world. For example, imprecision and uncertainty may sometimes be combined and used together. In this case, the actual fact, or the actual value of an attribute, is among a set of possible value–certainty pairs specified. It is also meaningful to consider imprecision and incompleteness in one setting. In such a case, possible values of an attribute may include, in an extreme case, the whole domain, indicating the state where the actual value is completely unknown.

Ignorance, yet another form of imperfection, is the state in which no information is available about the relevant values or about the relative certainties of facts. The terms *overspecified* and *underspecified* have also been used to refer, respectively, to inconsistent and ignorance states. Intuitively, these terms correspond, respectively, to where "too much" is said about a fact and where nothing is said about it.

As seen above, forms of imperfection in available information are diverse and literature on them is extensive. In this article, we confine ourselves to uncertainty and provide a survey of works on uncertainty in deductive databases and logic programming. These works, proposed over a period of about 15 years since the mid-1980s, are developed by extending the standard logic programming and deductive database systems to incorporate uncertainty. Interestingly, uncertain data management was identified as one of the important challenges for future database research in the 1991 NSF Workshop, by Silberschatz et al. (11): "Further research in uncertainty is essential, as we must learn not only to cope with data of *limited reliability*, but do so *efficiently*, with *massive amounts of data*." To be useful also in practice, a system developed to manage uncertain information is required to admit efficient implementation and perform efficient computations. This makes a survey of work in this important field particularly relevant.

The article is organized as follows. The next section gives an overview of deduction with uncertainty, collecting together the gist of the issues involved in any framework for deductive databases or logic programming with uncertainty. In section three, we present a classification of the various frameworks proposed for representing and reasoning with uncertainty in logic programming and deductive databases. In the fourth section, we give a detailed survey of important representative frameworks, and illustrate the formalisms with examples. As mentioned earlier, efficient computability is one of the key requirements for any framework supporting deduction and uncertainty. We consider two important questions surrounding this theme. The first of these, query optimization, is discussed in the subsection Query Containment and Equivalence. The second question has to do with a peculiar challenge posed by recursive queries. Although (recursive) queries in datalog can always be evaluated in polynomial time in the input database size, for some of the queries in the uncertain counterparts of datalog, bottom-up evaluation may not even terminate. This bizarre but important behavior is studied in the subsection Termination. Finally, in the sixth section, we enumerate several important problems for future research in this field and conclude the article. We assume the reader is familiar with the basics on deductive databases and logic programming. See Refs. 12–14 for excellent texts/surveys in these fields.

UNCERTAINTY AND DEDUCTION: A BIRD'S-EYE VIEW

Deductive databases and logic programming, with their advantages of clean declarative semantics coupled with powerful top-down and bottom-up query processing and optimization techniques, offer a framework in which applications can be developed rapidly. Building on these advantages, several researchers have proposed extended frameworks of deduction with various notions of uncertainty. A necessarily nonexhaustive but representative list of such works is Refs. 2, 10, 15–26, 51. In this section, we sketch some general principles that have gone into the design of many of these frameworks. Selected details of specific frameworks can be found in the next section.

Typically, these works propose a framework in which deduction can be combined with some kind of uncertainty. As in standard logic programming, these extended frameworks offer a declarative semantics of programs. On the operational side, this is supported by a sound and complete (or sometimes, just "weakly complete") proof procedure and a corresponding fix-point semantics. A common theme in these works is to lift, to deductive database frameworks with uncertainty, the rich body of theory and techniques from standard logic programming and datalog, the de facto standard language of deductive databases.

In a rule-based paradigm like deductive databases or logic programming, several issues arise in associating and manipulating uncertainty with data and rules, best captured by the following questions. (1) What uncertainty formalism should one employ? (2) Should uncertainty be associated with a rule as a whole, or with individual goals and subgoals? (3) How should uncertainty associated with subgoals in a rule be combined in a manner that corresponds to their conjunction? (4) How should the overall certainty associated with a rule body be propagated to the rule head? (5) The same conclusion can be obtained by multiple derivations. In classical logic programming, this is not a semantical issue. It is just an efficiency issue as one wants to minimize if not avoid duplicate derivations. When the same (uncertain) conclusion is derived using different derivations, we should really combine the associated certainties in a manner that reflects the intuition of taking their disjunction. How should this be done?

Frameworks differ based on the choices they make in answering the above questions. We shall quickly summarize the various choices that have been made.

Certainty may be modeled using means that are numeric, non-numeric, or a combination of the two (often referred to as hybrid). This can be further classified into the exact formalism used (e.g., certainty values, fuzzy logic, probabilities, and possibilities).

In some sense, uncertainty can be viewed as an extension of the notion of truth values, *true* and *false*, in the standard case, to collections of more (complex) elements. Examples of such extended truth values include the unit interval $\mathcal{V} = [0, 1]$, the product space $\mathcal{V} \times \mathcal{V}$, collection of subintervals of $\mathcal{V}$, or collection of pairs of such subintervals. In addition to lattices, semilattices and bilattices have also been employed (more on this

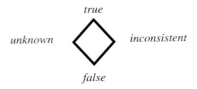

FIGURE 1   An example bilattice.

later; for now, see Figure 1 for an example bilattice). In the classical case, an *interpreta-tion* is a subset of the Herbrand case. To model uncertainty, an interpretation is defined as a mapping from the Herbrand case to one of the appropriate certainty domains, such as the above. Examples of non-numeric formalisms used include many-valued logics and annotated logics. The information source tracking (IST) model and situation model are two examples that adopt a hybrid means for modeling uncertainty. The idea in these models is to capture uncertainty in terms of conditions or situations under which a fact is supposed to hold (or not). This is decoupled from the numeric certainty associated with the fact, by assigning probabilities to the various atomic conditions (or primitive situations). As a quick example, we may know that according to sources s_1 and s_2, the bridge linking place A to place B is supposed to be intact (say, not damaged by bombing), whereas according to source s_3, it is broken. The IST and situation models allow conve-nient modeling of such information, by associating a vector (*true, true, false*) correspond-ing to the source of vector (s_1, s_2, s_3), with the fact "the bridge between A and B is intact."*

Certainty can be associated with a rule by associating it with the rule as a whole or, more precisely, with the implication itself. We can think of this as the confidence an expert has in the implication captured by the rule; for example, we can say with 60% certainty that if someone in a person's family has diabetes, and this person is middle aged, then s/he is prone to it as well. An alternative is to explicitly associate certainties with each subgoal of a rule as well as with its head; for example, we can say if the bridge connecting place A to B is undamaged by bombing with probability [60%, 70%] and the road connecting B to C continues to be navigable with probability [50%, 65%], then C is reachable from A with probability [40%, 55%]. Note the explicit association of certainties (probability intervals) with individual subgoals and the rule head. We call the former approach *implication based* (IB) and the latter approach *annotation based* (AB). The reason for this terminology will become clear later. In the AB approach, more gener-ally, we may wish to use variables ranging over certainty values and use functions to manipulate them and compute certainties for the conclusions. For example, we could say if the link between A and B is okay with probability [x, y] and that between B and C is okay with probability [z, w], then C is reachable from A with probability [$x \times z, y \times w$].

Next, we turn to combining certainties of subgoals in a rule body. One possibility often adopted in frameworks where the certainties come from a lattice is to treat the combination function as the lattice meet operator. The simplest example of this is

---

*References 25 and 27, in which these models were proposed, use a slightly different notation for the so-called source vectors. In the interest of homogeneity, we use a modified notation here.

the min function, which simply takes the minimum of the certainties associated with the subgoals being conjoined. In principle, any computable function can be used in place of the min function. However, it seems intuitive to insist that the result of conjoining subgoal certainties should not be greater (w.r.t. the partial order applicable on the certainty domain) than the individual subgoal certainties. In frameworks which make explicit certainty association with subgoals and rule head, this conjunction is often done using such computable functions.

Propagation of certainty from rule body to head is analogous, although not necessarily identical, to subgoal certainty conjunction. The similarity comes from the fact that it amounts to taking the "conjunction" of the rule's certainty with the body's certainty.

Finally, for combining the results of multiple derivations, we rely on (some form of) disjunction. Again, some frameworks base this disjunction on the underlying certainty lattice join operator. There are also frameworks where an arbitrary computable function is used instead to combine the certainties associated with multiple derivations of a fact. Here again, it makes sense to insist that the result of disjoining certainties associated with multiple derivations of a fact cannot be less than the individual derivation certainties.

In the next section, we discuss the IB and AB frameworks in detail, whereas the fourth illustrates several specific frameworks with examples.

ANNOTATION VERSUS IMPLICATION

As mentioned earlier, the various frameworks proposed for representing and reasoning with uncertainty in logic programming and deductive databases can be classified into the AB (annotation based) and IB (implication based) approaches on the basis of how certainties are associated with the facts and rules. In this section, we dwell on the general philosophy and computational models of these two approaches. Details of specific frameworks adopting either approach can be found in the next section.

In the AB approach, a rule r is an assertion of the form

$$r: \quad A: f(\beta_1, \ldots, \beta_n) \leftarrow B_1 : \beta_1, \ldots, B_n : \beta_n,$$

where A and B_i are atoms.* The underlying certainty domain could either be certainty values or certainty intervals, as discussed in the previous section. The above rule may then be read as saying "the certainty of A is at least (or is in, for intervals) $f(\beta_1, \ldots, \beta_n)$, whenever the certainty of B_i is at least (is in, for intervals) β_i, for $1 \leq i \leq n$." Each β_i is called an *annotation* because it specifies a certainty or certainty interval for individual atoms. An annotation may be constant or variable. The function f is any n-ary computable function over the appropriate certainty domain.

As an example, the rule

$$r_1: \text{canReach}(X, Y) : 0.6 \leftarrow \text{road}(X, Z) : 0.7, \quad \text{road}(Z, Y):0.8$$

says one can reach Y from X with certainty at least 0.6 provided the roads connecting X to some intermediate point Z and one connecting Z to Y are both intact with certainties at least 0.7 and 0.8, respectively. The underlying certainty domain is the unit interval

---

*Typically, one assumes every variable appearing in the head atom A necessarily appears in one of the B's in the body, an assumption called range-restrictedness in deductive database literature.

[0, 1]. The annotation function f is the one that always maps its arguments to the constant 0.6. As another example, the rule

$$r_2 : \text{canReach}(X, Y) : [V_1 \times V_3, V_2 \times V_4] \leftarrow \text{road}(X, Z) : [V_1, V_2],$$
$$\text{road}(Z, Y) : [V_3, V_4]$$

says that whenever the road linking X to Z is intact with a certainty that lies between V_1 and V_2 and the one from Z to Y has a certainty in the range $[V_3, V_4]$, then, overall, the certainty of reaching Y from X lies in the interval $[V_1 \times V_3, V_2 \times V_4]$. Here, the annotation function is the product function over interval endpoints. Note that the annotation function f plays the role of both conjunction and propagation functions mentioned earlier. In this example, variables such as V_1 are called annotation variables. An implicit assumption in annotation-based frameworks is that every annotation variable appearing in a rule head necessarily appears in the rule body. As a consequence, the annotation for a fact must be a constant annotation. More examples of AB frameworks can be found in the next section.

The semantics of a program in an AB framework is as follows. An interpretation is a mapping that assigns certainties to the ground atoms in the Herbrand base. For a ground atom A and a constant annotation β, satisfaction of $A : \beta$ by an interpretation is defined in the obvious way: The certainty assigned to A by the interpretation should be no less than β (or lie in β, if it is an interval). In classical logic programming, the semantics of a definite program P is formalized using a fix-point operator T_p that maps interpretations to interpretations. The same idea extends here, except our interpretations themselves are mappings. The intuition for such a mapping is as follows. Given a rule $r: A : f(\beta_1, \ldots, \beta_n) \leftarrow B_1 : \beta_1, \ldots, B_n : \beta_n$, we first check that each subgoal $B_i : \beta_i$ in the rule body is satisfied by the current interpretation. If this is the case, then the rule can be fired, assigning to the atom in the rule head the certainty defined by applying the computation of f to its arguments supplied. Each AB framework has an associated disjunction function. The function can vary from max to the interval intersection. Using max amounts to taking the best certainty for an atom among its many derivations, whereas taking the interval intersection amounts to deriving the sharpest possible bounds among those obtained from various derivations. This process, easily formalized, defines a fix-point operator on the space of interpretations. The fix-point operator induces natural bottom-up evaluation procedure similar to that for classical datalog or logic programs. For many AB frameworks, sound and complete (sometimes, "weakly complete") top-down proof procedures have been developed.

Subrahmanian (28) introduced the notion of *annotated logic programming*, the first AB framework proposed. This work was extended later by Kifer and Subrahmanian (22) to a generalized theory of annotated logic programming (GAP, for short). Instances of other AB frameworks include the work of Kifer and Li (10) and works of *probabilistic logic programming* by Ng and Subrahmanian (18–20). Examples illustrating some of these frameworks can be found in the next section. Note the considerable variety in the uncertainty formalisms by these various frameworks, a matter completely orthogonal to the fact that they are all annotation based.

In the IB approach, a rule r is an assertion of the form

$$r: \quad A \quad \xleftarrow{\quad \alpha \quad} \quad B_1, \ldots, B_n,$$

which may be read as saying "the certainty of the implication—$B_1, \ldots, B_n \rightarrow A$—is α." The certainty α of the rule may be viewed as "filtering" the "propagation" of truth from the body of the rule to its head by the uncertainty α. In any IB framework, each rule in a program has an associated conjunction and propagation function (which may be specified implicitly or explicitly). In addition, each derived predicate is associated with a disjunction function.

Semantics of programs adopting the IB approach can be formalized as follows. The notion of an interpretation is similar to that in the AB approach; that is, it is a mapping of the Herbrand base to an appropriate certainty domain. A fix-point operator on interpretations can be defined as follows. Recall that an interpretation assigns a certainty to each ground atom. First, the certainty of the rule body is determined by combining the certainties of the atoms in the body using the conjunction function associated with the rule. The result is then combined with the certainty α of the rule using the propagation function associated with r. This yields a certainty for the atom in the rule head. Finally, alternate derivations of the same (ground) atom, obtained possibly from different rules, are then combined, using the disjunction function associated with the head predicate. A key difference with the fix-point operator defined for AB frameworks has to do with the notion of satisfaction. Under the IB approach, a rule is true in an interpretation, provided the certainty of the head is no less than what is entailed by the rule under the interpretation, in the sense defined earlier. In case certainties are intervals, an AB rule is true in an interpretation provided the truth value assigned to the head by the interpretation lies in the certainty for the head that is entailed by the rule under the interpretation, this with the notion of satisfaction of a rule in the AB approach.

One of the pioneering works using the IB approach is that by van Emden (16), who formalized quantitative deduction and its fix-point theory. In his framework, the unit interval [0, 1] is used as the certainty lattice. Although a concrete example can be found in the next section, suffice it to observe for now that he uses min as the conjunction function, $\times$ as the propagation function, and max as the disjunction function. Other examples of the IB approach include the works of Fitting (2,17), which is based on bilattices as a certainty domain, Dubois et al. (21) based on possibility theory, Lakshmanan and Sadri (23,24), and Lakshmanan (25) which are based on formalisms ranging from probability theory to a hybrid between numerical and non-numerical formalisms of uncertainty.

REPRESENTATIVE IB AND AB FRAMEWORKS

In this section, we illustrate representative IB and AB frameworks through examples. This will show different ways of modeling and manipulating uncertainty. An important observation is that some of these frameworks (e.g., Refs. 2, 16, 17, 21, 23, and 24) amount to treating multiple derivations of an atom as a set, while others (e.g., Refs. 24 and 29) amount to treating them as a multiset.

Example IB Frameworks

We begin with a "generic" IB program, which we will instantiate by varying the choices of uncertainty formalism and of the functions.

Example 1 (A Generic Template). Let P be a "generic" IB program with the following rules:

$$r_1: \quad A \xleftarrow{\quad \alpha_1 \quad} B$$

$$r_2: \quad A \quad \xleftarrow{\quad \alpha_2 \quad} \quad C$$

$$r_3: \quad B \quad \xleftarrow{\quad \alpha_3 \quad}$$

$$r_4: \quad C \quad \xleftarrow{\quad \alpha_4 \quad}$$

For simplicity, we consider a propositional program. Thus, A, B, and C are propositions. Despite its simplicity, the program P suffices to illustrate most frameworks. Besides, many of the considerations can be lifted straightforwardly to first-order programs with uncertainty. Note that α_i, chosen from some underlying certainty lattice $\mathcal{V}$, is the certainty associated with rule r_i, for $1 \le i \le 4$. Using this program as a template, in the following we illustrate several IB frameworks via examples.   □

First, note that we can reduce P to classical deductive database framework by choosing the set of truth values (certainties) to be $\mathcal{V} = \{0, 1\}$, setting $\alpha_i = 1$, for $1 \le i \le 4$, letting both the propagation and conjunction functions associated with r_i be min and the disjunction function associated with every predicate symbol be max.* The reader is invited to verify that P is then a program in the standard framework of logic programming and deductive databases.†

Van Emden (16) was a pioneering work on extending deductive databases with a quantitative notion of uncertainty. It was also one of the earliest such works to propose a sound and complete proof theory with an equivalent fix-point theory. It corresponds to choosing the unit interval as the certainty domain, min as the conjunction function, × as the propagation function, and max as the disjunction function. The following example illustrates this.

Example 2 [van Emden (16)]. Let $\mathcal{V} = [0, 1]$, and suppose the rule certainly α_i is as defined in the previous example, for $1 \le i \le 4$. Also, suppose the conjunction and disjunction functions are as earlier, but the propagation function is ×, the product. Then, P is a program in van Emden's framework‡ (16), which is mathematically founded on the theory of fuzzy sets, proposed by Zadeh (30). Suppose $\alpha_1 = \alpha_4 = 0.8$ and $\alpha_2 = \alpha_3 = 0.7$. Then, in the least fix-point model, the certainties associated with A, B, and C are 0.56, 0.7, and 0.8, respectively.   □

Dubois et al. (21) proposed a framework for deductive databases with uncertainty modeled using possibility theory. The certainty domain in this case is the unit interval. Other parameters are essentially the same as for datalog. The following example illustrates this framework.

Example 3 [Dubois et al. (21)]. Let the certainty domain be the unit interval (i.e., $\mathcal{V} = [0, 1]$. Suppose $\alpha_1 = \alpha_4 = 0.8$ and $\alpha_2 = \alpha_3 = 0.7$ are possibility/necessity degrees associated with the rules. Also, suppose the conjunction, propagation, and disjunction functions are as in the previous example (i.e., respectively min, min, and max). Then, P is a program in the framework proposed by Dubois et al. (21), founded on the possibility theory, proposed by Zadeh (31). In the fix-point evaluation of P, the possibility degrees

---

*min would work too, although it is an unintuitive choice for disjunction, in general.
†Albeit propositional, but simulating datalog, for example, is straightforward.
‡Uninterpreted function symbols are allowed in Ref. 16, just as in Prolog, but in the context of databases, we only consider the function-free fragment of that framework, whenever we refer to it.

obtained for A, B, and C are 0.7, 0.7, and 0.8, respectively. Compare this with the result obtained in the van Emden framework. □

Example 4 [MYCIN (29)]. Let $\mathcal{V} = [0, 1]$, and suppose the α_i's are probability values defined as in the previous example. Suppose the propagation and conjunction functions associated with every rule in P are $\times$, and the disjunction function associated with every predicate symbol in P is $f(\alpha, \beta) = 1 - (1 - \alpha)(1 - \beta)$. Note that because f is associative, it is well defined on a collection of certainty values. Viewing each ground atom as an event, f returns the probability of the occurrence of an event, where different sources of occurrence (i.e., derivations) of the same event are assumed to be independent, in the probabilistic sense. The MYCIN expert system (29) uses f as the disjunction function.

Let us now consider a fix-point evaluation of P. In the first iteration, we derive B and C with probabilities 0.7 and 0.8, respectively. In the second iteration, there are two derivations of A: one by r_1 with certainty 0.56 and the other by r_2, with the same certainty. Therefore, the overall probability of A at iteration 2 is $f(0.56, 0.56) = 0.8064$. □

Two observations regarding MYCIN are particularly important. First, note the difference between MYCIN and the two preceding frameworks. The assumption of independence between different derivations of a ground atom sets it apart from other frameworks. Second, as Example 4 shows, it is important to treat the collection of derivations as a multiset; if the derivations were treated as a set, then the probability of A obtained would be 0.56—an incorrect result.

A limiting feature of the MYCIN approach is the across-the-board independence assumption it makes. In the above example, one may not *know* that B and C are independent. More seriously, if there were two rules for the same predicate whose bodies have at least one common predicate, assuming derivations coming from them are always independent is unrealistic.

We can set the parameters so that we get an IB framework founded on the *evidence theory*, as proposed by Dempster (32) and improved later by Shafer (33). The following example is adapted from the work of Ng and Subrahmanian (20), in the context of probabilistic logic programming.*

Example 5 (Dempster-Shafer). Let $\mathcal{V} = \mathcal{C}[0, 1]$ be the set of closed subintervals of $[0, 1]$, each of which is of the form [*Belief, Plausibility*]; for example, a certainty [0.6, 1] for an expression means that the expression is necessarily true with probability 0.6 and possibly true with probability 1. Suppose $\alpha_1 = [0.6, 1]$, $\alpha_2 = [0.7, 1]$, $\alpha_3 = [1, 1]$, and $\alpha_4 = [1, 1]$ are certainties associated with the corresponding rules in P. Further suppose that the propagation and conjunction functions associated with every rule are both $\cap$, which denotes interval intersection. For any pair of certainty elements $[\alpha, \beta]$, $[\sigma, \gamma]$ in $\mathcal{V}$, let $k \in \mathcal{V}$ be the *degree of conflict*, defined as $k = \alpha(1 - \gamma) + \sigma(1 - \beta)$. Using k, the disjunction function associated with every proposition is

$$h([\alpha, \beta], [\sigma, \gamma]) = \begin{cases} \left[\dfrac{\alpha\gamma + \beta\sigma}{1 - k}, \dfrac{\beta\gamma}{1 - k} \right] & \text{if } k \neq 1 \\ \varnothing & \text{otherwise,} \end{cases}$$

where $\varnothing$ is the empty interval, denoting the value "undefined."

---

*They had developed this as an AB framework.

The probability that A is true is h ([0.6, 1], [0.7, 1]) = [0.88, 1], indicating that these derivations, viewed as evidences, reinforce each other.   □

Fitting (2,17) developed an elegant IB framework by associating certainty values drawn from a bilattice with facts and rules and then employing the meet and join operators of the bilattice to serve as various combination functions. In the second section, we saw an example of a bilattice (Fig. 1). Although we have no space for formal definitions here, a bilattice is a set L with two partial orders such that it is a lattice w.r.t. each of the orders. Each order has its associated meet and join operations. In the bilattice of Figure 1, the order $\preceq_t$, defined by *false* $\preceq_t$ *unknown, inconsistent* $\preceq_t$ *true* can be regarded as the truth ordering. On the other hand, the order $\preceq_i$, defined by *unknown* $\preceq_i$ *false, true* $\preceq_i$ *inconsistent* can be regarded as the information ordering. Fitting shows that a logic programming framework can be developed using any bilattice by choosing the conjunction and propagation functions as the meet and the disjunction as the join w.r.t. either order. Because this framework is also entirely lattice-theoretic, we will not elaborate on it further.

Our next example illustrates the deductive IST framework developed by Lakshmanan and Sadri (23,34). We first quickly review the IST model proposed by Sadri (27), on which it is based. In Sadri's IST model, there is a fixed number, say k, of information sources, each of which may contribute to the information a database in a variety of ways: confirm it (indicated by the truth value *true*), deny it (*false*), be inconsistent about it (*inconsistent*), or be noncommittal (*unknown*). One may wonder why would a source give inconsistent opinions about some information. The reason is that even if relations in a database have only consistent contributions from sources, derived relations (involving minus) may contain inconsistent contributions. This leads to a certainty domain $\mathcal{V}$ which is the set of source vectors of the form $(a_1 \cdots, a_k)$, where $a_i \in L = \{$*true, false, unknown, inconsistent*$\}$. The partial ordering $<$ on the base lattice L is *unknown* $<$ *false* $<$ *inconsistent* and *unknown* $<$ *true* $<$ *inconsistent*. For example, the source vector (*true, false, unknown*) associated with a tuple t in relation R means that according to source s_1, t is in R, but not according to s_2, whereas s_3 is not sure about it. The following example illustrates the deductive IST framework.

Example 6 [Deductive IST (23,34)]. Suppose $k = 3$, and $\alpha_1 = ($*unknown true unknown*$)$, $\alpha_2 = ($*true unknown unknown*$)$, $\alpha_3 = ($*unknown unknown true*$)$, and $\alpha_4 = ($*true true unknown*$)$ are the certainties associated with the rules in P. The only propagation and conjunction function defined in this framework is $\overset{s}{\wedge}$, defined as follows. Given the source vectors $u = (a_1\ a_2\ a_3)$ and $v = (b_1\ b_2\ b_3)$, the conjunction or propagation of u and v is $u \overset{s}{\wedge} v = (\oplus(a_1, b_1)\ \oplus(a_2, b_2)\ \oplus(a_3, b_3))$, and for any sets of source vectors S_1 and S_2, $S_1 \overset{s}{\wedge} S_2 = \{u \overset{s}{\wedge} v \mid u \in S_1$ and $v \in S_2\}$, where $\oplus$ is the join operator on the certainty lattice $\mathcal{V}$. The disjunction function defined in this framework is $\vee$, which is essentially the set union. A fix-point evaluation of P delivers A, B, and C with certainties $\{($*unknown true true*$)$, (*true true unknown*$)\}$, $\{($*unknown unknown true*$)\}$, and $\{($*true true unknown*$)\}$, respectively.   □

In the above example, we treated uncertainty in qualitative terms in that a program tells what the conditions (on the contributing sources) are under which a tuple belongs to a relation. It is possible to turn this qualitative condition into quantitative terms by associating uncertainty about the veracity of the sources; for example, we may associate a probability of correctness with each source. Because source vectors and sets of source vectors represent complex conditions involving correctness of sources or its negation, we can then compute the probability of these conditions. In this process, we need to make assumptions about what we know regarding the interdependence of sources. As an example, the source vector (*true false unknown*) corresponds to the condition of source s_1 being correct and s_2 being incorrect. If we assume pairwise independence, we can calculate the reliability corresponding to this source vector as $p_1(1 - p_2)$, p_i being the probability of s_i being correct. We could make other assumptions such as positive or negative correlation, and even ignorance. So, in the most general case, the reliability may turn out to be a probability interval.

The situation-theoretic framework of Ref. 25 allows facts and rules to be associated with a pair of expressions (B, D) corresponding to belief and doubt. Instead of committing to any numerical domains for expressing belief and doubt, this framework uses propositional formulas over an abstract notion of (basic) scenarios, thus highlighting the structure of *reasoning* about which probabilistic reasoning is supposed to be. One can associate any appropriate probabilistic distribution over the basic scenarios to turn the abstract expressions into concrete probabilities, when needed. Reference 25 provides an epistemic foundation for reasoning with belief and doubt in this context, by relating the framework to extended modal logic S4. For more details, we refer the interested reader to that article.

Often, the agent contributing information may have incomplete knowledge, leading to a certain probability of belief and a certain probability of doubt. Exact probabilities are difficult to obtain in practice. Even if they could be obtained for basic events, as is well known, in the absence complete knowledge about the interdependence between various basic events, probabilities of complex events can only be estimated up to within lower and upper bounds. Consequently, it makes sense to work with a system for which an agent simultaneous associates a belief and a doubt with the information (say, a fact or a rule) he contributes, and each of these is a probability interval. Such a framework, called probabilistic deductive databases, was proposed by Lakshmanan and Sadri (24,35). Each certainty value is thus a pair of probability intervals $\langle[\alpha, \beta], [\gamma, \delta]\rangle$, called a confidence level. Interestingly, the underlying algebraic structure of confidence levels is a *trilattice*. Our next example illustrates this framework.

Example 7 [Probabilistic DDB (24,35)]. Let $\mathcal{V} = \mathcal{C}[0, 1] \times \mathcal{C}[0, 1]$. Each element in $\mathcal{V}$, called a confidence (level), is a pair of closed subintervals of $[0, 1]$. The meaning of confidence is as follows. If $\alpha = \langle[a_1, a_2], [a_3, a_4]\rangle$ is the confidence associated with an atom, say A, then it says the probability that "A is true" lies in the interval $[a_1, a_2]$, and the probability that "A is false" lies in $[a_3, a_4]$.

Suppose we have $\alpha_1 = \alpha_4 = \langle[0.7, 0.8], [0.1, 0.2]\rangle$, $\alpha_2 = \langle[0.8, 0.95], [0.05, 0.15]\rangle$, and $\alpha_3 = \langle[0.9, 0.95], [0, 0.15]\rangle$. Also, suppose the conjunction function associated with r_1 and r_2 is $\wedge_{pc}$, and the disjunction function associated with A is $\vee_{ind}$, where pc stands for the "positive correlation" mode and ind for the "independence," in the probabilistic sense. These modes are defined as follows. (See Ref. 24 for a full explanation of these modes.) Let $\alpha = \langle[a_1, a_2], [a_3, a_4]\rangle$ and $\beta = \langle[b_1, b_2], [b_3, b_4]\rangle$ be any intervals in $\mathcal{V}$. Then,

$$\wedge_{pc}(\alpha, \beta) = \langle[\min(a_1, a_2), \min(b_1, b_2)], [\max(c_1, c_2), \max(d_1, d_2)]\rangle$$

and

$$\vee_{ind}(\alpha, \beta) = \langle[a_1 + a_2 - a_1 a_2, b_1 + b_2 - b_1 b_2], [c_1 c_2, d_1 d_2]\rangle.$$

Let us consider a fix-point evaluation of P. Initially, each atom is assigned the least confidence, $\langle [0, 0], [1, 1] \rangle$ in $\mathcal{V}$, which corresponds to the truth value *false* in the standard logic. Then, in Step 1, we derive B and C with confidences $\langle [0.9, 0.95], [0, 0.15] \rangle$ and $\langle [0.7, 0.8], [0.1, 0.2] \rangle$, respectively. In Step 2, we obtain two derivations of A with the same confidence, $\langle [0.7, 0.8], [0.1, 0.2] \rangle$, which when combined, using $\vee_{\text{ind}}$, we obtain $\langle [0.91, 0.96], [0.01, 0.04] \rangle$ as A's confidence in this step. In Step 3, no new/better fact is derived, and hence P's evaluation terminates. $\qquad\square$

We illustrate the probabilistic deductive database framework with one more "real-life" example.

Example 8. Consider the following program, reproduced from Ref. 35:

1. *high-risk*$(X, D) \xleftarrow{\langle [\mathbf{0.65},\ \mathbf{0.65}],\ [\mathbf{0.1},\ \mathbf{0.1}] \rangle}$ *midaged*(X), *family-history*(X, D); $\langle ind,\_ \rangle$.

2. *takes*$(X, M) \xleftarrow{\langle [\mathbf{0.40},\ \mathbf{0.40}],\ [\mathbf{0},\ \mathbf{0}] \rangle}$ *high-risk*(X, D), *medication*(D, M); $\langle ign,\_ \rangle$.

3. *prognosis*$(X, D) \xleftarrow{\langle [\mathbf{0.70},\ \mathbf{0.70}],\ [\mathbf{0.12},\ \mathbf{0.12}] \rangle}$ *high-risk*(X, D); $\langle ign, pc \rangle$.

4. *prognosis*$(X, D) \xleftarrow{\langle [\mathbf{0.20},\ \mathbf{0.20}],\ [\mathbf{0.70},\ \mathbf{0.70}] \rangle}$ *takes*(X, M), *side-effects*(M, D); $\langle ind, pc \rangle$.

A patient can be at high risk for a disease based on his family history and his age. Patients are prescribed (and hence take) a medication out of many possible choices for a given disease. A patient's prognosis normally depends on the degree of risk. Sometimes, side effects caused by certain medications may be a contributing factor as well. The above program codifies this knowledge in the form of a probabilistic deductive database, where uncertainty is expressed in the form of confidence intervals (i.e., intervals of belief and doubt probabilities). In the program, rules 1 and 4 (respectively 2 and 3) specify that the subgoal certainties should be conjoined (together with the rule certainty itself) using the assuming independence (respectively, ignorance). Finally, rules 3 and 4 say that certainties associated with different derivations of the same prognosis for a patient should be disjoined assuming positive correlation. $\qquad\square$

As in the MYCIN example, the role of multisets is crucial in the above example; if the derivations were collected as sets, we would have obtained only one copy of A at iteration 2, resulting in an incorrect confidence level for A.

We illustrate some of the AB frameworks in the next section.

Examples of AB Frameworks

Annotated logic was first proposed by Subrahmanian (28) and was further investigated by other researchers. In this subsection, we illustrate representative frameworks following the annotation-based approach. Again, we start with a generic program.

Example 9 (A Generic Template). Let P be the following generic AB program:

r_1: $\quad A : f(\beta_1, \beta_2) \leftarrow B : \beta_1, C : \beta_2$
r_2: $\quad A : g(\beta_3, \beta_4) \leftarrow D : \beta_3, E : \beta_4$
r_3: $\quad B : \gamma_1 \leftarrow$

r_4: $C : \gamma_2 \leftarrow$
r_5: $D : \gamma_3 \leftarrow$
r_6: $E : \gamma_4 \leftarrow$

Here, $A, \ldots, E$ are ground atoms and β_i and γ_j are any uncertainty annotations (which may be constant or variable). Finally, f and g are annotation functions. $\quad\square$

We begin with Kifer and Li (10), who proposed a framework for rule-based systems with uncertainty based on annotated logic.

Example 10 [Kifer and Li (10)]. This was one of the early works using the AB approach, following Subrahmanian (28). To illustrate, let the certainty domain be the unit interval lattice [0, 1]. Kifer and Li allow arbitrary annotation functions. Let $\gamma_1 = 0.5$, $\gamma_2 = 0.6$, $\gamma_3 = 0.7$, $\gamma_4 = 0.8$, $\beta_1 = 0.4$, $\beta_2 = 0.5$, $\beta_3 = 0.6$, and $\beta_4 = 0.7$. Suppose f and g are both product. Let disjunction be max. Then, the certainty of A derived from the program P above is $\max\{0.4 \times 0.5, 0.6 \times 0.7\} = 0.42$. If, instead, disjunction was based on the independence assumption, A's certainty would be $1 - (1 - 0.4 \times 0.5)(1 - 0.6 \times 0.7) = 0.536$.

Ng and Subrahmanian were the first to propose a probabilistic framework for logic programming based on the AB approach. In its simplest form, the annotations tend to be constant certainty values (probability intervals), and the user can choose appropriate annotation functions. Interval intersection $\cap$ is chosen as the universal disjunction function for all programs in their framework. This corresponds to the join w.r.t. the precision ordering in the aforementioned trilattice. In their later works, the authors generalized annotations to allow variable annotations. The following example illustrates this framework.

Example 11 [Ng and Subrahmanian (18)]. Let $\gamma_1 = \gamma_4 = [0.6 \; 0.7]$, $\gamma_2 = \gamma_3 = [0.5, 0.6]$, $\beta_1 = \beta_2 = [0.4, 0.7]$, and $\beta_3 = \beta_4 = [0.3, 0.8]$. Finally, let f and g be the constant functions which map their arguments to the constants [0.3, 0.8] and [0.4, 0.9], respectively. Then, the certainty for A computed by the above program P would be $[0.3, 0.8] \cap [0.4, 0.9] = [0.4, 0.8]$. Recall that in this framework satisfaction of an annotated atom is based on interval inclusion.

Now, consider the variation where γ_i are as before, while $\beta_i = [V_1^i, V_2^i]$, $i = 1, \ldots, 4$. Finally, let $f([U, V], [W, X]) = g([U, V], [W, X]) = [U \times W, V \times X]$. Disjunction continues to be interval intersection, as in all annotated frameworks. Then, the certainty associated with A would be calculated as follows. From rule 1, we derive the certainty [0.3, 0.42], which is also the certainty derived using rule 2. Their disjunction is the same interval [0.3 0.42]. $\quad\square$

We illustrate the above probabilistic logic programming framework with one more example. The following real-life example is an adaptation of Example 8 to the framework of Ref. 19.

Example 12. Consider the following program:
1. *high-risk*$(X, D) : [0.8 * V_1 * V_3, 0.8 * V_2 * V_4] \leftarrow$
    midaged$(X) : [V_1, V_2]$, *family-history*$(X, D) : [V_3, V_4]$.
2. *takes*$(X, M) : [\max(0, 1 - (V_1 + V_3)), \min(V_2, V_4)] \leftarrow$
    high-risk$(X, D) : [V_1, V_2]$, *medication*$(D, M) : [V_3, V_4]$.

3. $prognosis(X, D) : [0.75 * V_1, 0.75 * V_2] \leftarrow$
        $high\text{-}risk(X, D) : [V_1, V_2].$
4. $prognosis(X, D) : [(V_1 + V_3)/2, (V_2 + V_4)/2] \leftarrow$
        $takes(X, M) : [V_1, V_2], side\text{-}effects(M, D) : [V_3, V_4].$

Note the difference with the program in Example 8. The use of annotation variables (V_i) and annotation functions lends considerable flexibility in the choice of conjunction and propagation functions. The conjunction/propagation functions can thus be more general than in the framework of Ref. 35. On the other hand, the disjunction function is anchored to be interval intersection.   □

As a last example, we consider the logic programming framework based on Dempster–Shafer theory, developed by Ng and Subrahmanian (20).

Example 13 (Dempster–Shafer). Consider the above program template P. Fix both the annotation functions f and g to be interval intersection {i.e., $f([U, V], [W, X]) = g([U, V], [W, X]) = [\max(U, W), \min(V, X)]$}. Choose the function h defined in Example 5 as the disjunction function. Then, we have a program in the Dempster–Shafer AB framework as proposed in Ref. 20. Its computation is fairly similar to that of the program illustrated in Example 5 and we omit this obvious detail.   □

Generalizations

There have been attempts at unifying the numerous proposed frameworks for deductive databases with uncertainty into a more general common foundation. The motivation was manifold: (1) Such unification often might give insight into the semantic underpinnings of the formalisms, illustrating common features as well as any subtle differences; (2) unification might lead one to tailor a framework for an application by "tuning" the parameters; (3) any study on query optimization conducted on the unifying framework would be applicable to specific instances of that framework. We comment on two such unifications in this section.

Kifer and Subrahmanian (22) developed a general lattice-theoretic framework called *generalized annotated programming* (GAP) for logic programming with uncertainty, which draws upon the AB approach. It is a powerful framework into which known proposals for multivalued logic programming and temporal reasoning can be embedded. In addition, it can simulate most known IB frameworks including van Emden (16) and Fitting (2). As an interesting by-product, the authors derive, for the first time, a model theory for the bilattice-based logic programming proposed by Fitting (2).

Debray and Ramakrishnan (36) propose an axiomatic basis for Horn clause logic programming, capturing a variety of "Horn-clause-like" computations, arising, for instance, in deductive databases, quantitative deduction, and inheritance systems, in terms of two operators. In the context of uncertainty reasoning, they show how their framework captures the computation in van Emden's language (16). In this context, it seems from their axioms that the proposed framework can also capture the fix-point computation of IB frameworks which have sets as the basis for their semantical structures (e.g., Refs. 23 and 34). However, their setting is incompatible with probabilistic frameworks, such as in Refs. 18, 19, 24, and 25, which require a first-class support for multisets.

Shiri (37) and Lakshmanan and Shiri (38) developed a so-called parametric framework as a unified framework into which most known IB (not AB) frameworks can be embedded. The main idea is that instead of committing to specific choices for the uncertainty domain, conjunction, propagation, and disjunction functions, they postulated the axioms that any meaningful choices must satisfy. Specific choices then lead to the various proposed frameworks, whereas new frameworks can be created by varying the choices. In particular, the framework provides support for multisets as well as sets. One of the highlights of this work was a comprehensive study of conjunctive query containment. We discuss query optimization in the next section.

QUERY OPTIMIZATION AND TERMINATION

One of the reasons for the success of the relational database technology is the rich body of sophisticated techniques developed for optimizing relational queries. Although termination is not an issue for relational and even deductive databases, for logic programs with function symbols, termination is an important problem. When uncertainty is associated with deductive databases (even without function symbols), as will become apparent in the subsection Termination, there are innocuous looking query programs whose bottom-up evaluation will not terminate in a finite number of steps. Thus, recognizing this problem and the conditions under which termination is guaranteed is important.

Query Containment and Equivalence

The main issue in query optimization is the ability to replace queries with equivalent ones which are expected to be more efficiently computable under a cost model. A key problem related to this is query equivalence. How can we efficiently test if two queries are equivalent? In the general case, this problem is undecidable for datalog. Indeed, in the classical case, testing the equivalence of conjunctive queries is regarded as a cornerstone of query optimization because such queries epitomize most practically occurring queries, and techniques for detecting their containment/equivalence are directly applicable for join elimination. It is well known that conjunctive query containment is completely characterized by the existence of containment mappings in the classical case. It is NP-complete to test containment in general, although when the contained query has no more than two occurrences of any relation/predicate, the existence of a containment mapping can be tested in polynomial time (see Ref. 12). What then can we say about containment of conjunctive queries in a framework with uncertainty?

In the relational model, we say a query Q_1 is contained in a query Q_2 provided for every input database D—$Q_1(D) \subseteq Q_2(D)$. Equivalence is then a two-way containment. In a framework with uncertainty, we can define containment by saying that on every input, the certainty associated with any tuple computed by Q_1 is no more than that associated with the same tuple by Q_2 on the same input. Formal definitions can be found in Refs. 34 and 38).

First, we discuss IB frameworks. Let us begin with the deductive IST framework. Recall that (deductive) IST associates qualitative conditions with facts and rules and the certainty domain is a lattice formed by sets of source vectors. Consequently, containment can be studied at two levels. The qualitative containment says $Q_1 \subseteq Q_2$, provided that for every input database D, and for every tuple t, $t \in Q_2(D)$ holds in every situation in which $t \in Q_1(D)$ holds. The quantitative containment is similar except that instead of conditions, we insist that the certainty computed by Q_2 for any tuple should be no less than that computed by Q_1 on any input database. It is known (34) that these two notions of containment coincide for deductive IST. Furthermore, the authors show that containment mappings completely characterize containment for conjunctive deductive IST queries. On the side of complexity, testing containment remains NP-complete provided the number of sources is constant, and co-NP-complete in the number of sources.

Actually, they establish results that are applicable to *recursive* query programs. As mentioned earlier, containment of recursive datalog query programs is undecidable. However, a restrictive notion of uniform containment is decidable, using a technique called chase (39). The idea is to treat the atoms appearing in the rule bodies of the contained program as constituting a database by "freezing" the variables, running the containing program on this database, and testing whether it derives the tuple corresponding to the (frozen) query tuple. Lakshmanan and Sadri showed that this technique extends to deductive IST. This is noteworthy, because, to our knowledge, no similar results are known about recursive query programs for other uncertainty frameworks.

Next, we briefly discuss the query containment results established in Ref. 38. As pointed out earlier, that article studies containment in the generic context of the parametric framework where the parameters (e.g., conjunction function, etc.) are not fixed but are merely known to satisfy certain postulates. Matters are considerably more complicated here because the choices of parameters can often influence the complexity of characterizing containment. The existence of a containment mapping (c.m.) continues to be necessary no matter what the parameters. It is in sufficiency that things can get quite complicated. This depends on whether the conjunction function is different from the certainty lattice meet operator and whether the disjunction function differs from the join operator. The key issue is that although existence of unconstrained c.m. is necessary, it might take the c.m. to satisfying some special conditions to achieve sufficiency in some cases. We give a few examples and refer the reader to Ref. 38 for a detailed classification of parameter choices and frameworks w.r.t. query containment.

When both the conjunction and disjunction functions of the containing query (Q_2) coincide with the lattice meet and join respectively, the existence of any c.m. is necessary and sufficient for containment. Note that choice of all other parameters is arbitrary. This situation holds for the works van Emden (16), Fitting (2), and Dubois et al. (21) and deductive IST (23), and to a restricted case of the probabilistic deductive database framework of Lakshmanan and Sadri (24,35).

When the disjunction function of Q_1 is different from the lattice join,* and the conjunction function of Q_2 coincides with the lattice meet, a variable onto c.m. is sufficient for containment, as long as Q_1 has distinct subgoals in its body. A variable mapping such as a c.m. is variable onto provided it is onto from the set of variables of Q_2 to those of Q_1. This result covers the probabilistic deductive database framework for many choices of disjunction function, provided conjunction corresponds to positive correlation.

Finally, when Q_1 and Q_2 both have identical parameters and their conjunction and disjunction functions are both different from the lattice meet† and join, a c.m. that is subgoal 1–1 and variable onto is sufficient for containment, as long as Q_1 has distinct subgoals in its body. This result is applicable to arbitrary choices of conjunction and disjunction functions in the probabilistic deductive database framework. Note that the

---

*The postulates require that it always be pointwise greater than or equal to the lattice join.
†Again, the postulates require that conjunction functions always be pointwise less than or equal to the lattice meet.

result is particularly relevant for determining whether joins can be eliminated from a conjunctive query in this framework.

As a final note, we remark that in all the results above the choice of the propagation function is left arbitrary.

Concerning AB frameworks, at this time of writing no major results on containment are known. We conjecture that most of the techniques developed for IB frameworks can be lifted for attacking query containment in AB frameworks.

We now consider a framework that is essentially implication based but is not covered by the parametric framework. What is different about this framework is that more than one notion of conjunction can be employed within the context of one query. This situation arises when programming with a bilattice, where there are two kinds of conjunction—the so-called truth conjunction (denoted $\wedge$) and knowledge conjunction (denoted $\otimes$). These are respectively the meet operator w.r.t. the truth ordering and the meet operator w.r.t. the knowledge ordering. One motivation for this may arise in the context of combining answers to subqueries coming from subsystems. The conjunction used by the subsystems may be different from that used for the combination itself. More specifically, each subsystem answers a subquery as an internal conjunction of atoms residing within itself. Different subqueries are combined using an external conjunction. An example is

$$Q(X) \leftarrow [A(X, \text{oscarPeterson}) \wedge E(X, \text{jazz})] \otimes [A(X, \text{oscarPeterson})$$
$$\wedge F(X, \text{jazz})]$$

This rule combines two subqueries processed by different subsystems computing a list of albums by Oscar Peterson sorted according to their jazziness. Here, $\wedge$ denotes internal conjunction and $\otimes$ denotes external conjunction. Grahne et al. (40) study the problem of conjunctive query containment in such a framework and extend the classical containment mapping (which is essentially a homomorphism) techniques to handle queries involving internal and external conjunction. In particular, they show that containment is Π_2^p-complete, essentially one level higher than the complexity for queries involving just one type of conjunction, for which containment remains NP-complete, just as for classical conjunctive query containment.

As a last remark, we point out that in recent work, Ioannidis and Ramakrishnan (41) study the containment of conjunctive queries for an extended relational model where each tuple has an associated label or annotation. Labels can be likened to, but do not have to be identical to, uncertainty. They identify several types of *label systems*, based on the algebraic properties of the label system, and provide sufficient (and necessary for some of the label types) conditions for query containment. As an example of the power of this framework, characterization of conjunctive query containment for the van Emden framework follows from their results. However, there are important differences with several of the uncertainty frameworks we have surveyed in this article. For more details on this, see Ref. 34.

Termination

Next, we turn our attention to termination of query program evaluation. For datalog, it is well known that the result of a recursive query program can be evaluated in a time polynomial in the size of the database. This nice property does not necessarily extend to deductive databases with uncertainty. Worse, there are frameworks in which one can write query programs whose bottom-up evaluation does not terminate in a finite number of steps! Here is an example.

Example 14 (Termination). Consider the following AB program in the framework of Refs. 18 and 19, computing the transitive closure of a relation e:

r_1: $p(X, Y) : [U \times W, V \times X] \leftarrow e(X, Z) : [U, V], p(Z, Y) : [W, X]$

r_2: $p(X, Y) : [U, V] \leftarrow e(X, Y) : [U, V]$

r_3: $e(1, 2) : [0, 1] \leftarrow$

r_4: $e(1, 1) : [0, 0.9] \leftarrow$

The last fix point of this program takes ω steps and $p(1, 2)$ and $p(1, 1)$ both have the probability interval $[0, 0]$ associated with it in the result. If we add the rule

r_5: $q(X, Y) : [1,1] \leftarrow p(X, Y) : [0, 0],$

then the least fix point of such a program cannot be computed in ω steps. The reason is that the fix-point operator T_P in this case is not continuous.   □

The problem of termination is not peculiar to AB frameworks; for example, if we choose ignorance as the mode for disjunction in the probabilistic DDB framework (24,35), the least fix point of programs like transitive closure can only be computed in ω steps. However, one advantage of IB frameworks is that even in this case, the least fix point can always be approximated to arbitrary precision with a large but finite number of iterations. The intuition is that for IB frameworks, the fix-point operator T_P is continuous.

We should point out the result in Ref. 35, that as long as the disjunction function for recursive predicates is chosen as positive correlation and/or the data is acyclic, query evaluation can be done on time polynomial time in the input database size, just as for datalog. Intuitively, this corresponds to basing disjunction on the lattice join. This termination and complexity result applies to a great majority of IB frameworks, including deductive IST and the works of van Emden, Dubois et al., and Fitting. Reference 37 contains some additional results on termination of recursive query programs in the parametric framework.

For AB frameworks, no corresponding results are known at this time.

SUMMARY AND OPEN PROBLEMS

Numerous formalism for reasoning with uncertain information have proposed in AI and in databases. Many of them have been extended to deductive databases, using one of two major approaches—annotation based or implication based. We provided a whirlwind tour of representative works in this important field. Our survey focused on the underlying semantic foundations as well as practical issues like query optimization (conjunctive query containment) and termination of recursive programs. Much work remains to be done, however, to make these frameworks usable for real-life applications. We now mention a few open problems which we believe are important.

A user is often unsure how to choose the various combination functions (conjunction, etc.). It is important to develop guidelines for their choice. As should be evident from our discussion on query optimization, the choices often impact on how complex query containment can get. However, this is only one guideline. Are there other general considerations that can help a user choose the various parameters for a given application?

For AB frameworks, it is important to develop techniques for basic problems like containment and termination. Although it is clear that techniques developed for IB frameworks should be useful, no concrete results have been established to date in this respect. This is an important direction for further work. Even for IB frameworks, with the exception of deductive IST, no techniques are known for optimizing recursive programs. One promising direction is to consider uniform containment of recursive programs.

There are far fewer implemented systems than there are proposals. FProlog (42) and the system for annotated logic programming developed at Maryland (43) are two interesting examples. Another landmark is the work by Kiessling and his colleagues (44–47). The main highlights of their work are the following: (1) they have developed efficient query processing strategies for van Emden's framework (44,45); (2) they have developed a framework called DUCK for reasoning with uncertainty. They provide an elegant logical axiomatic theory for uncertain reasoning in the presence of rules. For lack of space, we did not discuss this framework in detail, but a similar spirit is captured by our discussion of other probabilistic frameworks for deductive databases. Furthermore, the parametric framework of Refs. 26 and 38 covers many such frameworks as special cases.

For industry-strength performance, we need an implementation that espouses cost-based a physical access plan optimization similar to relational DBMS. This is currently a far cry for DDBs with uncertainty.

Last but not the least, there is a need for greater application pull. By this, we mean that uncertain DDB systems need to be deployed in real applications.

WHAT WE DID NOT COVER

There have been numerous works on manipulating uncertainty in relational databases, including extensions to SQL, based on any of the formalisms we have discussed. Similarly, researchers have discussed the interplay between uncertainty and object-oriented concepts like inheritance. We did not cover any of these issues. We refer the reader to Ref. 5 for a comprehensive survey of such works, which also discusses many works on uncertainty in AI. Finally, there are various probabilistic logics, some of which are surveyed by Halpern (48). Finally, various logics for dealing with inconsistency have been developed which may be usefully employed in the context of deductive databases with uncertainty. See Ref. 9 for an example.

Last, but not the least, even within the framework of probabilistic deductive databases, there has been recent work which addresses the use of multiple notions of conjunction and disjunction in the context of each rule in a query program. Dekhtyar and Subrahmanian (49,50) proposed the hybrid probabilistic logic programming framework and also study their efficient top-down evaluation using tabulation strategies.

REFERENCES

1. R. Chellappa, A. Rajput, S. Sirohey, and V. S. Subrahmanian, "The FIST Face Database System," unpublished work, 1995.
2. M. C. Fitting, "Bilattices and the Semantics of Logic Programming," *J. Logic Program.*, *11*, 91–116 (1991).

3. V. S. Subrahmanian, "Amalgamating Knowledge Bases," *ACM Trans. Database Syst.*, *19*(2), 291–331 (1994).

4. R. Fagin, "Combining Fuzzy Information from Multiple Systems," Proceedings of 15th ACM Symposium on Principles of Database Systems (*PODS*), 216–226 (1996).

5. S. Parsons, "Current Approaches to Handling Imperfect Information in Data and Knowledge Bases," *IEEE Trans. Knowledge Data Eng.*, *KDE-8*(3), 353–372 (1996).

6. P. P. Bonnissone and R. M. Tong, "Editorial: Reasoning with Uncertainty in Expert Systems," *Int. J. Man–Machine Studies*, *22*, 241–250 (1985).

7. J. D. Ullman, *Principles of Database and Knowledge-Base Systems*, Computer Science Press, MD, 1989, Vol. I.

8. J. Lobo, J. Minker, and A. Rajasekar, *Foundations of Disjunctive Logic Programming*. MIT Press, Cambridge, MA, 1992.

9. M. Kifer and E. L. Lozinskii, "RI: A Logic for Reasoning with Inconsistency," IEEE Symposium on Logic in Computer Science (*LICS*), 253–262 (1989).

10. M. Kifer and A. Li, "On the Semantics of Rule-Based Expert Systems with Uncertainty," in *2nd International Conference on Database Theory*, M. Gyssens, J. Paradaens, and D. van Gucht (eds.), Lecture Notes in Computer Science Vol. 326, Springer-Verlag, Berlin, 1988, pp. 102–117.

11. A. Silberschatz, M. Stonebraker, and J. D. Ullman, "Database Systems: Achievements and Opportunities," *Commun. ACM*, *34*, 110–120 (October 1991).

12. J. D. Ullman, *Principles of Database and Knowledge-Base Systems*, Computer Science Press, Maryland, 1989, Vol. II.

13. K. R. Apt, "Logic Programming," in *Handbook of Theoretical Computer Science, Volume B: Formal Models and Semantics*, J. van Leeuwen (ed.), Elsevier, Amsterdam, 1990, pp. 493–574.

14. J. W. Lloyd, *Foundations of Logic Programming*, 2nd ed., Springer-Verlag, New York, 1987.

15. E. Shapiro, "Logic Programs with Uncertainties: A Tool for Implementing Expert Systems," in Proceedings 8th International Joint Conference on Artificial Intelligence (IJCAI'83), Alan Bundy (ed.), William Kaufmann, 1983, pp. 529–532. According to the webpage of IJCAI'83 at dblp.uni-trier.de

16. M. H. van Emden, "Quantitative Deduction and Its Fixpoint Theory," *J. Logic Program.*, *4*(1), 37–53 (1986).

17. M. C. Fitting, "Logic Programming on a Topological Bilattice," *Fund. Inform.*, *11*, 209–218 (1988).

18. R. T. Ng and V. S. Subrahmanian, "Probabilistic Logic Programming," *Inform. Computat.*, *101*(2), 150–201 (1992).

19. R. T. Ng and V. S. Subrahmanian, "A Semantical Framework for Supporting Subjective and Conditional Probabilities in Deductive Databases," *Autom. Reason.*, *10*(2), 191–235 (1993).

20. R. T. Ng and V. S. Subrahmanian, "Relating Dempster–Shafer Theory to Stable Semantics," Technical Report UMIACS-TR-91-49 CS-TR-2647, Institute for Advanced Computer Studies and Department of Computer Science University of Maryland, College Park (April 1991).

21. D. Dubois Didier, J. Lang, and H. Prade, "Toward Possibilistic Logic Programming," in *Proceedings 8th International Conference on Logic Programming*, 1991, pp. 581–596.

22. M. Kifer and V. S. Subrahmanian, "Theory of Generalized Annotated Logic Programming and Its Applications," *J. Logic Program.*, *12*, 335–367 (1992).

23. L. V. S. Lakshmanan and F. Sadri, "Modeling Uncertainty in Deductive Databases," in *Proceedings International Conference on Database Expert Systems and Applications* (*DEXA '94*), Lecture Notes in Computer Science Vol. 856, Springer-Verlag, Berlin, 1994.

24. L. V. S. Lakshmanan and F. Sadri, "Probabilistic Deductive Databases," in *Proceedings International Logic Programming Symposium*, M. Bruynooghe (ed.) MIT Press, Cambridge, MA, 1994, pp. 254–268.

25. L. V. S. Lakshmanan, "An Epistemic Foundation for Logic Programming with Uncertainty," in *Proceedings 14th Conference on the Foundations of Software Technology and Theoretical*

Computer Science (*FST and TCS '94*), Lecture Notes in Computer Science Vol. 880, P. S. Thiagarajan (ed.) Springer-Verlag, Berlin, 1994.

26. L. V. S. Lakshmanan and N. Shiri, "A Parametric Approach to Deductive Databases with Uncertainty," in *Proceedings of the International Workshop on Logic in Databases* (*LID'96*), 1996, pp. 55–77.

27. F. Sadri, "Modeling Uncertainty in Databases," in *Proceedings of 7th IEEE International Conference on Data Engineering*, 1991, pp. 122–131.

28. V. S. Subrahmanian, "On the Semantics of Quantitative Logic Programs," in *Proc. 4th IEEE Symposium on Logic Programming*, Computer Society Press, Washington, DC, 1987, pp. 173–182.

29. B. G. Buchanan and E. D. Shortliffe, "A Model of Inexact Reasoning in Medicine," *Math. Biosci.*, *23*, 351–379 (1975).

30. L. A. Zadeh, "Fuzzy Sets," *Inform. Control*, *8*, 338–353 (1965).

31. L. A. Zadeh, "Fuzzy Sets as a Basis for a Theory of Possibility," *Fuzzy Sets and Syst.*, *1*(1), 3–28 (1978).

32. A. P. Dempster, "A Generalization of Bayesian Inference," *J. Roy. Statist. Soc., Series B*, *30*, 205–247 (1968).

33. G. Shafer, *A Mathematical Theory of Evidence*, Princeton University Press, Princeton, NJ, 1976.

34. L. V. S. Lakshmanan and F. Sadri, "Uncertain Deductive Databases: A Hybrid Approach," *Inform. Syst.*, *22*(8), 483–508 (1997).

35. L. V. S. Lakshmanan and F. Sadri, "On a Theory of Probabilistic Deductive Databases," *J. Theory Pract. Logic Program.* (in press).

36. S. Debray and R. Ramakrishnan, "Generalized Horn Clause Programs," unpublished work, 1994.

37. N. Shiri, "Towards a Generalized Theory of Deductive Databases with Uncertainty," Ph.D. thesis, Concordia University, Montreal (August 1997).

38. L. V. S. Lakshmanan and N. Shiri, "A Parametric Approach to Deductive Databases with Uncertainty," *IEEE Trans. Knowledge Data Eng.* (in press).

39. Y. Sagiv, "Optimizing Datalog Programs," 6th ACM Symposium on Principles of Database Systems (*PODS*), 349–362 (1987).

40. G. Grahne, N. Spyratos, and D. Stamate, "Semantics and Containment of Queries with Internal and External Conjunctions," in *6th International Conference on Database Theory* (*ICDT '97*), 1997, pp. 71–82.

41. Y. E. Ioannidis and R. Ramakrishnan, "Containment of Conjunctive Queries: Beyond Relations as Sets," *ACM Trans. Database Syst.*, *20*(3), 288–324 (1995).

42. T. P. Martin, J. F. Baldwin, and B. W. Pilsworth, "The Implementation of FProlog—A Fuzzy Prolog Interpreter," *Fuzzy Sets Syst.*, *23*, 119–129 (1987).

43. J. J. Lu and S. M. Leach, "Computing Annotated Logic Programs," in *Proceedings International Conference on Logic Programming*, Pascal van Hentenryck (ed.) MIT Press, Cambridge, MA, 1994.

44. H. Schmidt, N. Steger, U. Gntzer, W. Kieling, R. Azone, and R. Bayer, "Combining Deduction by Certainty with the Power of Magic," *DOOD*, 103–122 (1989).

45. N. Steger, H. Schmidt, U. Gntzer, and W. Kieling, "Semantics and Efficient Compilation for Quantitative Deductive Databases," Proceedings 5th International Conference on Data Engineering (*ICDE*), 660–669 (1989).

46. W. Kiessling, H. Thone, and U. Guntzer, *Database Support for Problematic Knowledge*, Lecture Notes in Computer Science Vol. 580, A. Pirotte, C. Delobel, and G. Gottlob (eds.) Springer-Verlag, Berlin, 1992, pp. 421–436.

47. H. Thone, W. Kiessling, and U. Guntzer, "On Cautious Probabilistic Inference and Default Detachment," *Ann. Oper. Res.*, *55*, 195–224 (1995).

48. J. Halpern, "An Analysis of First-Order Logic of Probability," *Artif. Intell.*, *46*(3), 311–350 (1990).
49. A. Dekhtyar and V. S. Subrahmanian, "Hybrid Probabilistic Programs," *J. Logic Program.*, *43*(3), 187–250 (2000).
50. A. Dekhtyar and V. S. Subrahmanian, "Tabulation Strategies for Hybrid Probabilistic Programs," Technical Report, University of Maryland (1999).
51. J. F. Baldwin, "Evidential Support Logic Programming," *Fuzzy Sets and Syst.*, *24*, 1–26 (1987).

LAKS V. S. LAKSHMANAN

NEMATOLLAAH SHIRI

MULTILAYER PERCEPTRONS AND FRACTALS

INTRODUCTION

A neural network (NN) can be viewed in a broad sense as both an optimization tool, capable of solving complex scientific problems, and as a statistical processor, one that makes probabilistic assumptions about data and data patterns. Interest in neural networks has grown rapidly in recent years, due to both pragmatic considerations (e.g., the availability of computational power) and theoretical results (e.g., backpropagation learning algorithm (1). They are currently used in numerous applications, many involving either classification of given observations or approximation of the observations' generating function (2). One of the most common NN models is the multilayer perceptron (MLP) which takes the neuron or perceptron as its basic processing unit. To arrive at a suitable solution for a given problem, MLPs use both backpropagation of error (3) and the gradient descent technique to optimize an objective function.

It has been postulated whether the optimization process of MLPs and the generation of fractals are related. There exist several definitions of fractals, but one useful definition is that fractals are self-similar mathematical objects which are usually generated by contractive maps (4). In other words, a group of contractive maps applied repeatedly to any collection of nonempty compact sets, as in the use of iterated function systems (IFSs), will ultimately force these sets to converge to a single set, called the attractor. The attractor is considered fractal.

Although seemingly unrelated, a theoretical relationship can be established between MLPs and fractals. This relationship is based on the observation that although the proof of convergence of the gradient descent technique to a local optimum is usually given in terms of results on Taylor's series (5), an alternative proof can be constructed by using elements of fractal theory—more specifically, theoretical results involving contractive maps.

The present article includes introductions to both multilayer perceptrons and fractals as well as a presentation of the alternative proof mentioned. A simple example is given in which steps from the aforementioned proof are used to find conditions under which a specific multilayer perceptron is guaranteed to converge.

MULTILAYER PERCEPTRONS

Neural Networks

Neural networks (NNs) have emerged and developed as a field of study through the efforts of not only researchers in artificial intelligence (AI) but also those in engineering, physics, mathematics, computer science, and neuroscience (6). Many strands of research exist in NNs, but there is a main underlying focus on developing mathematical models of brainlike systems and then studying these models to understand how such devices can be used to solve various computational problems in optimization and pattern recognition.

A neural network is a graph in which patterns are represented by numerical values at the nodes of the graph, and changes in the patterns are determined by node message-passing algorithms. The most common networks take the neuron as the basic processing unit (node), characterized by an activity level, an output value, a set of input connections, a bias level, and a set of output connections, all represented by real numbers. Each input connection has an associated weight which determines the effect of the incoming input on the activation level of the unit. Often, the inputs to a unit are assumed to sum linearly, yielding an activation for unit i at time t of

$$\alpha_i(t) = \sum_{j=1}^{k} w_{ij} x_{ij},$$

where k is the number of input connections and w_{ij} and x_{ij} are the weight and input value, respectively, on the connection from unit j to unit i. Weights can be positive (excitatory) or negative (inhibitory); the input/output function of the network can be adjusted by a learning algorithm, such as backpropagation (described in the subsection Error Backpropagation). The influence of unit i on unit j is determined by both the output value of unit i and the strength of its connection to unit j. The output level of a unit is often a nonlinear function of its activation value; one common function is the sigmoid function, defined as

$$f(\alpha_i(t)) = \frac{1}{(1 + e^{-k\alpha_i(t)})},$$

with $k > 0$, $0 < f(\alpha_i(t)) < 1$. Note that as $k \to \infty$, $f(\alpha_i(t)) \to$ Heaviside function.

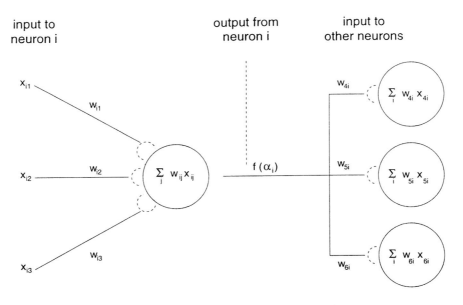

FIGURE 1   Basic network model. (From Ref. 7.)

The study of neural networks has its roots in the work of McCulloch and Pitts (8) over 50 years ago and Hebb's *Organization of Behavior* (9) published in 1949. However, in subsequent years, the symbol-processing view of intelligence (10) came to dominate work in AI, a concept of intelligence that could be represented on von Neumann computers instead of computers modeled after the human brain (11,12). The dominance of this view occurred partly because (1) the symbol-processing approach is well suited to implementation on serial digital computers, unlike the neural network models resembling Rosenblatt's parallel perceptron (11) and (2) the perceptron revealed limitations unforeseen by expectations, discouraging those in scientific research. As a result, despite the advances in neural network research in the 1970s by Amari, Anderson, Fukushima, Grossberg, Kohonen, Tsypkin, and Willshaw, among others, the field received relatively little attention until the 1980s.

The resurgence of interest in neural networks during the 1980s had both theoretical and practical motivations. Two dominant practical motivations were as follows:

- As the field of neuroscience continued to grow and develop, there emerged a desire to model and understand how complex biological neural networks function. It was hoped that the theory behind computational neural networks could assist in this endeavor.
- The increase in available computational power and capabilities allowed for the programming and simulation of larger, more interesting networks in scientific experimentation. The focus on parallel computational methods was also gaining momentum, and researchers believed that advances in the design and architecture of neural networks could help identify promising techniques for parallel processing.

Among the theoretical motivations, two of the more important are the following:

- The results of Hopfield (13) made it possible to relate how certain networks operate to point-attractor dynamics, making their behavior easier to understand and analyze. These results helped guide how networks could be structured to solve optimization problems through subsequent results achieved by Cohen and Grossberg (14) and Hinton et al. (15).
- The backpropagation algorithm for training multilayer perceptron networks was developed. By extending the work of Widrow and Hoff (16) who developed the ADALINE, or ADAptive LInear Element system) and Rosenblatt (11) (who designed and developed the perceptron), it was shown that gradient descent, in combination with a differentiable nonlinear function (like the sigmoid function described earlier), could be used for reliable learning in complex, multilayer networks (3). Werbos (17) developed and used the backpropagation learning method in 1974, but several years passed before this application was popularized.

It was later discovered (18,19) via reinterpretation that a classic mathematical result of Kolmogorov (20) proves that given a function $f : [0, 1]^n \subset \mathcal{R}^n \to \mathcal{R}^m$, there exists a three-layer neural network with n input nodes, $2n - 1$ hidden nodes, and m output nodes that approximates f exactly. This result was used to show that a backpropagation network could actually approximate any function of practical interest to any degree of accuracy (18), fueling the hopes that neural networks could be used to effectively approximate any given function.

Backpropagation Learning System

Backpropagation learning has had a major impact on the development of neurocomputing by providing a way by which networks may be reliably trained. Learning in neural networks is a question of finding the set of connection weights with which the network can solve the problem of interest, and backpropagation is one way in which such a set of weights can be found. Backpropagation was originally introduced by Werbos (17) in 1974, although its primary learning law can be shown to follow from the Robbins/ Monro technique of 1951 (21). Its widespread use is owed primarily to the work of Rumelhart, McClelland, Williams, and other members of the "Parallel Distributed Processing" group (22).

Backpropagation MLP Architecture

The backpropagation architecture is a hierarchical design consisting of several fully interconnected layers or rows of processing units. Backpropagation networks are designed to process information in such a way as to provide an approximation of a bounded function $f: B \subset \mathcal{R}^n \to \mathcal{R}^m$ defined on a compact subset B of n-dimensional Euclidean space to a bounded subset $f(B)$ of m-dimensional Euclidean space. This approximation is the result of learning from a training set of examples $\{(x_1, y_1), \ldots, (x_k, y_k)\}$, where $y_i = f(x_i)$, $i = 1,$ $\ldots, k$. It is often assumed that the training values $\{x_i\}_{i=1}^{k}$ and the values on which the network is to be used are selected randomly from the probability density function of x, $p(x)$.

In general, the MLP architecture consists of an initial row of input units connected through a set of hidden units to a final row of output units. There may be any number or configuration of hidden units and connections between units, but usually the hidden units are organized into layers—often one layer is sufficient—and all units are fully interconnected. The training set $\{(x_i, y_i)\}_{i=1}^{k}$ is presented to the network, and in response, the network modifies its connection weights in order to approximate the function f. The resulting network is then tested for its ability to generalize [i.e., its ability to predict or approximate the value of $f(x)$ for values of x not in the training set].

Generalizability can be a serious problem, just like "overfitting" in the statistical literature. A more general learning procedure places less restrictions on how the network develops and, hence, provides less assurance of the networks ability to work on yet unseen problems. Two popular approaches to dealing with this dilemma are (1) "Occam's razor"—the notion that the simplest network consistent with the data should be utilized and (2) cross-validation—the idea of training the network on one portion of the data, validating the training results and checking for overfit using a second portion of the data, then performing final testing and cross-validation on a third portion of the data. These methods are supported by findings which report not only better results for minimal-complexity networks versus more complicated networks (23) but also equivalent performance by cross-validated networks versus other networks despite less training time (24).

It should also be noted that other variants of the backpropagation neural network architecture exist; these include sigma–pi networks and networks which skip layers (22), as well as recurrent networks (25,26).

Error Backpropagation

As previously mentioned, during training, a set of inputs $\{x_i\}_{i=1}^{k}$ is entered into the network and a set of output values $\{z_i\}_{i=1}^{k}$ is generated. These values are then compared to the actual output values $\{y_i\}_{i=1}^{k}$ and a match is computed, generating an error value. Because the actual output is known, this type of learning is called "supervised learning." If there is no error, then no changes are made to the network; however, if an error does exist, then this error must be reduced by making changes to the network connections. The trick is to determine which connection weights need to be changed and by how much. For networks with hidden layers, this is a difficult problem, one that haunted neurocomputing until the 1980s, when a simple, powerful solution was developed. The basic idea is to define an overall measure of system performance, such as

$$E = \sum_p \sum_j (y_{pj} - z_{pj})^2,$$ [1]

where y_{pj} is the actual value for pattern p at output node j and z_{pj} is the network output for pattern p at output node j, summed over all output nodes and all patterns. The goal is then to minimize this quantity, and if the output function is differentiable, then this can be done by making the weight changes proportional to the derivative of the error with respect to the weights. In other words, weight changes should be proportional to

$$\Delta w_{ij} = \eta \frac{\partial E}{\partial z_{pj}} \frac{\partial z_{pj}}{\partial w_{ij}},$$ [2]

where w_{ij} is the connection weight between node i and node j. Hence, a reasonable learning law is

$$w_{\text{new}} = w_{\text{old}} - \Delta w.$$

This is the *generalized delta rule* and the value $\eta > 0$ incorporated into Δw is a small positive constant called the *learning rate* (small, so the process does not overshoot the minimum). Note that if node j is not an output node, then $\partial E/\partial z_{pj}$ is a function of the errors in subsequent units; hence, the error must be calculated first in the output nodes and then passed back to subsequent nodes for updating their weights. This is the reason why this particular learning law is referred to as backpropagation.

Generalized Delta Rule

The *error surface* of a backpropagation network is the mean squared error function E defined earlier but considered as a function of the weight vector w. The generalized delta rule is able to use the information provided by the training set to move the current weight vector w_0 of a network to a weight vector w_1 so that the error is decreased [i.e., $E(w_0) \geq E(w_1)$]. However, the following are known:

- Due to the combinatorial permutations of network weights which leave the error value unchanged, the backpropagation error surface often has many global minima.
- Many backpropagation error surfaces consist primarily of large flat areas and troughs with little slope in many dimensions. As a result, it may be necessary to move a considerable distance before any significant reduction in error is achieved. At the same time, because of the lack of slope across the surface, the generalized delta rule has a hard time determining in which direction to move the weights in order to reduce the error.
- The error surface can have local minima, points at which all first derivatives are zero, but the Hessian ($\partial^2 E/\partial w_i \, \partial w_j$) is strongly positive definite. The gener-

alized delta rule will be unable to move the weight vector from this point to any other point with lower error.

The reason that areas of little slope and local minima are of such concern is that the generalized delta rule essentially performs *gradient descent* on the error surface (27), using the fact that the error function E is differentiable as a function of w (28,29) and moving in the direction of maximum decrease; that is,

$$-\nabla_w E = - \left\{ \frac{\partial E}{\partial w_1}, \frac{\partial E}{\partial w_2}, \cdots \right\}.$$

As a consequence, learning laws based on this rule, even the momentum version (22), will move downhill in relatively short jumps, with the jumps getting shorter as a shallow area in the error surface is reached. In an attempt to speed the rate of descent, several variants of the above rule have been developed, incorporating such things as approximations to the pseudoinverse of the Hessian matrix (30,31) "annealing" schedules for the learning rate (32), and conjugate gradient methods (33,34). A discussion of numerous learning rule variants can be found in Refs. 35 and 36.

FRACTALS

Gradient descent is apparent not only in the generalized delta rule mentioned earlier but also in the creation of fractals. Mathematically speaking, fractals can be viewed as the supports of fractal measures associated with functional equations (37), but they are most often seen as powerful scientific tools with applications in areas such as biology, image compression, numerical function approximation, and chaotic systems (38–42). In our discussion of fractals, we will first discuss the concept of dimension and Mandelbrot's definition of a fractal (43). We then take the approach of Barnsley (4) and think of fractals as objects produced by overlaying copies of themselves and taking this process to the limit. We formalize this idea by saying that fractals are the *attractors* of *iterated function systems*. We then present some basic results concerning fractals and *contractive maps* before returning to the connection between fractals and neural networks.

Definition

The study of fractals, or *fractal geometry* (44), was founded upon the achievements of many great mathematicians of the last 200 years. Their works, once considered radical and sometimes dangerous, were gathered together by another mathematician, Benoit Mandelbrot, and used to form the foundation of fractal geometry. The word *fractal* was coined by Mandelbrot (43) using the Latin word "fractus," meaning broken or irregular. Mandelbrot formally defined a fractal as "a set for which the Hausdorff–Besicovitch dimension strictly exceeds the topical dimension." Although we are accustomed to working with objects that have integer Euclidean dimension, fractals generally have noninteger dimensions [e.g., the von Koch curve ("Koch curve," Fig. 2), a well-known fractal, has dimension ≈ 1.2618].

Other well-known fractals include the Mandelbrot set, the Sierpinski triangle, and the Julia sets. The Julia sets are named after Gaston Julia, who taught Mandelbrot at the Ecole Polytechnique in Paris in the 1940s.

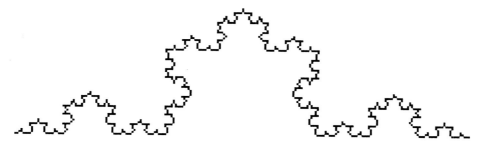

FIGURE 2   Koch curve.

An alternate view of fractals, adhered to by Barnsley and others, is that fractals are the attractors of iterated function systems. Generally speaking, the values which result from the iterative application of a specific set of functions F to a set A will converge to a set of values B. B is called the attractor of F and is considered fractal. For example, Newton's equation is used to find the roots of a polynomial. Given a polynomial, if Newton's equation is iteratively applied to a set of points, these points will converge to the roots of the polynomial. Hence, the roots of the polynomial are the attractor of Newton's equation.

In order to discuss in detail such sets of functions and related concepts, as well as the theory behind fractal generation, we must first discuss some of the basic results concerning fractals and *contractive maps*.

Contractive Maps and Attractors

Although the following results regarding contractive maps hold for any complete metric space, we will state them with respect to *n*-dimensional Euclidean space. Most of the results stated here can be found in Ref. 4.

Let $\mathcal{R}$ denote the real line. Let $\mathcal{R}^n$ denote the *n*-dimensional Euclidean plane and let A denote the set of all nonempty compact subsets of $\mathcal{R}^n$. $\rho(x, y)$ will denote the Euclidean distance between two points x and y in $\mathcal{R}^n$.

Definition 3.1. A function f defined from $\mathcal{R}^n$ to $\mathcal{R}^n$ is said to be *contractive* if there exists s, $0 \le s < 1$, such that

$$\rho(f(x), f(y)) \le s\rho(x, y) \quad \forall x, y \in \mathcal{R}^n.$$

s is said to be a *contractivity factor of f*. □

A contractive function (map) f will shrink any nonempty compact subset of $\mathcal{R}^n$. If there does not exist any $s < 1$ for which the above holds, then f is not contractive.

Result 3.1. Let f be a contractive map from $\mathcal{R}^n$ to $\mathcal{R}^n$. Then there exists a unique $x_0 \in \mathcal{R}^n$ such that

    1. $f(x_0) = x_0$
    2. $\lim_{l \to \infty} f^l(x) = x_0 \ \forall x \in \mathcal{R}^n$, where
       • $f^1(x) = f(x)$
       • $f^l(x) = f^{(l-1)}(f^1(x)) \quad \forall l > 1$ and $\forall x$

x_0 is said to be the *fixed point* of f. Repeated applications of f on any nonempty compact subset of $\mathcal{R}^n$ will eventually generate a set containing only x_0. □

We shall formally extend Result 3.1 to sets by using a metric between sets, namely the *Hausdorff metric*.

Definition 3.2. Let $\rho(x, A) = \inf_{y \in A} \rho(x, y)$. The *Hausdorff distance* between two sets A and B in $\mathbf{A}$ is defined as

$$D(A, B) = \max[\sup_{x \in A} \rho(x, B), \sup_{y \in B} \rho(y, A)].$$
□

It can be easily shown that the above D is a metric in $\mathbf{A}$.

Definition 3.3. Let f be a function from $\mathbf{A}$ to itself. Then, f is said to be *contractive* if there exists s, $0 \le s < 1$, such that

$$D(f(x), f(y)) \le sD(x, y) \quad \forall x, y \in \mathbf{A}.$$

s is said to be a *contractivity factor* of f. □

Result 3.2. Let f be a contractive map from $\mathbf{A}$ to $\mathbf{A}$. Then, there exists a unique $x_0 \in \mathbf{A}$ such that

1. $f(x_0) = x_0$
2. $\lim_{l \to \infty} f^l(x) = x_0 \; \forall x \in \mathbf{A}$, where
   - $f^1(x) = f(x)$
   - $f^l(x) = f^{(l-1)}(f^1(x)) \; \forall l > 1$ and $\forall x \in \mathbf{A}$

Here, the metric under consideration is the Hausdorff metric D. □

Result 3.3. Let $f_1, f_2, \ldots, f_m$ be m contractive maps defined from $\mathbf{A}$ to itself. Let $s_1, s_2, \ldots, s_m$ be their respective contractivity factors. For any $C \subseteq \mathbf{A}$, let

$$F_{(l+1)}(C) = \bigcup_i f_i(F_l(C)) \quad \forall l \ge 0$$

where

$$F_0(C) = C \quad \forall C \subseteq \mathbf{A}.$$

Then, there exists $A \subseteq \mathbf{A}$ such that

1. $F_1(A) = A$
2. $\lim_{l \to \infty} F_l(C) = A \; \forall C \subseteq \mathbf{A}$.

$(A: f_1, f_2, \ldots, f_m)$ is said to be a (*hyperbolic*) *iterated function system* (IFS) and A is said to be the *attractor* of the IFS. □

The word *fractal* is defined by various authors in various ways. As mentioned previously, Barnsley considers a fractal to be a set in $\mathbf{A}$; we will also consider fractals as such.

Fractals are usually generated by iterated function systems, systems which specify a discrete dissipative dynamical system (45). An iterated function system is a set of contractive functions (usually contractive affine transformations) which define a more complex contractive function, one that has an attractor. Given enough iterations of an IFS, any set will eventually converge to the attractor. This result and the existence of a fixed point are a result of Banach's *Contraction Mapping Theorem* (see Result 3.2, Theorem 3.1, and Ref. 4).

As a side note, in the design of a fractal model (i.e., an IFS), it is often desired that the attractor be close to a given set. For example, in fractal image compression, we would like to build a fractal model or, equivalently, design an IFS whose attractor is the image of interest. The following theorem, the *Collage Theorem*, is central to such designs.

Theorem 3.1 [Collage Theorem (46)]. *Let (A, d) be a complete metric space. Let $P \in \mathcal{H}(A)$ be given, where $\mathcal{H}(A)$ is the space of nonempty compact subsets of A. Let $\varepsilon > 0$ be given. Choose an IFS $(A: f_1, f_2, \ldots, f_m)$ with contractivity factor s, $0 \leq s < 1$, so that*

$$D(P, \cup_{k=1}^{m} f_k(P)) \leq \varepsilon,$$

where D is the Hausdorff metric. Then,

$$D(P, A) \leq \frac{\varepsilon}{1 - s},$$

where A is the attractor of the IFS. Equivalently,

$$D(P, A) \leq (1 - s)^{-1} D(P, \cup_{k=1}^{m} f_k(P)) \quad \text{for all } P \in \mathcal{H}(A). \qquad \square$$

Hence, given a target P and an $\varepsilon > 0$, the objective is to find an IFS such that the *collage distance* $D(P, \cup_{k=1}^{m} f_k(P))$ is less than ε. Further details regarding fractal image compression can be found in Refs. 37, 41, 42, and 47.

Mathematical Preliminaries

A definition and basic result from matrix algebra are stated below. These will be used in developing the relationship between the gradient descent technique and contractive maps.

Definition 3.4. For a real matrix **B** of order $n \times n$, the *norm* of **B**, denoted by $\|\mathbf{B}\|$, is defined as

$$\|\mathbf{B}\| = \sup_{(x: \|x\| \neq 0)} \frac{\|\mathbf{B}x\|}{\|x\|},$$

where $\|x\| = \sqrt{x_1^2 + \cdots + x_N^2}$ if $x = (x_1, \ldots, x_N)$. $\qquad \square$

Result 3.4. If **B** is a real symmetric positive definite matrix of order $n \times n$, then its norm is $\max[\alpha_1, \alpha_2, \ldots, \alpha_N]$, where α_i is the ith eigenvalue of the matrix **B**. $\qquad \square$

Note: If **B** is a real symmetric matrix, then the norm of **B** is the maximum of the modulus of the eigenvalues of **B**.

This completes the mathematical preliminaries. We shall now discuss the relationship among contractive maps, the essence of fractal generation, and gradient descent, the technique which underlies learning in backpropagation neural networks.

GRADIENT DESCENT TECHNIQUE AND CONTRACTIVE MAPS

Gradient descent is commonly used in neural network applications to find the minimum of a given objective function [9]. We describe the gradient descent technique next.

Gradient Descent Technique

Let g be a continuous, twice differentiable function from $\mathcal{R}^n$ to $\mathcal{R}$. Let $\partial g(\mathbf{y})/\partial x_i$ denote the partial derivative with respect to x_i of the function g at the point $\mathbf{y}$ in $\mathcal{R}^n$, where $i = 1, 2, \ldots, n$.

Let

$$\nabla g(\mathbf{y}) = \left(\frac{\partial g(\mathbf{y})}{\partial x_1}, \frac{\partial g(\mathbf{y})}{\partial x_2}, \ldots, \frac{\partial g(\mathbf{y})}{\partial x_n} \right)^t,$$

where t denotes the transpose. $\nabla g(\mathbf{y})$ is the *gradient* of $g(\mathbf{y})$.

Let f, a function from $\mathcal{R}^n$ to itself, be such that

$$f(\mathbf{y}) = \mathbf{y} - \eta \nabla g(\mathbf{y}), \qquad\qquad [3]$$

where $\eta > 0$ is a constant. Equation (3) represents the process of the gradient descent technique. In other words, let

$$f^1(\mathbf{y}) = f(\mathbf{y}) \quad \text{and} \quad f^l(\mathbf{y}) = f^{(l-1)}(f^1(\mathbf{y})) \quad \text{for all } l > 1 \text{ and for all } \mathbf{y} \in \mathcal{R}^n.$$

The limit of $f^l(\mathbf{y})$ as l goes to infinity is taken to be the solution for the minimization of g.

In terms of neural networks, $g(\mathbf{y})$ is usually the error function E [i.e., $\Sigma(\text{obs} - \text{exp})^2$], viewed as a function of the network weights [see Eq. (1)]. The objective is to find the choice of weights which minimizes $g(\mathbf{y})$. Note, however, that the result of the gradient descent technique depends on the choices of η and the initial weight vector.

We shall find the relationship between the gradient descent technique and the contractive maps below. Initially, we shall assume that $n = 1$ and, later, the results will be generalized to any n.

Let $n = 1$. Then, $g: \mathcal{R} \to \mathcal{R}$ and Eq. (3) can be written as

$$f(y) = y - \eta \frac{dg(y)}{dy}. \qquad\qquad [4]$$

Theorem 4.1. *Let g be a twice differentiable function with x_0 as a local minimum. Let $h(x) = d^2g(x)/dx^2$ be a continuous function where $h(x) > 0$ at $x = x_0$. Let v_2 be an open interval containing x_0 such that $dg(x)/dx \neq 0$ for all $x \neq x_0$ and $x \in v_2$. Then, there exists a closed interval v around x_0 such that the function f, defined in Eq. (4), is a contractive map on v and its fixed point in v is x_0.* $\square$

Proof: Note that h is continuous and $h(x_0) > 0$. Then, there exists an open interval v_1 around x_0 such that $h(x) > 0$ for all $x \in v_1$. Let y_1 and y_2 be in v_1 such that $y_1 \neq y_2$. Now,

$$|f(y_1) - f(y_2)| = \left| y_1 - y_2 - \eta \left(\frac{dg(y_1)}{dy} - \frac{dg(y_2)}{dy} \right) \right|$$

$$= \left| y_1 - y_2 - \eta \left(\frac{dg(y_1)/dy - dg(y_2)/dy}{y_1 - y_2} \right) (y_1 - y_2) \right|$$

$$= |y_1 - y_2||1 - \eta h(y_3)|.$$

[Here, y_3 is a convex combination of y_1 and y_2. This step follows from the Mean Value Theorem (48).]

Let v be a closed interval such that (a) v is contained in v_1 and v_2, (b) v contains x_0, and (c) v is bounded. Note that h is bounded on v.

Let $a = \inf_{x \in v} (1/h(x))$. Let

$$0 < \eta < a. \tag{5}$$

Then, note that $0 < |1 - \eta h(y)| < 1$ for all y in v. Then,

$$|f(y_1) - f(y_2)| = |y_1 - y_2||1 - \eta h(y_3)| < |y_1 - y_2|.$$

Thus, f is a contractive map on v. Its fixed point is the point y in v such that $f(y) = y$. Now,

$$f(y) = y$$

$$\Leftrightarrow y - \eta \frac{dg(y)}{dy} = y$$

$$\Leftrightarrow \eta \frac{dg(y)}{dy} = 0$$

$$\Leftrightarrow \frac{dg(y)}{dy} = 0 \quad (\text{because } \eta > 0).$$

Note that the only point in v for which $dg(y)/dy = 0$ is x_0 because v has been chosen in that way. ☐

Generally, the proof for the gradient descent technique is derived using results on Taylor's series. The above proof, in contrast, is based on the theory of contractive maps.

Remarks

1. Theorem 4.1 indicates that f is a contractive map in the compact interval, v and if f is iterated in v, it will eventually produce the local minimum x_0. The bound for η may also be noted in this regard. If η does not satisfy Eq. (5), then the function f may take values outside v for some values of x in v. Also, the selection of η is problematic if we want to get the global optimum.
2. The results hold in a certain interval containing the local optimum and the initial point for the iteration needs to be taken in that interval in order to get that particular local optimum. Thus, if we have more than one local optimum and the initial point is taken in the respective interval of one of these local optima, then, with the proper choice of η, the technique will converge to that optimum.
3. If the initial point is outside of the respective intervals of all local optima or η is not chosen properly, then f may not be contractive and hence the technique may not converge. In other words, the process may diverge to $+\infty$ or $-\infty$ or it may oscillate between $+\infty$ and $-\infty$.
4. Let the function g possess k local optima $x_1, x_2, \ldots, x_k$ for which $h(x_i) > 0$ $\forall_i = 1, \ldots, k$. Let v_i be a closed disk around x_i such that $dg(y)/dy \neq 0$ for all $y \neq x_i$ and $y \in v_i$. Let η_i be a choice of η which makes f contractive for $i = 1, \ldots, k$. Let $\lambda = \min[\eta_1, \ldots, \eta_k]$ and let

$$f(y) = y - \lambda \frac{dg(y)}{dy}. \tag{6}$$

Then, if y is an element of $\cup_i v_i$, the limit of $f^l y$ as l goes to infinity belongs to the set A, where $A = \{x_1, \ldots, x_k\}$. In other words, if Z is a nonempty compact subset of A, then

$$\lim_{l \to \infty} f^l(Z) \in A. \qquad \qquad \square$$

Because neural network applications involve data of higher dimensions, the generalization to the n-dimensional case is stated next.

Theorem 4.2. *Let g be a function from $\mathcal{R}^n$ to $\mathcal{R}$ with a local minimum at x_0. Let $b_{ij} = \partial^2 g/\partial x_i \, \partial x_j$ such that b_{ij} is continuous for each (ij) pair and b_{ij} (y) denotes the value of b_{ij} calculated at y. Let $\mathbf{H}$ be the Hessian matrix of g. Let v_2 be an open disk containing x_0 such that $\nabla g(x) \neq \mathbf{0}$ for all $x \neq x_0$ and $x \in v_2$. Let v_3 be an open disk containing x_0 such that $\mathbf{H}(c)$ is positive definite for all $c \in v_3$. Then, there exists a closed disk v around x_0 and a constant $\eta > 0$ such that the function f, defined in Eq. (3), is a contractive map on v and its fixed point in v is x_0.* $\qquad \square$

Proof: Note that for each $c \in v_3$, the eigenvalues of $\mathbf{H}(c)$ are all greater than zero, as $\mathbf{H}(c)$ is positive definite. Consider a closed disk v around x_0 such that $\nabla g(x) \neq \mathbf{0}$ for all $x \neq x_0$, $x \in v$ and $\mathbf{H}(c)$ is positive definite for all $c \in v$. Note that v is a subset of $v_2 \cup v_3$ and such a v exists.

Consider the equation

$$f(y) = y - \eta \nabla g(y). \qquad \qquad [7]$$

Let $a \neq b$ be two vectors in v. Now,

$$\|f(a) - f(b)\| = \|a - b - \eta(\nabla g(a) - \nabla g(b))\|$$

$$= \|a - b\| \cdot \left\| \left(\frac{a - b}{\|a - b\|} \right) \right.$$

$$\left. - \eta \left(\nabla \frac{g(a) - \nabla g(b)}{\|a - b\|} \right) \right\|$$

$$= \|a - b\| \cdot \left\| \left(\frac{a - b}{\|a - b\|} \right) \right.$$

$$\left. - \eta \mathbf{H}(c) \left(\frac{a - b}{\|a - b\|} \right) \right\|.$$

[Here, c is a convex combination of a and b, and c also lies in the set v. The existence of such a c is guaranteed from the literature (49).]

Let I represent the n-dimensional identity matrix. Then,

$$\|f(a) - f(b)\| = \|a - b\| \cdot \left\| (I - \eta \mathbf{H}(c)) \left(\frac{a - b}{\|a - b\|} \right) \right\|$$

$$\leq \|a - b\| \cdot \|T - \|\eta \mathbf{H}(c)\|.$$

Let $r(c) = \|I - \eta \mathbf{H}(c)\|$.

Now, if η is selected in such a way that $r < 1$ for each c in v, then f would be a contractive map and, thus, its fixed point would be x_0.

Let $t(c) = I - \eta \mathbf{H}(c)$. We observe that $t(c)$ is symmetric so the norm of $t(c)$ is the maximum of the modulus of its eigenvalues (from the subsection Mathematical Preliminaries). Hence, if $\mu_1(c)$, $\mu_2(c)$, ... , $\mu_n(c)$ are the eigenvalues of $\mathbf{H}(c)$, then the eigenvalues of $t(c)$ are $1 - \eta\mu_i(c)$ for $i = 1, 2, . . . , n$. Note that (a) $\mu_i(c) > 0 \ \forall_i = 1, 2, . . . , n$ and $\forall c \in v$ because $\mathbf{H}(c)$ is positive definite and (b) $\mu_i(c)$ is bounded for all $i = 1, 2, . . . , n$, and for all c in v because v is closed. Hence, η can be selected in such a way that

$$0 < 1 - \eta\mu_i(c) < 1 \quad \text{for } i = 1, 2, . . . , n \text{ and } \forall c \in v.$$

For this specific η, $\|t(c)\| < 1$. This makes f contractive in v; hence, the theorem. □

Remarks

1. Different proofs of the convergence of the gradient descent technique exist in the literature; see Ref. 5. However, this proof is unique in that it establishes a relationship between gradient descent and contractive maps.

2. The continuity of the Hessian matrix in the neighborhood of x_0 is one of the assumptions on which the above proof is based. The eigenvalues of $\mathbf{H}$ for different values of c are bounded because of this assumption.

3. The fixed points of the function f are different for different closed disks, for different values of η, and for different starting vectors. Note also that for the same η, the function $f^l(y)$ may oscillate as l goes to infinity for some values of y. The values of η for which $f^l(y)$ oscillates depends on y and the particular problem under consideration.

4. The selection of η is crucial to the performance of a neural network and its final result. The current methods for choosing η are heuristic, not theoretical. One such method is to choose a value of η which is very low. However, which values of η are considered low is the subjective choice of the researcher and may, in fact, be quite large relative to the problem of interest.

5. Let the function g possess k local optima $x_1, x_2, . . . , x_k$ for which the corresponding Hessian matrices are positive definite. Let v_i be a closed disk around x_i such that the corresponding Hessian matrices are positive definite for all $y \in v_i$ and for all $i = 1, 2, . . . , k$. Let η_i be a choice of η which makes f contractive for $i = 1, 2, . . . , k$. Set $\lambda = \min[\eta_1, \eta_2, . . . , \eta_k]$. Let

$$f(y) = y - \lambda \nabla g(y). \tag{8}$$

Then, the limit of $f^l y$ as l goes to infinity belongs to the set A, where $A = \{x_1, x_2, . . . , x_k\}$ is y is an element of $\cup_i v_i$. In other words, if C is a nonempty compact subset of A, then

$$\lim_{l \to \infty} f^l(C) \in A. \qquad \square$$

In the next section, the connection between MLP and Theorems 4.1 and 4.2 is described.

MLP AND CONTRACTIVE MAPS

As previously discussed, the multilayer perceptron (MLP) is a neural network model which is commonly used in supervised pattern classification. The connection weights in the network model are updated with the help of backpropagation (3). There are two ways of implementing MLP: batch mode and on-line. The following arguments do not depend on the mode of implementation. Some authors have considered adding a momentum term to the equation for updating the connection weights in MLP. The following discussion is confined to the MLP as described in Ref. 3 and, as such, does not include models with the momentum-term modification.

The connection weights in the MLP are modified with the help of Eq. (7) [i.e., Eq. (2)]. Note that if the vector y of the previous section represents the weight vector, $\eta \nabla g(y)$ represents the change in the weight vector, and $g(y)$ represents the error function, then a direct relationship can be drawn between the generalized delta rule (subsection Error Backpropagation) and gradient descent (section Gradient Descent Technique and Contractive Maps). In the batch mode learning algorithm, the connection weights are changed after **all** the patterns or values in the training set have been fed to the input layer, whereas in the online learning algorithm, the weights are changed after **each** pattern or value in the training set is fed to the input layer. In the backpropagation algorithm, initially the connection weights in the topmost layer are modified. Then, the connection weights in the next lower layer are modified and so on, until the weights in the bottommost layer are modified. The modification of connection weights in any layer is done using Eq. (7) [i.e., Eq. (2)]. It is expected that the backpropagation algorithm will provide a local optimal solution. It is not difficult to reach a stable value for g by making a few trials with η.

Theorem 4.2 establishes the relationship between MLP and fractals. It specifies that the gradient descent technique employed by MLP converges for certain values of η and certain starting values. For these values, f is a contractive map. Systems of contractive maps are often used to generate fractals. Note that the choice of η depends on the eigenvalues of the Hessian matrix. For this reason, given a real-life problem, it may be very difficult to use Theorem 4.2 (see the previous section). However, recent developments in neural network theory regarding the computation of the Hessian matrix for certain network models (50,51) may ease its implementation.

EXAMPLE

Preliminaries

We determined initially that constructing a hypothetical example involving the use of a MLP to build a mathematical model for minimizing an expression of the form $\Sigma(\text{obs} - \text{exp})^2$ would be extremely difficult (51). This is due primarily to two facts:

- Such an example would require the creation of a function $g : \mathcal{R}^{\text{weights}} \to \mathcal{R}$, where the superscript weights indicates the number of weights in the MLP and a choice of training sample points such that the expected results were known and could be compared to the experimental results.

- The function $\Sigma\,(\text{obs} - \text{exp})^2$ must have a positive-definite Hessian matrix, where the derivatives are taken with respect to the network weights. However, (a) this is often not the case in multilayer perceptron learning (35,51), hence the existence of modified Newton methods, and (b) determining whether the Hessian is positive definite requires the calculation of its eigenvalues, a computationally intensive task if the dimension of the Hessian is large.

The extreme difficulties in constructing a realistically complex example is highlighted by the dearth of such examples in the existing literature.

For these reasons, we chose instead to demonstrate the use of the above theory to minimize a function using a neural network of the form shown in Figure 3, where (a) x_1, $\ldots, x_m$ are the network weights as well as the function variables, (b) $h_1(x), \ldots, h_m(x)$ are factors of $g(x)$ [i.e., $g(x) = h_1(x) \cdot \cdots \cdot h_m(x)$], and (c) no transfer function is used. Nevertheless, if one has a function to be minimized which meets the assumptions of Theorems 4.1 and 4.2, then our methodology will work for solving problems of the type outlined in the previous section.

Construction

Let $x = (x_1, \ldots, x_m)$. The function $g(x)$ to be minimized was required to have a positive-definite Hessian matrix; that is, $\mu_i > 0 \;\forall i = 1, \ldots, m$, where $(\mu_1, \ldots, \mu_m)$ are the eigenvalues of

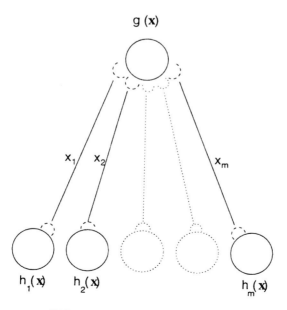

$$g\,(\mathbf{x})$$

$$x_1 \quad x_2 \qquad x_m$$

$$h_1(\mathbf{x}) \quad h_2(\mathbf{x}) \qquad h_m(\mathbf{x})$$

FIGURE 3   Neural network model.

$$H_g = \begin{bmatrix} \dfrac{\partial^2}{\partial^2 x_1}g(\boldsymbol{x}) & \dfrac{\partial^2}{\partial x_1\,\partial x_2}g(\boldsymbol{x}) & \cdots & \cdots & \dfrac{\partial^2}{\partial x_1\,\partial x_m}g(\boldsymbol{x}) \\[2ex] \dfrac{\partial^2}{\partial x_2\,\partial x_1}g(\boldsymbol{x}) & \cdots & & \cdots\ \cdots & \vdots \\ \vdots & \ddots & \vdots & \vdots & \vdots \\ \vdots & \vdots & \vdots & \ddots & \vdots \\ \dfrac{\partial^2}{x_1\,\partial x_m}g(\boldsymbol{x}) & \vdots & \vdots & \vdots & \dfrac{\partial^2}{\partial^2 x_m}g(\mathbf{x}) \end{bmatrix}.$$

We chose to minimize the function $g(x_1, x_2) = 5x_1^2 + 8x_1x_2 + 5x_2^2$. In this case, the Hessian matrix is

$$H = \begin{bmatrix} 10 & 8 \\ 8 & 10 \end{bmatrix}$$

with eigenvalues $\mu_1 = 2$ and $\mu_2 = 18$.

Our neural network may be diagrammed as seen in Figure 4. Note that the x_1 and x_2 are the input values as well as the network weights. Given an initial input/weight vector (x_1^0, x_2^0) and a learning parameter ν, the network will search for the value (x_1^*, x_2^*) which minimizes $g(x_1, x_2)$ by iteratively updating the set of weights. The updating equations are given by

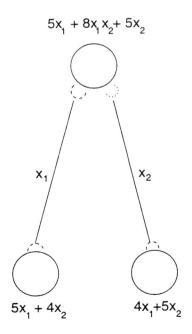

FIGURE 4   Example neural network.

$$\begin{pmatrix} x_1^{(l+1)} \\ x_2^{(l+1)} \end{pmatrix} = \begin{pmatrix} x_1^l \\ x_2^l \end{pmatrix} - \eta \left(\begin{array}{c} \dfrac{\partial g((x_1, x_2))}{\partial x_1} \\[2mm] \dfrac{\partial g((x_1, x_2))}{\partial x_2} \end{array} \right)_{(x_1^l, x_2^l)}$$

$$= \begin{pmatrix} x_1^l \\ x_2^l \end{pmatrix} - \eta \begin{pmatrix} 10x_1^l + 8x_2^l \\ 8x_1^l + 10x_2^l \end{pmatrix},$$

where $\left(x_1^l, x_2^l \right)$ denotes the value of (x_1, x_2) after the lth iteration and η is chosen such that

$$0 < 1 - \eta\mu_i < 1 \quad \text{for } i = 1, 2;$$

that is,

$$0 < 1 - \eta(2) < 1 \quad \text{and} \quad 0 < 1 - \eta(18) < 1 \Rightarrow 0 < \eta < \frac{1}{18}.$$

Note that

$$g(x_1, x_2) = 5x_1^2 + 8x_1 x_2 + 5x_2^2$$

$$= 5x_1^2 + 2\sqrt{5}\left(\frac{4}{\sqrt{5}} \right)x_1 x_2 + \frac{16}{5}x_2^2 + \left(5 - \frac{16}{5} \right)x_2^2$$

$$= \left(5x_1 + \frac{4}{\sqrt{5}}x_2 \right)^2 + \frac{9}{5}x_2^2$$

$$= \geq 0,$$

so $\left(x_1^*, x_2^* \right) = (0, 0)$. Hence, we wish to choose $\left(x_1^0, x_2^0 \right)$ as a value which lies within an open disk around $(0, 0)$.

Given that $g(x_1, x_2)$ has a positive-definite Hessian matrix, if we (1) choose η such that $0 < \eta < 1/18$, (2) choose $\left(x_1^0, x_2^0 \right)$ within an open disk around $(0, 0)$ and (3) update the network weights using the given formulas, then the above theory ensures that

$$\left(x_1^l, x_2^l \right) \to \left(x_1^*, x_2^* \right) \quad \text{as } l \to \infty.$$

Results

For our experiments, we chose three initial values for (x_1, x_2) and three values for η. The value $\eta = 0.2$ is outside of $(0, 1/18)$ and was chosen for comparison purposes. The program was written so that the algorithm was considered to have converged as soon as the updating values in the weight-updating equations dropped below a tolerance value. In other words, if τ denoted the tolerance value (supplied by the user), the program would stop when

$$10x_1^l + 8x_2^l < \tau \quad \text{and} \quad 8x_1^l + 10x_2^l < \tau.$$

Our experimental results are shown in Table 1. Note that n denotes the number of iterations for updating values to fall below tolerance (i.e., until the algorithm had reached desired convergence) and D denotes scientific notation (e.g., 8.05D-2 = 8.05×10^{-2}). No tolerance value was set for $\eta = 0.2$.

TABLE 1   Experimental Results

$\left(x_1^0, x_2^0\right)$	η	x_1^n	x_2^n	$g(x_1^n, x_2^n)$	τ	n
(1, 1)	0.05	9.99D-26	9.99D-26	1.8D-49	0.05D-5	<25
	0.10	2.037D-10	2.037D-10	7.47D-19	0.05D-5	<100
	0.20	3.14D + 41	3.14D + 41	1.778D + 84	—	<100
(2, −3)	0.05	6.64D-05	−6.64D-05	8.818D-09	0.05D-3	<100
	0.10	4.07D-10	−6.11D-10	7.05D-19	0.05D-6	<100
	0.20	−1.57D + 41	−1.57D + 41	4.44D + 83	—	<100
(−0.5, −1)	0.05	6.64D-06	−6.64D-06	8.81D-11	0.05D-4	<100
	0.10	−1.01D-10	−2.03D-10	4.25D-19	0.05D-6	<100
	0.20	−2.35D + 41	−2.35D + 41	1.00D + 84	—	<100

Our method did converge to the minimum function value for the given starting values and the values of η: $0 < \eta < 1/18$. Note that for $\eta = 0.20$, the algorithm diverged instead of converging to the minimum. This is consistent with the above theory.

Comments

1. At first glance, it may appear quite easy to find a function with a positive-definite Hessian matrix. However, many simple, "nice" functions do not have positive-definite Hessian matrices. For example, the function $f(x_1, x_2) = x_1^2 x_2^2$ has the Hessian matrix

$$\begin{bmatrix} 2x_2^2 & 4x_1x_2 \\ 4x_1x_2 & 2x_1^2 \end{bmatrix}$$

which is **not** positive definite. Note that with this function, it is not possible to chose a starting value $\left(x_1^0, x_2^0\right)$ which lies within an open disk of the minimum value. This is because when $x_1 = 0$ $(x_2 = 0)$, there are infinitely many values of x_2 (x_1) at which the function reaches its minimum. One must be careful when applying the above theory to any problem.

2. For a given starting value $\left(x_1^0, x_2^0\right)$, the method outlined above may still lead to the minimum value of a function $g(x)$ even when the learning parameter η does not meet the above specifications. Using the same function as above and a starting value of $\left(x_1^0, x_2^0\right) = (2, -2)$, we attained the results presented in Table 2. The algorithm converged when $\eta = 0.20$ even though this value is outside of our specifications. However, the algorithm is not guaranteed to converge for such values; only if η is chosen appropriately does the above theory guarantee convergence.

DISCUSSION

A relationship between the gradient descent technique and contractive maps has been derived. Noting that gradient descent is used in multilayer perceptron learning and the application of contractive maps gives rise to fractals, the above relationship is a connec-

TABLE 2   Example with η Outside Specifications

$\left(x_1^0, x_2^0\right)$	η	x_1^n	x_2^n	$g(x_1^n, x_2^n)$	τ	n
(2, −2)	0.05	5.31D-05	−5.31D-05	5.644D-09	0.05D-3	<100
	0.10	4.07D-10	−4.07D-10	3.319D-19	0.05D-7	<100
	0.20	1.306D-22	−1.306D-22	3.414D-44	0.05D-20	<100

tion between MLPs and fractals. Given the amount of research and attention being devoted to both neural networks and fractals, we hope that this connection will attract the attention of researchers and lead to advancements in both subjects.

Now that a connection has been made between these two subjects, this connection can be examined with future research. The similarity between gradient descent and fractal generation may lead to improvements in the gradient descent algorithm (hence enhancing MLP performance), as well as improvements in other optimization algorithms which use iterative techniques [such as genetic algorithms (52)].

The utility of Theorem 4.2 in modifying the connection weights for real-life problems needs to be explored. We would also like to examine what Theorem 4.2 can tell us about the selection of MLP parameters such as η (to avoid oscillation or divergence) and how recent advances in Hessian computation may ease implementation.

REFERENCES

1. D. Rumelhart, B. Widrow, and M. Lehr, "The Basic Ideas in Neural Networks," *Commun. ACM*, *37*, 87–92 (1994).
2. P. Antognetti and V. Milutinovic (eds.), *Neural Networks: Concepts, Applications and Implementations*, Prentice-Hall, Englewood Cliffs, NJ, 1991, Vols. 1–4.
3. D. E. Rumelhart and J. L. McClelland (eds.), *Parallel Distributed Processing: Explorations in the Microstructure of Cognition*, MIT Press, Cambridge, MA, 1986, Vol. I.
4. M. F. Barnsley, *Fractals Everywhere*, Academic Press, New York, 1993.
5. C. M. Bishop, *Neural Networks for Pattern Recognition*, Oxford University Press, Oxford, 1995.
6. M. Jordan and C. Bishop, "Neural Networks," *ACM Computing Surveys*, *28*, 73–75 (1996).
7. C. Stergiou and D. Siganos, "Neural Networks," http://www-dse.doc.ic.ac.uk/~nd/surprise_96/journal/vol4/cs11/report.html # References (1997).
8. W. McCulloch and W. Pitts, "A Logical Calculus of the Ideas Imminent in Nervous Activity," *Bull. Math. Biophys.*, *5*, 115–133 (1943).
9. D. Hebb, *The Organization of Behavior*, John Wiley & Sons, New York, 1949.
10. M. Minsky and S. Papert, *Perceptrons*, MIT Press, Cambridge, MA, 1969.
11. F. Rosenblatt, "The Perceptron: A Probabilistic Model for Information Storage and Organization in the Brain," *Psychol. Rev.*, *65*, 386–408 (1958).
12. O. Selfridge, "Pattern Recognition in Modern Computers," in *Proceedings of the Western Joint Computer Conference*, ACM, New York, 1955.
13. J. Hopfield, "Neural Networks and Physical Systems with Emergent Collective Computational Abilities," *Proc. Nat. Acad. Sci. USA*, *79*, 2554–2558 (1982).
14. M. Cohen and S. Grossberg, "Absolute Stability of Global Pattern Formation and Parallel Memory Storage by Competitive Neural Networks," *IEEE Trans. Syst., Man Cybern.*, *13*, 815–826 (1983).

15. G. Hinton, T. Sejnowski, and D. Ackley, "Boltzmann Machines: Constraint Satisfaction Networks That Learn," Carnegie Mellon University Technical Report CMU-CS-84-119, Carnegie Mellon University, Pittsburgh, PA (1984).

16. B. Widrow and M. E. Hoff, "Adaptive Switching Circuits," in *Institute of Radio Engineers, Western Electronic Show and Convention, Convention Record, Part 4*, Institute of Radio Engineers, 1960, pp. 96–104.

17. P. Werbos, "Beyond Regression: New Tools for Prediction and Analysis in the Behavioral Sciences," Doctoral dissertation, Applied Mathematics, Harvard University (1974).

18. R. Hecht-Nielsen, "Kolmogorov's Mapping Neural Network Existence Theorem," in *Proceedings of the International Conference on Neural Networks*, IEEE Press, New York, 1987, Vol. III, pp. 11–13.

19. K. Hornik, M. Stinchcombe, and H. White, "Multilayer Feedforward Networks Are Universal Approximators," *Neural Networks*, 2, 359–366 (1989).

20. A. Kolmogorov, "On the Representation of Continuous Functions of Many Variables by Superposition of Continuous Functions of One Variable and Addition," *Dokl. Akad. Nauk SSSR*, *108*, 179–182 (1956) (in Russian).

21. H. Robbins and S. Monro, "A Stochastic Approximation Method," *Ann. Math. Statist.*, 22, 400–407 (1951).

22. D. Rumelhart and J. McClelland, *Parallel Distributed Processing: Explorations in the Microstructure of Cognition*, MIT Press, Cambridge, MA, 1986, Vols. 1 and 2.

23. A. Weigund, D. Rumelhart, and B. Hubberman, "Generalization by Weight-Elimination with Applications to Forecasting," in *Advances in Neural Information Processing*, J. Lippman and D. Touretsky (eds.), Morgan Kaufman, San Mateo, CA, 1991, Vol. 3, pp. 875–882.

24. B. Curry and D. Rumelhart, "MSNET: A Neural Network That Classifies Mass Spectra," HPL Technical Report 90-161, MPL (1990).

25. F. Pineda, "Recurrent Backpropagation and the Dynamical Approach to Adaptive Neural Computation," *Neural Computat.*, *1*, 161–172 (1989).

26. R. Williams and D. Zipser, "A Learning Algorithm for Continually Running Fully Recurrent Neural Networks," *Neural Computat.*, *1*, 270–280 (1989).

27. M. Hirsch, "Dynamical Systems Review," tutorial presented at IEEE International Conference on Neural Networks, (1988); material available from IEEE Press, New York.

28. R. Hecht-Nielsen, *Neurocomputing*, Addison-Wesley, Reading, MA, 1990.

29. H. White, "Learning in Artificial Neural Networks: A Statistical Perspective," *Neural Computat.*, *1*, 425–464 (1989).

30. L. Ricotti, S. Ragazzini, and G. Martinelli, "Learning of Word Stress in a Sub-optimal Second Order Back-propagation Neural Network," in *Proceedings of the International Conference on Neural Networks*, IEE Press, New York, 1988, Vol. I, pp. 355–361.

31. R. Watrous, "Learning Algorithms for Connectionist Networks: Applied Gradient Methods of Nonlinear Optimization," in *Proceedings of the International Conference on Neural Networks*, IEEE Press, New York, 1987, pp. 619–627.

32. L. Malferrari, R. Serra, and G. Valastro, "Using Neural Networks for Signal Analysis in Oil Well Drilling," in *Proceedings of the Third Italian Workshop on Parallel Architecture Neural Networks*, World Scientific, Singapore, 1990.

33. G. Drago and S. Ridella, "An Optimum Weights Initialization for Improving Scaling Relationships in BP Learning," in *Proceedings of the International Conference on Artificial Neural Networks* (*ICANN-91*), 1991, pp. 1519–1522.

34. P. Williams, "A Morquordt Algorithm for Choosing the Step-Size in Back-propagation Learning with Conjugate Gradients," Preprint of the School of Cognitive and Computing Sciences, University of Sussex (February 13, 1991).

35. R. Battiti, "First- and Second-Order Methods for Learning: Between Steepest Descent and Newton's Method," *Neural Computat.*, *4*, 141–166 (1992).

36. F. Silva and L. Almeda, "Accelerating Backpropagation," in *Advanced Neural Computers*, R. Eckmiller, (ed.), Elsevier/North-Holland, Amsterdam, 1990.

37. M. Barnsley and L. Hurd, *Fractal Image Compression*, A. K. Peters, Wellesley, MA, 1993.

38. S. Balkin "Fractal and Chaotic Time Series Analysis," lecture notes presentation of August 5, Department of Statistics, the Pennsylvania State University (1996).

39. T. Bedford, F. Dekking, and M. Keane, "Fractal Image Coding Techniques and Contraction Operators," *Nieuw Archief Wiskunde*, 4, 185–217 (1992).

40. S. Chatterjee and M. Yilmaz, "Chaos, Fractals and Statistics," *Statist. Sci.*, 7, 49–68 (1992).

41. E. Vrscay, "A Hitchhiker's Guide to 'Fractal-Based' Function Approximation and Image Compression: Part 1," *Math Ties: Faculty of Mathematics Alumni News*, 10, 10–13, (1995); http://links.uwaterloo.ca/hitchiker.html

42. E. Vrscay, "A Hitchhiker's Guide to 'Fractal-Based' Function Approximation and Image Compression: Part 2," *Math Ties: Faculty of Mathematics Alumni News*, 10 (1995); http://links.uwaterloo.ca/hitchiker.html

43. B. Mandelbrot, *The Fractal Geometry of Nature*, W. H. Freeman, San Francisco, 1982.

44. D. Martin, "Fract-Ed from EALSoft: The Fract-Ed Information Pages," http://www.ealnet.com/ealsort/fracted.htm (1997).

45. E. Gröller, "Modeling and Rendering of Nonlinear Iterated Function Systems," Technical Report TR-186-2-94-12, Technical University Vienna, Institute for Computer Graphics (1998).

46. M. F. Barnsley and S. Demko, "Iterated Function Systems and the Global Construction of Fractals," *Proc. Roy. Soc. London, Series A*, 399, 243–275 (1985).

47. Y. Fisher, *Fractal Image Compression, Theory and Application*, Springer-Verlag, New York, 1995.

48. T. M. Apostol, *Mathematical Analysis*, Narosa Publishing House, Bombay, 1992.

49. J. E. Marsden and A. J. Tromba, *Vector Calculus*, W. H. Freeman and Company, New York, 1988.

50. C. M. Bishop, "Exact Calculation of the Hessian Matrix for the Multilayer Perceptron," *Neural Computat.*, 4, 494–501 (1992).

51. J. Wille, "On the Structure of the Hessian Matrix in Feedforward Networks and Second Derivative Methods," in *Proceedings of the ICNN*, 1997, pp. 1851–1855.

52. Z. Michalewicz, *Genetic Algorithms + Data Structures = Evolution Programs*, 3rd rev. and Extended Ed., Springer-Verlag, New York, 1996.

JENNIFER PITTMAN

MULTIMEDIA ABSTRACT MACHINE

INTRODUCTION

Multimedia technology changes the way humans interact with computers. With the technology improvements of audio/video hardware and large-capacity storage devices, the market price of a Multimedia Personal Computer (MPC) became reasonable. MPCs are widely accepted by the industrial world, business corporations, schools, government agents, and individuals. Most of the applications of MPCs include video conferencing systems, video-on-demand systems, news-on-demand systems, WWW software, and multimedia presentations. Among these applications, the needs of multimedia presentations, including most CD-ROM titles such as educational and entertainment software. Many authoring software were available for various spectra of users, from nonprogrammers to experienced software engineers, to produce quality multimedia presentations. Most of these authoring software systems are built with a friendly mechanism and a graphical user interface to assist the presentation designer in designing presentations. However, these presentations usually communicate with the audiences in a single direction manner; that is, most presentations do not consider user interactions as part of the presentation consequence. Even these presentations allow the user to select different navigation sequences as different demonstrations—all audiences still watch the same presentation every time. If a multimedia presentation can absorb user interactions as part of the presentation software, the presentation can learn from the audience; thus, the improved presentation can demonstrate a more suitable topic for the audiences.

The development of a multimedia presentation involves the analysis of a presentation script, the collection of multimedia resources, and the realization of a presentation's schedule/layout, as well as its navigation control flows. These presentation components (i.e., resources, layouts, navigation, etc.) are all predefined (i.e., static) by the designer. We aim to develop a system that allows these components to be changed by the presentation program at the run time. Therefore, the resulting presentation is dynamic. To create a dynamic presentation, we need an object composition mechanism which allows the designer to compose presentation windows from pictures, video clips, sound files, push buttons, navigation messages, and other parts. A dynamic multimedia-type system is thus essential for its use. We have developed such a type system and a dynamic script language for this purpose.

This is a research project integrating a number of multimedia systems that we have developed, with newly proposed underlying software architecture. The system is based on a timed Petri-net computation model, which runs pseudoassembly programs. We aim to provide a programming language and compilation techniques, which enable applications to be run under an abstract machine. Figure 1 illustrates the global view of our integrated system. We have developed an intelligent multimedia presentation system (IMMPS) (1–4) and a presentation automatic scheduling system (PreGen) (5,6). In this

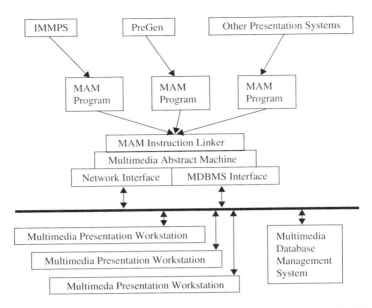

FIGURE 1   The environment of a multimedia abstract machine (MAM).

article, we present a concept of the specifications of multimedia applications, with a proposed spectrum of multimedia functionalities. The proposed language and our previous systems use pseudoassembly instructions, which are run under the Petri machine. The abstract machine is connected to an infrastructure of a local area network. Using a multimedia database system that we have proposed earlier (7), the machine accesses multimedia resources on the fly and multimedia demonstrations are broadcasted through the network to a number of workstations.

There are a number of systems related to multimedia presentations. Sony Corporation developed a hypermedia prototype system (SAL) (8) for multimedia authoring, which is based on a link and node model used in most authoring systems. The Layered Multimedia Data Model (LMDM) (9) allows the reuse of presentation templates, which are important for improving the efficiency of multimedia presentation designs. LMDM has a number of strengths, including the support of a general model of media synchronization, limited system dependencies, and the generalization of a traditional animation model. The work discussed in Ref. 10 proposes an architecture and data model for integrated multimedia presentations. The architecture provides a homogeneous strategy to access, process, and exchange multimedia documents generated by different authoring and presentation systems. Diamond (11) is a multimedia message system built on a distributed architecture for creating, editing, transmitting, and managing multimedia documents. Multimedia documents are stored in folders in a distributed database. An open hypermedia system is discussed in Ref. 12. The system supports heterogeneous multimedia data types and allows new types to be added. A platform-independent multimedia presentation composition system is discussed in Ref. 13. In the system, a script-based approach is used to model the object-oriented presentations as well as user interactions. We also looked at some well-known commercial products related to multimedia authoring or presentation designs, including Authorware Professional, Multimedia Toolbook, Action!, Multimedia Viewer, and Hypermedia Authoring and Playback System (by ITRI, Taiwan). None of the above systems, however, allows dynamic presentations; that is, a presentation generated by the above systems will stay in the form in it was created. Different audiences watch the same presentation over and over again. If a presentation can take user interactions and mutate itself, the presentation is more diversified: This is the main strength of our system.

This article is organized as the following. In the next section, the specification of a multimedia presentation, including five parts, is discussed. The third section describes the architecture of a multimedia abstract machine (MAM). The section also includes a new mechanism of multimedia presentation designs to overcome the drawbacks of some commercial authoring software. In this section, a type system to compose presentations from multimedia objects is addressed, a multimedia presentation script language is introduced, and a discussion of multimedia resource attributes is presented. The instruction set of MAM is briefly addressed in the fourth section. The fifth section is the discussion of the system interface and some algorithms. A short conclusion summarizes our contributions.

MULTIMEDIA PRESENTATION SPECIFICATIONS

A multimedia presentation, whether run on a stand-alone machine or across a multimedia network, has an environmental specification which describes the hardware/software configuration requirements that supports the presentation. The multimedia presentation also needs a resource specification, which describes what multimedia resources are to be used for demonstration. Also, the schedule and the layout of the multimedia presentation need to be decided before the presentation is put to use. An interactive presentation also needs a navigation specification, which describes the presentation flow. Conclusively, a multimedia presentation consists of the following five parts:

- **Environmental specification**: contains the necessary information describing the running environment of the presentation
- **Resource specification**: describes the amount of resources used in the presentation
- **Temporal specification**: provides the timing information for the presentation schedule
- **Spatial specification**: contains the layout of the presentation
- **Navigation specification**: states the presentation flow and controls possible user interactions

A multimedia language, whether specified visually or in text, should include the above components. The following is an example of such a specification:

Environmental Specification
The exact format of each representation is decided by an individual multimedia application. However, in general, the format should meet the requirement of the underlying supporting windowing system.

```
Author_Name = "ASCII_Text"
Copyright = "ASCII_Text"
Application_Software = "ASCII_Text"
Application_Directory = "ASCII_Text"

Screen_Resolution = (Integer, Integer)
Sound_Card_Specification = "ASCII_Text"
MPEG_Specification = "ASCII_Text"
CD_ROM_Specification = "ASCII_Text"
Pre-installed_Font_Specification = "ASCII_TEXT"
Graphic_Supporting_Drivers = "ASCII_Text"
MIDI_Sequencer = "ASCII_Text"
```

Resource Specification

Each variable describes a multimedia resource. The variables can be assigned to a value, which represents a location of the resource, the type of the resource, and other attributes of the resource. These variables are used in the run time while the multimedia application is presented.

```
Declare State Variable
    STRING        user_salary
    NUMBER        user_name
Declare Resource
    TEXT          title_text
    PICTURE       my_friend
    SOUND         explain
    MIDI          background_music
    VIDEO         tour_video
    ANIMATION     fast_train
```

Spatial Specification

Spatial specification contains area variables, which describe the location and size of a multimedia resource.

```
Declare Layout
    AREA   tour_video_dur, fast_train_dur
    AREA   title_text_area, my_friend_area
    AREA   ...
```

Temporal Specification

The temporal behavior of multimedia resources is declared by the temporal specification. It is necessary to have some operations or functions to provide such a temporal definition:

Operators and Functions

silent	_10 or _oo	keep silent for 10 time units, or forever
extension	r~10 or r~oo	extend for 10 time units or forever
truncate	r10! or !10 r	truncate for 10 time units at the beginning or at the end
concurrent	$(r1), $(r1, r2), or $(r1, r2, r3), etc.	concurrent events

| sequential | -(r1), -(r1, r2), or -(r1, r2, r3), etc. | sequential events |
| identical | #(r1), #(r1, r2), or #(r1, r2, r3), etc. | overlapped events |

A Specification Example

```
$(WallPaper,
  -($(-($(History, Explain), Tour), General), $(Map, Shopping)),
  -(Music1, Music2))
```

Navigation Specification

Navigation is controlled by message passing. In general, a multimedia presentation machine maintains a loop, which receives messages and performs actions until a close message is requested. The following is a sample section of multimedia presentation navigation.

```
Declare Activity
Start Up
  set user_name = "Timothy K. Shih"
  set title_text = "title.txt"
  set my_friend = "teresa.bmp"
  set explain = "explain.wav"
  set background_music = "sarasate.mid"
  set tour_video = "tour.avi"
  set fast_train = "train.fli"
  m1 = "open_next(next_frame, user_name)"
  m2 = "max_frame(this_frame)"
  m3 = "close_frame(this_frame)"
  explain_tour = [0, 30] /* start_time and video_length */
  title_text_dur = [0, 0, 500, 600] /* X1, Y1, X2, and Y2 */
  attach title_text_area to title_text
  play title_text


Loop
  on message open_frame(PAR1, PAR2, ...) perform {
    set user_name = "Mickey Mouse"
    set title_text = "mickey.txt"
    play title_text
    attach explain_dur to explain
    play fast_train
    ...
    send m3
  }

  on message open_frame(PAR1, PART, ...) perform {
    ...
  }


Close Up
  send m3
```

THE ARCHITECTURE OF MAM

The Petri net (14) has been used as a graph-based and mathematical tool for modeling concurrent systems, communication, multimedia synchronization, and other information systems. Many tools for Petri nets were available on PCs and workstations. Petri nets are very suitable for modeling the synchronization of multimedia events. However, there is no specific Petri-net tool especially designed for multimedia computation. For example, different multimedia resources have different computation needs. To display a bit-mapped picture usually involves four steps: prepare for an image device, read the picture to memory buffer, copy the picture from buffer to video RAM, and clean up the device. These steps can be handled in a specific subnet (i.e., the picture subnet). In our system, we have four subnets for different types of multimedia resource that are commonly used in multimedia presentations: picture, sound, animation, and video. In Figure 2, a multimedia Petri net and a video subnet are shown. The Petri net is used to model a presentation schedule and the subnet is used to run a video clip. In the video subnet, the image buffer and sound buffer are filled with data. Moving data to the video RAM and sound card is synchronized, in order to achieve lip synchronization. These two steps are repeated until a video clip is finished. This video subnet can be represented by a section of the pseudoassembly program. We also modified the timed Petri net to include an interrupt arc, which allows the execution to be suspended, stopped, or resumed. The interrupt arc can be specified by the interrupt instruction of our instruction set. Each place in our multimedia Petri net represents a multimedia resource demonstration. Each transition represents a synchronization point. We use a number of guard registers in our

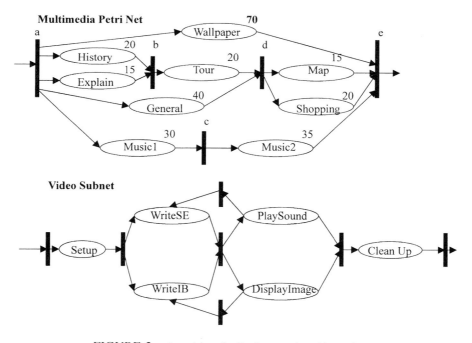

FIGURE 2   A multimedia Petri net and a video subnet.

machine to control synchronization. In this article, we briefly describe the components of the proposed abstract machine and a set of multimedia assembly instructions.

The main theme of our system is a timed-Petri-net-based MAM. The MAM is a software architecture and system for multimedia documentation demonstrations and interactions. We realized that most multimedia information processes consist of a sequence of atomic steps, such as opening a sound channel, transferring a block of video data from a buffer to the graphic memory page, closing a MIDI sequencer, and so forth. These atomic steps, from the perspective of multimedia computing, are nonseparable items. This concept is relatively similar to assembly language instructions, which are atomic steps of a procedural program. We have the MAM instruction set defined. Some instructions control multimedia hardware devices and others support user interactions. A multimedia presentation designed by using our multimedia DFD/CFD and Petri-net design tool has a number of Petri nets and navigation messages. These Petri nets are represented in a MAM assembly program, which is produced by an internal program translator. Therefore, the designed presentation can be run on the MAM. The system architecture for running multimedia applications will be presented from both software and hardware perspectives.

The development of MAM has multiple purposes. We have developed a multimedia script language. The language serves as an intermediate representation of various formats of multimedia presentations, which we have developed. These representations are compiled to the MAM instructions. Thus, it is possible to link multimedia presentations produced by different tools to make an integrated presentation. On the other side of the MAM is a multimedia database management system (MDBMS), which we integrated to the environment. The objective of this MDBMS, from the perspective of MAM, is to assist a presentation designer to quickly locate the multimedia resources required in the demonstration.

When a typical multimedia presentation is designed, the use of resources, the layout, and the navigation sequences are all fixed until the presentation is redesigned by the presenter. However, the audiences may have different learning speeds and backgrounds. We want to overcome the traditional presentation approach by allowing dynamic replacement of resources, layouts, and controls of the presentation. This gives the presentation generator have the ability to compute the next-step presentation at the run time. Possible dynamic changes include the following:

- Asserting/retracting of information (changing state variables)
- Changing the usages of multimedia resources (changing resource variables)
- Changing the presentation layout (changing layout variables)
- Changing the navigation controls (changing message variables)

A multimedia presentation script language (MScript) is designed for the realization of dynamic presentations. In this section, we start from the discussion of a multimedia type system that includes a number of type constructors allowing the composition of multimedia objects. Then, we address the script language that reveals various components of a multimedia presentation. A number of statements and actions that a multimedia presentation can act are then explained. The last subsection describes a number of multimedia resource attributes that help a user to select usable resources.

A Multimedia Type System

Multimedia presentations are collections of multimedia objects. These objects include sound files, video clips, buttons, or messages. Each multimedia object is associated with a type. A multimedia resource has a type, which describes what device needs to be used to present the resource. For instance, a sound resource file needs a sound card as its software driver. To ensure that the objects in the database are using the correct devices, type checking is necessary. Thus, we need a type hierarchy and type inference rules. The following is a type hierarchy used in our system:

> Composed Types
>   Collection
>   Structure
>   Union
> MMResource (Generic Type)
>   MMStatic (Generic Type)
>   Text
>   Picture
>   MMDynamic (Generic Type)
>   Sound
>   MIDI
>   Video
>   Animation
>   MMControl (Generic Type)
>   Data
>   Selection
>   MMAnnotation
>   Duration
>   Area
>   Message

In the hierarchy, MMResource is a generic type, which could be projected into either MMStatic or MMDynamic. These two types reveal the static and dynamic nature of basic type objects. An object of a basic type, such as MIDI, requires a specific hardware/software carrier to have the object presented correctly. Each basic type can have one or more type instances. Type instances of the same basic type can be converted to each other implicitly to meet the underlying hardware/software requirements of a presentation station. For instance, a picture of instance type "bmp" can be converted to a "gif" file if the presentation station can only display a GIF picture file. A resource object, when used in a presentation, must be deduced to fit a type instance. Each resource used in a presentation needs to be decorated with two annotations: the duration variable and the area variable. These two types of variable specify the temporal and spatial properties of that presentation resource. Annotation declarations are achieved via the attach action. To precisely define the type hierarchy, we use formal specification to declare the multimedia type system. The "==" sign denotes an abbreviation; that is, the symbol to the left of "==" is defined to be the expression to the right. We treat a basic type as a set of type instances. The six basic resource types are thus declared by the following abbreviations:

> *TEXT == { txt; doc; wri }*
> *PICTURE == { bmp; pcx; gif; tif ; pic; jpg }*

$SOUND == \{ wav \}$
$MIDI == \{ mid \}$
$VIDEO == \{ avi; mpg; mov \}$
$ANIMATION == \{ fli; flc \}$

Other standard file formats are incorporated in a similar manner. Next, the type hierarchy of resources needs to be defined. A given type is similar to a system-predefined type, such as the integer or the float type, of the C language. Not that a given type allows some fundamental objects to be declared without precise specifications of their detailed representations. A given type, such as RESOURCE NAME (i.e., a resource variable name), is declared in between a pair of square brackets. Generic types of multimedia resources are also declared via abbreviations. Finally, a RESOURCE object is a Cartesian product representing a resource declaration:

$[RESOURCE\_NAME\ ]$
$MMSTATIC == TEXT \cup PICTURE$
$MMDYNAMIC == SOUND \cup MIDI \cup VIDEO \cup ANIMATION$
$MMRESOURCE == MMSTATIC \cup MMYDNAMIC$
$RESOURCE\_TYPE == TEXT \cup PICTURE \cup SOUND \cup MIDI \cup VIDEO \cup$
$\qquad\qquad ANIMATION \cup MMSTATIC \cup MMDYNAMIC \cup MMRESOURCE$
$RESOURCE == RESOURCE\_TYPE * RESOURCE\_NAME$

Types are converted implicitly or explicitly. In general, a subtype can be converted implicitly to another type in an upper level of the type hierarchy (an upward coercion). Downward coercion occurs only if the type system can gather enough information of an object (e.g., the resource file format is detected). For instance, SOUND is converted to MMDYNAMIC, and TEXT is converted to MMSTATIC. We define a overloaded function, $\uparrow$, which performs an upward conversion. The following axiomatic definition specifies the $\uparrow$ function. An axiomatic definition is used to declare one or more global functions to be used in a formal specification:

$\uparrow\colon MMDYNAMIC \rightarrow MMRESOURCE$
$\uparrow\colon MMSTATIC \rightarrow MMRESOURCE$
$\uparrow\colon SOUND \rightarrow MMDYNAMIC$
$\uparrow\colon MIDI \rightarrow MMDYNAMIC$
$\uparrow\colon VIDEO \rightarrow MMDYNAMIC$
$\uparrow\colon ANIMATION \rightarrow MMDYNAMIC$
$\uparrow\colon TEXT \rightarrow MMSTATIC$
$\uparrow\colon PICTURE \rightarrow MMSTATIC$

Similarly, downward coercion is achieved by the $\downarrow$ function, which restricts a resource declaration to a more specific resource type:

$\downarrow\colon MMRESOURCE \rightarrow MMDYNAMIC$
$\downarrow\colon MMRESOURCE \rightarrow MMSTATIC$
$\downarrow\colon MMDYNAMIC \rightarrow SOUND$
$\downarrow\colon MMDYNAMIC \rightarrow MIDI$
$\downarrow\colon MMDYNAMIC \rightarrow VIDEO$
$\downarrow\colon MMDYNAMIC \rightarrow ANIMATION$
$\downarrow\colon MMSTATIC \rightarrow TEXT$
$\downarrow\colon MMSTATIC \rightarrow PICTURE$

In a multimedia presentation, a presentation window may use a number of multimedia resources. Thus, a presentation window has a composed type. Type composition is taken from two views: spatial type composition and temporal type composition. A spatial type describes the presentation layout with respect to a time slot. A temporal type, on the other hand, describes the presentation schedule with respect to an area on the screen. Three type constructors are used: collection, structure, and union. A collection constructor takes a number of objects of the same type and produces a composed type. For instance, a spatial collection constructor may take a number of text paragraphs and produce a text page, which is a collection of paragraphs. A temporal collection constructor may take, as input, a number of pictures and produce an animation, which is a collection of pictures. A structure constructor produces a composed type from a number of heterogenous objects. For instance, a spatial structure constructor takes a picture, a video, and a text paragraph and produces a presentation window. A temporal structure constructor may take two sound resources and a video and produce a presentation that presents those three resources sequentially. A union constructor also takes a number of heterogeneous objects. However, the composed type describes either an overlapped situation (for spatial composition) or a concurrent process (for temporal composition). For instance, a spatial union constructor takes a text resource and a picture resource and displays the text object on the top of the picture object as a text label. A temporal union constructor may take an animation and a MIDI resource and play them concurrently. We define the following functions for multimedia object compositions:

MakeSound : MIDI → SOUND
MakePicture : TEXT → PICTURE
MakeVideo : ANIMATION → VIDEO
Temporal_Collection_of : seq1 PICTURE → ANIMATION
Temporal_Collection_of : seq1 MIDI → MIDI
Temporal_Collection_of : seq1 SOUND → SOUND
Temporal_Union_of : seq1 MIDI → MIDI
Temporal_Union_of : seq1 SOUND → SOUND
*Temporal_Union_of : ANIMATION *Theta MIDI → VIDEO*
*Temporal_Union_of : ANIMATION *Theta SOUND → VIDEO*

Note that, seq1 X represents a nonempty sequence which contains objects of type X. In addition to multimedia resources, a multimedia presentation may also have push buttons, hot keys, menu selections, and data. The first three objects are for presentation navigation. The data object is to store presentation information either preassigned by the designer or entered by the presentation addressee. The following expressions define a SELECTION TYPE, which is a union of the three type instances. A SELECTION object is thus defined:

[SELECTION_NAME]
[BUTTON , KEY , MENU]
SELECTION_TYPE == BUTTON ∪ KEY ∪ MENU
*SELECTION == SELECTION_TYPE * SELECTION_NAME*

For a state variable holding presentation data, we allow two type instances: ASCII strings and numbers. A VAR object is defined in a similar manner:

[VAR NAME]
[NUMBER,STRING]
VAR_TYPE == NUMBER ∪ STRING
*VAR == VAR_TYPE * VAR_NAME*

Multimedia resources, navigation selections, and presentation information are stored in different kinds of variable. Each variable of a MScript program is declared with a type. The value of a variable may be mutated at the run time. In some situations, the value of a variable is undecided at the design time. In this case, a generic type is given to that variable. When the variable is bound to an object, an actual type is deduced. For instance, one can have a resource variable to store a text paragraph at a time spot and store a picture later. Thus, the variable is declared as a MMSTATIC object.

In addition to control elements, a multimedia presentation also has messages passed among presentation windows, as well as the schedule and layout of the window. These objects are declared as given types in our specification:

[MESSAGE , DURATION , AREA]

Note that these three object types are given with their internal representation omitted. In the implementation of a presentation, the representations will be considered. Therefore, the MMCONTROL and the MMANNOTATION types are declared as two abbreviations:

MMCONTROL == VAR ∪ SELECTION
MMANNOTATION == MESSAGE ∪ DURATION ∪AREA

After the multimedia type system and presentation components are defined, we use schemata to define a multimedia presentation. A schema denotes an object, an event, or a system the user wants to specify. Usually, a schema contains two parts: the variable declaration part and the axiom definition part. In the following schemata, we only use the first part:

PWin
pwin_name : PWIN_NAME
vars : P VAR
resources : P RESOURCE
selection : P SELECTION
start_section : seq ACTION
loop_section : seq1 MSG_STATEMENT
close_section : seq ACTION

Each presentation window (i.e., PWin) has a name, a number of data variables, resource variables, and selection variables. A PWin also contains three sections: start section, loop section, and close section. The start and close sections containing ACTION are executed only once when the presentation window is invoked or terminated. The loop section contains a number of message statements. Each statement contains a non-empty sequence of ACTIONs to be executed upon receiving the corresponding message. We also define the actions that can be used in our presentation language in the following abbreviations:

MSF_STATEMENT == MESSAGE → seq 1ACTION
ACTION ==

attach DURATION to RESOURCE_NAME V
attach AREA to RESOURCE_NAME V
attach MESSAGE to SELECTION_NAME V
set VAR_NAME = VALUE V
play RESOURCE_NAME V
send MESSAGE V
if COND then seq 1 ACTION else seq 1 ACTION V
if COND then seq 1 ACTION V
while COND perform seq 1 ACTION

Thus, a multimedia Presentation contains a set of presentation windows (i.e., PWins):

Presentation == P PWin

Programming in the MScript Language

An Mscript program is a collection of presentation window declarations. Each presentation window description consists of a number of divisions. Some divisions are written by the user in text windows; others may be generated by the graphical user interface. State variables are of type NUMBER or STRING, which holds a number or an ASCII string, respectively. For instance, a state variable declaration may look like

Declare State Variable
STRING user_salary
NUMBER user_name

These state variable declarations are held in the State Variable Dictionary of a presentation window. The declarations of multimedia resources are generated from the Resource Dictionary of a presentation window. Resources are selected via the resource browser of our system (7). The user is able to select suitable resources by issuing queries based on a number of multimedia resource attributes discussed in the subsection The Multimedia Resource Attributes. Each resource is given a name. For instance, the following is a resource declaration division:

Declare Resource
TEXT title_text
PICTURE my_friend
SOUND explain
MIDI background_music
VIDEO tour_video
ANIMATION fast_train

Each resource name is associated with a descriptor to a resource file on the disk. Resources are loaded when the presentation proceeds. Similarly, the declaration of presentation layout is generated from the information held in the Presentation Layout Window. These layout variables, similar to state variables, may be changed at run time:

Declare Layout
BUTTON next, back, start, stop
MENU new, open, save, print, exit
MESSAGE m1, m2, m3
DURATION explain_dur, background_music_dur

DURATION tour   ideo_dur, fast_train_dur
AREA title   ext_area, my_friend_area
AREA ...

The last division of an MScript program is the activity declaration division, which is programmed by the user in Script Program Window of a presentation window. Activities are divided into three groups: the start-up section, the loop section, and the close-up section. A start-up section or a close-up section is executed only once when the presentation window receives an open or a close message, respectively. A loop section repeats until a close message is received. The following is an example of activity declaration division:

```
Declare Activity
Start Up
set user_name = "Timothy K. Shih"
set title_text = "title.txt"
set my_friend = "teresa.bmp"
set explain - "explain.wav"
set background   usic = "sarasate.mid"
set tour_video = ◯qtour.avi"
set fast_train = "train.fli"
m1 = "open_next(next_frame, user_name)"
m2 = "max_frame(this_frame)"
m3 = "close_frame(this_frame)"
explain_tour = [0, 30] /* start_time and video_length */
title_text_dur = [0, 0, 500, 600] /* X1, Y1, X2, and Y2 */
attach title_text_area to title_text
play title_text
Loop
  on message open_frame(PAR1, PAR2, ...) perform {
  set user_name = "Mickey Mouse"
  set title_text = "mickey.txt"
  play title_text
  attach explain_dur to explain
  play fast_train
  ...
  send m3
  }
  on message open_frame(PAR1, PAR2, ...) perform {
  ...
  }
Close Loop
send m3
```

The MScript language has a number of statements and actions to control the navigation and demonstration of a multimedia presentation. In the next subsection, we address these statements and actions. Also, a number of type conversion functions are discussed.

Statements and Actions

The execution of presentation navigation is based on message passing. When a presentation window receives a message, a number of actions are performed sequentially. The on message statement receives a message with optimal parameters, except the first holding the name of the presentation window who should receive the message. The following is an example of the on message statement:

```
on message NAME(PWin, PAR1, PAR2, ...) perform
ACTION1
ACTION2
   }
```

We have defined a number of action statements, including the statements to change the execution states of a presentation, actions to control multimedia resources, and other control abstractions:

- Define the duration of a resource.
    Action syntax: attach DURATION_VAR to RESOURCE_VAR
- Define the layout of a resource.
    Action syntax: attach AREA_VAR to RESOURCE_VAR
- Define the message of a selection.
    Action syntax: attach MESSAGE_VAR to SELECTION_VAR
- Assign value to a variable.
    Action syntax: set DATA_VAR = VALUE
- Play a resource.
    Action syntax: play RESOURCE_VAR
- Send a message.
    Action syntax: send MESSAGE_VAR
- Conditional statement.
    Action syntax: if COND then ACTION1 else ACTION2
- Conditional statement.
    Action syntax: if COND then ACTION
- While statement.
    Action syntax: while COND perform {ACTION1, ACTION2, ...}

The attach action may provide a temporal or spatial specification to a resource. Thus, each resource is given a duration and area of display. The attach action may also attach a message to a selection. When the selection is fired, the associated message is sent. The set action assigns a value to a variable, which can be of an arbitrary type. The play and the send actions demonstrate a resource and send a message, respectively. We also have the if conditional statement and the while iterative statement, which are self-explanatory.

In addition to these actions, we also have a number of utilities. The following are functions for explicit type conversions:

- Sound <- Midi: converts a MIDI file to a sound file.
    Conversion function syntax:
    SOUND_VAR = MakeSound(MIDI_VAR)

- Picture <- Text: treats a text page as a picture.
  Conversion function syntax:
  PICTURE_VAR = MakePicture(TEXT_VAR)
- Video <- Animation: an animation is a silent video.
  Conversion function syntax:
  VIDEO<-AR = MakeVideo(ANIMATION_VAR)
- Animation <-Temporal Collection of Picture types: an animation consists of a number of pictures.
  Conversion function syntax:
  ANIMATION_VAR = Temporal_Collection_of(PICTURE_VAR1, PICTURE_VAR2, ...)
- Midi <-Temporal Collection of Midi types: concatenates two or more MIDI files yields another MIDI file.
  Conversion function syntax:
  MIDI_VAR = Temporal_Collection_of(MIDI_VAR1, MIDI_VAR2, ...)
- Sound <-Temporal Collection of Sound types: concatenates two or more sound file yielding another sound file.
  Conversion function syntax:
  SOUND_VAR = Temporal_Collection_of(SOUND_VAR1, SOUND_VAR2, ...)
- Midi <- Temporal Union of Midi types: mixes two or more MIDI files yielding another MIDI file.
  Conversion function syntax:
  MIDI <-AR = Temporal_Union_of(MIDI_VAR1, MIDI_VAR2, ...)
- Sound <- Temporal Union of Sound types: mixes two or more Sound files yielding another Sound file.
  Conversion function syntax:
  SOUND<-AR = Temporal_Union_of(SOUND_VAR1, SOUND_VAR2, ...)
- Video <- Temporal Union of Animation and Sound: a video file contains an animation and its background sound.
  Conversion function syntax:
  VIDEO_VAR = Temporal_Union_of(ANIMATION_VAR, SOUND_VAR)
- Video <- Temporal Union of Animation and Midi: a video file contains an animation and its background music.
  Conversion function syntax:
  VIDEO_VAR = Temporal_Union_of(ANIMATION_VAR, MIDI_VAR)

The Multimedia Resource Attributes

To make a good multimedia presentation, one has to use a set of multimedia resources. Multimedia resources are recorded or captured via camera, tape recorder, or video camera, converted to their digital formats, and saved on the disk. These resource files can be reused in different presentations. A resource is associated with a number of attributes. We consider the following attributes for multimedia resources:

- Name: a unique name of the resource
- Keyword: one or more keywords are used as the description of a multimedia resource; for instance, name of the city is a keyword of the bit-mapped picture of Paris.

- Usage: how the resource may be used (e.g., background, navigation, or focus)
- Medium: what multimedia device is needed to carry out this resource (e.g., hardware supports for sound, video, MPEG, or picture resources)
- Model: how the resource is presented (e.g., table, map, chart, or spoken language)
- Temporal endurance: how long the resource lasts in a presentation (e.g., 20 s or permanent)
- Synchronization tolerance: how a participant feels about the synchronization delay of a resource

For instance, a user usually expects an immediate response after pushing a button for the next page to text. However, the user might be able to tolerate a video playback being delayed for 2 s:

- Detectability: the intensity of the resource attracting a listener (e.g., high, medium, or low).
- Start-up delay: the time between sending a message and the presentation of the corresponding resource, especially when the resource is on a remote computer connected via network.
- Hardware limitation: what kind of hardware is essential for carrying out the resource (e.g., MPC level 1, level 2, level 3, or other limitations).
- Version: the version of this resource file.
- Date/time: the date and time this resource file was created.
- Resolution: the resolution of this resource file, specified by $X * Y$ (or $0 * 0$) screen units.
- Start/end time: for nonpermanent resources, the starting cycle and the ending cycle of the piece of video, sound, or other resource that can be used, especially as a presentation resource. A cycle can be a second, one-tenth of a second, or a frame number of a video/animation
- Resource descriptor: a logical descriptor to a physical resource data segment on the disk.

Because each resource has a number of attributes, it would be cumbersome to require each query searching for a resource to contain all of these attributes. Thus, we propose an intelligent mechanism to simplify a query. The system contains several inference rules. Each rule describes an if–then relation between two attributes. For example, the following are some of the rules used in our system:

```
If usage = focus then detectability = high
If model = illustration then medium = picture
If medium = picture then temporal endurance = permanent
If medium = MPEG then hardware limitation = MPEG_card
If model = map then medium = picture
If ... etc.
```

Some unspecified attributes can be deduced from others. Thus, a user does not need to specify all attributes of a resource when he/she is using a query to search for the resource.

Recently, data mining has became a hot research topic in the community of database systems. The existence of mutual dependence among the above multimedia attributes infers that it is possible to analyze these dependence and use data mining techniques to improve our system. For instance, we found that many presentation designers use a bit-mapped picture with a low detectability for background usage. A MIDI medium resource is usually used as background music. We are constructing an interactive database subsystem to collect the ways that presentation designers use our database. Therefore, the subsystem may later on suggests the user to use a good resource.

THE MAM INSTRUCTION SET

The MAM has a set of pseudoassembly instructions. The concept of pseudoassembly is that each instruction is a nonseparable step in running a multimedia application, which is similar to an assembly instruction serving as a atomic step in running a C program. However, multimedia pseudoinstructions are in a relatively higher level. The MAM also has some components. Conceptually, MAM uses a dual-bus architecture. Image and audio data are separated. The multimedia Petri net of MAM is controlled by a number of guard registers. A guard register serves as a switch-controlling multimedia synchronization. An instruction is executed only if all of its guarding registers are clear. After the execution, the instruction should release guard registers. This concept is similar to the blocking places in the timed Petri nets. The MAM has the following hardware components:

- Guard register array: G(n) is a collection of guard registers.
- Sound buffer array: SB(n) contains a number of cache buffers for sound data.
- Image buffer array: IB(n) contains a number of cache buffers for image data.
- Sound buffer index register: SBI is an index to SB(n).
- Image buffer index register: IBI is an index to IB(n).
- Sound channel status register array: SCS(n) controls the use of a number of sound channels.
- Image channel status register array: ICS(n) controls the use of a number of image channels.
- Sound channel index register: SCI is an index to SCS(n).
- Image channel index register: ICI is an index to ICS(n).
- Resource designator register: RD is a register holding a pointer to a multimedia resource.
- Device designator register: DD is a register holding a pointer to a multimedia device.
- File handler register array: FH(n) is a set of registers holding pointers to multimedia files.
- File handler index register: FHI is an index to FH(n).
- I/O status register: IOS controls the input/output status.

The set of instructions are divided into the following categories, with some instructions explained:

- **Instructions for user interactions and interrupts:** includes start, restart, stop, pause, resume, skip, reverse, mutate, and exception instructions. These instructions are to support interactive multimedia applications.
- **Instructions for network controls:** includes lock, unlock, remote copy, and others. These instructions are to control network activities.

- **Instructions for I/O, presenting resources, and timing controls:** includes the following instructions:

  - SetRD R, [Gi's], [Go's]: set resource designator register RD according to resource R. A resource could be a file name or a database descriptor.
  - Set DD D, [Gi's], [Go's]: set device designator register DD according to designator D. A designator could be a Windows 95 DC for image or video, or a sound channel.
  - GetFHI [Gi's], [Go's]: get available file handler. FHI is set to the available file handler, or set to 0 if no available handler is found.
  - PrepRes [Gi's], [Go's]: prepare presentation resource according to the designator specified in RD register, set FH(n) register and IOS register. This step is similar to opening a resource file.
  - GetSCI [Gi's], [Go's]: get available sound channel. SCI points to the available channel, or set to 0 if no available channel is found.
  - GetICI [Gi's], [Go's]: get available image channel. ICI points to the available channel, or set to 0 if no available channel is found.
  - GetSBI [Gi's], [Go's]: get available sound buffer. SBI points to the available buffer, or set to 0 if no available buffer is found.
  - PrepSC n, [Gi's], [Go's]: prepare the nth sound channel, set sound channel status register r, or set to 0 if no available buffer is found.
  - GetIBI [Gi's], [Go's]: get available image buffer. IBI points to the available buffer, SCS(n).
  - PrepIC n, [Gi's], [Go's]: prepare the nth image channel, set image channel status register ICS(n).
  - WriteSB FH(m), SB(n), [Gi's], [Go's]: move data from disk pointed by FH(m) to sound buffer SB(n).
  - WriteIB FH(m), IB(n), [Gi's], [Go's]: move data from disk pointed by FH(m) to image buffer IB(n).
  - PlaySound SB(m), n, [Gi's], [Go's]: move data from SB(m) to the nth sound channel.
  - DisplayImage IB(m), n, [Gi's], [Go's]: move data from IB(m) to the nth image channel.
  - WWFC [Gi's], [Go's]: wait until wave function complete.
  - UnPrepSC n, [Gi's], [Go's]: unprepare the nth sound channel, set sound channel status register SCS(n).
  - UnPrepIC n, [Gi's], [Go's]: unprepare the nth image channel, set image channel status register ICS(n).
  - UnPrepRES [Gi's], [Go's]: unprepare presentation resource pointed by FH(n) register and set IOS register.
  - Sync [Gi's], [Go's]: synchronization instruction does nothing except blocking other instructions to achieve synchronization. This is similar to the concept of transition in a timed Petri net.

- **Instructions for control abstractions:** includes conditional and unconditional branch instruction, assignments, and others. Note that [Gi's] and [Go's] are incoming and outgoing guard registers. They are represented by lists of integers pointing to guard registers. The integers are assigned by a register relocation algorithm in the multimedia specification language compiler. Using the set of instructions, for example, the video subnet discussed in Figure 3 can be coded as follows:

```
SetRD "Tour.avi", [Gi's], [Go's]
GetFHI [Gi's], [Go's]
PrepRes [Gi's], [Go's]
GetSCI [Gi's], [Go's]
PrepSC SCI, [Gi's], [Go's]
GetICI [Gi's], [Go's]
PrepIC ICI, [Gi's], [Go's]
GetSBI [Gi's], [Go's]
GetIBI [Gi's], [Go's]
WriteSB FH(FHI), SB(SBI), [Gi's], [Go's]
PlaySound SB(SBI), SCI, [Gi's], [Go's]
WriteIB FH(FHI), IB(IBI), [Gi's], [Go's]
DisplayImage IB(IBI), ICI, [Gi's], [Go's]
UnPrepIC, ICI, [Gi's], [Go's]
UnPrepSC SCI, [Gi's], [Go's]
UnPrepRes [Gi's], [Go's]
```

ALGORITHMS FOR MAM SIMULATION

In this section, we present the graphical user interface of our proposed multimedia presentation system. Figure 3 shows the main window, which has a toolbox containing some ICONs. The ICONs in the left column allows the designer to create Multimedia Resource, Resource Data link, Dynamic Mutation, and External Entity, respectively. The ICONs in the right column are to create State Variable, Navigation Message, text label, and Presentation Window, respectively. We also have two push buttons below the toolbox, which allows the user to choose a DFD/CFD or Petri net diagram and to navigate to an upper level of the diagram. A presentation designer has to use a drag-and-drop mechanism, similar to that of a standard windowing system, to create, insert, or delete diagram components. Clicking on a Presentation Window circle brings up the next level refinement of that window. Clicking on other objects results in other design windows. We have text and selection windows allowing the editing of individual type of diagram components. These windows contain text boxes and push buttons, which allow the user to enter specific information of each component.

In Figure 4, the toolbox on the left of the main window is changed for Petri-net diagram designs. ICONs in the left column are to create User Transition, Sync Arc, Transition, Selection, and Condition, respectively. ICONs in the right columns are for Place, User arc, text label, and Assignment, respectively. The mechanism to create the diagram is similar to that in Figure 3. We also have a navigation message window. Messages with optional parameters are entered by the users.

The layout design window shown in Figure 5 is a little complicated. The ruler below a number of place names indicates that the presentation is divided into five states. In a multimedia presentation, the start or the end point of a multimedia resource makes a state change. The change of state usually changes the presentation layout. While in a state, the layout is fixed. Clicking on a transition or user transition brings up the presenta-

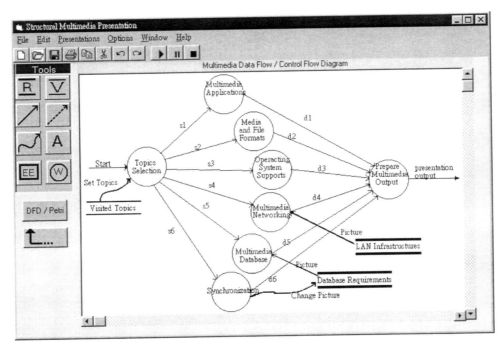

FIGURE 3   A structured multimedia presentation design tool.

tion layout starting from the transition. For example, clicking on the first transition in Figure 4 results in the layout design window in Figure 5. Presentation states are deduced from the propagation starting from a transition. Each presentation state is associated with a number of places (above the ruler). Clicking on a section of the ruler (representing the state) allows the designer to alter the location or size of objects of the state. However, Sound and MIDI objects do not have a layout. They are displayed as ICONs below the layout area. Each state in the ruler is given a number to indicate the number of executing cycles of the state.

In Figure 6, we show a multimedia resource browser. The browser is to help the designer select resources needed in a presentation. We use Microsoft Visual C^{++} (VC) and Visual Basic (VB) to implement our system. The graphical user interface is implemented in VB and the presentation running engine is implemented in VC with the supports from Media Control Interface (MCI) functions of Windows 95. In this section, we present algorithms of the presentation engine.

To run a presentation, its schedule must be decided first. Considering the Petri net with places and transitions shown in Figure 2, we want to construct a transition graph from the Petri net. Each place is associated with a number, which represents the duration of presenting a multimedia resource. Each transition has some incoming and outgoing arcs. We want to construct a transition graph such that the weighted edges represent places with durations and nodes represent transitions. From this transition graph, the schedule of presentation can be computed. However, the activation of a Petri net is due to receiving a navigation message. Therefore, a transition graph constructed with respect

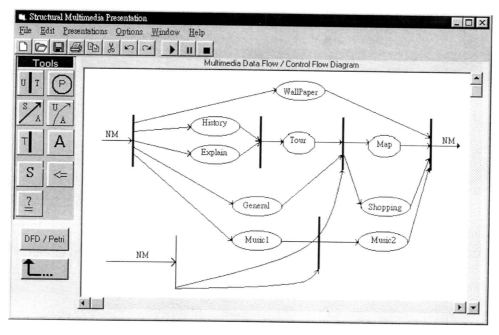

FIGURE 4   A multimedia Petri-net tool.

to the navigation message contains only those transitions (or nodes) reachable from the navigation message. Figure 7 shows such a graph corresponding to the Petri net shown in Figure 2, starting from transition "a." Note that in constructing the transition graph, a user arc has a weight equals to zero because a user transition causes the immediate firing of the corresponding transitions.

From the transition graph, the algorithm initials the node pointed by the message (i.e., node "a") to zero. Also, the nodes of the graph are sorted according to their topological order. Finally, the node time of each node is set to the maximum estimated time of all incoming edges of the node. An estimated time is computed from the node time of the source node and the duration of a multimedia resource. Algorithm Compute_ Node_Time presents the above process.

```
Algorithm: Compute_Node_Time
    Construct a Transition_Graph reachable from one of the starting
        Navigation_Messages
    Initial the node pointed by the Navigation_Message to Node_Time = 0
    Topological sort the Transition_Graph to a Transition_List
    For each node N in the Transition_List, except the first, do
        For each incoming edge, compute the
            Estimated_Time = Node_Time + Edge_Duration
        Set Node_Time of node N to the maximum of all
            Estimated_Time of incoming edges
```

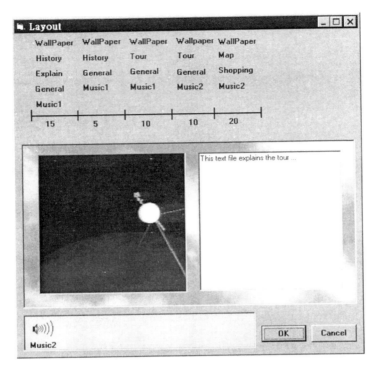

FIGURE 5   The layout design window.

From the transition shown in Figure 7, the algorithm computes a transition list with the node time of each transition:

```
Transition_List
    Node_Time(a) = 0
    Node_Time(b) = max{0+20, 0+15} = 20
    Node_Time(d) = max{20+20, 0+40} = 40
    Node_Time(c) = max{0+30} = 30
    Node_Time(e) = max{0+70, 40+15, 40+20, 30+35} = 70
```

The node time in the above transition list indicates the clock cycle in which a number of resources are to be demonstrated. The set of resources to be played with respect to a transition is collected from the outgoing sync arcs of the transition. For instance, the following sync sets are computed for the five transitions:

```
Syn_Sets:
    Sync_Set(a) = { WallPaper, History, Explain, General, Music1 }
    Sync_Set(b) = { Tour }
    Sync_Set(c) = { Music2 }
    Sync_Set(d) = { Map, Shopping }
    Sync_Set(e) = { }
```

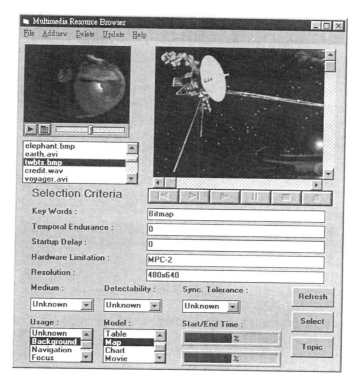

FIGURE 6   The Multimedia Resource Browser.

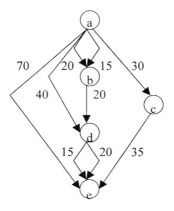

FIGURE 7   A transition graph reachable from a navigation message.

With the node time and sync sets, we know when and what resources to play, as shown in a presentation schedule chart in Figure 8.

The presentation engine is a concurrent program which is simulated by the multi-thread/multiprocess facility of Windows 98. The first process plays resources in the sorted transition list. The second process take cares in interrupt events, such as the receiving of another navigation message, as shown in algorithm Run_Petri_Net.

```
Algorithm: Run_Petri_Net
  For each node N in the Transition_List do
    Collect the Places pointed by Sync_Arcs from the Transition node N in
    Sync_Set(N)
  Sort the Transition_List according to Node_Time in a non-decreasing order
  CoBegin
    Process1:
      For each node N in the Transition_List do sequentially
        Play the resources in Sync_Set(N) at time Node_Time(N) concurrently
    Process2:
      LoopBegin
        If Process1 ends, then Process2 ends
        If there is a Navigation_Message of a User_Transition then
          Exits with the next starting Navigation_Message
        If there is a Selection, Assignment, or Condition then
          Perform the action accordingly
      LoopEnd
  Coend
```

Finally, algorithm Run_Presentation uses the above algorithms and serves as a presentation engine.

```
Algorithm: Run_Presentation
  LoopBegin
    If there is a starting Navigation_Message then
    Compute_Node_Time
```

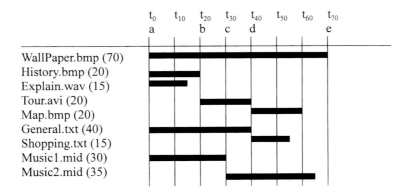

FIGURE 8   A presentation schedule.

```
        Run_Petri_Net
    else
        End Presentation
LoopEnd
```

SUMMARY

The MAM (15) is simulated under Microsoft Windows 95. Most instructions can be run. The most difficult part of implementing timing control instructions is to divide resources into chunks and to implement the necessary lower-level control. Our next research target is to implement the machine as hardware architecture. We believe that a dedicated machine should be built for multimedia computing. We also proposed a multimedia presentation script language for dynamic multimedia presentations. A presentation created in MScript allows the audience to change state variables, resources, layouts, and the navigation control sequences of the presentation. We use a simple recursive-descent parser to parse presentation programs. Our early experiences show that the MScript language is quite flexible in that many components of a presentation may be mutated at the run time. However, we are still working on the following issues in order to provide a better system for the designers:

- We are constructing a graphical user interface for the users to design presentations easily; for instance, the layout of the presentation should be drawn directly on the screen.
- So far, we rely on an event-based synchronization. We are looking at inter-stream-based synchronization mechanisms in order to allow the user to demonstrate multiple dynamic resources concurrently.

The system can be used for general-purpose presentations as well as education software, demonstrations, and others, With this system, we hope to bring the concept of dynamic multimedia presentations to the community of multimedia computing researchers.

REFERENCES

1. T. K. Shih, "An Artificial Intelligent Approach to Multimedia Authoring," in *Proceedings of the Second IASTED/ISMM International Conference on Distributed Multimedia Systems and Applications*, 1995, pp. 71–74.
2. T. K. Shih, "On Making a Better Interactive Multimedia Presentation," in *Proceedings of the International Conference on Multimedia Modeling*, 1995.
3. T. K. Shih, D.-A. Chiang, H.-C. Keh, and C.-C. Shis, "Formal Specification of Multimedia Authoring," in *Proceedings of the 1996 IEEE Workshop on Multimedia Software Development*, 1996.
4. T. K. Shih and R. E. Davis, "IMMPS: A Multimedia Presentation Design System," *IEEE Multimedia*, Summer 1997.
5. T. K. Shih, S. K. C. Lo, S.-J. Fu, and J. B. Chang, "Using Interval Temporal Logic and Inference Rules for the Automatic Generation of Multimedia Presentation," in *Proceedings of the IEEE International Conference on Multimedia Computing and Systems*, 1996, pp. 425–428.

6. T. K. Shih, L.-J. Hwang, and J.-Y. Tsai, "Formal Model of Temporal Properties Underlying Multimedia Presentations," in *Proceedings of the Third International Conference on Multimedia Modeling*, 1996.

7. T. K. Shih, C.-H. Kuo, and K.-S. An, "An Object-Oriented Database for Intelligent Multimedia Presentations," in *Proceedings of the IEEE International Conference on System, Man, and Cybernetics Information, Intelligence and Systems*, 1996.

8. A. Lundeberg, T. Yamamoto, and T. Usuki, "SAL, a Hypermedia Prototype System," in *Eurographic Seminars, Tutorials and Perspectives in Computer Graphics*, L. Kjelldahl (ed.), 1991.

9. G. A. Schloss and M. J. Wynblatt, "Presentation Layer Primitives for the Layered Multimedia Data Model," in *Proceedings of the IEEE 1995 International Conference on Multimedia Computing and Systems*, 1995, pp. 231–238.

10. H. Khalfallah and A. Karmouch, "An Architecture and a Data Model for Integrated Multimedia Documents and Presentational Applications," in *Multimedia Syst.*, *3*, 238–250 (1995).

11. R. H. Thomas and H. C. Forsdick, "Diamond: A Multimedia Message System Built on a Distributed Architecture," *IEEE Computer*, 65–78 (December 1985).

12. T. Kirsta and W. Hubner, "An Open Hypermedia System for Multimedia Applications," in *Eurographic Seminars, Tutorials and Perspectives in Computer Graphics*, L. Kjelldahl (ed.), 1991.

13. M. Vazirgiannis and C. Mourlas, "An Object-Oriented Model for Interactive Multimedia Presentations," *Computer J.*, *36*(1) (1993).

14. T. Murata, "Petri Nets: Properties, Analysis and Applications," *Proc. IEEE*, *77*(4) (1989).

15. T. K. Shih, C.-H. Kuo, Y.-H. Wang, Y.-S. Jeng, and Y.-C. Lin, "Structured Multimedia Presentation Designs," in *Proceedings of the ISCA 12th International Conference on Computers and Their Applications*, 1997.

16. J. M. Spivey, *Understanding Z: A Specification Language and Its Formal Semantics*, Cambridge Tracts in Theoretical Computer Science Vol. 3, Cambridge University Press, Cambridge, 1988.

17. J. M. Spivey, *The Z Notation: A Reference Manual*, International Series in Computer Science, Prentice-Hall, Englewood Cliffs, NJ, 1989.

TIMOTHY K. SHIH

ANTHONY Y. CHANG

JASON C. HUNG

PARALLEL COMPUTING

MOTIVATION FOR PARALLEL COMPUTING

The first ideas on parallel processors were published as early as the 1950s (1,2). Timid moves toward the first multiprocessor prototypes emerged at the end of that decade. In 1959, Sperry Rand built the *Larc* system consisting of three independent processors: one I/O processor and two general-purpose units. Built in the early 1960s, *ILLIAC IV* (3) already had the remarkable number of 64 processing elements operating in a SIMD mode (see the subsection Classification of Architectures). From there on, both numerous research prototypes and commercial systems have been designed and built. Today, parallel architectures represent a market segment ranging from large-scale supercomputers down to small desktop parallel systems.

Right from the beginning, the major incentive in parallel processing has been higher *performance*. Even the tremendous performance increase of monoprocessors (by a factor of 2 every year) has failed to satisfy the scientific user community. Larger and larger problems have been attacked; above all, numerical simulations (so-called Grand Challenge applications) in the fields of climate modeling, turbulent and viscous fluid dynamics, molecular dynamics, superconductor modeling, and VLSI design pushed technology toward billions and trillions of floating-point operations per second. Scientists and engineers have been interested in using improved models in order to gain results which approximate the corresponding natural phenomena as exactly as possible. Fortunately, these applications can be divided into multiple execution threads such that the calculations can be carried out on parallel machines. Thus, parallel computing has established a third pillar of science: the computational sciences.

However, raw computing power is not the only performance criterion. Other performance aspects that make parallel systems useful can be found in applications that have to meet real-time constraints and applications that are very data intensive (e.g., databases working with multiple disks in parallel), respectively.

Another motive with manifold practical applications have been *fault tolerance*. A key approach to enhancing availability in a system is to systematically avoid single points of failure (i.e., hardware or software components whose failure will bring down the entire system). This is achieved by increasing the number of corresponding components. Consequently, a multiprocessor with a suitable interconnection network and appropriate software will be able to carry on even if some of its components fail. Fault-tolerant parallel processing is not treated in this article (see Ref. 4).

An additional argument for parallel computing that has aroused controversy is *expressiveness*. Because the real world is parallel, parallel algorithms may be more natural to describe a problem solution and the derived parallel programs more expressive and easier to understand. Proponents of this thesis argue that many problems are inherently parallel and writing a sequential program to solve such problems boils down to artificially removing parallelism, whereas opponents point out the difficulties in parallel thinking and claim that parallel programming is always harder than sequential programming. Today, sequential programming is still the default, and parallel programming is considered to be an advanced topic. Whether and when this will change is an open issue.

BASIC CONCEPTS

Sequential, Concurrent, and Parallel Executions

The well-known *von Neumann computer* operates in a sequential manner. Data processing operations are executed one after another according to the *control flow* specified by the program. The *granularity* of the operations depends on the abstraction level under consideration: it can be a fine-grain machine instruction, a medium-grain assignment statement written in a high-level programming language, or a coarse-grain subroutine call, for example.

Control-flow principles can be modeled by (elementary) *Petri nets* (5). A Petri net consists of *places* that represent program states, *transitions* that correspond to data processing activities, and *links* that interconnect places and transitions. Places going to a transition are called its *input places*; those following a transition are called its *output places*. Places can contain *tokens*, which are markers for conditions. Finally, the dynamic behavior of a net is defined. A transition is called *fireable* if all its input places have at least one token; in this case, this transition can be *fired*, which causes a removal of a token from each input place and a placement of a token on each output place. Which of the fireable transitions really fires is defined by a control unit called a *demon*. To describe a sequential control flow, we restrict the net structure: Each transition has exactly one input and one output place and there is only a single token allowed which acts as a marker for the progress of a computation. In Figure 1a, the initial Petri net of a program consisting of a single loop is shown.

Corresponding to the sequential order of transitions at run time, such a program is called a *sequential process*. Two sequential processes are called *concurrent* if they can execute independently of each other. If there is at least one point in time where concurrent processes execute transitions simultaneously, they are called *parallel processes*. In order to model concurrency by a Petri net, a transition may have several input and output places. The change from sequential to concurrent program behavior (and the correspond-

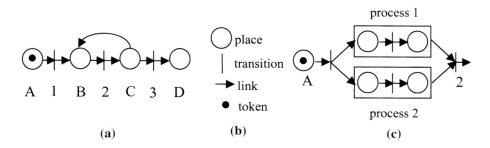

FIGURE 1   (a) Sequential process; (b) legend; (c) concurrent processes.

ing reverse step) is shown in Figure 1c. The firing of transition 1, called a *fork* operation, places a token on the first place of two independent net paths, called processes 1 and 2. Afterward, the two processes can progress independently until they both reach their final state. Next, transition 2, called a *join* operation, fires and the program continues in sequential mode.

Such a scenario of several independent concurrent/parallel processes is well known at the operating system level when jobs (defined by programs and corresponding data sets) are executed in a time-shared or parallel mode. Parallel processing, however, also deals with the more complicated (and interesting) case of *cooperating sequential processes*. Such processes interact, which requires the support of *communication* and *synchronization* activities. Communication is necessary in order to support data exchange and synchronization is necessary in order to specify control-flow restrictions for the sake of program correctness.

Communication

In general, cooperating activities must exchange data. Two fundamentally different communication techniques exist, using *shared variables* and *message passing*, respectively. In the first case, information is exchanged via memory which can be accessed by the communication partners. In the second case, messages and communication channels are used to transport information from the sending process to one or more receiving processes. Two variants of message passing exist: anonymous data exchange via channels (*process–channel model*) and direct data exchange by addressing the partner process (*sender–receiver model*).

A message consists of several entities: the actual information to be transmitted, the length of the message, information about the type of data, and the name of the receiver(s). In order to gain efficiency, data are collected in buffers and then sent as one packet. To achieve this, the sender composes the message in a send buffer and hands it over to the operating system by calling a send routine. The communication system delivers the message to the receiver(s). Each of the receivers takes over the information from its receive buffer by an explicit receive call.

We distinguish between *blocking* and *nonblocking* communication calls. When blocking routines are used, a sender process has to wait until the communication system has taken over the whole message; similarly, a receiver process has to wait until a message is written into its receive buffer. In a nonblocking communication mode, by contrast, processes immediately proceed after the corresponding call and later test whether the communication has been successfully completed. Nonblocking communication is more difficult to program but has more performance potential because of overlapping computation and communication.

Another classification feature is whether the communication system uses internal buffering or not. If buffering is not provided, the receiving process must take over the data immediately (*synchronous communication*). If not, the communication is called *asynchronous*.

Within the sender–receiver model, processes directly address a communication partner by its process identification (*point-to-point communication*). If several processes participate, the communication is called *collective*. Examples are the following:

- *Broadcast*: one process sends data to all the others
- *Multicast*: one process sends a message to some of the others

- *Gather*: information from other processes is collected by one of them
- *Scatter*: one process distributes data among others
- *Reduction* operations: global computations (e.g., calculations of the minimum, maximum, and sum) based on variables of other processes

Synchronization

In order to compute correct results, cooperating processes must synchronize their activities from time to time. Two types of synchronization are known:

- *Access control*: When some processes compete for a shared resource, the synchronization operation coordinates their access (e.g., it guarantees mutually exclusive access).
- *Sequence control*, also called *condition synchronization*: Processes can influence each other via blocking communication operations. Because processes usually execute with unpredictable speed, it is usually necessary to guarantee a certain order of communication events.

A frequent type of access control is the realization of *critical regions*. This means that for a given resource, concurrent access is forbidden and mutually exclusive access must be guaranteed. Corresponding techniques are well known from the operating systems literature (6–8): *locks, semaphores, critical regions*, and *monitors*. The shared resource can be data structures in common memory, but also other resources like I/O processors, buffers, and peripherals.

An example of sequence control is given in Figure 2a. Process 1 proceeds until place C. Transition 3 becomes fireable only when process 2 puts a token on place K. Afterward, process 1 can continue. Similarly, process 2 is blocked until a token is placed on place I. Such a process arrangement is called a *producer–consumer pattern*. If the communication is based on shared variables, the role of place I can be realized by a shared Boolean variable. This variable is called *spin lock* because process 2 is continuously testing this variable for a certain value which will be written by process 1 indicating that process 1 has finished activity 1. In the case of message passing, process 2 issues a blocking receive communication.

A *barrier* is another sequence control mechanism; it ensures that all processes have reached a common control-flow point. In order to achieve this, a barrier forces all pro-

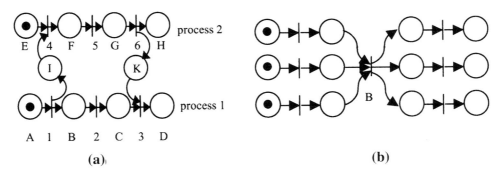

FIGURE 2   (a) Example sequence control; (b) barrier.

cesses to wait until each process reaches the barrier and then releases all of the processes. In Figure 2b, the corresponding Petri net for three processes and one barrier B is shown. Barriers are realized by software using locks or by special hardware support which combines individual "I'm here" signals to a global event.

Classification of Architectures

A *parallel system* is a set of processing elements which cooperate on solving a task. *Processing elements* can be pipelines, segments of pipelines, processors, and computer systems. These elements work in a coordinated manner and (at least partially) simultaneously.

According to this definition, all modern computers can claim to be parallel computers because they consist at least of a central processor, I/O processors, and a graphics unit, all working in parallel. However, in this article, we will only deal with parallel computers in the narrow sense. In order to explain this restriction, we will first introduce the well-known classification of Flynn (9). Other classification schemes can be found in the literature (10–12). Flynn's scheme is based on the multiplicity of instruction streams and data streams. Four classes can be distinguished:

SISD: Single Instruction–Single Data
SIMD: Single Instruction–Multiple Data
MISD: Multiple Instruction–Single Data
MIMD: Multiple Instruction–Multiple Data

The SISD class corresponds to the classical monoprocessor and the MISD class is empty. The two remaining classes represent the parallel systems. Vector processors and array processors are contained in the SIMD class. Because vector processing is based on pipelining and not on concurrency, only array processors are introduced in this article (see the section Array Processors). The members of the MIMD class are called multiprocessors because they consist of several processors which execute different programs or program parts at the same time. MIMDs are more flexible then SIMDs. They can operate as high-performance single-user machines, as machines running several tasks simultaneously (multiprogramming), and as a combination of these modes. For this reason, they have displaced array processors. Thus, this article mainly deals with multiprocessors. According to the architectural basis of information exchange, this class can be subdivided in the following:

- *Shared-memory architectures*. Processors have address space in common and can communicate via shared variables allocated in a shared memory.
- *Message-passing systems*. Each processor has only access to a private address space. The communication occurs by means of channel processors and messages.

Multiprocessors are treated in the sections Shared-Memory Machines and Message-Passing Systems. In these sections, we will introduce a more detailed classification (see Fig. 3).

Flynn classifies only so-called *control-flow-driven architectures* (i.e., systems where program counters steer the execution order to instructions). Other architectural principles have been investigated in research projects (13). In *data-flow machines*, the availability of data drives the execution of an instruction. Any instruction can be started

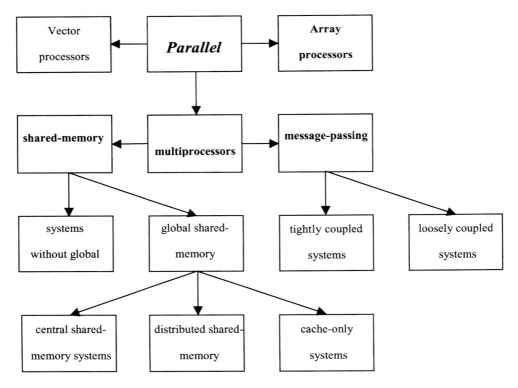

FIGURE 3   Classification of multiprocessors.

when the necessary operands have been calculated. Thus, data-flow machines can be considered as a direct hardware implementation of a given Petri net graph. In contrast, in *reduction machines*, computation is triggered by the demand for results. For instance, if the evaluation of an equation needs the results of other computations, then the necessary steps for obtaining these results are invoked. Application-oriented arrangements of *VLSI computing structures* (e.g., systolic arrays for matrix multiplication) represent another type of parallel system.

People are interested in machines that can grow as performance requirements increase. Therefore, scalability is a vital characteristic of parallel machines. An architecture is called *scalable* if it is possible to configure a machine of any desired size using the same hardware and software components. At the hardware level, this includes expandability of processors, memories, and the interconnection system. Because performance bottlenecks cannot be completely avoided, system scalability is possible only within certain limits.

With respect to scalability, message-passing machines are preferable, as these computers will be scalable to a large number of processors if the interconnection network is suitable (more information is given in the section Message-Passing Systems). On the other hand, it is easier to program shared-memory machines (see the subsection Basic Features and Main Types).

This apparent incompatibility of the advantages of memory and message coupling determined the evolution of multiprocessors (see also Fig. 3). The first systems were build with shared memory. At that time, it was not possible to realize systems of that kind at any size. Consequently, designers switched to message-passing multiprocessors which were built with up to some several thousand processors. With the appearance of NUMA and COMA computers (see the subsection Basic Features and Main Types), the advantages of both systems have been combined. Since that time, large parallel systems with a global shared memory can be built.

Programming Primitives

The sections Array Processors, Shared-Memory Machines, and Message-Passing Systems present the basic types of parallel systems together with programming examples. For the description of the basic paradigms, we introduce a hypothetical PASCAL-like language. In addition to well-known sequential programming elements, it offers support for creating concurrent processes and for synchronization purposes. The SIMD primitives will be introduced later. Concurrent MIMD execution can be defined using the following language constructs:

1. The creation of different concurrent processes is defined by the *parallel statement*: **PARALLEL** statement_sequence **END**. Within *statement_sequence*, those statements that can run concurrently are separated by the operator "‖." All processes will be started immediately and executed in parallel if multiple processors are available. The parallel statement terminates when all processes have terminated. A typical usage is the creation of parallel processes by means of subroutine calls.

    Example. PARALLEL Producer ‖ Consumer **END**

2. The creation of identical concurrent processes is defined by the *forall statement*: **FORALL** iter_expr **DO** statement_sequence **END**. Although all processes have identical process codes to be executed, each process gets a unique process identification, which is defined by a loop counter in *iter_expr*. The processes will immediately be started and executed in parallel if multiple processors are available. The forall statement terminates when all processes have terminated.

    Example. FORALL i := 0 **TO** max **DO** sum (i) **END**

3. For the definition of critical regions in shared-address systems, we introduce the data type Locktype and the operation pair Lock(lock:LockType) and Unlock(lock:LockType). Calling *Lock* guarantees exclusive entry into a statement sequence. Other processes which also call *Lock* are delayed until the first process has executed *Unlock*. Thus, a critical region is defined as a statement sequence with an initial *Lock* and a final *Unlock* statement.

4. For the sender–receiver model, processes directly address a communication partner by its process identification (*point-to-point communication*). We introduce the communication routines Sendp(pid:ident; info:Integer) and Receivep(pid:ident; VAR info:Integer). For a message exchange, the sender process calls *Sendp* while the receiver process calls *Receivep*. The first

calling process gets blocked until the communication partner arrives (*process rendevous*).

5. A parallel program is defined by parallel processes and their interaction via data channels. We introduce a data type `Channel` and the operations `Sendc (ch:Channel; info:Integer)` and `Receivec(ch:Channel; VAR info: Integer)`. When calling *Sendc*, a process deposits a message *info* in a channel variable *ch*. The message gets buffered internally in such a way that the sender gets blocked only if no more buffer space is available. Another process can receive this information by calling *Receivec*. If no message is stored, the process gets blocked.

Model Problem

In the following, an algorithm for numerically solving the Laplace equation under very simple conditions is introduced. This example will be used for demonstrating the different programming styles of different machines.

Problem. A square region G (see Fig. 4) is given. We search for a function $u(x, y)$ defined in G which fits the conditions as follows:

In the interior of G, the Laplace equation is true; that is

$$\frac{\delta^2 u(x,\ y)}{\delta x^2} + \frac{\delta^2 u(x,\ y)}{\delta y^2} = 0. \tag{1}$$

At the boundary of G, $u(x, y) = g(x, y)$ for a given function g.

Solution. The problem is solved by first discretizing and subsequently applying an iteration method. Therefore, the region G represented by a grid

$$K = \{(x_i,\ y_j):\ x_i = x_0 + ih,\ y_j = y_0 + jh,\ i,j = 0, 1, \ldots, n + 1\}$$

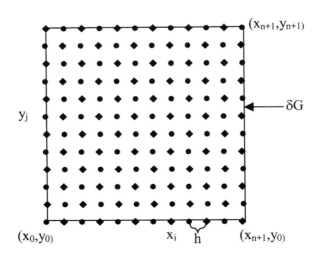

FIGURE 4   Grid covering a region G.

with a distance h between the grid points. Replacing the derivations in Eq. (1) by difference quotients, we get an approximation of that formula (we use the abbreviation $u_{i,j} = u(x_i, y_j)$),

$$(u_{i-1,j} + u_{i,j} - 2u_{i+1,j}) + (u_{i,j-1} + u_{i,j+1} - 2u_{i,j}) = 0 \quad \text{for } i,j = 1, 2, \ldots, n \qquad [2]$$

Given that $u_{i,j} = g_{i,j}$ for $i = 0, n + 1, j = 0, 1, \ldots, n + 1$ and $i = 0, 1, \ldots, n + 1, j = 0, n + 1$, the following iteration method will work if h is sufficiently small:

Example 1 PROCEDURE Jakobi(**VAR** u: **ARRAY**[1..n, 1-n] **OF** Real; n:Integer;
        eps: Real);
  VAR v: **ARRAY**[1..n, 1-n] **OF** Real; fault, fhelp: Real notConverged: Boolean;
BEGIN
  NotConverged := true;
  WHILE notConverged **DO**
    Fault := 0.0;
    FOR i:=1 **TO** n **DO**
      FOR j:=1 **TO** n **DO**
        v[i,j] = (u(i-1,j] + u[i+1,j] + u[i,j-1] + u[i,j+1])/4.0   (* derived from (2) *)
      END
    END;
    FOR i:=1 **TO** n **DO**
      FOR j:=1 **TO** n **DO**
        fhelp:= Abs(u[i,j] - v[i,j]);
        IF fhelp > fault **THEN** fault := fhelp **END**;
        u[i,j] := v[i,j]
      END
    END;
    IF fault <= eps **THEN** nonConverged:= false **END**;   (*maximum of changes
        <=eps*)
  END
END Jacobi

This method is a so-called stencil algorithm (see the subsection Grid and Torus Algorithms). In numerics, it is also known as a *relaxation* method. It is very easy to parallelize because the order of calculating the new values within one sweep is irrelevant. If we partition the grid into a red and a black set like a checkerboard (taking ◆ as red and ● as black in Fig. 4) and calculate in each sweep first the new black value and afterward the red values, then we obtain a much better converging method, called red–black relaxation. This method is also easy to parallelize, as the reds depend only on the black points and vice versa. We have only to guarantee that first all reds and afterward all blacks will be computed. It makes no difference in which order the various red and the various black points are calculated. Another advantage is that it is not necessary to restore the values using field *v*. Nevertheless, we will use only the Jacobi method because we want to avoid the additional effort of computing the indices necessary for red–black relaxation. Finally, it should be mentioned that, nowadays, people would use a multigrid method which is based on red–black relaxation but which will converge very much better by using several grids.

INTERCONNECTION NETWORKS

Features of Networks

In the following, we will use the term *node* for a unit consisting of one processor or processing element and one attached memory block. By a *module*, we mean either a node or a memory.

Interconnection networks enable the transportation of information between hardware units. In multiprocessors/array processors, they are used to connect nodes together or processors/processing elements to memories. Networks basically consist of *links* and *switches*. The availability of fast and efficient networks is crucial for achieving high performance. Some important characteristics are the following:

- *Topology*. To date, only regular interconnection networks have been used. According to Ref. 14, the following networks have been realized: bus (see Fig. 5), hierarchical systems of buses, rings, trees, grids (meshes; see Fig. 16) of two and three dimensions, pyramids, hypercubes (see Fig. 5b), crossbar switches, and multistage networks.

- *Dynamics*. In *static-interconnection networks*, there exist only fixed links between modules. The routing control is part of the module. It is performed by the processor or by a special router. A *dynamic network* is like a blackbox with I/O ports to which modules are attached. The routing is carried out by the network itself. Usually, the difference is hidden from the user by firmware.

- *Timing control*. This could be either *synchronous* or *asynchronous*.

- *Network control*. This can be either *centralized* or *distributed*. With centralized control, one special network unit manages the access to the network. In the distributed case, requests are handled by local devices independently. How the path is found (routing) depends very much on the topology.

- *Switching technique*. Two classes are known: *packet switching* or *circuit switching*. In circuit switching, a path connecting two nodes exists for the entire duration of data transfer. In packet switching, the data are broken into packets, each, individually, searching its way through the network. Each packet provided with address information is transported from node to node. Links between nodes are freed as soon as possible. Formerly the *store and forward* strategy was preferred. With this scheme, an arriving packet is stored in each node and

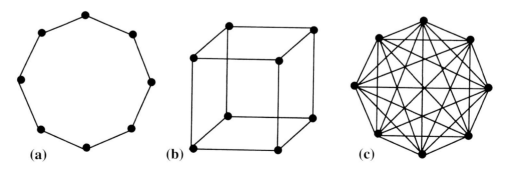

(a)   **(b)**   **(c)**

FIGURE 5   Static communication networks: (a) ring; (b) cube; (c) complete interconnection.

sent to the next node if a suitable link is free. Nowadays, *wormhole* routing has been accepted. Each packet is split into smaller parts, called flits. The first flit of a packet, the header, searches for a path through the network and the other flits must follow immediately. Thereby something like asynchronous pipelining takes place. If the header is blocked, the flits of one packet will remain in different nodes of the network. The main advantage in comparison with store and forward is that the latency is almost independent of the distance between the source and the destination (13). Very similar to this method is the *virtual cut-through* approach. The only difference occurs in the case of blocking, where the whole packet is stored in one node.

- *Blocking.* A network is called *nonblocking* if any two free modules can be connected independently of the existing connections. If not, it is a *blocking* network.
- *Costs.* The number of switches and links plus the bandwidth and the length of the links.
- *Performance.* Bandwidth is the amount of data that can be sent over the network per unit time. The (*total*) *bandwidth* is given by the sum of the bandwidths of all links. This value represents the maximum which can be reached. The worst case is approximated by the *bisection bandwidth*. In order to calculate this measure, the net is split into two nearly equal parts and, afterward, the bandwidth of the links between parts 1 and 2 is summed up. Also of great interest is the *latency*, which is given by the time a message needs to cross the net. Static networks with 64 modules are compared in Table 1 [the bandwidth is given in multiples of the bandwidth provided by one link (15)].
- *Scalability.* This feature of a network is the essential condition for a scalable parallel computer. In particular, the bandwidth has to grow with increasing size of the system. Representatives of well-scaling nets are rings and grids used by many commercial multiprocessors, mostly in a hierarchical manner.

Examples of Dynamic Networks

The simplest way to interconnect modules is offered by a single bus (see Fig. 5a). It makes no sense to build too large a system of this kind because the number of modules is restricted. The limitation arises because a bus becomes saturated when the traffic overwhelms the bandwidth and, consequently, the waiting times increase.

With regard to volume, the other extreme is a *crossbar* (Fig. 6a). It is a nonblocking network and offers high communications performance. To connect n processors

TABLE 1   Static Networks

		Bus	Ring	2D-grid	6D-cube	Complete connectivity
Performance	Total bandwidth	1	64	112	192	2016
	Bisection bandwidth	1	2	8	32	1024
Costs	Ports per switch	—	3	5	7	64
	Number of links	1	128	176	256	2080

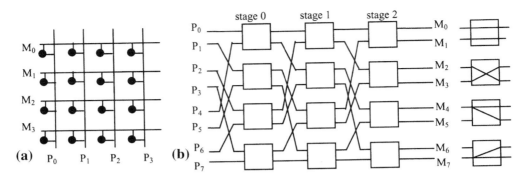

FIGURE 6   Network examples: (a) crossbar switch; (b) multistage Omega network. (● corresponds to a switch.)

to n memories, n^2 switches are necessary. Because the volume rises more than proportionally as the number of modules increases, a crossbar is not scalable. However, it is possible to realize crossbar switches by VLSI circuits in such a way that the limitation is essentially a function of the number of pins (16). At present, crossbars connecting 256 units together are commercially available (Fujitsu VPP 700). Figure 6a shows a crossbar linking processors P_i to memory units M_i. If nodes are to be interconnected, then each node corresponds to one of the processors, say P_i, and one memory block, say M_i. Accordingly, there are two ports per node: one output and one input port.

In *multistage networks* (17), connections among modules are realized by a fixed number of stages. Each stage consists of a number of $a \times b$ switches which can link each of the a inputs either to one or to several of the b outputs. Adjacent stages are connected according to a fixed pattern. The switches can be set dynamically to establish a desired path between any input module and any output module. Different classes of multistage network differ in the switch types and in how the stages are connected.

A well-known example is the *Omega network* (Fig. 6b). The switches are 2×2 crossbars which can realize four different interconnection patterns, shown at the right side of Fig. 6b. The one to two interconnections are used for broadcast purposes. Each switch is individually controlled. The pattern between the $\log_2 n$ stages corresponds to the perfect shuffle. An Omega network with n inputs and n outputs requires only $n/2 \log_2 n$ switches. Therefore, the amount for building an Omega network is considerably smaller than for a crossbar. However, the network is blocking. This can be seen from Figure 6b, where paths from P_0 to M_0 and from P_2 to M_1 cannot simultaneously exit because the path between each processor and each memory is unique.

In order to avoid such conflicts, each switch can be provided with additional buffers. Nevertheless, the well-known *hot-spot* problem may occur. A hot spot is a memory bank M_i to which the number of accesses is higher than to the other banks. This situation causes all buffers which are part of a path from a processor to that hot spot to fill up. Especially, this is true for all switches of level 0. As a consequence, the throughput of the system decreases dramatically (18). In many cases, *combining* will help. This is a technique where several requests to the same memory cell or line (e.g., in the case of caching) detected by a switch will be combined to one access by that switch. Another way of reducing the drawbacks of a hot spot is to increase the complexity of the network in such a way that more than one path between each source and each sink is offered (19).

Figure 6b shows an Omega network connecting processors and memory blocks. Such nets have been built with up to 1024 input and output ports.

During the last years, many new high-speed networks have been developed. Most of them consist of components (switches and interfaces between host and the real network) which enable the designer to build various types of network. The network interconnect is usually located at the I/O bus. They range from local/wide area networks (LAN/WAN) like Fast Ethernet and ATN, to system area networks (SAN) like Myrinet and Memory Channel.

Fast Ethernet is a family of high-speed LANs running at about 100 Mbit/s. It represents an upgrade of the standard Ethernet. It uses the same protocol (CSMA/CD).

Asynchronous Transfer Mode (ATM) was designed for wide area. It delivers many advantages over existing LAN and WAN technologies. It promises scalable bandwidths and Quality of Service.

Scalable Coherent Interface (SCI) is an IEEE standard with provides the programmer with an systemwide shared memory (there is one address room which can be accessed by all active devices). Therefore, the communication is done by variables and not by messages (see the subsection Communication).

Myrinet is a relatively inexpensive gigabit-per-second network. The communication latencies between computing nodes is very small and is nearly comparable with that of supercomputer interconnects. One main advantage is the onboard programmable microcontroller enabling the users to fit the interconnect to their special needs. The switches have up to 16 ports.

The Memory Channel provides a physical bandwidth of 100 Mbyte/s and virtual shared memory among nodes.

For a more detailed overview of such networks, see Ref. 20.

ARRAY PROCESSORS

Architecture

An *array processor* consists of a monoprocessor called a *control unit* (CU) and a large number of *processing elements* (PEs) (Fig. 7). The PEs are basically arithmetic logical units. A local memory is attached to each PE. These memory blocks are interconnected in a regular manner. Usually, a static interconnection network between PEs is implemented, which enables each PE to communicate with other neighborhood PEs. An example is the grid interconnection (Fig. 7b), often called a NEWS scheme (Northern, Eastern, Western, and Southern neighbors). The interconnection hardware supports the simultaneous transportation of data between nodes (e.g., shift of data in a certain direction). Some array processors offer an additional network for global communication.

Example. CM-200
Producer: Thinking Machines Corporation
2–64K 1-bit PEs
An arithmetic processor attached to every 32 PEs

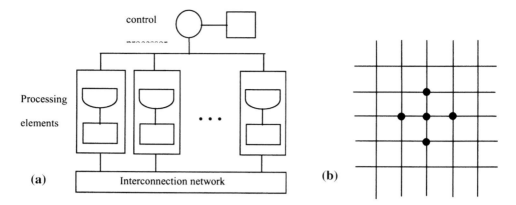

FIGURE 7   (a) General structure of an array processor; (b) neighbors. (● is a PE in a grid.)

256 KBytes of memory and several I/O channels are attached to every 32 PEs
Interconnection networks: one NEWS grid and one cube of dimension 12

At the moment, no commercial system is available. The reason for SIMD computers disappearing seems to be that they are less flexible than MIMD systems. The scope of applications where SIMD can be successfully used is relatively small. However, where it makes sense, the results are very good due to the usually very large number of processing elements. Furthermore, there is one area which is not well covered by multiprocessors—associative processing (parts of the content of an object are used for addressing). New investigations try to reanimate array processors by integrating SIMD operation principles into memory.

An example is computational RAM (C · RAM) (21). This integrated circuit implements a "smart memory" whereby processing elements are integrated into the memory chip. C·RAM can function either as a conventional memory chip or as a SIMD computer. With this approach, the scope of application for such devices is extended.

Programming Issues

The machine language of an array processor divides into two classes of instructions: CU-type and PE-type instructions, respectively. The first class comprises instructions executed by the CU (e.g., program flow control and scalar operations); the second covers instructions to be executed by the PEs (arithmetic, logical, and communication operations). Program execution consists of alternating phases of sequential and parallel activities according the following scheme: The next instruction to be executed is fetched and decoded by the CU. If it is of CU-type, it is directly executed; if it is of PE-type, it is broadcast to the PEs which synchronously perform the same operation, each on different data (SIMD mode). Whether a PE participates in a computation or remains inactive can be specified by the CU, using special masking operations.

In our model language, we introduce a *PAR statement* for operations to be executed on the PEs. By default, all other statements are executed on the control unit. The allocation of PE variables is signaled by means of the *PLURAL* keyword. We assume a grid

PE interconnection. Data exchange is done via the function *Shift*, which can send data in the four grid directions. Finally, a PE variable is accessible from the CU by means of the PE coordinate *proc*[*x, y*].

Example 2 deals with our model problem 1. To minimize overhead, we assume that the grid is distributed onto a PE grid of the same size (i.e., each PE holds exactly one grid value). If it is smaller, then some PEs are locked. On the other hand, if the number of the grid points is larger than the number of processors, then some of the processors have to manage more than one grid point. Furthermore, we assume that the word width of the PEs is equivalent to a real.

The calculation of the new values is very similar to that of the origin. The maximum of the changes is computed in the procedure FindMaximum. The way in which the maximum is obtained is quite different from the method used in the monoprocessor version. In the first program phase, the local maximum within each row is computed; in the second phase, similar computations result in the global maximum, which is located at the left lower PE.

Note that the program is executed by the CU. During the entire computation all PEs, are active except when explicitly disabled by a mask sent to the PEs. This mask contains one bit for each PE. The first PAR statement after the WHILE is more detailed than usual. This makes it easier to understand how the machine works. In reality, a shorter description is used. A possible version—it depends on the language—is

v_value = (u_value[−1,.] + u_value[+1,.] + u_value[.,−1] + u_value[.,+1]/4.0.

Example 2 Program example: Laplace problem on SIMD

```
PROCEDURE Jakobi(VAR u: ARRAY[1..n] OF Real; n:Integer; eps: Real);
   VAR v: ARRAY[1..n] OF Real; max: Real notConverged: Boolean;
   PLURAL u_value, v_value, fault: Real;

PROCEDURE FindMaximum (VAR max: Integer);
   BEGIN
     FOR i:=1 TO n-1 DO (* compute maximum within rows *)
     PAR
       buffer:= fault;
       Shift(west, buffer);
       IF buffer > fault THEN fault:=buffer END
     END;
     FOR i:=1 TO n-1 DO (* compute maximum within columns *)
     PAR
       buffer:= fault;
       Shift(south, buffer);
       IF buffer > fault THEN fault:=buffer END
     END;
     max:= proc[0,0]. fault
   END FindMaximum

BEGIN
Distribute matrix a onto PEs and store in uvalue;
NotConverged := true;
WHILE notConverged DO
```

```
Fault := 0.0;
PAR
    buffer: =u_value; (* u[i,j] -> buffer *);
    Shift(east, buffer); (* u[i-1,j] -> buffer *);
    v_value := buffer;
    buffer: =u_value; (* u[i,j] -> buffer *);
    Shift(east, buffer); (* u[j+1,j] -> buffer *);
    v_value := v_value + buffer;
    buffer: =u_value; (* u[i,j] -> buffer *);
    Shift(east, buffer); (* u[i,j-1] -> buffer *);
    v_value := v_value + buffer;
    buffer: =u_value; (* u[i,j] -> buffer *);
    Shift(east, buffer); (* u[i,j+1] -> buffer *);
    v_value := (v_value + buffer)/4.0;
END;
deactive(boundary processors); (* mask
PAR
    fault := Abs(u_value − v_value);
    u_value := v_value
END;
activate(boundary processors)
END;
FindMaximum(max);
IF max <= eps THEN nonConverged:= false END (*maximum of changes
        <=eps*)
END
END Jacobi
```

SHARED-MEMORY ARCHITECTURES

Basic Features and Main Types

Such architecture processors share memory space and can communicate via shared variables allocated in a shared memory (Fig. 8). Mostly, a global shared space is realized, which means that all processors have access to the whole shared memory. Sometimes, additional private memory is available, which allows efficient access to local data. Of course, information exchange between processors is done via the shared memory. Peripherals are also shared in some fashion.

Shared-memory machines have a number of advantages:

- They are more flexible because they support shared variables as well as message passing.
- It is easier to port sequential code to machines with shared memory than to those based on message passing. This issue has been proved by experiments.
- The mapping of data to the memory is less critical. Especially, load balancing can be realized much more easily.
- Shared-memory communication is done with simple load/store instructions and, therefore, it has relatively low communication latency.

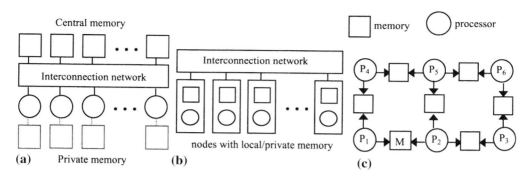

FIGURE 8 Multiprocessors: (a) central shared memory; (b) distributed shared memory: (c) restricted neighborhood.

In the past, shared memory has often been implemented as a system with restricted neighborhoods. This means that each processor can directly communicate only with some of the processors but not with all. The consequence is shown by an example (see Fig. 8c). Processors P_1 and P_2 are able to exchange information via memory M. If P_1 needs data from P_3, P_2 is necessary for that purpose. In other words, remote communication is much more expensive than local. If the communication pattern of a parallel task shows the same locality as given by the restricted neighborhood (one example: our model problem in the subsection Model Problem), then such machines have advantages over systems with global shared memory because, in this case, the number of network conflicts can be kept to a low level (22). Unfortunately, these computers are relatively difficult to program and therefore they did not succeed.

Nowadays, nearly all systems possess a *global address space* common to all processors. Usually, such a multiprocessor is addressed by the term *shared-memory architecture*. Furthermore, the whole address space is global in all commercial systems, which means that there is no private memory available.

A single address space for all processors has several advantages. Two of them are as follows:

- Any processor can access any memory location and any I/O device.
- There is only one copy of the operating system or other program residing in shared memory.

Although programming would be a little more troublesome, private memory, which could be added to all the machines mentioned later (see Fig. 8a), would reduce network traffic. Because caches have become so large now, this no longer seems necessary. For this reason, we will discuss only systems without private memory.

Now, we will use the different ways in which shared memory can be organized to classify these multiprocessors in more detail.

Multiprocessors provided with only one *central* memory (see Fig. 8a without private memory) are called *UMA* machines (*uniform memory access*). They were given this name because each memory access needs the same time if network conflicts do not occur. A synonym for UMA is *symmetrical multiprocessor* (SMP).

The easiest way to build an UMA is to take several processors and a central memory and connect these components via a shared bus (see Fig. 9a). Each processor has its own cache for minimizing the average memory access time (see the next subsection). Problems with SMPs are as follows:

- Although caches significantly reduce the requirements for bus bandwidth, such a system is reasonable only up to a relatively small number of processors. The demand for bandwidth increases more than proportionally with each additional processor. The main bottleneck is the memory bus. This situation will not change during the next few years, since the memory bandwidth has not kept and will not keep pace with the increase in processor speed.
- A further problem is latency. Compared to message passing systems shared memory systems have low latency, but even without contention the latency per memory access is hundreds of processor cycles in modern systems.
- The availability of such a multiprocessor is low since at least the bus is a single point of failure. If the bus is defective, the whole system will break down.

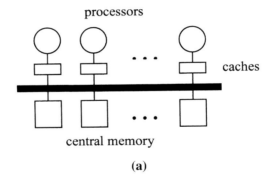

(a)

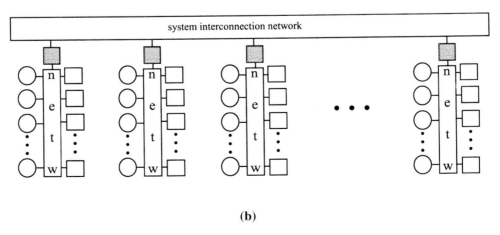

(b)

FIGURE 9   (a) SMP with bus interconnect; (b) NUMA based on SMP clusters.

Typical representatives of this type are a large number of commercial servers (e.g., systems based on the Intel board) (see the subsection Examples of Shared-Memory Machines). High-performance SMPs use a crossbar to interconnect the components (see, e.g., DEC Alphaserver GS60E also in the subsection Examples of Shared-Memory Machines).

In contrast to SMPs, in NUMA (*nonuniform memory access*) machines, the access time depends on where the corresponding data are located. Many NUMAs feature a two-level access hierarchy. Some memory accesses (local accesses) do not pass the system network; others (remote accesses) must use that network, causing an additional delay.

One implementation technique is to attach a local memory to each processor. Each processor can access its local memory directly. If it wants to read or write from or to other memory locations (local to other processors), a delay caused by the network will occur. All the local memories represent a part of the global address space. Nowadays, in most shared-memory architectures, the global memory is realized as the union of all local memories (Fig. 8b). In other words, there is no central memory. By this measure, it is possible to build shared-memory multiprocessors which are scalable up to a large number of processors (of the order of thousands) if the interconnection network is scalable as well. These multiprocessors are called *distributed shared-memory machines*.

Modern NUMAs feature a slightly different organization. Instead of modules consisting of one processor and its attached local memory, full SMPs (processors, memories blocks, and I/O facilities) are interconnected by the system network (see Fig. 9b). Usually, an additional memory, a so-called remote cache, is attached to each SMP in such a system. When at least one processor in SMP A intends to access a data block located in another (remote) SMP, this block is first copied into A's remote cache. Furthermore, this class can be split into two subclasses depending on whether cache coherence is supported by hardware or not (see the subsection The Cache Coherence Problem).

One essential task in the NUMA context is the mapping of data onto the distributed memories. For that, most modern machines use the following mechanism. When a cache line forming part of a page is first addressed by some processor, that page is assigned to that processor's local memory, which becomes its home memory. When a processor P subsequently accesses the cache line, P temporarily stores the line in its local cache, but, if necessary, the line has to be written back into the home memory. In spite of the caching mechanism, it could happen that a lot of communication is required over the network. In any case, this situation will occur if, for a process in node P, those parts of its working set which are assigned to remote home memories are larger than the remote cache of P. Therefore, all NUMAs have in common that the programmer interested in efficient programs has to think about where data should be stored. The average access time will be reduced only if data is positioned in favorable locations (see Program Example 4).

One answer to the question of how to free the user from this task is given by COMA machines (*cache-only memory architecture*). In those machines, the whole local memory of each processor is implemented as one large cache. According to the usual behavior of caches, a memory block is loaded if it is required. Therefore, the memory is often addressed as *attraction memory* (AM). All the caches form a global memory space. Distributed cache directories help to perform remote accesses. Here, the initial data placement is not critical because data will migrate to where it will be needed. However, another difference from NUMA architecture is unpleasant. Memory blocks are not assigned to a unique main memory location. If a processor calls for a memory block and there is no copy inside its local cache, the block must be searched for. Furthermore, if the block is overwritten, the system is eventually forced to find a suitable location. The only fixed position for a memory block exists in virtual memory, which is implemented on the disk. In other words, a COMA demands more hardware support than a NUMA; in particular, it must integrate cache management with virtual memory management.

Kendall Square's KSR2 (see the subsection Examples of Shared-Memory Machines) was an example of COMA architecture. In such a machine, up to 32 processors together with a 32-MB cache were interconnected by a ring (level 0). Larger systems were generated by interconnecting rings of level 0 using another ring (level 1). Then, a partial directory was located at the interfaces between the levels. Such a partial directory reflected the placement of blocks in the whole memory of the corresponding ring of level 0. Applying this technique recursively, a tree hierarchy of rings was possible. Each level in the hierarchy contained a partial directory with information about the states of the blocks contained in the branches up to that level. In order to find a block, the processor issued a request that went up successively from one level to the next higher, until the partial directory provided the information that the corresponding subtree contained the desired block. This type of COMA was called *Hierarchical COMA*. A design similar to KSR2 is the data-diffusion machine DDT developed at the Swedish Institute of Computer Science (24).

One answer to the problem of finding a block is to fix the directory entries in their home node, which is determined by their physical address as in NUMA, unlike the memory blocks which can migrate. One essential advantage of this approach would be that any high-speed network can be used. As no network hierarchy is necessary, this type of multiprocessor is therefore called *Flat COMA* (25).

In contrast to Hierarchical and Flat COMAs which implement block replacement and relocation in hardware, Simple COMA partially transfers the corresponding mechanisms into software and, as a consequence, hardware complexity is reduced (26).

More about COMA architectures and their performance, especially in comparison to NUMA systems can be found in Ref. (27).

Multiple Copies of Data

A potential bottleneck is the system network. It could be reduced by allowing multiple copies of data and by storing one copy closer to some processor calling for it. Thereby the granularity of shared data is usually a cache line in the case of NUMA and COMA and a page in the case of SC-NUMA The methods used are very similar. Therefore, we restrict the discussion to caches.

It is well known that in monoprocessor systems, caches considerably reduce the access rate to memory or rather to the memory bus. Naturally, this applies just as much to multiprocessors. The number of accesses is much less with caches than without. Furthermore network contention will be reduced if the (system) programmer exploits *cache coherence*. Before we demonstrate this issue by an example, we have to look at the feature in question.

The Cache Coherence Problem

As different processors may access the same memory location, it is possible that copies of the same memory block exist in different caches. Consequently, any local write can cause a globally inconsistent view of memory if nothing is done about it. There are two classes of protocols which will help and which can be distinguished with respect to their behavior if a write operation occurs:

- Write-invalidate: If any processor intends to write, then all other copies will be invalidated.
- Write-update: This type demands that the new block content be broadcast to all cache copies.

It is obvious that the specific protocol depends on whether a write-through or a write-back cache is implemented. Furthermore, we can distinguish between snoopy protocols and directory-based protocols.

Snoopy Protocols: So-called *snoopy protocols* are typically used in SMPs. In order to explain the principle, we assume an UMA with a single bus used as interconnect. The basic idea is to achieve data consistency among shared memory and data caches through a bus watching mechanism. Therefore, a snooper is attached to each cache to control the actions performed on the bus and start the necessary action if need be. If a write-invalidate protocol is used, any processor which intends to write an item will set a corresponding signal on the bus. This signal leads the snoopers of all caches to check whether they possess a copy. If so, the snoopers will invalidate their copy. In contrast, the write-update case demands the new block content to be broadcast to all cache copies via bus (also under the snoopers' control).

More information is given in Ref. 28.

Directory-Based Protocols: In larger NUMA machines, snoopy protocols are not adequate, because the number of messages for informing all local memories or all caches about activities would be very large and the network would thus be overloaded. In order to avoid this, such systems implement a logically central *directory*, which contains information about the state of each block and where a copy of this block exists in the system. To avoid memory contention caused by the directory, it is usually physically distributed over the memories. If a shared object is to be changed, the controller of the directory part concerned will send commands to all and only those processors which possess a copy in their environment. If the system preserves sequential consistency (see the subsection Multiple Copies of Data), the controller must also wait for acknowledgement from its partners before the write is performed.

In order to reduce the additional load on the network, such machines are often organized in two levels. Instead of single nodes, *clusters* of processors are connected by the network. Each cluster represents a multiprocessor with a central shared memory. Within the cluster, a snoopy protocol is used for coherence purposes. To achieve system coherence, a partial directory exists for each cluster. The controller of this partial directory listens to all activities performed on the cluster bus and triggers the corresponding actions as required. Multiprocessors providing copies only in caches and implementing most of the directory protocol in hardware are called *CC-NUMA* (cache coherent). A well-known example is the Dash (29), designed and build in Stanford. A commercial representative is the SGI Origin 2000. A well-known machine which does not support cache coherence is CRAY T3E. Such architectures are referred as *NCC-NUMA* (non-cache-coherent). More information about these systems is given in the subsection Examples of Shared-Memory Machines. If shared-memory computing is enabled on NCC-NUMA and NORMA systems (see the section Message-Passing Multiprocessors) by means of software extensions, this is called SC-NUMA.

Using Cache Coherence for Synchronization

Cache coherence can be used to reduce the demands imposed on the system network. We give the following program realizing a lock as an example. Without caches such a lock could impose a heavy burden on the network, because each processor trying to gain the lock would make one attempt after another.

A processor, say A, tries to gain the lock. This is achieved by calling a program as follows (taken from Ref. 15). As a simplification, we assume that exactly one process resides at each processor.

```
PROCEDURE Lock (VAR S: LockType);
VAR k: Boolean;

BEGIN
  repeat
    repeat () until S=false; (*false means the lock is open, true it is set*)
    k:=true;
    exchange (k, S) (*a special indivisible instruction equivalent to: H:=S; S:=k;
      k:=H*)
  until k = false (* false signals: lock gained*)
END Lock
```

The interior repeat implies that a copy of S is stored into the cache. If the lock is set by another processor, say B, A must wait until B unlocks S. This waiting is done by continuously testing that value. Because A accesses only the copy of S in its cache, the network is not stretched. When B writes a false to S, the consequence is that A gets a new copy of S. Now, A makes an attempt to execute the exchange instruction. Because this operation contains a write access, the processor A needs and calls for an exclusive copy of S. Perhaps A has to wait for that copy, because there could be several competitors. If A is not the first that is provided with an exclusive copy, then another competitor locks S and A recognizes k = true and, therefore, it waits at the inner repeat again. If A gets an exclusive copy, then the lock is open and after the exchange instruction k = false. In either case, S is locked after the exchange. The exchange instruction must be an indivisible operation provided by the hardware. If not, it is possible that, immediately after reading S, another processor reads the unchanged variable. Both processors would find the value false and both would think that they have set the lock after their writes.

Programming Shared-Memory Systems

Before we look at our model problem, we give an example in which the programmer explicitly splits a process into two parallel processes during the program run. Where these processes will be located is the responsibility of the system.

Program Example 3 computes the minimum and maximum of positive integer values which are stored in a vector *a*. Two processes each compute half of the array and store their local minimum and maximum in variables *locMin* and *locMax*. Within a critical region, the global minimum *min* and global maximum *max* is computed by comparing the values of *min* and *max* with the corresponding local values.

Example 3 Program Example. Minimum and maximum of vector elements

```
PROCEDURE FindMinMax(a: ARRAY[1..n] OF Integer; n:Integer; VAR min,
        max: Integer);
VAR critReg: LockType;                    (* lock variable *)

  PROCEDURE MinMax(start, end :Integer);
  VAR locMin, locMax, j: Integer;    (* local variables *)
  BEGIN
    locMin:= a[start]; locMax:= locMin;
    FOR j:= start + 1 TO end DO
      IF a[j] < locMin THEN locMin:= a[j] END;
      IF a[j] > locMax THEN locMax:= a[j] END;
    END;
    Lock(critReg);                        (* begin of critical region *)
      IF locMin < min THEN min := locMin END;
      IF locMax > max THEN max := locMax END;
    Unlock(critReg)                       (* end of critical region *)
  END MinMax;

BEGIN                                     (* FindMinMax *)
  min:= maxInt; max:=0;
  PARALLEL
    MinMax(1, n DIV 2)
      ||                                  (* creation of two concurrent processes *)
    MinMax(n DIV 2 + 1, n)
  END
END FindMinMax
```

Program example 4 is a Jacobi solver for our model problem written for a CC-NUMA based on SMPs. The program is of type SPMD (*single program multidata*); that is, the same program is running at each processor, only the data is partitioned. The system will generate identical processes, each attached to exactly one processor.

The partitioning of data is well done if load balancing is achieved as far as possible. In our case, we divide the interior of the region G into squares of nearly the same size (see Fig. 10). On the right-hand side, we see the enlarged part that one process has to manipulate (light gray). The dark grid points belong to neighboring processes and are needed for the calculation. In order to reduce remote communication between clusters, we inform the system that we want processes to be arranged like a grid. This implies that the processes loaded into one cluster (SMP) are neighboring with respect to the grid of processes (see the think lines on the left).

For all processes, the system will start the main program. After some setup work (e.g., setting the boundary grid points to the desired values and several more), all processes reach a barrier of a special type: The last and only the last process reaching that barrier will execute the statements between BARRIER and END (see, e.g., the statement marked by (*O*) in Program Example 4. At this first barrier, only notConverged := true and notConvergedTest = false are executed by the last process. Then, each processor will call the following procedure.

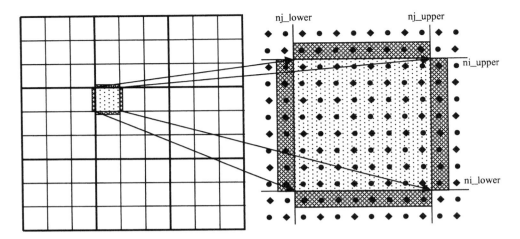

FIGURE 10   Model problem: partitioning data.

Example 4 Program Example. Model problem on CC-NUMA based on SMPs

```
PROCEDURE Jakobi (k_pid, I_pid, kmax, Imax, Integer;
          VAR u: ARRAY[1..n, 1..n] OF Real n:Integer; eps: Real,
          notConverged, notConvergedTest: Boolean);
   VAR ni_lower, ni_upper, nj_lower, nj_upper: Integer; fhelp: Real;
       v ARRAY[ni_lower..ni_upper,nj_lower..nj_uper] OF Real;

PROCEDURE CalculateLimits (VAR ni_lower, ni_upper, nj_lower, nj_upper:
          Integer);
BEGIN ..... END       (*computation of the part of u which is manipulated by this
          process*)

BEGIN
   CalculateLimits (ni_lower, ni_upper, nj_lower, nj_upper);
   WHILE notConverged DO
     Fault := 0.0;
     FOR i:= ni_lower TO ni_upper DO
       FOR j:= nj_lower TO nj_upper DO
        v[i,j] = (u[i-1,j] + u[i+1,j] + u[i,j-1] + u[i,j+1])/4.0     (* relax point *)
       END
     END;
     FOR i:= ni_lower TO ni_upper DO
       FOR j:= nj_lower TO nj_upper DO
         fhelp:= Abs(u[i,j] - v[i,j]);
         IF fhelp > faultTHEN fault:= fhelp END;
         u[i,j] := v[i,j]
       END
     END;
     IF fault > eps THEN notConvergedTest := true END
```

Barrier (* **O** *)
    IF not notConvergedTest **THEN** notConverged := false **END;**
    notConvergedTest := false
  END barrier;
END
END Jacobi

The size of the process(or) grid is given by kmax and lmax. The position within this grid is given by k_pid, l_pid. All these values are provided by the system and are first used to determine that part of the region each process has to relax. The synchronization is as follows. The variable notConverged signals whether an additional iteration step is necessary or not. At the beginning of each step, the variable notConveredTest is set to false. Each processor calculates the changes to the values while relaxing the grid points. If the maximum in its part of data is too large, the processor then sets notConvergedTest to true. At the barrier **O**, the last process, say A, checks that variable. If at least one process has stored a true in notConvergedTest, then A resets this variable and a new iteration step is started. Otherwise, A sets notConverged to false and all processes will return from the procedure.

If a red–black relaxation method is used, the program is very similar, but within each iteration step, there is an additional barrier after relaxing the red points to guarantee that in the second part of the step, the new values of the red points are used. In principle, the program looks as follows. More details are given in Program Example 6.

Example 5 Program Example. Red–black relaxation on CC-NUMA based on SMPs

    relax redpoints
    BARRIER END;
    Relax black points;
    Barrier statements as in example (4) **END;**

One additional advantage of the red–black algorithm is that it is not necessary to store the interim values in v, because if a new value is calculated, it will never be used.

Techniques for Reducing the Average Access Time in Shared-Memory Architectures

Memory accesses which have to pass any network are expensive. The read latencies measured in Origin 2000 (see Ref. 1) give an idea of the cost (Table 2).

In other machines, the situation is similar: The more remote the access is with

TABLE 2   Read Latencies in Origin 2000

Data stored in	Read latency in clocks
Register	0
Cache on chip	1–3
Level-2 cache (off chip)	10
Local memory	61
Remote memory	117–157

respect to the memory hierarchy, the more cycles are necessary. Especially, an access passing the system interconnect causes a large delay. It is obvious that it is desirable to reduce or even better to hide this delay. Several *latency-hiding* techniques are known:

- One approach for reducing latency is based on the idea of dynamically distributing data in such a way that most accesses are local. Two main techniques are used: It is accepted that copies of the same data block exist either in several local memories or several caches. We discuss this approach in the subsection Multiple Copies of Data.
- Using reflective memory achieves very good results. These memory systems make it possible to declare parts of a local memory to be part of a virtual shared memory. Any writing to a virtual memory address causes the new data to be sent to all copies. In other words, the information in the caches is updated by word. This is the main difference from other NUMA machines. As an example of a multiprocessor with reflective memory we cite Merlin (30), a computer provided with a grid interconnection network. Digital Equipment sells a workstation cluster which is interconnected by a so-called Memory Channel. The Memory Channel realizes the reflective memory.
- Data prefetching tries to avoid latency by causing the data to be transported to the cache before they are really needed. Prefetching can be controlled by hardware (based on the detection of memory reference patterns) or by software (by inserting additional instructions into the code). More information is given in Ref. 31.
- Another approach for hiding latency is the use of *multithreaded processors*. Here, there are two main approaches. The first is to support many threads and to switch every cycle from one thread to next without penalty, thereby hiding the latency (32). The other idea is only in case of a remote access instead of waiting for the result of that access to perform a context switch. A good overview of recent findings concerning such systems is given in Ref. 33.
- Relaxed-memory models provide quite a different approach. In contrast to the other methods, the user must be aware of the use of such a model and adapt his programming style accordingly. Some comments are presented in the subsection Relaxed-Memory Models. First, we must discuss memory consistency.

Memory-Consistency Models

Cache coherence provides a mechanism to propagate a newly written value. Memory-consistency models represent an additional constraint on when a value can be sent to a given processor. For example, the processor has to wait for the completion of previous write operations even if it finds a copy of the desired value in its cache.

In order to understand why an additional restriction is necessary, we look at the following code fragments written for two processors to run in parallel.

Processor A	Processor B
(Initially x: = y: = 0*)†	
x:= 1;	y:= 1;
IF y=0 **THEN** EntercritReg **END**;	**IF** x=0 **THEN** EntercritReg **END**;

---

†Initially memory cells x and y contain zeros and the registers R1 of A and B each contain the value 1*.

After compilation, the corresponding code fragments may look as follows:

a: store register R1 to x   d: store register R1 to y
b: load register R2 with y   e: load register R2 with x
c: branch if r2-0 to critReg   f : branch if r2=0 to critReg

Usually, programmers suppose that both processors will never be in the critical region at the same time. However, if no care is taken, it may happen that both processors execute their first statement, thus sending a "1" to x and y, respectively, and afterward they load y or x, respectively, getting the old value "0." The reason is there are contentions in the network and the read requests reach the memory earlier than the writes. If the values to be read are still in caches, then the signals for the changes have not reached the caches before the read operations have been performed.

Sequential Consistency

This situation cannot occur if the hardware fits the sequential-consistency model of memory. Lamport (34) defined this as follows:

> A multiprocessor is *sequentially consistent* if the result of any execution is the same as if the operation of all the processors were executed in some sequential order, and the operations of each individual processor appear in this sequence in the order specified by its program.

The scenario given above does not fulfill these conditions. Any sequential order of the statements causing that mentioned effect (e.g., "b, c, e, a, d, f") does not preserve the program order of either processor A or B or both, as at least operations a and b or d and e are not performed in the right order. Thus, we see that program order is essential. Atomicity is also important, as the following example for three processors demonstrates.

Processor A	Processor B	Processor C
	(*Initially x: = y: = 0*)	
x:= 1;	**while** x=0 **do** () **END**;	**while** y=0 **do** () **END**;
	y:= 1;	z:= x;

If no special care is taken, it is possible that the value 0 is written to z. Given sequential consistency, it is guaranteed that the effect of processor A's write is seen by the entire system at the same time.

In connection with sequential consistency, a corresponding model of the shared memory exists (see Fig. 11) which helps one to understand this type of consistency. The model looks like a single global memory with one port to which an arbitrary processor is connected at any time and which provides a global serialization among all memory operations. The key aspect is that any memory operation is performed atomically or instantaneously with respect to other memory operations.

This model differs essentially from the reality of the underlying hardware, where several memory blocks and many ports exist. Consequently, more hardware is necessary and much additional work has to be done. Measures for maintaining sequential consistency are very time-consuming (see, e.g., the actions necessary in connection with cache coherence). It is obvious that people are interested in renouncing sequential consistency if possible. In many cases, this strong memory-access model of sequential consistency will not be necessary if the programmer has the new situation in mind. The waiting periods in connection with memory accesses can rather be bridged by overlapping communication and execution if the conditions for the behavior of the memory are relaxed.

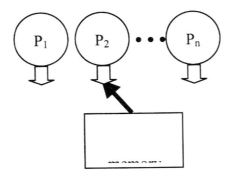

FIGURE 11   Sequential-consistency memory model.

Relaxed-Memory Models

There are several proposals for relaxing the sequential constraints. One of these models is *weak consistency*, which was derived by Dubois et al. (35). In this case, each program contains special synchronization points which are subjected to three conditions:

- All previous synchronization accesses must be performed before a read or a write access is allowed with respect to any other process.
- All previous reads and writes must be performed before a synchronization access is performed with respect to any other processor.
- Synchronization accesses are sequentially consistent with respect to one another.

Here is a very simple example. We assume that a multiprocessor without sequential consistency is available and that this machine supports barriers satisfying the above conditions. Now, we consider only programs which represent a strict sequence of megasteps. Each megastep consists of a computational phase completed by a barrier. The barrier forces the processors (processes) to wait until all processors have finished their megastep before any of them can proceed. Under these conditions, many programs will run more quickly than a corresponding implementation on a sequentially consistent machine. We demonstrated this by means of our model problem (see subsection Model Problem, especially look at Program Examples 4 and 5).

Example 6 Model Problem: Red–black solver using weak consistency (slightly abbreviated)

```
....
  WHILE notConverged DO
    Fault := 0.0;
    FOR all red points of processor's part of the grid Do
        fhelp := u[i,j]
        u[i,j](u[i-1,j] + u[i+1,j] + u[i,j-1] + u[i,j+1])/4.0;        (* relax point *)
        fhelp:= Abs(u[i,j] - fhelp);
        IF fhelp > fault THEN fault:= fhelp END
    END;
```

```
BARRIER END barrier;
FOR all black points of processor's part of the grid DO
        fhelp := u[i,j]
        u[i,j] = (u[i-1,j] + u[i+1,j] + u[i,j-1] + u[i,j+1])/4.0;      (* relax point *)
        fhelp:= Abs(u[i,j] - fhelp);
            IF fhelp > fault THEN fault:= fhelp END
END;
IF fault > eps THEN notConvergedTest := true END
Barrier
    IF not notConvergedTest THEN notConverged := false END;
    notConvergedTest := false
END barrier
END
```

If this program is run on a sequentially consistent multiprocessor, latency problems will arise when values are written to addresses located near the boundary. There are cache lines of which a copy exists in some neighboring processor. If a new value is written into such a line, the sequentially consistent processor has to wait until an acknowledgment arrives for invalidating the line or accepting the new value. However, this delay is not necessary because this value will be used by the neighbor after the next barrier at the earliest. Thus, weak consistency is sufficient.

More information about *relaxed-memory consistency models* (especially about *processor* and *release consistency*) is given in Refs. 26 and 36. In the former article, there is especially recorded which models are supported by modern machines like CRAY T3E and Compaq Alphaserver.

Examples of Shared-Memory Machines

In this section, we given some characteristics about one typical representative of each class of shared-memory multiprocessor.

SMP with bus interconnect (see Fig. 9a): Compaq Alphaserver GS60E
    Processor: Up to 8 Alpha21264A 700 MHz
    Cache: 8 MB
    Memory: 28 GB
    Bus bandwidth: 1.49 GB/s
SMP with several busses: IBM RS/6000 S80/7020
    Processors: Up to 8 Power 604E 332MHz
    Cache: 8 MB
    Memory: 3 GB
    System interconnect: 8 Buses to memory and I/O, 2 processors share 2 buses
    Bus bandwidth: 1.49 GB/s for 8 Buses
SMP with crossbar: HP V2250
    Processors: Up to 32 PA 8500 440 MHz
    Cache: 1 MB
    Memory: 32 GB
    System interconnect: 8×8 crossbar
    Bandwidth   15.36 GB/s

CC-NUMA: Sequent NUMA-Q

Nodestructure:	SMP with bus: so-called quad
Processors:	4 Pentium Pro 200 MHz
Cache/remote cache:	512 KB/32 MB
Memory:	4 GB
Bus bandwidth:	500 MB/s
System interconnect:	IQ-links between quads realizing a daisy chain, 1 GB/s

NCC-NUMA:Cray T3E 1200E

Processors:	Up to liquid cooled 2048 Alpha 21264A 600 MHz
Memory:	2 GB/processor
Bus bandwidth:	500 MB/s
System interconnect:	3D bidirectional torus
Bisectional bandwidth:	122 GB/s
Peak performance:	Maximum: 2.5 Tflops

Hierarchical COMA: Kendall Square's KSR 2

Processors:	Up to 2048 Alpha 264a 600 MHz
Memory:	2 GB/processor
Bus bandwidth	500 MB/s
System interconnect	
Level 0:	32 processor on ring plus 32 MB remote cache
Level i:	Ring interconnection of all level $i - 1$ rings

MESSAGE-PASSING MULTIPROCESSORS

A message-passing multiprocessor consists of a network which interconnects nodes containing at least one processor with memory, E/A subsystem, and an interface to the network (i.e., the communications hardware). In a block diagram (Fig. 12), it looks like a NUMA system (Fig. 8b). The essential difference is that a message-passing machine possesses only private memory. Consequently, information exchange is possible only via messages. These machines are often called *distributed-memory machines*.

To relieve the processors of the burden of transporting messages as far as possible,

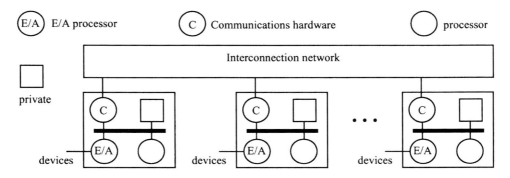

FIGURE 12   Diagram of a message-passing computer.

each node is provided with special communications hardware which performs most of the work occurring in context with messaging, which gives the processor the opportunity to proceed in executing its program. Nevertheless, the so-called setup time cannot be hidden. This loss is caused by the process switches necessary for starting a message send or for taking over a message which has still been received by the communications hardware.

A further difference from shared-memory machines is that the I/O facilities are individual to the nodes. In a shared-memory machine, the I/O is mostly connected to the system using the network.

From the user's point of view, a program consists of multiple processes, each having its private address space. Communication must explicitly be done by means of messages. The structure of the interconnection is hidden from the user. He has the impression that there is a complete interconnection between nodes.

Advantages of message-passing systems are as follows:

- Scalability is the main benefit of this kind of machine. Because there are only private address spaces, a data-consistency problem does not exist.
- For the same reason, no special actions are necessary to prevent undesired access to data by other processors.
- Because any synchronization is done by messages, these processes are easier to understand than in the case of shared data.

On the other hand there are several disadvantages:

- The programmer himself must control communications using send and receive statements and has to think about how to distribute data over the system. In recent years, many efforts have been made to assign this to the compiler and to provide the programmer with programming model which is equivalent to that of a shared-memory architecture (see the subsection High-Performance Fortran on recent Fortran developments).
- Due to setup times, the cost of communication is higher than for systems with central memory.

We distinguish two classes of message-passing computers:

- *Massively Parallel Systems* (MPP). These systems are the high-speed version of message-passing machines.
- *Cluster of Workstations* (COW): These machines are the low-cost variation.

Massively Parallel Systems

This term refers to very large computer systems. Here, we interpret MMP in a narrow sense: a massively parallel message-passing system. This meaning was the original one. Up to now, machines of this type are among the very fastest systems in the world (37). Essential features are as follows:

- Each node contains one or more microprocessors and powerful communications hardware.
- A high-speed memory bus interconnects these elements within a node.
- The nodes are interconnected by a high-speed network.

Example. Intel/Sandia ASCI Option Red. This research architecture (38) was developed by Intel and Sandia within the scope of the ASCI (Accelerated Strategic Computing Initiative) project, a 10-year $1 billion program for building Tflop/s supercomputers launched by the U.S. Department of Energy. These machines are to be used for solving grand challenge problems like weather prediction and so forth.

Option Red has been the fastest MPP for several years. It is continually being improved. At the moment, it consists of 4816 nodes, each having two Pentium II XEON processors. Sixteen nodes are used for system service and 74 for disk traffic (storage capacity: 12.5 TB). The system interconnect is made up of two planes, each realizing a grid network ($38 \times 38 \times 2$). At each node of these meshes, there is one node board. Corresponding nodes of the two planes are connected by a link. Each link in the network provides a bidirectional bandwidth of 800 MB/s. The total size of the RAM adds up to 606 GB. The peak performance of the whole multiprocessor is 3.15 TOPS (terraoperations per second). (See Figure 13.)

Cluster of Workstations

According to Hwang, the main features of such clusters are as follows:

1. Each node of a COW is a complete workstation. Sometimes, a node may be a SMP or a PC.
2. The nodes Each node of a COW is a complete workstation. Sometimes, a node may be a SMP or a PC.
3. There is always a local disk in each node.
4. A complete operating system resides on each node, whereas in some MPPs, only a microkernel exists. Usually, a UNIX is installed which is extended by an software layer for supporting a single-system image, parallelism, communication, and, perhaps, load balancing.
5. The network interface is loosely coupled to the I/O bus in the node. This is in contrast to the memory bus coupling in an MPP node.
6. The nodes are interconnected by a low-cost commodity network like Ethernet.

If the cluster is homogeneous (i.e., all nodes are equal), then the programming is similar to that of MPPs. The main difference results from the weaker communication

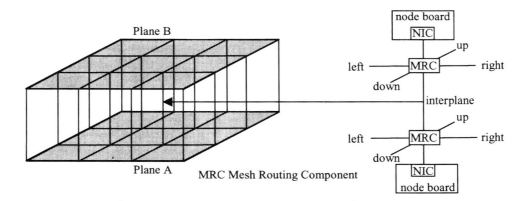

FIGURE 13   Interconnection architecture of Intel/Sandia ASCI Option Red.

performance of COWs. In case of heterogeneous systems—often called distributed systems—the problem of load balancing is extremely challenging.

Due to the evolution of technology, point 6 has become obsolete in many modern COWs where high-speed networks are used like Myrinet and Memory Channel (see the subsection Examples of Dynamic Networks).

The COWs have some advantages over specialized parallel computers:

- Workstations are less expensive and are widespread.
- They are easy to integrate into existing networks.
- Standard tools are available.

Due to the increasing power of workstation and decreasing network, latency become more and more an alternative to specialized multiprocessors.

Programming Message-Passing Systems

The techniques for writing programs for both MPPs and COWs are similar. They mainly depend on the software support provided by the system. Before outlining the solution to our model problem, we describe two sample programs using the primitives of the subsection Programming Primitives.

Process–Channel Model

Program Example 7 shows the cooperation of two processes, *Producer* and *Consumer*. *Producer* generates *n* information elements by calling subroutine *Generate* and sends the data to channel *c*. *Process Consumer* receives all data and outputs them.

Example 7 Program Example. Producer–consumer processes

```
PROCEDURE ProducerConsumer(n: Integer);
VAR c : Channel;                        (* channel variable *)

  PROCEDURE Producer;                   (* Process Producer *)
  VAR i, info: Integer;
    PROCEDURE Generate (VAR info: Integer);
    BEGIN ... END Generate;             (* details to be specified *)
  BEGIN
    FOR i:= 1 TO n DO
      Generate(info); Sendc(c, info)
    END
  END Producer;

  PROCEDURE Consumer;                   (* Process Consumer *)
  VAR i, info: Integer;
  BEGIN
    FOR i:= 1 TO n DO
      Receivec(c, info); Write(info)
    END
    END Consumer;

BEGIN
  PARALLEL Producer || Consumer END     (* creation of processes *)
END ProducerConsumer
```

```
BEGIN
   PARALLEL Producer ‖ Consumer END      (* creation of processes *)
   END ProducerConsumer
```

Sender–Receiver Model

As an example, we compute prefix sums of a given vector of numbers v_i $(i = 0, \ldots, n -$
$1; n = 2^d)$. Prefix sums are partial sums $S_i = \Sigma_{j=0}^{i} v_j$ $(i = 0, \ldots, n - 1)$. The program starts
n processes P_i which have a unique process identifier $i(i = 0, \ldots, n - 1)$. Process P_i computes prefix sum S_i. Figure 14 displays the corresponding computation and communication steps for a vector of length $p = 8$ and vector elements $v_i = i + 1$ $(i = 0, \ldots, 7)$.

Program Example 8 computes prefix sums in $\log_2 n$ loop iterations. Note that parallel execution is heavily restricted because of the rendezvous demands introduced; for
example, communication between processes 4 and 5, abbreviated as (4,5), is possible
only if the two communications (6,7) and (5,6) are completed. Nonblocking send and
receive operations provide a higher potential for parallelism and are thus supported by
modern message-passing libraries (see the subsection Message-Passing Libraries).

Example 8 Program Example: Computation of prefix sums

```
PROCEDURE PrefixSums (VAR v:ARRAY[0 ..n–1] OF Integer; n: Integer);
VAR max: Integer;
   PROCEDURE Sum(pid:Integer);
   VAR i, dist, val, tmp: Integer;
   BEGIN
      val:= v[pid];
      dist:=1;                              (* initial distance = 1 *)
```

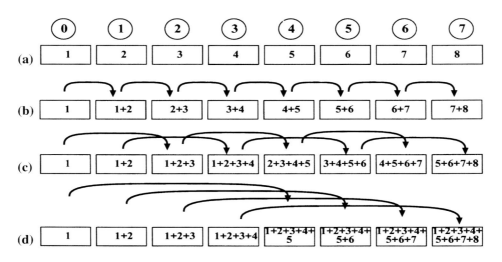

FIGURE 14   Prefix sum computation: (a) initial values; (b–d) communication steps for distances 1, 2, and 4, respectively.

```
    FOR i:= 1 TO log(n) DO
        IF pid <= max-dist THEN        (* select sender processes *)
            Sendp(pid + dist, val);
        END;
        IF pid >= dist THEN            (* select receiver processes *)
            Receivep(pid - dist, tmp);  (* receive in buffer variable *)
            val:=val + tmp              (* update current value *)
        END;
        dist:=dist*2;                  (* double the distance *)
    END;
    v[pid]:=val
    END Sum;
BEGIN
    max:= n-1;
    FORALL i:= 0 TO max DO             (* creation of processes *)
        Sum(i)
    END;
END PrefixSums
```

Model Problem

The sender–receiver model is relevant for this solution, too. We assume that the processors are logically arranged like a grid by the system, as in Program Example 4. The variables k_pid, l_pid, kmax, lmax have the same meaning as in that example. The code is abbreviated. The line marked by ♣ corresponds to three sends equivalent to the previous line. The same is true for the line with ♥ but with receives instead of sends.

Although all processes execute the same program, one of them is distinguished from all others: process (1,1) takes the part of the coordinator. At the end of each iteration step, it waits for messages from all others containing the local fault. After calculating the global fault, it broadcasts the decision on whether a new step is necessary or not.

Example 9 Jacobi Method for Model Problem on MPP

```
PROCEDURE Jakobi (VAR u: ARRAY[1..n, 1..n] OF Real n: Integer; eps;
Real)
    VAR v ARRAY[1..n, 1..n] OF Real; fault: Real; notConverged, help: Boolean;

BEGIN
    NotConverged := true;
    WHILE notConverged DO
        fault := 0.0;      (* Local_Fault *)
        FOR i:= 1TO n DO
            FOR j:= 1 TO n DO
                v[i,j] = (u[i-1,j] + u[i+1,j] + u[i,j-1] + u[i,j+1])/4.0      (* relax point *)
            END
        END;
        Calculate_Local_Fault and Copy_v_to_u; (*see example (4)*)
        IF k_pid /= 1THEN send((k_pid – 1, l_pid), u(1,j)(j=1..n)) END;
                                    (*send left boundary to left neighbor *)
```

(*♣*) send_to_upper,_lower,_and_right_neighbor_the_corresponding_boundary_
            data;
        IF k_pid /= 1**THEN** receive((k_pid - 1, l_pid), u(0,j)(j=1..n)) **END**;
                                            (*receive from left neighbor its right boundary*)
(*♥*) receive_from_lower,_upper,_and_left_neighbor_their_boundary_data;
        IF k_pid=1 and l_pid=1 **THEN**
            IF fault > eps **THEN** notConverged:= true **ELSE** notConverged:= false
END;
            FOR k:= 1**TO** kmax **DO**
            FOR l:= 1 **TO** lmax **DO**
                IF not(k_pid=1 and l_pid=1) **THEN**
                    receive((k,l), help);
                    NotConverged := notConverged or help
                END
            END;
            IF notConverged **THEN** send(all_but_me, true) **ELSE** send(all_but_me,
                false) **END**
        ELSE IF fault > eps **THEN** send((1,1),true) **ELSE** send((1,1),false) **END**;
        END;
            receive((1,1),notConverged)
    END
END Jacobi

PARALLEL ALGORITHMS

Parallel algorithms are characterized by concurrent threads of execution. Efficient parallel algorithms maximize the number of execution threads and minimize the amount of communication between them. Because these are usually conflicting goals, a compromise needs to be found.

There is a dilemma that has not been solved so far: for its general applicability, a parallel algorithm aims at an architecture-independent formal description. The more abstract its definition, though, the less accurately it models performance. Thus, current literature on parallel algorithms reveals two tracks: one based on an idealized machine model (e.g., the PRAM model) and one describing more realistic algorithms to be used on certain process(or) topologies.

Knowledge of parallel algorithms is poor compared to their sequential counterparts. However, for some problem areas, such as graph algorithms, matrix computations, and sort algorithms, detailed results are available. Significant improvements are expected from computational sciences, which combine real-life applicability and the need for high performance.

PRAM Model

The *random-access machine* (RAM) model has been successful for the description and analysis of sequential algorithms. The parallel extension is the *parallel random-access machine* (PRAM). All processors have access to a common memory and execute instructions synchronously. Regarding simultaneous access to the common memory, different types have been proposed: *concurrent read* (CR), *concurrent write* (CW), *exclusive read* (ER), and *exclusive write* (EW). Program Example 10 computes prefix sums on a CREW PRAM.

Example 10 Program Example. Prefix computation on PRAM

```
PROCEDURE PrefixSums (VAR v:ARRAY[0..n-1] OF Integer; n: Integer);
VAR dist, i, j : Integer;
BEGIN
  dist:=1;
  FOR i:= 1 TO log(n) DO
    FORALL j:= dist TO n-1 DO
      v[j]:= v[j] + v[j-dist]
    END;
    dist:= dist*2
  END
END PrefixSums
```

Performance analysis of PRAM algorithms is done using asymptotic costs: $cost(n) = p(n) \, t(n)$; n is the problem size, $p(n)$ is the number of processors used, and $t(n)$ is the resulting execution time. Algorithmic cost for Program Example 10 is $O(n \log n)$. This particular algorithm can easily be implemented on a distributed-memory system as shown in Program Example 8.

Topology-Oriented Algorithms

Parallel algorithms can be classified in different ways. Reference 39 lists 13 criteria for the description of parallel algorithms. Reference 40 introduces algorithmic classes such as Compute-Aggregate-Broadcast, Systolic, and Divide-and-Conquer. Most references classify according to the process topology used (i.e., the direct neighborhoods used for efficient data exchange).

In this subsection, we concentrate on regular parallelism (i.e., algorithms which make use of regular configurations of processes operating on partitioned datasets). For a treatment of irregular algorithms and related issues, see Ref. 41.

Farm Algorithms

A *farm* is a set of processes. Each process has a unique process identification. One of the processes is selected as the master process and manages task distributions as well as input and output operations. The other processes are worker processes and compute solutions of problems assigned. Task management is done by either common task list or collective communication (broadcast).

Many parallel algorithms use farm topologies. Computing the definite integral of a non-negative function $f(x)$ is often used as a reference example (42–44).

The following example computes the transitive closure of a directed graph (45). Graphs are often represented by an $n \cdot n$ *adjacency matrix A* of Boolean values, where n is the number of graph nodes. If element A_{ij} has the value *true*, a direct connection from node i to node j exists. The *transitive closure* is a related matrix which indicates reachability, both directly and via intermediate nodes. The main idea of the Warshall algorithm is as follows: If a node j can reach a node i, node j can also reach the nodes k which can be reached starting at node i. Figure 15a shows an example graph and the computed

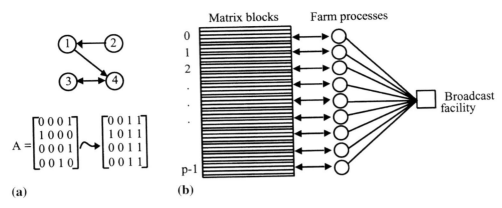

FIGURE 15 Warshall algorithm: (a) sample graph, adjacency matrix, and transitive closure; (b) parallelization.

transitive closure; Program Example 11 describes the sequential algorithm. Note that the transitive closure can be computed *in situ* (i.e., it is stored within the array initially used for the adjacency matrix).

Example 11 Program Example. Transitive closure

```
PROCEDURE TransitiveClosure (VAR A:ARRAY[1 ..n, 1 ..n] OF Boolean; n:
                Integer);

VAR i, j, k : Integer;
BEGIN
  FOR i:= 1 TO n DO
    FOR j:= 1 TO n DO
      IF A[j,i] THEN
        FOR k:= 1 TO n DO
          A[j,k]:=A[j,k] OR A[i,k]
        END
      END
    END
  END
END TransitiveClosure
```

The program can be parallelized by rowwise partitioning of A into *p* blocks and distribution of the blocks among *p* farm processes (Fig. 15b). Like the sequential program, the parallel program consists of *n* iterations of the following steps:

1. The "owner" of line *i* broadcasts line *i* in iteration step *i*. Processes store the data received in an auxiliary variable.
2. The transitive closure is computed in parallel in all matrix blocks with the aid of the auxiliary variable.

Grid and Torus Algorithms

Grid and *torus* are two-dimensional arrays of processes (Fig. 16a). Each process (except the border processes of a grid) has four direct neighbors, usually identified by the NEWS direction scheme. For collective communication, data exchange within rows and columns is supported. Application areas for grid and torus topologies are manifold: simulations, image processing, and computations on cellular automata, for example.

As an example, we describe a parallel algorithm for multiplying two dense matrices A and B using a torus of size $p \cdot p$ (46). Both matrix A (of size $h_A \cdot w_A$) and matrix B (of size $h_B \cdot w_B$; $w_A = h_B$ must hold) are partitioned and subblocks are distributed among the p^2 processes. The algorithm uses one-to-all broadcasts of A blocks within process rows and single-step circular upward shifts of B blocks along process columns. The algorithm performs p iterations of the following loop body:

1. Broadcast the selected A block and store in local buffer $\hat{A}$. In the first step, select A^{ii}; if A^{ij} is selected in the current step, select $A^{i(j+1) \bmod p}$ for the next step.
2. Multiply the $\hat{A}$ block received with the resident block of B and store in matrix C.
3. Send the block of B to the process directly above it and receive a new block of B from the process below it (both communications with wraparound at borders).

Figure 17 shows the execution steps of this algorithm ($p = 2$). References 47 and 43 describe corresponding PVM and MPI programs (see the subsection Message-Passing Libraries.). Reference 48 analyzes the complexity of the algorithm.

Stencil algorithms represent another class of algorithm based on grid partitioning.

Grid

Torus

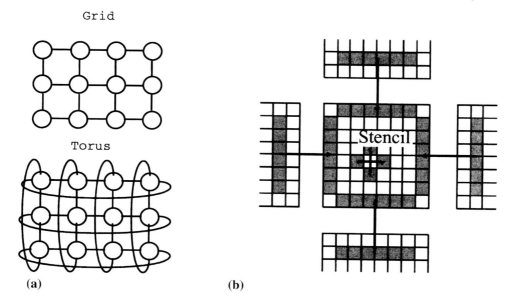

(a) **(b)**

FIGURE 16   Grid and torus: (a) process topologies; (b) data exchange for stencil algorithm.

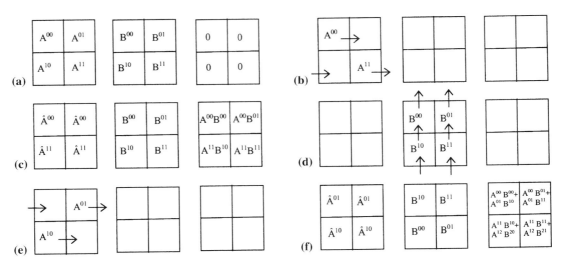

FIGURE 17   Execution steps of matrix multiplication: (a) initial values; (b) first broadcast; (c) first multiplication; (d) first upward shift; (e) second broadcast; (f) second multiplication.

These algorithms are popular in scientific computing and are applied when discretization is the method used to solve a problem (e.g., solving partial differential equations). Just as in the matrix multiplication example, arrays are partitioned and distributed as rectangular data blocks. During the update of an individual data cell, the values of surrounding neighbor cells are taken and a new value is computed according to a given formula (this regular computation pattern is called a *stencil*). Although updates in the inner parts of a block can be done independently of other processes, computing the stencil at the borders requires data exchange (Fig. 16b). In order to use communication time efficiently, it is better to communicate whole border rows and columns instead of individual cell values.

Hypercube Algorithms

A *hypercube* is a process topology consisting of 2^d processes. d is called the *hypercube dimension*. Each process has a unique process identifier with a binary encoding b. The hypercube of dimension $d = 0$ is a single node with a binary encoding $b = 0$. The hypercube of dimension $d = 1$ consists of two nodes with a binary encoding $b = 0$ and $b = 1$, respectively. Hypercubes of dimensions $d > 1$ are constructed as follows: Corresponding nodes (i.e., having the binary coding b) of two hypercubes of dimension $d = 1$ are directly connected; one node gets coding $0b$, the other one coding $1b$. Figure 18a shows hypercubes for small dimensions.

The following algorithm computes the sum of integer data. The program consists of $p = 2^d$ parallel processes organized as a hypercube of dimension d. The number of integers to be added is $p \cdot n$. The algorithm has three basic phases: reading of data values into an array a, computation of local sums, and computation of the final sum by d reduction steps. Figure 18b shows an example for $d = 3$. In Figure 18b, for the sake of simplicity, local sums are set to the value of the process encoding (i.e., process 5 gets local sum 5). All circles shaded gray denote active processes that fetch the value from

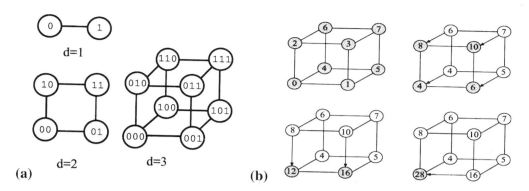

FIGURE 18   (a) Hypercubes for dimensions 1–3; (b) computation of sum.

the corresponding neighbor and add it to their value. Program Example 12 is the corresponding program.

Example 12 Program Example. Adding integers on a hypercube

```
PROCEDURE HypercubeSum (d,n: Integer; VAR res: Integer);
VAR p: Integer;
  PROCEDURE Sum(pid:Integer);
  VAR a: ARRAY[1 ..n] OF Integer;
       locSum, dist, tmp, i: Integer;
  BEGIN
    Read data into array a;                    (* left unspecified *)
    locSum:= 0; dist:=p;
    FOR i:= 1 To n DO locSum:=locSum+a+[i] END;
    FOR i:= 1 TO d DO                          (* d reduction steps *)
      dist:=dist DIV 2;
      IF pid < dist THEN                       (* process remains active *)
        Receivep(pid + dist, tmp);
        locSum:=locSum + tmp
      ELSE                                     (* process becomes inactive *)
        Sendp(pid - dist, locSum);
        RETURN
      END
    END;
      res:=locSum;                             (* return final sum *)
  END Sum;
BEGIN
  p:= 2**d;
  FORALL i:= 0 TO p-1 DO
    Sum(i)
  END
END HypercubeSum
```

Many other computations on a hypercube of dimension d follow the same basic steps: independent local computations, followed by d reduction steps. Other algorithms [e.g., Batcher's *bitonic sorting* algorithm (49)] have a slightly more complicated scheme of data exchange.

Further Algorithms

Examples of further process topologies often used in parallel programming are the following:

- Linear arrays: These are linearly ordered sequences of process nodes. For instance, in a *ring*, all nodes have exactly one direct predecessor and successor that data can be transferred from and to, respectively. It is easy to support more generalized process abstractions, such as access to the nth predecessor and nth successor node. Prefix sums can be elegantly computed in a linear array (50).
- Hierarchies: A *tree* is a topology which represents an hierarchical arrangement of process nodes. Each node (except so-called leaf nodes) has a fixed number of child processes. Topology-specific abstractions comprise information regarding position (level and child information) and neighborhood (subtree processes). Divide-and-conquer algorithms are well-known examples using process hierarchies (51).

Transformations Between Topologies

Ideally, the process topology of the algorithm to be implemented matches the interconnection topology of the target system. With different process topologies, there is a need for a *reconfigurable interconnection* system. Today's systems, though, have fixed interconnections such as buses, rings, grids, and hypercubes (see the Section Interconnecting Networks). Thus, either the hardware architecture is already taken into consideration when the algorithm is developed or subsequent mapping between topologies is needed. For example, Figure 19 shows how ring and torus topologies can be mapped onto a hypercube topology.

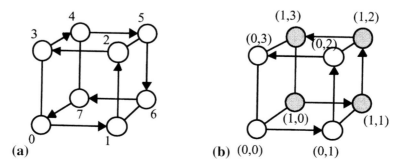

FIGURE 19   Mapping topologies onto an hypercube: (a) ring; (b) torus.

PERFORMANCE ISSUES

In this section, we introduce basic performance measures and laws used for analyzing parallel program performance. We also discuss the basic sources of performance loss and give an overview of performance analysis tools. We restrict our discussion to a dedicated usage of a parallel system; that is, a single application program is executed and analyzed.

Run Time, Communication Time, and Bandwidth

The *run time* of a parallel program is the length of the time interval, which is defined from the start of the first process until termination of the last process. During the run time of a program, operations such as computations, input/output requests, synchronization, and interprocess communication are executed and the performance of these routines determine the overall performance. For instance, in a system with distributed memory, the *communication time* t_{com} is essential. The main factors affecting it are a constant start-up time t_l (also called *latency*), the *transmission time* t_d for a single data value, and the *message length n*.

Example 13 $t_{com} = t_l + nt_d$

For very large values of n, the latency can be neglected and the *bandwidth* $1/t_d$ is used for characterizing the communication performance.

Speedup and Efficiency

Speedup defines the performance win (or loss) of a parallel program executed on a multiprocessor in comparison to a single-processor solution. Strictly speaking, two different measures exist: relative and absolute speedup. The *relative speedup* is the ratio of the run time t_1 of an parallelized program executed on a single processor compared to the run time t_p of the same program when executed on p processors.

Example 14 Relative speedup $= t_1/t_p$

Because the parallel program contains parallelization overhead, a stricter measure (*absolute speedup*) is defined. For comparison, the run time t_s of the fastest sequential program is used.

Example 15 Absolute speedup $= t_s/t_p$

In literature, this difference is often neglected and t_s/t_p is implicitly used. also different terminology can be found (e.g., true speedup and rough speedup).

High relative speedup values do not guarantee "best performance." As an example, program A has a run time of 1000 s on 1 processor and 2 s on 1000 processors. Program B solves the same task within 100 s on 1 processor and within 0.5 s on 1000 processors. Hence, the relative speedup values are 500 and 200, respectively. Although program A has a higher speedup value, one would prefer program B because it solves the problem four times faster.

It is uneconomic to use an additional processor for getting only a very small speedup increase (or even an decrease). *Efficiency* defines the portion of processor performance effectively used. Again, *absolute* and *relative efficiency* can be distinguished.

Example 16 Efficiency $=$ Speedup/p

A program runs 10 s on 1 processor and 5 and 4 s on 3 and 4 processors, respectively.

The relative speedup values are 2 and 2.5; the relative efficiency values are 0.66 and 0.62, respectively. Thus, the processor performance effectively used decreases from 66% to 62%.

Amdahl's Law

Amdahl's law predicts the maximum speedup one can expect with p processors in comparison to a single-processor run (52). The following assumptions hold: (1) The problem size is constant (i.e., the same program with the same datasets is used for getting single-processor and multiprocessor performance results; (2) the program execution time is divided into two parts: a sequential part of length t_{seq} and a parallel part of length t_{par}. Thus, the execution time on a single-processor system is $t_{seq} + t_{par}$ (normalized to 1), whereas on a parallel system of p processors, the parallel work load is assumed to be ideally distributable with a resulting run time of length $t_{seq} + t_{par}/p$ (Fig. 20a).

Example 17 Maximum relative speedup $= \dfrac{t_{seq} + t_{par}}{t_{seq} + t_{par}/p} = \dfrac{p}{1 + (p-1)t_{seq}}$

Figure 20b presents performance values for different values of p and t_{seq}. According to Amdahl's law, the sequential part is a performance bottleneck that cannot be overcome: Even with an infinite number of processors, for a program with a sequential percentage of, say, 10% one can only expect a speedup value of 10. This frustrating result has for a long time been accepted as a performance barrier.

Gustafson–Barsis Law

With the widespread usage of distributed-memory architectures in the mid-1980s it was recognized that with an increasing number of processors, one also gets more memory, which can be used for increasing the problem size. Like Amdahl's law, the Gustafson–Barsis law (53) predicts the maximum speedup one can expect, but it does not use Assumption 1. We again divide the program execution into a sequential part t_{seq} and a parallel part t_{par}, but first analyze the multiprocessor execution. There, after a time interval

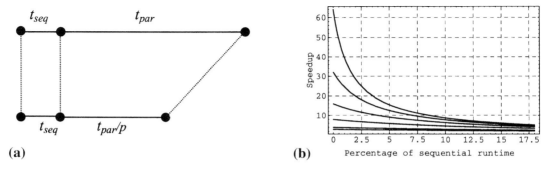

(a)   **(b)**

FIGURE 20   Amdahl's law: (a) Top: run-time for 1 processor; bottom: run time for $p = 2$ processors. (b) Speedup for different values of p (64, 32, 16, 8, 4, and 3 from top to bottom) in relation to percentage of sequential execution time.

of length t_{seq}, each of the processors runs a parallel program component of length t_{par}. If such a computation has to be executed on a single-processor system, $t_{seq} + pt_{par}$ time units are needed (Fig. 21a). $t_{seq} + t_{par}$ is again normalized to 1.

Example 18 Maximum relative speedup $= \dfrac{t_{seq} + pt_{par}}{t_{seq} + t_{par}} = p + (1 - p)t_{seq}$

Figure 21b reveals only a linear speedup decrease. Therefore, we must target for algorithms which have an increase regarding the problem size.

Scalability and Isoefficiency

A program is called *scalable* if, for increasing processor numbers, efficiency can be kept constant by increasing the problem size. The *isoefficiency* function defines the dependency between the number of processors used and the problem size needed.

Example. We analyze the hypercube program example introduced in the subsection Hypertube Algorithms. The number n of vector elements to be added represents the problem size; p is the number of processors used. We assume that the time needed for adding two numbers and the time needed for doing a point-to-point communication are identical (normalized to one time unit). For the parallel program, we get one program phase for the local computations, followed by $\log p$ phases consisting of a communication and a sum.

Example 19 Speedup $S\dfrac{n - 1}{(n/p) - 1 + 2 \log p} \approx \dfrac{np}{n + 2p \log p}$ (for large values of n)

Example 20 Efficiency $E = \dfrac{n}{n + 2p \log p}$

If the efficiency target is 0.8, Eq. (20) can be rewritten and the isoefficiency function is derived as $n = 8\, p \log p$. All data values (n, p) which fulfill this equation guarantee the required efficiency. Examples are (64, 4), (192, 8), and (512, 16).

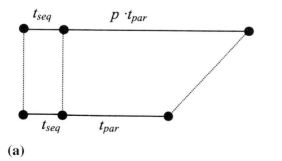
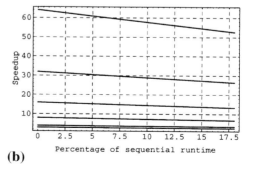

(a)　　　　　　　　　　　　　　**(b)**

FIGURE 21　Gustafson–Baris law: (a) top: run time for 1 processor: bottom: run time for $p = 2$ processors. (b) Speedup for different values of p (64, 32, 16, 8, 4, and 3 from top to bottom) in relation to percentage of sequential execution time.

Performance Anomalies

Performance anomalies are situations in which behavior differing from that expected is found. For instance, superlinear speedup describes a scenario where p processors are used, but the resulting speedup value is greater than p. This is not only a theoretical aspect but can occur in practice. For instance, branch-and-bound algorithms solve a problem by traversing a decision tree. The resulting run times in the branches are usually different. If the problem tree of Figure 22a is traversed in depth-first order, the sequential run time is 15 time units (Fig. 22b). If two processors traverse in parallel, the problem is solved within three time units. The resulting relative speedup is 5!

Another well-known situation for superlinear speedup is caused by the memory hierarchy of computer systems. In addition to main memory, cache memories offer fast and transparent access to data. If a program is very data intensive, data will be placed both in cache and main memories. If the same problem is solved on a parallel system, all data can be held in the distributed caches, which can result in a superlinear speedup.

Performance Loss

Any program execution that results in a program efficiency of less than 1 indicates a performance loss. A major contributing factor is the presence of *sequential program parts*. The discussion of the Amdahl and Gustafson–Barsis laws has shown the consequences for the overall performance when processors tend to be idle.

Data locality (i.e., the placement of data within the memory hierarchy) is another source of inefficiencies. Memory-coupled multiprocessors usually have additional private memory segments, which offer faster access. In message-passing systems, time-consuming communication operations are necessary to access remote data. As a consequence, data placement is crucial for the resulting overall performance.

Further sources are, for instance, *extra computations* (i.e., computations not done in the monoprocessor runs) and *overheads* (i.e., process creation and termination times). Detailed information can be found in Refs. 54 and 55.

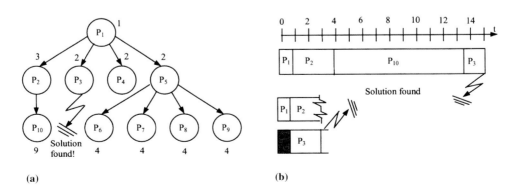

FIGURE 22 Superlinear speedup: (a) problem tree and execution times; (b) top: run time for one processor, bottom: run time for two processors.

PARALLEL SOFTWARE

Hundreds of experimental programming languages, libraries, and tools have been introduced over the years. We sketch a few of those which have found widespread usage. Further information (including sample programs and tutorials) is available at several sites on the Internet (56–60).

Message-Passing Libraries

Under the message-passing paradigm, processes exchange data and thus cooperate by using explicit send and receive operations. These operations are included in a subroutine library (the so-called *message-passing library*) which the programmer calls from well-known sequential languages (such as C and Fortran 77). As a result, initial learning efforts required for writing first parallel programs tend to be moderate (no new programming language required). However, parallel programming is not at all easy, as every aspect of parallelism must explicitly be managed by the programmer. Even worse, the abstraction level is operating-system-oriented and considered as rather low. Today, explicit message passing is the dominant programming model used on distributed-memory multiprocessors and computer networks.

Early libraries were target-system-specific. More recently, program portability has been emphasized and certain (*de facto*) standards have been developed. For an overview, see Ref. 61.

Parallel Virtual Machine

The *parallel virtual machine* (PVM) supports the simultaneous usage of a dynamic set of computers that are connected by a network. Each computer executes an operating system extension, the so-called *PVM demon*. All demons together manage the parallel virtual machine (for instance, they know where parallel processes are allocated). PVM comprises around 60 routines which provide support for process control, process information, event handling, communication, and group operations (47).

The strength of PVM is the support of heterogeneous networks of computers, its wide distribution, and the existence of programming tools. Although first releases were limited to UNIX systems, new developments (PVM 3.4) also support an interfacing of Windows-based systems. C and Fortran 77 were the two host languages offered right from the beginning. In the meantime, further language support is available. For up-to-date information, see Ref. 62.

Message-Passing Interface

The *message-passing interface* (MPI) is a specification of a library for programming distributed-memory multiprocessors (43,63). MPI is a successor of PVM with a focus on standardization and efficient implementation on multiprocessors. The standardization process has been driven by the Message-Passing Interface Forum, a consortium representing most of the major vendors of concurrent computers, along with researchers from universities and government laboratories.

The first standard (MPI-1) includes features such as a *communicator* (a safe communication space in which unrelated messages are separated from each other), manifold send and receive modes, Cartesian and graph process topologies, group communication, barriers, and derived data types. MPI-1 can be considered as being large because it has more than 125 functions; on the other hand, it can be considered as being small because useful SPMD programs can be developed with as few as 6 functions. These six primary functions are: MPI_Init (initialization routine), MPI_Comm_size (returns number of processes that can cooperate), MPI_Comm_rank (returns unique process identification), and MPI_Finalize (finalization routine). More recently, the forum has released a set of extensions (MPI-2). New features include dynamic process creation, one-sided communication, extended collective operations, and input and output support.

As with PVM, C and Fortran 77 were the two host languages offered right from the beginning. In the mean time, further language facilities have become available. For up-to-date information, see Ref. 64.

Programming Shared-Memory Systems

Thread Packages

Today's high-end workstations have a multiprocessor architecture. Operating-system extensions (*thread packages*) support the development of concurrent programs. *POSIX Threads* (PThreads; ISO/IEC 9945-1 : 1996) is such a well-known UNIX extension. PThreads support task parallelism but not data parallelism. Because the programmer has to work on a rather system-oriented abstraction level, PThreads and other thread packages have not found widespread usage in the high-performance community.

OpenMP

OpenMP is a set of compiler directives and run-time-library routines that extend Fortran (and separately, C and C++) to express shared-memory parallelism. The goal of the standard envisaged is program portability among shared-memory architectures (44). Because they address different target architectures, OpenMP and MPI complement each other.

OpenMP is a continuation of earlier standardisation activities that failed (project ANSI X3H5). It supports both fine-grain loop parallelism and coarse-grain process parallelism. A major design goal is the support of incremental parallelization of programs: Few textual directives are inserted at program parts where an earlier performance analysis has revealed performance bottlenecks. The language extensions proposed fall into one of three categories: control structures, data environment, and synchronization. For up-to-date information, see Ref. 65.

Parallel Programming Using Fortran

Fortran has always been the primary language for scientific programming. Compute-intensive applications can be implemented either by a combination of Fortran 77 (a sequential language) and a message-passing library (e.g., PVM and MPI), or by the usage of Fortran language variants (e.g., Fortran 90 and High Performance Fortran) that include language features for parallel programming.

Fortran 90/Fortran 95

Fortran 90 (66) is an extension of Fortran 77. Whole arrays or array sections can be used directly in expressions. This makes programs both compact and readable and allows a compiler to make target-specific optimizations (e.g., generating code for parallel execution). An *activity mask* (where directive) can be used to specify computation restrictions (e.g., exclude all computations that cause a division by zero). The language also contains several *intrinsic functions* for array computations. Examples are MINVAL and MAX-VAL (minimum and maximum value of an array) and SUM and PRODUCT (sum and product of array values).

Fortran 90 has been standardized as ISO/IEC 1539 : 1991 and ANSI X3.198-1992. Implementations exist for different architectures including parallel processors. Its successor Fortran 95 (ISO/IEC 1539-1 : 1997) offers further elements such as FORALL-statement (67).

High Performance Fortran

High Performance Fortran (HPF) (68,69) is an extension of Fortran 90. Its focus is on code generation for data parallel programs executed on distributed-memory systems. Language extensions, called *directives*, are structured comments all beginning with the same character sequence !HPF$. By means of these directives, a programmer gives hints to the compiler about essential program properties. The key notion is *data locality*: Data objects which are closely related and accessed in computation phases shall be allocated to the same processor node. The core of HPF thus comprises directives which support the mapping of array data structures to processor arrays. This mapping process is threefold (Fig. 23a): *alignment* of data arrays, creation of *abstract processor arrays*, and *distribution* of arrays to abstract processors. Figure 23b shows two examples for the alignments of vectors.

High Performance Fortran has been developed by the High-Performance Fortran Forum taking results from other research projects [e.g., Fortran D (70) and Vienna Fortran (71)] into account. For up-to-date information regarding implementations and support tools, see Ref. 72.

Java

Java (73) proliferates both in academia and industry. It is a fully object-oriented programming language designed for Internet applications (applets). Java supports concurrent programming (74,75). Processes (called threads) can be created either by inheritance from system class Thread or by implementing interface Runnable. All threads share a common address space. For synchronization purposes, Java uses the monitor concept. Mutual exclusion can be specified at the level of individual statements (synchronized

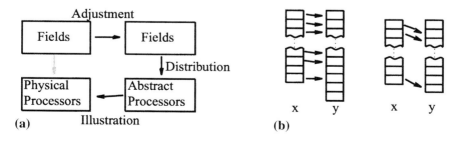

FIGURE 23   High Performance Fortran: (a) data mapping; (b) alignment of two vectors.

statement) and at the function level (synchronized modifier). A thread can block itself inside a critical region by calling wait. The event which will enable this process to continue is signalled by notify.

Java for high-performance computing is under investigation. Both language bindings to PVM and MPI, and data parallel language extensions à la HPF have been proposed. For up-to-date information, see Ref. 76.

Languages Based on Theoretical Frameworks

Communicating Sequential Processes and Occam

Communicating Sequential Processes (CSP) (77) is a theoretical framework for the design of parallel programs. CSP is based on the channel model of message parallelism process. A process can await messages arriving in multiple channels; thus, a generalized producer (e.g., consumer program) can be easily specified.

The first language design based on CSP was Occam (78). Occam and the *transputer* (a processor architecture which closely matches the programming model of CSP) were popular in the 1980s. CSP has, however, also been integrated in other sequential host languages. For example, recent implementations for Java exist (79,80). Many algorithms that were once developed under Occam are thus reusable in a modern language context.

Tuple-Space Parallelism and Linda

A *tuple space* is a data storage common to all processes. It stores a collection of tuples, each of which is a finite, ordered list of data elements. For data exchange, processes put tuples to the data space (operation Out) or get tuples from the data space (operation In). *Tuple templates* are used when data values are requested. These templates represent search masks, as certain data positions can be left open. During the search process, all data vectors in the tuple space are compared and those that match the specifications of the search pattern are retrieved. Thus tuple search has similarities to *query by example*, a search technique proposed for relational databases.

Tuple-space parallelism was pioneered by Linda (81). Linda is not a stand-alone programming language but extends a sequential host language (e.g., C and Modula-2) by the tuple space and its access operations. Recent developments use the tuple space concept for the realization of persistent messages (PVM 3.4).

Programming Tools

Programming tools support the software development. They can improve program quality, increase programmers' productivity, and optimize system performance. Tools can be classified by the application area addressed (82):

- Compilers and transformers
- Specification and software construction tools
- Static analyzers
- Debuggers
- Performance analyzers/visualizers

We give some more information about three of these points in the following subsections.

Specification and Software Construction Tools

Tools for specifying and constructing parallel programs affect different program aspects, including grouping of subtasks to processes, specifying interaction between processes, and distributing data to processes. The following subsections concentrate on tools for specifying data distributions.

Data should be distributed among parallel processes in such a way that good load balancing is achieved and interprocess communication is minimized. The second issue is relevant only if data are physically distributed among the nodes of a parallel computer. Because automatic specification of data distributions, which is performed by several parallelizing compilers, is restricted to a few regular problems, tools are required for the general case.

Data distribution tools concentrate on multidimensional data arrays because such data structures are predominantly used in performance-demanding programs. The tools provide a number of distribution strategies, ranging from regular strategies like block or cyclic to arbitrary, so-called irregular distributions. Data distribution strategies have been formalized through the design of high-performance languages such as High Performance Fortran or Vienna Fortran. Consequently, most data distribution tools provide distribution of arrays using HPF distribution functions. Furthermore, many tools provide visualization capabilities in order to show the impact of a distribution on load balance and interprocess communication.

A tool that supports specification of data distributions is GDDT (Graphical Data Distribution Tool) (83). The tool parses programs written in Fortran 77, extracts array definitions, and allows the user to specify array distributions using regular and irregular distribution functions of Vienna Fortran. The distributions specified can be written back to file, so that a user-driven migration from Fortran 77 to Vienna Fortran is possible. Furthermore, the tool provides visualization and evaluation of specified distributions using several two-dimensional and three-dimensional displays. The displays allow fast and easy exploration of mapping relationships between data arrays and logical processor arrays, which represent abstractions of the physical processor set. Array representations can be scaled, translated, rotated, and sliced. Mapping relationships can be shown at the level of single-array elements, element groups, slices, or distribution blocks. Finally, the displays show the impact of a distribution on load balance and interprocess communication. The latter facility is restricted to cases where distributed arrays are accessed using n-point stencils.

Another tool for specification and visualization of data distributions is HPF-Builder (84). This tool extracts array definitions from programs written in Fortran 90, allows the user to specify array distributions interactively, and writes array distributions back as HPF source text. It thus provides user-driven migration from Fortran 90 to HPF. Specification of distributions is more restricted than with GDDT because the base part of HPF allows just regular distributions. On the other hand, HPF-Builder provides a more sophisticated evaluation of the communication impact than GDDT, because it handles arbitrary loop nests with affine loop bounds and affine array access functions.

Debuggers

The group of debuggers consists of tools that support users in analyzing program behavior in order to track down, isolate, and remove bugs from software (85). In addition to the problems of sequential debugging, parallel debuggers have to cope with the increased complexity due to parallelism, the potentially huge amount of debugging data from such programs, and additional anomalous effects due to communication and synchronization of concurrently executing processes. In consequence, many different approaches to parallel debugging have been proposed in the past, and debugging is still a field with many ongoing research projects. Consequently, it is probably impossible to capture all existing techniques and approaches, or even to distinguish among pure theoretical achievements, actual tool prototypes, and tools available for end users. (An overview is given in Ref. 86).

An important input in this area is expected from the High-Performance Debugging Forum HPDF (87), which was established in 1997 and is officially sponsored by the Ptools consortium (88). Its goal is the definition of a useful and appropriate set of standards relevant to debugging tools for high-performance computing (89). Yet, although a first version of the HPD standard was released in 1998, actual implementations of its functionality are still not available to data and it remains to be seen whether the efforts of HPDF can yield substantial benefits for parallel debugging users.

Of the set of tools that are actually available to the user community, the Totalview (90) debugger is probably the most widely used commercial representative. Other example tools in this area available by research groups include P2D2 (91), Panorama (92), PDBG (93), and PDT (94). An important characteristic of these tools is that every approach applies several instances of a sequential debugger in order to perform the debugging task on the participating processes. Thus, their idea is to offer a user interface for managing the features of these base debuggers (92). Consequently, they are based on a textual representation of the source code and resemble sequential debuggers in many aspects. However, it has been noted earlier that textual representations are inadequate for expressing the complexity established in such programs (95). Therefore some projects investigate techniques in the area of software visualization for parallel program debugging.

An example of a debugging tool that uses a graphical representation as the main interface for debugging is the MAD environment (96). All the debugging features are applied on the event graph display, a space–time diagram that represents the parallel processes of a program, and their interactions through communication and synchronization (97). In addition, the MAD environment can be used to study the effects of race conditions, which may occur in nondeterministic parallel programs and represent one of the most tedious sources for errors in parallel programs. Other tools that offer specialized solutions for anomalous effects in parallel programs are described in Refs. 98–101.

Performance Analyzers/Visualizers

In contrast to debugging, performance analysis and tuning tools are almost always based on graphical representations (see overview in Ref. 102). One of the best-known examples in this area is ParaGraph (103), which includes space-time diagrams, utilization counts, Kiviat diagrams, Gantt charts, and many others. Following its success, many vendors announce similar sets of performance analysis tools [e.g., ParAide for Intel's Paragon, MPP Apprentice for Cray's T-3D, Prim for TMC's CM-5, PV for IBM's SP2, and CX-Trace for Convex's SPP1 (104)]. Other tools developed in research centers and academic institutions include AIMS (105), XPVM (106), Trapper (107), and VAMPIR (108).

One remarkable approach is the Paradyn performance analysis toolset (109), because it applies dynamic instrumentation to program monitoring, making it possible to determine the amount of analysis data during program observation. The problem of scalability is addressed in the visualization tool VISTOP (110), which offers a selection mechanism for "interesting" objects and "interesting" phases of a program in order to limit the display to the key scenes of a program. Other interesting solution in this area are provided by tools that apply three-dimensional representations (111), or even virtual reality techniques (112).

CURRENT RESEARCH ISSUES AND TRENDS

Parallel computing is a field still under development. We give an overview of current research issues that are likely to influence the future of parallel computing.

Architecture-Independent Programming Models

Sequential programming is, to a large degree, architecture independent. The acceptance of a generalized machine model (von Neumann computer), high-level programming models (imperative, functional, logic, and object oriented), and corresponding programming languages resulted in an improvement and productivity increase of software development. For parallel programming, the situation is less satisfactory. As the previous sections have shown, it is still architecture dependent. We list a few of the proposals for abstract machine models which have been published:

- Most of the literature on parallel algorithms (51,113) is based on the PRAM machine model. The original PRAM model has been criticized because of its lack of reality, and several variants have been proposed (see also the subsection PRAM Model).
- Snyder has proposed an integrated approach consisting of a machine model (*candidate-type architecture*, CTA), a programming model (*phase abstractions*), and programming languages (ORCA language family) (114).
- LogP is a machine model for distributed-memory multiprocessors based on four parameters: latency, overhead, gap, and processor (115). Using these parameters, a cost model predicts expected performance during algorithm design.
- *Bulk Synchronous Parallel Computer* (BSP) is a similar approach with emphasis on a realistic cost model (116,117). The machine abstraction consists of processor-memory modules which are interconnected both point-to-point and via an efficient broadcast mechanism. The programming model is based on algorithmic phases (*supersteps*) (118). In each superstep, a process executes a bounded number of computation operations which access only variables of its local memory and a communication operation for information exchange via messages or shared variables. The superstep ends with a barrier. The memory model is sequentially consistent.

Software Engineering for Parallel Systems

The price to be paid for the performance gain of parallel processors has been high: Time-consuming programming, nonreusable programs, and lack of suitable standards are among the arguments that characterize a rather immature software development. To overcome this "dilemma," software engineering techniques have been proposed:

- High-level programming languages,
- Skeleton-oriented programming,

- Object-oriented parallel programming,
- Interoperable parallel programming.

Information about these techniques can be found in Refs. 119–122.

Metacomputing

There are several sometimes conflicting interpretations of the term metacomputing. Here, we will follow the definition given by Barker and Fox (123):

> Metacomputing is the use of computing resources transparently available to the user via a networked environment. In other words, metacomputing use computers sharing and acting together to solve common problems. The key difference to a parallel computer is the behavior of individual computational nodes. A metacomputer is a dynamic environment that has some informal pool of nodes that can join or leave the environment whenever they desire. The nodes can be viewed as independent machines.

A metacomputer can be compared with the electricity grid. You get the necessary power without knowing from where it explicitly comes. In the same manner, a metacomputer is a similarly easy-to-use collection of networked computers that can work together. Therefore, such a system is often called "Computational Grid." Naturally, such a system is based on parallelism but the user does not see it. For more information, see Refs. 123 and 124.

Hardware Trends

Advances in integrated circuit technology will play an important role in future multiprocessors (see, e.g., Refs. 125 and 126). Because one million transistors will be soon integrated on one chip, symmetric multiprocessors consisting of up to eight processors and a shared large second-level cache will be placed on such a chip.

Consequently, future NUMA and COMA machines will be organized on a cluster base. Furthermore, the relative cost of a remote memory access is likely to increase in the future. Therefore, reducing the proportion of remote memory accesses in a way transparent to the programmer will become an important research issue. Therefore, replication and migration techniques have to be improved.

Very important would be a possible breakthrough in optical computing (127). Especially, optical interconnection networks would help to reduce the problem of remote memory accesses.

In any case, the peak performance of parallel processors will exceed the Petaflops (billion Megaflops) boundary in the next years. Within the scope of the Peta Flops Project, IBM announced such a system for 2005 (128). The range of applications which require such gigantic performance will become smaller and smaller. On the other hand, a situation like that provides the chance to use parts of that power for improved software.

How quickly the performance of parallel machines is improved can be seen by looking at the TOP500 list published every 6 months (129). Many members of that list are removed with the appearance of a new one. Only the special MPP Intel ASCI Red has remained at the first position for an extended period, due to the fact that this machine is continually being improved as part of the well-known ASCI program.

Although a NORMA computer has been leading that list for many months, the shared-memory machines will win in the future, due to the advantages of that type of systems. The question is, "Will NUMA or COMA win?" Despite of the fact that at the moment no COMA is commercially available, these computers have a lot of merits. COMA will outperform a CC-NUMA if the application runs without special tuning and requires many remote accesses. Only if much work is investigated in program structure which fits the memory hierarchy of a NUMA will such a system provide better results. Thus, much investigation is in progress on merging COMA and NUMA (130,131). In Ref. 132, an approach is presented where the hardware switches between COMA and NUMA, depending on the demands of the active program. The proposed system is called reconfigurable.

Many research activities are performed in the field of reconfigurable architectures (133). This will help to adjust a given machine to the needs of given application. A well-known project is RAW (134). The idea is to implement on a single chip a parallel architecture consisting of hundreds of very simple processors, each with some reconfigurable logic. Thereby, the design burdens the software alone with parallel execution and communication.

REFERENCES

1. K. Zuse, German Patent 1122748, February 25, 1956; see also http://www.zib.de/zuse/
2. J. H. Holland, "A Universal Computer Capable of Executing an Arbitrary Number of Sub-programs Simultaneously," *Proc. East Joint Computer Conf.*, *16*, 108–113 (1959).
3. G. H. Barnes, R. M. Brown, M. Kato, D. J. Kuck, D. L. Slotnick, and R. A. Stokes, "The ILLIAC IV Computer," *IEEE Trans. Computers*, *17*, 746–757 (August 1968).
4. http://www.tandem.com
5. G. Michelis, L. Pomello, E. Battiston, F. De Cindio, and C. Simone, "Formal Methods: A Petri Net Approach," in *Parallel and Distributed Handbook*, Zomaya (ed.), McGraw Hill, New York, 1996.
6. E. W. Dijkstra, "Cooperating Sequential Processes," in *Programming Languages*, F. Gennys (ed.), Academic Press, New York, 1968.
7. C. A. R. Hoare, "Monitors: An Operating System Structuring Concept," *Commun. ACM*, *17*, 549–557 (1974).
8. P. B. Hansen, *The Architecture of Concurrent Programs*, Prentice-Hall, Englewood Cliffs, NJ, 1977.
9. M. Flynn, "Some Computer Organizations and Their Effectiveness," *IEEE Trans. Computers*, *21*(9), 948–960 (1972).
10. G. A. Blaauw and W. Händler (eds.), *Workshop on Taxonomy in Computer Architecture*, Friedrich Alexander Universität, Erlangen–Nürnberg, 1981.
11. K. M. Kavi and H. G. Gragon, "A Conceptional Framework for the Description and Classification of Computer Architecture," in *Proceedings IEEE International Workshop on Computer Systems*, 1983, pp. 10–19.
12. D. B. Skillicorn, "A Taxonomy for Computer Architecture," *IEEE Computer*, *21*(11), 46–57 (1988).
13. K. Hwang, *Advanced Computer Architecture*, McGraw-Hill, New York, 1993.
14. G. Lerman, L. Rudolph, *Parallel Evolution of Parallel Processors*, Plenum Press, New York, 1993.
15. J. L. Hennessy and D. A. Patterson, *Computer Organization & Design. The Hardware/Software Interface*, Morgan Kaufmann, San Mateo, CA, 1994.
16. U. Brünning and K. Waldschmidt, "Grundlagen paralleler Architekturen," in *Parallelrechner: Architeckturen—Systeme—Werkzeuge*, K. Waldschmidt (ed.), Teubner, Stuttgart, 1995.

17. H. J. Siegel, *Interconnection Networks for Large-Scale Parallel Processing*, McGraw-Hill, New York, 1998.

18. G. F. Pfister and V. A. Norton, "'Hot Spot.' Contention and Combining in Multistage Interconnection Networks," *IEEE Trans. Compl.*, C-34(10) XXX (1985).

19. M.-C. Wang, H. J. Siegel, M. A. Nichols, and S. Abraham, "Using a Multipath Network for Reducing the Effects of Hot Spots," *IEEE Trans. Parallel Distrib. Syst.*, PDS-6(3), 252–268 (1995).

20. B. Nagendra and L. Rzymianowics, "High Speed Networks," in *High Performance Cluster Computing*, R. Buyya (ed.), Prentice-Hall, Englewood Cliffs, NJ, 1999.

21. E. Duncan, M. Stumm, M. Snelgrove, C. Cojocaru, and R. McKenzie, "Computational RAM," *IEEE Design Test Computers*, 16(1) (1999).

22. W. Henning and J. Volkert, "Datentransporte in einem hierarchischen Multiprocessor mit verteilten lokalen Speichern," *PARS Mitteilungen*, 4, 100–113 (1987).

23. J. Laudon and D. Lenoski, "The SGI Origin: A ccNUMA Highly Scalable Server," in *Proc. of the 24th Intern. Symp. Computer Architecture* 1997, pp. 241–251.

24. E. Hagersten, A. Landin, and S. Haridi, "DDM—A Cache-Only Architecture," *Computer*, 44–54 (September 1992).

25. T. Mowry, "Tolerating Latency Through Software-Controlled Data Prefetching," Doctorial dissertation, Computer Systems Laboratory, Stanford University, Stanford, CA, 1994.

26. S. V. Adve and K. Gharachorloo, "Shared Memory Consistency Models: A Tutorial," *Computer*, 66–76 (December 1996).

27. F. Dahlgren and J. Torellas, "Cache-Only Memory Architectures," *Computer*, 72–79 (June 1999).

28. K. Hwang and X. Zhiwei, *Scalable Parallel Computing*, McGraw-Hill, New York, 1998.

29. D. Lenoski, et al., "The Stanford Dash Multiprocessor," *IEEE Computer*, 63–79 (March 1992).

30. C. Maples and L. Wittie, *Merlin: A Superglue for Multicomputer Systems Compapcon 90*, CS Press, 1990.

31. A. Gupta, J. Hennessy, K. Gharlachorloo, T. Mowry, and W.-D. Weber, "Comparative Evaluation of Latency Reducing and Tolerating Techniques," in *Proc. of the 18th Intern. Symp. Computer Architecture*, 1991, pp. 532–533.

32. S. V. Alversion, et al., "The Terra Computer System," in *Proceedings 1990 International Conference on Supercomputing*, IEEE Computer Science Press, Los Alomitos, CA, 1990, pp. 1–6.

33. *Journal of Parallel and Distributed Computing*, 37(1) (1996); special issue on multithreading for multiprocessors.

34. L. Lamport, "How to Make a Multiprocessor Computer That Correctly Executes Multiprocess Programs," *IEEE Trans. Computers*, 28(9), 241–248 (1979).

35. M. Dubois, C. Scheurich, and F. A. Briggs, *Synchronization, Coherence and Event Ordering in Multiprocessors, IEEE Computer*, 21(2), (1988).

36. I. Tartalja and V. Milutinovic, "A Survey of Software Solutions for Maintenance of Cache Consistency in Shared Memory Multiprocessors," in *Proceedings of Twenty-Eighth Hawii International Conference on System Sciences*, IEEE, Washington, DC, 1995.

37. http://www.top500.org

38. http://www.sandia.jov/ASCI/Red/RedFacts.him

39. L. H. Jamieson, in *The Characteristics of Parallel Algorithms*, L. H. Jamieson, D. Gannon, and R. J. Douglass (eds.), MIT Press, Cambridge, MA, 1988, pp. 65–100.

40. P. A. Nelson and L. Snyder, in *The Characteristics of Parallel Algorithms*, L. H. Jamieson, D. Gannon, and R. J. Douglass (eds.), MIT Press, Cambridge, MA, 1988, pp. 3–20.

41. A. Ferreira and J. Rolim (eds.), *J. Parallel Distrib. Computing*, 50 (1988); special issue on irregular problems in supercomputing applications.

42. R. G. Babb (ed.), *Programming Parallel Processors*, Addison-Wesley, New York, 1988.

43. P. Pacheco, *Parallel Programming with MPI*, Morgan Kaufman, San Francisco, 1997.
44. L. Dagum and R. Menon, "OpenMP: An Industry-Standard API for Shared-Memory Programming," *IEEE Computat. Sci. Eng.*, 5, 46 (1998).
45. S. Warshall, "A Theorem on Boolean Matrices," *J. ACM*, 9, 11 (1962).
46. G. Fox, M. Johnson, G. Lyzengen, S. Olto, J. Salmon, and D. Walker, *Solving Problems on Concurrent Processors*, Prentice-Hall, Englewood Cliffs, NJ, 1988, Vols. I and II.
47. A. Geist, A. Beguelin, J. Dongarra, W. Jiang, R. Manchek, and V. Sunderam, *PVM—Parallel Virtual Machine*, MIT Press, Cambridge, MA, 1994.
48. V. Kumar, A. Grama, A. Gupta, and G. Karypis, *Introduction to Parallel Computing*, Benjamin/Cummings, Redwood City, CA, 1994.
49. K. Batcher, "Sorting Networks and Their Applications," in *AFIPS Spring Joint Computing Conference*, 1968, pp. 307–314.
50. S. G. Akl, *Parallel Computation: Models and Methods*, Prentice-Hall, Englewood Cliffs, NJ, 1997.
51. J. JaJa, *An Introduction to Parallel Algorithms*, Addison-Wesley, Reading, MA, 1992.
52. G. Amdahl, "Validity of the Single-Processor Approach to Achieving Large-scale Computing Capabilities," in *Proc. AFIPS Conf.*, 30, 483 (1967).
53. J. L. Gustaffson, "Reevaluating Amdahl's Law", *Commun. ACM*, 31, 532 (1988).
54. J. Bull, "A Hierarchical Classification of Overheads in Parallel Programs," in *Software Engineering for Parallel and Distributed Systems*, I. Jelly, et al. (eds.), Chapman & Hall, London; 1996, pp. 208–219.
55. H. Burkhart and R. Millen, "Performance-Measurement Tools in a Multiprocessor Environment," *IEEE Trans. Computers*, 38, 725–737 (1989).
56. Parascope, www.computer.org/parascope/
57. Schaller Nan's Parallel Computing Page; www.cs.rit.edu/~ncs/parallel.html
58. Yahoo, Yahoo Guide Supercomputing and Parallel Computing: www.yahoo.com/Computers/Supercomputing_and_Parallel_Computing/
59. NetLib, www.netlib.org/
60. IPCA Internet Parallel Computing Archive, unix.hensa.ac.uk.parallel/
61. R. Hempel, A. Hey, O. McBryan, and D. Walker, *Parallel Computing 20* (1994); special issue on Message-passing interfaces.
62. PVM www.epm.ornl.gov/pvm/pvm_home.html
63. W. Gropp, E. Lusk, and A. Skjellum, *Using MPI: Portable Parallel Programming with the Message Passing Interface*, MIT Press, Cambridge, MA, 1995.
64. www.mpi-forum.org/
65. www.openmp.org.
66. J. Adams, W. Brainerd, J. Martin, B. Smith, and J. Wagener, *Fortran 90 Handbook*, McGraw-Hill, New York, 1992.
67. J. Adams, W. Brainerd, J. Martin, B. Smith, and J. Wagener, *Fortran 95 Handbook*, MIT Press, Cambridge, MA, 1997.
68. Ch. Koelbel, D. Loveman, R. Schreiber, G. Steele, and M. Zosel, *The High Performance Fortran Handbook*, MIT Press, Cambridge, MA, 1994.
69. D. Loveman, "High Performance Fortran," *IEEE Parallel Distrib. Technol.*, 1, 25–42 (1993).
70. S. Hiranandani, K. Kennedy, C. Koelbel, U. Kremer, and C. Tseng, "An Overview of the Fortran D Programming System," in *Languages and Compilers for Parallel Computing*, Springer-Verlag, Berlin, 1992.
71. B. Chapman, P. Mehrotra, and H. Zima, "Programming in Vienna Fortran," *Sci. Program.*, 1, 31–50 (1992).
72. www.erc.msstate.edu/hpff/home.html
73. J. Gosling, B. Joy, and G. Steele, *The Java Language Specification*, Addison-Wesley, Reading, MA, 1996.

74. S. Hartley, *Concurrent Programming: The JAVA Programming Language*, Oxford University Press, Oxford, 1998.
75. D. Lea, *Concurrent Programming in Java*, ACM Press, New York, 1996.
76. www.javagrande.org
77. C. Hoare, *Communicating Sequential Processes*. Prentice-Hall, Englewood Cliffs, NJ, 1984.
78. J. Wexler, *Concurrent Programming in OCCAM 2—Computers and Their Applications*, John Wiley & Sons, New York, 1989.
79. P. Austin, JCSP web page: www.cs.ukc.ac.uk/projects/ofa/jcsp/
80. G. Hilderink, JavaPP web page: www.rt.el.utwente.nl/javapp/
81. N. Carriero and D. Gelernter, "How to Write Parallel Programs: A Guide to the Perplexed," *ACM Computing Surveys*, *21*, 323–357 (1989).
82. B. Appelbe and D. Bergmark, "Software Tools for High-Performance Computing: Survey and Recommendations," *Sci. Program.*, *5*, 239–249 (1996).
83. R. Koppler, S. Grabner, and J. Volkert, "Visualization of Distributed Data Structures for HPF-like Languages," *Sci. Program.*, *6*(1), 115–126 (1997).
84. J.-L. Dekeyer and Ch. Lefebvre, "HPF-Builder: A Visual Environment to Transform Fortran 90 Codes to HPF," *Int. J. Supercomputing Applic. High Perform. Computing*, *11*(2), 95–102 (1997).
85. J. B. Rosenberg, *How Debuggers Work: Algorithms, Data Structures, and Architecture*, John Wiley & Sons, New York, 1996.
86. C. M. Pancake and R. H. B. Netzer, "A Bibliography of Parallel Debuggers, 1993 Edition," in *Proc. of the 3rd ACM/ONR Workshop on Parallel and Distributed Debugging*, 1993; reprinted in *ACM SIGPLAN Notices*, *28*(12), 169–186 (1993).
87. High-Performance Debugging Forum, http://www.ptools.org/hpdf
88. Ptools consortium, http://www.ptools.org
89. J. Brown, J. Francioni, and C. Pancake, "White Paper on Formation of the High Performance Debugging Forum," available at http://www.ptools.org/hpdf/meetings/mar97/white-paper.html (February 1997).
90. Dolphin Interconnect Solutions Inc., "TotalView 3.8," available via WWW at http://www.dolphinics.com/tw/download/tv3.8.0-webdocs/User_Guide.ps (1998).
91. R. Hood, "The p2d2 Project: Building a Portable Distributed Debugger," in *Proc. SPDT'96, ACM SIGMETRICS Symp. on Parallel and Distributed Tools*, 1996, pp. 127–136.
92. J. May and F. Berman, "Panorama: A Portable, Extensible Parallel Debugger," in *Proc. 3rd ACM/ONR Workshop on Parallel and Distributed Debugging*, 1993; reprinted in *ACM SIGPLAN Notices*, *28*(12), 96–106 (1993).
93. J. C. Cunha, J. M. Lourenço, J. Vieira, B. Moscão, and D. Pereira, "A Framework to Support Parallel and Distributed Debugging," in *Proc. of HPCN'98*, 1998.
94. C. Clemencon, J. Fritscher, and R. Rühl, "Visualization, Execution Control and Replay of Massively Parallel Programs within Annai's Debugging Tool," in *Proc. High Performance Computing Symposium, HPCS '95*, 1995, pp. 393–404.
95. C. M. Pancake, "Visualization Techniques for Parallel Debugging and Performance-Tuning Tools," in *Parallel Computing: Paradigms and Applications*, A. Y. Zomaya (ed.), *Thomson Computer Press*, London, 1996, pp. 376–393.
96. D. Kranzlmüller, S. Grabner, and J. Volkert, "Debugging with the MAD Environment," *Environments and Tools for Parallel Scientific Computing III*, J. J. Dongarra and B. Tourancheau (eds.), Elsevier, Amsterdam, 1997, pp. 199–217.
97. D. Kranzlmüller, S. Grabner, and J. Volkert, "Event Graph Visualization for Debugging Large Applications," in *Proc. SPDT'96, ACM SIGMETRICS Symposium on Parallel and Distributed Tools*, 1996, pp. 108–117.
98. J. M. R. Martin and S. A. Jassim, "A Tool for Providing Deadlock Freedom," in *Parallel Programming and Java, Proceedings of the 20th World Occam and Transputer User Group Technical Meeting*, IOS Press, 1997.

99. Ch. E. McDowell and D. P. Helmbold, "Debugging Concurrent Programs," *ACM Computing Surveys*, *21*(4), 593–622 (1989).

100. R. H. B. Netzer and B. P. Miller, "Optimal Tracing and Replay for Debugging Message-Passing Parallel Program," in *Proc. Supercomputing 92*, 1992, pp. 502–511; reprinted in *J. Supercomputing*, *8*(4), 371–388 (1994).

101. S. K. Damodaran-Kamal and J. M. Francioni, "Nondeterminacy: Testing and Debugging in Message Passing Parallel Programs," in *Proc. 3rd ACM/ONR Workshop on Parallel and Distributed Debugging*, 1993; reprinted in *ACM SIGPLAN Notices*, *28*(12), 118–128 (1993).

102. A. Hondroudakis, "Performance Analysis Tools for Parallel Programs," Version 1.0.1, Edinburgh Parallel Computing Centre, The University of Edinburgh; available at http://www.epcc.ed.ac.uk/epcc-tec/documents.html (July 1995).

103. M. T. Heath and J. A. Etheridge, "Visualizing the Performance of Parallel Programs," *IEEE Software*, *8*(5), 29–39 (1991).

104. J. C. Yan and S. R. Sarukkai, "Analyzing Parallel Program Performance Using Normalized Performance Indices and Trace Transformation Techniques," *Parallel Computing*, *22*(9), 1215–1237 (1996).

105. J. C. Yan, S. Sarukkai, and P. Mekra, "Performance Measurement, Visualization and Modelling of Parallel and Distributed Programs using the AIMS Toolkit," *Software: Pract. Exper.*, *25*(4), 429–461 (1995).

106. G. A. Geist, J. Kohl, and P. Papadopoulos, "Visualization, Debugging and Performance in PVM," in *Proc. of Visualization and Debugging Workshop*, 1994.

107. T. Born, W. Obelöer, L. Schäfers, and C. Scheidler, "The Monitoring Facilities of the Graphical Parallel Programming Environment TRAPPER," in *Proc. 3rd Euromicro Workshop on Parallel and Distributed Processing*, 1995, pp. 555–562.

108. W. E. Nagel, A. Arnold, M. Weber, H.-C. Hoppe, and K. Solchenbach, "VAMPIR: Visualization and Analysis of MPI Resources," *Supercomputer 63*, *12*(1), pp. 69–80 (96).

109. B. P. Miller, M. D. Callaghan, J. M. Cargille, J. K. Hollingsworth, R. B. Irvin, K. L. Karavanic, K. Kunchithapadam, and T. Newhall, "The Paradyn Parallel Performance Measurement Tool," *IEEE Computer*, *28*(11), 37–46 (1995).

110. T. Bemmerl and P. Braun, "Visualization of Message Passing Parallel Programs with the TOPSYS Parallel Programming Environment," *J. Parallel Distrib. Computing*, *18*(2), 118–128 (1993).

111. J. Y. Vion-Dury and M. Santana, "Virtual Images: Interactive Visualization of Distributed Object-Oriented Programming Systems," in *Proc. OOPSLA '94, Conference on Object-Oriented Systems, Languages, and Applications*; reprinted in *ACM SIGPLAN Notices*, *29*(10), 65–84 (1994).

112. D. A. Reed, K. A. Shields, W. H. Scullin, L. F. Tavera, and C. L. Elford, "Virtual Reality and Parallel Systems Performance Analysis," *IEEE Computer*, *28*(11), 57–67 (1995).

113. S. Akl, *Design and Analysis of Parallel Algorithms*, Prentice-Hall, Englewood Cliffs, NJ, 1989.

114. L. Snyder, "Foundations of Practical Parallel Programming Languages," in *Portability and Performance for Parallel Processing*, T. Hey and J. Ferrante (eds.), John Wiley & Sons, New York, 1994, pp. 1–19.

115. D. Culler, et al., "LogP: Toward a Realistic Model of Parallel Computation," in *ACM SIGPLAN Symposium on Principles and Practive Parallel Computing*. ACM Press, New York, 1993, pp. 1–12.

116. L. Valiant, "A Bridging Model for Parallel Computing," *Commun. ACM*, *33*, 103–111 (1990).

117. W. McColl, "An Architecture Independent Programming Model for Scalable Parallel Computing," in *Portability and Performance for Parallel Processing*, T. Hey and J. Ferrante (eds.), John Wiley & Sons, New York, 1994, pp. 43–69.

118. T. Cheatham, A. Fahmy, D. Stefanescu, and L. Valiant, "Bulk Synchronous Parallel Computing—A Paradigm for Transportable Software," in *Proc. HICCS'95*, IEEE Press, Washington, DC, 1995, Vol. II, pp. 268–275.

119. D. Skillicorn and D. Talia (eds.), *Programming Languages for Parallel Processing*, IEEE Computer Science Press, Los Alamitos, CA, 1995.

120. I. Forster, R. Olson, and St. Tuecke, "Productive Parallel Programming: The PCN Approach," *Sci. Program.*, *1*, 51–66 (1992).

121. H. Burkhart, R. Frank, and G. Hächler, "Structured Parallel Programming: How Informatics Can Help Overcome the Software Dilemma," *Sci. Program.*, *5*, 33–45 (1996).

122. M. Cole, *Algorithmic Skeletons—Structured Management of Parallel Computation*, Pitman, London; 1989.

123. M. Baker and J. Fox, "Metacomputing: Harnessing Informal Supercomputers," in *High Performance Cluster Computing*, R. Buyya (ed.), Prentice-Hall, Englewood Cliffs, NJ, 1999.

124. I. Foster and K. L. Kesselmann, *The Grid: Blueprint for a New Computing Infrastructure*, Morgan Kaufmann, San Francisco, 1999.

125. D. Burger and J. Goodman, "Billion-Transistor Architectures," *Computer*, 46–47 (September 1997).

126. C. E. Kozyrakis and D. A. Patterson, "A New Direction for Computer Architecture Research," *Computer*, 24–32 (November 1998).

127. Y. L. Kyungsook, L. Guoping, and H. Jordan, "Hierarchical Networks for Optical Communications," *J. Parallel Distrib. Computing*, *60*, 1–16 (2000).

128. http://pavel.physics.sunysb.edu/RSFQ/Research/PetaFLOPs/references.html

129. http://www.top500.de/

130. E. Ekanadham, et al., "PRISM: An Integrated Architecture for Scalable Shared Memory," in *Proceedings 4th International Symposium on High-Performance Computer Architecture*, IEEE Computer Science Press, Los Alamitos, CA, 1998, pp. 140–151.

131. E. Hagersten and M. Koster, "Wildfire: A Scalable Path for SMPs," in *Proceedings 5th International Symposium on High-Performance Computer Architecture*, IEEE Computer Science Press, Los Alamitos, CA, 1999, pp. 171–181.

132. B. Falsavi and D. Wood, "Reactive NUMA: A Design for Unifying S-COMA and CC-NUMA," in *Proceedings 5th Annual International Symposium on Computer Architecture*, ACM Press, New York, 1997, pp. 229–239.

133. http://www.cis.unisa.edu.au/~raw2000

134. E. Waingold, M. Taylor, D. Srikrishna, and V. Sarkar, "Baring It All to Software: Raw Machines," *IEEE Computer Mag.*, *30*, 86–93 (1997).

HELMAR BURKHART

JENS VOLKERT

REAL-TIME CONSTRAINTS

INTRODUCTION

Should *real time* be fast? No, that is a myth! In fact, real time is *just in time*. For example, an avionics flight control system must spend 2.5 ms for attitude control every 50-ms period and 0.28 ms for flutter control every 4-ms period. The period restriction must be strictly abided, no faster and no slower, otherwise an airplane might crash! These just-in-time aspects constitute what are called *real-time constraints*.

With the increased use of intelligent everyday-life systems, such as electric home appliances, office automation contrivances, and medical equipments, it has become increasingly important to assimilate knowledge on how real-time constraints can be *specified*, *modeled*, *implemented*, and *verified*. Without trying to be exhaustive, this article tries to cover most aspects of real-time constraints, such that both a novice and an expert may benefit from referring to it.

Informally speaking, a real-time constraint is any condition on the timing of events, including event enabling, firing, initiation, resource usage, synchronization, and termination. A real-time constraint may be as simple as the specification of a deadline for a particular task to complete execution. A periodic real-time task may be further associated with a period constraint. For example, task *A* must execute once every 50-ms period with a deadline of 60 ms. Further details on the specification of real-time constraints are given in the section Real-Time Constraints.

Constraints may be classified in several ways (1). As far as strictness of timing is concerned, constraints may be classified as *hard* or *soft*. Hard constraints *must* be satisfied, the failure of which results in system crashes or serious consequences. Soft constraints *may* be satisfied and have tolerance ranges associated, the violation of which merely degrades a system behavior, without endangering it or the environment. Hard real-time constraints are found in high-assurance systems, such as nuclear reactors, avionics, power systems, medical emergency equipment, and space navigation systems. Soft real-time constraints are found in low-assurance systems, such as telecommunication systems, network systems, electric home appliances, flexible manufacturing systems, and office automation systems.

Constraints can also be classified based on the type of specification. There are two types: (1) *abstract* specifications in the form of an assertion language that is independent of the design or implementation language and (2) *integrated* specifications that are inseparable from the implementation language and make use of language variables like actual time and resource status.

Timing constraints can be evaluated in different ways: (1) *static* evaluation (i.e., pre-run-time), which implies that the timing specifications are implementation independent, (2) *dynamic* evaluation (i.e., at run time), which is necessary if priorities are specified, and (3) *hybrid* evaluation, which is a combination of 1 and 2 and is necessary in off-line schedulability analysis with exact runtimes.

The time domain in a real-time system can be *discrete* or *dense*. Discrete time allows simpler analysis and instrumentation procedures because the tasks in a real-time system may then be simply taking turns as in a card game of poker. Examples of such systems are telephone networks, communication protocols, and manufacturing systems, where automatic control can be applied by enabling and disabling of system events. Here, the domain of integers is used to model time (2,3). A smallest measurable time unit is specified a priori in the discrete-time model. The *fictitious clock* approach includes an explicit tick transition making time a global state variable (4,5). Each tick increments time by some predetermined time quantum. In this model, events between the ith and $(i + 1)$st clock ticks are assumed to occur at some unspecified time between times i and $i + 1$. Thus, it is impossible to know the exact time delay between any two events. The model can be interpreted as an approximation to real time, where events between times i and $i + 1$ have their occurrence times truncated to i.

The dense-time domain makes analysis and instrumentation procedures much more complex due to the requirement of exact timeliness. Some systems must be analyzed and implemented using the dense-time model for it to correctly satisfy given real-time constraints. Examples of such systems include automation of transport systems, such as railway and flight control, which depends critically on reaction times. Computer networks demand a maximal response time (6). There are four strong reasons why a dense model of time is necessary (7). A dense model of time is needed for *correctness*. It is more *expressive* than the others. The *composition* of processes is straightforward in the dense-time model. Finally, some important problems for finite-state systems have the same *complexity* using a dense-time model as for the other models.

This article is organized as follows. The second section introduces differences between untimed and real-time systems along with system models. The third section presents real-time constraints, specification methods, language constructs, and constraint checker. The fourth section deals with real-time system design, including hardware, software, and their models. The fifth section covers real-time system verification, including model checking, verification tools, and verification techniques. The sixth section concludes this article with pointers to future research directions and technology improvements.

UNTIMED AND REAL-TIME SYSTEMS

Control systems such as certain flexible manufacturing systems perform a sequence of tasks based on external events, such as the push of a switch or a lever. The correctness of such systems depends on the execution sequence and not on time. Thus, they are called *untimed systems*. Although untimed systems do not depend on time for task execution, their overall performance may still be related to time. For example, a scheduling criterion for an untimed flexible manufacturing system may be the minimization of total execution time or the maximization of total throughput. However, often such types of timing constraints affect neither the correctness nor the stability of a system. These timing constraints are thus not real-time constraints and are out of the scope of our discussion in this article.

From the above discussion, it can be stated that real-time constraints include only those constraints that actually affect a system's correctness, feasibility, or stability. Real-time systems are control systems that have constraints on the exact timing of task executions, which are expressed as real-time constraints. For example, as shown in Figure 1, an Autonomous Intelligent Cruise Controller (AICC) developed by Swedish Road Transport Informatics Programme and installed in a Saab automobile (8) requires traffic light and speed information to be polled every 200 ms, information processing to be performed every 100 ms, and final coordination control to be performed ever 50 ms. In Figure 1, SRC stands for Short Range Communication and EST stands for Electronic Servo Throttle. This is an example of a typical embedded real-time system.

In the remainder of this section, different models of real-time systems will be introduced and compared, including timed variants of Petri nets, timed automata, process algebra, and object-oriented models.

Petri Nets

Petri nets are a graphical form of a formal system model, which can be used to efficiently model transition systems characterized by concurrency, nondeterminism or conflicts, synchronization, merging, confusion, mutual exclusion, and priority (9). We first define a standard Petri net and then introduce its timed versions, which can be used to model real-time systems.

In the following, the set of integers and non-negative real numbers are denoted by N and $R_{\geq 0}$, respectively. A standard Petri net can be defined as follows.

Definition 1: A *Petri net* is a 5-tuple (P, T, I, O, M_0), where

- $P = \{p_1, p_2, \ldots, p_m\}$ is a finite set of *places*.
- $T = \{t_1, t_2, \ldots, t_n\}$ is a finite set of *transitions*, $P \cup T \neq \varnothing$, and $P \cap T = \varnothing$.
- $I: (P \times T) \to N$ is an *input function* that defines directed *arcs* from places to transitions.
- $O: (P \times T) \to N$ is an *output function* that defines directed arcs from transitions to places.

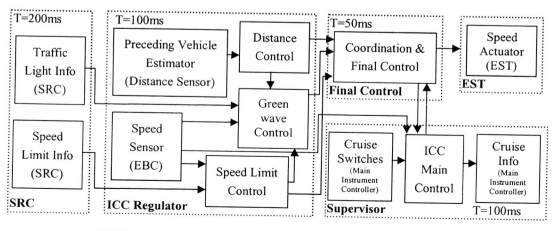

FIGURE 1 Autonomous intelligent cruise controller. (From Ref. 8.)

- M_0: $P \rightarrow N$ is the initial *marking*, where a marking is an assignment of *tokens* to the places of a Petri net.

A token is a primitive concept for Petri nets (like places and transitions). Tokens are assigned to, and can be thought to reside in, the places of a Petri net. The number and position of tokens may change during the execution of a Petri net. The tokens are used to define the execution of a Petri net.

A Petri net can be graphically represented as shown in Figure 2, where a circle represents a place, a bar or a box represents a transition, an arrow represents an arc connecting a place and a transition, and a black dot represents a token. If $I(p_j, t_i) = k$ [or $O(p_j, t_i) = k$], then there exist k arrows connecting place p_j to transition t_i (or connecting transition t_i to place p_j). An arc may be labeled by an integer, which represents its multiplicity or weight.

A transition t is said to be enabled if each input place p of t contains at least the number of tokens equal to the weight of the directed arc connecting p to t [i.e., $M(p) \geq I(p, t)$ for any p in P, where M is the current marking]. An enabled transition t may or may not fire depending on additional interpretation. A firing of an enabled transition t removes from each input place p the number of tokens equal to the weight of the directed arc connecting p to t. It also deposits in each output place p the number of tokens equal to the weight of the directed arc connecting t to p.

Petri nets can be used to analyze system properties such as reachability, boundedness, conservativeness, and liveness. Analysis methods of Petri nets include the coverability tree, incidence matrix and state equation, invariant analysis, and reduction rules.

The standard Petri net has been extended into high-level Petri nets by several domain experts, including extensions such as fuzzy, object oriented, stochastic, generalized, colored, and timed. Three timed versions of Petri nets are introduced here, namely Deterministic Timed Petri Nets (DTPN), Time Petri Nets (TPN), and Timing Constraint Petri Nets (TCPN).

There are three types of DTPN, depending on where deterministic time labels (representing time delays) are placed. If time labels are associated with transitions, then it is called Deterministic Timed Transitions Petri Nets (DTTPNs) (10). If time labels are associated with places, then it is called Deterministic Timed Places Petri Nets (DTPPN). If time labels are associated with arcs, then it is called Deterministic Timed Arcs Petri

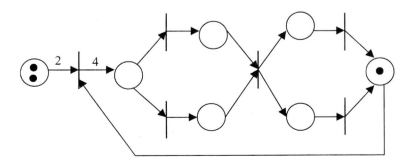

FIGURE 2   A standard Petri net.

Nets (DTAPN). Only DTTPNs are defined here, because the other DTPNs can be defined similarly.

Definition 2. A *deterministic timed transitions Petri net* (DTTPN) is a 6-tuple (P, T, I, O, M_0, D), where (P, T, I, O, M_0) is a standard Petri net and $D: T \rightarrow R_{\geq 0}$ is a function that associates transitions with deterministic time delays. A transition t_i in a DTTPN can fire at time d if and only if

- In any input place p of t_i, $w(p, t)$ tokens have resided for the time interval $[d - d_i, d]$, where $w(p, t)$ is the weight associated with arc connecting p to t and d_i is the associated firing time of t_i.
- After a transition fires, tokens are produced at output places at time d.

Depending on a given real-time system, different DTPNs may be used to model it. DTAPN is more general and can thus be used to model complex real-time systems.

Merlin and Farber (11) proposed time Petri nets (TPN), in which two time values are associated with each transition. The values constitute a time interval within which a transition is enabled and may fire. A formal definition is as follows.

Definition 3. A *time Petri net* (TPN) is a 6-tuple (P, T, I, O, M_0, S), where (P, T, I, O, M_0) is a standard Petri net, and $S: T \rightarrow Q^+ \times (Q^+ \cup \infty)$ is a mapping called a static interval, where Q^+ is the set of positive rational numbers.

If a transition t_i has an interval (a, b) associated with it, then a is the minimum time t_i must wait for after it is enabled and before it is fired, and b is the maximum time the transition can wait for before firing if it is still enabled. Transition firing is instantaneous; that is, firing a transition takes no time to complete. When a pair (a, b) is not defined, then it is implicitly assumed that the corresponding transition is a classical Petri net transition and $(a = 0, b = \infty)$.

Sloan and Buy (12) developed a set of reduction rules for TPNs, such as serial fusion, prefusion, postfusion, and lateral fusion. These reduction rules can reduce the size of the exponentially large state spaces and thus help in analyzing TPNs. Further compositional TPNs are also defined for augmenting Petri nets with module constructs. A compositional TPN consists of two basic elements: component TPN models and inter-component connections.

One more type of timed Petri nets is called timing constraint Petri nets (TCPN) (13), which was inspired from DTPN and TPN. The major difference is that TCPN assume a *weak firing mode*, in contrast to the *strong firing mode* of the other two types of timed Petri nets. The weak firing mode does not force any enabled transition to fire. The strong firing mode forces an enabled transition to fire immediately. The strong firing mode is not suitable for some nets with conflict structures, which results in contradictions.

Definition 4. A *timing constraint Petri net* (TCPN) is a 7-tuple (P, T, I, O, M_0, C, D), where (P, T, I, O, M_0) is a standard Petri net, C is a set of integer pairs $(TC_{min}(pt_j), TC_{max}(pt_j))$, where $TC_{min}(pt_j) \leq TC_{max}(pt_j)$ and pt_j is either a place or a transition, and D is a set of firing durations, $\{FIRE_{dur}(pt_j)\}$.

A transition t_j with a time pair, $(TC_{min}(t_j), TC_{max}(t_j))$, is said to be enabled if each of its input places has at least one token. A transition t_j, which is enabled at time t, is said to be firable during the time period $t + TC_{min}(t_j)$ to $t + TC_{max}(t_j)$. A firable transition can fire but there is no guarantee that the firing will complete successfully because the firing of a transition takes a period of time $\text{FIRE}_{dur}(t_j)$.

Timed Automata

When real-time systems are more control oriented, they can be modeled by *timed automata* (TA), which are a timed extension of finite-state machines. Before defining TA, some necessary terms are defined as follows, where the set of integers and non-negative real numbers are denoted by N and $R_{\geq 0}$, respectively.

Definition 5. Given a set C of clock variables and a set D of discrete variables, the syntax of a *mode predicate* η over C and D is defined as $\eta := \text{false} \,|\, x{\sim}c \,|\, x{-}y{\sim}c \,|\, d{\sim}c \,|\, \eta_1$. $\wedge \eta_2 \,|\, \neg\eta_1$, where $x, y \in C, \sim \in \{\leq, <, =, \geq, >\}$, $c \in N$, $d \in D$, and η_1 and η_2 are mode predicates.

Let $B(C, D)$ represent the set of all mode predicates over C and D. A TA is composed of various *modes* interconnected by *transitions*. Variables are distinguished into *clock* and *discrete*. Clock variables increment at a uniform rate and can be reset on a transition. Discrete variables change values only when assigned a new value on a transition.

Definition 6. A *timed automaton* (TA) is an 8-tuple $A = (M, m^0, C, D, X, E, T, R)$ such that M is a finite set of modes, $m^0 \in M$ is the initial mode, C is a set of clock variables, D is a set of discrete variables, $X: M \to B(C, D)$ is an invariance function that labels each mode with a condition true in that mode, $E \subseteq M \times M$ is a set of transitions, $T: E \to B(C, D)$ defines the transition triggering conditions, and $R: E \to 2^{C \cup (D \times N)}$ is an assignment function that maps each transition to a set of assignments such as resetting some clock variables and setting some discrete variables to specific integer values.

We further define the semantics of a TA by defining its state, mode transition, and a feasible computation run as follows.

Definition 7. Given a TA, $A = (M, m^0, C, D, X, E, T, R)$, a *state* s of A is defined as a mapping from $C \cup D$ to $R_{\geq 0} \cup N$ such that for all x in C, $s(x) \in R_{\geq 0}$ is the reading of clock x in s, and for all d in D, $s(d) \in N$ is the value of d in s.

Definition 8. Given two states s_1 and s_2, there is a *mode transition* from s_1 to s_2, in symbols $s_1 \to s_2$, iff both s_1 and s_2 belong to some defined modes, mode invariants are satisfied by the states, there is a transition between the two modes, the triggering condition of the transition is satisfied by s_1, and for all clocks x in C, $s_2(x) = 0$ when x is in the reset assignment of the transition and all other clocks are unchanged.

A real-time system is often modeled as a network of communicating TA. The TA may share global variables, including clock and discrete. State spaces of a real-time system modeled by a set of TA are generally very large and grows exponentially with the large time constant and the system degree of concurrency.

Process Algebra

Process algebra (14,15) is a term-based formal specification language for system design and analysis. Calculus of communicating systems (CCS) (14) was extended in several works to model real-time systems, resulting in real-time process algebras (15,16). Another recent work tackles state-space explosions by using dynamic priorities, called CCS with dynamic priority, which extends CCS by assigning priority values to actions. Unlike other real-time process algebras, CCS with dynamic priority avoids the unfolding of delay values into sequences of elementary steps, each consuming one time unit, thereby providing a formal foundation for efficiently implementing real-time semantics. CCS with dynamic priority has been proved to be bisimilar to CCS with real-time.

The syntax of CCS with real-time and with dynamic priority can be defined as follows.

Definition 9. The syntax of *CCS with real-time and dynamic priority* is defined as follows:

$$P ::= \mathbf{0} \,|\, x \,|\, \alpha{:}k.P \,|\, P + P \,|\, P \Diamond P \,|\, P \,|\, P \,|\, P[f] \,|\, P \backslash L \,|\, \mu x.P$$

where x is a variable taken from some countable domain V, α is an action, $k \in N$, the mapping $f\colon A \to A$ is a relabeling, $L \subseteq A \backslash \{\tau\}$ is a restriction set, A is the set of all actions, and τ is an internal action. As far as the binary operators are concerned, $+$ is a nondeterministic choice, $\Diamond$ is a disabling operator, $|$ is a parallel operator, and $\backslash$ is the set subtraction operator.

The semantics can be defined by action transitions and clock transitions. Here, in CCS with real time, $\alpha{:}k.P$ means the action α has a delay equal to k time units associated with it and the resulting process is P. In CCS with dynamic priority, $\alpha{:}k.P$ means the action has a priority k associated with it and the priority can be changed dynamically. The labeled transition system for a process P is a 4-tuple $(\mathbf{P}, A \cup \{1\}, \to P)$, where $\mathbf{P}$ is the set of states, $A \cup \{1\}$ is the alphabet, $\to$ is the transition relation, and P represents the start state. Maximal progress is assumed here; that is, no idling is allowed when a communication can take place. Further in CCS with dynamic priority, higher-priority processes can preempt lower-priority tasks.

Object-Oriented Techniques

Real-time systems can be modeled by object-oriented techniques (17,18), which have been widely accepted in the software as well as the hardware design community. Object orientation has many benefits not found in traditional structured design. In a real-time system, each process thread can be modeled by a class and each resource can also be modeled by a class. Encapsulations of data and time in a class result in safer systems, which can be upgraded more easily than conventional systems.

A standard for object-oriented modeling language, called Unified Modeling Language (UML) (19) has been extended with a real-time profile. Real-time UML (20) is currently a well-received design modeling paradigm in the real-time community (21). Further, programming languages like Java has also been recently extended for real-time application design, with a Real-Time Specification for Java (22), by the Real-Time for Java Experts Group. CORBA is another standard in designing distributed object-oriented real-time applications (23).

In real-time UML modeling resources (24), QoS (quality of service) characteristics are taken as the basic for quantitative analysis. These characteristics are given as constraints to model elements that specify behavior at run time, including use cases, interactions, operations, state machine transitions, activities, and individual actions. A *realization mapping* is used to compare QoS characteristics. This mapping is a syntactical declaration that a particular resource supports a particular logical element in some un-specified way. The user must determine the realization's semantics and validity. More formal and more sophisticated forms, such as standard stereotypes, involve semantic knowledge of the nature of the logical and engineering model elements being bound. For example, a CORBA or a COM channel can realize a communication link between two objects in a logical model. A *realization package* is modeled as a UML package and represents a consistent set of mappings that are mutually compatible and nonexclusive. A given logical model can have any number of realization packages, each of which represents one distinct mapping of the logical model to exactly one engineering model.

The *real-time specification for Java* (RTSJ) was recently proposed by the Real-Time for Java Experts Group (RTJEG), which begin development in March 1999 under the Java Community Process. The programming language Java was left untouched. The specification merely enhances Java by defining new classes that provide real-time behavior. Seven areas were proposed that required new specification, namely *scheduling*, *memory management*, *synchronization*, *asynchronous event handling*, *asynchronous transfer of control*, *asynchronous thread termination*, and *physical memory access*. Each area was considered as the state-of-the-art technology in real-time system and application development.

For scheduling, the only specification was that a *fixed-priority preemptive scheduler* with no fewer than 28 priorities was required. For memory management, several areas of memory were newly defined, namely scoped memory, immortal memory, and Java heap. For synchronization, the *priority inheritance protocol* was required to be implemented by default, and wait queues were defined for communication among regular Java threads, real-time (RT) threads, and no-heap real-time (NHRT) threads. For asynchronous event handling, two new classes were defined: *AsyncEvent* and *AsyncEventHandler*, where the former represents something that can happen (e.g., a *Posix* signal) and the latter is a schedulable object that handles an asynchronous event. A *Clock* class is also specified for modeling time. More than one clock may also be implemented. For asynchronous control transfer, *AsynchronouslyInterruptedException* (AIE) is specified asynchronously transfer control. For asynchronous thread termination, safe stopping of threads is implemented. For physical memory access, RTSJ defines two classes: *RawMemoryAccess*, which allows memory access in terms of byte, word, long, and multiple-byte granularity, and *PhysicalMemory*, in which Java objects can be located.

REAL-TIME CONSTRAINTS

A *real-time constraint* is defined as a Boolean condition on the values of clock variables. Clock variables are variables whose value increases with time. Clock variables, or clocks in short, may be either *global* or *local*. The values of global clocks are visible to all processes of a system and those of local clocks are visible only to their owner processes. Clocks may be either *absolute* or *relative*. Absolute clocks take values from a global timer, which is never reset after initialization. Relative clocks take values from a timer, which could be a difference of two other clock values. Clocks may be *discrete* or *dense*. Discrete clocks increase value by integral increments, whereas dense clocks increase value by real-time quantums. In a single real-time system, all clocks are discrete or all clocks are dense, but absolute and relative clocks, just as global and local clocks, may coexist in a system. Because different models propose different syntaxes for real-time constraint specification, the exact syntax of a Boolean condition on clock variables is dependent on the system model used. In general, the condition evaluates to either true or false in a system state. For example, in a timed automation, $x < 3 \land y \geq 8$ is a Boolean condition on clock variables x and y, such that it evaluates to true in a particular system state only when both of the clocks have values satisfying the two predicates, respectively, in the condition.

In the following subsection, real-time extensions to existing programming and modeling languages are described such that real-time constraints can be specified. Real-time languages often add statements about the temporal constraints of computations to the syntax of the language. However, most current real-time languages using the process model for programming also assume the conventional run-time model which manages a set of processes preempting one another according to their execution priority, competing for resources, and blocking when resources are already in use, which tends to limit their ability to predict execution behavior. In the final subsection, constraints checking for temporal correctness is described and an associated real-time logic (RTL) is introduced.

Real-Time Languages

Real-time Euclid (25) was one of the earliest real-time languages, which is an extension of Euclid. It restricts language constructs such as recursion and dynamic memory allocation. Concurrency can also be controlled through **signal** and **wait** constructs. Real-time Euclid was designed mainly for schedulability analysis under a number of assumptions on the system and process behavior.

Real-time Mentat (26) is an object-oriented real-time language, which is an extension of C++. In real-time Mentat, a programmer may specify timing constraints in the statement level. Both soft and hard deadlines can be specified. A block with a soft deadline may be skipped if the hard real-time tasks cannot meet their deadlines. It does not support preemption of objects.

RTC++ (17) is an object-oriented real-time language, which is also an extension of C++. It supports preemption, but not soft deadlines. Active objects are introduced and active objects with timing constraints are called real-time objects. It supports inheritance in active objects, synchronous communications among active objects, and exception handling. Time is encapsulated in an active object so as to specify timings for an operation. A critical region is realized in RTC++ by implementing an object with a guard expression. Rate monotonic scheduling is assumed.

The programming language for the Maruti system, MPL (27), also extends C++. MPL provides several ways to specify temporal constraints on blocks of code within an object. Loop bounds are specified and recursion forbidden to increase predictability.

Kenny and Lin describe the Flex language (28), another extension of C++, which includes a number of timing-constraint expressions and exception-handling clauses. A polymorphism analogous to operator overloading is adopted for approximate processing (29). Here, polymorphism refers to providing several routines implementing the same function, which have different properties in space and/or time. Flex also supports monotonic algorithms, which support computations with unpredictable behavior by establishing an initial result early and then iteratively refining it until the deadline is reached.

Real-Time Concurrent C (30) extends Concurrent C by providing facilities for building systems with strict timing constraints. Real-Time Concurrent C allows processes to execute activities with specified periodicity or deadline constraints, to seek dynamic guarantees that timing constraints will be met, and to perform alternative actions when either the timing constraints cannot be met or the guarantees are not available.

Spring System's real-time system description language, SDL (31), explicitly supports specifying a computation's real-time behavioral constraints, end-to-end constraints, concurrency, and details of the hardware–software platform that are required to accurately analyze the system and achieve predictability. The programming language, Spring-C (32), works in concert with the specification language. Its structure constrains the programmer in ways which ensure that worst-case execution behavior, including execution times, can be automatically predicted for the particular hardware platform being used. Of course, such platforms should have predictable instruction execution times. A key aspect of the Spring-C compiler is that it automatically identifies all of a computation's potential blocking points (i.e., points during execution when it can block for resources or wait for synchronous communication to occur) (33).

Constraints Checking and Real-Time Logic

A *reactive real-time system* has to compute a result to an external trigger event within certain timing constraints even in the presence of faults. It has to initiate some adaptive reactions when an assumption is violated (34). Possible reactions include the activation of standby resources, a rescheduling of the remaining resources, or the execution of alternative algorithms for solving the problem under certain emergency conditions. For a reaction to be made, a system has to be informed of the occurrence of a violation. Run-time monitoring and checking of constraints are thus a part of such reactive systems. A *constraint checker* is the required facility.

Major work in the area of checking timing constraints in a real-time system were done by Jahanian and Mok, which was initiated by proposing Real-time Logic (RTL) language (35) for the specification of real-time systems. The semantics of RTL is based on the occurrence of events, which result on the execution of a real-time system, such as the start and the end of code blocks or the assignment of values to state variables. Algorithms for checking safety assertions (36) and for partial event traces (37) against RTL specifications were developed. A distributed on-line monitoring and checking tool, which allows one to specify timing assertions in a subset of RTL and to check whether these assertions are violated or not, was later developed (38,39). Events storing, definition of timing constraints, and evaluation of constraints in a distributed environment are all handled by the monitoring tool. Later, the work was extended to object-oriented models, integrated into standard programming languages like C++, and code instrumented with event triggers (34).

As far as constraints checking is concerned, RTC++ and Flex provide schedulability analysis, but do not provide static worst-case execution-time analysis. Real-time Euclid provides static worst-case execution-time analysis. Using a real-time language cannot guarantee that timing violations will not happen. To cope with such violations, most real-time languages contain a checker for deadline violations and an exception-handling mechanism. In Ref. 34, a new component called "constraint" section, is added to a class description. This section contains a list of named RTL-like formulas, which are composed out of basic events such as "start" and "end" of code sections and changes of state variables. When a constraint is violated, the object produces an event with the static name of the constraint, the dynamic context of the object that violated the constraint, and a time stamp that is the earliest point in time when the checker could evaluate that the constraint will be violated. This independence of functional and timing specifications avoids inheritance anomalies and it allows the construction of two separate systems: the object-oriented real-time system and its constraint checker.

As shown in Figure 3, there are two constraints in the constraints section of a class description. Constraint 1, named max_time states that an execution of the member function compute ( ) must not take longer than 8 ms. The expression @(compute. start, -1) denotes the start time of the most recent execution of the member function compute ( ) and @(compute.end, -1) evaluates to the end time of the same execution. Constraint 2, named recovery, expresses that two successive calls to compute ( ) must have a distance of at least 2 s.

For constraints checking, a compile-time and run-time support is required. A compiler for a proposed language extension has to do two additional tasks in addition to the production of the object code. It has to translate the timing constraints into (1) an instrumentation of the object-oriented program in order to produce the required events and (2) a representation of the constraints that can be evaluated by the constraint checker. An eventing system is the run-time support. It has to receive event records from code instrumentations, it has to provide time stamps from a global clock, and it has to filter out irrelevant events. It then collects the events from the different nodes of a distributed system and merges them into a global event stream according to the total order imposed by the time stamps. The constraint checker has to receive static information about the structure of the timing constraints from the compiler. During run time, it has to react to incoming events. It maintains a global event dispatch table that maps other incoming events to the objects and the constraints that might be affected. A constraint violation is

```
class sensor {
public:
    int compute();

    :

    [[ // The Constraint Section
    // Constraint 1:
    // compute() must not take longer than 8 ms
        max_time: @(compute.start, -1) >= @(compute.end, -1) - 4ms;
    // Constraint 2:
    // compute() must not be called more than once per second
        recovery: @(compute.start, -2) <= @(compute.end, -1) - 2s;
    ]]

}
```

FIGURE 3   A C++ class with constraints section.

detected by constructing a current instance of a graph out of the graph templates. Upon detection of a constraint violation, the checker itself produces a corresponding event, which will immediately be checked (because it is the next event in the total order of events).

There are three possible modes in which a checker can be used: *off- line*, *on-line*, and *real time*. In the off-line mode, performance of the checker has no effect on the system being checked. An on-line checker has to cope with the average event rate, so that it can keep track of a running system. If it is a real-time checker, then all of its parts must have known worst-case execution times and they must be scheduled with the application itself.

REAL-TIME SYSTEM DESIGN

Real-time system design deals with how real-time constraints may be feasibly implemented in working systems that might contain pure hardware, pure software, or both hardware and software. In general, a real-time system is designed as follows. A set of system specifications, including real-time constraints, is specified by a designer. A synthesis methodology uses some kind of system models, performance models, estimation models, and exploration models to design a system that satisfied all of the system's specifications. The final design is then validated through simulation, testing, or rapid prototyping. A target design could be a sequential system, consisting of either one CPU or one ASIC, or a parallel system, consisting of multiple CPUs or multiple ASICs. The latter is much more complex to design than the former, as described in the subsection Hardware System Design. Irrespective of hardware or software implementations, real-time scheduling of multiple tasks on a single CPU or ASIC is essentially the most validated and theoretically proven. Real-time scheduling will be discussed briefly in the subsection Real-Time Scheduling. Hardware design is introduced in the subsection Hardware System Design. Different paradigms for software design are discussed in the subsection Software System Design. Hardware–software codesign methodologies are presented in the subsection Hardware–Software Codesign.

Definition 10. Synthesis of multiple tasks hard real-time multiprocessor systems. Given a set of tasks with hard real-time constraints such as period, start time, and finish time or deadline, design a system consisting of multiple CPUs or multiple ASICs such that the set of tasks is partitioned into several subsets, each subset is implemented on one dedicated CPU or ASIC, all the given real-time constraints are satisfied, and the overall system cost is minimal.

The above-defined optimization design problem is NP-complete (40). Even several subproblems of the above problem are NP-complete, such as scheduling of a single task on minimal resources (41), minimization of only one type of resource (42), or register minimization (42). This layering of computationally intractable subproblems does not affect overall worst-case asymptotic computational complexity, but it makes the synthesis problem exceptionally challenging in practice because numerous contradictory effects along several hardware dimensions, at both process and task granularity levels, must be taken into account.

Real-time Scheduling

A real-time system generally needs to process various concurrent tasks. *Real-time scheduling* is defined as assigning the exact execution times for a set of real-time tasks such that all temporal constraints including period, phase, deadline, priority, and resource requirements are satisfied.

A *task* is a finite sequence of computation steps that collectively perform some required action of a real-time system and may be characterized by its execution time, deadline, and so forth. *Periodic* tasks are tasks that are repeatedly executed once per period of time. Each execution instance of a periodic task is called a *job* of that task.

In a processor-controlled system, when a processor is shared between time-critical tasks and non-time-critical ones, efficient use of the processor can only be achieved by careful scheduling of the tasks. Here, time-critical tasks are assumed to be preemptive, independent, and periodic and having constant execution times with hard, critical deadlines.

Scheduling may be *time driven* or *priority driven*. A time-driven scheduling algorithm determines the exact execution time of all tasks. A priority-driven scheduling algorithm assigns priorities to tasks and determines which task is to be executed at a particular moment.

In the following, we mainly discuss time-critical periodic tasks with the above assumptions and scheduled using priority-driven scheduling algorithms. Depending on the type of priority assignments, there are three classes of scheduling algorithms: *fixed-priority*, *dynamic-priority*, and *mixed-priority* scheduling algorithms. When the priorities assigned to tasks are fixed and do not change between job executions, the algorithm is called a fixed-priority scheduling algorithm. When priorities change dynamically between job executions, it is called a dynamic-priority scheduling. When a subset of tasks is scheduled using fixed-priority assignment and the rest using dynamic-priority assignment, it is called mixed-priority scheduling.

Before going into the details of scheduling algorithms, we define the task set to be scheduled as a set of n tasks $\{\phi_1, \phi_2, \ldots, \phi_n\}$ with computation times $c_1, c_2, \ldots, c_n$, request periods $p_1, p_2, \ldots, p_n$, and phasings $h_1, h_2, \ldots, h_n$, respectively. A task ϕ_i is to be periodically executed for c_i time units once every p_i time units. The first job of task ϕ_i starts execution at a time h_i. The worst-case phasing, called a *critical instant*, occurs when $h_i = 0$, for all i, $1 \leq i \leq n$.

Liu and Layland (43) proposed an optimal fixed-priority scheduling algorithm called the *rate-monotonic* (RM) scheduling algorithm and an optimal dynamic-priority scheduling algorithm called *earliest-deadline first* (EDF) scheduling.

The RM scheduling algorithm assigns higher priorities to tasks with higher request rates (i.e., smaller request periods). Liu and Layland proved that the worst-case utilization bound of RM was $n \times (2^{1/n} - 1)$ for a set of n tasks. This bound decreases monotonically from 0.83 when $n = 2$ to $\log_e 2 = 0.693$ as $n \rightarrow \infty$. This result shows that any periodic task set of any size will be able to meet all deadlines all of the time if the RM scheduling algorithm is used and the total utilization is not greater than 0.693.

The exact characterization for RM was given by Lehoczky et al. (44). They proved that given periodic tasks $\phi_1, \phi_2, \ldots, \phi_n$ with request periods $p_1 \leq p_2 \leq \cdots p_n$, computation requirements $c_1, c_2, \ldots, c_n$ and phasings $h_1, h_2, \ldots h_n$, ϕ_i is schedulable using RM iff

$$\text{Min}_{\{t \in G_i\}} \frac{W_i(t)}{t} \leq 1,$$
[1]

where $W_i(t) = \Sigma_{j=1}^{i} c_j \lceil t/p_j \rceil$, the cumulative demands on the processor by tasks over $[0, t]$, 0 is a critical instant (i.e., $h_i = 0$ for all i), and $G_i = \{k \times p_j | j = 1, \ldots, i, k = 1, \ldots, \lfloor p_i/p_j \rfloor \}$. Liu and Layland discussed the case when task deadlines coincide with request periods, whereas Lehoczky (45) considered the fixed-priority scheduling of periodic tasks with *arbitrary* deadlines and gave a feasibility characterization of RM in this case: Given a task set with arbitrary deadlines $d_1 \leq d_2 \leq \cdots \leq d_n$, ϕ_i is RM schedulable iff $\text{Max}_{k \leq N_i} W_i(k, (k-1)p_i + d_i) \leq 1$, where $W_i(k, x) = \min_{t \leq x} ((\Sigma_{j=1,\ldots,i-1} c_j \lceil t/p_j \rceil + k \times c_i)/t)$ and $N_i = \min\{k | -W_i)k, k \times p_i) \leq 1\}$.

The worst-case utilization bound of RM with arbitrary deadlines was also derived in Ref. 45. This bound ($U\infty$) depends on the common deadline postponement factor Δ (i.e., $d_i = \Delta p_i$, $1 \leq i \leq n$):

$$U\infty(\Delta) = \Delta \; \log_e \left(\frac{\Delta + 1}{\Delta} \right), \quad \Delta = 1, 2, \ldots . \qquad [2]$$

For $\Delta = 2$, the worst-case utilization increases from 0.693 to 0.811, and for $\Delta = 3$, it is 0.863. Recently, the timing analysis for a more general hard real-time periodic task set on a uniprocessor using fixed-priority methods was proposed by Härbour et al. (46).

Considering the earliest-deadline first dynamic-priority scheduling, Liu and Layland (43) proved that given a task set, it is EDF schedulable iff

$$\sum_{i=1,\ldots,n} \frac{c_i}{p_i} \leq 1 \qquad [3]$$

and showed that the processor utilization can be as high as 100%.

Liu and Layland also discussed the case of *mixed-priority* (MP) scheduling, where given a task set $\phi_1, \phi_2, \ldots, \phi_n$, the first k tasks $\phi_1, \ldots, \phi_k$, $k < n$, are scheduled using fixed-priority assignments and the remaining $n - k$ tasks $\phi_{k+1,\ldots,} \phi_n$ are scheduled using dynamic-priority assignments. It was shown that considering the accumulated processor time from 0 to t available to the task set ($a_k(t)$), the task set is mixed-priority schedulable iff

$$\sum_{i=1,\ldots,n-k} \lfloor t/p_{k+i} \rfloor c_{k+i} \leq a_k(t) \qquad [4]$$

for all t which are multiples of p_{k+1} or $\cdots$ or p_n. Here, $a_k(t)$ can be computed as follows:

$$a_k(t) = t - \sum_{j=1,\ldots,k} c_j \lceil t/p_j \rceil .$$

Although the EDF dynamic priority scheduling has a high processor utilization, in recent years fixed-priority scheduling has received great interests from both academy and industry (44–51).

Summarizing the above scheduling algorithms, we have five different cases of schedulability considerations:

- RM-safe: All task sets are schedulable as long as the server utilization is below $\log_e 2 = 0.693$.
- RM-exact: All task sets satisfying Eq. (1) are schedulable.
- RM-arbitrary: All task sets are schedulable as long as the server utilization is below $\Delta \log_e[(\Delta + 1)/\Delta]$ [Eq. (2)].
- EDF: All task sets satisfying Eq. (3) are schedulable.
- MP: All task sets satisfying Eq. (4) are schedulable.

Hardware System Design

As far as hardware system design is concerned, Potkonjak and Wolf (40) recently developed a new two-domain iterative refinement multiresolution synthesis strategy to help manage the complexity of the above-defined synthesis problem (Definition 10). The final solution implements the set of processes into a partitioned system of multiple ASICs.

Each process is initially considered in a single process domain. Estimations are made using the Hyper high-level synthesis system (52) through area–time trade-off curves for three types of hardware resources: execution units, interconnect, and registers. Estimations are then made for each partition with respect to the required hardware resources and feasibility of timing constraints. In the single process domain, augmented Hyper-LP estimations are made for all hardware components and complete implementations obtained. Inferior and nonfeasible solutions are discarded. Finally, the complete single process and task-level schedules are obtained using the Hyper scheduler and a task-level scheduler. The proposed design methodology is a basis for an optimal worst-case exponential-time branch and the bound synthesis algorithm as well as the fast heuristic synthesis algorithm.

Software System Design

Designing a software system to solve the real-time synthesis problem (Definition 10) is a scheduling problem, such that a given set of tasks is to be scheduled on a set of processors while simultaneously satisfying real-time constraints and using the processor and memory resources as efficiently as possible (53). As mentioned at the beginning of this section, this problem itself is NP-complete. Hence, many software scheduling strategies have been proposed.

Formal Software Synthesis

Scheduling of software can be accomplished based on data computations and control structures in a system specification. Three types of scheduling can be combined to obtain an ideal scheduling technique. First, *static* scheduling can be used to exploit fixed dependencies between blocks of operation. Second, *quasistatic* scheduling can be used to identify data-dependent operations with the same rate and schedule them. Third, *dynamic* scheduling can be used to determine which tasks should be executed.

For the synthesis of software executing on a single processor, several studies are still ongoing. Buck (54) proposed a quasistatic schedule computation algorithm based on the *Boolean Data Flow* (BDF) network model. Theon et al. (55) proposed a technique to exploit static information in the specification and extract from a constraint graph description of the system statically schedulable clusters of threads. Lin (56,57) used intermediate Petri net models to generate a software program from a concurrent process specification. Here, it is assumed that the Petri nets are *safe* (i.e., buffers can store at most one data unit, and hence cannot handle multirate specifications, like FFT computations and down sampling). Zhu and Lin (58) then proposed a compositional approach to software synthesis such that the size of the resulting C program was directly proportional to the size of the original specification. Later, Sgroi et al. (53) proposed a software synthesis method based on quasistatic scheduling (QSS) of Free Choice Petri Nets (FCPN). The proposed algorithm is complete, in that it can solve QSS for any FCPN that is quasistatically schedulable. Recently, an approach that maximizes the amount of static scheduling to reduce the need for context switching and operating system intervention was proposed by Cortadella et al. (59).

Formal *real-time* software synthesis based on Petri nets is still at a premature stage and research work is ongoing in this area. Some work on using timed Petri nets to schedule flexible manufacturing systems have been proposed. Onaga et al. (60) proposed a linear-programming-based heuristic approach for generating minimal time strict periodic schedules. Qadri and Robbi (61) used a Timed Petri Net Simulation tool (TPNS) (62) to model the performance of a flexible manufacturing cell arrangement with different scheduling approaches. Later, Zuberek (63) used invariant analysis of timed Petri nets to provide performance characteristics of manufacturing cells with composite schedules. Recently, Di Natale et al. (64) proposed an iterative solution to schedule reactive real-time transactions modeled by a network of Codesign Finite-State Machines (CFSM). It offers a priority assignment scheme together with a tight worst-case analysis.

Object-Oriented Application Frameworks

Another paradigm of software development for real-time systems is Object-Oriented Application Frameworks (OOAFs). An OOAF is a reusable, "semicomplete" application that can be specialized to produce custom applications (65). Examples include MacApp, ET++, Interviews, ACE, Microsoft's MFC and DCOM, Javasoft's RMI, and implementation of OMG's CORBA. Compared to other application domains, *real-time* OOAFs are limited in number. Currently, there are Real-Time Framework (RTFrame), which is also called SESAG (66) and Object-Oriented Real-Time System Framework (OORTSF) (67).

SESAG is modularized into five components, namely *Specifier*, *Extractor*, *Scheduler*, *Allocator*, and *Generator*. Two different views of SESAG were presented: a *components–patterns* view and a *class* view. Application domain objects are specified using the Specifier. Real-time constraints are either specified separately or coupled with the application domain objects. In the latter case, Extractor is used for extracting constraints. Extractor is also used to extract tasks from the given domain objects. Scheduler schedules the tasks using some scheduling algorithm and Allocator allocates resources among the tasks that are running concurrently. Finally, Generator is used to generate the application code based on the decisions made in the other components. Through applications on avionics and cruiser controls, SESAG has been shown to decrease design efforts to less than 5% of that required without using SESAG. The evaluation was made based on a *relative design effort* metric.

OORTSF emphasizes on high-level design reuse. Several design patterns and schedulers have been implemented into OORTSF. A five-step process is defined for developing real-time applications using OORTSF. First, domain task objects are identified and defined. Second, real-time requirements for each domain task object are generated. Third, schedulability check is performed on the set of tasks. Fourth, OORTSF is used to generate the target system code. Fifth, the generated target system is validated and verified. Currently, it has also been extended into a framework for developing distributed real-time applications. Three components called *AppNode*, *AppControl*, and *RemotePipeDirector* have been defined for a distributed application environment. Its integration with CORBA (68) and with Java RMI (69) has also been discussed. OORTSF has been used to design an airborne-vehicle flight-path-control real-time application.

Real-Time Operating Systems

Last but not least, in real-time software development is Real-Time Operating Systems (RTOS), which are stripped down and optimized versions of time-sharing operating systems. Some features of RTOS include fast context switch, small size, quick response to external interrupts, minimal interrupt–disable intervals, no virtual memory, code and data locking in memory, and fast accumulation of data through special sequential files (33). RTOS kernels maintain a real-time clock, provide priority-scheduling mechanisms, provide for special alarms and timeouts, and permit tasks to pause/resume execution. In general, RTOS kernels are multitasking, and intertask communication and synchronization are achieved via standard primitives such as mailboxes, events, signals, and semaphores. Many real-time UNIX OS (70) and a standard for RTOS, called RT POSIX (71), have been developed. There are also over 70 commercial proprietary RTOS, including QNX, LynxOS, OS-9, VxWorks, and VRTXsa. Real-Time Mach (18) is a RTOS developed in academia.

Hardware–Software Codesign

An embedded system often contains both *hardware* in the form of one or more ASICs or ASIPs and *software* executable on one or more microprocessors. Several works have been done on synthesizing a hardware–software system (72), but there are relatively fewer results targeted at hardware–software *real-time* systems. In the following, a recently proposed methodology, called Distributed Embedded System Codesign (DESC) methodology (73) is briefly presented.

The DESC methodology uses three types of semantically equivalent models, namely Object Modeling Technique (OMT) (74) models for system description and input, Linear Hybrid Automata (LHA) (75) models for system evaluation during partitioning and for formal verification, and SES/workbench simulation (76) models for performance evaluation after partitioning. A *hierarchical partitioning* algorithm (77) is proposed specifically for distributed systems. Software is synthesized by task scheduling and hardware is synthesized by *object-oriented* design techniques (78–80). Design alternatives for synthesized hardware–software systems are then checked for design feasibility through rapid prototyping using hardware–software emulators. Timing coverification of real-time constraints is performed using LHA models (81,82). DESC methodology has been applied to a case study on a Vehicle Parking Management System (VPMS) (73), which shows the benefits of object-oriented codesign and the benefits of considering physical restrictions.

REAL-TIME SYSTEM VERIFICATION

Because the correctness of real-time systems depends on whether the specified real-time constraints are satisfied or not, the validation or verification of such systems are all the more crucial. Validation of real-time systems can be done in the following ways: *simulation, testing, emulation, rapid prototyping*, and *worst-case execution-time analysis*. Validation is not a *complete* or *full* technique, in the sense that after validation, a system designer still cannot guarantee 100% system correctness. Often, statistical or probabilistic figures are cited after a real-time system is validated. For example, one can say that, after validation, a real-time system is 99.99% correct with a 95% confidence range, or that it is correct for 99.5% of execution time.

In contrast, *formal verification* or *analysis* is complete; that is, a real-time system is verified to be 100% correct, with respect to some kind of temporal specification. In the recent few years, *model checking* (83) has gained wide recognition due to its algorithmic approach at verifying real-time systems. In the following, model checking is presented based on the *timed automata* (TA) system model and *timed computation tree logic* (TCTL) specification, as defined in Definitions 6 and 11, respectively.

Definition 11: A *timed computation tree logic* formula has the following syntax.

$$\phi ::= \eta \, | \, \exists \Box \phi' \, | \, \exists \phi' U_{\sim c} \phi'' \, | \, \phi' \, | \, \phi' \vee \phi'' \tag{5}$$

Here, η is a mode predicate (Definition 5), ϕ' and ϕ'' are TCTL formulas, $\sim \in \{<, \leq, =, \geq, >\}$, and $c \in N$. $\exists \Box \phi'$ means there exists a computation, from the current state, along which ϕ' is always true. $\exists \phi' U_{\sim c} \phi''$ means there exists a computation, from the current state, along which ϕ' is true until ϕ'' becomes true, within the time constraint of $\sim c$. Traditional shorthand like $\exists \Diamond$, $\forall \Box$, $\forall \Diamond$, $\forall U$, $\wedge$, and $\rightarrow$ can all be defined (84).

Model checking is an automatic procedure to verify that a given system satisfies a given temporal property. A dense real-time system can be described using a set of timed automata and a property specified in TCTL. In the following, a brief introduction to the intrinsic of model checking is given.

A symbolic model-checking procedure is given in Figure 4, where two data structures are maintained: a queue of regions (*Unvisited*) and a set of reachable regions (*Reach*). The former keeps a record of which regions are yet to be explored, whereas the latter keeps a record of all the regions reached. The procedure starts from an initial region, R_{init}, which is a Cartesian product of the initial modes of all the TA in the input set of TA, B. Initially, the initial region is queued in *Unvisited* and recorded in *Reach*. A region, R', is dequeued from *Unvisited*, and corresponding to each outgoing transition, e, of R', a successor region, R'', is constructed by the function **Successor_Region**(R', e) (see Fig. 5). If R'' is consistent and is not already in *Reach*, then it is recorded in *Reach* and queued in *Unvisited* for further exploration of its successors. The procedure loops until all regions in the queue have been explored. Finally, the regions in *Reach* are labeled according to the labeling algorithm **Label_Reach**(*Reach*, ϕ) (see Fig. 6), where ϕ is a TCTL formula, such that all regions in *Reach* satisfy ϕ. The procedure finally outputs the initial region label, R_{init}.

As detailed in Figure 5 [**Successor_Region**( )], the successor region is constructed as follows. Given a region R and an outgoing transition e, the successor region R' is constructed by first advancing [**Advance**( )] all clock values until it satisfies the triggering condition (*e.Trigger*) of e, while still satisfying the clock condition R, *R.ClockCond*. This first step gives an intermediate symbolic condition $R'.ClockCond$ for the successor region R'. Second, the clock resets in *e.Assign* are applied to $R'.ClockCond$ by **Assign**( ). Third, the clock conditions of all subregions of R' have also to be satisfied by $R'.Clock$ *Cond*. Finally, the discrete variable values are assigned to *R.DvarCond* to obtain the new symbolic condition $R'.DvarCond$. In this way, both the clock and discrete variable symbolic conditions of the successor region R' are computed.

The labeling algorithm, **Label_Region**( ), is presented in Figure 6. This algorithm assigns a label, $L(R, \phi)$, to each region, R, in the set of regions *RSet*. The label indicates if the region R satisfies ϕ. This labeling is computed as follows. For a mode predicate

Symbolic_Mcheck(B, ϕ)

Set of TA B;

TCTL formula ϕ,

{

    Let *Reach* = *Unvisited* = {R_{init}};

    While (*Unvisited* ≠ NULL) {

        R' = **Dequeue**(*Unvisited*);

        For all out-going transition e of R' {

            R'' = **Successor_Region**(R', e);

            If R'' is consistent and $R'' \notin Reach$ {

            Reach = *Reach* ∪ {R''};

            Queue(R'', *Unvisited*); }}}

    Label_Region(*Reach*, ϕ);

    Return L(R_{init});

}

FIGURE 4   Symbolic model-checking procedure.

Successor_Region(R, e)
region R;
transition e;

{

    R' = **New_Region**();

    $R'.ClockCond$ = **Advance**($R.ClockCond$) ∧ $e.Trigger$ ∧ $R.ClockCond$;

    $R'.ClockCond$ = **Assign**($R'.ClockCond$, $e.Assign$);

    $R'.ClockCond$ = $R'.ClockCond$ ∧ ($\wedge_i$ $R'.SubRegion_i.ClockCond$);

    $R'.DvarCond$ = **Assign**($R.DvarCond$, $e.Assign$);

    Return R';

}

FIGURE 5   Successor region function.

Label_Region(*RSet*, ϕ)

set of region *RSet*;

TCTL formula ϕ;

{

    For each $R \in RSet$, calculate recursively the label of R, $L(R)$, as follows.

    case $\phi = x \sim c$: $L(R, \phi):= true$, if $x \sim c$ is true in R; *false* otherwise;

    case $\phi = x - y \sim c$: $L(R, \phi):= true$, if $x - y \sim c$ is true in R; *false* otherwise;

    case $\phi = d \sim c$: $L(R, \phi):= true$, if $d \sim c$ is true in R; *false* otherwise;

    case $\phi = \eta_1 \wedge \eta_2$: $L(R, \phi):= true$, if both η_1, η_2 are true in R; *false* otherwise;

    case $\phi = \eta_1$: $L(R, \phi):= true$, if η_1 is false in R; *false* otherwise;

    case $\phi = \exists \Diamond \phi' \mathbf{U}_{\sim c} \phi''$: $L(R, \phi):= true$, if there is a successor R' of R such that

        $L(R', \phi')$ is true, there is a path, π, from R to R' such that for all regions

        R'' along π, $L(R'', \phi')$ is true, and $time_\pi(R, R') \sim c$ is true; *false* otherwise;

    Similarly, for the other cases:

        $\phi = \exists \Box \phi \mathbf{U}_{\sim c} \phi''$, $\phi = \forall \Diamond \phi \mathbf{U}_{\sim c} \phi''$, and $\phi = \forall \Box \phi \mathbf{U}_{\sim c} \phi''$.

}

FIGURE 6   Label region function.

(see Definition 5), the label is *true* if the region satisfies the mode predicate, and it is *false* otherwise. For a TCTL path formula, ϕ, the label is computed recursively according to the semantics of the formula.

    Model-checking-based tools can be mostly found in academia. Verification tools that can be used to specify and verify real-time systems include UPPAAL (85), Kronos (86), SGM (87,88), NuSMV (89), RED (90), XTL (91), and several others. Besides model checking, there are also process algebra-based (92) and logic-based (93) verification for real-time systems. For hardware–software coverification, there are some recently proposed works (81,82,94).

CONCLUSION AND FUTURE WORK

At the turn of a new century, computer technology is no longer confined in the laboratories of academia and research institutes. In the last few years, the world has experienced a burgeoning widespread increase of embedded systems in intelligent appliances and high-assurance systems, which are mostly *real time*. Software and hardware standards in modeling and programming languages are all being extended to cover the realm of the *real-time* domain. Some examples include real-time UML, real-time Java, and real-time CORBA. Real-time constraints have permeated from highly advanced systems, such as nuclear reactors and spacecrafts, to everyday-life systems such as telecommunications, transportation systems, and home appliances. Real-time constraints have even entered the wireless technology such as the *Bluetooth technology*, which allows users to make effortless, wireless, and instant connections between various communication devices, such as mobile phones and desktop and notebook computers. Because it uses radio transmission, transfer of both voice and data is in real-time. This article comes at a time when real-time constraints are here to stay, both in academy and in industry, for a very long period into the future of computer science history. Real-time constraints have been specified, modeled, designed, and verified in this article. This introductory material is not intended to be exhaustive and the technology is still developing! A major future work is the integration of the Internet with real-time constraints. *Real-time Internet* is still a dream, although real-time networking has already matured to some stage today with the use of *Video-On-Demand* systems and other real-time multimedia applications and systems. Another major breakthrough that most information technologists are awaiting for is *gigabit real-time wireless*. This is currently a dream, too. Nevertheless, progressive works are being carried out with an ambitious goal. Although the verification of real-time systems has seen some breakthroughs through the automatic model-checking procedure, some more efficient methods, either improved model-checking or other formal methods, are required to really attack the large exponential state spaces of complex real-time systems.

REFERENCES

1. D. K. Hammer, L. R. Welch, and O. S. van Roosmalen, "A Taxonomy for Distributed Object-Oriented Real-Time Systems," *ACM OOPS Messenger*, 7(1) (1996).
2. Y. Brave and M. Heymann, "Formulation and Control of Real-Time Discrete Event Processes," in *Proceedings of 27th Conference on Decision and Control*, 1988.
3. C. H. Golaszewski and P. J. Ramadge, "On the Control of Real-Time Discrete Event Systems," in *Proceedings of 23rd Conference on Information Sciences and Systems*, 1989, pp. 98–102.
4. J. S. Ostroff, "Synthesis of Controllers for Real-Time Discrete Event Systems," in *Proceedings of 28th Conference on Decision and Control*, 1989, pp. 138–144.
5. J. S. Ostroff and W. M. Wonham, "A Framework for Real-Time Discrete Event Control," *IEEE Trans. Autom. Control*, AC-35(4), 386–397 (1990).
6. H. Wong-Toi and G. Hoffmann, "The Control of Dense Real-Time Discrete Event Systems," Technical Report STAN-CS-92-1411, Stanford University, Stanford, CA, 1992.
7. R. Alur, "Techniques for Automatic Verification of Real-Time Systems," Technical Report STAN-CS-91-1378, Department of Computer Science, Stanford University, Stanford, CA, (1991) (Ph.D. thesis).
8. H. A. Hansson, H. W. Lawson, M. Stromberg, and S. Larsson, "BASEMENT: A Distributed Real-Time Architecture for Vehicle Applications," *Real-Time Syst.*, 11(3), 223–244 (1996).
9. J. Wang, *Timed Petri Nets—Theory and Application*, Kluwer Academic, Boston, 1998.
10. C. Ramamoorthy and G. Ho, "Performance Evaluation of Asynchronous Concurrent Systems Using Petri Nets," *IEEE Trans. Software Eng.*, SE-6(5), 440–449 (1980).
11. P. Merlin and D. Farber, "Recoverability of Communication Protocols—Implication of a Theoretical Study," *IEEE Trans. Communications*, 1063–1043 (September 1976).

12. R. Sloan and U. Buy, "Reduction Rules for Time Petri Nets," *Acta Inform.*, *33*, 687–706 (1996).
13. J. J. P. Tsai, S. J. Yang, and Y.-H. Chang, "Timing Constraint Petri Nets and Their Application to Schedulability Analysis of Real-Time System Specifications," *IEEE Trans. Software Eng.*, *SE-21*(1), 32–49 (1995).
14. R. Milner, *Communication and Concurrency*, Prentice-Hall, London, 1989.
15. F. Moller and C. Tofts, "A Temporal Calculus of Communication Systems," in *Proceedings of CONCUR '90 (Concurrency Theory)*, J. Baeten and J. Klop (eds.), Lecture Notes in Computer Science Vol. 458, Springer-Verlag, Berlin, 1990, pp. 401–415.
16. W. Yi, "CCS + Time = an Interleaving Model for Real-Time Systems," in *Automata, Languages, and Programming (ICALP'91)*, J. L. Albert, B. Monien, and M. R. Artalejo (eds.), Lecture Notes in Computer Science Vol. 510, Springer-Verlag, Berlin, 1991, pp. 217–228.
17. Y. Ishikawa, H. Tokuda, and C. Mercer, "Object-Oriented Real-Time Language Design: Constructs for Timing Constraints," *Proceedings of OOPSLA/ECOOP*, ACM Press, New York, 1990.
18. H. Tokuda, T. Nakajima, and P. Rao, "Real-Time MACH: Towards a Predictable Real-Time System," in *Proceedings of the USENIX MACH Workshop*, 1990.
19. Object Management Group, *The Unified Modeling Language Specification*, http://www.omg.org (November 1999).
20. B. P. Douglass, *Real-Time UML*, Addison-Wesley, Reading, MA, 1999.
21. B. P. Douglass, *Doing Hard Time*, Addison-Wesley, Reading, MA, 1999.
22. Bollella et al. (Real-Time for Java Experts Group), *The Real-Time Specification for Java*, Addison-Wesley, Reading, MA, 2000.
23. Object Management Group, *The Common Object Request Broker: Architecture and Specification, Version 2.3*, 1999.
24. B. Selic, "A Generic Framework for Modeling Resources with UML," *IEEE Computer*, 64–69 (June 2000).
25. E. Kligerman and A. D. Stoyenko, "Real-Time Euclid: A Language for Reliable Real-Time Systems," *IEEE Trans. Software Eng.*, *SE- 12*(9), 941–949 (1986).
26. A. S. Grimshaw, A. Silberman, and J. W. S. Liu, "Real-Time Mentat: A Data-Driven, Object-Oriented System," in *Proceedings of IEEE Globecom*, 1989, pp. 141–147.
27. V. Nirkhe, S. Tripathi, and A. Agrawala, "Language Support for the Maruti Real-Time System," in *Proceedings of the IEEE Real-Time Systems Symposium*, 1990.
28. K. Kenney and K. Lin, "Building Flexible Real-Time Systems Using the Flex Language," *IEEE Computer*, *24*(5), 70–78 (1991).
29. J. Liu, K. Lin, W. Shih, A. Yu, J. Chung, and W. Zhao, "Algorithms for Scheduling Imprecise Calculations," *IEEE Computer*, *24*(5), 58–68 (1991).
30. N. Gehani and K. Ramamritham, "Real-Time Concurrent C (C++): A Language for Programming Dynamic Real-Time Systems," *Real-Time Syst.*, *3*(4), 377–405 (1991).
31. D. Niehaus, J. A. Stankovic, and K. Ramamritham, "A Real-Time System Description Language," in *Proceedings of the IEEE Real-Time Technology and Applications Symposium*, 1995.
32. D. Niehaus, "Program Representation and Execution in Real-Time Multiprocessor Systems," Ph.D. dissertation, University of Massachusetts, Amherst, MA (1994).
33. J. A. Stankovic, K. Ramamritham, D. Niehaus, M. Humphrey, and G. Wallace, "The Spring System: Integrated Support for Complex Real-Time Systems," Technical Report CS-98-18, University of Virginia (August 1998).
34. M. Gergeleit, J. Kaiser, and H. Streich, "Checking Timing Constraints in Distributed Object-Oriented Programs," *ACM OOPS Messenger*, *7*(1) (1996), special issue on object-oriented real-time systems.
35. F. Jahanian and A. Mok, "Safety Analysis of Timing Properties in Real-Time Systems," *IEEE Trans. Software Eng.*, *SE-12*(9), 890–904 (1986).

36. F. Jahanian and A. Mok, "A Graph-Theoretic Approach for Timing Analysis and Implementation," *IEEE Trans. Computers* C-36(8) (1987).

37. F. Jahanian and A. Goyal, "A Formalism for Monitoring Real-Time Constraints at Run-Time," in *Proceedings of IEEE Fault-Tolerant Computing Symposium*, 1990, pp. 148–155.

38. S. E. Chodrow, F. Jahanian, and M. Donner, "Run-Time Monitoring of Real-Time Systems," in *Proceedings of Real-Time Systems Symposium* (*RTSS*), 1991, pp. 74–83.

39. F. Jahanian, R. Rajkumar, and S. Raju, "Runtime Monitoring of Timing Constraints in Distributed Real-Time Systems," *Real-Time Syst.*, 7(3), 247–274 (1994).

40. M. Potkonjak and W. Wolf, "A Methodology and Algorithms for the Design of Hard Real-Time Multi-tasking ASICs," *ACM Trans. Design Autom. Electron. Syst.*, 4(4), 430–459 (1999).

41. R. L. Graham, E. L. Lawler, J. K. Lenstra, and A. H. G. Rinnooy Kan, "Optimization and Approximation in Deterministic Sequencing and Scheduling: A Survey," *Ann. Discrete Math.*, 5, 287–326 (1979).

42. M. R. Garey and D. S. Johnson, *Computers and Intractability: A Guide to the Theory of NP-Completeness*, W. H. Freeman, New York, 1979.

43. C.-L. Liu and J. Layland, "Scheduling Algorithms for Multiprogramming in a Hard-Real Time Environment," *J. Assoc. Computing Mach.*, 20, 41–61 (1973).

44. J. Lehoczky, L. Sha, and Y. Ding, "The Rate Monotonic Scheduling Algorithm: Exact Characterization and Average Case Behavior," in *Proceedings of the Real-Time Systems Symposium*, 1989, pp. 166–171.

45. J. Lehoczky, "Fixed Priority Scheduling of Periodic Task Sets with Arbitrary Deadlines," in *Proceedings of the Real-Time Systems Symposium*, 1990, 201–209.

46. M. Harbour, M. Klein, and J. Lehoczky, "Timing Analysis for Fixed-Priority Scheduling of Hard Real-Time Systems," *IEEE Trans. Software Eng.*, SE-20(1) (1994).

47. L. Sha and J. Goodenough, "Real-Time Scheduling Theory and Ada," *IEEE Computer*, 23, 53–62 (April 1990).

48. M. Harbour, M. Klein, and J. Lehoczky, "Fixed Priority Scheduling of Periodic Tasks with Varying Execution Priority," in *Proceedings of the Real-Time Systems Symposium*, 1991, pp. 116–128.

49. L. Sha, M. Klein, and J. Goodenough, "Rate Monotonic Analysis for Real-Time Systems," in *Foundations of Real-Time Computing: Scheduling and Resource Management*, Kluwer Academic Publishers, New York, 1991, pp. 129–155.

50. K. Tindell, A. Burns, and A. Wellings, "Mode Changes in Priority Pre-emptively Scheduled Systems," in *Proceedings of the Real-Time Systems Symposium*, 1992, pp. 100–109.

51. D. Katcher, H. Arakawa, and J. Strosnider, "Engineering and analysis of fixed priority scheduler," *IEEE Transactions on Software Engineering*, Vol. 19, pp. 920–934, September 1993.

52. J. Rabaey, C. Chu, P. Hoang, and P. Potkonjak, "Fast Prototyping of Datapath-Intensive Architectures," *IEEE Design Test Computers*, 8(2), 40–51 (1991).

53. M. Sgroi, L. Lavagno, Y. Watanabe, and A. Sangiovanni-Vincentelli, "Synthesis of Embedded Software Using Free-Choice Petri Nets," in *Proceedings of the Design Automation Conference*, ACM Press, New York, 1999, pp. 805–810.

54. J. Buck, "Scheduling Dynamic Dataflow Graphs with Bounded Memory Using the Token Flow Model," Ph.D. dissertation, UC Berkeley (1993).

55. F. Theon, et al., "Intellectual Property Re-use in Embedded System Codesign: An Industrial Case Study," in *Proceedings of the International System Synthesis Symposium*, 1995.

56. B. Lin, "Software Synthesis of Process-Based Concurrent Programs," in *Proceedings of Design Automation Conference*, ACM Press, New York, 1998, pp. 502–505.

57. B. Lin, "Efficient Compilation of Process-Based Concurrent Programs Without Run-Time Scheduling," in *Proceedings of the Conference on Design and Test in Europe* (*DATE*), 1998, pp. 211–217.

58. X. Zhu and B. Lin, "Compositional Software Synthesis of Communicating Processes," in *Proceedings of the International Conference on Computer Design*, 1999, pp. 646–651.

59. J. Cortadella, A. Kondratyev, L. Lavagno, M. Massot, S. Moral, C. Passerone, Y. Watanabe, and A. Sangiovanni-Vincentelli, "Task Generation and Compile-Time Scheduling for Mixed Data-Control Embedded Software," in *Proceedings of Design Automation Conference*, ACM Press, New York, 2000, pp. 489–494.

60. K. Onaga, M. Silva, and T. Watanabe, "On Periodic Schedules for Deterministically Timed Petri Net Systems," in *Proceedings of the 4th International Workshop on Petri Nets and Performance Models (PNPM'91)*, 1991, pp. 210–215.

61. F. Qadri and A. Robbi, "Timed Petri Nets for Flexible Manufacturing Cell Design," in *Proceedings of the IEEE International Conference on Humans, Information, and Technology*, 1994, Vol. 2, pp. 1695–1699.

62. J. Siddiqi, Y. Chen, and A. Robbi, "A Timed Petri Net Simulation Tool," in *Proceedings of the 9th International Conference on CAD/CAM, Robotics, and Factories of the Future*, 1993.

63. W. M. Zuberek, "Composite Schedules of Manufacturing Cells and Their Timed Petri Net Models," in *Proceedings of the IEEE International Conference on Systems, Man, and Cybernetics*, 1996, Vol. 4, pp. 2990–2995.

64. M. Di Natale, A. Sangiovanni-Vincentelli, and F. Balarin, "Task Scheduling with RT Constraints," in *Proceedings of Design Automation Conference*, ACM Press, New York, 2000, pp. 483–488.

65. R. Johnson and B. Foote, "Designing Reusable Classes," *J. Object- Oriented Program.*, *1*, 22–35 (June 1988).

66. P.-A. Hsiung, "RTFrame: An Object-Oriented Application Framework for Real-Time Applications," in *Proceedings of the 27th International Conference on Technology of Object-Oriented Languages and Systems (TOOLS'98)*, IEEE Computer Society Press, Los Alamitos, CA, 1998, pp. 138–147.

67. W.-B. See and S.-J. Chen, "Object-Oriented Real-Time System Framework," in *Domain-Specific Application Frameworks*, M. E. Fayad and R. E. Johnson (eds.), John Wiley & Sons, New York, 2000, pp. 327–370.

68. D. C. Schmidt and F. Kuhns, "An Overview of the Real-Time CORBA Specification," *IEEE Computer*, *33*(6), 56–63 (2000).

69. Sun Microsystems, "RMI specifications and tutorials," http://java.sun.com/products/jdk/1.2/docs/guide/rmi

70. B. Furht, D. Grostick, D. Gluch, G. Rabbat, J. Parker, and M. McRoberts, *Real-time Unix Systems, Design and Application Guide*, Kluwer Academic Publishers, Boston, MA, 1991.

71. B. Gallmeister, *POSIX.4: Programming for the Real World*, O'Reilly and Associates, 1995.

72. P.-A. Hsiung, "CMAPS: A Cosynthesis Methodology for Application-Oriented Parallel Systems," *ACM Trans. Design Autom. Electron. Syst.*, *5*(1), 51–81 (2000).

73. T.-Y. Lee, P.-A. Hsiung, and S.-J. Chen, "A Case Study in Hardware–Software Codesign of Distributed Systems—Vehicle Parking Management System," in *Proceedings of the International Conference on Parallel and Distributed Processing Techniques and Applications (PDPTA'99)*, 1999, Vol. 6, pp. 2982–2987.

74. J. Rumbaugh, M. Blaha, W. Premerlani, F. Eddy, and W. Lorensen, *Object-Oriented Modeling and Design*, Prentice-Hall, Englewood Cliffs, NJ, 1991.

75. T. A. Henzinger, P.-H. Ho, and H. Wong-Toi, "HyTech: The Next Generation," in *Proceedings of the 16th Real-Time Systems Symposium*, IEEE Computer Society Press, Los Alamitos, CA, 1995, pp. 56–65.

76. Scientific and Engineering Software, Inc., *SES/Workbench User's Manual, Release 2.0*, January 1991.

77. T.-Y. Lee, P.-A. Hsiung, and S.-J. Chen, "Hardware–Software Multi-level Partitioning for Distributed Embedded Multiprocessor Systems," *IEICE Trans. Fundam. Electron. Commun. Computer Sci.* (in press).

78. P.-A. Hsiung, S.-J. Chen, T.-C. Hu, and S.-C. Wang, "PSM: An Object-Oriented Synthesis Approach to Multiprocessor System Design," *IEEE Trans. VLSI Syst.*, *4*(1), 83–97 (1996).

79. P.-A. Hsiung, C.-H. Chen, T.-Y. Lee, and S.-J. Chen, "ICOS: An Intelligent Concurrent Object-Oriented Synthesis Methodology for Multiprocessor Systems," *ACM Trans. Design Autom. Electron. Syst.*, *3*(2), 109–135 (1998).

80. P.-A. Hsiung, "POSE: A Parallel Object-Oriented Synthesis Environment," *ACM Trans. Design Autom. Electron. Syst.*, *6*(1) (2001).

81. P.-A. Hsiung, "Timing Coverification of Concurrent Embedded Real-Time Systems," in *Proceedings of the 7th IEEE/ACM International Workshop on Hardware/Software Codesign (CODES'99)*, ACM Press, Los Alamitos, CA, 1999, pp. 100–114.

82. P.-A. Hsiung, "Hardware–Software Timing Coverification of Concurrent Embedded Real-Time Systems," *IEE Proc. Computers Digital Tech.*, *147*(2), 81–90 (2000).

83. R. Alur, C. Courcoubetis, N. Halbwachs, and D. Dill, "Model Checking for Real-Time Systems," in *Proceedings of IEEE International Conference on Logics in Computer Science (LICS)*, 1990.

84. T. A. Henzinger, X. Nicollin, J. Sifakis, and S. Yovine, "Symbolic Model-Checking for Real-Time Systems," in *Proceedings of IEEE Logics in Computer Science (LICS)*, 1992.

85. J. Bengtsson, F. Larsen, K. Larsson, P. Petterson, Y. Wang, and C. Weise, "New Generation of UPPAAL," in *Proceedings of the International Workshop on Software Tools for Technology Transfer (STTT'98)*, 1998.

86. C. Daws, A. Olivers, S. Tripakis, and S. Yovine, "The tools KRONOS," in *Hybrid Systems III*, Lecture Notes in Computer Science Vol. 1066, Springer-Verlag, Berlin, 1996, pp. 208–219.

87. P.-A. Hsiung and F. Wang, "A State-Graph Manipulator Tool for Real-Time System Specification and Verification," in *Proceedings of the 5th International Conference on Real-Time Computing Systems and Applications (RTCSA '98)*, 1998.

88. P.-A. Hsiung and F. Wang, "User-Friendly Verification," in *Proceedings of the International Conference on Formal Description Techniques for Distributed Systems and Communication Protocols & Protocol Specification, Testing, and Verification (FORTE/PSTV'99)*, 1999.

89. A. Cimatti, F. Clarke, E. Giunchiglia, and M. Roveri, "NuSMV: A Reimplementation of SMV," in *Proceedings of the International Workshop on Software Tools for Technology Transfer (STTT'98)*, July 1998.

90. W. Farn, "Region Encoding Diagram for Fully Symbolic Verification of Real-time Systems," in *Proceedings of IEEE Computer Software and Applications Conference (COMPSAC'2000)*, IEEE Computer Science Press, Los Alamitos, CA, 2000.

91. R. Mateescu and H. Garavel, "XTL: A Meta-language and Tool for Temporal Logic Model Checking," in *Proceedings of the International Workshop on Software Tools for Technology Transfer (STTT'98)*, 1998.

92. R. Cleaveland, J. Parrow, and B. Steffen, "The Concurrency Workbench: A Semantics-Based Tool for the Verification of Finite-State Systems," *ACM Trans. Program. Lang. Syst.*, *15*, 36–72 (1993).

93. J. Gulmann, J. Jensen, M. Jorgensen, N. Klarlund, T. Rauhe, and A. Sandholm, "Mona: Monadic Second-Order Logic in Practice," in *Proceedings of the 1st International Workshop on Tools and Algorithms for the Construction and Analysis of Systems (TACAS'95)*, Lecture Notes in Computer Science Vol. 1019, Springer-Verlag, Berlin, 1995.

94. J.-M. Fu, T.-Y. Lee, P.-A. Hsiung, and S.-J. Chen, "Hardware–Software Timing Coverification of Distributed Embedded Systems," *IEICE Trans. Inform. Syst.* (in press).

PAO-ANN HSIUNG

SHAPE MODELING

INTRODUCTION

According to *Longman Dictionary of Contemporary English* (1), the word *shape* means the outer form of something, that you see or feel. Reasoning about the shape is a common way of describing, representing, and visualizing real and abstract objects in computer science, engineering, mathematics, biology, physics, chemistry, medicine, entertainment applications, and even daily life. *Shape modeling* includes methods and tools of creation, storage, and manipulation of digital representations of shapes by means of computer. Shape modeling is an interdisciplinary area composing theoretical and experimental results from mathematics, physics, computer graphics, computer-aided design, computer animation, and other fields. Examples of shape-modeling applications are visualization, rapid prototyping, virtual reality, gaming and entertainment, and computer art. Recently, interactive shape-modeling applications are extended via force-feedback or haptic technology that lets users feel and control such factors as hardness and friction of designed shapes.

Unfortunately, there is no method or system that is ideally suited to all tasks, and researchers are still focusing on the development of sophisticated algorithms to discover the essential rules of generating and representing shapes. The scope of shape modeling is so wide that it is impossible even to mention all available bibliographies. In this article, we try to present methods, main ideas, examples, and problems of describing and representing real and abstract objects from the computer graphics (CG) and geometric point of view. Methods of modeling curves, surfaces, solids, and volumetric objects will be discussed.

Computer-aided geometric design (CAGD) based on parametric shape models now pervades many areas. Using CAGD tools, designers can create and refine their ideas to produce complex shapes by combining large numbers of curve and surface segments into boundary shells of three-dimensional solids. However, in spite of elaborate user interfaces, this is very routine work that leads to long training.

Free-form deformations are controlled by user-defined point lattices and, sometimes, are too global and depend on user intuition. Large amount of effort has been put into solving blending and offsetting problems. However, now we can ascertain that this problem is far from the solution, especially for set-theoretic operations.

Constructive solid geometry (CSG) deals with a collection of simple primitives and now is looking as most promising direction in the geometric modeling. However, it suffers from the difficulties connected with free-form modeling. It is quite difficult to solve such important problems as collision detection and rendering for CSG trees, including free-form shapes.

Polygonal representation is rather popular in the animation field. However, we have to note that polygonal patches, in fact in many cases, are the result of another representations or processing data. Also, there are tremendous problems with transformations or metamorphosis of shapes, free-form deformations, set-theoretic and any operations under objects, and level of details question.

TABLE 1   Dimensions in Shapes

$k \leq n,\ n = 1\text{–}4$	Shape
0	Point
1	Curve
2	Surface
3	Solid
$k = 3,\ n = 4$	Volume

Geometric objects defined by real functions of several variables (so-called implicit models), with the help of procedural techniques (physically based modeling, L-systems, particle systems), have proven to be useful in CG, geometric modeling, and animation. Objects of this kind can be created with skeleton-based surfaces, so-called R-functions for set-theoretic operations, and by processing range or volume data. Blended implicit surfaces use an unstructured collection of key points and provide excellent local control, but practical modeling with implicit surfaces is an arcane art with no discernible system. The main problems of this technique are the performance, interface, and interactivity.

Physics-based modeling is essentially an approach based on the finite-element method, which has a history in the application of structural analysis of materials. This method is used in CAD applications, and different tissue simulations were performed for computer animation goals and surgery planning.

In the following sections, we discuss different types of shape and method of modeling them, provide mathematical details and illustrations where it is necessary, and provide extensive list of references for further reading.

SHAPE DIMENSION AND DEFINITION

We consider a shape to be a point set in n-dimensional geometric space (e.g., in Euclidean space). A shape is k dimensional if there is continuous one-to-one mapping of the k-dimensional cube (ball) on this shape. Table 1 shows dimensions of the shapes in geometric spaces with $n = 1$ to 4. A shape can exist in the space if $k \leq n$. How can one define such shapes? There are several basic ways to do this:

1. Make a list of all elements (points) of the point set. It is obvious that only finite point sets can be defined in this way and no continuous shape (such as curve or surface) can be defined.
2. Mapping from a known set $\mathbf{M}$: $\mathbf{A} \rightarrow \mathbf{B}$. If the set $\mathbf{A}$ is defined, mapping $\mathbf{M}$ establishes one-to-one correspondence between the set $\mathbf{A}$ and the new set $\mathbf{B}$

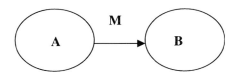

FIGURE 1   Mapping from a known set to a new set.

FIGURE 2   Point membership rule.

(Fig. 1). Parametric curves, surfaces, and volumes presented in the next section are defined in this way.

3. Point membership rule. A rule may be established which allows for any given point to judge if it belongs to the newly defined set or not (Fig. 2). Implicit curves and surfaces and functionally defined solids and volumes are introduced in this way.

4. Generation rule. A rule can be specified to generate shape in a recursive manner, starting with some initial shape and use the current shape as input at the following generation step (Fig. 3). Fractals, L-systems, and other procedural models can be defined in this way.

MODELING SCHEMES

Basic modeling schemes for shapes of different dimensions are characterized in this section. More details can be found in Refs. 2–6.

Parametric Modeling

Parametric curves, surfaces, and solids are defined by equations of x, y, and z in terms of auxiliary parameters t, u, and v depending on the shape dimension. These parametric equations can be thought as mappings of one-, two-, and three-dimensional space of parameters onto a geometric space as illustrated by Figure 4. See specific models in the subsection Parametric Models.

Implicit Modeling

Implicit curves and surfaces are defined using the continuous function of two or three point coordinates, respectively. For example, a set of points with $f(x, y) = 0$ defines an

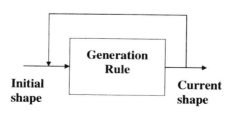

FIGURE 3   Generation rule.

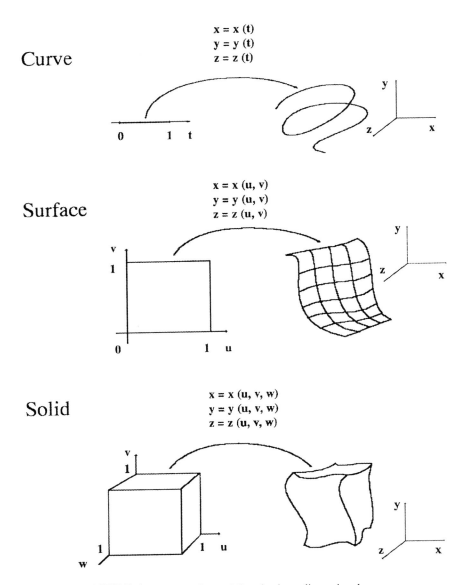

FIGURE 4   Parametric modeling in three-dimensional space.

implicit curve, which is a boundary between two other sets of points on a plane: inside points with positive function values and outside points with negative function values (circle in Fig. 5). See specific models of implicit surfaces in the subsection Implicit Models. Functionally defined solids are defined with the inequality $f(x_1, x_2, \ldots, x_n) \geq 0$ and are n-dimensional objects in n-dimensional space as a two-dimensional disk in the two-dimensional space in Figure 5 (see the section Solid Modeling). Volumes should be distinguished from solids. A volume can be defined by an explicit function $x_4 =$

$$f(x,y) = R^2 - x^2 - y^2$$

Disk (k=2) $f(x,y) \geq 0$

Circle (k=1) $f(x,y) = 0$

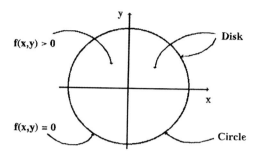

FIGURE 5   Implicit modeling on the plane: circle and disk.

$f(x_1, x_2, x_3)$ and is a three-dimensional object in four-dimensional space (see the section Volume Modeling).

Discrete Modeling

A discrete model can be thought as the approximation of a continuous shape by a collection of adjoining shapes that are more primitive than the original shape; for example:

- In spatial enumeration, a shape is approximated by a union of rectangular shapes of uniform size (voxels) or varying sizes (space partitioning with quad-trees and octrees).
- In cell decomposition, primitives are disjoint cells with distinct shapes (block, pyramid, prism, etc.).
- In ray representation, the original shape is represented by a set of spatial samples (e.g., line segments) augmented with some symbolic data (e.g., half-space equations at endpoints) (7).

See the subsection Spatial Partitioning and the section Volume Modeling for more details.

Physics-Based and Procedural Modeling

Deformable models based on concepts from physics in accordance with Newtonian mechanics are widely used for computer animation (for instance, in facial and cloth modeling). Physics-based modeling mainly uses the finite-element method (FEM), which is a technique to approximate the solution of a continuous function with a series of shape functions. The advantage of the FEM is that the discrete equations can be derived for almost any arbitrary geometry. A continuous physical problem is transformed into a discrete finite-element problem with unknown nodal values. For a linear problem, a system of linear algebraic equations should be solved. Values inside finite elements can be recovered using nodal values.

Two features of the FEM are worthy of mention:

- Piecewise approximation of physical field on finite elements provides good precision even with simple approximating functions (increasing the number of elements, we can achieve any precision).
- Locality of approximation leads to equation systems for a discrete problem. This helps to solve problems with very large number of nodal unknowns.

A continuum meshing, necessary for FEM computation, is created and elastic properties are passed to elements.

Great number of shapes, especially in the simulation of natural phenomena, can be designed with the help of procedural modeling. Procedural modeling includes different techniques such as fractal modeling, L-systems, and particle-based models. The complexity of the natural shapes requires an approximation of the processes seen in nature. Such surfaces depend on many factors that lead to the use of a combination of many calculating methods and procedural approximations to attain a good visual appearance of designed objects. Such objects as water waves or flows can be modeled by solving the Navier–Stokes equations; clouds may be approximated by a fractal function or particle systems. See the sections Physics-Based Modeling and Procedural Modeling for more details.

Topological Modeling

In topological modeling, shapes are considered on a higher abstraction level. It aims at providing most fundamental shape characteristics (genus, connectedness, critical points, etc.) that are invariant from specific geometric instancing and do not change under deformation (3,8).

In topology, surfaces can be classified in terms of the numbers of "handles" on them. The number of handles in the object is defined by its *genus* (e.g., a sphere is classified as genus 0, as there is no handle). The surface is called orientable if clockwise rotation stays clockwise on any closed loop on a surface. If the surface is bounded and complete, it is called a compact one. An infinite cylinder is an example of the noncompact surface; see Ref. 9.

A generalized model, called the homotopy model, was proposed and developed by Shinagawa and Kunii (10) and can be referred to as the topological modeling. The toroidal graph representation is used to reconstruct surfaces from cross-sectional data. See more information on topological modeling in the book by Fomenko and Kunii (3).

MODELING CURVES AND SURFACES

Parametric Models

The theory of parametric models splits naturally into consideration of parametric curves and parametric surfaces. Curves are easier to consider and their relevant properties extend without difficulty to parametric surfaces.

A parametrically defined curve in three dimensions is given by three univariate functions:

$$Q(u) = (X(u), Y(u), Z(u)),$$

where $0 \leq u \leq 1$. Similarly, a parametric surface is defined by three bivarate functions.

$$Q(u) = (X(u, v), Y(u, v), Z(u, v)),$$

where $0 \leq u \leq 1$ and $0 \leq v \leq 1$. The main idea situated in the base of the parametrical approximation is the following. A polynomial of degree $n - 1$ can be made to pass through n given data points. The resulting curve is generally not a smooth curve through the points, because such a function would not only include the "noise" in the data but would also very likely fluctuate considerably between the data points. In many instances, a smooth curve can be obtained by passing a drafter's spline through all of the given data points.

In a cubic spline fit, it is assumed that the approximating function between any two adjacent data points is a third-degree polynomial. A general problem statement of spline approximation (11–15) should be considered. Let us note that cubic splines conforms to the following minimum condition:

$$\int_a^b [u''(x)]^2 \, dx$$

which is equal to the minimization of a bending energy.

The development of the theory was to construct the interpolation spline function $U(P_i) \in W_2^m (\Omega)$, where W_2^m is the set of all functions whose squares of all derivatives of order $\leq m$ are integrable over $\mathbf{R}^n$, so that $U(P_i) = r_i$, $i = 1, 2, \ldots, N$, and the spline has minimum energy of all functions that interpolate the values r_i. It leads to the utilization of differential operator L and using the more general minimum condition

$$\int_a^b [Lu(x)]^2 \, dx$$

instead of double differentiation. Such an approximation accompanied developments in smoothing technique. General theorems of the existence and uniqueness of spline functions were proved and it was shown that minimization of the functionals results in system of linear algebraic equations.

B-spline

We assume (see Ref. 16) that a point in 4-space (E^4) is given by its coordinates $[x, y, z, w]$. It can be shown that an nth-degree rational Bezier curve is given by

$$\mathrm{x}(u) = \frac{w_0 \mathbf{b}_0 B_0^n(u) + \cdots + w_n \mathbf{b}_n B_n^n(u)}{w_0 B_0^n(u) + \cdots + w_n B_n^n(u)}, \quad \mathrm{x}(u), \, \mathbf{b}_i \subseteq E^3.$$

The w_i are called weights, the b_i form the control polygon, and $B_i^n(t)$ are B-spline basis functions (Bershtein polynomials).

The weights w_i are typically used as shape parameters. If we increase one w_i, the curve is pulled toward the corresponding $\mathbf{b}_i$. The effect of changing a weight is different from that of moving a control vertex. If all weights equal 1, we obtain the standard nonrational Bezier curve.

The rational B-spline curve is defined in direct way analogy to the rational Bezier. A three-dimensional (3D) rational cubic B-spline curve is the projection through the origin of a 4D nonrational cubic B-spline curve to a space of lower dimension. The form of a rational B-spline curve is

$$\mathrm{x}(u) = \sum_{i=0}^{L+n-1} w_i \mathbf{d}_i N_i(u) \left(\sum_{i=0}^{L+n-1} \mathbf{d}_i N_i(u) \right)^{-1}.$$

Here, the $\mathbf{d}_i$ are the de Boor points, L is the number of polynomial segments of the B-spline curve, and $N(t)$ is the B-spline basis functions. The w values represent the weight associated with de Boor points.

The rational form of the nonuniform B-spline is called NURBS; see Ref. 17. The NURBS model provides an exact representation of conic sections.

Implicit Models

A wide variety of curves and surfaces exist apart from parametrically defined types. There is a large body of surfaces that are defined implicitly; that is, geometric objects are considered as closed subsets of n-dimensional Euclidean space E^n with the definition $f(x_1, x_2, \ldots, x_n) = 0$, where f is a real continuous function defined on E^n. Recent work has shown the usefulness and advantages related to implicit form of definition; see Ref. 18.

Three major lines in of work in implicit models are as follows:

- *Algebraic surfaces.* Algebraic methods define surfaces with polynomial functions of three variables. Typically, these are low-degree polynomials (2 to 4). The most popular algebraic surfaces are surfaces with polynomials of degree 2 or so-called "quadrics" (sphere, cylinder, cone, ellipsoid, etc.). They can be used as separate shapes or as initial primitives in Constructive Solid Geometry (see the subsection Constructive Solid Geometry). Simplicity of these surfaces made it possible to architect and implement special-purpose hardware (7) for processing complex shapes composed of quadratic surfaces. Algebraic patch-based methods provide meshing tiny subsets of quadratic surfaces with smooth continuity to model complex free-form shapes (19,20).
- *Skeleton-based implicit surfaces.* A surface is considered as a zero set of the scalar field generated by some "skeleton" field source (discrete set of points, lines, triangles, etc.). Combining individual field functions of skeletal elements can be implemented with the algebraic sum or integration technique (convolution surfaces).
- *Function representation.* The function representation defines an entire shape by a single continuous real-valued function $f(x_1, x_2, \ldots, x_n)$, where $(x_1, x_2, \ldots, x_n)$ is a vector of point coordinates. Functions are not restricted—they have to be at least C^0 continuous. The function is defined by an evaluation procedure, which evaluates functions of basic shapes and applies different functional operations to them. The inequality $f \geq 0$ defines an F-rep solid and the equation $f = 0$ defines its surface (or so-called isosurface of the function f). See the subsection Real-Function Representation for details.

Skeleton-Based Implicit Surfaces

A skeleton-based implicit surface is defined as follows:

$$F(X) = 0 \quad \text{with } F(X) = \sum_k f(r_k) - T,$$

where $f(r_k)$ is a field function of an individual skeletal element, r_k is the distance between a given point X and the kth skeletal element, and T is a threshold value. Figure 6 illustrates the simplest case of the point skeleton.

A skeleton-based blobby model was introduced in Ref. 21 with the following field function:

$$f(r_k) = b_k e^{-a_k r_k^2},$$

which is a Gaussian bell-shaped function centered in the skeletal point, with height b_k and standard deviation a_k. Exponential field function decay does not provide an opportunity to localize influence of each skeletal point. Metaballs (22) and soft objects (23) employ polynomial field functions, which decay completely in a given finite distance.

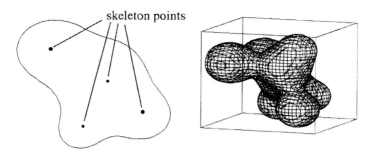

skeleton points

FIGURE 6 Skeleton points placement inside the surface (left) and a typical point skeleton-based surface (right).

A skeleton can include other elements (lines, curves, triangles, etc.) with individual distance function r_k applied to each type of elements. Algebraic sums between individual field functions provide natural shape blending. Skeleton-based surfaces support intuitive modeling of natural shapes such as molecules, liquid and melting objects, and animal and human bodies.

Convolution Surfaces

Convolution surfaces were introduced in Ref. 24 as a generalization of skeleton-based implicit surfaces. A field function for a convolution surface is obtained by spatial convolution between a skeletal element and a Gaussian-type kernel:

$$f(X) = \int_{R^3} s(P)h(X - P) \, dP,$$

where X is a vector of point coordinates, $s(X)$ is a predicate function defining the geometry of the skeletal element [$s(X) = 1$ for points of the element and $s(X) = 0$ for other points in space], and $h(X)$ is a convolution kernel.

Properties of convolution, such as superposition, make modeling with convolution surfaces quite intuitive. Analytical solutions for the above-mentioned integral can be found only for simple skeletal elements and kernels. In Ref. 25, such solutions were found for the kernel $h(X) = 1/(1 + a^2\|X\|^2)^2$ and for several skeletal elements such as line segment, circular arc, triangle, and plane (see the example in Fig. 7).

SHAPE TRANSFORMATIONS

Shape transformation is one of basic operations in computer graphics. In CAD, shape-transformation methods become also important because allow to generate custom objects according to some measurement data; see Ref. 26. The problem concerns transformation of a given geometric shape into another in a continuous manner. We consider shape transformation as a general operation type, including space mappings, metamorphoses, and others. Examples of applications can be found in such fields as animation and computer-aided design.

FIGURE 7   A hand model using convolution surfaces.

Most existing shape transformation techniques fall into one of the following three categories:

1. Mapping the space onto itself
2. Metamorphosis
3. Modification of defining functions

Linear Transformations

The basic 2D and 3D geometrical transformations (translation, scaling, and rotation) are used quite widely in different geometry packages. The 2D and 3D linear transformations can be represented by 3×3 and 4×4 matrices correspondingly using homogeneous coordinates; see, for instance, Ref. 27. Thus, instead of representing a point as (x, y, z), we represent it as (x, y, z, W). Transforming the point to this form is called homogenizing. A point with a zero W coordinate is called a point at infinity. Each point in 3-space is represented by a line through the origin in 4-space, and the homogenized representations of these points form a 3D subspace of 4-space that is defined by the single equation $W = 1$. The composition of transformations or a combination of the fundamental translation, scaling, and rotation matrices produces desired general result. The basic purpose of composing transformations is to gain efficiency by applying a single composed transformation to a point, rather than applying a series of transformations, one after the other.

Global and Local Transformations

Global and Local Deformations of Solid Primitives

Global and local deformations of solid primitives were introduced by Barr (28). The chief result is that the normal vector of an arbitrarily deformed smooth surface can be calculated directly from the surface normal vector of the undeformed surface and a transformation matrix.

A globally specified deformation of a 3D solid is a mathematical function F that explicitly modifies the global coordinates of points in space.

A locally specified deformation modifies the tangent space of the solid. Tangent vectors and normal vectors are the two most important vectors used in modeling. The former is for constructing the local geometry, and the latter for obtaining surface orientation.

The algebraic manipulations for the transformation rules involve a single multiplication by the Jacobian matrix J of the transformation function F and is calculated by taking partial derivatives of F with respect to the coordinate vector **x**:

$$J_i(x) = \frac{\partial F(\boldsymbol{x})}{\partial x_i} .$$

Examples of deformations are scaling, tapering, axial twists (see an example in Fig. 8).

> *Tapering.* One of the simplest deformations is a change in the length of the three global components parallel to the coordinate axes.
> *Global tapering along the Z axis* is similar to scaling, by differentially changing the length of two global components without changing the length of the third.
> *Global axial twists* can be approximated as differential rotation, just as tapering is a differential scaling of the global basis vectors.

Transformations of Objects Represented by Generalized Implicit Functions

These transformations were proposed by Sclaroff and Pentland (29). They used natural vibration modes to express a wide range of deformations. If the transformation is not degenerate, an inverse matrix can be calculated and used for the inverse mapping, which is necessary to transform implicit surfaces. An implicit function representation defines a surface as a level set of points for which $f(x) = 0$. For instance, the superquadric ellipsoid, before rotation, translation, or deformation, is

$$f(\boldsymbol{x}) = [(x^{2/e2} + y^{2/e2})^{e2/e1} + z^{2/e1}]^{e1/2} - 1$$

A solid defined in this way can be easily positioned and oriented by transforming the implicit function:

FIGURE 8   Twisting a solid about a vertical axis.

$$x^\wedge = Mx + b,$$

where M is a rotation matrix and b is a translation vector. Similarly, the implicit function's positioned and oriented inside–outside function becomes

$$f(x) = f(M^{-1}(x^\wedge - b)).$$

The basic set of functions can be generalized further by defining an appropriate set of global deformations D with parameters u. For particular values of u, the new deformed surface is defined using a deformation matrix D_u:

$$x^\wedge = MD_u x + b,$$

where $x^\wedge$ is the position vector after rotation, deformation, and translation. Similarly, the inside–outside function becomes:

$$f(x) = f(D_u^{-1} M^{-1}(x^\wedge - b)).$$

This function is valid as long as the inverse deformation D_u^{-1} exists. So the main idea is to select a set of deformations that can be easily inverted and to expend the class of shapes that can be described using an implicit function representation.

Deformation matrix D_u, referred to as the modal deformation matrix, whose entries are polynomials which mimic the free vibration modes found in real objects. The linear superposition of these deformation polynomials allows an accurate description of the dynamic, nonrigid behavior of real objects.

Metamorphosis

Metamorphosis (or shape averaging, shape blending, in-betweening, morphing) is an operation on two geometric objects resulting in a new object with intermediate shape. It can also be thought of also as a transformation of the initial object controlled by another one. Morphing was first introduced in image processing and animation to generate intermediate images by transformation of one image into another; for more References, see Ref. 30.

Shape metamorphosis for 3D polyhedral objects is quite well elaborated. An interesting combination of representations has been shown by Payne and Toga (31). Initial polyhedra are converted into distance-field volumetric data, then these data are interpolated and the resulting isosurface is polygonized. More sophisticated metamorphosis of volumetric objects has been proposed by Hughes (32), who used the Fourier transforms of two volumetric objects to interpolate between low frequencies with the high frequencies of the first object gradually removed.

Lerios et al. (33) generalize image metamorphosis to the case of 3D volume data and combine warping and cross-dissolving. Shape in-betweening for soft objects (34) applies gradually changing weighting of the force property of each source key. The skeleton of the intermediate shape can be constructed by applying the Minkowski sum to initial skeletons (35).

Metamorphosis for implicit objects can be defined as a transformation between two functions:

$$f_3(x) = f_1(x)(1 - t) + f_2(x)t,$$

where $0 \le t \le 1$. Figure 9 presents a femur reconstructed from 2D cross sections using metamorphosis between neighboring cross sections with the z coordinate (vertical axis) serving as a parameter t of the metamorphosis.

FIGURE 9   Reconstruction of a femur from cross sections using metamorphosis between neighboring cross sections with the z coordinate (vertical axis) serving as a parameter of the metamorphosis.

Although metamorphosis for implicit objects is simple and useful for many applications, the fact that the intermediate stages of the transformation do not provide a *homeomorphism* limits its use. Two objects are said to be *homeomorphic*, or *topologically equivalent*, if a continuous, invertible, one-to-one mapping between points on the surface of two objects exists.

Much attention is paid to development of efficient algorithms for solving metamorphosis or the shape-transformation problem for polyhedral objects in computer graphics. For recent references, see, for instance, Refs. 37 and 38. A common approach to transforming one shape into another is to divide the problem into two steps:

- The first step is referred to as the *correspondence problem*, more specifically, the problem is to establish a homeomorphism between two shapes.
- The second step is referred to as *interpolation problem*.

As an example illustrating the problem, consider the discrete-event approach of homotopic shape deformation for polygons proposed by Fujimura and Makarov (39). Figure 10 illustrates this deformation as a dynamic triangulation over a given set of feature points. As a feature point moves, the triangulation changes its shape. An event is said to occur when a triangle in the triangulation satisfies a certain condition (e.g., becomes flat, ceases to be optimal, etc.). For a mapping between Figures 10a and 10b, the triangulation can be used, because quadrilaterals in Figures 10a and 10b have the same (i.e., isomorphic) structure. However, between Figures 10a and 10d, the flipping of a diagonal occurs. To maintain one-to-one correspondence, another triangulation ($\triangle$ABC and $\triangle$ADC) will

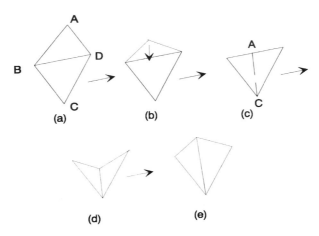

FIGURE 10   Homotopic transformation from shape (a) to shape (e). Steps: (a,b) vertex **A** moving down; (c) "event" and creation of a new edge **AC**; (d,e) vertex **A** moving up.

have to take place at some point. To switch between the two triangulations smoothly, a dual representation of barycentric coordinates is used.

Space Mappings and Free-Form Transformations

A space mapping establishes one-to-one correspondence between points of the space. If applied to some point set in the space, it changes this set to a different one. A mapping can be defined by functional dependence between new and old coordinates of a point. Mappings can be controlled by numerical parameters of functions, by control points, and by differential equations. Fournier and Wesley (40) and Barr (28) have proposed specific functions for bending, tapering, and twisting operations. Interactive control of these deformations by a single curve in 3D space has been implemented by Lazarus et al. (41). General deformation techniques (42,43), providing forward and inverse mapping, are better suited to implicit surfaces. Most of the above-mentioned deformation methods are too global to provide a series of small bumps defined by arbitrary points. Although the method of Borrel and Rappoport (43) has been designed for localized space mappings, it can lead to nonintuitive results when bounding spheres of several control points intersect. The survey (44) discusses common mathematical foundations of the mentioned space deformation techniques.

In a different approach, scattered data interpolation techniques such as thin-plate spline (45), distance-weighted interpolants (46), volume spline based on Green's function (47), or multiquadrics (48) are applied. The authors of the last article attempt to combine space mappings with metamorphosis. Their method does not provide a solution in 3D space but relies on 2D image morphing.

Free-form deformations (FFD) proposed by Sederberg and Perry (49) and extended in Refs. 50–52 are controlled by user-defined point lattices. Forward space mapping is described by trivariate Bezier volumes and can be effectively applied to polygonal and parametric surfaces. Alternatively, inverse mapping for implicit surfaces requires a time-consuming iterative search or subdivisions (53). Chang and Rockwood (54) presented an intuitive approach to control free-form deformations by a single Bezier curve. Their algorithm works faster than standard FFD, because the problem dimension has been reduced from three to one.

Free-form deformation can be thought of as a method for sculpturing solid models. A good physical analogy for FFD is to consider a "brick" of clear, flexible plastic in which is embedded an object, or several objects, which we wish to deform. The object is imagined to also be flexible, so that it deforms along with the plastic that surrounds it. FFD involves a mapping from R^3 to R^3 through a trivariate tensor-product Bernstein polynomial.

A space mapping can be defined using displacements of arbitrarily selected feature points. Volume spline functions derived for multidimensional scattered data on the base of the Green's function can be applied to interpolate the displacements (55,56). The main advantage of this spline is the minimum bending energy of all functions that interpolate given scattered data. In the 2D case, it is a so-called "thin-plate" spine (57–59).

The example of three-dimensional coordinate space mapping (with volume splines interpolating x, y, and z displacements) applied to a block is shown in Figure 11.

Extended Space Mappings

Modification of Defining Functions

Descriptions of skeleton-based implicit surfaces (see the subsection Implicit Models) are essentially based on algebraic sums of defining functions, which allow deformation of an object by adding new primitives to its skeleton. Deformations of distance surfaces in collisions by algebraic difference of defining field functions have been proposed by Gascuel (60). A blend surface can be described in terms of algebraic operations on defining functions (61). These operations are applied in practice to solid primitives but not to constructive solids (see, for example, Ref. 62). The theory of R-functions (63,64) provides a means of function representation of solids constructed by the standard (nonregularized) set operations (see Ref. 65 for a survey). Shapiro (65) applies algebraic difference to construct a real function defining a regular solid required in constructive solid geometry (see the section Solid Modeling). Blending, offsetting, and other operations

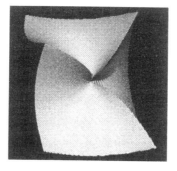

FIGURE 11 Shape transformation of a block using coordinate space mapping defined by one displaced control point and eight fixed boundary points.

have been defined in Ref. 66 by algebraic sums applied to R-function-based exact descriptions of constructive solids.

Shape reconstruction from given points can be thought as a special case of transformation. Muraki (67) proposes to apply the blobby model to fit scattered points. To fit an algebraic surface to given points, Bajaj et al. (68) solve a constrained minimization problem for distance criteria. Savchenko et al. (55) used algebraic sums of an initial defining function and a volume spline to reconstruct a solid from scattered surface points.

Figure 12 illustrates modeling the pricking effect with control points placed inside a 3D solid defined by the set-theoretic and blending operations. One can note the local nature of deformations that is practically impossible to achieve by other existing deformation methods.

If the displacement function $d(x)$ interpolates defining function values in control points more smoothly (without local extreme points), more global deformation can be obtained. This can be achieved with the volume spline based on the Green's function. An algebraic sum of a sphere and a volume spline can be used to reconstruct 3D solids from given scattered surface points (55).

A general mathematical framework called *extended space mapping* was proposed in Ref. 69 for transforming functionally defined shapes. This framework generalizes the above-discussed transformations: space mappings and modification of defining functions. This model also introduces several new transformations, such as *function-dependent space mapping* and *combined mappings*.

Function-Dependent Space Mappings

In this case, coordinate space mapping depends on the defining function and, therefore, on the shape of the initial object. Consider, for example, the following formulation of the offsetting "along the normal" operation:

$$\xi' = f(x' + d\mathbf{N}),$$

where d is a given offset distance and $\mathbf{N}$ is a gradient vector of the function f in a given point x'. The vector $\mathbf{N}$ is a normal vector for a point on the surface.

FIGURE 12   Local deformations with function mappings: pricking effect with arbitrarily placed control points.

FIGURE 13   Offsettting "along the normal": offset of a 3D solid with the distance modulated by the depth data.

This operation is illustrated by Figure 13. Note that for application of the offsetting for object with an arbitrary geometry, the notion of the offsetting "along the normal" should be reformulated by substituting the function gradient instead of the surface normal.

Combined Mappings

A combined mapping is a mixture of function mappings and space mappings. Figure 14 illustrates the 3D application of combined mappings to the well-known problem: to obtain the visually smooth transformation between the initial (ellipsoidal in this example) shape and the final shape during motion in presence of obstacles. Here, the space mapping provides constraints for collision avoidance and the function mapping defines metamorphosis between two implicitly defined shapes.

SOLID MODELING

The main characteristic of a solid is homogeneous three dimensionality. It means that a solid must have an interior, and a solid's boundary cannot have isolated or dangling portions. There are several different ways to digitally represent solids. Each representa-

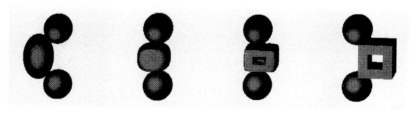

FIGURE 14   Combined mapping in 3D space: metamorphosis and collision-free motion.

tion has to provide the determination of point membership: Given any point, it must be possible to determine whether it is inside, outside, or on the surface of a solid. In this section, we describe the following representational schemes: constructive solid geometry, boundary representation, sweeping, spatial partitioning, medial axis, and parametric and real function representations. Formal definitions and more details on solids and solid representations can be found in Refs. 4–6 and 70.

Constructive Solid Geometry

To design a shape, one can select simple shapes (primitives), specify their parameters and position in space, and construct a more complex shape of them by applying union, intersection, or subtraction set operations (see Fig. 15). This modeling paradigm and the corresponding representation is called constructive solid geometry (CSG). Traditional CSG primitives are block, cylinder, cone, sphere, and torus. Linear transformations (translation and rotation) can be used together with regularized set operations. A regularized set operation includes removing lower-dimensional parts of the standard set operation result such as dangling surfaces, curves, or points.

A CSG object is represented as a binary tree (or CSG tree) with operations at the internal nodes and primitives at the leaves (see Fig. 16). The point membership classification algorithm defines whether a given point is inside, outside, or on the boundary of the solid. This algorithm recursively traverses the CSG tree starting from the root. In the nodes with linear transformations, the inverse of the transformation is applied to the current point coordinates. When the recursion reaches the leaves, the point is tested against the corresponding primitives. Then, the classification results are combined in the internal nodes with set-theoretic operations.

Boundary Representation

A solid can be represented by its boundary. To define a boundary surface, one can introduce points (vertices), curves (edges), and surface patches (faces) and stitch them together (Fig. 17, left). This boundary representation (or B-rep) has two parts (Fig. 17, right): topological information of the connectivity of vertices, edges, and faces; geometric information embedding these boundary elements in three-dimensional space. Topological information specifies incidences and adjacencies of boundary elements. Geometric information specifies coordinates of vertices or the equations of the surfaces containing the

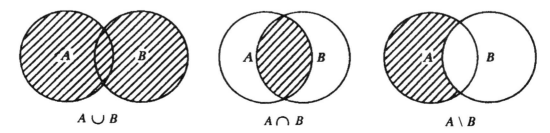

$A \cup B$ $A \cap B$ $A \setminus B$

FIGURE 15   Set operations between two 2D disks: union ($\cup$), intersection ($\cap$), and subtraction ($\setminus$). The result of each operation is shown as a hatched area.

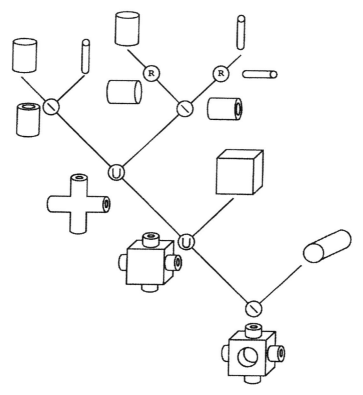

FIGURE 16   Example of a CSG tree. Operations: R (ration), \ (subtraction), and ∪ (union).

faces. The boundary of the solid is a two-dimensional manifold. Each point of the bound-ary has a neighborhood with one-to-one correspondence to a disk in the plane.

A polyhedral solid is bounded by a set of planar polygons such that each edge connects two vertices and is shred by exactly two faces, at least three edges meet at each vertex, and faces do not interpenetrate. A simple polygon can be deformed into a sphere. The B-rep of a simple polyhedron satisfies Euler's formula:

$$V - E + F = 2,$$

where V is the number of vertices, E is the number of edges, and F is the number of faces. The B-rep including faces with holes satisfies the generalized Euler's formula:

$$V - E + F - H = 2(C - G),$$

where H is the number of holes in the faces, C is the number of solid disjoint compo-nents, and G is the surface genus (for a sphere, $G = 0$; for a torus, $G = 1$). Local modifications of the boundary are performed using tweaking operations such as the moving vertex, edge, or face. Topological modifications are performed using Euler operators, which include adding and removing vertices, edges, and faces. These operators satisfy Euler's formula and thus ensure topological validity of the resulting solids.

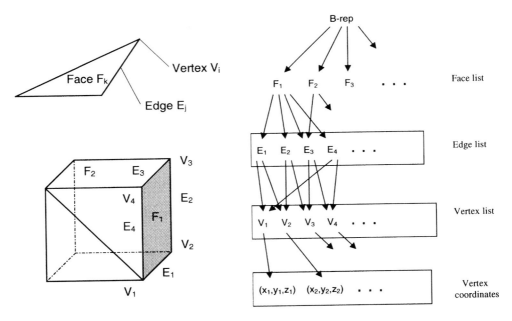

FIGURE 17 Boundary representation of a cube is based on surface faces (triangles and/or quadrangles), edges, and vertices.

Sweeping

A sweeping operation defines a set of points visited by a generator (curve, surface, or solid) moving along a trajectory (see Fig. 18). In the translational sweep, the trajectory is a line segment orthogonal to the plane containing the generator planar patch, as is shown in Figure 18. In the rotational sweep, a circular arc serves as the trajectory and directs the rotation of each point of the generator around the rotation axis by the given angle. A parametrized planar cross section with a variable shape swept along an arbitrary curve defines a generalized cylinder. General sweeping allows for the arbitrary generator, including curvilinear surfaces and set-theoretic solids. Shape variations of the generator

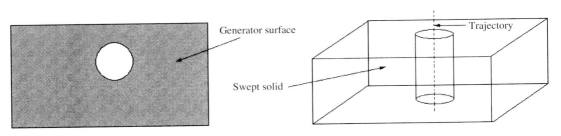

FIGURE 18 Elements of sweeping: generator surface, trajectory, and swept solid.

during the motion may include deformations, topology changes, and appearance of disconnected components.

Spatial Partitioning

In spatial-partitioning (spatial decomposition) representations, a solid is decomposed in a finite set of more primitive nonintersecting solids. The primitives can be different in type, size, position, or parametrization. Table 2 shows different types of primitives and corresponding representational schemes.

Spatial occupancy enumeration decomposes a bounding box of a solid into a set of identical cells arranged in a fixed, regular grid. For each cell, only its presence or absence in the grid is defined. A cell is presented in the grid if it is occupied by the solid. No concept of partial occupancy is employed. An *octree* divides a cube in eight subcubes recursively. A subcube can be completely inside the solid, outside the solid, or can be subdivided again, if it is partially occupied by the solid. *Boundary space partition* (BSP) *trees* are also based on the recursive subdivision of space. Each node of the tree represents a plane that separates space into two disjoint point sets. The leaves of the BSP tree represent cells that are inside or outside the solid.

A *ray representation* (7) of a solid is a set of segments resulting from the intersection of the solid with a ray grid (a finite set of regularly spaced parallel lines). In general, spatial partitioning schemes provide the approximation of solids. The ray representation can include special tags with descriptive symbolic information on the primitives in the solid's CSG or the boundary surfaces.

Medial Axis

The definition of *medial axis transform* (MAT) comes from Blum (71). Medial axis (or medial surface in 3D) is a locus of centers of maximal disks (spheres in 3D) inscribed within the solid. An inscribed disk (sphere) is maximal if no other inscribed disk (sphere) contains it. With the radius of a sphere given in any point of the medial surface, an unambiguous solid is represented. An example of a 2D shape and its medial axis is shown in Figure 19.

The MAT is powerful in that the following is true (72):

- Morphological analysis might be simpler.
- It captures the overall shape characteristics of an object in a simple form.
- Objects can be recovered efficiently from their skeleton representation. How-

TABLE 2   Types of Primitives and Corresponding Representational Schemes

Primitive	Representational scheme
Cells (cube, prism, hyperpatch)	Cell decomposition
Cube (fixed size)	Spatial occupancy enumeration or voxel representation
Cube (variable size)	Quadrees (2D), octrees (3D)
Planar half-spaces	Binary space partitioning (BSP) tree
Line segments	Ray representation

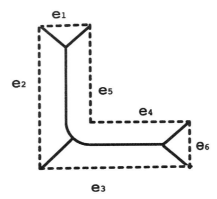

FIGURE 19   The medial axis of a planar *L* shape.

ever, reconstruction of the solid's B-rep from the medial surface in 3D is a difficult problem.

*   Some meshing algorithms use the medial axis and the medial surface to construct cell decomposition (finite-element mesh) of the solid.

Parametric Function Representation

The parametric function representation is an extension and generalization of sweeping (see the subsection Sweeping). It was introduced in the most general form in the *generative modeling* approach (73). Shapes are represented by multidimensional, continuous, piecewise-differentiable parametric functions

$$F : R^n \to R^m,$$

where R^n is parameter space and R^m is object space. For $n = 3$ and $m = 3$,

$$[x(u, v, w), y(u, v, w), z(u, v, w)]$$

defines a solid in 3D space.

Generative modeling provides a closed set of operators, including the standard geometric transformations (rotate, translate, etc.), set-theoretic operations (intersection, union, subtraction), and operators for creating time-dependent shapes (sweep operators, differentiation, integration, inverse functions, constraint solution, constrained minimization). These operators are based on the mathematical technique of interval analysis.

Real-Function Representation

The *function representation* (or F-rep) defines a whole geometric object by a single real-valued continuous function of several variables as $F(X) \geq 0$ (66). F-rep combines together many different models like algebraic and skeleton-based implicits (see the subsection Implicit Models), set-theoretic solids (see the subsection Constructive Solid Geometry), sweeps (see the subsection Sweeping), voxel objects (see the subsection Spatial Positioning), and procedural models (see the section Procedural Modeling).

Modeling concepts include sets of objects, operations, and relations. Any operation has to be closed on the representation (i.e., generate a continuous real function as a result). Set-theoretic operations are closed on F-rep with the use of C^k continuous R-functions introduced by Rvachev (64) (see also the survey in Ref. 65). The main restriction of well-known min/max operations is that they are C^1 discontinuous. This can yield unexpected results in further operations on the object.

The simplest R-functions are

$$f_1 \ \& \ f_2 = f_1 + f_2 - \sqrt{f_1^2 + f_2^2}$$

for the intersection of two objects described by f_1 and f_2, and

$$f_1 \ \& \ f_2 = f_1 + f_2 + \sqrt{f_1^2 + f_2^2}$$

for the union. These functions have C^1 discontinuity only in the points where $f_1 = f_1 = 0$. C^k continuous R-functions are also available. Other basic analytically defined operations are blending (Fig. 20a), offsetting, and Cartesian product. Advanced procedurally defined operations are sweeping by a moving solid (Fig. 20b) (74), different types of deformation defined by extended space mappings (see the subsection Extended Space Mappings), reconstruction from surface points and contours (55), and metamorphosis, which produces an intermediate shape between two given objects (Fig. 21).

VOLUME MODELING

The research in volume modeling with voxel data includes Boolean operations and linear transformations (75,76), scattered data interpolation (77), transformation from one voxel data structure to another by manual 3D painting and carving (78–80), volume sculpting (81–83), metamorphosis (84.85), and morphological operations (86). For example, Ref. 76, presenting a voxel-based approach to volume modeling, offers a powerful methodol-

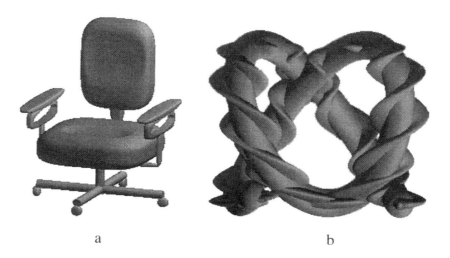

a   b

FIGURE 20   F-rep operations: (a) set-theoretic and blending; (b) sweeping by a moving solid.

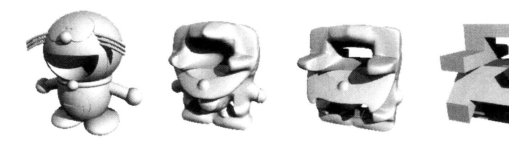

FIGURE 21   Metamorphosis between two constructive solids of differing topology. In F-rep, metamorphosis can be expressed as the weighted interpolation between two defining functions.

ogy for layered manufacturing. It has several advantages over conventional modeling methods, stemming chiefly from the close resemblance between a voxel model of an object and the object fabricated using layered manufacturing technology. The modeling system is based on the compressed form of voxel data, voxelization algorithms are used when necessary, and a voxel-based approach to CSG is implemented.

Traditionally, voxel data collected from the real world are represented by scalar values in the nodes of a regular 3D grid and can be displayed by rendering hardware based on a volume buffer. However, "very little has yet been done on the topic of volume modeling" (87). There are such problems here, as pointed by Kaufman et al. (88):

- Sculpturing in discrete space
- Feature mapping and warping
- Morphing and changing of the model
- Intermixing volumetric and analytically defined geometric objects

In fact, these topics were intensively investigated in geometric modeling. Nowadays, CAGD tools and software are restricted in the above-mentioned capabilities; ideally, volume modeling software will be able to deal with data from different sources (e.g., analytically defined objects and natural objects) and produce models according to the user specifications or ideas. The traditional areas such as solid modeling and volume graphics also can benefit from this approach: For solid modeling, a new source of shapes appears. Instead of voxelization of exactly represented objects such as spheres, tori, and others (as discussed in Ref. 89), a solid modeler keeps as high accuracy as possible while dealing with volumetric objects. Research results can be examined in new application fields such as surgery planning, prosthesis design, and even virtual hairdressing. The rich set of operations can be used for modeling volumes. Temporal transformation or metamorphosis can be useful in different applications (e.g., artistic animation or recognition tasks). Shapes can be constructed by the linear interpolation of two shapes by using a linear blending function which specifies the relative contribution of each shape on the resulting blended shape (examples of using nonlinear blending function are given, for example, in Ref. 90). In Ref. 74, sweeping defined with real functions was studded to solve several problems that could not find a general solution in other models earlier. The authors were able to define a complex swept solid with any arbitrary CSG object moving by any complex trajectory with self-intersections. This approach can be expanded to sweeping by a volumetric object. There is a problem that lies in the nature of volumetric data used. These data, normally, do not have a distance property that is very important for the implementation of the method of sweeping.

We illustrate here the following operations on volumetric objects: set-theoretic operations and hypertexturing. All operations result in a new procedurally defined real function of three variables.

Set-Theoretic Operations

In Figure 22, a complex object made of a volumetric head, and simple CSG primitives was created. The head is applied set-theoretic operations and affine transformations to make a drawer that is filled with CSG primitives.

Hypertexturing

A general approach to hypertexturing was presented by Perlin and Hoffert in Ref. 91. The 3D hypertexture can be defined by a real function $f(x, y, z) \geq 0$. With this method, one could define moss, corrosion, snow, fur, and hair. This approach was extended to voxel objects. The improved hair-modeling technique that allows the user to grow and style solid hair on a volumetric head was presented in Ref. 36. Figure 23 presents an example of intermixing volumetric and analytically defined geometric objects to form a solid object with complex surfaces. In this example volume data of a voxel head is used with simulated hair in a synthetic carving on a solid ball.

PHYSICS-BASED MODELING

Spring Networks and Finite-Element Methods

The finite-element method (FEM) is a numerical technique for solving problems, which are described by partial differential equations or can be formulated as functional minimization. A domain of interest is represented as an assembly of finite elements. Approximating functions in finite elements are determined in terms of nodal values of a physical

FIGURE 22   Volumetric head is applied set-theoretic operations and unified with CSG primitives.

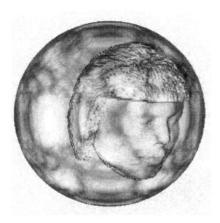

FIGURE 23   Volumetric head and hair unified with a sphere.

field, which is sought. A continuous physical problem is transformed into a discrete finite-element problem with unknown nodal values. For a linear problem, a system of linear algebraic equations should be solved. Values inside finite elements can be recovered using nodal values.

Two features of the finite-element method are worthy of mention:

- Piecewise approximation of physical filed on finite elements provides good precision, even with simple approximating functions (by increasing the number of elements, we can achieve any precision)
- Locality of approximation leads to sparse equation systems for a discrete problem. This helps to solve problems with very large number of nodal unknowns. The FEM is the standard technique for simulating the dynamic behavior of an object. In the FEM, the continuous variation of displacements throughout an object is replaced by displacements at a finite number of so-called nodal points. Energy equations are then derived in terms of the nodal unknowns, and the resulting set of simultaneous differential equations are then iterated to solve for displacements as a function of impinging forces.

Modeling an elastic boundary can be achieved by a mesh of N virtual masses on the grid or on the contour. Each mass is attached to its neighbors by perfect identical springs of stiffness K and natural length l. Generalizing the model to 3D surfaces is straightforward.

The system under study is made of the N virtual masses located at time t at points $M_1(t)$, $M_2(t)$, . . . , $M_N(t)$. The fundamental equation of dynamics states that the vector addition of all applied forces on M_i is equal to its mass m_i multiplied by its acceleration. Finally, in 3D, the deformation of the system is governed by the $3N$-dimensional differential matrix equation:

$$Mu'' + Cu' + Ku = F(t),$$

where u is a $3N$ vector of the (x, y, z) displacements of the N nodal points, M, C, and K are $3N \times 3N$ matrices describing the mass, damping, and material stiffness between each point within the body, respectively, and F is $3N$ vector describing the (x, y, z) components of the forces acting on the nodes. The major drawback of the FEM is its large computational expense. In $3D$, the $3N$-order matrix equations decouple into three directional matrix equations of order N. Modal analysis is a standard engineering technique allowing effective computations. This technique based on transformation of the equilibrium equations by a change of basis. FEMs are computationally expensive and it is worthwhile to note a physically based algorithm for deformable object simulation suitable for real time applications developed by James and Pai (92). Their approach is based on a Boundary Element Method.

Elastically deformable models can be applied for modeling different structures—in particular, for computer simulating legless figures such as snakes and worms (93), which have complex internal structures. Naturally, greatly simplified models can be used. Each segment of the creature was modeled as a cube of masses with springs along each edge and across the diagonal of each face. For each time interval, the spring lengths and spring-length velocities were used to compute the forces exerted on the masses at the end of each spring.

The use of a physically based technique to calculate the draping of textiles are described in Refs. 94 and 95; for more references, see the special issue on Computer Graphics in Textiles and Apparel (96). Eberhardt (97) presented the use of a particle system to compute minimal surfaces and their dynamical behavior. The main idea of the approach is to represent a particle by taking a subdivision of some initially given surface and apply spring forces from each particle to its neighbors for modeling almost all rubberlike materials. This approach is useful for blending objects with rubberlike materials.

Human facial modeling has been the subject of much investigation and the interested reader can find a lot of material in the book of Parke and Waters (98).

Level Set Methodology

Surface deformation as we mentioned earlier actually can be considered as a main instrument for the shape design. There have been a number of attempts to simulate a variety of shapes based on an idea of an evolution of boundaries. Reference 99 provides detailed descriptions and overview of the algorithms, numerical/theoretical analysis, and implementation details of level set or partial differential methods, which view surface generation as a boundary-value problem. Applications of the level set methods are 3D surface morphing, filleting and blending, 3D reconstruction from range data, and computer vision (100,101). A list of references and examples of the application of level set methods can be found in Ref. 102.

The essential feature of level set methods according to Sethian (99) is that deformable models are parametrized. A geometry model is often referred to as being parametric if it is controlled by the values of a certain number of parameters which can be chosen so as to determine the shape. An alternative to a parametric model is an implicit model (i.e., specifying a model as a level set of a scalar function F). Such a strategy rises the question of how to represent F which may depend on many factors for producing an adequate model. Actually, this offers a variety of new modeling tools. Sethian (99) has defined that function F depends on three major factors:

- *Local properties* are those determined by local geometric information, such as curvature and normal direction.
- *Global properties* of the front are those that depend on the shape and position

of the front. For example, the speed might depend on integrals along the front and/or associated differential equations.

- *Independent properties* are those that are independent of the shape of the front.

A well-founded mathematical model leads to a set of rules that describe how a model can be manipulated to create deformation in the level sets. However, level set models have some drawbacks. In particular, they are computationally burdensome. The development of level set level methods is extended mainly in two directions. The first is overcoming shortcomings in level set modeling through improved numerical algorithms. The second is the development of local deformation processes to solve problems in computer graphics and geometric modeling.

PROCEDURAL MODELING

Fractals

Fractals, introduced by Mandelbrott, have become significant tools in natural sciences and they are of great interest to graphics designers for their ability to simulate most of the natural phenomenon. The word fractal is derived from the Latin adjective "fractus," which means broken or fragmented; see Ref. 103. The following statements describe a fractal:

- Fractal objects are entities that cannot be represented with Euclidean methods.
- Fractals have fractional dimension, a number that agrees with our intuitive notion of dimension
- Fractals have the property of self-similarity; they are invariant under change of scale.
- The basic principle of generating fractals involves repetitive application of a specified transformation function to points within a region of space.

See Refs. 27 and 104–107 for further discussions.

Deterministic Fractals

Sometimes in applications, point sets are studied that consist of "extremely many," "very small" subsets (e.g., systems of very small pores). Such sets are called "dusts." Examples of deterministic fractals are well-known *Cantor Dusts C*, where the set *C* is a subset of the real axis obtained by deleting step-by-step open subintervals of [0,1], and *Square Dust Q*; the Q is a planar set obtained by taking from the unit-square step-by-step cross shaped subsets. This set contains unaccountably many disconnected points; *von Koch Snow Flakes*. What we mean by self-similarity is best illustrated by an example, the von Koch snowflake. In every step, suitably diminished generators replace all line segments of the figure, where the vertices always point outward.

The notion of *fractal dimension* is associated with the notion of self-similarity. In 1919, Hausdorf proposed noninteger dimensions (see Ref. 9). Although a line has a dimension of 1 and a square a dimension of 2, many sets have an in-between dimension related to the varying amounts of "material" they contain. To define fractal dimension, the formula for calculating traditional dimensions is simply extended. For instance, when the von Koch snowflake is divided into four pieces (the pieces associated with original scaled four segments), each resulting piece looks like the original scaled down by a factor of 3. It has a dimension D and the value of D must be $\log(4)/\log(3) = 1.26$.

Algebraic fractals are obtained from iterations of some algebraic transformation functions. Algebraic fractals are used to display the dynamical systems. Mandelbrot considered a self-squared function $f(z) = z^2 + c$, where z and c are complex numbers. The basic principle of generating algebraic fractals is as follows. An initial value of z and of c are chosen. For this value of c, the function is iterated ($z_n \leftarrow z_{n-1}^2 + c$) until the value of z_n reaches a preselected limiting value or the number of iterations reaches a maximum allowable value. The number of iterations carried out for this value of c is used to assign a color to the corresponding point in the region.

Random fractals exhibit statistical self-similarity. The statistical self-similarity refers to the property in which the magnification of a smaller portion of a fractal results into a fractal, which is seemingly but not exactly similar to the original fractal itself. Fractal geometry methods produce the most realistic rocky terrain displays. Mainly, developed algorithms are based on recursive subdivision; see, for instance, Ref. 108. For terrain generation, subdividing the ground plane is applied.

Many examples of modeling biological objects can be found in Ref. 109.

L-Systems and Shape Grammars

Grammar-based models, L-systems, first developed by Lindenmayer to describe biological processes, are well documented (110,111). An L-system is based on an alphabet, an axiom, and a set of rewriting rules or productions. Each production gives a rule for changing a character belonging to the alphabet into another character or word (consisting of a sequence of characters). Characters in the alphabet of an L-system can be related to elements in the biological structure of a growing form. For computer graphics use, each character can also be used to drive a drawing device. A simple method for doing this is to use "turtle graphics" commands (see Ref. 112), which typically use alphabet characters such as "*F*" to indicate drawing a forward step of a given length, "+" to turn left by a given angle, "[" to initiate a branch, and "]" to end a branch process.

The use of computer graphics for the generation of realistic images of biological growth is a mature research area; several examples of plant models and more references can be found in Ref. 113. Parametric L-systems are developed to model the growth and structure of a plant. The models use biological understanding of the flow many additional parameters to control the simulation of growth. The use of parametric L-system could be extended to similarly constructed models in other disciplines (e.g., the modeling of traffic flow and city growth).

Smith (114) introduced a method called "graftals" for fractal object modeling in computer graphics. An approach to adapt Constructive Solid Geometry operations over iterated function systems is presented in Ref. 115.

Particles

Traditionally, a method for modeling natural objects such as clouds, smoke, fire, and clumps of grass is called a particle system; see Ref. 116. Particle systems were designed by Reeves (117). Particle shapes can be small spheres, ellipsoids, boxes, or other irregular shapes. The size and shape of particles may vary randomly over time. In some applications, particle motion may be controlled by specified forces such as gravity field or solar radiation. Oriented particles (118) defined by a normal vector can be considered as a surface element. They prove to be useful for modeling complex 3D objects.

FEATURE-BASED AND CONSTRUCTIONS-BASED MODELING

Feature concepts were developed for integration of geometric modeling and knowledge representation, in which the geometry of an object is interpreted in terms of geometric elements of engineering significance.

The word feature conjures up different entities presented to engineers from different backgrounds. A number of definitions exist to clarify matters; for examples, "A *feature* is a region of interest on the surface of a part." A feature can be defined as a geometric entity that defines the attributes of a part's nominal size and shape.

It is apparent that although there is much interest in developing feature-based modeling techniques, the problem of integration or how to establish an analogy between geometric modeling and knowledge representation is an open issue (4,119–122).

One of the ways to attack the problem proposed in Ref. 123 is the following:

- To create an exhaustive library of design features based on technical and non-technical terms for shape and form together with the vocabulary for their modification and use
- To classify the features by topology and form
- To define them parametrically
- To produce suitable feature surface models based on incomplete specification of parameters

Geometric Constraints for CAD

According to Hoffmann and Peters (124), constraint-based sketching has become a major design paradigm in mechanical computer-aided design (MCAD). Conceptually, a rough sketch is prepared by the user and annotated with geometric constraints such as distance, angle, parallelism, tangency, concentricity, and so forth. The sketch is then instituted to the precise specifications implied by the constraints and is interpreted as a profile. This profile, in turn, defines a solid or solid operation through lofting or sweeping, such as a linear extrusion or a general sweep along a space curve.

Solving a system of geometric constraints is a problem that has been considered by several communities and using differently approaches. For example, the constraints can include the physical constraints imposed by the machine tool and the cutting process. Physical constraints are maximal and minimal feed rate, depth of cut, cutting power, and force. For more references, see also Ref. 125.

The CAD of different objects subjected to composite constraints (e.g., optical devices) is, nowadays, an attractive research area with some encouraging examples of applications. Recently, a number of articles were published in which authors considered a long-standing problem of CAD of geometric shapes with constrains: to find optimal designs for optical systems (126–128).

Genetic algorithms (GA) introduced by Holland et al. (129) are programs used to deal with optimization problems. Their goal is to find optimum of a given function F on a given search space S. It seems to us that an attractive and a possible way to solve many shape-modeling problem is to use optimization techniques based on GAs, as was shown in Ref. 130.

Goel and Thompson (130) presented an elegant example of using evolutionary optimization technique to create the curved refractive interface in the eye of a certain type of trilobite, the phacopid. More references about applications of GAs can be found in Ref. 131.

ACKNOWLEDGMENTS

Our sincere thanks to our colleagues Valery Adzhiev, Eric Fausett, and Alexei Sourin for their help with preparing illustrations.

REFERENCES

1. *Longman Dictionary of Contemporary English*, Longman Dictionaries, London, 1995.
2. A. Bowyer and J. Woodwark, *Introduction to Computing with Geometry*, Information Geometers, Winchester, UK, 1993.
3. A. Fomenko and T. Kunii, *Topological Modeling for Visualization*, Springer-Verlag, Tokyo, 1997.
4. C. Hoffmann, *Geometric and Solid Modeling. An Introduction*, Morgan Kaufmann, San Mateo, CA, 1989.
5. M. Mortenson, *Geometric Modeling*, 2nd ed. John Wiley & Sons, New York, 1997.
6. J. Shah and M. Mäntylä, *Parametric and Feature-based CAD/CAM. Concepts, Techniques, and Applications*, John Wiley & Sons, New York, 1995.
7. J. Menon, R. Marisa, and J. Zagajac, "More Powerful Solid Modeling Through Ray Representation," *IEEE Computer Graphics Applic. CGA-14*(3), 22–35 (1994).
8. J. Hart, "Computational Topology for Shape Modeling," in *Shape Modeling and Applications, Proceedings of Shape Modeling International '99 Conference*, IEEE Computer Society Press, Los Alamitos, CA, 1999, pp. 36–43.
9. S. G. Hoggar, *Mathematics for Computer Graphics*, Cambridge University Press, Cambridge, 1992, p. 472.
10. Y. Shinagawa and T. L. Kunii, "The Homotopy Model: A Generalized Model for Smooth Surface Generation from Cross Sectional Data," *Visual Computer*, 7(2–3), 72–86 (1991).
11. J. H. Ahlberg, E. N. Nilson, and J. L. Walh, "Extremal Orthogonality and Convergence of Multidimensional Splines," *J. Math. Applic.*, 11, 27–48 (1965).
12. P. M. Anselone and P. J. Laurent, "A General Method for Construction of Interpolating or Smoothing Spline Functions, *Numer. Math.*, 12(1), 66–82 (1968).
13. J. C. Holladay, "Smoothest Curve Approximation," *Math. Tables Aids Comput.*, 11, 233–243 (1957).
14. I. J. Schonberg, "On Polya Frequency Functions and Their Laplace Transforms," *J. Anal. Math.*, 1, 331–374 (1951).
15. I. J. Schonberg, "Contributions to Problem of Approximation of Equidistant Data by Analytic Functions," *J. Appl. Math.*, 4, 45–99, 112–141 (1946).
16. G. Farin, *Curves and Surfaces for Computer-Aided Geometric Design*, Academic Press, New York, 1997, p. 429.
17. L. Piegle and W. Tiller, *The Book of NURBS*, Springer-Verlag, New York, 1995.
18. J. Bloomenthal (ed.), Morgan Kaufman, *Introduction to Implicit Surfaces*, Morgan Kaufman, San Mateo, CA, 1997, p. 332.

19. C. Bajaj, "Implicit Surface Patches," in *Introduction to Implicit Surfaces*, J. Bloomenthal (ed.), Morgan Kaufmann, San Mateo, CA, 1997, pp. 98–125.

20. J. Menon, "Constructive Shell Representations for Free-Form Surfaces and Solids, *IEEE Computer Graphics Applic.*, *14*(2), 24–36 (1994).

21. J. Blinn, "A Generalization of Algebraic Surface Drawing," *ACM Trans. Graphics*, *1*(3), 235–256 (1982).

22. H. Nishimura, M. Hirai, T. Kawai, T. Kawata, I. Shirakawa, and K. Omura, "Object Modeling by Distributed Function and a Method of Image Generation," *Trans. IECE Japan*, *J68-D*(4), 718–725 (1985) (in Japanese).

23. G. Wyvill, C. McPheeters, and B. Wyvill, "Data Structure for Soft Objects," *Visual Computer*, *2*(4), 227–234 (1986).

24. J. Bloomenthal and K. Shoemake, "Convolution Surfaces, SIGGRAPH'91 Proceedings," *Computer Graphics*, *25*(4), 341–355 (1991).

25. J. McCormack and A. Sherstyuk, "Creating and Rendering Convolution Surfaces," *Computer Graphics Forum*, *17*(2), 113–120 (1998).

26. T. Varady, R. R. Martin, and J. Coxt, "Reverse Engineering of Geometric Models—An Introduction," *CAD*, *29*(4), 255–268 (1997).

27. J. D. Foley, A. van Dam, S. K. Feiner, J. F. Hughes, and R. L. Phillips, *Introduction to Computer Graphics*, 1994, p. 559.

28. A. H. Barr, "Global and Local Deformations of Solid Primitives," *Computer Graphics*, *18*(3), 21–30 (1984).

29. S. Sclaroff and A. Pentland, "Generalized Implicit Functions for Computer Graphics," *Computer Graphics*, *25*(4), 247–250 (1991).

30. G. Wolberg, *Digital Image Warping*, IEEE Computer Society Press, Los Alamitos, CA, 1990, p. 319.

31. B. Payne and A. Toga, "Distance Field Manipulation of Surface Models," *IEEE Computer Graphics Applic.*, *12*(1), 65–71 (1992).

32. J. F. Hughes, "Scheduled Fourier Volume Morphing," *Computer Graphics*, *26*(2), 43–46 (1992).

33. A. Lerios, C. D. Garfinkle, and M. Levoy, "Feature-Based Volume Metamorphosis," *SIGGRAPH'95, Computer Graphics Proceedings*, 1995, pp. 449–456.

34. B. Wyvill, "A Computer Animation Tutorial," in *Computer Graphics Techniques. Theory and Practice*, D. F. Rogers and R. A. Earnshaw (eds.), Springer-Verlag, New York, 1990, pp. 235–282.

35. E. Galin and S. Akkouche, "Blob metamorphosis based on Minkowski sums, EURO-GRAPHICS '96," *Computer Graphics Forum*, *15*(3), 143–153 (1996).

36. V. V. Savchenko, A. A. Pasko, A. I. Sourin, and T. L. Kunii, "Volume Modeling: Representations and Advanced Operations," in *Proceedings Computer Graphics International'98*, F. E. Wolter and N. M. Patrikalakis (eds.), 1998, pp. 4–13.

37. M. Alexa, "Merging Polyhedral Shapes with Scattered Features," in *Proceedings Shape Modeling International '99 Conference*, 1999, pp. 202–218.

38. K. Singh and R. Parent, "Implicit Function Based Deformations of Polyhedral Objects," *Implicit Surfaces '95*, 1995, pp. 113–128.

39. K. Fujimura and M. Makarov, "Homotopic Shape Deformation," in *Proceeding ISM'97 Conference*, 1997, pp. 215–225.

40. A. Fournier and M. A. Wesley, "Bending Polyhedral Objects," *Computer-Aided Design*, *15*(2), 79–87 (1983).

41. F. Lazarus, S. Coquillart, and P. Jancene, "Interactive Axial Deformations," in *Modeling in Computer Graphics*, B. Falcidieno and T. L. Kunii (eds.), Springer-Verlag, New York, 1993, pp. 241–254.

42. P. Borrel and D. Bechmann, "Deformation of *N*-Dimensional Objects," *Int. J. Computat. Geom. Applic.*, *1*(4), 427–453 (1991).

43. P. Borrel and A. Rappoport, "Simple Constrained Deformations for Geometric Modeling and Interactive Design," *ACM Trans. Graphics*, *13*(2), 137–155 (1994).

44. D. Bechmann, "Space Deformation Models Survey," *Computers Graphics*, *18*(4), 571–586 (1994).

45. F. L. Bookstein, *Morphometric Tools for Landmark Data*, Cambridge University Press, Cambridge, 1991.

46. C. W. A. M. van Overveld, "Beyond Bump Maps: Nonlinear Mappings for the Modeling of Geometric Details in Computer Graphics," *Computer-Aided Design*, *24*(4), 201–209 (1992).

47. V. V. Savchenko and A. A. Pasko, "Shape Transformations of 3D Geometric Solids," in *Proceedings of the International Workshop "Shape Modeling: Parallelism Interactivity and Applications,"* 1994, pp. 47–53.

48. D. Ruprecht, R. Nagel, and H. Muller, "Spatial Free-Form Deformation with Scattered Data Interpolation Methods," *Computers Graphics*, *19*(1), 63–71 (1995).

49. T. W. Sederberg and S. R. Parry, "Free-Form Deformation of Solid Geometric Models," *Computer Graphics*, *20*(4), 151–160 (1986).

50. S. Coquillart, "Extended Free-Form Deformation: A Sculpting Tool for 3D Geometric Modeling," *Computer Graphics*, *24*(4), 187–196 (1990).

51. S. Coquillart and P. Jancene, "Animated Free-Form Deformation: An Interactive Animation Technique," *Computer Graphics*, *25*(4), 23–26 (1991).

52. W. M. Hsu, G. F. Hughes, and H. Kaufman, "Direct Manipulation of Free-Form Deformations," *Computer Graphics*, *26*(2), 177–184 (1992).

53. T. Nishita, T. Fujii, and E. Nakamae, "Metamorphosis Using Bezier Clipping," in *Computer Graphics and Applications, Proceedings of Pacific Graphics '93*, World Scientific, Singapore, 1993, pp. 162–175.

54. Y.-K. Chang and A. P. Rockwood, "A Generalized de Casteljau Approach to 3D Free-Form Deformation," *Computer Graphics Proceedings, Annual Conference Series*, 1994, pp. 257–260.

55. V. Savchenko, A. Pasko, O. Okunev, and T. Kunii, "Function Representation of Solids Reconstructed from Scattered Surface Points and Contours," *Computer Graphics Forum*, *14*(4), 181–188 (1995).

56. V. A. Vasilenko, *Spline-Functions: Theory, Algorithms and Programs*, Nauka Publishers, Novosibirsk, 1983 (in Russian).

57. J. Duchon, "Splines Minimizing Rotation-Invariant Semi-norms in Sobolev Spaces," in *Constructive Theory of Functions of Several Variables*, A. Dodd and B. Eckmann (eds.), Springer-Verlag, New York, 1977, pp. 85–100.

58. P. Alfeld, "Scattered Data Interpolation in Three or More Variables," in *Mathematical Methods in Computer Aided Geometric Design*, T. Lyche and L. Schumaker (eds.), Academic Press, New York, 1989, pp. 1–33.

59. G. M. Nielson, T. A. Foley, B. Hamann, and D. Lane, "Visualizing and Modeling Scattered Multivariate Data," *IEEE Computer Graphics Applic.*, *11*(3), 47–55 (1991).

60. M. P. Gascuel, "An Implicit Formulation for Precise Contact Modeling Between Flexible Solids," in *Computer Graphics Proceedings, Annual Conference Series*, 1993, pp. 313–320.

61. J. R. Woodwark, "Blends in Geometric Modeling," in *The Mathematics of Surfaces II*, R. R. Martin (ed.), Oxford University Press, Oxford, 1987, pp. 255–297.

62. A. Bowyer, *SVLIS Set-Theoretic Kernel Modeller. Introduction and User Manual*, Information Geometers, Winchester, UK, 1994.

63. V. L. Rvachev, "On the Analytical Description of Some Geometric Objects," *Rep. Ukrainian Acad. Sci.*, *153*(4), 765–767 (1963) (in Russian).

64. V. L. Rvachev, *Theory of R-functions and Some Applications*, Naukova Dumka, Kiev, 1987 (in Russian).

65. V. Shapiro, "Real Functions for Representation of Rigid Solids," *Computer Aided Geom. Des.*, *11*(2), 153–175 (1994).

66. A. Pasko, V. Adzhiev, A. Sourin, and V. Savchenko, "Function Representation in Geometric Modeling: Concepts, Implementation and Applications," *Visual Computer*, *11*(8), 429–446 (1995).

67. S. Muraki, "Volumetric Shape Description of Range Data Using 'Blobby Model,' " *Computer Graphics*, *25*(4), 227–235 (1991).

68. C. Bajaj, I. Ihm, and J. Warren, "High Order Interpolation and Least-Squares Approximation Using Implicit Algebraic Surfaces," *ACM Trans. Graphics*, *11*(4), 327–347 (1992).

69. V. Savchenko and A. Pasko, "Transformation of Functionally Defined Shapes by Extended Space Mappings," *Visual Computer*, *14*, 257–270 (1998).

70. A. A. G. Requicha, "Representations of Rigid Solids: Theory, Methods, and Systems," *Computing Surveys*, *12*(4), 437–465 (1980).

71. H. Blum, "A Transformation for Extracting New Descriptors of Shape," in *Models for the Perception of Speech and Visual Form*, W. Whaten-Dunn (ed.), MIT Press, Cambridge, MA, 1967, pp. 362–380.

72. C. Hoffmann, "Computer Vision, Descriptive Geometry, and Classical Mechanics," in *Computer Graphics and Mathematics*, B. Falcidieno et al. (eds.), Springer-Verlag, Berlin, 1992, pp. 229–243.

73. J. Snyder, *Generative Modeling for Computer Graphics and CAD*, Academic Press, New York, 1992.

74. Sourin and A. Pasko, "Function Representation for Sweeping by a Moving Solid," *IEEE Trans. Visualiz. Computer Graphics*, *2*(1), 11–18 (1996).

75. K. J. Udupa and D. Odhner, "Fast Visualization, Manipulation, and Analysis of Binary Volumetric Objects," *IEEE Computer Graphics Applic.*, *11*(6), 53–62 (1991).

76. V. Chandru, S. Manohar, and C. E. Prakash, "Voxel-Based Modeling for Layered Manufacturing," *IEEE Computer Graphics Applic.*, *15*(6), 42–47 (1995).

77. G. M. Nielson, T. A. Foley, B. Hamann, and D. Lane, "Visualizing and Modeling Scattered Multivariate Data," *IEEE Computer Graphics Applic.*, *11*(3), 47–55 (1991).

78. T. A. Galyean and J. F. Hughes, "Sculpting: An Interactive Volumetric Modeling Technique," *SIGGRAPH'91, Computer Graphics Proc.*, *25*(4), 267–274 (1991).

79. D. R. Ney and E. K. Fishman, "Editing Tools for 3D Medical Imaging," *IEEE Computer Graphics Applic.*, *11*(6), 63–71 (1991).

80. R. Avila and L. Sobierajski, "A Haptic Interaction Method for Volume Visualization," in *IEEE Visualization '96*, R. Yagel and G. Nielson (eds.), IEEE Computer Society Press, Los Alamitos, CA, 1996.

81. S. Wang and A. Kaufman, "Volume sculpting," in *Symposium on Interactive 3D Graphics*, ACM Press, New York, 1995, pp. 151–156.

82. J. Bærentzen, "Octree-Based Volume Sculpting," in *IEEE Visualization '98, Late Breaking Hot Topics Proceedings*, IEEE Computer Society Press, Los Alamitos, CA, 1998, pp. 9–12.

83. H. Arata, Y. Takai, N. Takai, and T. Yamamoto, "Free-Form Shape Modeling by 3D Cellular Automata," in *Shape Modeling International '99*, IEEE Computer Society Press, Los Alamitos, CA, 1999, pp. 242–247.

84. J. Hughes, "Scheduled Fourier Volume Morphing," in *SIGGRAPH '92, Computer Graphics*, 1992, pp. 43–46.

85. Lerios, C. D. Garfinkle, and M. Levoy, "Feature-Based Volume Metamorphosis, in *SIGGRAPH'95, Computer Graphics Proceedings*, 1995, pp. 449–456.

86. N. Ozawa and I. Fujishiro, "A Morphological Approach to Volume Synthesis of Weathered Stones," *Volume Graphics Workshop '99*, 1999, Vol. II, pp. 207–220.

87. G. M. Nielson, "Visualization Takes Its Place in the Scientific Community," *IEEE Trans. Visualiz. Computer Graphics*, *1*(2), 97–98 (1995).

88. Kaufman, K. H. Hohne, W. Kruger, L. Rosenblum, and P. Shroder, "Research Issues in Volume Visualization," *IEEE Computer Graphics Applic.*, *14*(2), 63–67 (1993).

89. N. Shareef and R. Yagel, "Rapid Previewing via Volume-Based Solid Modeling," in *Third Symposium on Solid Modeling and Applications*, C. Hoffmann and J. Rossignac (eds.), ACM Press, New York, 1995, pp. 281–291.

90. DeCarlo and D. Metaxas, "Blended Deformable Models," *IEEE Trans. Pattern Anal. Machine Intell., PAMI-18*(4), 443–448 (1996).

91. K. Perlin and E. M. Hoffert, "Hypertexture," *Computer Graphics, 23*(2), 253–262 (1989).

92. D. R. James and D. K. Pai, "Accurate Real Time Deformable Objects," in *SIGGRAPH'99*, 1999, pp. 65–72.

93. G. S. P. Miller, "The Motion Dynamics of Snakes and Worms," *Computer Graphics, 22*(4), 169–173 (1988).

94. Terzopoulos, J. C. Platt, A. H. Barr, and K. Fleisher, "Elastically Deformable Models," *Computer Graphics, 21*(4), 205–214.

95. Eberhard, A. Weber, and W. Strasser, "A Fast, Flexible, Particle-System Model for Cloth Dropping," *IEEE Computer Graphics Applic., 16*(5), 52–60 (1996).

96. Computer Graphics in Textiles and Apparel, *IEEE Computer Graphics Applic., 16*(5) (1996).

97. B. Eberhardt, "Computing Minimal Surfaces with Particle Systems," in *Geometric Modeling: Theory and Practice*, W. Strasser, R. Klein, and R. Rau (eds.), Springer-Verlag, New York, 1997, pp. 52–58.

98. F. I. Parke and K. Waters, *Computer Facial Animation*, A. K. Peters Wellesley, MA, 1996, p. 365.

99. J. A. Sethian, *Level Set Methods*, Cambridge University Press, Cambridge, 1996, 218.

100. M. I. G. Bloor, M. J. Wilson, Z. Knudsen, C. Knudsen, and A. Holden, "Time-Dependent Parametric Surface Models of the Human Heart," in *Proceedings Computer Graphics International '99*, 1999, pp. 174–179.

101. R. T. Whitaker and D. E. Breen, "Level-Set Models for the Deformation of Solid Objects," in *Proceedings Implicit Surface '98*, J. Bloomental and D. Saupe (eds.), 1998, pp. 19–35.

102. M. Bertalmio, G. Sapiro, and G. Randall, "Region Tracking on Level-Sets Methods," *IEEE Trans. Med. Imaging, 18*(5), 448–451 (1999).

103. S. G. Hoggar, *Mathematics for Computer Graphics*, Cambridge University Press, Cambridge, 1992, p. 472.

104. D. Stoyan and H. Stoyan, *Fractals, Random Shapes and Point Fields*, John Wiley & Sons, New York, 1994, p. 387.

105. J. C. Russ, *Fractal Surfaces*, Plenum Press, New York, 1994, p. 309.

106. J. L. Encarnacao, et al. (eds.), *Fractal Geometry and Computer Graphics*, Springer-Verlag, New York, 1992.

107. T. Vicsek, *Fractal Growth Phenomena*, World Scientific, Singapore, 1992.

108. K. Koh and D. D. Hearn, "Fast Generation and Surface Structuring Methods for Terrain and Other Natural Phenomena," *EUROGRAPHICS '92, 11*/3, 169–180 (1992).

109. J. A. Kaandorp, *Fractal Modelling: Growth and Form in Biology*, Springer-Verlag, New York, 1994, p. 208.

110. P. Prusinkiewicz and A. Lindenmayer, *The Algorithmic Beauty of Plants*, Springer-Verlag, New York, 1990.

111. de Reffye, P. C. Edelin, J. Francon, M. Jaeger, and C. Puech, "Plant Models Faithful to Botanical Structure and Development," in *SIGGRAPH 88*, 1988, pp. 151–158.

112. H. Adelson and A. A. diSessa, *Turtle Geometry*, MIT Press, Cambridge, MA, 1982.

113. J. L. Power, A. J. Bernheim Brush, P. Prusinkiewich, and D. H. Salesin, "Interactive Arrangement of Botanical L-System Models," in *Proceedings 1999 Symposium on Interactive 3D Graphics*, ACM Press, New York, 1999, pp. 175–182.

114. A. R. Smith, "Plants, Fractals and Formal Languages," in *SIGGRAPH 84*, 1984, pp. 1–10.

115. J. Thollot and E. Tosan, "Constructive Fractal Geometry: Constructive Approach to Fractal

Modeling Using Language Operations," in *Proceedings Graphics'95 Interface*, Canadian Human–Computer Communication Society, Quebec, 1995, pp. 196–203.

116. Hearn and M. P. Baker, *Computer Graphics*, Prentice Hall, Englewood Cliffs, NJ, 1994, p. 652.

117. W. T. Reeves, "Particle System—A Technique for Modeling a Class of Fuzzy Objects," *Computer Graphics*, *17*(3), (1983).

118. R. Szelisky and D. Tonnesen, "Surface Modeling with Oriented Particle Systems," *Computer Graphics*, *26*(2), 185–194 (1992).

119. R. Klein, "A Knowledge Representation Perspective on Geometric Modeling," in *Geometric Modeling: Theory and Practice*, W. Strasser, R. Klein, and R. Rau (eds.), Springer-Verlag, New York, 1997, pp. 175–196.

120. J. R. Woodwark, "Some Speculations on Feature Recognition," *Computer-Aided Design*, *20*(4), 189–196 (1988).

121. J. Han and A. A. G. Requicha, "Feature Recognition from CAD Models," *IEEE Computer Graphics Applic.*, *18*(2), 80–94 (1998).

122. Z. Dong (ed.), *Artificial Intelligence in Optimal Design and Manufacturing*, PTR Prentice Hall, London, 1994, p. 375.

123. Gandhi, A. Myklebust, "A Natural Language Approach to Feature Based Modeling," in *Proceedings Conference on CAD and Computer Graphics*, International Academic Publisher, Beijing, 1989, pp. 245–254.

124. M. Hoffmann and J. Peters, "Geometric Constraints for CAGD," in *Mathematical Methods in CAGD III*, M. Daehlen et al. (eds.), 1995, pp. 1–16.

125. W. Bouma, I. Fudos, C. Hoffman, J. Cai, and R. Paige, "A Geometric Constraint Solver," Report CSD-TR-93-054 (August 1993).

126. J. Loos, Ph. Slusallek, and H.-P. Seidel, "Using Wavefront Tracing for the Visualization and Optimization of Progressive Lenses," *Computer Graphics Forum*, *17*(3), 225–265 (1998).

127. J. Loos, G. Greiner, and H.-P. Seidel, "A Variational Approach to Progressive Lens Design," *Computer-Aided Design*, *30*(8), 595–602 (1998).

128. M. Halstead, B. Barsky, S. Klein, and R. Mandell, "Reconstructing Curved Surfaces from Specular Reflection Patterns Using Spline Surface Fitting of Normals," in *SIGGRAPH 96 Conference Proceedings*, H. Rushmeier (ed.), Addison-Wesley, Reading, MA, 1996, pp. 335–342.

129. J. H. Holland, K. J. Holyoak, R. E. Nisbett, and P. R. Thagard, *Induction: Processes of Inference Learning and Discovery*, MIT Press, Cambridge, MA, 1986.

130. M. Goel and R. L. Thompson, "The Evolution of the Trilobite Eye," in *Computer Simulations of Self-Organization in Biological Systems*, *Part 11*, Croom Helm, London, 1988, pp. 275–290.

131. P. Bentely, *Evolutionary Design by Computers*, Morgan Kaufman, San Mateo, CA, 1999, p. 446.

VLADIMIR SAVCHENKO

ALEXANDER PASKO

STATISTICAL LANGUAGE MODELING

INTRODUCTION

Modeling language using statistics and mathematics rather than grammar has grown rapidly in importance in the last 10 years mainly because of its application to speech recognition. Almost all of the many speech recognition systems which one can buy in computer stores and use to dictate documents or e-mails (1) use statistical language models to improve the performance of their acoustic recognition modules (2–5). For this type of task, statistical models outperform the grammatical models of language which dominated language research in the previous decades, following the seminal work of Chomsky (6). Their successes cast doubt on Chomsky's underlying assumption that language is a rule-based structure which humans are genetically predisposed to learn at birth (7).

The problem with purely grammatical models is illustrated by the following two sentences which might be two possible alternative sentences matching a distorted acoustic signal:

1. "The cat sat on the mat."
2. "The mat sat on the cat."

Both are equally correct and equally probable in a grammatical model, so a grammatical model cannot distinguish between them; of course, the reason is that the semantic information within the sentences is not included, only their grammatical structure. However, in statistical language models, both semantic and syntactic information are modeled and any well-designed and well-trained statistical language model would be able to deduce, as any human can do, that the first sentence is very much more likely than the second.

Statistical models work by measuring and sorting the frequencies of word sequences from large text corpora (i.e., training corpora) and using these to measure the probability that a particular sequence of words occurs in a meaningful sentence. Thus, statistical language models can measure the relative probabilities of the sequences of words in the two sentences in our example and can thus calculate that "The cat sat on the mat" has a very much higher probability than the second sentence.

Another example is a missing word experiment in which the word "think" is removed from the sentence "What do you *think* you are doing." A simple statistical language model trained on a million-word corpus (which did not include this sentence) is asked to find the missing word. The possible words and their probabilities from the model are shown in Table 1. Note that all but 1 of the first 10 words is a verb; this illustrates that statistical models generally model syntax as well as semantics.

A statistical model works at a basic word level by calculating the probability that a word follows or is part of a given sequence of words. Although this is a long way from one which can help with an ultimate goal of artificial intelligence (i.e., language understanding), it can still be a powerful tool in several more limited but important

TABLE 1   List of the 10 Words Chosen
by a Trigram Statistical Language Model to
Replace the Word "think" in the Sentence
"What do you *think* you are doing"

Word	Rank	Probability
Think	1	0.292004
Know	2	0.177287
Feel	3	0.166881
Mean	4	0.058612
Do	5	0.053928
Want	6	0.038776
Expect	7	0.016576
Tell	8	0.014156
That	9	0.012439
Say	10	0.012207

applications, particularly in speech recognition (8), but also in speech synthesis (9), optical character recognition (10), automatic translation (11,12), dialogue systems (13), word classification systems (14,15), and in document analysis and information retrieval systems (16,17). Statistical language models are also of interest to cognitive scientists, who build computational models of the human ability to process language (18,19); however, this review is only indirectly concerned with these cognitive aspects of language modeling.

For those interested in building their own statistical language model, a toolkit is available from Cambridge University in England (20).

N-GRAM LANGUAGE MODEL

The basic requirement of a statistical language model is to calculate the probability of a word, w_k, following a sequence of words $w_1 \ldots w_{k-1}$ (sometimes written w_1^{k-1}). One of the simplest ways of doing this is to use an *N*-gram model (21) in which it is assumed that the probability of w_k depends only on the previous N-1 words, which we write as

$$P(w_k) = P(w_k \mid w_{k-N+1}^{k-1}) \qquad \text{if } k > N - 1. \tag{1}$$

The simplest form of this model is the trigram model, which we write as

$$P(w_k) = P(w_k \mid w_{k-2}w_{k-1}) \qquad \text{if } k > 2, \tag{2}$$

in which the probability of w_k depends only on the two previous words. Although this is very simple, it works remarkably well and no other model, statistical or grammatical, performs significantly better. Indeed, the success of this simple model and our difficulty in improving on it is one of the quandaries of language modeling (22).

To explore how the *N*-gram model works, we illustrate first with an example of the probability that the word "mat" follows the two words "on the." In the training corpus, the frequencies of all of the trigrams (i.e., three-word phrases) in the corpus are measured. These include the frequency for the trigram "on the mat." Let us assume that it occurs 12 times. The frequencies of all of the bigrams are also measured, including the bigram "on the"; let us assume that "on the" occurs 10,000 times. Then, the probability that "mat" occurs after "on the" is computed as

$$P(\text{mat} \mid \text{on the}) = \frac{\text{Frequency (on the mat)}}{\text{Frequency (on the)}} = \frac{12}{10,000} = 0.0012. \tag{3}$$

This is called the *maximum likelihood probability*, which approximates to the true probability, which can only be found theoretically from an infinitely large corpus. The word "maximum" does not mean that this probability is the maximum possible, but rather that it is the probability with the maximum likelihood (i.e., the most likely probability). However, as we see later, Turing has shown that it is generally slightly larger than the true probability.

For the two sample sentences discussed, let us compare the two halves of the sentences separately. The second half of sentence 1 is the phrase "on the mat", and of sentence 2, it is the phrase "on the cat"; these are likely to have similar probabilities and therefore will not help us much in distinguishing between the two sentences. However, looking at the first half of the sentences, the first three words of sentence 2, "the mat sat," are likely to have a very much lower probability compared with "the cat sat" of sentence 1. However, to calculate the relative probabilities of both of the two sentences, we would need to compare not only both halves of the two sentences together, but all of the words in sequence. This is done by combining them using Bayesian statistics as follows.

If S is a sentence made up of the words $w_1 w_2 \ldots w_m$, then the Bayesian probability of S is given by

$$P(S) = P(w_1) \ P(w_2 \mid w_1) \ P(w_3 \mid w_1 w_2) \cdots P(w_m \mid w_1 \cdots w_{m-1}). \tag{4}$$

For simplicity, if we ignore the fact that w_1 is the first word in a sentence, then the first term in Eq. (4), $P(w_1)$, is the unigram probability for word w_1, which is approximated by the maximum likelihood value:

$$P(w_1) = \frac{\text{Frequency of } w_1}{T} \tag{5}$$

where T is the total size of the corpus in words (i.e., in tokens). The second term $P(w_2 \mid w_1)$ is a bigram probability (i.e., the probability that w_2 follows w_1); the third term is a trigram probability; and so on.

In the trigram model, this simplifies to

$$P^{(3)}(S) = P(w_1) \ P(w_2 \mid w_1) P(w_3 \mid w_1 w_2) \cdots P(w_m \mid w_{m-2} w_{m-1}) \tag{6}$$

(i.e., each probability after the first two terms is a trigram probability). This formula was used to obtain the results for the missing word "think" in Table 1. For the sentence, $S =$ "The mat sat on the cat," Eq. (6) becomes

$$P(S) = P(\text{the}) \ P(\text{mat} \mid \text{the}) P(\text{sat} \mid \text{the mat}) P(\text{on} \mid \text{mat sat}) P(\text{the} \mid \text{sat on})$$
$$P(\text{cat} \mid \text{on the}). \tag{7}$$

It is likely to be the third, fourth, as well as the sixth low-probability terms in this produce that give this sentence a very low probability compared with the equivalent expression and probabilities of sentence 1. Normally, if an incorrect or unusual word, x, occurs in a sentence, it causes three terms in the trigram expression for the probability of a sentence in Eq. (6); that is, if the sentence is

$$w_1 \ldots w_{i-2}w_{i-1} \; x \; w_{i+1}w_{i+2} \ldots w_m$$

the three terms are

$$P(x \mid w_{i-2}w_{i-1}), \; P(w_{i+1} \mid w_{i-1} \; x), \quad \text{and} \quad P(w_{i+2} \mid xw_{i+1}).$$

For higher N-grams, there are generally N low terms in such an example.

The greatest difficulty with this application of the N-gram model is that the N-gram maximum likelihood probabilities are unreliable if the frequencies are low; even worse, they may be zero because a particular N-gram has not occurred in the training text. This can give a zero probability to a perfectly understandable and meaningful sentence to a human; for example, "The lynx sat on the mat" may be given a zero probability, either because the word "lynx" does not occur in the training text or because it does not occur before the word "sat." This perfectly correct and understandable sentence would then be rejected. So, all of the maximum likelihood probabilities for rare N-grams are unreliable because of the finite size of corpora. This has led to a number of modifications of the N-gram model to try to overcome this sparse data problem.

LANGUAGE METRICS

Before beginning to describe the numerous modifications of the N-gram model to overcome this sparse data problem (and other problems), we need first to describe some of the metrics used to compare language models. Some of these in this article are now used internationally by different laboratories, enabling researchers to compare different variants of the models.

Corpora

All metrics comparing statistical language models are based on known corpora of text. Each of these is broken into a training corpus on which the language models are trained and a separate test corpus on which tests are performed. Some of the best known early corpora are the Brown Corpus (23,24) of about 1 million words of American English taken from a wide range of sources by Brown University in Rhode Island in the 1970s. About the same time, a similar-sized corpus was compiled by the Universities at Lancaster, Oslo, and Bergen, called the LOB corpus (25,26). This had the advantages of being tagged with the grammatical type of each word. Although these corpora are still widely used, it is more common today to use larger corpora, such as one based on the *Wall Street Journal* with 40 million words (27) or one based on spontaneous speech from numerous broadcasts, called the "Broadcast News" corpus, with 130 million words (28,29). Some smaller but restricted domain corpora have also been built and used, such as corpora built by DARPA on air travel information systems (30,31) and a similar railway timetable corpus in England by British Telecom and others called the Vodis corpus (32). A list of commonly used corpora is given in Table 2.

TABLE 2   Some Major Text Corpora

Corpus name	Size (in words)	Description	Ref.
Brown	1 million	American English; Real and fictional topics	23, 24
LOB	1 million	Press reportage, fictional and real	25, 26
WSJ	87–89: 40 million 90–92: 35 million	Articles from the *Wall Street Journal* newspaper	27
Broadcast News	130 million	Spontaneous speech	28, 29
ATIS	150,000	Air travel information	30, 31
Vodis	100,000	Railway travel information	32
London–Lund Corpus	1 million	Spoken and written English	33
Switchboard	2 million	Spontaneous speech	34
Penn Treebank	4.5 million	American English corpus; annotated for part-of-speech (POS) information	35
Verbmobil	278,000	Business text in German; used for translations	36
British National Corpus	100 million	Written and spoken British text	37

Missing-Word Error Rate

When a language model has been trained on a particular training corpus, the tests are carried out on a separate test corpus. The simplest tests are based on missing-word tests. In one form of this test, a word is removed at random from the test text and the language model is required to estimate which word has been removed. In a large sample, the percentage of words estimated incorrectly is called the missing-word error rate (ε):

$$\varepsilon = \frac{\text{No. of words incorrect}}{\text{Total number of words considered}} \qquad [8]$$

In another form of the same test, all of the words in the test text are examined rather than randomly selected words before calculating ε.

For any removed or missing word, the language model can calculate the probabilities of all possible replacement words and put them in a rank order. If the removed word is found in this set of words, it is given a rank number. The number of words with rank 1 is the same as the number used to calculate ε. The number with rank 2, rank 3, and so on is counted and a graph can then be drawn of the number of words with rank ≤1, ≤2, ≤3, and so on, as shown in Figure 1. The higher the curve, the better the model.

Information

A problem with missing-word error rates is that all words are treated equally, which they are not. For example, if a language model replaces a common word, like "the," incorrectly, it is generally (although not always) a less important error than missing an uncommon word like "lynx," which contains a great deal of precise information. A measure of the importance of a word, called its information content or value, is given by information theory due to Shannon (38). He developed a now well-known method of measuring the

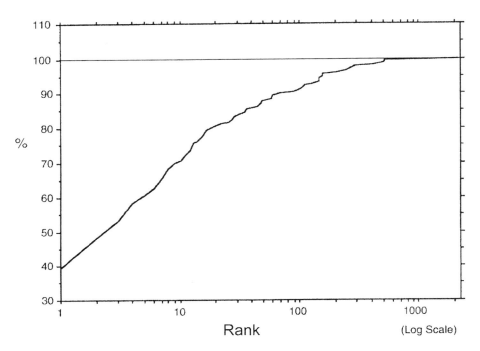

FIGURE 1   Percentage of words correctly selected in a rank list to replace words removed at random from unseen text from the VODIS corpus.

information value $I(w)$ of a symbol w obtained from some source in terms of the probability $P(w)$ of the symbol from the source, using the equation

$$I(w) = \log_2\left(\frac{1}{P(w)}\right). \tag{9}$$

(In information theory, the log function is usually calculated to the base 2 and information is then measured in bits.) For language modeling, the "symbol" is a word and the source of words is the training text. For example, for the word "the," which has a high probability, (299,429 occurrences out of 5,946,585 tokens for a part of the Wall Street Journal; i.e., about 1 in 20), the information value $I(\text{the}) = 4.3$ bits. However, an uncommon word like "lynx" in the corpus has a very low probability (4 times in 5.9 million, $P = 6.7 \times 10^{-7}$) and it has a high information content $I(\text{lynx}) = 20$ bits. Unfortunately, it may not occur even once in the training corpus; then $P(w) = 0$ and $I(w)$ is, in theory, infinite. We discuss this again later.

Although this simple measure of information is very effective in optimizing communications networks, it is not how a human perceives it; a human would perceive the difference in information content of "lynx" and "the" in most cases (although not always) to be greater than the ratio of $20 : 4$; however, it is the best measure available and is better than a measure treating every word equally.

Thus, using information theory, the missing-word error rate obtained by counting only the percentage of words which the language model estimates incorrectly can be improved by calculating the total information content of all of the incorrect words and measuring this against the total information content of all words, correctly estimated or not; that is, the information error rate (IER) is

$$\text{IER} = \frac{\sum\limits_{w_i \in x} \log[1/P(w_i)]}{\sum\limits_{\text{all } w_i} \log[1/P(w_i)]} , \qquad [10]$$

where $w_i \in x$ refers to a summation over all words w_i in the training text which belong to the set x of words which have been incorrectly estimated in the model. The probabilities $P(w_i)$ are probabilities obtained from the language model trained on the training corpus.

Perplexity

Another measure, based on information theory, is obtained by first calculating the total information of each sentence of the test corpus. This is obtained from the expression for the probability $P(S)$ of a sentence S in Eq. (4) based on N-grams. The information content of sentence S_i is given by

$$I(S_i) = \log\left(\frac{1}{P(S_i)}\right)$$

$$\log\left(\frac{1}{P(w_1)}\right) + \log\left(\frac{1}{P(w_2 \mid w_1)}\right) + \cdots + \log\left(\frac{1}{P(w_m \mid w_1 \ldots w_{m-1})}\right) \qquad [11]$$

for the m words in the sentence, where $P(w_1)$ is the probability that w_1 starts a new sentence. The information content of the whole test corpus, $I(C)$, is obtained by assuming that the sentences are independent and adding the total information of all the sentences of the corpus:

$$I(C) = \sum_{i=1}^{n_s} I(S_i), \qquad [12]$$

where n_s is the number of sentences in the corpus. The average information per word, $H(C)$, called the entropy, is next calculated by dividing by the number of words in the corpus, m:

$$H(C) = \frac{1}{m} I(C) \qquad [13]$$

A measure called the perplexity (PP) is defined (21) as

$$PP = 2^H \qquad [14]$$

This is used rather than the entropy, $H(C)$, as it is roughly equal to the number of likely alternative words which can be computed by the model. This is evident by noting that if the language consists of N equally likely words, independent of one another, then the probability of each word is $1/N$. The average information per word then equals $\log(N)$ and the perplexity equals N, the number of words.

The perplexity measure has been very widely used by all language modelers over the last two decades. Clearly, the perplexity is lower if the probabilities of the words in the test corpus are higher (i.e., for a better language model); so, in general, the best language model obtains the lowest perplexity. Perplexity values vary in practice between about 50 for a single-domain training corpus with a limited vocabulary and about 300 or more for an inadequately trained model on a general training corpus.

Difficulties with Perplexity

A difficulty with perplexity is that it is based on Shannon's definition of information (38), which, as we have already stated, is suited to communications but is different from the human perception of information in language. Another major difficulty with perplexity arises when a word (or *N*-gram) occurs in a test which has not appeared in the training corpus. This gives a probability of zero. Unfortunately, as we have already explained, the information value of a word with zero probability is infinite: so, it has to be excluded from the calculation in Eq. (11) or given an arbitrarily high limiting value. This is related to the sparse data problem which bedevils all language models.

Another difficulty with perplexity, that it depends only on the probabilities of words contained in the test text and not to the probabilities of alternatives to these words, was pointed out by Clarkson and Robinson (39). This leads to a disparity between the two common measures, word error rate WER [obtained from a speech recognition system which uses a language model (40)] and perplexity. These sometimes give different orders in a comparison of two models for a test text. Clarkson and Robinson proposed a new measure similar to perplexity which obtains results closer to the WER. This was based partly on an earlier measure proposed by Chen et al. (41). Other variants on these measures are due to Eide et al. (42), Iyer et al. (43), and Ito et al. (44). Whether these are better than perplexity and WER or combinations of the two is still not clear.

IMPROVED *N*-GRAM MODELS

A question of which *N*-gram to use in a particular circumstance or what combination of N-gram models to use arises. This is made difficult by the sparse data problem. If a word *x* occurs only once in a training corpus and another word *y* only twice, the maximum likelihood probability (according to a unigram model) of *y* is twice that of *x*. However, we know this is only approximately true, as a precise jump of 2 from $P(x)$ to $P(y)$ is unlikely. The same is true for all models. Thus, modifications have been made to combine models to overcome this difficulty. The techniques used to combine models, called smoothing, has been the subject of a wide range of publications (21,45–48) since N-gram models were first proposed by Turing in the 1950s (49). The subject has been reviewed by Chen and Goodman in 1999 (50). We now describe some of these.

Turing–Good

The first attempt to improve on the maximum likelihood probabilities for rare events such as rare words or *N*-grams was due to Turing and probably used by him to help decipher German codes in the war. It was first reported by Good (49). If an event (i.e., a word) occurs *f* times in an *T*-event sequence (i.e., *T* is the total number of word tokens in a corpus), then the maximum likelihood probability is $P_{ML} = f/T$; however, Turing stated that the probability is more accurately represented by $P_T = f^*/T$, where

$$f^* = (f + 1)\frac{n_{f+1}}{n_f}$$ [15]

in which n_f is the number of words which occur f times in the corpus. Nadas (51) gave various statistical derivations of this formula. The discounted frequencies f^* are generally less than the actual counted frequencies f (see Table 3); thus, the sum of probabilities for all words which occur in the text is

$$\sum \frac{f^*}{T} < \sum \frac{f}{T} = 1 .$$ [16]

It can be shown that the difference M, which is the total probability mass of all words which do not occur in the corpus, is given by

$$M = \sum_{(all\ words)} \frac{f - f^*}{T} = \frac{n_1}{T} .$$ [17]

In general, the number of missed words, n_0, is much greater than n_1, the number occurring once, but their total probabilities are approximately equal. Thus, the Turing–Good model has the advantage that all words, including those which do not occur in the training text, can be given a nonzero probability; so improved results are obtained. The same formulas are applied both to N-gram probabilities and to individual words.

Other methods of dealing with the sparse data problem, which are related to the Turing–Good method, are interpolated estimation (45), deleted interpolation by Jelinek and Mercer (52), and a held-out estimate by Church and Gale (47) attributed to Jelinek.

One limitation with these methods is that they assign the same probability to all

TABLE 3   Frequency: f; Number of Words with Frequency f: n_f; Turing Discounted Frequency f^* for Bigrams in a 6-Million-Word Corpus from the WSJ and a Vocabulary of 71837 Words

f	n_f	f^*
1	851,542	0.36
2	155,068	1.26
3	65,230	2.22
4	36,185	3.21
5	23,263	4.21
6	16,320	5.13
7	11,961	6.18
8	9,238	7.26
9	7,457	8.13
10	6,065	8.98
11	4,953	10.36
12	4,277	11.08
13	3,645	12.27
14	3,195	13.13
15	2,797	13.85

events which occur zero times (or once, twice, and so on). Church and Gale suggest a way of allowing us to partition the set of bigrams which occur f times by using a second source of information-component unigram frequencies; that is, although words clearly are not generated independently, the product $P(w_1)P(w_2)$ is still a useful source of information about the zero-frequency bigram w_1w_2. This has been shown to work well for bigrams, but not for higher N-grams (50). The deleted estimate method generally performs slightly better than the others, although computationally expensive. However, the most important application of the Turing–Good expression is the back-off method, which we discuss next.

Back-off Model

In a 5-gram model, the 5-gram

"Lynx sat on the mat"

is unlikely to occur in any corpus, even a very large one. Therefore, the maximum likelihood probability for "mat" following "lynx sat on the" will be zero. However, to any human, even if this phrase has not been read or heard before, the probability is clearly not zero.

One approach to deal with the problem is the back-off method due to Katz (46). If the probability of a word is zero in a 5-gram model, then back off to the next lower N-gram (i.e., 4-gram) and use a fraction α of this probability instead. Thus,

$P(\text{mat} \mid \text{lynx sat on the})$ is replaced by $\alpha P(\text{mat} \mid \text{sat on the})$.

This process is repeated until a positive probability is obtained. To ensure that the sum of all probabilities equals 1, the fractional weight α is chosen based on the Turing–Good expressions in Eqs. (15) and (17). The formal mathematical description of this relatively simple principle is complicated and need not be given here. However, it is easy to put in a program although it involves a lot of computation. It is still probably the most widely used method of dealing with trigram maximum likelihood probabilities today and is often the baseline model against which other models are tested.

More advanced models based on the discounting principle of the Turing–Good formula and on the Katz algorithm have been developed by Ney (53–55) and by Kneser and Ney (56). In Kneser–Ney smoothing, a unigram probability is not proportional to the number of occurrences of a word but to the number of different words which follow it. It is not easy to describe mathematically, although the principle is straightforward. Recently, it has been found (57) to be particularly important for large corpora and as part of combined models (which we discuss later).

Combined *N*-grams by Linear Interpolation

Another common method for partially overcoming the sparse data problem is by the combination of models by linear interpolation. For example, although the 5-gram "lynx sat on the mat" may not have occurred in the training corpus and, therefore, could not be used to compute the probability $P(\text{mat} \mid \text{lynx sat on the})$, statistics on the 4-gram "sat on the mat" and on the 3-gram "on the mat," bigram "the mat," and, finally, unigram "mat" would likely be available from a large corpus. By changing the N-gram model to the linear combination of contributions from N-grams, $(N-1)$ grams, and so on, the sparse data problem can thus be reduced. In general, the N-gram model is changed to a weighted sum (45), which, for the trigram, has the form

$$P(w_k) = \lambda_1 P(w_k) + \lambda_2 P(w_k \mid w_{k-1}) + \lambda_3 (P(w_k \mid w_{k-2}w_{k-1}),$$ [18]

where the λs must be chosen to normalize the probability:

$$\lambda_1 + \lambda_2 + \lambda_3 = 1.$$ [19]

Optimization

The λs should also be chosen to optimize the performance of the model; the reestimation algorithm of Baum et al. (58) can be used iteratively to optimize a set of initial parameter values to an arbitrary degree of significance to give the lowest perplexity. The recursive equation for the jth weight, λ_j, out of m N-gram probabilities is as follows:

$$\lambda_j' = \sum_{i=1}^{n} \frac{\lambda_j P_j(w_i)}{\sum_{k=1}^{m} \lambda_k P_k(w_i)} ,$$ [20]

where a held-out training corpus is n words long and $P_k(w_i)$ is the maximum likelihood probability of word w_i, using the k-gram probability. This procedure has been shown to lead to Markovian language models where $P^t(w_1^n) \geq P^{t-1}(w_1^n)$, where t is the iteration number; that is, given that the held-out text is a sufficiently representative sample of the language being modeled, then the algorithm makes the held-out text iteratively more likely and, therefore, a better language model.

Unfortunately, training times for this model are increased by an order or orders of magnitude over simpler methods such as the back-off method, with only marginally better results, although a method of speeding this up has been suggested by O'Boyle et al. (59).

With the more complicated interpolated language model, where λ values depend on frequencies, $\lambda_j'(f)$ is calculated using an equation similar to Eq. (20), except that only those words w_i are used which come after a word whose frequency is f. This obtains only slightly better results than other methods.

Variable N-gram Models

Theoretically, an improvement in the language model occurs as the size of the N-gram model increases from 3 to 5 or 7 or higher. As the N-gram size increases, the number of parameters, the calculation and storage, rise very rapidly if we attempt to store all combinations of possible N-grams. To avoid these problems, variable N-gram language models have been studied.

Variable N-gram language models are based on an increase in size of the N-gram selectively, depending on the context (60,61); that is, statistics on the 4-gram "a b c d" are stored only if the 3-gram "a b c" occurs more than a threshold value (2 or greater). In this way, statistics on N-grams of any length can be calculated; N-grams up to $N = 22$ have been used (62). A variable-length N-gram model can also be created by creating a full N-gram model and decreasing the size of the N-gram depending on the impact of those N-grams in the model (63). In Figure 2, we show how the perplexity of a test text for an N-gram model trained on part of the *Wall Street Journal* (6 million words) decreases as the length N of the N-gram increases. Clearly, contributions for 6-grams and higher are very small and can be neglected.

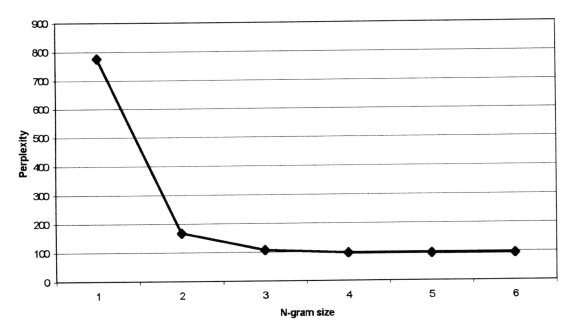

FIGURE 2   Typical dependence of perplexity on the size of the *N*-gram.

Weighted-Average Model

A simple and computationally efficient way of combining models, which is also automatically a variable length *N*-gram model, is to use an empirical formula to represent the λ's and use experiment to optimize the formulas using text corpora (48). This results in the definition of weights for the *m*-gram contribution to a weighted-average sum:

$$P(w_k) = \lambda_1 P(w_k) + \lambda_2 P(w_k \mid w_{k-1}) + \cdots + \lambda_m P(w_k \mid w_{k-m+1}^{k-1}) \quad \text{if } k > m - 1, \quad [21]$$

where the coefficients λ_m, $1 \leq m \leq n$, are calculated from a weighting function μ_m:

$$\mu_m = e^{m-1} \log[f(w_{k-m+1} \ldots w_{k-1})]. \quad [22]$$

In this formula, *f* is the frequency of the previous $(m - 1)$-gram. The λ's are then chosen to normalize these weights:

$$\lambda_m = \frac{\mu_m}{\mu_1 + \mu_2 + \cdots + \mu_n}. \quad [23]$$

The log (frequency) term equals zero when the frequency equals 1 and automatically cuts off infrequent higher *N*-grams, making it a variable *N*-gram model. The maximum size of the *N*-gram, *n*, is generally chosen to be 5 or larger. This gives results just below the optimum perplexity while being computationally efficient and allows extra data to be added to the training text easily, even during the computation of probabilities, a feature not possible with most methods.

Phrase-Based Models

Another technique to improve the *N*-gram language model is to use phrases. Phrase-based language models are based on the idea that some pair of words $w_i w_j$ give more context information than the words w_i and w_j independently. Examples of these phrases are "United States of America," "I would like to," or "I am going to."

One of the methods for finding those phrases was to select pairs of words w_i and w_j with high frequency and rewrite each occurrence of the pair in the training corpus as $w_{i\_}w_j$ (64,65). Although the perplexity decreases for these languages models, this language model has some problems. For example, by merging words in the training corpus, the size of the training corpus decreases, and for some infrequent words, the probability estimate will be poorer. Heeman and Damnati (66) found some solutions for these problems by combining 2-gram, 3-gram, and 4-gram probabilities. However, it is not clear that any of these methods bring about large improvements.

Overlapping *N*-grams

In the normal computation of *N*-grams, there is a great deal of overlap between the *N*-grams in a model. For example, the first three words of this paragraph

"in the normal"

includes one trigram (the whole phrase), two bigrams "in the," and "the normal," which overlaps with the word "the" and three unigrams. So, these three words yield 10 words combined in different ways in a typical *N*-gram language model and there is further overlap with the following words.

This overlapping causes obvious errors in the language model. For example, consider the most probable word following the phrase "she went riding." It might be "home" or "back." However, if the training text includes the children's story about "little red riding hood," the bigram "riding hood" will occur frequently and the language model might return "hood" not "home," which is clearly incorrect. Removing the overlap corrects this. The resulting smaller number of *N*-grams have been called "reduced" *N*-grams (67), "complete phrases" (68), and more recently "complemented *N*-grams" (56,69). They result in slightly improved language models if the training text is large. If the training text is small (less than 10 million words), the reduced size of the language model causes problems with zero and low frequencies.

Skipping and Distance *N*-grams

Skipping is best illustrated with an example. Consider the phrase "on the bus." There would be a high probability for $P(\text{bus} \mid \text{on the})$ in most training corpora. However, the phrase "on the red bus" would give a lower probability to "bus." This is solved in a trigram model for the word sequence $w_1 w_2 w_3 w_4$ by storing probabilities for a word w_4 following $w_1 w_2$, $w_1 w_3$, as well as $w_2 w_3$. Goodman (57) used this to get improvements of 7–10% in the baseline model depending on the size of the training corpus. It is similar to distance *n*-grams, which look at the probabilities w_4 (or w_5, w_6, etc.) following $w_1 w_2$ Rosenfeld (69) obtained an 8% improvement using this idea, similar to Goodman.

DYNAMIC OR ADAPTIVE LANGUAGE MODELS

The previous models are static models in that the model is trained on a training corpus which does not alter as the model is being used. Clearly, this is not ideal. For example, in a language model trained on a general corpus, the phrase

"on the green . . ."

would be followed in a static 4-gram model by a noun such as "door" or "grass." However, if the previous sentences were concerned with golf, "green" would likely be a noun (i.e., a "putting green" not an adjective) and it would probably be followed by a preposition phrase such as "at the fifth tee" or "with an iron." Humans automatically make such adjustments in their expectations of words depending on the context; indeed, humans might not be able to understand a conversation without recognizing domains and taking into account the more limited diction of the domains. Thus, to imitate humans, language models must be able to recognize and use domains dynamically and several attempts at doing this have been developed in what are called dynamic or adaptive language models.

Therefore, adaptive language modeling is based on the idea of capturing long dependencies in style and topic of the corpus. In order to capture these dependencies, a small number of parameters is added to the model to allow the extraction of information from further back in the document history; the models then adapt their expectations and probabilities.

These dynamic or adaptive language models have four different approaches: cache-based language models (70–72), trigger-based language models (73), domain-based language models (74–77), and, recently, individual word domain models (78,79). These are discussed individually below.

Cache-Based Language Models

In a conversation or text, a word used in the immediate past, stored in a cache, is much more likely to be used again. The cache-based language models increase the unigram probabilities of these words. Suppose the word sequence "The Gulf . . ." has just been recognized and the word "war" followed these two words 10% of the time in the static training text, whereas the word "stream" followed them 1% of the time. In an isolated sentence, the trigram with the highest probability will then be "The Gulf war." However, if we have several previous sentences concerned with geography containing the word "stream" and none contains the word "war," a cache-based model would change the probabilities and assign a higher probability to the word "stream." A human would do something similar.

This cache-based model approach has been widely used for adapting N-gram models (70–72). It is calculated as follows:

$$P_{combined}(w \mid h) = \lambda P_{global}(w \mid h) + (1 - \lambda) P_{cache}(w \mid h), \qquad [24]$$

where $P_{global}(w \mid h)$ is the conditional probability of the word w in the global or general training corpus, $P_{cache}(w \mid h)$ is the conditional probability of the word w in the cache, and $0 < \lambda \le 1$ is the interpolation parameter chosen to optimize the perplexity using a held-out training text. This has been shown to give considerable improvements over a global model, reducing the perplexity by 30% or more for small corpora and 10–20% for large corpora (39,57,69,77). It is easy to apply and is now widely used.

Trigger-Based Language Model

A model similar to cache-based models goes further by including trigger pairs. Trigger pairs (A → B) are pairs of associated words that when word A appears in the document history, it is often associated with word B (i.e., it triggers B) and therefore increases the probability estimate of word B. The trigger pairs are measured in the training text, possibly at a long distance of 100 words or more (73,74). Usually, this improvement is modest, but Rosenfeld in 1996 (69) obtained an improvement of 25% in perplexity over the baseline Katz trigram model using triggers (in a maximum entropy approach discussed later).

Sometimes, cache-based models are also called trigger-based models, as a content word triggers a change in probability of subsequent occurrences of the word. The most advanced form of a trigger model is one in which a word triggers a whole minilanguage model for that word, not just a set of trigger pairs. This is also discussed later.

Domain-Based Language Models

Language models are usually trained on large training corpora of 10 million to 100 million words or more. These corpora usually cover many subject areas or styles (i.e., domains). It is known that language models built with highly restricted domains obtain low perplexities even with small training text; for example, a perplexity of about 68 can be obtained with the VODIS train timetable enquiry corpus, although it is less than 100,000 words long (48).

Domain-based language models are based on the idea of producing a language model adapted to each particular topic or domain. These domains can include subdomains. For example, the domain "sports" may include "golf," "football," and "tennis," and these may also be broken down into smaller subdomains (e.g., the football domain may be made up of subdomains from American football, soccer, and rugby). So, a hierarchy of domains can be constructed. Models based on these domains try to improve the language model by adding more focused information on the language being used and by adding extra parameters in the calculation of the probability of a sequence that takes into account the possible domain to which that word belongs.

A hierarchical domain-based language model can be defined as follows:

$$P_{\text{combined}}(w \mid h) = \lambda_0 P_{\text{global}}(w \mid h) + \lambda_1 P_1(w \mid h) + \cdots + \lambda_k P_k(w \mid h), \qquad [25]$$

where $P_{\text{global}}(w \mid h)$ is the conditional probability of the word w in the global or general training corpus for context h, $P_i(w \mid h)$ is the conditional probability of the word w in the training corpus for the subdomain at level i, and where λ_i is the interpolation weight. Often, there is only one level (i.e., one domain with no subdomains).

As in class-based language models, an important factor is the creation of the domain. For example, Clarkson and Robinson (80) created a set of domains through clustering articles, Iyer and Ostendorf (77) clustered sentences, Donnelly et al. (76) created similar domains by clustering documents (mostly small documents), and Mahajan et al. (81) created a domain language model using information retrieval methods for clustering. A language model is then created from each domain or subdomain corpus. The parameters λ_k in Eq. (25) are optimized to produce the language model using a held-out corpus.

Domain-based language models have improved the performance of the baseline model by 25% by Donnelly et al. (76), 25% by Bellegarda (82), and 21% by Iyer and Ostendorf (77). These improvements are disappointing. There are two difficulties with these domain models based on clustering. First, a document may cover more than one domain but be in only one cluster (i.e., recognized as in one domain and not in the other). If the wrong domain is chosen, the result may be degradation rather than an improvement on the basic global model. Second, it is difficult to define the best domain to use without a long cache. A human can recognize the precise domain of a conversation before a first sentence is finished, but not a computer. Therefore, the idea of domain-based language models has been extended by creating a language model for each significant word; that is, each significant word spawns a domain for itself, discussed next.

Individual Word Domains

The Individual Word-Domain model (78) should overcome the two difficulties of domain models mentioned earlier. The precise domain of a conversation should be determined after one or two sentences. Also, it has been found that when building global models, that the smaller or more precise the global model, the better the result obtained. These considerations led to the idea of the smallest possible domain, one of which could normally always be chosen correctly, a domain language model of an individual word.

A few years ago, this concept would have been impractical, but with recent technology, it is just possible in the year 2001. If there are 100,000 word types in a corpus and each word has a language model averaging in size 10,000 words and phrases, stored in 100,000 bytes, this can be stored on a PC with 10 gigabytes of disk space. Each language model can still each be accessed in milliseconds using a hash index.

Individual word-domain language models are derived from a corpus for each word. This corpus is made up of text extracts from all the occurrences of the word in a large global corpus. These extracts might be the sentences or paragraphs containing the word. These pieces of text are collected together and comprise the corpus from which statistics of the word language model are calculated. This will include not only unigram probabilities but also *N*-gram probabilities.

These probabilities have to be combined to obtain a final probability; for example, for the sentence "The climate of Norway is affected by the Gulf . . . ," there would be four probabilities for an unknown word following "Gulf": probabilities from the word domains for "climate," "Norway," and "Gulf," and from the overall global domain. These would be combined as follows:

$$P = \lambda_{global}P_{global} + \lambda_{climate}P_{climate} + \lambda_{Norway}P_{Norway} + \lambda_{Gulf}P_{Gulf},$$ [26]

where

$$\lambda_{global} + \lambda_{climate} + \lambda_{Norway} + \lambda_{Gulf} = 1.$$ [27]

In other models, the λ values would be chosen to optimize the model using a held-out text, but in this case, it is not possible in real time, as the words in Eq. (26) at each step cannot be known beforehand. It has been found that using equal weights for the word models gives a 10% improvement and using weights which fall-off exponentially with word distance gives a 17% improvement in perplexities compared with a baseline model in initial experiments. A more complex Union model gave a 20% improvement (79).

It is also possible to combine weighted frequencies in this model before combining probabilities. This is possible to do dynamically with the weighted-average model described earlier and is simpler and easier to normalize. The initial results with this idea are encouraging and are as good as Eq. (26) and an order of magnitude faster.

MAXIMUM ENTROPY MODELS

Entropy, defined in Eq. (13), is the basis of the maximum entropy (ME) principle, which was developed for speech recognition by Jaynes (83) and first applied to language modeling by Della Pietra et al. (84) and Lau et al. (85). The subject was recently reviewed by Chen and Rosenfeld (86). Unlike earlier methods of combining models, which compute the individual models first and then combine them afterward, in the maximum entropy approach, a more integrated single model is constructed. Every information source (e.g., trigram or trigger word) is represented by a set of constraints which are then imposed in the estimation of the ME model. The intersection of these constraints yields a set of probability functions which are consistent with all of this information. The model that maximizes the entropy subject to those constraints is the maximum entropy model.

The constraints are expressed in terms of constraints functions $f_S(h \mid w)$ for models S, environment h, and word w. For example, the constraint function for the bigram $\{w_1 w_2\}$ is

$$f_{\{w_1, w_2\}}(h, w) = \begin{cases} 1 & \text{if } h \text{ ends in } w_1 \text{ and } w = w_2 \\ 0 & \text{otherwise.} \end{cases} \qquad [28]$$

Similar constraint functions can be readily defined for the other models discussed earlier. Each constraint limits the values of the desired ME probability function, $P(h, w)$ and can be written as

$$\sum_{(h, w)} P(h \; w) f_S(h, w) = K_S, \qquad [29]$$

where K_S is the expected value of f_S. For example, for the bigram, this becomes

$$\sum_{h \in h_1} P(h) \left(\sum_{w = w_2} P(w \mid h) \right) [f_{\{w_1, w_2\}}(h, w)] = K_{\{w_1, w_2\}}, \qquad [30]$$

where h_1 represents all word sequences ending in w_1 and

$$K_{\{w_1, w_2\}} = \frac{\text{freq}(w_1 w_2)}{\text{freq}(w_1)}, \qquad [31]$$

where $\text{freq}(w_1)$ is the frequency count for w_1 in the training corpus (i.e., $K_{\{w_1 w_2\}}$ is the maximum likelihood probability).

The unique maximum entropy solution that satisfies Eq. (29) can be shown to be also the maximum likelihood solution (87). It can be described in a parametric form as follows:

$$P_\lambda(w \mid h) = \frac{1}{C} \exp\left(\sum_S \lambda_S f_S(h, w) \right), \qquad [32]$$

where C is a normalization constant. The λ's are optimized (as in previous models), but using a different algorithm [e.g., the Brown algorithm (88) or the Iterative Scaling Algorithm of Darroch and Ratcliff (89)].

Experiments show that the ME approach outperforms the previous back-off or linear interpolation models. For example, Rosenfeld (69) found that combining a unigram, bigram, and trigram with a trigger model based on six triggers gave a reduction in perplexity of 25% from a baseline back-off trigram model based on part of the *Wall Street Journal* corpus. Using a linear interpolation gave only a 2% reduction. Other experiments gave a similar performance.

One difficulty with the ME model is that training is computationally expensive. For example, Rosenfeld reports that an experiment with 38 million words took about 200 days on an alpha computer reported in 1996 (69). This was in spite of the use of high N-grams thresholds to reduce the training time. Other methods, such as the use of larger corpora, can produce an 18% improvement in a much shorter time.

CLASS-BASED LANGUAGE MODELS

Some words are similar to other words either in their meaning (semantic) or grammar (syntactic). For example, the word "Red" is semantically similar to the word "Blue." The word "sit" is syntactically similar to the word "see" because both are verbs. In both cases, the two words can be said to belong to the same class. So, a class can be defined as a group of words semantically or syntactically similar; examples are given in Table 4.

Classification

The process of word classification where a word is assigned to a syntactic class is usually called "part of speech" (POS) tagging. Many systems are available for automatic POS tagging, including those by Church (9), Brill et al. (90), Kupiec (91), and Brill and Marcus (92). These can achieve a typical 96% tagging accuracy using a form of Markov modeling (not unlike language modeling). The difficulty is that many word types can take several grammatical forms depending on context.

Assigning words to semantic classes is usually carried out by some method of clustering (21,60,69,93–97). Finding an optimal assignment of words to classes is computationally difficult and multiple techniques have been described during the past 10 years (14,98–100).

Explicit information-theoretic approaches to automatic word classification are common. Some researches have used various measures taken from information theory as the bases of their systems (14,54,101). Connectionist networks are also well attested: Kiss (18), Elman (102), and Finch and Chater (103) present interesting systems, couched mainly in a cognitive scientific perspective. Finch and Chater (104) also investigate a word classification system based on a more traditional statistic: Spearman's rank sum correlation coefficient. Several other researchers have also resorted to standard statistical measures; these include Schütze (105) and Hughes and Atwell (106). Brill et al. (90) designed a word classification measure based explicitly on early structural linguistic theory.

TABLE 4   Examples of Word Classes

Semantic classes	Syntactic classes
published publication author writer	you he she they
school classroom teaching grade math	sit see say thank use

Many automatic word classification systems begin with word associations which can be extracted from corpora by borrowing the information theoretic measure of *mutual information* (8,107); if $P(x)$ and $P(y)$ are the independent probabilities of words x and y, then the mutual information, $M(x, y)$, is

$$M(x, y) = \log\left(\frac{P(x, y)}{P(x)P(y)}\right). \tag{33}$$

This measure compares how likely x and y are to occur together; in the case of words, this means serial occurrence, so that $M(x, y)$ is not usually the same as $M(y, x)$. The higher the likelihood of the co-occurrence of events x and y, the larger the mutual information value. Church and Hanks (108) describe some initial analyses of corpora using mutual information. Most of their results are close examinations of particular word relations and syntactic constructions.

The system described in Brown et al. (14) makes use of mutual information and works by a process of local optimization. The mutual information between two random variables, X and Y, is the expectation of Eq. (33):

$$M(X, Y) = \sum_{x,y} P(x, y) \log\left(\frac{P(x, y)}{P(x)P(y)}\right), \tag{34}$$

where x and y are discrete values of the random variables X and Y, respectively, and $P(x)$ is the probability of event x. Brown embeds this metric in a bottom-up agglomerative algorithm, the results of which can be used to produce an interesting classification of the vocabulary. Brown's algorithm discovered, among others, the following classes:

"mother wife father son husband brother daughter sister boss uncle"
"had hadn't hath would've could've should've must've might've"
"head body hands eyes voice arm seat eye hair mouth"

McMahon and Smith (97) used a top-down approach with the same algorithm, arguing its advantages and obtained clustering results similar to those of Brown. One interesting "discovery" was the linking of the words "of" and "de" in one class: there was apparently some French text in the corpus!

The variety of approaches in automatic word classification makes evaluation and comparison of systems difficult. However, the work of McMahon and Smith (97) contains experimental evaluations for the systems of Brown (14), McMahon and Smith (97), Elman (102), Finch and Chater (103), and Hughes and Atwell (106).

Class-Based Modeling

The class-based language models are defined as follows. Let w_i be a word in the test set. The probability that w_i follows the sequence $\{w_{i-2}, w_{i-1}\}$ in a class-based 3-gram language model is defined as the product of two terms:

either

$$P(w_i \mid w_{i-2}w_{i-1}) = P(w_i \mid c_i)P(c_i \mid w_{i-2}w_{i-1}) \tag{35}$$

or

$$P(w_i \mid w_{i-2}w_{i-1}) = P(w_i \mid c_i)P(c_i \mid c_{i-2}c_{i-1}) \tag{36}$$

where c_i is the class of the word w_i. The first term in these equations is the maximum likelihood probability of the word w_i given the current word class c_i; that is,

$$P(w_i \mid c_i) = \frac{\text{freq}(w_i)}{\text{freq}(c_i)} ,$$ [37]

where $\text{freq}(c_i)$ is the number of words in the training test for which the class is c_i. The second term in Eq. (36) is calculated from

$$P(c_i \mid c_{i-2}c_{i-1}) = \frac{\text{freq}(c_{i-2}c_{i-1}c_i)}{\sum_c \text{freq}(c_{i-2}c_{i-1}c)}$$ [38]

and similarly for Eq. (35).

Simple application of these formulas for dates, days of the week, and so forth can give useful improvements to a language model with little cost. For example, a phrase

"The exam in March"

may have few occurrences. But if "March" is replaced by MONTH, then

"The exam in MONTH"

will have a higher frequency and the probability

$$P(\text{March} \mid \text{exam in}) = P(\text{MONTH} \mid \text{exam in})P(\text{March} \mid \text{MONTH})$$

$$= P(\text{MONTH} \mid \text{exam in})\left(\frac{1}{12}\right)$$ [39]

will be more reliable.

Unfortunately class-based language models (97,100,109–112) have not shown significant improvement in performance on their own, although they contribute to large compound models, which we discuss later. However, in a series of articles (60,113–115), Niesler and Woodland explored the models and obtained perplexity reduction of 12–15% compared with a trigram model, which is the best result recorded with this type of model.

One reason for the poor performance is that many words belong to more than one class. For example, the word "work" is a noun or a verb. However, class-based language models are usually under the constraint that each word belongs to a single class; if it does not, it is difficult to assign each token to the correct class. Another reason is the loss of specificity for those words whose frequency is high. To overcome this problem, different approaches had been proposed by using different techniques of tagging (54,116) or by interpolating with traditional N-gram techniques (97).

COMBINED MODELS

In the previous section, a dozen or more approaches to the combination of basic statistical language models have been proposed and, in the best of them, improvement of 20–25% in perplexity over a baseline trigram model is obtained. The only systems which have improved on this are combined models which combine several different approaches in large systems. For example, Rosenfeld in 1996 (69), using a maximum entropy model on a corpus of 5 million words, combined trigrams and triggers to obtain a 25% improvement. However, by combining this model with a trigram model, he got a 27% improvement, and by including caches, he obtained a 37% improvement. This was the highest improvement over the baseline model reported until 2000, when a large combined model by Goodman (57) obtained the best result yet in the literature, a fall in perplexity from 66 to 36 (i.e., a reduction of 45% in perplexity over the baseline model for the *Wall Street Journal* corpus of 260 million words). He combined a 5-gram model with caching, classes, Kneser–Ney smoothing, and "skipping" into one large model. However, he obtained a reduction in the speech recognition word error rate of only 8.26%, which is surprising.

COMPARISON WITH HUMANS

There have been many attempts over the last 20 years to improve on the baseline trigram model, but improvements in perplexity have rarely improved by more than 30%, except in large and complex combined models. Improvements in word error rates have been even less convincing, all less than 10%. As stated early in this article, the fact that we find it so difficult to improve on a simple trigram model is one of the central quandaries of statistical language modeling.

The question of what improvements are possible when the best optimized language model has been discovered arises. It appears obvious that evolution dictates that this "best" language model should not perform better than human performance. Thus, an experiment with humans that compares their performance with the performances of the basic trigram language model and with more advanced models should determine what is possible and what room remains for improvement.

The first experiments similar to this were conducted by Mercer and Roukos in 1992 (117) in a game asking humans to predict the next word in a document given a long prior context. Experiments have more recently been performed with missing-word tests by Owens et al. (118,119) varying the length of context from two words to three sentences. A suite of missing-word tests based on text extracts selected randomly from two different text corpora (Vodis and London-Times) were used in the evaluation of human performance compared to the language model performance. Two main patterns became clear from the results illustrated in Figure 3. Surprisingly, for tests where the context consisted of six words or less, the language model outperformed humans; humans only outperformed the language model when the size of context given for the missing word exceeded six words, and not by a great margin.

The design of these experiments is open to criticism and the dataset was not large enough to be conclusive. Further experiments are underway, and if these confirm the above results, then possible improvements in language modeling may be limited and speech recognition should look for improvements in acoustic modeling rather than improvements in language modeling.

CONCLUSIONS: THE NEED FOR GRAMMAR

Research in statistical language modeling has been growing very rapidly in the last 5 years, particularly because of its possible applications to speech recognition, optical character recognition, handwriting documents, and machine translation. However, to come

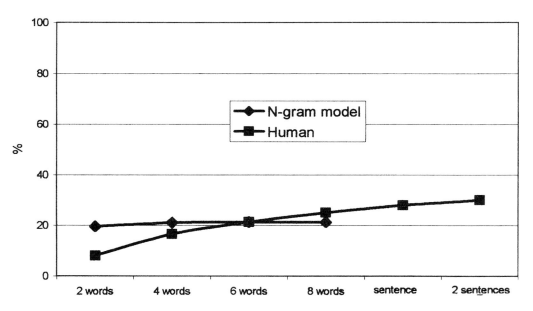

FIGURE 3   Percentage of words guessed correctly by 48 humans in 2400 tests compared with those computes with an *N*-gram model for different contexts.

close to model human performance, the models will have to include more than just *N*-grams. For example, in current models, the words "cat" and "cats" are quite separate and the fact that both belong to the same lemma is not used. The inclusion of simple grammar lemmatization as in this example and the recognition of noun phrases, prepositions phrases, and verb phrases are needed. At least the unconscious understanding of grammar and grammatical word order known to a 5-year-old child should be included before statistical language modeling can be said to have begun as a mature branch of science. A few articles have appeared in 2000 beginning to study the combination of statistical with grammatical models (120–123). It is too early to comment on their success, but this is where the future lies for statistical language modeling.

REFERENCES

1. V. Zue, "Talking with Your Computer," *Sci. Am.*, *281* 56–57 (1999).
2. S. J. Young, "Large Vocabulary Continuous Speech Recognition: A Review," *IEEE Signal Process. Mag.*, *13*(5), 45–57 (1996).
3. H. Ney and S. Ortmanns, "Dynamic Programming Search for Continuous Speech Recognition," *IEEE Signal Process. Mag.*, *16*(5), 64–83 (1999).
4. J. R. Bellegarda, "Large Vocabulary Speech Recognition with Multispan Statistical Language Models," *IEEE Trans. Speech Audio Process.*, *SAP-8*(1), 76–84 (2000).
5. R. Zhang, E. Black, A. Finch, and Y. Sagisaka, "Integrating Detailed Information into Language Model," in *IEEE ICASSP 2000*, 2000, Vol. 3, pp. 1595–1598.
6. N. Chomsky, *Syntactic Structures*, Mouton & Co., London, 1957.
7. D. Shanks, "Breaking Chomsky's Rules," *New Scientist*, *137*(1858), 26–30 (1993).

8. F. Jelinek, "The Development of an Experimental Discrete Dictation Recogniser," *Proc. IEEE, 73*(11), 1616–1624 (1985).

9. K. W. Church, "A Stochastic Parts Program and Noun Phrase Parser for Unrestricted Text," *ANLP–ACL, 88,* 136–143 (1988).

10. J. J. Hull, "Combining Syntactic Knowledge and Visual Text Recognition: A Hidden Markov Model for Part of Speech Tagging in a Word Recognition Algorithm," in *Intelligent Probabilistic Approaches to Natural Language Papers, 1992 Fall Symposium American Association for Artificial Intelligence*, AAAI Press, Cambridge, MA, 1992, pp. 77–83.

11. P. F. Brown, J. Cocke, V. J. Della Pietra, S. A. Della Pietra, F. Jelinek, J. D. Lafferty, R. L. Mercer, and P. S. Roosin, "A Statistical Approach to Machine Translation," *Computat. Linguist., 16*(2), 79–85 (1990).

12. H. Ney, S. Nießen, F. J. Och, H. Sawaf, C. Tillmann, and S. Vogel, "Algorithms for Statistical Translation of Spoken Language," *IEEE Trans. Speech Audio Process., SAP-8*(1), 24–36 (2000).

13. G. Riccardi and A. L. Gorin, "Stochastic Language Adaptation over Time and State in Natural Spoken Dialog System," *IEEE Trans. Speech Audio Process., SAP-8*(1), 3–10 (2000).

14. P. F. Brown, V. J. Della Pietra, P. V. De Souza, J. C. Lai, and R. Mercer, "Class-Based *n*-gram Models of Natural Language," *Computat. Linguist., 18*(4), 467–479 (1992).

15. J. McMahon and F. J. Smith, "Structural Tags, Annealing and Automatic Word Classification," *Artif. Intell. Simul. Behav. Q., 90,* 5–14 (1994).

16. K. W. Church, W. A. Gale, P. Hanks, and D. Hilde, "Using Statistics in Lexical Analysis," in *Lexical Acquisition: Exploiting On-Line Resources to Build a Lexicon*, edited by U. Zernik, Lawrence Erlbaum Associates, Hillsdale, NJ, 1991, pp. 115–164.

17. K. Ng and V. Zue, "Subword Unit Representations for Spoken Document Retrieval," in *EUROSPEECH 97*, 1997, Vol. 3, pp. 1607–1610.

18. G. R. Kiss, "Grammatical Word Classes: A Learning Process and Its Simulation," *Psychol. Learning Motiv., 7,* 1–41 (1973).

19. N. Chater, "Neural Networks: The New Statistical Models of Mind," in *3rd Neural Computation and Psychology Workshop*, edited by C. J. van Rijsbergen, UCL Press, London, 1994.

20. P. Clarkson and R. Rosenfeld, "Statistical Language Modeling Using the CMU-Cambridge Toolkit," in *EUROSPEECH 97*, 1997, Vol. 5, pp. 2707–2710.

21. R. Bahl, F. Jelinek, and R. L. Mercer, "A Maximum Likelihood Approach to Continuous Speech Recognition," *IEEE Trans. Pattern Anal. Machine Intell., PAMI-5*(2), 179–190 (1983).

22. F. Jelinek, "Up from Trigrams: The Struggle for Improved Language Models," in *EUROSPEECH 91*, 1991, Vol. 3, pp. 1037–1040.

23. W. N. Francis, "Manual of Information to Accompany a Standard Sample of Present-Day American English for Use with Digital Computers," Department of Linguistics, Brown University, Providence, RI (1964).

24. H. Kucera and W. N. Francis, "Computational Analysis of Present-Day American English," Brown University, Providence, RI (1967).

25. S. Johansson, G. Leech, and H. Goodluck, "Manual of Information to Accompany the Lancaster-Oslo/Bergen Corpus of British English, for Use with Digital Computers," Department of English, University of Oslo (1978).

26. S. Johansson, E. Atwell, R. Garside, G. Leech, *The Tagged LOB Corpus Users' Manual,* Norwegian Computing Centre for the Humanities, Bergen, Norway, 1986.

27. D. B. Paul and J. M. Baker, "The Design for the *Wall Street Journal*-Based CSR Corpus," in *ICSLP 92*, 1992, pp. 899–902.

28. D. Graff, "The 1996 Broadcast News Speech and Language-Model Corpus," in *ARPA Workshop on Human Language Technology*, 1996.

29. D. S. Pallett, J. G. Fiscus, and M. A. Przybocki, "1996 Preliminary Broadcast News Benchmark Tests," in *DARPA Speech Recognition Workshop*, 1997, pp. 11–14.

30. R. Moore, M. Cohen, V. Abrash, D. Appelt, H. Bratt, J. Butzberger, L. Cherny, J. Dowding, H. Franco, M. Gawron, and D. Moran, "SRI's Recent Progress on the ATIS Task," in *Spoken Language Systems Technology Workshop*, 1994, pp. 72–75.

31. H. Bratt, J. Dowding, and K. Hunicke-Smith, "The SRI Telephone-based ATIS System," in *ARPA Workshop on Spoken Language Technology*, 1995.

32. S. Cookson, "Final Evaluation of VODIS," in *SPEECH 88, Seventh FASE Symposium*, 1988, pp. 1311–1320.

33. S. Greenbaum and J. Svartvik, "The London Corpus of Spoken English: Description and Research," in *Lund Studies in English 82*, edited by J. Svartvik, Lund University Press, Lund, 1990.

34. J. J. Godfrey, E. C. Holliman, and J. McDaniel, "SWITCHBOARD: Telephone Speech Corpus for Research and Development," *IEEE ICASSP*, *1*, 517–520 (1992).

35. M. Marcus, B. Santorini, and M. Marcinkiewicz, "Building a Large Annotated Corpus of English: The Penn Treebank," *Computat. Linguist.*, *19*(2), 313–330 (1992).

36. N. Reithinger and E. Maier, "Utilizing Statistical Dialogue Act Processing in Verbmobil," in *ACL 95*, 1995, pp. 116–121.

37. L. Burnard, *User Reference Guide for the British National Corpus*, Oxford University Computing Services, Oxford, 1995.

38. C. E. Shannon, "Prediction and Entropy of Printed English," *Bell Sys. Technol. J.*, *30* (1951).

39. P. Clarkson and A. J. Robinson, "Towards Improved Language Models Evaluation Measures," in *EUROSPEECH 99*, 1999, Vol. 4, pp. 1927–1930.

40. D. Johnston (BT Research Laboratories. Martlesham, England, private communication, 1991).

41. S. F. Chen, D. Beeferman, and R. Rosenfeld, "Evaluation Metrics for Language Models," in *DARPA Broadcast News Transcription and Understanding Workshop*, 1998.

42. E. Eide, H. Gish, P. Jeanrenaud, and A. Mielke, "Understanding and Improving Speech Recognition Performance Through the Use of Diagnostic Tools," *IEEE ICASSP 95*, 1995, Vol. 1, pp. 221–224.

43. R. Iyer, M. Ostendorf, and M. Meteer, "Analyzing and Predicting Language Model Improvements," in *IEEE Workshop on Modelling Pronunciation Variation for Automatic Speech Recognition*, 1998, pp. 7–12.

44. A. Ito, M. Kodha, and M. Ostendorf, "A New Metric for Stochastic Language Model Evaluation," in *EUROSPEECH 99*, 1999, Vol. 4, pp. 1591–1594.

45. F. Jelinek and R. L. Mercer, "Interpolated Estimation of Markov Source Parameters from Sparse Data," in *Workshop on Pattern Recognition in Practice*, edited by E. S. Gelsema and L. N. Kanal, North-Holland, Amsterdam, 1980, pp. 381–397.

46. S. M. Katz, "Estimation of Probabilities from Sparse Data for the Language Model Component of the Speech Recognizer," *IEEE Trans. Acoustic Speech, Signal Process.*, ASSP-35(3), 400–401 (1987).

47. K. W. Church and W. A. Gale, "A Comparison of the Enhanced Good–Turing and Deleted Estimation Methods for Estimating Probabilities of English Bigrams," *Computer Speech Lang.*, *5*, 19–54 (1991).

48. P. O'Boyle, M. Owens, and F. J. Smith, "A Weighted Average *N*-gram Model of Natural Language," *Computer Speech Lang.*, *8*, 337–349 (1994).

49. I. Good, "The Population Frequencies of Species and the Estimation of Population Parameters," *Biometrika*, *40*(3&4), 237–264 (1953).

50. S. F. Chen and J. Goodman, "An Empirical Study of Smoothing Techniques for Language Modeling," *Computer Speech Lang.*, *3*, 359–394 (1999).

51. A. Nadas, "On Turing's Formula for Word Probabilities," *IEEE Trans. Acoustic Speech Signal Process.*, *ASSP-33*(6), 1414–1416 (1985).

52. F. Jelinek and R. L. Mercer, "Probability Distribution Estimation from Sparse Data," *IBM Tech. Disclosure Bull.*, *28*, 2591–2594 (1985).

53. H. Ney and U. Essen, "On Smoothing Techniques for Bigrams-Based Natural Language Modelling," in *IEEE ICASSP 91*, 1991, Vol. 2, pp. 825–829.

54. H. Ney, U. Essen, and R. Kneser, "On Structuring Probabilistic Dependences in Stochastic Language Modelling," *Computer Speech Lang.*, *8*, 1–38 (1994).

55. H. Ney, U. Essen, and R. Kneser, "On the Estimation of "Small" Probabilities by Leaving-One-Out," *IEEE Trans. Pattern Anal. Machine Intell.*, *PAMI-17*(12) (1995).

56. R. Kneser and H. Ney, "Improving Backing-Off for M-Gram Language Modeling," in *IEEE ICASSP 95*, 1995, Vol. 1, pp. 181–184.

57. J. Goodman, "Putting It All Together in Language Model Combination," in *IEEE ICASSP 2000*, 2000, Vol. 3, pp. 1647–1650.

58. L. E. Baum, T. Petrie, G. Soules, and N. Weiss, "A Maximization Technique Occurring in Statistical Analysis of Probabilistic Functions in Markov Chains," *Ann. Math. Statist.*, *41*(1), 164–171 (1970).

59. P. O'Boyle, J. Ming, M. Owens, and F. J. Smith, "Adaptive Parameter Training in an Interpolated *N*-gram Language Model," *Quant. Linguist.*, *6*(1), 10–13 (1999).

60. T. R. Niesler and P. C. Woodland, "A Variable-Length Category-Based *N*-gram Language Model," in *IEEE ICASSP 96*, 1996, Vol. 1, pp. 164–167.

61. M. Siu and M. Ostendorf, "Variable *N*-grams and Extensions for Conversational Speech Language Modeling," *IEEE Trans. Speech Audio Process.*, *SAP-8*(1), 63–75 (2000).

62. F. J. Smith and P. O'Boyle, "The N-gram Language Model," in *The Cognitive Science of Natural Language Processing Workshop*, 1992, pp. 51–58.

63. R. Kneser, "Statistical Language Modeling Using a Variable Context Length," in *ICSLP 96*, 1996, Vol. 1, pp. 494–497.

64. K. Ries, F. D. Buo, and A. Waibel, "Class Phrase Models for Language Modelling," in *ICSLP 96*, 1996, Vol. 1, pp. 398–401.

65. G. Riccardi, A. L. Gorin, A. Ljolje, and M. Riley, "A Spoken Language System for Automatic Call Routing," in *IEEE ICASSP 97*, 1997, Vol. 2, pp. 1143–1146.

66. P. A. Heeman and G. Damnati, "Deriving Phrase-Based Language Models," in *IEEE Workshop on Speech Recognition and Understanding*, 1997.

67. P. Craig, "An Investigation of Zipf's Law for Phrases," Graduate Diploma thesis, Queen's University of Belfast (1983).

68. P. O'Boyle, "A Study of an *N*-gram Language Model for Speech Recognition," Ph.D. thesis, Queen's University of Belfast (1993).

69. R. Rosenfeld, "Adaptive Statistical Language Modelling: A Maximum Entropy Approach," *Computer Speech Lang.*, *10*(3), 187–228 (1996).

70. R. Kuhn and R. De Mori, "A Cache-Based Natural Language Model for Speech Recognition," *IEEE Trans. Pattern Anal. Machine Intell.*, *PAMI-12*(6), 570–583 (1990).

71. R. Kuhn and R. De Mori, "Corrections to a Cache-Based Natural Language Model for Speech Recognition," *IEEE Trans. Pattern Anal. Machine Intell.*, *PAMI-14*(6), 691–692 (1992).

72. F. Jelinek, B. Merialdo, S. Roukos, and M. Strauss, "A Dynamic Language Model for Speech Recognition," in *Speech and Natural Language DARPA Workshop*, 1991, pp. 293–295.

73. R. Lau, R. Rosenfeld, and S. Roukos, "Trigger-Based Language Models: A Maximum Entropy Approach," in *IEEE ICASSP 93*, 1993, Vol. 3, pp. 45–48.

74. R. Rosenfeld and X. D. Huang, "Improvements in Stochastic Language Modeling," in *Speech and Natural Language DARPA Workshop*, 1992.

75. R. Kneser and V. Steinbiss, "On the Dynamic Adaptation of Stochastic Language Models," in *IEEE ICASSP 93*, 1993, Vol. 2, pp. 586–589.

76. P. G. Donnelly, F. J. Smith, E. I. Sicilia-Garcia, and J. Ming, "Language Modelling with Hierarchical Domains," in *EUROSPEECH 99*, 1999, Vol. 4, pp. 1575–1578.

77. R. Iyer and M. Ostendorf, "Modeling Long Distance Dependence in Language: Topic Mixture Vs. Dynamic Cache Models," *IEEE Trans. Speech Audio Process.*, SAP-17(1), 30–39 (1999).

78. E. I. Sicilia-Garcia, F. J. Smith, and P. Hanna, "A Dynamic Language Model Based on Individual Word Models," in *AICS 99*, 1999, pp. 222–229.

79. E. I. Sicilia-Garcia, J. Ming, and F. J. Smith, "A Dynamic Language Model based on Individual Word Domains," in *COLING 2000*, 2000, pp. 789–794.

80. P. Clarkson and A. Robinson, "Language Model Adaptation Using Mixtures and an Exponentially Decaying Cache," in *IEEE ICASSP 97*, 1997, Vol. 2, pp. 799–802.

81. M. Mahajan, D. Beeferman, and X. D. Huang, "Improved Topic-Dependent Language Modeling Using Information Retrieval Techniques," in *IEEE ICASSP 99*, 1999, Vol. 1, pp. 541–544.

82. J. R. Bellegarda, "Speech Recognition Experiments Using Multi-Span Statistical Language Models," in *IEEE ICASSP 99*, 1999, Vol. 2, pp. 717–720.

83. E. T. Jaynes, "Information Theory and Statistical Machines," *Phys. Rev.*, 106, 620–630 (1957).

84. S. A. Della Pietra, V. J. Della Pietra, R. Mercer, and S. Roukos, "Adaptive Language Modeling Using Minimum Discriminant Estimation," in *IEEE ICASSP 92*, 1992, Vol. 1, pp. 633–636.

85. R. Lau, R. Rosenfeld, and S. Roukos, "Adaptive Language Modeling Using the Maximum Entropy Principle," *ARPA Human Language Technology Workshop*, 1993, pp. 108–113.

86. S. F. Chen and R. Rosenfeld, "A Survey of Smoothing Techniques for ME Models," *IEEE Trans. Speech Audio Process.*, SAP-8(1), 37–50 (2000).

87. A. L. Berger, S. A. Della Pietra, and V. J. Della Pietra, "A Maximum Entropy Approach to Natural Language Processing," *Computat. Linguist.*, 22(1), 39–71 (1996).

88. D. Brown, "A Note on Approximations to Discrete Probability Distributions," *Inform. Control*, 2, 386–392 (1959).

89. J. N. Darroch and D. Ratcliff, "Generalized Scaling for Log-Linear Models," *Ann. Math. Statist.*, 43, 1470–1480 (1972).

90. E. Brill, D. Magerman, M. Marcus, and B. Santorini, "Deducing Linguistic Structure from the Statistics of Large Corpora," in *DARPA Speech and Natural Language Workshop*, 1990, pp. 275–282.

91. J. Kupiec, "Robust Part-of-Speech Tagging Using a Hidden Markov Model," *Computer Speech Lang.*, 6, 225–242 (1992).

92. E. Brill and M. Marcus, "Tagging an Unfamiliar Text with Minimal Human Supervision," in *Probabilistic Approaches to Natural Language*, AAAI Press, Cambridge, MA, 1992, pp. 10–16.

93. F. Jelinek, R. Mercer, and S. Roukos, "Classifying Words for Improved Statistical Language Models," in *IEEE ICASSP 90*, 1990, Vol. 1, pp. 621–624.

94. F. Jelinek, "Self-Organized Language Modeling for Speech Recognition," in *Readings in Speech Recognition*, edited by A. Waibel and K. F. Lee, Morgan Kaufmann Publishers, San Mateo, CA, 1990, pp. 450–506.

95. R. Kneser and H. Ney, "Improved Clustering Techniques for Class-Based Language Modelling," in *EUROSPEECH 93*, 1993, Vol. 2, pp. 973–976.

96. B. Suhm and A. Waibel, "Towards Better Language Modelling for Spontaneous Speech," in *ICSLP 94*, 1994, Vol. 2, pp. 831–834.

97. J. McMahon and F. J. Smith, "Improving Statistical Language Performance with Automatically Generates Word Hierarchies," *Computat. Linguist.*, 22(2), 217–247 (1996).

98. M. Meteer, R. Schwartz, and R. Weischedel, "POST: Using Probabilities in Language Processing," in *International Joint Conference on Artificial Intelligence*, 1991, pp. 960–965.

99. A. Ratnaparkhi, "A Maximum Entropy Part-of-Speech Tagger," in *Empirical Methods in Natural Language Processing Conference*, 1996, pp. 133–142.

100. A. Farhat, J-F. Isabelle, and D. O'Shaughnessy, "Clustering Words for Statistical Language Models Based on Contextual Word Similarity," in *IEEE ICASSP 96*, 1996, Vol. 1, pp. 180–183.

101. F. Pereira and N. Tishby, "Distributional Similarity, Phase Transitions and Hierarchical Clustering," in *Intelligent Probabilistic Approaches to Natural Language Papers from the 1992 Fall Symposium. American Association for Artificial Intelligence*, AAAI Press, Cambridge, MA, 1992, pp. 108–112.

102. J. L. Elman, "Finding Structure in Time," *Cognitive Sci.*, *14*(2), 179–211 (1990).

103. S. Finch and N. Chater, "Learning Syntactic Categories: A Statistical Approach," in *Neurodynamics and Psychology*, edited by M. Oaksford and G. Brown, Academic Press, New York, 1994.

104. S. Finch and N. Chater, "Bootstrapping Syntactic Categories Using Statistical Methods," in *Background and Experiments in Machine Learning of Natural Language*, edited by W. Daelemans and D. Powers, Institute for Language Technology and AI, 1992, pp. 229–235.

105. H. Schütze, "Part-of-Speech Induction from Scratch," in *ACL 93*, 1993, pp. 251–258.

106. J. Hughes and E. Atwell, "The Automated Evaluation of Inferred Word Classifications," in *11th European Conference on Artificial Intelligence*, 1994, pp. 535–539.

107. T. M. Cover and J. A. Thomas, *Elements of Information Theory*, Wiley & Sons, New York, 1991.

108. K. Church and P. Hanks, "Word Association Norms, Mutual Information, and Lexicography," *Computat. Linguist.*, *16*(1), 22–29 (1990).

109. S. Mori, M. Nishimura, and N. Itoh, "Word Clustering for a Word Bi-Gram Model," in *ICSLP 98*, 1998, Vol. 6, pp. 2467–2470.

110. R. Blasig, "Combination of Words and Word Categories in Varigram Histories," in *IEEE ICASSP 99*, 1999, Vol. 1, pp. 529–532.

111. H. Yamamoto and Y. Sagisaka, "Multi-Class Composite *N*-gram Based on Connection Direction," in *IEEE ICASSP 99*, 1999, Vol. 1, pp. 533–536.

112. C. Samuelsson and W. Reichl, "A Class-Based Language Model for Large-Vocabulary Speech Recognition Extracted from Part-of-Speech Statistics," in *IEEE ICASSP 99*, 1999, Vol. 1, pp. 537–540.

113. T. R. Niesler and P. C. Woodland, "Combination of Word-Based and Category-Based Language Models," in *ICSLP 98*, 1998, Vol. 1, pp. 220–223.

114. T. R. Niesler and P. C. Woodland, "Modelling Word-Pair Relations in a Category-Based Language Model," in *IEEE ICASSP 97*, 1997, Vol. 2, pp. 795–798.

115. T. R. Niesler, E. W. D. Whittaker, and P. C. Woodland, "Comparison of Part-of-Speech and Automatically Derived Category-Based Language Models for Speech Recognition," in *IEEE ICASSP 98*, 1998, Vol. 1, pp. 177–180.

116. J. Uerbela, "More Efficient Clustering of *N*-grams for Statistical Language Modelling," in *EUROSPEECH 95*, 1995, Vol. 1, pp. 1257–1260.

117. R. Mercer and S. Roukos, unpublished "Shannon Game" reported by Rosenfeld [69], 1992.

118. M. Owens, P. O'Boyle, J. McMahon, J. Ming, and F. J. Smith, "A Comparison of Human and Statistical Language Model Performance Using Missing-Word Tests," *Lang. Speech*, *40*(4), 377–389 (1997).

119. M. Owens, A. Kruger, P. G. Donnelly, F. J. Smith, and J. Ming, "A Missing-Word Test Comparison of Human and Statistical Language Model Performance," in *EUROSPEECH 99*, 1999, Vol. 1, pp. 145–148.

120. F. Jelinek and C. Chelba, "Putting Language into Language Modeling," in *EUROSPEECH 99*, 1999, pp. KN-1–6.

121. M. Siu and M. Ostendorf, "Integrating a Context-Dependent Phrase Grammar in the Variable *N*-Gram Framework," in *IEEE ICASSP 2000*, 2000, Vol. 3, pp. 1643–1646.

122. J. Wu and S. Khudanpur, "Syntactic Heads in Statistical Language Modelling," in *IEEE ICASSP 2000*, 2000, Vol. 3, pp. 1699–1702.

123. Y. Wang, M. Mahajan, and X. Huang, "A Unified Context-Free Grammar and *N*-gram Model for Spoken Language Processing," in *IEEE ICASSP 2000*, 2000, Vol. 3, pp. 1639–1642.

BASIC READING FOR FURTHER STUDY

1. Charniak, *Statistical Language Learning*, MIT Press, Cambridge, MA, 1993, pp. 1–170.

2. *IEEE Transactions on Speech and Acoustic Processing.* 8(1) (2000), Special Issue in Language Modelling and Dialogue Systems.

3. Jelinek, F., *Statistical Methods for Speech Recognition*, MIT Press, Cambridge, MA, 1997, pp. 1–283.

4. Young, S., and Bloothooft, G. (eds.), *Corpus-Based Methods in Language and Speech Processing*, Kluwer Academic, Dordrecht, 1997, pp. 1–234.

5. "Breaking Chomsky's Rules," *New Scientist*, 137 1858, 26–30 (1993).

ELVIRA I. SICILIA-GARCIA

F. JACK SMITH

SYSTEMS DOCUMENTATION

Systems documentation refers to a highly detailed description of the internal architecture of an information processing system. It may also involve descriptions of both the user-level interactions and a specification of the hardware characteristics as they relate to the software design. It is different from *user documentation* in that it goes beyond the contexts of the end-user's interaction with the technology and discusses in detail the underlying components and interactions between them that implement the functionality provided by the information system.

Systems documentation can be defined as

the collection of information that exists for the purpose of documenting a device, a process, or a system in sufficient detail to permit quality assurance, maintenance, and further development.

In terms of information technology, systems documentation mainly focuses on *software*, because, unlike *hardware*, the flexible nature of software is what makes it amenable to change, customization, and improvements over a long period of time. The most complete forms of systems documentation include some documentation of the hardware as well as the software components, but this is not a strict requirement for software projects that will be deployed on highly standardized hardware platforms running well-understood operating systems. Supporting software engineering was the original motivation behind systems documentation, as the main people who used systems documentation were other programmers, now referred to as *software engineers*.

However, systems documentation is more than comments inside a source code. It takes different forms and levels of abstraction depending on the scope or context of the software project. Object-oriented software development methodologies (1), social changes such as the open source movement (2), the emergence of networked and distributed computing, and wireless ubiquitous computing have expanded the traditional audience from software engineers to include system integrators, network administrators, and even end users who wish to connect a wide array of computing devices to achieve their information technology or interoperability objectives. As programming paradigms evolved in response to these and other factors, so have the methods for systems documentation, culminating in the creation of the Unified Modeling Language (UML).

Systems documentation has becoming increasingly important as computer technology has become more pervasive and intertwined. Although it is not generally perceived as the most important task of the software or systems engineer, it is an essential skill to acquire and institute as part of an integrated and consistent software engineering process.

BRIEF HISTORICAL DISCUSSION ON SOFTWARE AND SYSTEMS DOCUMENTATION

In an industry that changes faster than any other in terms of hardware infrastructure, the time and cost of developing functional and robust software represents a significant investment by a company that relies on it for internal use or in products or services it renders. Software is, in many cases, the digital embodiment of the intellectual property of an organization in an increasingly knowledge-based world. Although it is an intangible in most respects, software that implements a solution to a problem or meets an information processing need is improved and periodically recompiled as hardware becomes faster. This process results in continued value and productivity, as long as the software remains able to meet the needs of its users. However, as programs have gotten larger to add new functionality while supporting existing and legacy code, it has become more difficult to manage, maintain, or extend source code without incurring risk. Software has gotten so complex that it is nearly impossible to know all of the subtle interactions that can occur or to provide adequate testing to uncover them.

In earlier paradigms, such as procedural programming, it was not easy to reorganize program code as it grew more complex. Once a function or subroutine had been made to work and additional code was written around it, the software routines became tightly bound, highly dependent on one another, and very sensitive to change. Any subsequent alteration to the internals or structure of previously existing code may break operability with other parts of the program.

Understandably, there was great resistance to reorganizing the software for fear of introducing subtle new defects or making the code nonfunctional. Programming at that time was more concerned with the issue of fitting a program into the very small amounts of RAM available, which meant merging as much of the program code together, eliminating (where possible) calls to routines to save memory, and, sometimes, programming in assembly language, because compilers at the time did not generate particularly efficient machine code from high-level language sources. These pressures kept procedural programming the norm for many years.

Change was strongly discouraged in the past because code dependencies had to be tracked manually—a daunting task once the project reached any significant size. Thus, the prevailing strategy was to graft code onto the existing source code tree, and in that way try to mitigate any unexpected interactions between software routines.

Despite these conditions in the late 1950s and early 1960s, the sustained need for scientific computing led to the development of some of the world's most advanced software. Scientific software such as NASTRAN (3) has been refined and extended up to the present day. Legacy software systems, enhanced through the efforts of many programmers totaling upward of a century of programmer-years, now consist of millions of lines of code. Much of this code has minimal or no available documentation to clearly indicate the information flow and dependencies between blocks of code.

Procedural programming was the norm during a time when computers did not have the memory or computing power to support the much richer integrated development environments enjoyed by contemporary C++ and Java programmers, as shown in Figure 1.

PROBLEM DOMAIN ABSTRACTION AND THE NEED FOR MULTIPLE VIEWS OF SOFTWARE

For any digital machine that is programmable, software for that machine can be defined as

> an ordered set of states, representing both machine instructions and their operands, that trigger state transitions in the computing device, which, in turn, perform any of a range of Boolean combinational logic operations, such as arithmetic, logic, loading, or storing.

FIGURE 1   A modern integrated software development environment.

Most modern computers are functionally equivalent to a theoretical model called the *Turing machine*, which, by virtue of it being able to run recursive algorithms, is the most general automaton. (For an overview of the Turing machine, see Ref. 4.) However, this view of software is the most specific to the architecture of the machine being programmed and is generally used by compiler writers, embedded system programmers, or those who write device drivers. This is called the *machine* or *assembly language* programming model. For more information on the programming model, see Ref. 5.

Software written with higher-level computing languages strive to be as general as possible and independent of the underlying hardware, as most of the optimizations for a given platform will be performed by the compiler. Therefore, most modern programming languages presume an idealized computing model with a flat memory space and an orthogonal register architecture. It is up to the compiler to analyze the source code, generate and optimize assembly language for a given processor, and produce a binary program that can be run on a particular computer. A background discussion of processor register architecture is provided in Ref. 6.

Higher-level procedural programming languages such as Fortran and C do include constructs to more easily *express* program flow and data processing, but they do not necessarily provide easy ways to *unify program code and data* into coherent and independent units easily, along with structured ways to group code together to derive more advanced functionality. This kind of software organization is possible, but it requires great scrutiny by the software designer to create the richer data structures and functions to succeed. The ability to combine blocks of organized code together in an ordered way to model objects is the basis for *object-oriented software engineering* and is a cornerstone for current programming idealogy.

Programming a computer, however, demands both correctness and precision, in order to get valid, meaningful, and useful answers from any software that is written or used. However, the complexity can be overwhelming, unless the means is there to clearly map programming logic to separate blocks of code and data, that communicate and share data with other blocks of code and data through well-defined and controlled means. This requires viewing the code at both a very detailed level and manipulating data structures and algorithms, as well as the ability to take a *bird's-eye view* of the project to ensure that the functional requirements of the software are being met.

Object-Oriented Software Design

Object-oriented design is a valuable methodology for modelling a problem domain. It is important to recognize that the human mind does not normally think in terms of the binary, octal, and hexadecimal numbers used at the lowest levels of digital computing and processor instruction sets. Most people assess the world in terms of more continuous values, real numbers, fuzzy and imprecise reasoning, partitioning the world into separate elements, and making extensive use of metaphor in creating the semantics of their view of the world and in communicating it to other people. Indeed, models of knowledge representation in the field of artificial intelligence use what is called a *semantic network* to categorize both procedural and declarative knowledge. Like the semantic network, object-oriented design distributes the processing to be done across many independent software objects that relate to the project. Because people have many different criteria for viewing the world, they will also have different methods of partitioning a problem domain in order to better comprehend the information processing task and, eventually, the programming to be done.

Is there a *best way* to decompose a programming problem to minimize risk of error and maximize correctness, reliability, and run-time efficiency? Perhaps there is, but until software engineering matures to the extent that other fields of mathematics and engineering have, the exact means to calculate the most effective way to subdivide a problem domain will remain a research topic and not be readily known for some time. Already, trends in computing such as scientific parallel processing have expanded the programming envelope in ways that will keep computer theoreticians busy for years trying to quantify the computational properties of these systems, much less develop rigorous programming methodologies and models.

For the present and the foreseeable future, a great deal of software quality and maintainability can be grained by simply ensuring that the problem domain is partitioned in an *intuitive* manner that is in some obvious way an analog to a domain in the physical world. This is the basic idea of *object-oriented design* and, done correctly, offers a viable means of approaching even the largest software projects and managing the complexity of the programming by carefully delegating the programming logic among various *classes*, which become the blueprint for software *objects* that then interact to perform the desired computation. Distributing the programming logic and data structures in this way makes the overall software project more intelligible because the structure is in some way analogous to a tangible problem domain. In areas where the problem domain is more abstract, where there may not exist a real-world analogy, the exact design hierarchy becomes more subjective, but should still be done in a manner that furthers understanding.

The software design process requires that an engineer be able to specify details both *inside the classes* and the *interactions between classes*. To do this in a relatively complete and precise way that captures the *design intent* of the software engineer has come together in the Unified Modeling Language (UML) which is a first indication that software engineering as a formal discipline is coming of age. UML is an evolution toward a pervasive design standard.

SOFTWARE REVERSE ENGINEERING: A RATIONAL RESPONSE TO A LACK OF SYSTEMS DOCUMENTATION

Finding a way to distill the overall software structure of large project in the absence of any documentation has created, out of necessity, a subdiscipline of software engineering called *software reverse engineering*. Its practitioners (7) developed advanced lexical analysis software to examine source codes from earlier languages such as Fortran or C and they generated detailed reports showing the logical organization and dependencies between blocks of code. The immediate benefits of such an endeavor are to increase the maintainability of the software by knowing the proper places to add additional functionality.

The long-term goal is to be able to automatically migrate code based on procedural programming paradigms to object-oriented languages while retaining all of the functionality of the original code. Doing this via an algorithm in a manner that results in a class hierarchy which is both natural and intuitive to a human programmer who may wish to extend the source code is a serious undertaking. This is because software reverse engineering is, in essence, an attempt to automate what a human software designer would do when migrating legacy code to an object-oriented language, using various heuristics and statistics derived from the source code analysis to infer the most logical class hierarchy. Very advanced metrics must be used to determine the most appropriate reorganization of the code based on a search space involving call-graph path lengths, data structure usage patterns, or minimization of function call overhead. Even with such criteria, there is the risk that none of these may reveal the underlying semantic relationships conducive to an anthropocentrically well-ordered class hierarchy.

SCOPE OF SYSTEMS DOCUMENTATION

Software engineering is done at many levels of analysis. Therefore, different views of the software project are necessary in order to properly document it for the purposes of maintenance or future work. The following sections suggest some of the possible ways to view parts of a software project, after which there will be a brief introduction to the emerging standard for documentation methodologies, the Unified Modeling Language (UML).

MATHEMATICAL/ABSTRACT LEVEL OF SYSTEMS DOCUMENTATION

In terms of the microstructure of a software project, some of the most important and complex forms of software development are implementations of a more abstract mathematical representation of a domain. Applied mathematical computing such as scientific visualization or engineering analysis are examples of these. Implementations of these kinds of algorithms can sometimes lead to subtle errors in logic, rather than syntax, because the data structures involved in research computing can become very complex, with millions of such structures in memory, all of which may be sharing data with each other in order to compute a realistic solution to an already complex problem.

Hence, for maintainability of code that models sophisticated phenomena, there is the additional issue of ensuring that the software is not only well written and easy to understand but also the imperative to describe the mathematical foundations on which the code is based.

The intent is to convey to the programmer the algorithm in its most general way, which is usually a mathematical one. Advances in efficiency for this kind of programming are found at the abstract level, where modifications of the *algorithm itself* come from the research literature, rather than more efficient source code, or better compiler optimizations. Hence, before perusing actual code (which may not be easy to reverse engineer into its general aspects) constituting the algorithm, an exposure to the algorithm in its original mathematical form can be of use.

Example: Derivation of a Learning Algorithm

Below are excerpts from a neural network learning rule derivation to illustrate how mathematical models relate to the program which implements the algorithm. If a programmer is given the means to understand the mathematics *behind the programmed implementation*, then they are much better equipped to add extra functionality in the appropriate way as variations or improvements, or to create test cases to validate the correctness of the implementation. Such detail is not necessary in most programming assignments, but this representation of how the algorithm's key components were inferred will make it much more obvious why the program is structured in a particular way and in that sense constitutes admissible systems documentation.

Where possible, additional commentary is provided in italics that explains the implications for data structures and algorithms. the derivation is as follows:

For any node in the network, the weighted sum input into the *j*th node from *n* other nodes is

$$\text{net}_j = w_{j0} + \sum_{i=1}^{n} w_{ji}o_i.$$

This would tell the programmer that some manner of looping structure exists, as well as an array to hold numerical values. This is a good time to think about whether single precision or double-precision floating point should be used.

This is passed through a transfer function f_j to produce the *output* value for the *j*th node:

$$o_j = f_j(\text{net}_j).$$

Here, the programmer would know that some kind of separate routine could be used to compute the transfer function. An enterprising programmer might realize that this is an opportunity to add a choice of transfer functions to choose from or, seeing that an exponential is involved, might want to find ways of avoiding having to use a relatively slow routine, albeit with high accuracy. One solution might be to use a precomputed array of values, which would avoid having to repeatedly call the slow library function.

A *differentiable* transfer function makes it possible to adjust the weights according to the derivative of the transfer function and, therefore, is absolutely critical to resolving the limitations of perceptrons and the credit assignment problem. Note that the derivative of the sigmoid function is as follows:

$$f'_j(\text{net}_j) = f_j(\text{net}_j)[1 - f_j(\text{net}_j)].$$

This particular transfer function has an easy to compute derivative, which could also be stored in a large array as well.

Learning is accomplished by the changing of weights in the neural network. The change for a given weight should be proportional (α) to the contribution of that weight on the total error (E):

$$\Delta w_{ji} = -\alpha \frac{\partial E}{\partial w_{ji}} .$$

The learning algorithm also uses a parameter that adjusts the weight change, setting the learning rate.

[. . .]

Then, the amount to change the weight is given by

$$\Delta w_{ji} = -\alpha \delta_j o_i.$$

This tells the programmer that the weight change is proportional to the learning rate and the extent to which that weight contributed to the total computed error.

[. . .]

Hence, the "credit" for the jth node (an output) is

$$\delta_j = (t_j - o_j) f'_j(\text{net}_j).$$

This is one of the first dichotomies in the algorithm. The error is computed at the output nodes using the difference between the target pattern and the output the network has produced.

If the jth node is a hidden node, then the "credit" is defined by

$$\frac{\partial E}{\partial o_j} = \sum_k^{\kappa} \frac{\partial E}{\partial \text{net}_k} \frac{\partial \text{net}_k}{\partial o_j} = -\sum_k^{\kappa} \delta_k w_{kj},$$

$$\delta_j = f'_j(\text{net}_j) \sum_k^{\kappa} \delta_k w_{kj},$$

where $k-\kappa$ are the indices of nodes *to which* the jth nodes connect.

This is the second scenario, where the weight change is a function of the pre-viously computed error values in the subsequent layers.

To extend the basic algorithm, an *inertia* or *momentum* term can be added to smooth the weight changes over time. The weight-change equation is modified to include an inertia constant (γ) in the interval [0, 1]:

$$\Delta w_{ji}(t) = -\alpha\delta_j(t) + \gamma\Delta w_{ji}(t-1),$$
$$w_{ji}(t) = w_{ji}(t-1) + \Delta w_{ji}(t).$$

Other options cover special cases, such as biasing the derivative to speed conver-gence, thus avoiding cases where the derivative is exactly zero.

These offer additional options to consider in the design for future development.

The preceding derivation is an example of the additional knowledge that would be required to understand the structure of a program based on this algorithm and to extend or improve it. Because a computer program must necessarily make trade-offs from the mathematical ideal, some of the more subtle aspects of the algorithm will not be present in a computer implementation. So, documentation that discusses some algorithms at a very high level of abstraction will provide the generality required to extend the capability of the procedure in a way that retains its elegance and clean design.

DATA STRUCTURE DOCUMENTATION

Most programming involves an algorithm that acts on data structures which reside in memory or in a file. Often, the run-time efficiency and maintainability as well as extensi-bility of the computing algorithm is directly related to the choice of data structures used at the outset of the programming project.

A *data structure* is a representation of the logical relationship among individual elements of data. The data structures chosen sets the precedent for the organization, methods of access, degree of associativity, and processing alternatives for information. The organization and complexity of a data structure is based on the preferences of the designer and their logical breakdown of the software project class hierarchy. In an object-oriented programming project, data structures are usually documented in UML diagrams and in the source code itself. When perusing source code, naming conventions for identi-fiers that access data structures can be used to more easily imply what kind of informa-tion is held in the data structures, as shown in Table 1.

The following basic data structures form the building blocks of most constructs used in a computer program or class definitions for holding information to be processed.

Scalar Data Structures

Figure 2 is the simplest of data structures. A scalar item represents a single element of information that may be addressed by an identifier, meaning that the identifier refers to a single item at a particular location in memory. The size and format of a scalar item may vary within bounds defined by the programming language. A scalar can be a logical entity as small as 1 bit, or as large as 64 bits, or even a character string thousands of bytes long.

[scalar value]

FIGURE 2   A scalar can represent a character, integer, or floating-point data type.

These should be documented with a name that indicates its role as well as its data type. In that way, it is easier to infer what the identifier is and how it should be used. Constants should be in capital letters.

Sequential Vectors

Scalars organized into a list result in *sequential* vectors. Vectors are also known as (single-dimension) arrays, and allow indexing of information in the array (see Fig. 3). For example, vector [5] would access a particular scalar in the list; vector [4] would reference a different item in the same list.

Array Structures

Vectors arranged into an *n-dimensional space* of elements is an *array* (see Fig. 4). The most familiar example of an array is a two-dimensional matrix. If the data to be organized are richer in associativity, more indexes will be required, which reference data along different axes in the array.

Linked Lists

A linked list is a data structure that encapsulates noncontiguous scalars, vectors, or arrays into *nodes* that enables them to be processed as a list (see Fig. 5). Each node contains both the data structure being held and one or more *pointers* that indicate the memory address of the next node in the list. Because the pointers provide a level of indirection between nodes, insertion of an object at any point in the linked list is easily done by simply modifying the pointer of a node in the linked list to the new node and having the pointer in the new node point to the next item in the list. In contrast, inserting an item into a sequential vector, which does not use pointers, would require manually copying elements in the vector from one part of the array to the other in order to make room for the item to be inserted. For large vectors, this can be time-consuming and would indicate a bad design decision if a data need to be moved about often.

Summarizing Data Structures

Some documentation refers to the variables and data structures used by a particular segment of code. Usually, its purpose is to provide a more specific way of describing the algorithm than a mathematical description, but still independent of any particular computer language. Once the data structures are defined, then it is possible to write algo-

⟨[scalar value],[scalar value], . . . ,[scalar value]⟩

FIGURE 3   A vector data structure is built from a sequence of scalars.

$$\begin{bmatrix} [\text{scalar value}] \ldots [\text{scalar value}] \\ \vdots \qquad \ddots \qquad \vdots \\ [\text{scalar value}] \ldots [\text{scalar value}] \end{bmatrix}$$

FIGURE 4   Arrays can be *n* dimensional and are built from vectors.

rithms around these data structures to manipulate information. Often, the ease and efficiency of an algorithm implementation is determined by the data structures and types used to hold the information.

Thus, it is important to choose carefully the size and type of data structures that will hold the data to be processed, in order to ensure that the algorithm will be easy to maintain and extend, without requiring fundamental changes to the data structures. If structural changes are required in the future, incompatibilities with earlier versions will result, necessitating costly and time-consuming conversion utilities and customer support.

PSEUDOCODE LEVEL OF DESCRIPTION

In order to aid in conceptual understanding and to prevent major program restructuring later in development, many programmers will "sketch" their programs in *pseudocode*. Pseudocode is not a formal language by any means. It is a very generic, loose sort of *software colloquialism* that is used when describing how an algorithm is to work. Pseudocode is less precise than a mathematical specification of an algorithm and also not as well defined in terms of variable types, but it shows the *design intent* of the algorithm. Pseudocode is created by programmers en route to the highly structured code of an actual computer program, where both the program and its variables are explicitly stated.

In this example of pseudocode, the programmer is describing the algorithm which was derived in the section Example: Derivation of a Learning Algorithm.

The Multilayer Perceptron Algorithm in Pseudocode

The algorithm for the multilayer perceptron that implements the back-propagation training rule is shown below. It requires the units to have thresholding nonlinear functions that are continuously differentiable (i.e., smooth everywhere). We have assumed the use of the sigmoid function,

$$f(\text{net}) = \frac{1}{1 + e^{-k\,\text{net}}}$$

because it has a simple derivative.

$$\langle [\text{scalar value}\langle\text{pointer}\rangle], [\text{scalar value}\langle\text{pointer}\rangle], \ldots, \\ [\text{scalar value}\langle\text{unused pointer}\rangle] \rangle$$

FIGURE 5   A linked list uses pointers to "point to" the next item in the list.

Learning Algorithm

1. Initialize weights and thresholds: Set all weights and thresholds to small random values.

2. Present input and desired output: Present input $X_p = x_0, x_1, x_2, \ldots, x_{n-1}$ and target output $T_p = t_0, t_1, t_2, \ldots t_{m-1}$, where n is the number of input nodes and m is the number of output nodes. Set w_0 to be be $-\theta$, the bias, and x_0 to be always 1.

   For pattern association, X_p and T_p represent the patterns to be associated. For classification, T_p is set to zero except for one element set to 1 that corresponds to the class that X_p is in.

3. Calculate the actual output. Each layer calculates:

$$y_{pj} = f\left[\sum_{i=0}^{n-1} w_i x_i\right]$$

   and passes that as input to the next layer. The final layer outputs values o_{pj}

4. Adapt weights: Start from the output layer, and work backward:

$$w_{ij}(t + 1) = w_{ij}(t) + \eta\delta_{pj}o_{pj},$$

   where $w_{ij}(t)$ represents the weights from node i to node j at time t, η is a gain term, and δ_{pj} is an error term for pattern p on node j.
   For output units,

$$\delta_{pj} = ko_{pj}(1 - o_{pj})(t_{pj} - o_{pj})$$

   For hidden units,

$$\delta_{pj} = ko_{pj}(1 - o_{pj}) \sum_{k} \delta_{pk}w_{jk}$$

   where the sum is over the k nodes in the layer above the node.

SOURCE CODE LEVEL OF SYSTEMS DOCUMENTATION

Documentation within source code helps increase comprehension when immersed in the microstructure of a software project. Comments interspersed throughout the source files can be of immense value when another software engineer must quickly familiarize himself with the routines that comprise a software project.

Every file that contains source code should be documented with an introductory comment that provides information on the file name and its contents. All files must include contact and copyright information. Every function should be preceded with descriptive comments regarding its role and purpose and any other relevant maintenance information.

Source code documentation should be consise and brief, explaining any aspects that may not be immediately obvious. By properly choosing names for variables, functions, and classes and by properly structuring the code, there is less need for comments withing the code. A suggested notation is provided in Table 1.

With C++, comments in *include files* are meant for the *users of classes*, while comments in *implementation files* are meant for those who *maintain the classes*.

TABLE 1   Example of a Variable Prefix and Naming Convention

Prefix	Data type
b	BOOL (Boolean: 0 or 1, TRUE or FALSE)
by	BYTE, or unsigned char
c	char
cx, cy	integer used as x or y length, c stands for "count"
dw	DWORD (double word; unsigned long)
g_	Variable global in scope
h	Handle or event handler
l	LONG
n	Integer: "n"teger
p	pointer
str	string
sz	string terminated by 0 byte (null terminated string)
w	WORD (unsigned short)
m_	member variable of a class
CONSTANT	Constants should be declared using all uppercase

Documentation of a C++ Source Code File

```
//
//   File:              backprop.cc
//   Description:       backpropagation neural net learning algorithm
//   Revision:          A
//   Created:           Monday November 20, 2000, 12:30:14
//   Author:            Sanjay Singh
//   E-Mail:            ssingh@area51.uwaterloo.ca
//   Phone:             519.888.4567 Ext: 6165
//
//   Copyright 2000     University of Waterloo
//                      200 University Avenue
//                      Waterloo ON N2L3G1
//                      Canada
//
//   The copyright to the computer program(s) herein
//   is the property of the University of Waterloo.
//   The program(s) may be used and/or copied only with
//   the written permission of the University of Waterloo
//   or in accordance with the terms and conditions
//   stipulated in the agreement/contract under which
//   the program(s) have been supplied.
//
```

Strategic and Tactical Comments in Source Code

In-line comments are often said to be either *strategic* or *tactical*. A strategic comment describes what a function or section of code is intended to do and is placed before this code. A tactical comment describes what a single line of code is intended to do and is placed, if possible, at the end of this line. Unfortunately, too many tactical comments can make code unreadable. For this reason, it is recommended that a programmer primarily use strategic comments, unless trying to explain very complicated code, which necessitates tactical comments for greater clarity.

Example of strategic and tactical comments (in italics):

```
//  strategic comment goes in this space, before the function
int ComplicatedFunction( int i )
{
     int index = i++ + ++i * i-- - --i; // tactical comment goes here
     return index;
}
```

Java and Generation of Online Documentation

The Java language supports three kinds of comments (8), regular C-style comments, Java-specific documentation comments, and C++ style comments.

In this example, the compiler ignores everything between /* and */. This is identical to the C programming language:

```
/* put your comments here */
```

The following is a *documentation comment*. The Java compiler also ignores this kind of comment. However, the *javadoc* tool that comes with the Java Development Kit (JDK) uses these comments when preparing automatically generated on-line documentation, suitable for viewing with a browser.

```
/** documentation comment that will be used by javadoc */
```

Finally, there is the standard comment delimiter used in C++ that is also usable in Java:

```
// this is a good way to do a quick 1 line comment
```

For more information on javadoc, a visit to the Sun Microsystems (9) website would be the authoritative place for the current standard.

PROJECT ORGANIZATION LEVEL OF SYSTEMS DOCUMENTATION

When a manager leaves the details of the source code behind and considers the many files that constitute a typical program, an overall picture of how the different modules of the program link together emerges.

This view comprises the total application and is needed in order to easily comprehend the relationship of the program components to each other. Stated more simply, the emphasis shifts from what is inside each file or routine to the *organization of the project files* and also *how the routines and classes interact* with one another, as shown in Figure 6.

In this way, parts of the program can be improved, independently of others, and the related issues of program design and maintainability can be properly regulated. Program routines pass information to each other via variables, and the purpose behind organization levels of systems documentation is to ensure that information transfer is easily trackable and variables are passing only the correct values to other parts of the program. At this level, function arguments and return values are to be clearly documented, so that

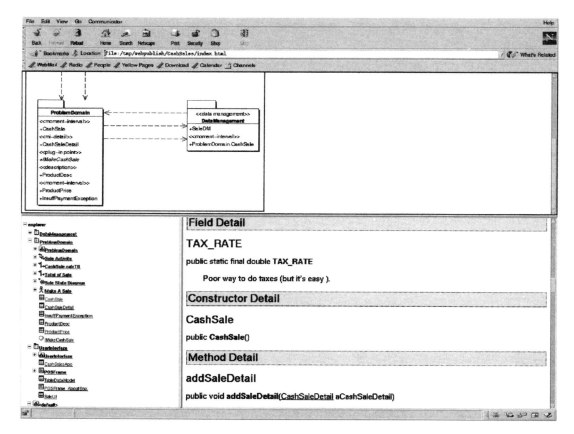

FIGURE 6   Systems documentation generated by the Together Enterprise UML tool, showing project structure.

other programmers can properly use this functionality, without being mired down in the details of how the routine is actually written.

For the largest and most complex projects, information not only moves between the different parts of the program but also into and out of the boundaries of the software project. For example, software can interact with CORBA middleware, Java applets or servlets, IP services, SQL, or HTTP servers. This is especially true if software components or libraries of routines are used which come from the Java Development Kit (JDK) API (10) because of its extensive support for a broad range of technologies. In cases such as these, source code to these libraries are often not available or too voluminous to go through, but calling usage conventions and return values are provided so that they can be *used* properly.

Leveraging third-party class libraries rather than creating this functionality from scratch is the norm, especially in graphical programming, where programs use the routines and services provided by the operating system or run-time system in order to interact with the user and to communicate with peripherals. This trend is part of the mandate of object-oriented software design, which advocates reusing software components that have the required basic functionality and then customizing through inheritance or polymorphism as needed.

However, in order to isolate problems and find solutions in situations when a manager does not have complete control over the design of the software, project level documentation can be a valuable aid in software quality assurance and in reducing the workload of the programmers by being able to use already existing code.

UNIFIED MODELING LANGUAGE: A MODERN SYNTHESIS OF SYSTEMS DOCUMENTATION CONCEPTS AND METHODOLOGIES

Effective management of large-scale software projects requires a notation that allows the rigorous specification of the design and implementation of a software project. The emergence of the Unified Modeling Language (UML) is a convergence of ideas from Grady Booch (11) (Booch methodology), Dr. Ivar Jacobsen (12) (objectory process), and Dr. James Rumbaugh (13) (OMT methodology).

The result is the UML becoming the *de facto* standard language (14) for specification, visualizing, constructing, and documenting the artifacts of software systems. UML is the common nomenclature for business analysts, software designers, and programmers to use when designing *software blueprints*. The diagrams in the subsequent sections were created with Together Enterprise, a multiplatform UML modeling tool written in Java, from Togethersoft (15).

Unified Modeling Language is applicable to object-oriented problem-solving. Anyone interested in learning UML should be familiar with the underlying philosophy of object-oriented modeling and problem solving, as discussed in the section Object-Oriented Software Design.

Unified Modeling Language begins with the construction of a model. A software model is an abstraction of the underlying problem that captures the information flow between objects in order to implement a solution to an information processing problem. The *domain* is the actual world from which the problem comes. Models consist of software *objects* that interact by sending each other *messages*, upon which the objects then act. This is usually done within an *event-driven* run-time environment, where messages can be received from outside of the software project as well. Objects have things they know and internal data structures, called *attributes*, and things they can do, referred to as *behaviors*, *operations*, or *methods*. The values of an object's attributes determine its *state*. Classes are the *templates* for objects. A class wraps attributes (data) and behaviors (methods or functions) into a single distinct entity. Objects are *instances* of classes.

Unified Modeling Language makes possible the complete specification of a software system at many levels of abstraction and relates the different aspects of the design so that a comprehensive and complete picture emerges that shows the way toward an implementation that fulfills the requirements of the software project.

Use Case Diagrams

Use case diagrams describe what a system does from the standpoint of an external observer, called an *actor* (see Fig. 7). An actor is *who* or *what* initiates the events involved in that task. Actors are simply roles that people or objects play. In most cases, the actor

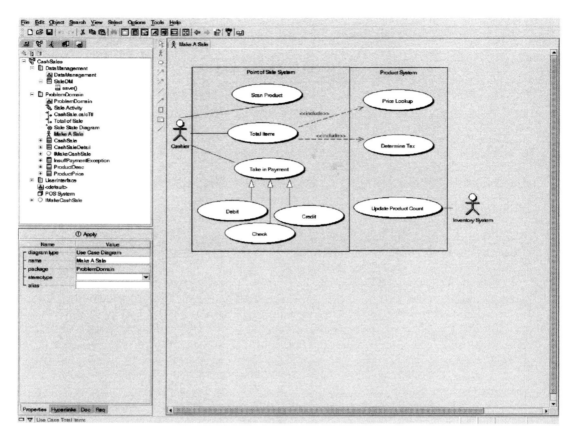

FIGURE 7   A use case diagram enumerates the main high-level interactions between users.

is a person, such as an end user. However, it is important to note that an actor can, in some situations, be another software system, with a well-defined set of interactions with the system under construction. Examples of actors as software would include the operating system, Internet services, or a database system.

With use case diagrams, though, the emphasis is on *what a system does* rather than the specifics of how it is to be done. In that sense, the use case diagram enumerates the user-level interactions, thus showing the way toward the content that would be required in *user documentation* in projects where there is an interaction between an actor and software.

A use case diagram is a collection of actors, use cases, and their communications. Actors are represented by stick figures. Use cases are shown by ovals. Communications are lines that link actors to use cases. Note that a single use case can have *multiple* actors.

Use case diagrams also play an important role in *setting the agenda* for the software design itself because they specify the set of interactions that define the *functional requirements* of the system. Ideally, these requirements will be fulfilled by the software design when it is complete.

The finer algorithmic and data structure details implied by each scenario are best specified by other UML diagrams, but their general aspects should be captured in the use case diagram.

Use case diagrams are helpful in the following areas:

- Determining features (requirements). New use cases often generate new requirements as the system is analyzed and the design takes shape.
- Communicating with clients. Their notational simplicity makes use case diagrams a good way for developers to communicate with clients.
- Generating test cases. The collection of scenarios for a use case may suggest a suite of test cases for those scenarios.
- Preparing user documentation. The use cases may also show the procedures that should be documented for a user manual.
- User interface design (16). Diligent consideration of the logical groupings of the user interactions can assist with a clean, consistent, and intuitive graphical user-interface design.

Class Diagrams

A class diagram gives an overview of a system by showing its classes and the relationships among them. Class diagrams are static, meaning they display *what interacts* but *not what happens when they do interact*. (See Figure 8.)

Unified Modeling Language class notation is a rectangle divided into three parts: class name, attributes, and operations. Names of abstract classes (classes with method signatures but *no implementation*; to be provided in subclasses) are in italics. Relationships between classes are the connecting links.

Three kinds of relationship between classes are possible:

- *Association*: a relationship between instances of the two classes. There is an association between two classes if an instance of one class must know about the other in order to perform its work. In a diagram, an association is a link connecting two classes.
- *Aggregation*: an association in which one class belongs to a collection. An aggregation has a diamond end pointing to the part containing the whole. In our diagram, Order has a collection of OrderDetails.
- *Generalization*: an inheritance link indicating one class is a superclass of the other. A generalization has a triangle pointing to the superclass.

Every class diagram has classes, associations, and multiplicities. Navigability and roles are optional items placed in a diagram to provide clarity. Table 2 gives the most common multiplicities.

Package and Object Diagrams

To simplify complex class diagrams, classes can be grouped into *packages*. A package is a collection of logically related UML elements.

Packages appear as rectangles with small tabs at the top (see Fig. 9). The package name is on the tab or inside the rectangle. Any dotted arrows would indicate dependencies. One package depends on another if changes in the other could possibly force changes in the first.

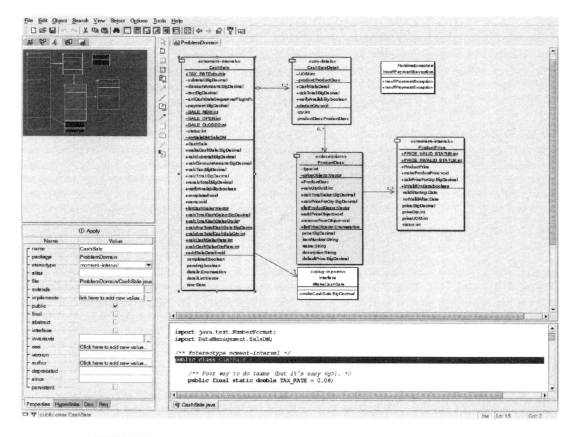

FIGURE 8   A UML class diagram shows the static structure between classes.

Object diagrams, which are related to package and class diagrams, show instances instead of classes. They are useful for explaining small pieces with complicated relationships, especially recursive relationships.

Each rectangle in the object diagram corresponds to a single instance. Instance names are underlined in UML diagrams. Class or instance names may be omitted from object diagrams as long as the diagram meaning is still clear.

TABLE 2   Multiplicities and Their Meanings

Multiplicities	Meaning
0..1	Zero or one instance. The notation n . . m indicates n to m instances.
0..* or *	No limit on the number of instances (including none)
1	Exactly one instance
1..*	At least one instance

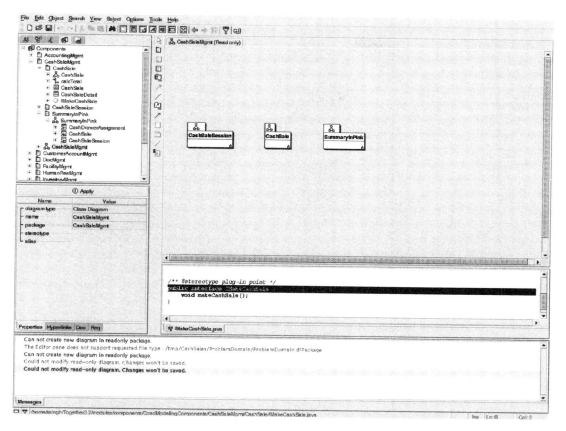

FIGURE 9   A simple package diagram illustrating the logical grouping of classes for a project.

Interaction Diagrams: Sequence and Collaboration Diagrams

Class and object diagrams are *static* model views. Interaction diagrams are *dynamic*. They describe how objects collaborate. A *sequence diagram* is an interaction diagram that details how operations are carried out, and what messages are sent and when (see Fig. 10). Sequence diagrams are organized according to time. The time progresses as one goes down the page. The objects involved in the operation are listed from left to right according to when they take part in the message sequence.

Each vertical dotted line is a *lifeline*, representing the time that an object exists. Each arrow is a message call. An arrow goes from the sender to the top of the activation bar of the message on the receiver's lifeline. The activation bar represents the duration of execution of the message.

Collaboration diagrams are also a form of interaction diagram. They convey the same information as sequence diagrams, but they focus on object roles instead of the times that messages are sent. In a sequence diagram, object roles are the vertices and messages are the connecting links.

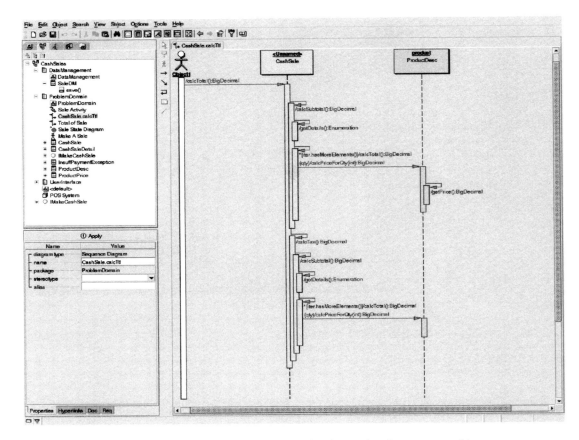

FIGURE 10   A sequence diagram illustrating interactions between two objects.

State Chart Diagrams

Objects have *behaviors* and *internal states*. The state of an object depends on its current activity or condition. (For an introduction to state machines, see Ref. 17.) A *statechart diagram* (or simply a *state diagram*) shows the possible states of the object and the transitions that cause a change in the states of the object.

        States are diagrammed as rounded rectangles. Transitions are represented by arrows from one state to another. Events or conditions that trigger transitions are written beside the arrows. The initial state (black circle) is a proxy entry point to the state machine. Final states are also proxy states that terminate the action.

Activity Diagrams

An activity diagram is a modern reimplementation of the historical *flowchart*. Activity diagrams and statechart diagrams are related. Whereas a statechart diagram focuses attention on an object undergoing a process (or on a process as an object), an activity diagram focuses on the *flow of activities* involved in a single process. The activity diagram shows the how those activities depend on one another. (See Figure 12.)

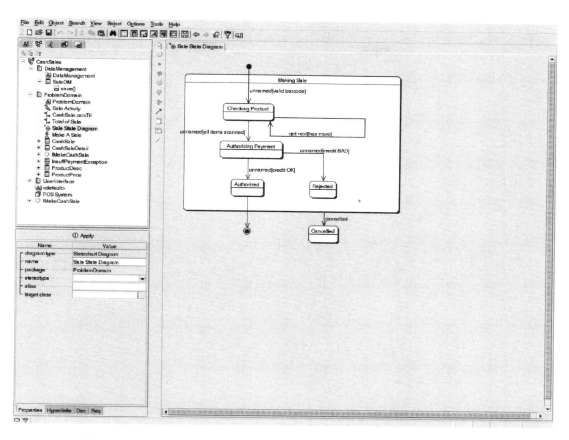

FIGURE 11   A state diagram models algorithms at a fundamental level within a class.

Activity diagrams can be divided into *object swimlanes* that determine what object is responsible for which activity. A single transition comes out of each activity, connecting it to the next activity.

A transition may branch into two or more mutually exclusive transitions. Guard expressions (inside [ ]) label the transitions coming out of a branch. A branch and its subsequent merge marking the end of the branch appear in the diagram as hollow diamonds.

A transition may fork into two or more parallel activities. The fork and the subsequent join of the threads coming out of the fork appear in the diagram as solid bars.

Component and Deployment Diagrams

A *component* is a code module. Component diagrams are physical analogs of class diagrams. Deployment diagrams show the physical configurations of software and hardware.

The deployment diagram in Figure 13 shows the relationships between software and hardware components involved in a point-of-sale system. The physical hardware is

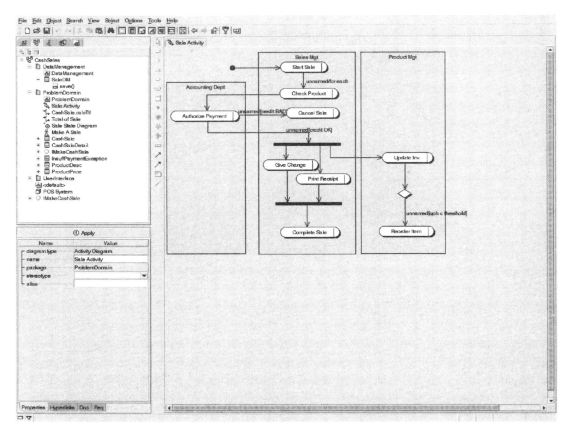

FIGURE 12   An activity diagram is a flowchart with *swimlanes* that chronicles the interactions among several classes.

made up of nodes. Each software component is mapped to node to indicate where it will eventually run.

CONCLUSIONS AND FUTURE DIRECTIONS

The fields of computer science and software engineering involve the study and application of data structures and algorithms. The research aspect of algorithms concerns itself with exploring the properties of a particular model of computation and determining the quantitative properties of various standard algorithms, such as their resource requirements, and scalability to large amounts of data. The applied field of software engineering teaches people to apply the current methodologies of software design requirements, along with maintenance issues, correctness criteria, performance metrics, and reliability assessments. There is some overlap between the research and application aspects of software engineering, and the two fields complement one another.

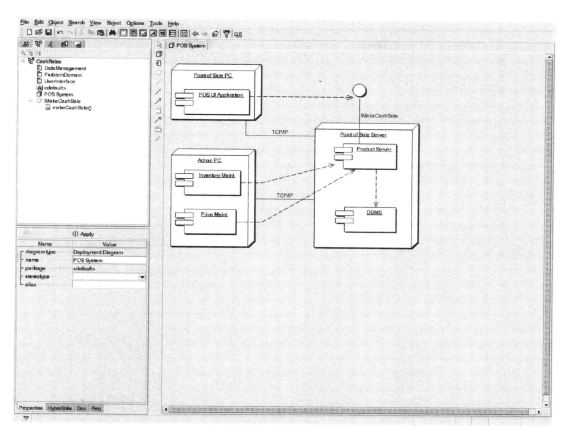

FIGURE 13   A deployment diagram for a point-of-sale system.

Software engineering is qualitatively different from other engineering disciplines because the laws governing its design and quality assessments are entirely abstract constructs. In that sense, it has more in common with mathematics. However, software design is still a new discipline relative to other fields of mathematics and engineering. The standards and methodologies to ensure that software will perform reliably have not been officially defined, because unlike a mathematical proof, it is not practical to test the software under all possible scenarios to provide a rigorous assurance of design integrity. Therefore, well-managed software projects will include a standardized design and documentation system as part of an overall proactive risk management strategy that will facilitate easy change and maintenance to evolve the software to a more perfect level of refinement in an iterative fashion.

The qualities of correctness, reliability, maintainability, and robustness (18) must continue to be strived for within the context of object-oriented software development. If this is done at many levels of a project, both in *process* and *product* assessments, computer systems can be deployed in more mission-critical (19) areas to enhance the quality of life for all members of society in a new era of ubiquitious computing. Software design, engineering, analysis, and documentation will remain important computer science and software engineering topics for the foreseeable future. For its part, systems documentation will continue to play a critical role in the design and maintenance of information systems as software development methodologies continue to be refined and perfected.

REFERENCES

1. Object Management Group, Unified Modeling Language Resource Page, http://www.omg.org/uml
2. T. O'Reilly and E. Dyson, "The Open Source Revolution" http://www.edventure.com/release1/1198.html
3. NASA Structural Analysis Branch homepage: http://www.lerc.nasa.gov/WWW/sab4320/
4. D. Wood, *Theory of Computation*, John Wiley & Sons, New York, 1987, pp. 280–337.
5. S. Singh, "User Documentation" in *Encyclopedia of Computer Science & Technology*, edited by A. Kent and J. G. Williams, Marcel Dekker, Inc., New York, 19XX, Vol. 41, Suppl. 26, p. 272.
6. S. Singh, "User Documentation," in *Encyclopedia of Computer Science & Technology*, edited by A. Kent and J. G. Williams, Marcel Dekker, Inc., New York, 19XX, Vol. 41, Suppl. 26, pp. 270–272.
7. K. Kontogiannis, "From Legacy Code to Modern Architecture," http://www.swen.uwaterloo.ca/~kostas/cser-desc.html
8. M. Campione and K. Walrath, *The Java Tutorial*, Addison-Wesley/Longman, Boston, 1996.
9. Sun Microsystems website. http://www.sun.com/forte/ffj/ce/features.html
10. P. Chan, *The Java Developer's Almanac*, Addison-Wesley/Longman, Boston, 1998.
11. Rational Software website: http://www.rational.com/university/rubios.jsp#booch
12. Rational Software website: http://www.rational.com/university/rubios.jsp#jacobson
13. Rational Software website: http://www.rational.com/university/rubios.jsp#rumbaugh
14. G. Booch, et al., "The Unified Modeling Language User Guide" Addison Wesley Longman 1999.
15. Togethersoft website: http://www.togethersoft.com. Screen shots used with permission.
16. R. S. Pressman, *Software Engineering: A Practitioner's Approach*, McGraw-Hill, New York, 1992, pp. 457–479.
17. D. Wood, *Theory of Computation*, John Wiley & Sons, New York, 1987, pp. 95–110.
18. C. Ghezzi, et al., *Fundamentals of Software Engineering*, Prentice-Hall, Englewood Cliffs, NJ, 1991, p. 19.
19. They Write the Right Stuff: http://www.fastcompany.com/online/06/writestuff.html

SANJAY SINGH

VISUAL INFORMATION QUERYING

INTRODUCTION

Computers have become our companions in many of the activities we pursue in our life. They assist us, in particular, in searching relevant information that is needed to perform a variety of tasks, from professional usage to personal entertainment. They hold this information in a huge number of heterogeneous sources, either dedicated to a specific user community (e.g., enterprise databases) or maintained for the general public (e.g., websites and digital libraries). Whereas progress in basic information technology is nowadays capable of guaranteeing effective information management, information retrieval and dissemination has become a core issue that needs further accomplishments to achieve user satisfaction. The research communities in databases, information retrieval, information visualization, and human–computer interaction have already largely investigated these domains. However, the technical environment has so dramatically evolved in recent years, inducing a parallel and very significant evolution in user habits and expectations, that new approaches are definitely needed to meet current demand.

One of the most evident and significant changes is the human–computer interaction paradigm. Traditional interactions relayed on programming to express user information requirements in formal code and on textual output to convey to users the information extracted by the system. Except for professional data-intensive application frameworks, still in the hands of computer specialists, we have basically moved away from this pattern both in terms of expressing information requests and conveying results. The new goal is direct interaction with the final user (the person who is looking for information and is not necessarily familiar with computer technology). The key motto to achieve this is "go visual." The well-known high bandwidth of the human-vision channel allows both recognition and understanding of large quantities of information in no more than a few seconds. Thus, for instance, if the result of an information request can be organized as a visual display, or a sequence of visual displays, the information throughput is immensely superior to the one that can be achieved using textual support. User interaction becomes an iterative query–answer game that very rapidly leads to the desired final result. Conversely, the system can provide efficient visual support for easy query formulation. Displaying a visual representation of the information space, for instance, lets users directly point at the information they are looking for, without any need to be trained into the complex syntax of current query languages. Alternatively, users can navigate in the information space, following visible paths that will lead them to the targeted items. Again, thanks to the visual support, users are able to easily understand how to formulate queries and they are likely to achieve the task more rapidly and less prone to errors than with traditional textual interaction modes.

The two facets of "going visual" are usually referred to as visual query systems, for query formulation, and information visualization, for result display. Visual Query

Systems (VQSs) are defined as systems for querying databases that use a visual representation to depict the domain of interest and express related requests. VQSs provide both a language to express the queries in a visual format and a variety of functionalities to facilitate user–system interaction. As such, they are oriented toward a wide spectrum of users, especially novices who have limited computer expertise and generally ignore the inner structure of the accessed database.

Information visualization, an increasingly important subdiscipline within the field of Human–Computer Interaction (HCI) (1), focuses on visual mechanisms designed to communicate clearly to the user the structure of information and improve on the cost of accessing large data repositories. In printed form, information visualization has included the display of numerical data (e.g., bar charts, plot charts, pie charts), combinatorial relations (e.g., drawings of graphs), and geographic data (e.g., encoded maps) (2–4). In addition to these "static" displays, computer-based systems, such as the Information Visualizer (5) and Dynamic Queries (6), have coupled powerful visualization techniques (e.g., 3D, animation) with near real-time interactivity (i.e., the ability of the system to respond quickly to the user's direct manipulation commands). Information visualization is tightly combined with querying capabilities in some recent database-centered approaches (7–9). More opportunities for information visualization in a database environment may be found today in data mining and data warehousing applications, which typically access large data repositories. The enormous quantity of information sources on the World-Wide Web (WWW) available to users with diverse capabilities also calls for visualization techniques [see, for instance, the ACM report on Strategic Directions in HCI (1), the reports of the "FADIVA" Working Group (10), and the work presented in Refs. 11 and 12].

In this article, we survey the main features and main proposals for visual query systems and touch upon the visualization of results mainly discussing traditional visualization forms. A discussion of modern database visualization techniques may be found elsewhere (13). Many related articles by Daniel Keim are available at http://www.informatik.uni-halle.de/dbs/publications.html.

VISUAL QUERY SYSTEMS

One of the most compelling mandates for any kind of interactive system is aiming the interaction at the user who will work with the system, rather than at the system itself [by "user," we refer in this article to the "end user" (i.e., the person working with the VQS)]. The system should be tailored to help users in performing the tasks they have in mind. Therefore, the characteristics of the classes of users that will be working with a particular interface and the tasks such users need to perform should be well understood.

The purpose of VQSs is to provide access to the information contained in a database. The main users' tasks are understanding the database content, focusing on meaningful items, finding query patterns, and reasoning on the query result. These tasks require specific techniques to be effectively accomplished, and such techniques involve typical activities such as pointing, browsing, filtering, and zooming. Consequently, we can say that a visual user interface is the most adequate for the above tasks, at least from the user's point of view (see also Ref. 14).

It is worth noting that most people interacting with computers see only the system interface. Thus, interfaces are a very important component of a software system from the design phase onward. This is in contrast with the old-fashioned developmental approach, where the interface was considered only from an aesthetic point of view and therefore was added only at the last stage of the system development.

Recently, the growth of database users, both expert and novice, has led to the development of a number of interfaces based on different principles whose main purpose is to facilitate human–computer interaction. One of the most interesting approaches is based on using *direct manipulation* languages (15), characterized by both the visibility of objects of interest and the replacement of a command language syntax by the direct manipulation of displayed objects. Such an interaction style is widely used in existing commercial interfaces. In fact, the availability of low-cost graphical devices has given rise in recent years to a widespread diffusion of products that have gained popularity due to their increased visual content. A rapid visual feedback, another feature of direct manipulation interfaces, provides evaluative information for every executed user action. Several authors singled out a number of usability features that can be obtained with direct manipulation visual techniques:

- Shorter distance between the user's mental model of reality and the representation of such reality proposed by the computer
- Reduced dependency on the native language of the user
- Ease in learning of the basic functionality of the interaction
- High efficiency rate obtained also by expert users, partly because of the possibility of defining new functions and features
- Significant reduction in the error rate (16)

Direct manipulation is successfully used in conjunction with windows, icons, menus, and pointers in the so-called WIMP (Window, Icon, Menu, Pointer) interfaces (17), where metaphors are also adopted to increase the initial familiarity between users and computer applications (18). Once WIMP interfaces are designed for querying databases, the query language operators have to be rendered in terms of appropriate direct manipulation sequences. Such sequences cannot be applied on the formal data model concepts, but on a proper external *representation* of such concepts, which must be easily perceived by the user (see also Ref. 9). As such, the representation has to be close to the reality in which the user lives. When the chosen representation is visual, we can say that we are in the presence of a *visual query language* (VQL). VQLs are the languages implemented by VQSs.

CLASSIFICATION CRITERIA FOR VQSs

In this section, we introduce criteria for a VQS taxonomy that may help readers understand the differences among the many VQSs that have been recently proposed in the literature. A first attempt to classify query languages dates back to 1981: The criterion adopted was *ease-of-use* and referred to human factors only (19). A few years later, another taxonomy was proposed (20), separating traditional from new-generation query languages, where the use of more senses for the interaction is the main distinguishing factor between the two classes. In this study, all query languages are evaluated on the basis of two dimensions: functional capabilities and usability. The former is related to both the language power (how much a user can do with the language) and the alternatives the user has for output presentation. The latter is related to the query formulation effort (i.e., the user's effort to work with the system).

We concentrate specifically on VQSs, not including textual query languages in this survey. We classify VQSs according to two criteria. The first one is the *visual representation* that the VQS adopts to present the reality of interest, the applicable language operators, and the query result. The query representation is generally dependent on the data-base representation, because the way in which the query operands (i.e., data in the database) are presented constrains the query representation. For example, given a query on a relational database, we may state the query in terms of several representations (e.g., filling some fields in tables visualizing the relations, or following paths in a hypergraph that visualizes the relational schema). In this case, the table and the hypergraph are two possible representations associated with the relational database. Therefore, we will consider a unique classification schema for both database and query representations. Based on such a schema, VQSs are organized into four classes depending on the adopted visual formalism: form, diagram, icon, or a combination of them. On the other hand, the visual representation used to display the query result can be different from the database representation, giving rise to a different classification. This is mainly due to the fact that what is visualized for the query purpose most often is the schema of the database, whereas the actual database instances constitute the query result to be displayed to the user.

The second criterion for the proposed VQS classification refers to the *interaction strategies* provided to retrieve data. Data retrieval through interaction with a VQS is usually accomplished through the following two main activities:

1. *Understanding the reality of interest.* The goal of this activity is the precise identification of the fragment of the schema to which the query refers. Generally, the schema is much richer than the subset of concepts that are involved in the query. The result of this step is a query subschema (i.e., the static representation of all schema items that are needed to solve the query).

2. *Formulating the query.* The query subschema can be manipulated in several ways, according to which query operators are provided. The goal of query formulation is to formally express the operations and operands that eventually make up the query.

Visual Representations

Form-based representations are the simplest way to provide users with friendly interfaces for data manipulation. They are very common as application or system interfaces to relational databases, where the forms are actually a visualization of the tables. In query formulation, prototypical forms are visualized for users to state the query by filling appropriate fields. In systems such as QBE (21), only the intensional part of relations is shown: The user fills the extensional part to provide an example of the requested result. The system retrieves whatever matches the example. In more recent form-based representations, the user can manipulate both the intensional and the extensional part of the database. (See Figure 1.)

Diagrammatic representations are also widely used in existing systems. Typically, diagrams represent data structures displayed using visual elements that correspond to the various types of concepts available in the underlying data model. Diagrammatic representations adopt as typical query operators the selection of elements, the traversal on adjacent elements, and the creation of a bridge among disconnected elements. (See Figure 2.)

Iconic representations use icons to denote both the objects of the database and the

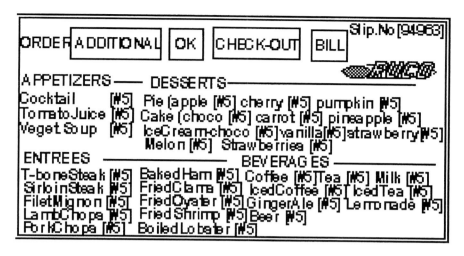

FIGURE 1   Example of form-based representation in EMBS. (From Ref. 22.)

operations to be performed on them. (See Figure 3.) A query is expressed primarily by combining operand and operator icons. For example, icons may be vertically combined to denote conjunction (logical AND) and horizontally combined to denote disjunction (logical OR) (24). In order to be effective, the proposed set of icons should be easily and intuitively understandable by most people. The need for users to memorize the semantics of the icons makes the approach manageable only for somehow limited sets of icons.

The *hybrid* representation is a combination of the above representations. Often, diagrams are used to describe the database schema, whereas icons are used either to

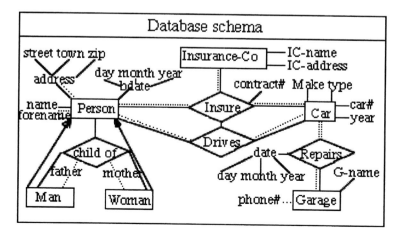

FIGURE 2   Example of diagrammatic representation. (From Ref. 23.)

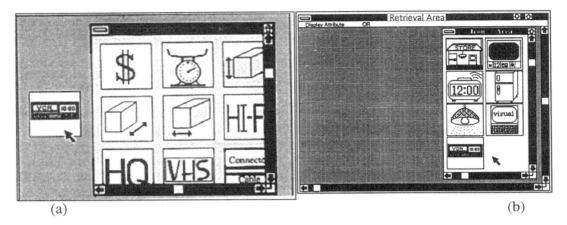

(a)   (b)

FIGURE 3   Example of iconic representation. (From Ref. 4.)

represent specific prototypical objects or to indicate actions to be performed. Forms are mainly used for displaying the query result.

All of the above representations present complementary advantages and disadvantages. In traditional VQSs, still the majority of existing VQSs, only one type of representation is available to the user. More modern approaches aim at supporting multiparadigm interfaces. As an example of this trend, we briefly describe the main features of a system that is a good representative for this trend, the VENUS project (25).

The main idea in VENUS is to allow different classes of users to access multiple, heterogeneous databases by means of a uniform interface. The most notable VENUS features are the following:

- The existence of a common formalism, named the Graph Model (26), which, in principle, is sufficiently abstract to represent database schemata expressed in any of the most common data models as well as most frequently used visual representations. The Graph Model is equipped with suitable constraints to better organize the presentation of the query result.
- The definition of a set of elementary graphical actions (such as selection of nodes and drawing of edges), called graphical primitives, having a clear semantics and in terms of which more complex visual interaction mechanisms may be defined.
- The precise definition of suitable translations among different representations in terms of both database content and visual interaction mechanisms.
- The construction and management of an effective user model that allows the system to propose the most appropriate visual representation according to the user's skill and needs.

On one hand, the Graph Model is powerful enough to express the semantics of most of the common data models, so it is suitable as a unifying canonical model. The user is thus oblivious to the existence of the underlying databases and need not be concerned with their specific storage formats or query languages. On the other hand, the semantics of the query operations as expressed in the various representations is uniformly defined in terms of the graphical primitives, so the user can change visual representation during the query formulation. As the user can switch among different visual representations while formulating the query, it is also possible to switch when visualizing the result produced by query execution. Again, several representations are available, and the one used to display the query result can be different from the one used in the query phase.

Examples of other similar approaches aiming at providing users with multiple visual representations and possibly generating the most effective one are DARE (27), OPOSSUM (9), and DOODLE (28). The idea of the graphical presentation module originated from a pioneering system for information display, which automatically draws graphical presentations of information (29).

Result Visualization

Similar to most graphical user interfaces, the VQSs that have been developed so far have mainly stressed the user input aspects of the interaction and have given little thought to the visualization of output data. The results are usually presented by means of structured text, without considering other possible display formats. Conversely, an appropriate visualization of the query result allows the user to better capture the relationships among the output data.

Under *form-based* visualization, we enclose all systems that show the result organized in tables, or more generally in lists that can easily be scrolled. This class contains most of current VQSs, because the table is the typical representation of the relational model. As an example, QBD* (30) presents the query results as relational tables in a compact form, by visualizing only distinct values (31). Useless and sometimes confusing duplication of values are avoided (see Fig. 4), and the user can request to visualize all attribute values at any moment, by a simple click of the mouse.

With reference to *diagram-based* techniques, we use the word diagram with a broad meaning, referring to any graphics that encodes information by using the position and shape of geometrical objects. Several kinds of diagram are used by the different VQSs also to visualize the query result. Some VQSs (e.g., Ref. 32) show the query result through the same kind of graph used for formulating the query, by filling graph nodes with appropriate values. AMAZE is one of the very few VQSs employing 3D graphs (33). The data are shown as a 3D snapshot of the *n*-dimensional results. Different meth-

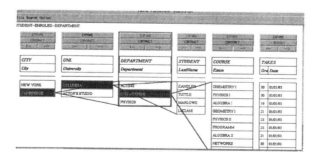

FIGURE 4   Example of form-based visualization.

ods of result visualization are also planned to be available to the user. One of these employs tree structures, based on the cone-tree approach (5). Powerful result visualizations are those provided in Refs. 6 and 9. The work presented in Ref. 9 refers to a real-estate database about houses in the Washington, DC area. Retrieved houses are indicated by bright points on the Washington map that is displayed on the screen. The FilmFinder system (6) visualizes information about movies by means of *starfield displays*, which show database objects as small selectable spots (either points or 2D figures). The displayed data can be filtered by changing the range of values on both of the Cartesian axes. The query result fits on a single screen and the system quickly (i.e., within 1 s), computes the new data display in response to the user's requests. This property, called near real-time interactivity, ensures high usability (1).

Icon-based representations use icons to visualize the query result. An example is SICON (34), which shows a set of occurrences of an entity by means of copies of the same icon representing that entity; an identification label (attached to each copy of the icon) is used to distinguish the occurrences. This is very effective if we want to quickly know the kind of data retrieved. Moreover, when the user finds an entity occurrence of special interest, he or she can obtain the connected relationship occurrences represented in terms of icons.

As we already stated, the *hybrid* representation offers to the user various alternative visualizations. In SUPER (23), a browser that provides two data display modes is implemented. The result of a query is returned to such a browser in order to be presented to the user. In the form-based mode, occurrences of the object or relationship types are displayed through formlike representations; in the graphical mode, ER-like diagrams show the currently examined occurrences which can then be directly manipulated by the users.

Mulitmodal systems are most effective in adapting the presentation to the current task, domain, and user, using different presentation modalities and knowledge of the above three elements (task, domain, and user). In this way, the information will be presented in the best modality to be fully perceived and understood. MIMESIS, which actually proposes a multimodal interface using both a visual interaction style and a natural language style, is one of the first VQSs implementing a graphical presentation module that chooses the graphics that better express the data to be visualized (35). Such a module also allows the graphs displayed in the output window to be manipulated using graphical operators. Because MIMESIS is the interface to a system that collects and visualizes data on air pollution, the output graphics consist of thematic maps of cities, graphs such as bar charts, XY plots, area plots, multibar charts, pie charts, and also map animation.

A different approach is to use virtual-reality techniques to present the query result with a stimulation of a real environment (i.e., a virtual one) that depicts a situation familiar to the user. VQRH (36) is one of the systems that provide the user with several visual representations for both query formulation and result visualization. One possibility is to use 3D features to present the results in the simulated reality setting. For example, if the database refers to the books in a library, a virtual library can be represented in which the physical locations of the books are indicated by icons in a 3D presentation of the book stacks of the library. Similarly, Ref. 37 provides a very suggestive visualization, thanks also to the power of specialized graphic workstations.

Interaction Strategies

In this section, we classify the VQSs according to the specific strategy they use to accomplish the two activities that make up data retrieval (i.e., understanding the reality of interest and formulating the query). Note that some VQSs allow more than one strategy for each activity.

Understanding the reality of interest may be a complex task when the database schema is made of hundreds or thousands of concepts and/or the extension of the database is made of millions or billions of instances. What is needed is a mechanism to filter the information considered significant by the user. This may be achieved by means of a *top-down* strategy, where general aspects of the reality are first perceived, and then specific details may be viewed. The top-down strategy is implemented in several ways. The first one can be seen as a sequence of iterative refinements; that is, the system provides a library of top-down refinements for each schema. Each refinement can be obtained from the previous one by means of transformations, which, when applied to atomic objects, result in more detailed structures (30). A similar approach is based on the idea of providing either selective or hierarchical zoom. In the case of selective zoom, the schema is unique, and the concepts are layered in terms of levels of importance; the schema can be examined at several levels, so that only objects above a specified importance level are visible. The user can also graphically edit the schema, so that irrelevant objects can be removed from the screen.

Another well-established technique for learning about the information content of a schema is *browsing*. In this case, browsing is essentially a viewing technique aimed at gaining knowledge about the database. In principle, it can handle both schemata and instances in a homogeneous way without any distinction (38). The main hypothesis is that the user has only a slight knowledge about the database and the interaction techniques. Within this hypothesis, the user starts the interaction by examining a concept and its neighborhood (adjacent concepts can be considered as a first level of explanation of the examined concept). Next, a new element is selected by the user from neighboring concepts to be the current one, and its neighborhood is also shown: this process proceeds iteratively.

An alternative approach to top-down refinement and browsing is *schema simplification*. The idea here is to "bring the schema close to the query." This is done by building a user view resulting from aggregations and transformations of concepts of the original schema. Whereas in the top-down approach, it is possible to locate concepts that exactly match the initial schema (at different levels of abstraction), in the schema simplification approach, the user may build a proper view of the original schema which cannot be extracted by the schema itself at any of its levels of abstraction.

Query formulation is the fundamental activity in the process of data retrieval. The query strategy *by schema navigation* has the characteristic of concentrating on a concept (or a group of concepts) and moving from it in order to reach other concepts of interest, on which further conditions may be specified. Such a strategy differs according to the type of path followed during the navigation (see Fig. 5 for an example of unconnected path).

A second strategy for query formulation is *by subqueries*. In this case, the query is formulated by composing partial results. The third strategy for query formulation is *by*

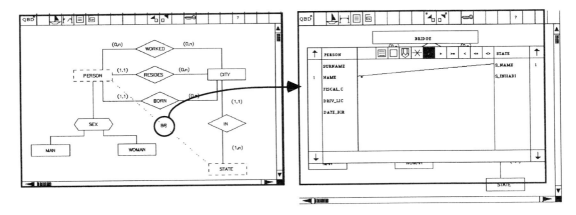

FIGURE 5   Unconnected path in QBD*. (From Ref. 30.)

matching. It is based on the idea of presenting the structure of a possible answer that is matched against the stored data.

The last strategy for query formulation is *by range selection*, allowing a search on multikey datasets conditioned by a given range to be performed. The query is formulated through direct manipulation of graphical widgets, such as buttons, sliders, and scrollable lists, with one widget being used for every key. An interesting implementation of such a technique has been proposed in Ref. 39 and is called *dynamic query*. The user can either indicate a range of numerical values (with a range slider) or a sequence of names alphabetically ordered (with an alpha slider). Given a query, a new query is easily formulated by moving the position of a slider with a mouse: this is supposed to give a sense of power but also of fun to the user, who is challenged to try other queries and see how the result is modified. Usually, input and output data are of the same type and may even coincide.

VQS USABILITY

Visual Query Systems are basically interactive systems, aiming at facilitating the extraction from databases the information users need. As such, VQSs should be developed following a user-centered design methodology (40). In order to be user-centered, the development of a VQS, as well as any interactive system, should be carried out by emphasizing the following three points:

1. The identification of the users and their needs
2. The usage of this information to develop a system which, through a suitable interface, meets the user's needs
3. The usability evaluation and validation tests of the system

Unfortunately, the above guidelines do not seem to be completely followed in actual VQS developments. In particular, little attention has been given to the range of users that might interact with a system and how the system should adapt to the different types of users. Also, not many usability experiments have been reported in the VQS literature.

A well-known definition of usability is given as "the extent to which a product can be used with efficiency, effectiveness and satisfaction by specific users to achieve specific goals in specific environments" (41). More precisely, effectiveness refers to the extent to which the intended goals of the system can be achieved; efficiency is the time, the money, and the mental effort spent to achieve these goals; satisfaction depends on how comfortable the users feel using the system.

From this point of view, usability is a major criterion in assessing the quality of interactions between the user and the overall system. Usually, at least one measurement must be provided for each usability factor. The effectiveness can be evaluated by relating the goals or subgoals of using the system to the accuracy and completeness with which these goals can be achieved. In the case of VQSs, the main goal is to extract information from the database by performing queries, and the accuracy in achieving such a goal is generally measured in terms of the accuracy of query completion (i.e., user's correctness rate when writing the queries). Measures of efficiency relate the level of effectiveness achieved at the expense of various resources, such as mental and physical effort, time, financial cost, and so forth. In principle, both the user's and the organization's point of view should be considered. However, the user's efficiency is most frequently measured in terms of the time spent to complete a query.

The above two measures (i.e., query accuracy and response time) can be evaluated quite precisely. Frequently, this is done either by recording real users performing predefined tasks with the system and then analyzing the recorded data or by directly observing the user. The most common tasks are *query writing* and *query reading*, both of which are performed by investigating the relationships between database queries expressed in natural language and the same queries expressed in the system under study. In query writing, the question is: "Given a query in natural language, how easily can a user express it through the query language statements?" The question for query reading is: "Given a query expressed through the query language statements, can the user express the query easily in natural language?" Moreover, other kinds of measure can be defined and evaluated, although with less precision.

Measures of satisfaction describe the comfort and acceptability of the overall system used. The learnability of a product may be measured by comparing the usability of a product handled by one user along a time scale. Measuring usability in different contexts can assess the flexibility of a product.

Usability of query languages has first been studied through the comparison between QBE and SQL (42,43). The former study (42) showed better user performances when using QBE with respect to SQL, both in query reading and query writing tests. However, a later study (43) also comparing QBE and SQL took into account several factors, such as the use of the same database management system, a similar environment, and so forth. It is interesting to note that the query language type affected user performance only in "paper and pencil" tests, in which case QBE users had higher scores than SQL users. In on-line tests, the user's accuracy was not affected by the type of the language adopted, but the user's satisfaction was much greater with QBE, and his or her efficiency much better.

In Ref. 39, a language based on the above-mentioned *dynamic queries* was tested against two other query languages, both providing form fill-in as the input method. One of these languages (called FG) has a graphical visualization output, and the other one (called FT) has a fully textual output. The alternative interfaces were chosen to find out which aspect of dynamic queries makes the major difference, either the input by sliders or the output visualization. The tasks to be performed by the user concerned basically the selection of elements that satisfy certain conditions. However, the subjects were also asked to find a trend for a data property and to find an exception for a trend. The hypothesis that the dynamic query language would perform better than both the FG and the FT interfaces was confirmed. Similarly, the FG interface produced faster completion times than the FT interface. In particular, for the task of finding a trend, the possibility of getting an overview of the database (in the dynamic and FG interfaces) made the major difference. In searching for an exception, the dynamic interface performed significantly better than the FG and FT ones. This was due to the advantages offered by both the visualization and the sliders. The visualization allowed subjects to see exceptions easily when they showed up on the screen, and the sliders allowed them to quickly change the values to find the correct answer.

   Other experiments have been conducted (44,45) to compare a diagrammatic query language, namely QBD* (30), against both SQL and QBI (46), an iconic query language. The overall objective of the studies was measuring and understanding the comparative effectiveness and efficiency with which subjects can construct queries in SQL or in the diagrammatic or iconic languages. The experiments were designed to determine if there is a significant correlation between (1) the query class and the query language type and (2) the type of query language and the experience of the user. The subjects were undergraduate students, secretaries, and professionals having different levels of expertise. The results of the comparison between QBD* and SQL confirmed the intuitive feeling that a visual language is easier to understand and use than a traditional textual language, not only for novice users but also for expert ones. The experts' errors when using SQL were mainly due to the need of remembering table names and using a precise syntax. Working with QBD*, users can gain from looking at the E-R diagrams. Davis (47) proved the advantage of the availability of E-R diagrams for users with some database background, as opposed to traditional textual representations.

   On the basis of the figures which have been obtained when comparing QBD* and QBI, one can say that expert users perform better using the QBD* system, and a small difference exists concerning the performance of nonexpert users (slightly better using QBI). There are, however, noticeable differences between the class of queries containing cycles (these are better performed in QBI) and the class of queries containing paths (better performed in QBD*). Such differences involve both time and accuracy and are totally independent from the skill of the users. In the second case, the difference could be due to the fact that paths are explicitly represented in the E-R schema (whereas in QBI, there are only sequences of icons) and the user perceives the whole path not as a unique complex function, but as a sequence of single steps. Considering the queries containing cycles, one may note that whenever a query involves two attributes belonging to the same concept, the QBD* users became much more confused than the QBI ones. This could be due to the fact that in QBD*, the user navigates in the E-R diagram, and for any concept, there is only one graphical symbol, even if it is met twice. However, in QBI, when a query contains a concept twice, the user sees two distinct icons on the screen and is not misled when manipulating the right occurrence of the concept (i.e., the right icon).

NEW REALMS FOR VQSs

Visual Query Systems mainly deal with traditional databases, i.e., databases containing alphanumeric data. However, in recent years the application realms of databases have raised a lot in terms of both number and variety of data types. As a consequence, specialized systems have been proposed for accessing such new kinds of database, containing nonconventional data such as images, videos, temporal series, maps, and so forth. Furthermore, the idea of an information repository has been deeply influenced by the beginning of the Web age. Different visual systems have been proposed to cope with the need for extracting information residing on the Web. In this section, we overview interfaces to temporal and spatial databases and interfaces to the Web and to digital libraries.

Temporal Databases

There are a growing number of applications dealing with data characterized by the temporal dimension (e.g., medical records, biographical data, financial data, etc.). Still, visual interfaces for querying temporal databases have been less investigated than their counterpart in traditional databases. Typically, end users of these data are competent in the field of the application but are not computer experts. They need easy-to-use systems able to support them in the task of accessing and manipulating the data contained in the databases. In this case, typical interactions with the data involve the visualization of some of their characteristics over some timeframe or the formulation of queries related with temporal events, such as the change of status of an employee or the inversion of the tendency of stock exchanges. Noticeable proposals for temporal VQSs include (48), ERT/vql (49), TVQL (50), and TVQE (51).

Very often, VQSs for temporal databases do not provide the user with satisfactory mechanisms for analyzing the retrieved data. This is also due to the fact that traditionally what is visualized for the query purpose is the schema of the database, whereas the actual database instances constitute the query result to be displayed to the user. Sometimes, what is visualized is the result of a previous query, which was expressed interacting with a different visualization of the data. In the remainder of this section, we first recall examples of temporal VQSs, and then mention more visualization-oriented systems.

Temporal Visual Queries

To cope with temporal data, VQSs need to be extended with effective visual representations of the time dimension and visual constructs to express temporal queries. An example of such extended VQSs is MMVIS (50), which integrates a temporal visual query language (TVQL) with a temporal visualization of results. TVQL contains dynamic query (6) filters (i.e., the temporal visualization is dynamically updated as the time selection is changed). Similarly, TVQE (51) is a visual query system which provides the user with a friendly environment to interact with temporal databases. The system adopts a diagrammatic representation of the database schema (including temporal classes and relationships) and a "graphical notebook" as interaction metaphor. The TVQE interface contains two panels, namely Schema and Interaction Windows. The Schema window is a panel on which the database schema is visually represented as a top-down tree, as a graph (database schema), and as a subgraph (database subschema), where the three representations share the same panel. Through the Schema window, the user has a global view of the classes of the schema and their interrelationships. The Interaction window is a panel on which a database schema is visually displayed as a "graphical notebook."

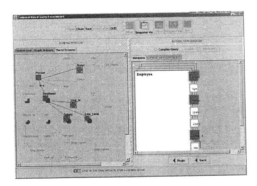

FIGURE 6   Graphical notebook in TVQE.

The user interacts with the graphical notebook by selecting its indices, as shown in Figure 6. The two windows are synchronized: For each selected index, the corresponding node in the Schema window is also selected. Next, the system displays the subschema, as shown in Figure 7. Through the use of dialog boxes, the user specifies the query condition.

Time-Oriented Data Visualization

Visualization of time-related data is more than ordering them along on an axis. Indeed, temporal extensions of existing visualization techniques or new techniques have mainly focused on time-oriented interactive exploration and visualization of large datasets. Most of them address a particular notion of time (e.g., linear or branching time, discrete or continuous time) in domain-specific applications, as it is difficult to represent the different aspects of temporal data in a single visual structure.

In Ref. 52, the following classification for time-oriented visualizations is proposed:

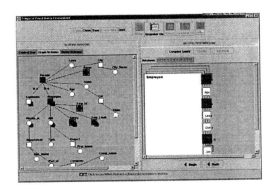

FIGURE 7   Selected schema.

- *Slice Visualization*, which corresponds to a visualization of valid history [i.e., a visualization of one or more entities (and their attributes and interrelationships) valid at discrete (continuous) instants or intervals in a *linear* order]
- *Periodic Slice Visualization*, which corresponds to a visualization of valid history at specific discrete (continuous) patterns of time (calendar)
- *Multislice Visualization*, which corresponds to a visualization of valid history at discrete (continuous) instants or intervals in a *branching* order
- *Snapshot Visualization*, which corresponds to a visualization of event history [i.e., a visualization of one or more entities valid at a single discrete (continuous) instant or interval].

The most used slice visualization technique is the timeline. A timeline is a graphical or textual display of events in chronological order (53). It also allows the user to explore relationships among historical events. Interactive timelines are displayed on a computer screen and may be directly manipulated by the user, so as to make easier the chronological navigation of a large temporal dataset. Interactive timeline systems proposed in the literature mainly use 2D visualizations, where the time dimension is represented by a slider labeled with discrete periods at specific time granularities (scrollbars are needed when all periods do not fit on the screen).

Most timeline systems are particularly suitable for a specific domain. An interesting system is *Lifelines* (54), which implements a technique for visualizing individual history in a 2D layout. In *Lifelines*, two types of histories are presented: medical patient records and youth criminal histories. The screen is horizontally divided into regions, which are visualized by alternate background colors, where each region represents a specific phase of a person's life.

Innovative timelines have been proposed to enrich the visualization offered by "traditional" timelines. They make use of distortion techniques, modeling features, visual metaphors, and interactive visualization of video and spatiotemporal data, in order to better visualize huge amounts of data on the screen and provide the user with more effective mechanisms to explore such data.

The *Perspective Wall* (55) is a well-known distortion technique that makes better use of the available screen space, by integrating detailed and contextual views of large amount of linear information. Mackinlay et al. argue that large datasets are often linearly structured by some metric (e.g., time), but they are not efficiently displayed in a 2D layout (with extensive scrolling), which results in loss of context.

The solution is distorting such a 2D layout into a 3D visualization, on which the user visualizes the information on a perspective wall, as shown in Figure 8. Data (contextual information) outside the center area (detailed information) are reduced in size and represented in two perspective areas, in accordance with the technique known as Fisheye view (56). The user directly interacts with the wall by selecting an object in one of the three panels. A smooth transition among different views of the wall is pursued. Perspective wall visualizes several entities at a time but has the limitation of visualizing only one entity attribute.

Other time-related visualizations (e.g., the periodic slice visualization) are deeply related with the notion of calendar. For instance, the Calendar Visualizer (57) comprises two visualizers that enhance the exploration of personal and group scheduling events. The *Spiral Calendar* is used for accessing an individual daily schedule in a 3D spiral and the *Time Lattice* for analyzing the temporal relationships among the schedules of

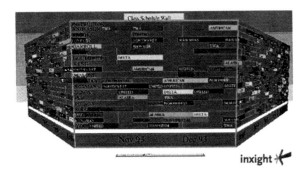

FIGURE 8   Perspective Wall. [From http://www.parc.xerox.com/istl/projects/uir/images/ (copyright inxight software corporate web site, http://www.inxight.com).]

groups. Figure 9 illustrates the Spiral Calendar. Note that different calendars are visible at multiple levels of detail (depth) and are connected by transparent pyramids, similar to a spiral lap. The user may focus on a detail of any calendar (e.g., week) by clicking on it and the selected calendar becomes the closest one on the spiral. The calendars with thinner time granularities (e.g., day) are not visualized. Information detail and context are tightly integrated through the 3D spiral.

Finally, in some applications, such as personal histories, image sequences, and so forth, an additional functionality is needed that allows the snapshot visualization of an information [i.e., visualization of data valid at a single discrete (continuous) instant or interval]. The snapshot visualization is very useful in presenting current and past instantaneous facts, highlighting a facet of a current view or a past state of an information.

The TimeScape system (58) visualizes past and future desktop states of personal information in a desktop environment in three different ways: snapshot, timeline, and calendar views. The snapshot view visualizes the desktop items (file and application icons, etc.) at a time instant. The instant is visually represented as a "time-travel" dial, successor and predecessor instants may be accessed by navigation buttons, as shown in

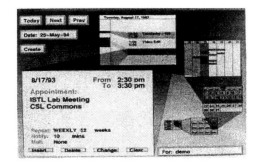

FIGURE 9   The Spiral Calendar. (From Ref. 57.)

FIGURE 10   TimeScape. (From http:/www.csl/sony.co.jp/person/rekimoto.html, copyright 1999, Sony Computer Science Laboratories, Inc.)

Figure 10. The system restores the computer state at a specific instant, by allowing a "time–traveling" interaction.

Geographical Databases

Geographical information is most naturally conveyed in visual format. Maps and diagrams (i.e., schematic maps such as a bus network map) are the core means in user interactions, both for querying the database and displaying the result of a query. A typical query would be "show me on a city map where the post office that is closest to this location is". The query itself would most likely be expressed using preformatted forms and menus to select the city and the reference location. The result would be a blinking or otherwise highlighted point in the displayed map. Once a map is displayed, as a result of a previous query or as an initial background screen in a query formulation interaction, the map can be used to specify a new query. This typically supports queries such as "give me more information on *this*," where the value of the *this* parameter is specified by pointing in some way to a location in the map (i.e., a point on the screen). Thus, in some sense, visual interaction is common practice in GIS systems, due to the intrinsically spatial reference that is associated to the data.

Although not yet implemented in commercial systems, the research literature has proposed different ways to support query formulation in a more visual approach than just forms and menus. The issue itself is actually more complex than for traditional databases. Formulating a query visually implies using the space on the screen to display the query elements. In traditional databases, the way query elements are positioned within the screen is irrelevant: a person-owns-car schema diagram has the same semantics whether the person type is on the right-hand side and the car type is on the left-hand side, or vice versa. The only thing that matters is to know whether the query is looking for persons or for cars. In a geographical database, a query to retrieve cities that have a lake within 5 km of the city limits will similarly require that city and lake types are displayed on the screen. But now the question arises: Is the relative positioning of the city and lake visual notations relevant or not to the query? Does the fact that city has been positioned left of lake on the screen mean that the user is looking for cities that have a lake east of the city, or is the relative positioning irrelevant? To correctly understand the query that is formulated as a configuration of set of objects on a screen, the system has to be able to determine to what extent the organization of the space in the screen corresponds to a search criterion versus the organization of the database objects in the geographical space to which they belong. An unambiguation interaction with the user is needed, for which different techniques may be used (e.g., resorting to additional specifications, entering a dialogue with the user, or having the query reformulated by the system in natural language for validation by the user).

One well-known proposal is an iconic interface called CIGALES (59,60). In this approach, each object type in the database has an associated icon. To formulate a query, the user selects the icons of interest and positions the icons along axis that represent directions supported by the system (e.g., North, East, West, and South). Icons positioned adjacent to each other express an adjacency topological relationship that must hold between the selected instances. Icons that do not touch each other imply that corresponding instances are separated by some metric distance that can be separately specified if a distance criterion is to be part of the query. Although very intuitive, CIGALES has two obvious limitations. The first is intrinsic to iconic systems and is the difficulty to define a large number of icons that can be recognized and understood by users. This makes iconic interfaces best adapted for databases with a relatively small number of object types, which is definitely not the case for many geographical databases. The second limitation is in expressive power and is due to the limited number of positions available on the screen to dispose the icons that participate into the query. For instance, an icon can only be adjacent to four other icons (one in each direction), and only two icons may visually intersect on the screen. Menus can be used to overcome such limitations, but this degrades the visual quality of the interface. LVIS, an iconic approach similar to CIGALES, has been recently developed for spatiotemporal databases (61).

Figure 11 shows two examples from this proposal. The first one (Fig. 11a) shows how the query "Which paths from Paris to Vienna avoid towns of more than 1000 inhabitants?" is formulated. Two labeled town icons are used to denote Paris and Vienna, and one more is used to state the predicate that restricts towns to those with requested population. Geometries of Town and Road objects are drawn as an area for Towns and as a line for Road. Putting those two geometries apart is meant to express a disjointedness

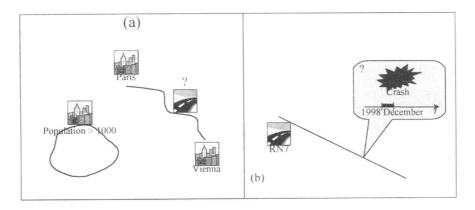

FIGURE 11   Visual Queries in LVIS. (From Ref. 61.)

predicate. Finally, a question mark on the Road icon shows that the query is to retrieve roads that satisfy the selection criterion (i.e., being disjoint from towns with population greater than 1000). Referring to the previous discussion on the ambiguity of spatial configurations in visual query, it is worthwhile noting that, in this example, the relative position of the road line and the town area are irrelevant as far as they are disjoint. Also irrelevant is the distance between the road and the town. The second query (Fig. 11b) shows a labeled road icon, denoting road RN7, whose geometry is associated with a balloon that includes a question mark, a crash icon, and a timeline with the December 1988 interval highlighted. This configuration conveys the spatial and temporal query "Where did crashes occur on road RN7 in December 1988?" Finally, Figure 12 shows a spatiotemporal query involving both moving objects and object's life cycle. The query is "Which trucks did drive in a riverside expressway five hours before a flood?" The query is split into two parts. Figure 12a represents the requested spatial configuration (i.e., the road and the river being adjacent). Figure 12b holds the temporal configuration (i.e., the requested 5 h delay between the passing of the truck and the flood). The labeled anchors in Figure 12a link the temporal events to the spatial configuration.

A different paradigm aims at supporting query by sketch (62). Sketches do not use predefined icons, but let users draw a sketch of the geographical configuration for which they are looking. Forms drawn by the user are considered to denote regions, lines, and point features. The exact shape that is drawn is not considered (the form is rather a symbolic notation than an approximate drawing of an existing shape). The semantics of these features (i.e., to which object types they correspond) has to be separately specified. Further specifications are also needed to distinguish relevant spatial combinations from accidental ones, as discussed earlier. Based on pragmatic rules, topological relationships are considered first, and metric conditions are seen as second-order criteria. The approach is clearly rooted in similar sketching facilities provided by some well-known query systems for image databases, where the sketch is used as a prototypical skeleton to select images from the database.

A similar symbolic interface has been proposed in Ref. 63. In this work, however, the focus is on a set of algebraic operations that the user can denote by adequately disposing the symbolic objects. The sketch is eventually translated into SQL-like statements.

Whereas most interfaces, as most GIS developments, focus on topological relationships, some efforts have been directed toward support of orientation relationships (e.g., north of). Pictorial Query-By-Example is a good representative from this class (64). These relationships are often used in multimedia databases for image retrieval by content.

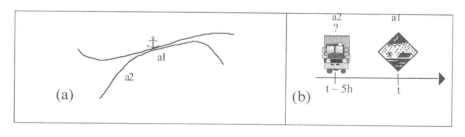

FIGURE 12   A visual spatiotemporal query in LVIS. (From Ref. 61.)

They allow selection predicates such as "images where an object of type A appears northeast of an object of type B" (e.g., a picture showing the moon over a palm tree).

Web Visual Access

Nowadays, the Web is the widest information repository. However, to find the information of interest among the mass of uninteresting ones is a very hard task. In order to help the user in retrieving information scattered everywhere in the Web, several proposals have been made by different research communities, such as those of database, artificial intelligence, and human–computer interaction (see Ref. 65 for a short survey). A limited amount of proposals relate to visual querying and information visualization, which we briefly discuss in the remaining of this section.

Visual Web Querying

An approach providing the user with mechanisms for querying (instead than browsing) the Web involves the development of Web query languages, somehow similar to database query languages (see, e.g., Refs. 66 and 67). Note that, at least in the first generation of such languages, the main idea is to model the Web document network topology and to provide the user with a query language enriched with primitives for specifying query conditions on both the structure of single documents and their locality on the network. However, the user has no chance to query the Web information content.

Such a first generation of Web languages still presents many of the problems one encounters using indexes, such as information changes or lack of representation of document structures. However, the possibility of capturing the structure of a hypermedia network, explicitly describing links between documents, and the introduction of the "query locality" concept to measure the cost of answering a query are important elements that need to be taken into account in the development of effective and efficient systems.

The second generation of Web query languages exhibits a powerful feature with respect to the above ones, namely they provide access to the structure of the Web objects they manipulate, modeling the internal as well as the external links of the documents and supporting some semistructured data modeling features. Also, they have the ability to define new complex structures as query result, but also have a quite complex SQL-like syntax. Finally, the recent growth of XML has caused the development of another class of languages explicitly thought for XML documents, but somehow similar to Web query languages.

From the user's point of view, all of these languages are too difficult to be used. SQL itself is too difficult to be used by a casual user (14), so very recent proposals aim at putting visual query interfaces on top of Web query languages [e.g., XML-GL (68), which uses graphs as visual representation, and EquiX (69), based on forms]. Such proposals claim to offer easy-to-use alternatives to textual Web query languages. Unfortunately, no usability experiment results are presented, thus there is no evidence supporting such a claim. Also, one of the usability problems that users could have with such languages is the lack of a "user-oriented" interaction strategy. Indeed, even if the languages employ visual elements, the proposed interaction styles seem to be one-to-one with the traditional (textual) query formulation. For instance, in Figure 13, from XML-GL, the user wants to express the query: "Select all orders not containing any item priced more than $25 and shipped to an address in Los Angeles." In order to do this, s/he has to

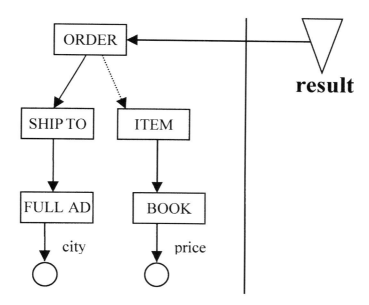

FIGURE 13   A query in XML-GL.

construct the graph represented in the figure, in which a dotted edge means negation and the circles will contain the selection predicates (="Los Angeles," >25).

Web Visualization

One of the basic ideas underlying the sophisticated visualization mechanisms proposed for the Web is representing the data in a form that matches the user's perceptual capabilities, so that s/he may easily grasp the information of interest. Proposed visualizations range from sophisticated techniques to visualize large networks in a screen shot (70), to animated spaces where related information may be organized, analyzed, and linked by means of different visual mechanisms (71), to sense-making tools, which help users understanding information by associating and combining it. Such tools re-represent retrieved information to make patterns visible, or they allow the construction of new information patterns from old ones by exploiting the power of visual attributes of the representation, which may be quickly detected by the eye (72).

One of the most used technique to support Web navigation and avoid the "being lost in hyperspace" problem is the so-called "focus + context." If, while surfing through the Web, the user comes to a particular node and feels lost, some idea of the position of the node in the overall information space will help orient her/him. In Ref. 73, a technique to develop focus + context views of Web documents is discussed. The views show the details of a particular node (document); nodes in the immediate neighborhood (i.e., those directly reachable from the document) are also displayed. This is for the local detail. To place the node in the global context, which is a large and complex network, the paths to and from the important (landmark) nodes are only shown. This recalls usual geographical navigation strategy: a lost person will try to find where she is using her immediate neighborhood and important geographical landmarks. (See Fig. 14 for an example.)

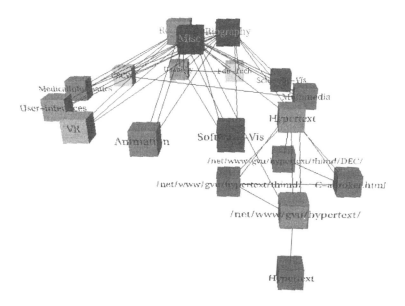

FIGURE 14   Focus and context.

Visualization mechanisms may help even when dealing with single documents. For instance, the WebBook (74) (see Fig. 15) lets users group pages of document(s) into a simulated physical book and fan them for rapid scanning. CyberMap (75) automatically generates overview maps for textual documents. CyberMap creates a graph of a collection of nodes by clustering related documents by content into nodes and automatically

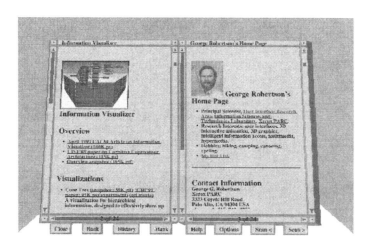

FIGURE 15   The WebBook.

generating links between semantically related nodes. The resulting graph can be viewed in multiple representations, providing for quick access to information and data filtering in the Web. In addition to several visual techniques, CyberMap builds a personal user profile and tracks the user interaction history to offer personalized views of the various documents.

Recently, the information-foraging theory has been proposed to elicit and precisely define the role of visualization with respect to Web information searching (76). Information foraging refers to activities associated with assessing, seeking, and handling information sources, in analogy with the optimal foraging theory found in biology and anthropology. As animals adapt their behavior and their structure through evolution in order to survive the changes of the environment, so humans adapt for gaining and making sense out of information. Optimality models developed for studying the animals' behavior can be extended to model the information foragers in order to provide them with better interfaces and data distribution strategies.

Visually Querying Digital Libraries

The main purpose of a digital library (DL) is to help the users to easily access the enormous amount of globally networked information, which includes preexisting public libraries, catalog data, digitized document collections, and so forth. Thus, it is fundamental to develop both the infrastructure and the user interface to effectively access the information via the Internet. The key technological issues are how to search and how to display desired selections from and across large collections (77). A DL interface must support a range of functions including query formulation, presentation of retrieved information, relevance feedback, and browsing (78). Unfortunately, user interfaces encountered in many digital libraries and archives allow the user just to access catalogs by submitting queries through HTML fill-in forms and, in most cases, offer the choice between "simple" and "advanced" query modes. The "browsing by argument" function is almost always offered, and links to other library catalogs are often provided. In practice, the bibliographic search seems to be usually considered a quite easy task, which does not deserve very sophisticated user interfaces. However, careful analyses of users' requirements and tasks seem to contrast this assumption (7). Notwithstanding, during the last years, digital library systems have not made many efforts to solve the user-interaction problems. Only recently, new projects [e.g., University of Stanford (http://www-diglib. stanford.edu/diglib/) and University of Michigan (http://http2.sils.umich.edu/UMDL/) DL Projects] are developing a more complex model of information-seeking tasks. Similar to the general case of accessing Web data, display of information, visualization of, and navigation through large information collections as well as linkages to information manipulation/analysis tools can be identified as key areas for research.

The AQUA (79) project proposes a visual interface for querying DLs, which supports the idea of incrementally refining the query and decomposing it in a series of suboperations. For visualizing chains of operations, AQUA uses a set of panels (i.e., form-based interfaces). Each panel represents the operation used to generate the next result. Final and intermediate query results are also visualized in the panels. Panels can support not only simple search mechanisms but also more sophisticated methods, such as document clustering and relevance feedback. Visualizations of clusters and key words is also supported.

LAURIN (7) is a EU-funded project dealing with digital libraries of newspaper clippings, whose key point is assuring an easy and effective access to the stored clip-

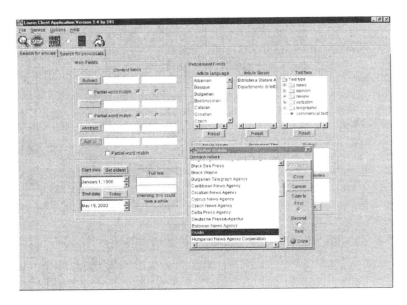

FIGURE 16   The Laurin query interface.

pings. The LAURIN system is equipped with different visual interfaces supporting the indexing tasks of librarians and the retrieval tasks of the generic users. The query interface is mainly form based (see Fig. 16) but is enriched with a tridimensional visualization space for further analyzing and filtering retrieved clippings based on their properties and clustering similarities. Besides traditional key-word-based search methods, the interface also offers the possibility of browsing the clipping collection by argument, organizing the document space in a manner that is readily understood by users. Such activity is supported by the use of an integrated multilingual thesaurus, which plays a central role in the system. The user will see a unified search space; therefore, s/he can ignore the existence of different information sources (i.e., libraries). However, s/he will also be able to select a library on demand, based on the description of its characteristics, in order to restrict her/his attention to specific topics covered by a certain library only.

Requests can be formulated in any of the languages supported by the system (currently English, French, German, Italian, Norwegian, Spanish, and Swedish) and the system will provide translations for the purpose of key-word- and content-based search.

CONCLUSION

In the world of information technology today, it looks like the only users that are happy with textual interaction are computer scientists and computer professionals in charge of software development. Out of this relatively restricted community, nobody would give a dime for using an application or software that only supports textual interfaces. Young students in computer science look at textual interfaces as old-fashioned grandpa technology. Just like kids asking their parents how could they live without TV.

As shown in this article, research on visual interfaces to databases has been going on for a long time [a good starting point is Zloof's paper on QBE which dates back to 1977 (21)] and has produced a large number of prototypes and a few commercial softwares. The diversity of the proposed approaches motivated our effort to produce a survey that would help in organizing the ideas about issues and solutions in this rich domain. We have discussed generic tools and techniques to access data, such as visual query systems for traditional alphanumeric databases as well as for temporal and spatial databases. We have also analyzed visual query systems for access to Web data and to digital libraries. We did not explicitly analyze multimedia database systems, as, in this domain, many publicly available products are accessible on the Web and the diversity is in the details rather than in the general approach. Basically, these systems support query-by-example (i.e., using an example image as input to a query for similar images) or query by physical features such as color and texture.

Our overview shows that a large know-how is available, so that it should be easy today to design and implement new visual query systems. However, the accumulated knowledge is not easily formalized in a way that makes it immediately reusable. Some rules are well known to HCI designers, such as ergonomics rules or rules about user behavior and capacity to face complexity. Some rules are well known to designers of database languages, such as how to provide expressive power and how to avoid ambiguities in formal languages. Some rules are known to everybody but rarely enforced, such as the need for early usability tests before the full implementation of the interface starts. More interdisciplinary teams may well be the best guarantee for the successful development of advanced visual systems.

A major step forward in visual query systems may be expected though their interleaving with information visualization techniques. What would, indeed, be the benefit of smart query formulation interfaces if coupled with poor result visualization? Information visualization has bloomed tremendously over the last decade, both as a research field and in practical applications. It offers, for instance, an excellent support for interactive data mining or even simply information retrieval. Considering that the wealth of information that is available today tends to move the data access issue from database technology to information retrieval technology, information visualization certainly has a bright future.

The last comment we address is about application interfaces versus database interfaces. Many people still think that visual query facilities belong to the application world (i.e., they can only be application-specific and designed and produced by application developers). Certainly, applications are best served by interfaces that are customized for their users. However, such a customization has also a negative side, as it only allows users to access data through preformulated queries (most often, predefined forms). Free access to data requires more flexibility and openness to unexpected combinations of data items and interconnections in any query, and scrollable menus (to present users with what is available) are of no help when dealing with thousands of data items. Generic tools such as visual query systems are capable of supporting such requirements. We therefore expect their importance to grow steadily over the short-term future.

REFERENCES

1. B. Myers, J. Hollan, and I. Cruz (eds.), "Strategic Directions in Human Computer Interaction," *ACM Computing Surveys, 28*(4) (1996).
2. J. Bertin, *Semiology of Graphics*, University of Wisconsin Press, Madison, 1983.

3. E. R. Tufte, *The Visual Display of Quantitative Information*, Graphics Press, Cheshire, CT, 1983.

4. E. R. Tufte, *Envisioning Information*, Graphics Press, Cheshire, CT. K. Tsuda, A Yoshitaka, M. Hirakawa, M. Tanaka, and T. Ichikawa, "Iconic Browser: An Iconic Retrieval System for Object-Oriented Databases, *J. Visual Lang. Computing*, *1*(1), 59–76 (1990).

5. G. G. Robertson, S. K. Card, and J. D. Mackinlay, "Information Visualization Using 3D Interactive Animation," *Commun. ACM*, *36*(4), 57–71 (1993).

6. C. Ahlberg and B. Shneiderman, "Visual Information Seeking: Tight Coupling of Dynamic Query Filters with Starfield Displays," in *Proc. of ACM Conference on Human Factors in Computing Systems CHI'94*, 1994, pp. 313–317.

7. D. Calvanese, T. Catarci, and G. Santucci, "Building a Digital Library of Newspaper Clippings: The LAURIN Project," in *Proc. of the IEEE Int. Forum on Research and Technology Advances in Digital Libraries (ADL2000)*, 2000.

8. I. F. Cruz, "User-defined Visual Query Languages," in *Proc. IEEE Symposium on Visual Languages (VL '94)*, 1994, pp. 224–231.

9. E. M. Haber, Y. E. Ioannidis, and M. Livny, "OPOSSUM: Desk-Top Schema Management through Customizable Visualizations," in *Proc. of the XXI VLDB Conference*, 1995, pp. 527–538.

10. "Foundations of Advanced 3D Information Visualization," European (ESPRIT) Working Group Technical Reports available at http://www-cui.cs.darmstadt.gmd.de:80/visit/activities/IEEE/Fadiva, 1996.

11. P. Pirolli and S. Card, "Information Foraging in Information Access Environments," *Proc. ACM SIGCHI'95*, 1995, pp. 51–58.

12. S. K. Card, J. D. Mackinlay, and B. Shneiderman, *Readings in Information Visualization*, Morgan Kaufmann, San Mateo, CA, 1999.

13. D. A. Keim and H.-P. Kriegel, "Issues in Visualizing Large Databases," in *Proc. Conf. on Visual Database Systems (VDB'95)*, 1995; *Visual Database Systems*, Chapman & Hall, London, 1995, pp. 203–214.

14. T. Catarci, M. F. Costabile, S. Levialdi, and C. Batini, "Visual Query Systems for Databases: A Survey," *J. Visual Lang. Computing*, *8*(2), 215–260 (1997).

15. B. Shneiderman, "The Future of Interactive Systems and the Emergence of Direct Manipulation," *Behav. Inform. Technol.*, *1*, 237–256 (1982).

16. J. E. Ziegler and K. P. Fahnrich, "Direct Manipulation," in *Handbook of Human–Computer Interaction*, edited by M. Helander, North-Holland, Amsterdam, 1988, pp. 123–133.

17. A. Dix, J. Finlay, G. Abowd, and R. Beale, *Human–Computer Interaction*, Prentice-Hall International, London, 1993.

18. T. Catarci, M. F. Costabile, and M. Matera, "Visual Metaphors for Interacting with Databases," *ACM SIGCHI Bull.*, *27*(2), 15–17 (1995).

19. P. Reisner, "Human Factors Studies of Database Query Languages: A Survey and Assessment," *ACM Computing Surveys*, *13* (1981).

20. M. Jarke and Y. Vassiliou, "A Framework for Choosing a Database Query Language," *ACM Computing Surveys*, *17*(3), 313–340 (1985).

21. M. M. Zloof, "Query-by-Example: A Database Language," *IBM Syst. J.*, *16*(4), 324–343 (1977).

22. Y. Shirota, Y. Shirai, and T. L. Kunii, "Sophisticated Form-Oriented Database Interface for Non-Programmers," in *Visual Database Systems*, edited by T. L. Kunji, North-Holland, Amsterdam, 1989, pp. 127–155.

23. Y. Dennebouy, M. Andersson, A. Auddino, Y. Dupont, E. Fontana, M. Gentile, and S. Spaccapietra, "SUPER: Visual Interfaces for Object + Relationship Data Models," *J. Visual Lang. Computing*, *6*(1), 74–99 (1995).

24. S. K. Chang, "A Visual Language Compiler for Information Retrieval by Visual Reasoning," *IEEE Trans. Software Eng.*, *16*, 1136–1149 (1990).

25. T. Catarci, S. K. Chang, M. F. Costabile, S. Levialdi, and G. Santucci, "A Graph-based Framework for Multiparadigmatic Visual Access to Databases," *IEEE Trans. Knowledge Data Eng.*, *KDE-8*(3), 455–475 (1996).

26. T. Catarci, G. Santucci, and M. Angelaccio, "Fundamental Graphical Primitives for Visual Query Languages," *Inform. Syst.*, *18*(2), 75–98 (1993).

27. T. Catarci, G. Santucci, M. F. Costabile, and I. Cruz, "Foundations of the DARE System for Drawing Adequate Representations," in *Proceedings of the International Symposium on Database Applications in Non-Traditional Environments* (*DANTE'99*), IEEE Press, New York, 1999.

28. I. F. Cruz, "DOODLE: A Visual Language for Object-Oriented Databases," in *Proc. of the ACM SIGMOD Conf. on Management of Data*, 1992.

29. J. D. Mackinlay, "Automating the Design of Graphical Presentations of Relational Information," *ACM Trans. Graphics*, *5*, 110–141 (1986).

30. M. Angelaccio, T. Catarci, and G. Santucci, "QBD*: A Graphical Query Language with Recursion," *IEEE Trans. Software Eng.*, *SE-16*, 1150–1163 (1990).

31. G. Santucci and F. Palmisano, "A Dynamic Form-Based Data Visualiser for Semantic Query Languages," in *Interfaces to Database Systems*, edited by P. Sawyer, Series Workshop in Computing, Springer-Verlag, London, 1994, pp. 249–265.

32. M. P. Consens and A. O. Mendelzon, "Hy$^+$: A Hygraph-based Query and Visualization System," in *Proc. of the ACM SIGMOD Conf. on Management of Data*, 1993, pp. 511–516.

33. J. Boyle, S. Leishman, and P. M. D. Gray, "From WIMP to 3D: The Development of AMAZE," *J. Visual Lang. Computing*, *7*, 291–319 (1996).

34. I. P. Groette and E. G. Nilsson, "SICON: An Icon Presentation Module for an E-R Database," in *Proc. of the 7th Int. Conf. on Entity–Relationship Approach*, 1988, pp. 271–289.

35. P. Marti, M. Profili, P. Raffaelli, and G. Toffoli, "Graphics, Hyperqueries, and Natural Language: An Integrated Approach to User-Computer Interfaces," in *Proceedings of the International Workshop on Advanced Visual Interfaces*, AVI'92, World Scientific, Singapore, 1992, pp. 68–84.

36. S. K. Chang, M. F. Costabile, and S. Levialdi, "Reality Bites—Progressive Querying and Result Visualization in Logical and VR Spaces," in *Proc. of the 1994 IEEE Symp. on Visual Languages*, 1994, pp. 100–109.

37. A. Massari and L. Saladini, "Virgilio: A VR-based System for Database Visualization," in *Proceedings of the International Workshop on Advanced Visual Interfaces*, AVI'96, edited by T. Catarci, M. F. Costabile, S. Levialdi, and G. Santucci, ACM Press, New York, 1996, pp. 263–265.

38. A. D'Atri and L. Tarantino, "From Browsing to Querying," *IEEE Data Eng. Bull.*, *12*(2), 46–53 (1989).

39. C. Ahlberg, C. Williamson, and B. Shneidermann, "Dynamic Queries for Information Exploration: An Implementation and Evaluation," in *Proc. of the ACM Conference on Human Factors in Computing Systems CHI'92*, 1992, pp. 619–626.

40. D. Norman and S. Draper (eds.), *User Centered System Design*, Lawrence Erlbaum Associates, Hillsdale, NJ, 1986.

41. N. Bevan and M. Macleod, "Usability Assessment and Measurement," in *The Management of Software Quality*, edited by M. Kelly, Ashgate Technical/Gower Press, 1993.

42. P. Reisner, "Query languages," in *Handbook of Human-Computer Interaction*, edited by M. Helander, North-Holland, Amsterdam, 1998, pp. 257–280.

43. M. Y. Yen and R. W. Scamell, "A Human Factors Experimental Comparison of SQL and QBE," *IEEE Trans. Software Eng.*, *19*(4), 390–402 (1993).

44. T. Catarci and G. Santucci, "Diagrammatic vs Textual Query Languages: A Comparative Experiment," in *Proc. of the IFIP W.G. 2.6 Working Conference on Visual Databases*, 1995, pp. 57–85.

45. A. N. Badre, T. Catarci, A. Massari, and G. Santucci, "Comparative Ease of Use of a Dia-

grammatic Vs. an Iconic Query Language," in *Interfaces to Databases*, edited by J. Kennedy and P. J. Barclay, Electronic Series Workshop in Computing, Springer-Verlag, London, 1996.

46. A. Massari and P. K. Chrysanthis, "Visual Query of Completely Encapsulated Objects," in *Proc. of the Fifth Int. Workshop on Research Issues on Data Engineering*, 1995, pp. 18–25.

47. J. S. Davis, "Experimental Investigation of the Utility of Data Structure and E-R Diagrams in Database Query," *Int. J. Man–Machine Studies, 32*, 449–459 (1990).

48. V. Kouramajian and M. Gertz, "A Visual Query Editor for Object-Oriented Databases," in *Proc. 14th Int. Conf. on O–O and E–R Modeling*, 1995, pp. 388–399.

49. B. Theodoulidis, et al., "Interactive Querying and Visualization in Temporal Databases," in *Proc. Reasoning Workshop of the 4th DOOD Conference*, 1995.

50. S. Hibino and E. A. Rundensteiner, "MMVIS: Design and Implementation of a Multimedia Visual Information Seeking Environment," in *Proc. of ACM Multimedia 96*, 1996, pp. 75–86.

51. S. Fernandes Silva and T. Catarci, "Graphical Interaction with Historical Databases," in *Proc. 11th Int. Conf. on Scientific and Statistical Database Management (SSDBM'99)*, 1999.

52. S. Fernandes Silva and T. Catarci, "Visualization of Linear Time-Oriented Data: A Survey," in *Proc. of the 1st Int. Conf. on Web Information System Engineering (WISE'2000)*, 2000.

53. V. Kumar, R. Furuta, and R. B. Allen, "Metadata Visualization for Digital Libraries: Interactive Timeline Editing and Review," in *Proc. of ACM Digital Libraries*, 1998, pp. 126–133.

54. C. Plaisant, B. Milash, A. Rose, S. Widoff, and B. Shneiderman, "Lifelines: Visualizing Personal Histories," in *Proc. of ACM CHI'96*, 1996, pp. 221–227.

55. J. D. Mackinlay, G. G. Robertson, and S. K. Card, "The Perspective Wall: Detail and Context Smoothly Integrated," in *Proc. of ACM CHI'91*, 1991, pp. 173–179.

56. G. W. Furnas, "Generalized Fisheye Views," in *Proc. of ACM CHI'86*, 1986, pp. 16–23.

57. J. D. Mackinlay, G. G. Robertson, and R. DeLine, "Developing Calendar Visualizers for the Information Visualizer," in *Proc. of ACM UIST'94*, 1994, pp. 109–118.

58. J. Rekimoto, "TimeScape: A Time-Machine for the Desktop Environment," in *Proc. of ACM CHI'99 Extended Abstracts*, 1999, pp. 180–181.

59. M.-A. Aufaure, "A High-Level Interface Language for GIS," *J. Visual Lang. Computing, 6*(2), 167–182 (1995).

60. D. Calcinelli and M. Mainguenaud, "Cigales, a Visual Language for Geographical Information System: the User Interface," *J. Visual Lang. Computing, 5*(2), 113–13 (1994).

61. C. Bonhomme, M.-A. Aufaure, and C. Trépied, "Metaphors for Visual Querying of Spatio-Temporal Databases," in *Proc. Fourth Int. Conf. on Visual Information Systems—Visual 2000*, 2000.

62. M. J. Egenhofer, "Spatial-Query-by-Sketch," in *Proceedings of VL'96 (IEEE Symposium on Visual Languages)*, 1996, pp. 60–67.

63. F. Di Loreto, F. Ferri, F. Massari, and M. Rafanelli, "A Pictorial Query Language for Geographic Databases," in *Proc. AVI'96 Workshop on Advanced Visual Interfaces*, 1996, pp. 233–244.

64. T. Dalamagas, T. Sellis, and L. Sinos, "A Visual Database System for Spatial and Non-spatial Data Management," in *Visual Database Systems 4*, edited by Y. Ioannidis and W. Klas, IFIP Chapman & Hall, London, 1998.

65. T. Catarci, "Web-based Information Access," in *Proc. of the Int. Conf. on Cooperative Information Systems (CoopIS'99)*, 1999.

66. S. Abiteboul, "Querying Semi-structured Data," in *Proc. ICDT'97*, 1997.

67. D. Florescu, A. Levy, and A. Mendelzon, "Database Techniques for the World-Wide-Web: A Survey," *Sigmod Record, 27*(3), 59–74 (1998).

68. S. Ceri, S. Comai, E. Damiani, P. Fraternali, S. Paraboschi, and L. Tanca, "XML-GL: A Graphical Query Language for Querying and Restructuring XML Documents," http://www.w3.org/TandS/QL/QL98/pp/xml-gl.html, 1998.

69. S. Cohen, Y. Kanza, Y. Kogan, W. Nutt, Y. Sagiv, and A. Serebrenik, "EquiX—Easy Querying in XML Databases," in *Proc. WebDB*, 1999.

70. N. Gershon and J. Brown (eds.), "Special Report on Computer Graphics and Visualization in the Global Information Infrastructure," *IEEE Computer Graphics*, *16*, 2 (1996).

71. M. Czerwinski, S. Dumais, G. Robertson, S. Dziadosz, S. Tiernan, and M. van Dantzich, "Visualizing Implicit Queries for Information Management and Retrieval," in *Proc. ACM CHI'99*, 1999.

72. E. H. Chi, J. Mackinlay, P. Pirolli, R. Gossweiler, and S. K. Card, "Visualizing the Evolution of Web Ecologies," in *Proc. ACM CHI'98*, 1998.

73. S. Mukherjea and Y. Hara, "Focus + Context Views of World-Wide Web Nodes," in *Proc. Hypertext 97*, 1997, pp. 187–196.

74. S. K. Card, G. Robertson, and W. York, "The WebBook and the Web Forager: An Information Workspace for the World Wide Web," in *Proc. ACM CHI'96*, 1996.

75. P. A. Gloor and S. B. C. Dynes, "Cybermap: Visually Navigating the Web," *J. Visual Lang. Computing*, *9* (1998).

76. P. Pirolli and S. K. Card, "Information Foraging," *Psychol. Rev.* (1999).

77. C. Lynch and H. Garcia-Molina, "Interoperability, Scaling, and the Digital Libraries Research Agenda: A Report," in *Proc. of IITA Digital Libraries Workshop*, 1995.

78. W. B. Croft, "What Do People Want from Information Retrieval? (The Top 10 Research Issues for Companies that Use and Sell IR Systems," *D-Lib. Mag.* (November 1995).

79. L. Kovács, A. Micsik, and B. Pataki, "AQUA: Query Visualization for the NCSTRL Digital Library," in *Proc. DL'99*, 1999, pp. 230–231.

TIZIANA CATARCI

STEFANO SPACCAPIETRA

WARDS AND UPGMA CLUSTERING OF DATA WITH VERY HIGH DIMENSIONALITY

INTRODUCTION

Over the last few decades, clustering analysis has been applied in a number of scientific fields, including medicine, biology, chemistry, and social sciences in order to help classify and group diseases and chemical compounds, as well as to determine population statistical data and trends (1). Cluster analysis, known also as mathematical taxonomy, consists of a variety of mathematical tools that are applied in order to determine families of *similar* objects. This similarity is derived from a number of features that directly describe and/or characterize the objects involved in the process. Depending on the number of participating features in the analysis, we may have clustering of one or more dimensions (2). For instance, one could try to classify available PCs—for market research purposes—using features such as CPU clock rates, memory size, disk size, average disk access time, size of video-card RAM, and speed of the system bus. In this case, data objects of five dimensions participate in the process which works in the following intuitive manner: A distance metric among objects is introduced and is calculated based in the values of the various domains; subsequently, the *closest* objects are grouped together to form the clusters sought.

The role of clustering is manifold: It groups, displays, summarizes, predicts, and provides a basis for understanding. Objects are grouped to create more general and abstract entities that share properties and have identical behavior in the context of the system from which they are derived. Clusters are displayed so that differences and similarities become apparent. In this regard, clustering can be used as an effective tool to determine similar and dissimilar objects. Although sorting can be used to determine the latter, matters become challenging when multiple dimensions are involved. In general, properties of clusters are highlighted by hiding properties of individuals. What is expected in general from a mathematical taxonomy is that clusters present *similar* properties. Thus, clusters easily isolated offer a basis for understanding and speculating about the structure of the system. Unusual formulations frequently do reveal anomalies.

In recent years, a considerable volume of work in clustering algorithms has appeared in areas that involve data-intensive processing environments (2–7). Such systems involve significant movement of data elements throughout the memory hierarchy, yielding considerable delays for user requests. Here, the main rationale of using clustering techniques is to be able to place data objects that demonstrate *similar* behavior in the same page and/or data segment. In doing so, costly I/O operations can be avoided while related objects are simultaneously brought in the main memory for CPU processing (5,8). In a similar fashion, clustering has been used in a host of other areas in data management to improve performance. These areas include organization of data structures and semantic networks, buffer and storage managers, design of distributed databases, generalized clustered I/O subsystems, and distributed computing systems. The application of clustering in all of these diverse fields attempts to mix the effects of access pattern behavior of user requests and clustering methods used with the internal organization and the memory and caching policies to provide good response rates.

For each application area, a number of important considerations have to be resolved in order for clustering to be applied in a fruitful manner. Three vital areas that need to be defined and/or addressed are as follows:

- The computation of the degree of association between different objects
- The designation of an acceptable criterion to evaluate how good and/or successful a clustering method is
- The adaptability of the clustering method used under different statistical distributions of data, including random, skewed, concentrated around certain regions, and so forth.

Various clustering algorithms have been proposed to date (1,9,10) to perform object groupings. These approaches mostly depend on the rationale upon which the clustering is conducted. In that respect, each such technique has a different theoretical basis and is only applicable to specific field(s) (6,11,12). In this study, our emphasis is on the nature of the objects and their multifaceted characteristics. In contrast to prior work (2,13), where a limited number of dimensions for data features is considered (typically up to three), in this study we investigate the effect of very high-dimensional data in the clustering process and the stability of the used algorithms. In this regard, we extend our previous work in several ways. One major extension is the use data dimensions ranging from 50 to 200. It is our opinion that for most contemporary and future applications, this number of dimensions represents a practical upper bound. In investigating this core theme, we vary the algorithms used in the mathematical taxonomy as well as the statistical distribution of values that articulate the various data object dimensions. It is worth pointing out that previous findings with data with limited numbers of dimensions show little differences in the behavior and stability of the considered clustering methods (2,13,14).

The organization of this article is as follows. The second section provides an overview of the usage of clustering techniques in data-intensive applications. The third section discusses the clustering techniques used in our evaluation and describes the various distributions used to derive our experimental data. The fourth section outlines the experimental methodology and the fifth section presents a summary of our results. Finally, conclusions can be found in the last section.

CLUSTERING IN SYSTEMS FOR DATA-INTENSIVE APPLICATIONS

Two early pieces of algorithmic work (15,16) provided the basis for a number of proposals in data-intensive and database environment that have appeared during the last two decades. In Ref. 15, an efficient heuristic procedure for partitioning graphs is discussed. The algorithm solves the following combinatorial problem: Given a graph G with costs on its edges, partition the nodes of G into subsets no larger than a given maximum size, so as to minimize the total cost of the edges that interconnect the partitions. The proposed algorithm is used to place the components of electric circuits on circuit boards (VLSI chips) in order to minimize the number of connections between boards. In Ref. 16, the Lukes' algorithm for computing an optimal partitioning for the vertices of a tree is proposed. The algorithm is designed for clustering of logic circuits onto integrated-circuit chips and mapping of computer information onto physical blocks of storage. For the optimal solution, the algorithm adopts a dynamic programming technique to a tree-partitioning problem. Lukes' algorithm exploits the trees' acyclic nature in order to find a globally optimal partition. Based on the aforementioned algorithms, many efforts that investigated clustering in various areas of data management appeared over the last two decades. Below, we provide an overview of a number of such efforts.

In Ref. 17, Schkolnick proposed an efficient algorithm to partition a hierarchical structure. The algorithm is used to compute an optimal clustering of an IMS-type hierarchical database tree into dataset groups with respect to a predefined access pattern and an underlying cost model. In order to obtain a near optimal clustering, Stamos proposes a presort order trace that sorts objects according to their first appearance in the access trace of a specific application (18). Stamos also evaluated the behavior of different memory architectures in a nondistributed, single-user object manager and used different strategies for clustering. Stamos also evaluated the behavior of different memory architectures in a nondistributed, single-user object manager and used different strategies for clustering. The "adaptive record clustering" algorithm (19) places frequently coreferenced records on the same pages so that a minimal number of pages are accessed in query processing. The proposed algorithm is capable of detecting sudden changes in users' access patterns and then creating an appropriate clustering for the access patterns. It does not require classification of queries into types and avoids the collection of individual query statistics. In Ref. 20, Banerjee et al. proposed a clustering algorithm that makes use of a directed acyclic graph (DAG) in computer-aid design (CAD) databases. The key objective is that all descendants of a node of a DAG are fetched in a single forward scan of the DAG. Such graphs typically arise in design hierarchies where nodes represent design artifacts, and edges represent relationships among these design artifacts. The proposed traversal algorithm is "children-depth-first" in nature and is a hybrid of the depth-first and breadth-first traversal algorithms.

In Ref. 21, Chang and Katz examined the effect of clustering and buffering on the average response time for an object-oriented database. They proposed a run-time algorithm, called "smart-clustering," that considers the structural and inheritance semantics as well as user-hints. Using this information, the algorithm defines a set of candidate pages for the placement of a new or an updated object. The page with minimum cost is chosen from the set. If the page is full, then it can be split or the next page with maximum cost will be selected. Cheng and Hurson (8) investigated the effects of modifications in clustering and proposed a dynamic reclustering scheme that reorganizes related objects on the disk. The benefits and overheads of reclustering are determined with the help of a suggested cost model. The latter assists in the decision on whether reclustering is warranted. In addition, a multipass clustering scheme is proposed to handle the situations in which multiple relationships exist among objects. Tsangaris and Naughton addressed the problem of partitioning a given object base while taking into account the application behavioral information (5,22). Discrete-time Markov chains are used for characterizing and predicting the access patterns of clients. By representing access patterns as stochastic processes, clustering is formulated as an optimization problem. Gerlhof et al. proposed a new class of greedy object-graph partitioning algorithms in Ref. 23. The goal is to provide an adaptable clustering strategy that synergistically works with features of an object-oriented database, including the size of objects and the degree of object sharing. In the introduced new class of greedy object graph (GGP) partitioning algorithms running-time complexity is moderate and furnishes good clustering results.

In Ref. 6, McIver and King presented an architecture that performs reclustering over composite objects in an on-line manner, which is adaptive to changing usage patterns. The architecture decomposes the clustering process into three concurrently operating components: statistics collection, clustering, and reorganization. The proposed clustering algorithm is designed to group objects according to their traversal types (e.g., set- oriented, navigational access, etc.). To this end, they utilize the database statistics proposed in Cactis (24). In Ref. 25, Shrufi addressed the problem of clustering graphs in object databases. Unlike other related work which focused only on a workload consisting of a class of operations, Shrufi examined the problem when the workload is a set of operation classes that occur with a certain probability. To resolve the problem of clustering graphs in object-oriented database systems (OODBS), Shrufi proposed a new clustering policy based on the "nearest-neighbor" graph partitioning algorithm. The objective of the algorithm is to minimize the expected cost of an operation in the workload while maintaining a similarly low cost for each individual operation class.

The common thread in all of the above efforts is that they cluster items while using only few features. Emerging environments and applications such as data warehousing, data mining, spatio-temporal databases, and so on need to efficiently handle very high-dimension data. It is rather evident that prior work has not sufficiently addressed the effects of very high-dimension data in clustering.

CLUSTERING ANALYSIS ELEMENTS

The primary goal of clustering is to produce homogeneous entities. Homogeneity refers to the common properties of the objects to be clustered. Properties of clusters are highlighted by hiding properties of individuals. Clusters can be represented in the measurement space in the same way as the objects they contain. From that point of view, a single object is a cluster containing exactly one object. There are generally two ways to represent clusters in a measurement space:

- As a hypothetical point which is not an object in the cluster
- As an existing object in the cluster, called centroid or cluster representative

A means of quantifying the degree of associations between items is needed to cluster data objects. This can be a measure of distances or similarities. There is a number of similarity measures available and the choice may have an effect on the results obtained. Multidimensional objects may use relative or normalized weight to convert their distance to an arbitrary scale so they can be compared. Once the objects are defined in the same measurement space as the points, it is then possible to compute the degree of similarity. In this respect, the smaller the distance, the more similar two objects are. The most popular choice in computing distance is the Euclidean distance: $d(i, j) = \sqrt{\sum_{k=1}^{n} (x_{i_k} - x_{j_k})^2}$, where n is the number of dimensions.

Coefficients of correlation are the measurements that describe the strength of the relationship between two variables $\mathcal{X}$ and $\mathcal{Y}$. It essentially answers the question "how similar are $\mathcal{X}$ and $\mathcal{Y}$." The values of the coefficients of correlation range from 0 to 1, where the value 0 points to *no similarity* and the value 1 points to *high similarity*. The coefficient of correlation is used to find the similarity among (clustering) objects. The correlation r of two random variables $\mathcal{X}$ and $\mathcal{Y}$, where $\mathcal{X} = (x_1, x_2, x_3, \ldots, x_n)$ and $\mathcal{Y} = (y_1, y_2, y_3, \ldots, y_n)$, is given by the formula

$$r = \frac{|E(\mathcal{X},\mathcal{Y}) - E(\mathcal{X})E(\mathcal{Y})|}{\sqrt{(E)(\mathcal{X}^2) - E^2(\mathcal{X})} \sqrt{(E(\mathcal{Y}^2) - E^2(\mathcal{Y})}},$$

where $E(\mathcal{X}) = (\sum_{i=1}^{n} x_i)/n$, $E(\mathcal{Y}) = (\sum_{i=1}^{n} y_i)/n$, and $E(\mathcal{X},\mathcal{Y}) = (\sum_{i=1}^{n} x_i\, y_i)/n$.

Clustering methods can be classified according to the type of the group structure they produce: partitioning and hierarchical. Here, we focus on hierarchical methods which work in a bottom-up approach and are appropriate for a data-intensive environment (26). The algorithm proceeds by performing a series of successive fusion. This produces a nested dataset in which pairs of items or clusters are successively linked until every item in the dataset is linked to form one cluster, known also as a hierarchical tree. This tree is often presented as a *dendrogram*, in which pairwise couplings of the objects in the dataset are shown and the length of the branches (vertices) or the value of the similarity is expressed numerically. In this study, we focus on two methods that enjoy wide usage (1,27): Unweighted Pair-Group using Arithmetic Averages (UPGMA) and Ward's.

- Unweighted Pair-Group Using Arithmetic Averages: This method uses the average values of pairwise distance, denoted $\mathcal{D}_{X,Y}$, within each participating cluster to determine similarity. All participating objects contribute to intercluster similarity. This method is also known as one of "average linkage" clustering methods (1,27,28). The distance between two clusters is $\mathcal{D}_{X,Y} = (\sum \mathcal{D}_{x,y})/(n_X\, n_Y)$, where X and Y are two clusters, x and y are objects from X and Y, $\mathcal{D}_{x,y}$ is the distance between x and y, and n_X and n_Y are the respective size of the clusters.

- Ward's Method: This method is based on the statistical minimization of clustering expansion (26). In the course of every step, the central point is calculated for any possible combination of two clusters. In addition, the sum of the squared distances of all elements in the clusters from their central points is computed. The two clusters that offer the smallest possible sum are used to formulate the new cluster. The notion of distance used here has no geometric nature.

Before the grouping commences, objects following the chosen probabilistic functions are generated. In this article, objects are randomly selected and are drawn from the interval $[0, 1]^n$, where n is the number of data dimensions. Subsequently, the objects are compared to each other by computing their distances. The distance used in assessing the similarity between two clusters is called the *similarity coefficient*. This is not to be confused with *coefficients of correlation*, as the latter are used to *compare* outcomes (i.e., hierarchical trees) of the clustering process. The way objects and clusters of objects coalesce together to form larger clusters varies with the approach used. Below, we outline a generic algorithm that is applicable to all clustering methods (initially, every cluster consists of exactly one object):

1. Create all possible cluster formulations from the existing ones.
2. For each such candidate, compute its corresponding similarity coefficient.
3. Find the minimum of all similarity coefficients and then join the corresponding clusters.
4. If not all clusters have coalesced into one entity, then go to Step 1.

Essentially, the algorithm consists of two phases. The first phase records the similarity coefficients. The second phase computes the minimum coefficient and then performs the clustering.

There is a case when using average-based methods that ambiguity may arise. For instance, let us suppose that when performing Step 1 (of the above algorithmic skeleton), three successive clusters are to be joined. All three clusters have the same minimum similarity value. When performing Step 2, the first two clusters are joined. However, when computing the similarity coefficient between this new cluster and the third cluster, the similarity coefficient value may now be different from the minimum value. The question at this stage is what the next step should be. There are essentially two options:

- Continue by joining clusters using a recomputation of the similarity coefficient every time we find ourselves in Step 2.
- Join *all* those clusters that have the same similarity coefficient at once and do not recompute the similarity in Step 2.

In general, there is no evidence that one is better than the other (27). For our study, we selected the first alternative.

As mentioned earlier, objects that participate in the clustering process are randomly selected from a designated area (i.e., $[0, 1] \times [0, 1] \times [0, 1] \cdots$). We use three distributions for the creation of data, namely uniform, piecewise (skewed), and, finally, Gaussian distribution. Below, we describe these statistical distributions in terms of density functions:

- *Uniform distribution*, whose density function is $f(x) = 1$ for all x in $0 \le x \le 1$.
- *Normal distribution*, whose density function is

$$f(x) = \frac{1}{\sqrt{2\pi}} \frac{\mu - x}{\sigma^3} \exp \left(-\frac{(\mu - x)^2}{2\sigma^2} \right).$$

  This is a two-parameter (σ and μ) distribution, where μ is the mean of the distribution and σ^2 is the variance; $0 \le x \le 1$.
- *Exponential distribution*, whose density function is

$$f(x) = \lambda e^{-\lambda x}, \text{ where } \lambda > 0 \text{ and } 0 \le x \le 1.$$

EXPERIMENTAL METHODOLOGY

In this study, data objects are generated in a high-dimensional space (10–100 with step 10) using various statistical distribution methods. The dimensions represent the attributes of a relation in the relational model. The experiments use different data sizes ranging from 50 to 200 objects. For brevity, we will focus in the Discussion section on the case of 200 objects. The value of each attribute value ranges from 0 to 1 inclusive. The seed of the statistical distributions is the system time. Each experiment goes through the following steps that result in a clustering tree:

- Generate lists of objects with a statistical distribution method (uniform or Normal or exponential). We first generate 100 objects for the first dimension. Then, the seed is generated again and we generate another 100 objects for the second dimension, and so on.
- Initiate the clustering process with a clustering method (UPGMA or Wards).

For statistical validation, each experiment is repeated 50 times. The seed selection is important because we would like to generate different data objects.

The remainder of the experiments consists of comparing clustering trees. We use coefficients of correlation as a means to compare two trees. There are two main methods to determine how correlated two clustering trees are. We use two types of distance to capture the relatedness of two sets of objects and decide how much their clustering resemble each other. We use the linear (Euclidean) distance and the minimum number of edges in a tree needed to join two objects. In this study, we call the former type of distance the linear distance and the latter distance is called the edge distance.

As can be seen, there are several parameters to generate clustering trees. These parameters include the clustering method, statistical distribution method, distance method, as well as dimension size and input size. They are all listed in the following tables. Essentially, there are 12 ($2 \times 3 \times 2$) possible combinations, where each combination will be used to compute a number of coefficients of correlation to study the clustering techniques behavior. The possible choices can be easily established in Figure 1.

For every combination above (e.g., Wards, Normal, linear), 10 coefficients of correlation (situations) have been isolated to assess clustering technique behaviors. In addition, the three last coefficients of correlation are not always computed because of the intrinsic symmetry. We believe that these combinations closely represent what may influence the choice of a clustering method.

We divide these 10 coefficients of correlation into three blocks, where each block tests a key behavior of a clustering method. For instance, the first block (consisting of four coefficients of correlation) tests the influence of the context on how objects are clustered. The description of each type of coefficient of correlation in this block follows.

The **first block** of four coefficients of correlation tests the influence of the context in which the clustering takes place. In that regard, we test the cases of one single context and two different contexts. The context defines the set from which the data objects are drawn.

1. The coefficient of correlation is between pair of objects drawn from a set S and pairs of objects drawn from the first half of the same set S. The first half of S is used for clustering before the set is sorted on a random dimension.
2. The coefficient of correlation is between pairs of objects drawn from S and pairs of objects drawn from the second half of S. As in the first type, the second half of S is used for clustering before the set is sorted on a random dimension.
3. The coefficient of correlation is between pairs of objects drawn from the first half of S, say $S1$, and pairs of objects drawn from the first half of another set SS, say $SS1$. The two sets are given ascending identifiers after being sorted. The sorting is dependent on the value of one randomly chosen dimension of the data object. Then, the first object of $S1$ is given the number 1 as identifier. All other involved objects run through the same process.
4. The coefficient of correlation is between pairs of objects drawn from the second half of S, say $S2$, and pairs of objects drawn from the second half of SS, say $SS2$. The two sets are given ascending identifiers after being sorted in the same way as the previous case.

The **second block**, consisting of three coefficients of correlation, is to check the influence of the data size. The main procedure to test is to add controlled "noise" to a set of data objects and then assess the clustering behavior.

5. The coefficient of correlation is between pairs of objects drawn from S and pairs of objects drawn from the union of a set X and S, where X contains 20% newly randomly generated objects.

6. The coefficient of correlation definition is the same as in the previous case except that X now contains 30% newly randomly generated objects.

7. The coefficient correlation definition is the same as the fifth case except that X now contains 40% newly randomly generated objects.

The **final block**, consisting of three coefficients of correlation, focuses on the investigation of statistical distributions on clustering.

8. The coefficient of correlation is between pairs of objects using the exponential distribution and pairs of objects using the Normal distribution.

9. The coefficient of correlation is between pairs of objects using the uniform distribution and pairs of objects using the exponential distribution.

10. The coefficient of correlation is between pairs of objects using the Normal distribution and pairs of objects using the uniform distribution.

Finally, to validate the results, the average of 50 coefficients of correlation and standard deviation values are computed. Then, the least-squares approximation is applied to gauge the acceptability of the results. We do not present the results here, but they show all coefficients of correlation to be within the standard deviation of the linear least-squares approximation.

RESULTS AND INTERPRETATION

We annotate Figures 2–10 using a shorthand notation. For example, the abbreviation WNE is used to represent the input with the following parameters: Wards, Normal distribution, and edge distance. The abbreviations for the parameters are listed in Table 1. The line types in Figures 2–10 identify the different types of coefficients of correlation. Table 2 shows the mapping between the coefficients of correlation and line types. The Figures 6–10 depict the average execution time of each experiment. The meaning of the line types is described in Table 3.

In what follows, we provide a thorough interpretation of the results. We first look at the first four coefficients of correlation. From Figure 1 (UPGMA), we can see that the

TABLE 1   List of Abbreviations

Term	Shorthand
UPGMA	U
Wards	W
Normal distribution	G
Exponential distribution	P
Uniform distribution	U
Linear distance	L
Edge distance	E

TABLE 2 Graphical Representation of the
Types of Correlation Coefficient

Type	Line
First, third, sixth, ninth	Dashed
Second, fourth, fifth, eight	Solid
Seventh, tenth	Dash-dotted

choice of the distance type does not have any noticeable influence. Indeed, the difference between the two curves across the figures spanning the correlation types and distribution is negligible. For the first two coefficients of correlation, the choice of distribution does not seem to have any influence in the clustering process. However, the distance type seems to have a small impact on the clustering. Indeed, we note that the correlations are a bit stronger in the case of the Euclidean distance. This can be explained by the fact that the distance between the members of two clusters is the same for all members under the linear (Euclidean) distance. Note that the edge distance value represents the number of edges between members of two clusters. It is also the shortest path between them in the created tree. Usually, the resulting tree is not balanced, so the distance between members of two clusters may be different under E. Because of the high correlation in all cases depicted in Figure 2, the context in this specific case does not seem to make any significant difference in the clustering process. If we look at Figure 3, which depicts the clustering possibilities using Wards method, the results are very similar. The most notable difference is in the correlation values, which are slightly less in the case of Wards. However, the correlation values are high in both cases. This strengthens the conjecture that no matter what the context of the clustering is, the outcome is almost invariably the same.

The experiments regarding the second and third types of coefficients of correlation show some surprising results. The previous study results using low dimensionality show above-average correlation. In contrast, in this study, as shown in Figures 4 (UPGMA) and 5 (Wards), the correlation values are low. It is a strong indication that in high dimensions, almost no correlation exists between the two sets of objects. In the case of the first and second coefficients of correlation, the data objects are drawn from the same initial set. However, the third and fourth coefficients correlation draw the values from different initial sets. The difference from the previous study is that we now randomly select one dimension from multiple dimensions as our reference dimension. As a result, the order of data points is dependent on the value of the selected dimension.

The next three coefficients of correlation check the influence of the data size on

TABLE 3 Line Types Used in Figure 10

Clustering method	Line
UPGMA	Dash-dotted
Wards	Dashed-dotted-dotted-dotted

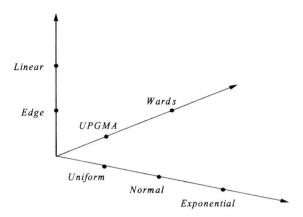

FIGURE 1   Twelve combinations of clustering, distance computation, and distribution methods.

clustering. They are shown in Figures 6 and 7. There are no significant differences when using these two clustering methods, respectively. When using L and E, no substantial differences are found in these cases. Therefore, these results indicate that Wards and UPGMA are relatively stable for multidimensional objects. The perturbation represented by the insertion of new data objects does not seem to have any significant effect on the clustering process.

The final three coefficients of correlation are used to check the influence of the statistical distributions on the clustering process. We also use one randomly selected dimension to sort all objects. Figures 8 (UPGMA) and 9 (Wards) show the result of the experiments. It is quite obvious that almost no correlation can be drawn between the two differently generated lists of objects. Simply put, the clustering process is influenced by the statistical distribution used to generate objects. We also note that there is a small difference between using linear (L) and edge (E) distances.

In order to validate our interpretation of the results, we ran the same experiments for different input sizes (50, 100, 150). The results show the same type of behavior as for the input size of 200. Therefore, these experiments indicate that the data size has essentially no role in the clustering process.

As a final set of measurements, we also recorded the computation time for various methods. Figure 10 shows the average logarithmic computation time of all experiments varying the dimensions. The considered data input sizes are 50, 100, 150, and 200. The time unit is in (logarithmic) seconds. We can see that UPGMA is computationally more attractive than Wards. This is expected, as Wards needs to compute the distance for every possibility of combinations in each step. Therefore, Wards variance clustering methods is not computationally good to use for large datasets with multiple attributes. It is interesting to note that both methods exhibit the same computational behavior when varying the dimensions and data input size.

The results obtained in this study confirm several findings from previous studies focusing on low-dimension data objects (1D, 2D, and 3D). The major finding is the following: If we consider unique sets of data objects, there is a basic inherent way for data objects to cluster and independently of the clustering method used. Especially, the

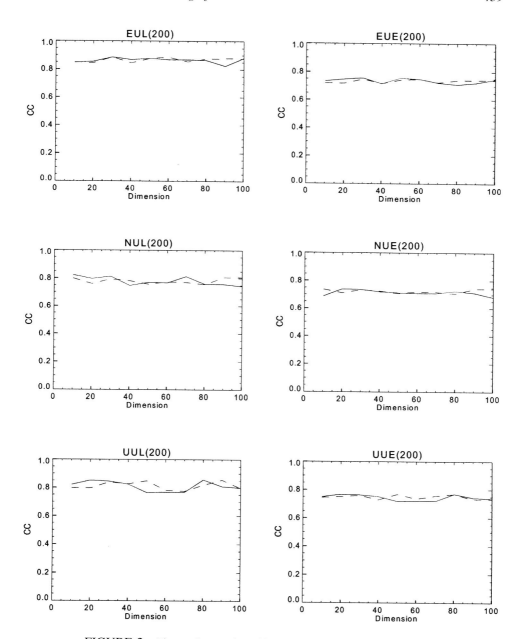

FIGURE 2   First and second coefficients of correlation for UPGMA.

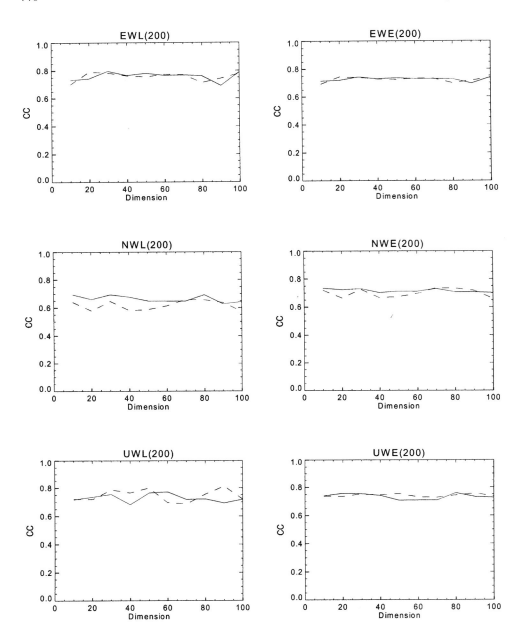

FIGURE 3   First and second coefficients of correlation for Wards.

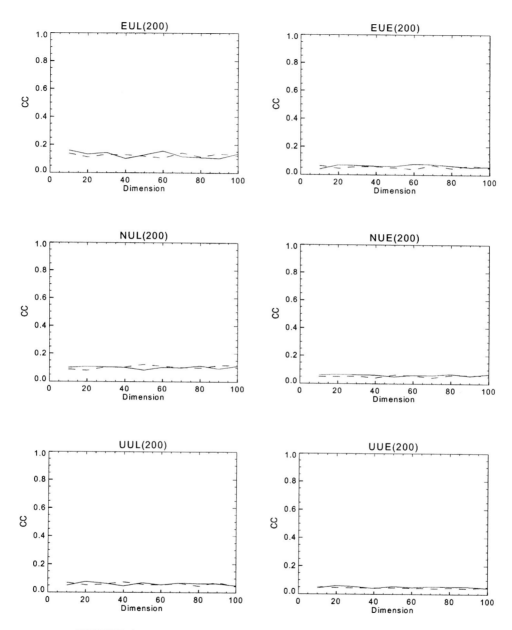

FIGURE 4   Third and fourth coefficients of correlation for UPGMA.

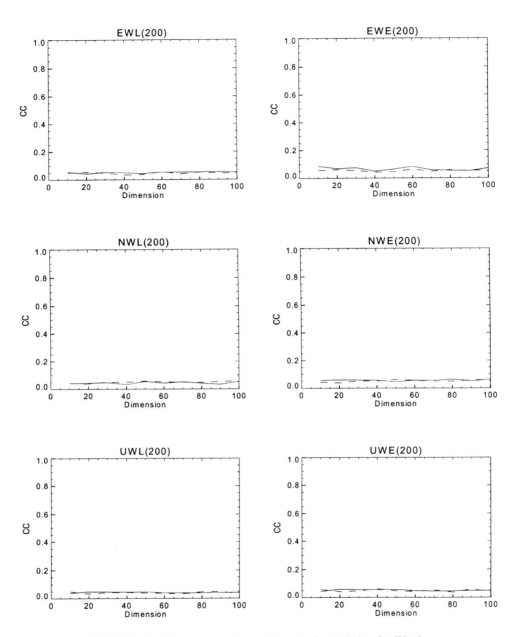

FIGURE 5   Third and fourth coefficients of correlation for Wards.

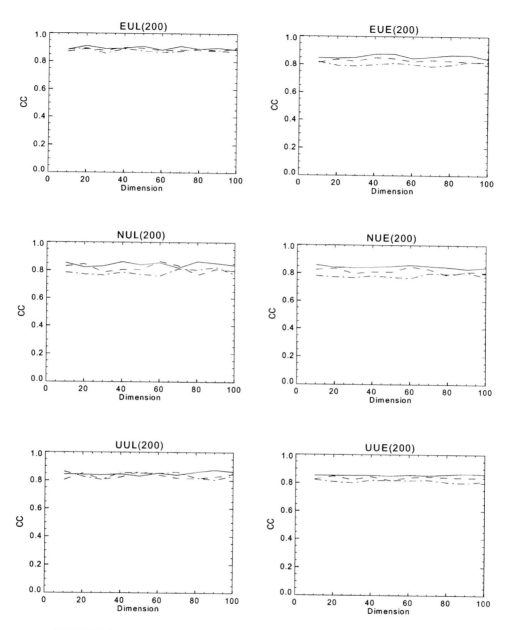

FIGURE 6   Fifth, sixth, and seventh coefficients of correlation for UPGMA.

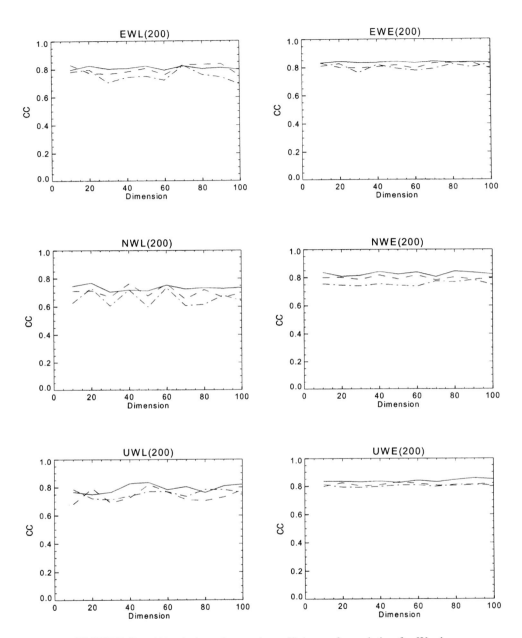

FIGURE 7   Fifth, sixth, and seventh coefficients of correlation for Wards.

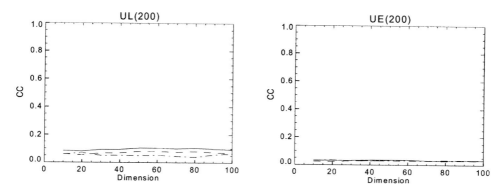

FIGURE 8   Eighth, ninth, and tenth coefficients of correlation for UPGMA.

dimensionality does not have a significant role in the clustering of data objects. This is compelling evidence that clustering methods, in general, do not seem to influence the outcome of the clustering process. It is worth indicating that the experiments presented in this article were computationally intensive. We used 10 Sun Workstations running Solaris 7.0. The complete set of experiments for each clustering methods took an average of 3 days to complete.

CONCLUSIONS

In this study, we analyzed two clustering methods, UPGMA and Wards. We ran a wide array of experiments to test the stability of sensibility of the clustering methods for high-dimensional data objects. The obtained results strengthen a previous study result considering low-dimensional data objects. The results seem to suggest that if the data

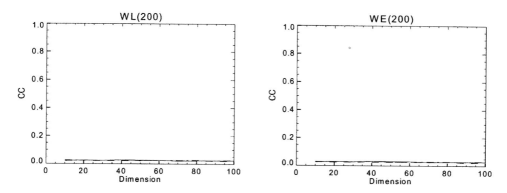

FIGURE 9   Eighth, ninth, and tenth coefficients of correlation for Wards.

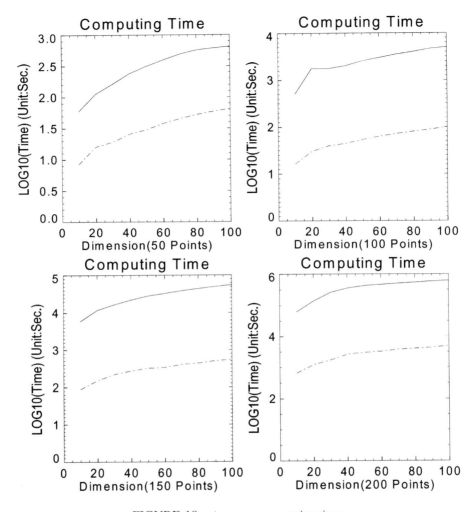

FIGURE 10   Average computation times.

are drawn from the same context, then any clustering methods will yield approximately the same highly correlated outcome. However, if the correlation values seem to indicate that the choice of a clustering technique (UPGMA and Wards) should be based solely on computational merit. When the contexts are different, the results are the same for the two clustering techniques. However, in this case, the correlation values are quite low. This is indicative of the significance of choosing different contexts for clustering. The other factors, including the choice of a clustering techniques, did not have any bearing on the outcome. We plan on further generalizing our findings by considering data input sizes ranging from the thousands to hundreds of thousands.

ACKNOWLEDGMENTS

This work was supported in part by the National Science Foundation under Grant NSF IIS-9733642 and the Center for Advanced Technology in Telecommunications, Brooklyn, NY.

REFERENCES

1. B. Everitt, *Cluster Analysis*, Heinemann, Yorkshire, 1977.
2. A. Bouguettaya, "On-Line Clustering," *IEEE Trans. Knowledge Data Eng.*, *KDE-8*(2) (1996).
3. M. S. Alderfer and R. K. Blashfield, *Cluster Analysis*. Sage Publication, San Francisco, CA, 1984.
4. M. F. Hornick and S. Zdonick, "A Shared Segmented Memory System for an Object-Oriented Database," *ACM Trans. Office Inform. Syst.*, *5*(1) (1987).
5. M. Tsangaris and J. F. Naughton, "A Stochastic Approach for Clustering in Object Bases," in *Proceedings of the International Conference on the Management of Data (SIGMOD)*, 1991.
6. J. McIver and R. King, "Self-Adaptive, On-Line Reclustering of Complex Object Data," in *Proceedings of the International Conference on Management of Data*, ACM Press, New York, 1994, pp. 407–418.
7. B. Salzberg and V. J. Tsotras, "A Comparison of Access Methods for Time-Evolving Data," *ACM Computing Surveys*, 31(2) (1999).
8. J. R. Cheng and A. R. Hurson, "Effective Clustering of Complex Objects in Object-Oriented Databases," in *Proceedings of the International Conference on the Management of Data (SIGMOD)*, 1991.
9. L. Kaufman and P. J. Rousseeuw, *Finding Groups in Data, an Introduction to Cluster Analysis*, John Wiley & Sons, London, 1990.
10. J. A. Hartigan, *Clustering Algorithms*, John Wiley & Sons, London, 1975.
11. A. Kemper and G. Moerkotte, *Object-Oriented Database Management: Applications in Engineering and Computer Science*, 1994.
12. K. Shannon and R. Snodgrass, "Semantic Clustering," in *Proceedings of the Conference on Principles of Database Systems*, 1990.
13. A. Bouguettaya and Q. L. Viet, "Data Clustering Analysis in a Multidimensional Space," *Inform. Sci.*, *112*(1–4), 267–295 (1998).
14. A. Bouguettaya, Q. LeViet, and A. Delis, "Data Education," in *Encyclopedia of Electrical and Electronics Engineering*, edited by J. Webster, John Wiley & Sons, New York, 1999.
15. B. Kerninghan and S. Lin, "An Efficient Heuristic Procedure for Partitioning Graphs," *Bell Syst. Tech. J.*, *49*(2), 291–307 (1970).
16. J. Lukes, "Efficient Algorithm for the Partitioning of Trees," *IBM J. Res. Dev.*, *18*(3), 217–224 (1974).
17. M. Schkolnick, "A Clustering Algorithm for Hierarchical Structures," *ACM Trans. Database Syst.*, *2*(1), 27–44 (1977).
18. J. Stamos, "Static Grouping of Small Objects to Enhance Performance of Paged Virtual Memory," *ACM Trans. Computer Syst.*, *2*(2) (1984).
19. C. T. Yu, C. Suen, K. Lam, and M. K. Siu, "Adaptive Record Clustering," *ACM Trans. Database Syst.*, *10*(2), 180–204 (1985).
20. J. Banerjee, W. Kim, S-J. Kim, and J. F. Garza, "Clustering a DAG for CAD Databases," *IEEE Trans. Software Eng.*, *SE-14*(11) (1988).

21. E. E. Chang and R. H. Katz, "Exploiting Inheritance and Structure Semantics for Effective Clustering and Buffering in an Object-Oriented DBMS," in *Proceedings of the 1989 ACM SIGMOD International Conference on the Management of Data*, 1989, pp. 348–357.

22. M. Tsangaris and J. F. Naughton, "On the Performance of Object Clustering Techniques," in *Proceedings of 20th ACM SIGMOD Conference on the Management of Data*, 1992, pp. 144–153.

23. G. A. Gerlhof, A. Kemper, C. Kilger, and G. Moerkotte, "Partition-Based Clustering in Object Bases: From Theory to Practice," in *Proceedings of the International Conference on Foundations of Data Organization*, 1993.

24. S. E. Hudson and R. King, "Cactis: A Self-Adaptive, Concurrent Implementation of an Object-Oriented Database Management System," *ACM Trans. Database Syst.*, *14*(3), 291–321 (1989).

25. A. Shrufi, "Performance of Clustering Policies in Object Bases," in *Proceedings of the Conference on Information and Knowledge Management*, 1994.

26. J. Zupan, *Clustering of Large Data Sets*, Research Studies Press, Letchworth, UK, 1982.

27. H. C. Romesburg, *Cluster Analysis for Researchers*, Krieger, Malabar, FL, 1990.

28. G. N. Lance and W. T. Williams, "A General Theory for Classification Sorting Strategy," *Computer J.*, *9*(5), 373–386 (1967).

ATHMAN BOUGUETTAYA

HONGMING QI

JE-HO PARK

ALEX DELIS

ISBN 0-8247-2298-1

90000